ADVENTURES
FOR READERS
BOOK TWO

The ADVENTURES IN LITERATURE *Program*

ADVENTURES FOR READERS: BOOK ONE
Teacher's Manual
Tests
Reading/Writing Workshop A

ADVENTURES FOR READERS: BOOK TWO
Teacher's Manual
Tests
Reading/Writing Workshop B

ADVENTURES IN READING
Teacher's Manual
Tests
Reading/Writing Workshop C

ADVENTURES IN APPRECIATION
Teacher's Manual
Tests
Reading/Writing Workshop D

ADVENTURES IN AMERICAN LITERATURE
Teacher's Manual
Tests

ADVENTURES IN ENGLISH LITERATURE
Teacher's Manual
Tests

CURRICULUM AND WRITING

Fannie Safier
Formerly teacher of English
New York City Schools, New York, New York
Kathleen T. Daniel
Secondary English Editorial Staff
Harcourt Brace Jovanovich, Publishers

ADVENTURES
FOR READERS
BOOK TWO

HERITAGE EDITION REVISED

HBJ **Harcourt Brace Jovanovich, Publishers**
Orlando   New York   Chicago   San Diego   Atlanta   Dallas

Acknowledgments

For permission to reprint copyrighted material, grateful acknowledgment is made to the following sources:

The Bodley Head: "Hints on Pronunciation for Foreigners" from *A Flock of Words,* edited by David Mackay.

Brandt & Brandt: "The Sea Devil" by Arthur Gordon. Originally published by the *Saturday Evening Post.* Copyright 1953 by the Curtis Publishing Company.

Curtis Brown Ltd., London: The Ugly Duckling by A. A. Milne. Copyright © 1941 by A. A. Milne.

Don Congdon Associates, Inc.: "The Gift" by Ray Bradbury. Copyright © 1952 by Ray Bradbury; renewed 1980.

Coward-McCann, Inc: "Calling in the Cat" from *Compass Rose* by Elizabeth Coatsworth. Copyright 1929 by Coward-McCann, Inc.; renewed © 1957 by Elizabeth Coatsworth.

Joan Daves: From "I Have a Dream" by Martin Luther King, Jr. Copyright © 1963 by Martin Luther King, Jr.

Delacorte Press: "The Valentine" from *The Ice-Cream Headache and Other Stories* by James Jones. (Abridged)

Doubleday & Company, Inc.: "Raymond's Run" from *Tales and Stories for Black Folks* by Toni Cade Bambara. Copyright © 1971 by Doubleday & Company, Inc. "Child on Top of a Greenhouse" from *The Collected Poems of Theodore Roethke* by Theodore Roethke. Copyright 1946 by Editorial Publications, Inc. "A Retrieved Reformation" from *Roads of Destiny* by O. Henry.

Farrar, Straus & Giroux, Inc.: "Charles" from *The Lottery* by Shirley Jackson. Copyright 1948, 1949 by Shirley Jackson; renewed 1976 by Laurence Hyman, Barry Hyman, Mrs. Sarah Webster and Mrs. Joanne Schnurer.

Granada Publishing Ltd.: "Antigone" from *Men and Gods* by Rex Warner. Published by Granada Publishing Ltd.

Harcourt Brace Jovanovich, Inc.: "For My Sister Molly Who in the Fifties" from *Revolutionary Petunias and Other Poems* by Alice Walker. Copyright © 1972 by Alice Walker. "How Dictionaries Are Made" from *Language in Thought and Action,* 3rd Edition, by S. I. Hayakawa. Copyright © 1972 by Harcourt Brace Jovanovich, Inc. "Dialogue—Earth and Moon" from *Earth Shine* by Anne Morrow Lindbergh. Copyright © 1969 by Anne Morrow Lindbergh. "Twelve: Winter" from *Cress Delahanty* by Jessamyn West. Copyright 1948; renewed 1976 by Jessamyn West. Originally published in *The New Yorker* under the title "Then He Goes Free." "old age sticks" from *Complete Poems 1913–1962* by E. E. Cummings. Copyright 1958 by E. E. Cummings. "The Emperor's New Clothes" from *It's Perfectly True and Other Stories* by Hans Christian Andersen, translated by Paul Leyssac. Copyright © 1938 by Paul Leyssac; renewed 1966 by Mary Rehan. From *The Diary of Anaïs Nin, 1947–1955* (Titled "Forest Fire") by Anaïs Nin. Copyright © 1974 by Anaïs Nin. "The Apprentice" from *A Harvest of Stories* by Dorothy Canfield. Copyright 1947 by the Curtis Publishing Company.

Harper & Row, Publishers, Inc.: Adaptation of "The Kamiah Monster" from *Nine Tales of Coyote* by Fran Martin. Copyright 1950 by Harper & Row, Publishers. "The Bean Eaters" in *The World of Gwendolyn Brooks* (1971) by Gwendolyn Brooks. Copyright © 1959 by Gwendolyn Brooks. "The Celebrated Jumping Frog of Calaveras County" from *Sketches New and Old* by Mark Twain. "Cub Pilot on the Mississippi" from *Life on the Mississippi* by Mark Twain. Abridged from pp. 128–131, 136–137 in *The Names* (Titled: "It Will Not Be Seen Again") by N. Scott Momaday. Copyright © 1976 by N. Scott Momaday. From *Black Boy* (Titled: "The

Critical Readers

We wish to thank the following people, who helped to evaluate materials in this book:

Garry E. Burris, Mifflin Middle School, Columbus, Ohio

Vicki Hartman, Clinton High School, Clinton, Mississippi

Dorothy D. Hendry, Huntsville High School, Huntsville, Alabama

Virginia Irwin, Simonsen Junior High School, Jefferson City, Missouri

Carol Kuykendall, Houston Independent School District, Houston, Texas

Genevieve Murguia, South Pasadena Junior High School, South Pasadena, California

Bette B. Perlmutter, Arlington Junior High School, Poughkeepsie, New York

Jerome Smiley, Alva T. Stanforth Junior High School, Elmont, New York

Russell Thompson, Olle Middle School, Houston, Texas

Francelia Butler, University of Connecticut, Storrs, Connecticut

W. T. Jewkes, University of Arizona, Tucson, Arizona

Richard J. Smith, University of Wisconsin, Madison, Wisconsin

David Thorburn, Massachusetts Institute of Technology, Cambridge, Massachusetts

David Wagoner, University of Washington, Seattle, Washington

Special Acknowledgment

Irene M. Reiter, Northeast High School, Philadelphia, Pennsylvania

We also wish to thank

Madeline Hendrix, Librarian, Alva T. Stanforth Junior High School, Elmont, New York, for assistance in compiling bibliographies

Lee A. Jacobus, University of Connecticut, Storrs, Connecticut, for developing the Guide to Literary Terms and Techniques

Contents

See page xv for the contents of *Reading and Writing About Literature*

Part One   *Themes in Literature*

PROVING GROUNDS

THE VIEW FROM HERE

IMAGES OF AMERICA

Part Two   Forms of Literature

SHORT STORIES

DRAMA

NONFICTION

POETRY

Less Is More

Sound Effects

Sense and Nonsense

Part Three   Tales from Many Lands

Proving grounds are places where new theories or new pieces of equipment are tested. In this unit, "proving grounds" are situations where individual courage, honesty, strength, and intelligence are challenged. The "tests" in this unit take many forms. In one story, a man wages a life-and-death battle with a gigantic sea monster. In another story, a woman fights against many dangers in order to lead people out of slavery. In another story, a boy wages a battle in his own mind as he struggles to make a painful decision. All of the people in this unit are "tested" and all prove themselves to be winners. You might find that some of their tests are ones that you yourself have already faced.

PROVING GROUNDS

Plummer was as tone-deaf as boiled cabbage. But he was determined to win a place with the A Band. All it finally took was a smart business deal — and an eight-foot bass drum.

The No-Talent Kid

Kurt Vonnegut

It was autumn, and the leaves outside Lincoln High School were turning the same rusty color as the bare brick walls in the band-rehearsal room. George M. Helmholtz, head of the music department and director of the band, was ringed by folding chairs and instrument cases; and on each chair sat a very young man, nervously prepared to blow through something, or, in the case of the percussion section, to hit something, the instant Mr. Helmholtz lowered his white baton.

Mr. Helmholtz, a man of forty, who believed that his great belly was a sign of health, strength and dignity, smiled angelically, as though he were about to release the most exquisite sounds ever heard by men. Down came his baton.

"*Blooooomp!*" went the big sousaphones.

"*Blat! Blat!*" echoed the French horns, and the plodding, shrieking, querulous[1] waltz was begun.

Mr. Helmholtz's expression did not change as the brasses lost their places, as the woodwinds' nerve failed and they became inaudible rather than have their mistakes heard, as the percussion section shifted into a rhythm pattern belonging to a march they knew and liked better.

"A-a-a-a-ta-ta, a-a-a-a-a-a, ta-ta-ta-ta!" sang Mr. Helmholtz in a loud tenor, singing the first-cornet part when the first cornetist, florid and perspiring, gave up and slouched in his chair, his instrument in his lap.

"Saxophones, let me hear you," called Mr. Helmholtz. "Good!"

This was the C Band, and, for the C Band, the performance was good; it couldn't have been more polished for the fifth session of the school year. Most of the youngsters were just starting out as bandsmen, and in the years ahead of them they would acquire artistry enough to move into the B Band, which met in the next hour. And finally the best of them would gain positions in the pride of the city, the Lincoln High School Ten Square Band.

The football team lost half its games and the basketball team lost two thirds of its, but the band, in the ten years Mr. Helmholtz had been running it, had been second to none until last June. It had been first in the state to use flag twirlers, the first to use choral as well as instrumental numbers, the first to use triple-tonguing extensively, the first to march in breathtaking double time, the first to put a light in its bass drum. Lincoln High School awarded letter sweaters to the members of the A Band, and the sweaters were deeply respected—and properly so. The band had won every statewide high school band competition in the last ten years—every one save the one in June.

As the members of the C Band dropped out of the waltz, one by one, as though mustard gas[2] were coming out of the ventilators, Mr. Helmholtz continued to smile and wave his baton for the survivors, and to brood inwardly over the defeat his band had sustained in June, when Johnstown High School had won with a secret weapon, a bass drum seven feet in diameter. The judges, who were not musicians but politicians, had had eyes and ears for nothing but this eighth wonder of the world, and since then Mr. Helmholtz had thought of little else. But the school budget was already lopsided with band expenses. When the school board had given him the last special appropriation he'd begged so desperately—money to wire the plumes of the

---

1. **querulous** (kwĕr′ə-ləs): fretful; complaining. In other words, it wasn't much like a waltz. (A key to the pronunciation of words in the footnotes appears in the glossary at the back of this book.)

2. **mustard gas**: a poisonous gas.

bandsmen's hats with flashlight bulbs and batteries for night games—the board had made him swear that this was the last time.

Only two members of the C Band were playing now, a clarinetist and a snare drummer, both playing loudly, proudly, confidently, and all wrong. Mr. Helmholtz, coming out of his wistful dream of a bass drum bigger than the one that had beaten him, administered the *coup de grâce*[3] to the waltz by clattering his stick against his music stand. "All righty, all righty," he said cheerily, and he nodded his congratulations to the two who had persevered to the bitter end.

Walter Plummer, the clarinetist, nodded back soberly, like a concert soloist receiving an ovation led by the director of a symphony orchestra. He was small, but with a thick chest developed in summers spent at the bottom of swimming pools, and he could hold a note longer than anyone in the A Band, much longer, but that was all he could do. He drew back his tired, reddened lips, showing the two large front teeth that gave him the look of a squirrel, adjusted his reed, limbered his fingers, and awaited the next challenge to his virtuosity.

This would be Plummer's third year in the C Band, Mr. Helmholtz thought, with a mixture of pity and fear. Nothing, apparently, could shake Plummer's determination to earn the right to wear one of the sacred letters of the A Band, so far, terribly far away.

Mr. Helmholtz had tried to tell Plummer how misplaced his ambitions were, to recommend other fields for his great lungs and enthusiasm, where pitch would be unimportant. But Plummer was blindly in love, not with music, but with the letter sweaters, and, being as tone-deaf as boiled cabbage, he could

detect nothing in his own playing to be discouraged about.

"Remember, now," said Mr. Helmholtz to the C Band, "Friday is challenge day, so be on your toes. The chairs you have now were assigned arbitrarily.[4] On challenge day it'll be up to you to prove which chair you deserve." He avoided the narrowed, confident eyes of Plummer, who had taken the first clarinetist's chair without consulting the seating plan posted on the bulletin board. Challenge day occurred every two weeks, and on that day any bandsman could challenge anyone ahead of him to a contest for his position, with Mr. Helmholtz as utterly dispassionate judge.

Plummer's hand was raised, its fingers snapping urgently.

"Yes, Plummer?" said Mr. Helmholtz, smiling bleakly. He had come to dread challenge days because of Plummer, and had come to think of it as Plummer's day. Plummer never challenged anybody in the C Band or even in the B Band, but stormed the organization at the very top, challenging, as was unfortunately the privilege of all, only members of the A Band. The waste of the A Band's time was troubling enough, but infinitely more painful for Mr. Helmholtz were Plummer's looks of stunned disbelief when he heard Mr. Helmholtz's decision that he hadn't outplayed the men he'd challenged. And Mr. Helmholtz was thus rebuked not just on challenge days, but every day, just before supper, when Plummer delivered the evening paper. "Something about challenge day, Plummer?" said Mr. Helmholtz uneasily.

"Mr. Helmholtz," said Plummer coolly, "I'd like to come to A Band session that day."

"All right—if you feel up to it." Plummer

---

3. *coup de grâce* (kŌŌ′ də gräs′): finishing stroke (strictly speaking, the blow that ends suffering).

4. **arbitrarily** (är′bə-trěr′ə-lē): without any rules or standards.

always felt up to it, and it would have been more of a surprise if Plummer had announced that he wouldn't be at the A Band session.

"I'd like to challenge Flammer."

The rustling of sheet music and clicking of instrument-case latches stopped. Flammer was the first clarinetist in the A Band, a genius that not even members of the A Band would have had the gall to challenge.

Mr. Helmholtz cleared his throat. "I admire your spirit, Plummer, but isn't that rather ambitious for the first of the year? Perhaps you should start out with, say, challenging Ed Delaney." Delaney held down the last chair in the B Band.

"You don't understand," said Plummer patiently. "You haven't noticed I have a new clarinet."

"H'm'm? Oh—well, so you do."

Plummer stroked the satin-black barrel of the instrument as though it were like King Arthur's sword, giving magical powers to whoever possessed it. "It's as good as Flammer's," said Plummer. "Better, even."

There was a warning in his voice, telling Mr. Helmholtz that the days of discrimination were over, that nobody in his right mind would dare to hold back a man with an instrument like this.

"Um," said Mr. Helmholtz. "Well, we'll see, we'll see."

After practice, he was forced into close quarters with Plummer again in the crowded hallway. Plummer was talking darkly to a wide-eyed freshman bandsman.

"Know why the band lost to Johnstown High last June?" asked Plummer, seemingly ignorant of the fact that he was back to back with Mr. Helmholtz. "Because," said Plummer triumphantly, "they stopped running the band on the merit system. Keep your eyes open on Friday."

Mr. George Helmholtz lived in a world of music, and even the throbbing of his headaches came to him musically, if painfully, as the deep-throated boom of a cart-borne bass drum seven feet in diameter. It was late afternoon on the first challenge day of the new school year. He was sitting in his living room, his eyes covered, awaiting another sort of thump—the impact of the evening paper, hurled against the clapboard of the front of the house by Walter Plummer.

As Mr. Helmholtz was telling himself that he would rather not have his newspaper on challenge day, since Plummer came with it, the paper was delivered with a crash that would have done credit to a siege gun.

"Plummer!" he cried furiously, shaken.

"Yes, sir?" said Plummer solicitously[5] from the sidewalk.

Mr. Helmholtz shuffled to the door in his carpet slippers. "Please, my boy," he said plaintively,[6] "can't we be friends?"

"Sure—why not?" said Plummer, shrugging. "Let bygones be bygones, is what I say." He gave a bitter imitation of an amiable chuckle. "Water over the dam. It's been two hours now since the knife was stuck in me and twisted."

Mr. Helmholtz sighed. "Have you got a moment? It's time we had a talk, my boy."

Plummer kicked down the standard on his bicycle, hid his papers under shrubbery, and walked in sullenly. Mr. Helmholtz gestured at the most comfortable chair in the room, the one in which he'd been sitting, but Plummer chose instead to sit on the edge of a hard one with a straight back.

Mr. Helmholtz, forming careful sentences in his mind before speaking, opened his newspaper, and laid it open on the coffee table.

"My boy," he said at last, "God made all

---

5. **solicitously** (sə-lĭs′ə-təs-lē): with concern.
6. **plaintively:** sadly.

kinds of people: some who can run fast, some who can write wonderful stories, some who can paint pictures, some who can sell anything, some who can make beautiful music. But He didn't make anybody who could do everything well. Part of the growing-up process is finding out what we can do well and what we can't do well." He patted Plummer's shoulder gently. "The last part, finding out what we can't do, is what hurts most about growing up. But everybody has to face it, and then go in search of his true self."

Plummer's head was sinking lower and lower on his chest and Mr. Helmholtz hastily pointed out a silver lining. "For instance, Flammer could never run a business like a paper route, keeping records, getting new customers. He hasn't that kind of a mind, and couldn't do that sort of thing if his life depended on it."

"You've got a point," said Plummer, looking up suddenly with unexpected brightness. "A guy's got to be awful one-sided to be as good at one thing as Flammer is. I think it's more worthwhile to try to be better-rounded. No, Flammer beat me fair and square today, and I don't want you to think I'm a bad sport about that. It isn't that that gets me."

"That's very mature of you," said Mr. Helmholtz. "But what I was trying to point out to you was that we've all got weak points, and——"

Plummer charitably waved him to silence. "You don't have to explain to me, Mr. Helmholtz. With a job as big as you've got, it'd be a miracle if you did the whole thing right."

"Now, hold on, Plummer!" said Mr. Helmholtz.

"All I'm asking is that you look at it from my point of view," said Plummer. "No sooner'd I come back from challenging A Band material, no sooner'd I come back from playing my heart out, than you turned those C Band kids loose on me. You and I know we were just giving 'em the feel of challenge days, and that I was all played out. But did you tell them that? Heck, no, you didn't, Mr. Helmholtz; and those kids all think they can play better than me. That's all I'm sore about, Mr. Helmholtz. They think it means something, me in the last chair of the C Band."

"Plummer," said Mr. Helmholtz evenly, "I have been trying to tell you something as kindly as possible, but apparently the only way to get it across to you is to tell it to you straight."

"Go ahead and quash[7] criticism," said Plummer, standing.

"Quash?"

"Quash," said Plummer with finality. He headed for the door. "I'm probably ruining my chances for getting into the A Band by speaking out like this, Mr. Helmholtz, but frankly, it's incidents like what happened to me today that lost you the band competition last June."

"It was a seven-foot bass drum!"

"Well, get one for Lincoln High and see how you make out then."

"I'd give my right arm for one!" said Mr. Helmholtz, forgetting the point at issue and remembering his all-consuming dream.

Plummer paused on the threshold. "One like the Knights of Kandahar use in their parades?"

"That's the ticket!" Mr. Helmholtz imagined the Knights of Kandahar's huge drum, the showpiece of every local parade. He tried to think of it with the Lincoln High School black panther painted on it. "Yes, sir!" When he returned to earth, Plummer was on his bicycle.

Mr. Helmholtz started to shout after Plummer, to bring him back and tell him bluntly that he didn't have the remotest chance of

---

7. **quash** (kwäsh): put a stop to.

getting out of C Band ever; that he would never be able to understand that the mission of a band wasn't simply to make noises, but to make special kinds of noises. But Plummer was off and away.

Temporarily relieved until next challenge day, Mr. Helmholtz sat down to enjoy his paper, to read that the treasurer of the Knights of Kandahar, a respected citizen, had disappeared with the organization's funds, leaving behind and unpaid the Knights' bills for the past year and a half. "We'll pay a hundred cents on the dollar, if we have to sell everything but the Sacred Mace," the Sublime Chamberlain of the Inner Shrine was on record as saying.

Mr. Helmholtz didn't know any of the people involved, and he yawned and turned to the funnies. He gasped suddenly, turned to the front page again, looked up a number in the phone book, and dialed feverishly.

"Zum-zum-zum-zum," went the busy signal in his ear. He dropped the telephone clattering into its cradle. Hundreds of people, he thought, must be trying to get in touch with the Sublime Chamberlain of the Inner Shrine of the Knights of Kandahar at this moment. He looked up at his flaking ceiling in prayer. But none of them, he prayed, were after a bargain in a cart-borne bass drum.

He dialed again and again, always getting the busy signal, and walked out on his porch to relieve some of the tension building up in him. He would be the only one bidding on the drum, he told himself, and he could name his own price. If he offered fifty dollars for it, he could probably have it! He'd put up his own money, and get the school to pay him back in three years, when the plumes with the electric lights in them were paid for in full.

He lit a cigarette, and laughed like a department-store Santa Claus at this magnificent stroke of fortune. As he exhaled happily, his gaze dropped from heaven to his lawn, and he saw Plummer's undelivered newspapers lying beneath the shrubbery.

He went inside and called the Sublime Chamberlain again, with the same results. To make the time go, and to do a Christian good turn, he called Plummer's home to let him know where the papers were mislaid. But the Plummers' line was busy too.

He dialed alternately the Plummers' number and the Sublime Chamberlain's number for fifteen minutes before getting a ringing signal.

"Yes?" said Mrs. Plummer.

"This is Mr. Helmholtz, Mrs. Plummer. Is Walter there?"

"He was here a minute ago, telephoning, but he just went out of here like a shot."

"Looking for his papers? He left them under my spiraea."[8]

"He did? Heavens, I have no idea where he was going. He didn't say anything about his papers, but I thought I overheard something about selling his clarinet." She sighed and then laughed nervously. "Having money of their own makes them awfully independent. He never tells me anything."

"Well, you tell him I think maybe it's for the best, his selling his clarinet. And tell him where his papers are."

It was unexpected good news that Plummer had at last seen the light about his musical career, and Mr. Helmholtz now called the Sublime Chamberlain's home again for more good news. He got through this time, but was momentarily disappointed to learn that the man had just left on some sort of lodge business.

For years Mr. Helmholtz had managed to smile and keep his wits about him in C Band

8. **spiraea** (spī-rē′ə): a shrub in the rose family.

practice sessions. But on the day after his fruitless efforts to find out anything about the Knights of Kandahar's bass drum, his defenses were down, and the poisonous music penetrated to the roots of his soul.

"No, no, no!" he cried in pain, and he threw his white baton against the brick wall. The springy stick bounded off the bricks and fell into an empty folding chair at the rear of the clarinet section—Plummer's empty chair.

As Mr. Helmholtz, red-faced and apologetic, retrieved the baton, he found himself unexpectedly moved by the symbol of the empty chair. No one else, he realized, no matter how untalented, could ever fill the last chair in the organization as well as Plummer had. He looked up to find many of the bandsmen contemplating the chair with him, as though they, too, sensed that something great, in a fantastic way, had disappeared, and that life would be a good bit duller on account of it.

During the ten minutes between the C Band and B Band sessions, Mr. Helmholtz hurried to his office and again tried to get in touch with the Sublime Chamberlain of the Knights of Kandahar, and was again told what he'd been told substantially several times during the night before and again in the morning.

"Lord knows where he's off to now. He was in for just a second, but went right out again. I gave him your name, so I expect he'll call you when he gets a minute. You're the drum gentleman, aren't you?"

"That's right—the drum gentleman."

The buzzers in the hall were sounding, marking the beginning of another class period. Mr. Helmholtz wanted to stay by the phone until he'd caught the Sublime Chamberlain and closed the deal, but the B Band was waiting—and after that it would be the A Band.

An inspiration came to him. He called Western Union, and sent a telegram to the man, offering fifty dollars for the drum, and requesting a reply collect.

But no reply came during B Band practice. Nor had one come by the halfway point of the A Band session. The bandsmen, a sensitive, high-strung lot, knew immediately that their director was on edge about something, and the rehearsal went badly. Mr. Helmholtz was growing so nervous about the drum that he stopped a march in the middle because of a small noise coming from the large double doors at one end of the room, where someone out-of-doors was apparently working on the lock.

"All right, all right, let's wait until the racket dies down so we can hear ourselves," he said.

At that moment, a student messenger handed him a telegram. Mr. Helmholtz beamed, tore open the envelope, and read:

DRUM SOLD STOP COULD YOU USE A STUFFED CAMEL ON WHEELS STOP.

The wooden doors opened with a shriek of rusty hinges, and a snappy autumn gust showered the band with leaves. Plummer stood in the great opening, winded and perspiring, harnessed to a drum on wheels that could have contained a dozen youngsters his size.

"I know this isn't challenge day," said Plummer, "but I thought you might make an exception in my case."

He walked in with splendid dignity, the huge apparatus grumbling along behind him.

Mr. Helmholtz rushed to meet him, and crushed Plummer's right hand between both of his. "Plummer, boy! You got it for us! Good boy! I'll pay you whatever you paid for it," he cried, and in his joy he added rashly, "and a nice little profit besides. Good boy!"

Plummer laughed modestly. "Sell it?" he said. "Heck fire, I'll give it to you when I grad-

uate," he said grandly. "All I want to do is play it in the A Band while I'm here."

"But, Plummer," said Mr. Helmholtz uneasily, "you don't know anything about drums."

"I'll practice hard," said Plummer reassuringly. He started to back his instrument into an aisle between the tubas and the trombones — like a man backing a trailer truck into a narrow alley — backing it toward the percussion section, where the amazed musicians were hastily making room.

"Now, just a minute," said Mr. Helmholtz, chuckling as though Plummer were joking, and knowing full well he wasn't. "There's more to drum playing than just lambasting[9] the thing whenever you take a notion to, you know. It takes years to be a drummer."

_____

9. **lambasting** (lăm-băst'ĭng): beating or pounding.

"Well," said Plummer cheerfully, "the quicker I get at it, the quicker I'll get good."

"What I meant was that I'm afraid you won't be quite ready for the A Band for a little while."

Plummer stopped his backing. "How long?" he asked suspiciously.

"Oh, sometime in your senior year, perhaps. Meanwhile, you could let the band have your drum to use until you're ready."

Mr. Helmholtz's skin began to itch all over as Plummer stared at him coldly, appraisingly. "Until hell freezes over?" Plummer said at last.

Mr. Helmholtz sighed resignedly. "I'm afraid that's about right." He shook his head sadly. "It's what I tried to tell you yesterday afternoon: nobody can do everything well, and we've all got to face up to our limitations. You're a fine boy, Plummer, but you'll never be a musician—not in a million years. The only thing to do is what we all have to do now and then: smile, shrug, and say, 'Well, that's just one of those things that's not for me.' "

Tears formed on the rims of Plummer's eyes, but went no farther. He walked slowly toward the doorway, with the drum tagging after him. He paused on the doorsill for one more wistful look at the A Band that would never have a chair for him. He smiled feebly and shrugged. "Some people have eight-foot drums," he said kindly, "and others don't, and that's just the way life is. You're a fine man, Mr. Helmholtz, but you'll never get this drum in a million years, because I'm going to give it to my mother for a coffee table."

"Plummer!" cried Mr. Helmholtz. His plaintive voice was drowned out by the rumble and rattle of the big drum as it followed its small master down the school's concrete driveway.

Mr. Helmholtz ran after him with a floundering, foot-slapping gait. Plummer and his drum had stopped at an intersection to wait for a light to change, and Mr. Helmholtz caught him there, and seized his arm. "We've got to have that drum," he panted. "How much do you want?"

"Smile," said Plummer. "Shrug! That's what I did." Plummer did it again. "See? So I can't get into the A Band, so you can't have the drum. Who cares? All part of the growing-up process."

"The situations aren't the same!" said Mr. Helmholtz furiously. "Not at all the same!"

"You're right," said Plummer, without a smile. "I'm growing up, and you're not."

The light changed, and Plummer left Mr. Helmholtz on the corner, stunned.

Mr. Helmholtz had to run after him again. "Plummer," he said sweetly, "you'll never be able to play it well."

"Rub it in," said Plummer, bitterly.

"But you're doing a beautiful job of pulling it, and if we got it, I don't think we'd ever be able to find anybody who could do it as well."

Plummer stopped, backed and turned the instrument on the narrow sidewalk with speed and hair-breadth precision, and headed back for Lincoln High School, skipping once to get in step with Mr. Helmholtz.

As they approached the school they both loved, they met and passed a group of youngsters from the C Band, who carried unscarred instrument cases and spoke self-consciously of music.

"Got a good bunch of kids coming up this year," said Plummer judiciously.[10] "All they need's a little seasoning."

---

10. **judiciously** (jōō-dǐsh′əs-lē): wisely and carefully, like a judge.

SEEKING MEANING

1. In this humorous story, Mr. Helmholtz has a problem: he wants to beat Johnstown High School in the next statewide band competition. What does he think he needs in order to accomplish this?

2. Plummer has a problem, too. Why does he want so much to be a member of the A Band?

3. How does Plummer plan to solve both problems?

4. Like all other comedies, this one ends with everyone happy and all problems solved. What compromise does Mr. Helmholtz finally propose? By accepting this offer, what will Plummer get?

5. Plummer may be "as tone-deaf as boiled cabbage," but he is certainly *not* a "no-talent kid." Tell what you think Plummer's talents are.

DEVELOPING VOCABULARY

Using Footnotes, Glossary, and Dictionary

There are several methods you can use to find the meaning of an unfamiliar word in this book. You can check to see whether it is footnoted, as the word *querulous* is on page 3. Footnotes, however, do not give all the possible meanings of a word. In this book, they tell what a word means in a particular sentence.

If an unfamiliar word isn't footnoted, it may be in the glossary in the back of this book. For example, you might not have known the meaning of the word *florid*, used on page 3 to describe the cornetist. The glossary defines *florid* in this way:

florid (flôr′ĭd) *adj.* Red-faced; ruddy.

The abbreviation *adj.* tells you that the word is an adjective. You will find a key to the pronunciations in the glossary at the back of this book.

A dictionary contains more information than either the footnotes or the glossary. A dictionary not only cites all the meanings a word has, but also tells something about the history of the word. For example, here is a complete dictionary entry for the word *florid* from *Webster's Ninth New Collegiate Dictionary.* (Like all dictionaries, this one uses its own symbols to indicate pronunciation.)

flor·id \′flȯr-əd, ′flär-\ *adj* [L *floridus* blooming, flowery, fr. *florēre*] (ca. 1656) **1 a** *obs*: covered with flowers **b** : excessively flowery in style : ORNATE **2** : tinged with red : RUDDY <a ~ complexion> **3** *archaic* : HEALTHY **4** : fully developed : manifesting a complete and typical clinical syndrome <the ~ stage of a disease> — **flo·rid·i·ty** \flə-′rid-ət-ē, flȯ-\ *n* — **flor·id·ly** \′flȯr-əd-lē, ′flär-\ *adv*

The information in brackets tells the history of the word. The abbreviation *L* stands for "Latin." What Latin word does *florid* come from? What is its *obsolete* (*obs*) meaning—that is, a meaning that is no longer in use? What is its *archaic*, or old-fashioned, meaning? What other meanings for *florid* are listed in this dictionary entry?

Use the glossary to find the pronunciations and meanings of the italicized words in the following quotations from "The No-Talent Kid." Compare these definitions with what a dictionary tells you.

> . . . or, in the case of the *percussion* section, to hit something . . . .
> . . . to brood inwardly over the defeat his band had *sustained* in June . . . .
> . . . the days of *discrimination* were over. . . .

ABOUT THE AUTHOR

Kurt Vonnegut (1922–   ) tried many jobs before he finally became a writer. He studied biochemistry in college, and was a police reporter, a public-relations man, and a teacher. During World War II, when he served in the infantry, he was captured by the Germans and sheltered underground in a slaughterhouse in Dresden. He was in Dresden when that city was firebombed by the Allied forces. Vonnegut used his war experiences as the basis for *Slaughterhouse-Five*, one of his best-known novels.

Vonnegut's writing has won him a strong following among college students. He has written another story about Mr. Helmholtz, called "The Kid Nobody Could Handle." He has also written many science-fiction stories. One of these that you might enjoy is "EPI-CAC," which is about a computer that falls in love with a mathematician.

Elizabeth Blackwell (1821–1910) was a real person. She seemed ordinary in every way except one—she wanted to do what no American woman had ever done before.

Elizabeth Blackwell   *Eve Merriam*

What will you do when you grow up,
nineteenth-century-young-lady?
Will you sew a fine seam and spoon dappled cream
under an apple tree shady?

Or will you be a teacher   5
in a dames' school°
and train the little dears
by the scientific rule
that mental activity
may strain   10
the delicate female brain;
therefore let
the curriculum stress music, French, and especially
etiquette:
teach how to set   15
a truly refined banquet.
Question One:
What kind of sauce
for the fish dish,
and pickle or lemon fork?   20
Quickly, students,
which should it be?

Now Elizabeth Blackwell, how about you?
Seamstress or teacher, which of the two?
You know there's not much else that a girl can do.   25
Don't mumble, Elizabeth. Learn to raise your head.
"I'm not very nimble with a needle and thread.
I could teach music—if I had to," she said,
"But I think I'd rather be a doctor instead."

6. **dames' school:** a school in which children are taught by a woman in her home.

"Is this some kind of joke?"   30
asked the proper menfolk.
"A woman be a doctor?
Not in our respectable day!
A doctor? An M.D.! Did you hear what she said?
She's clearly and indubitably out of her head!"   35

"Indeed, indeed, we are thoroughly agreed,"
hissed the ladies of society all laced in and prim,
"it's a scientific fact a doctor has to be a him.
Yes, sir,
'twould be against nature   40
if a doctor were a her."

Hibble hobble bibble bobble
widdle waddle wag
tsk tsk
    twit twit   45
       flip flap flutter
           mitter matter mutter
moan groan wail and rail
    Indecorous!
       Revolting!!   50
         A scandal
           A SIN
their voices pierced the air like a jabbing hat-pin.
But little miss Elizabeth wouldn't give in.

To medical schools she applied.   55
In vain.
And applied again
and again
and again
and one rejection offered this plan: 60
why not disguise herself as a man?
If she pulled back her hair, put on boots and pants,
she might attend medical lectures in France.
Although she wouldn't earn a degree,
they'd let her study anatomy.   65

Elizabeth refused to hide
her feminine pride.
She drew herself up tall
(all five feet one of her!)
and tried again.
And denied again.   70
The letters answering no
mounted like winter snow.

Until the day
when her ramrod will   75
finally had its way.
After the twenty-ninth try,
there came from Geneva, New York
the reply
of a blessed   80
Yes!

Geneva,
Geneva,
how sweet the sound;
Geneva,   85
Geneva,
sweet sanctuary found . . .

. . . and the ladies of Geneva
passing by her in the street
drew back their hoopskirts   90
so they wouldn't have to meet.

Psst, psst,
hiss, hiss
this sinister scarlet miss.
Avoid her, the hoyden, the hussy,   95
lest we all be contaminated!
If your glove so much as touch her, my dear,
best go get it fumigated!

When Elizabeth came to table,
their talking all would halt;   100
wouldn't so much as ask her
please to pass the salt.

In between classes
without a kind word,
Elizabeth dwelt   105
like a pale gray bird.

In a bare attic room
cold as stone,
far from her family,
huddled alone   110

studying, studying
throughout the night
warming herself
with an inner light:

don't let it darken,   115
the spark of fire;
keep it aglow,
that heart's desire:

the will to serve,
to help those in pain—   120
flickered and flared
and flickered again—

until
like a fairy tale
(except it was true!)   125
Elizabeth received
her honored due.

The perfect happy ending
came to pass:
Elizabeth graduated . . .   130
. . . at the head of her class.

And the ladies of Geneva
all rushed forward now to greet
that clever, dear Elizabeth,
so talented, so sweet!   135

Wasn't it glorious
she'd won first prize?

Elizabeth smiled
with cool gray eyes

and she wrapped her shawl   140
against the praise:

how soon there might come
more chilling days.

Turned to leave
without hesitating.   145

She was ready now,
and the world was waiting.

SEEKING MEANING

1. This poem seems light and humorous, but it tells a dramatic story about a woman who made an unusual decision when she was twenty-three years old. What did Elizabeth want to do? What did other people think she *should* do?

2. Like many heroic people, Elizabeth Blackwell had to go through her ordeal alone. What details in this poem describe how Elizabeth became an outcast?

3. In lines 113–114, the poet says that Elizabeth warmed herself "with an inner light." How do the next eight lines explain this light? What lines in the poem use "cold" to describe Elizabeth's experiences?

4. After Elizabeth graduated at the head of her class, the ladies of Geneva changed their minds and praised her. What do you think the poet means when she says that Elizabeth "wrapped her shawl / against the praise" (lines 140–141)?

DEVELOPING SKILLS IN READING

Responding to Words That Suggest Sounds
Eve Merriam uses several words that echo or suggest sounds. For example, in line 37 she says that the society ladies "hissed" as they mocked Elizabeth's desire to be a doctor. The word *hissed* suggests that the ladies are expressing disapproval, perhaps something like a crowd hissing at an umpire it doesn't like. *Hissed* also might suggest the sound a snake makes when it rears to strike. You get a picture of the society ladies acting like hissing snakes, trying to strike at Elizabeth. What else could these angry hissing ladies remind you of?

What words in lines 92–93 echo the sounds made by the Geneva ladies?

In lines 42–48 the poet uses a string of words to suggest sounds, and movements and gestures as well. What kind of talk or movements do you think the poet is suggesting when she uses such expressions as "hibble hobble," "widdle waddle," "tsk tsk," and "flip flap flutter"?

DEVELOPING SKILLS OF EXPRESSION

Giving a Dramatic Reading
Most poems are only half alive until they are read aloud. Prepare "Elizabeth Blackwell" for a dramatic reading in your class. How many voices will be necessary to dramatize this poem, in addition to the voices of the narrator and of Elizabeth Blackwell herself? In a dramatic reading, each voice in the poem should have a distinct character. Which voices will sound disapproving? Will some sound stuffy and dull? Will some sound mean? Will any voice sound quiet and determined?

ABOUT THE AUTHOR

Eve Merriam (1916–   ) has written poetry, plays, song lyrics, and fiction for children and adults. One of her unusual books is *The Inner City Mother Goose,* a collection of verses that imitate the old nursery rhymes, using urban settings and characters. Some of the rhymes in this collection are called "Sing a Song of Subways," "You'll Find Mice," and "Twelve Rooftops Leaping."

Now at last he knew how the fish must feel when it is dragged to its doom. Now he knew.

The Sea Devil

Arthur Gordon

The man came out of the house and stood quite still, listening. Behind him, the lights glowed in the cheerful room, the books were neat and orderly in their cases, the radio talked importantly to itself. In front of him, the bay stretched dark and silent, one of the countless lagoons that border the coast where Florida thrusts its green thumb deep into the tropics.

It was late in September. The night was breathless; summer's dead hand still lay heavy on the land. The man moved forward six paces and stood on the sea wall. He dropped his cigarette and noted where the tiny spark hissed and went out. The tide was beginning to ebb.

Somewhere out in the blackness a mullet jumped and fell back with a sullen splash. Heavy with roe,[1] they were jumping less often, now. They would not take a hook, but a practiced eye could see the swirls they made in the glassy water. In the dark of the moon, a

---

1. **roe:** fish eggs.

skilled man with a cast net might take half a dozen in an hour's work. And a big mullet makes a meal for a family.

The man turned abruptly and went into the garage, where his cast net hung. He was in his late twenties, wide-shouldered and strong. He did not have to fish for a living, or even for food. He was a man who worked with his head, not with his hands. But he liked to go casting alone at night.

He liked the loneliness and the labor of it. He liked the clean taste of salt when he gripped the edge of the net with his teeth as a cast netter must. He liked the arching flight of sixteen pounds of lead and linen against the starlight, and the weltering crash[2] of the net into the unsuspecting water. He liked the harsh tug of the retrieving rope around his wrist, and the way the net came alive when the cast was true, and the thud of captured fish on the floor boards of the skiff.

He liked all that because he found in it a reality that seemed to be missing from his twentieth-century job and from his daily life. He liked being the hunter, skilled and solitary and elemental. There was no conscious cruelty in the way he felt. It was the way things had been in the beginning.

The man lifted the net down carefully and lowered it into a bucket. He put a paddle beside the bucket. Then he went into the house. When he came out, he was wearing swimming trunks and a pair of old tennis shoes. Nothing else.

The skiff, flat-bottomed, was moored off the sea wall. He would not go far, he told himself. Just to the tumbledown dock half a mile away. Mullet had a way of feeding around old pilings after dark. If he moved quietly, he might pick up two or three in one cast close to the dock. And maybe a couple of others on the way down or back.

He shoved off and stood motionless for a moment, letting his eyes grow accustomed to the dark. Somewhere out in the channel a porpoise blew with a sound like steam escaping. The man smiled a little; porpoises were his friends. Once, fishing in the Gulf, he had seen the charter-boat captain reach overside and gaff[3] a baby porpoise through the sinewy part of the tail. He had hoisted it aboard, had dropped it into the bait well, where it thrashed around, puzzled and unhappy. And the mother had swum alongside the boat and under the boat and around the boat, nudging the stout planking with her back, slapping it with her tail, until the man felt sorry for her and made the captain let the baby porpoise go.

He took the net from the bucket, slipped the noose in the retrieving rope over his wrist, pulled the slipknot tight. It was an old net, but still serviceable; he had rewoven the rents[4] made by underwater snags. He coiled the thirty-foot rope carefully, making sure there were no kinks. A tangled rope, he knew, would spoil any cast.

The basic design of the net had not changed in three thousand years. It was a mesh circle with a diameter of fourteen feet. It measured close to fifteen yards around the circumference and could, if thrown perfectly, blanket a hundred fifty square feet of sea water. In the center of this radial trap[5] was a small iron collar where the retrieving rope met the twenty-three separate drawstrings leading to the outer rim of the net. Along this rim,

2. **weltering crash:** a crash that causes a great disturbance in the water.

3. **gaff:** spear.
4. **rents:** holes.
5. **radial** (rā′dē-əl) **trap:** The drawstrings of the net lead out from a small iron collar, like spokes from the center of a wheel.

spaced an inch and a half apart, were the heavy lead sinkers.

The man raised the iron collar until it was a foot above his head. The net hung soft and pliant and deadly. He shook it gently, making sure that the drawstrings were not tangled, that the sinkers were hanging true. Then he eased it down and picked up the paddle.

The night was black as a witch's cat; the stars looked fuzzy and dim. Down to the southward, the lights of a causeway made a yellow necklace across the sky. To the man's left were the tangled roots of a mangrove swamp; to his right, the open waters of the bay. Most of it was fairly shallow, but there were channels eight feet deep. The man could not see the old dock, but he knew where it was. He pulled the paddle quietly through the water, and the phosphorescence[6] glowed and died.

For five minutes he paddled. Then, twenty feet ahead of the skiff, a mullet jumped. A big fish, close to three pounds. For a moment it hung in the still air, gleaming dully. Then it vanished. But the ripples marked the spot, and where there was one there were often others.

The man stood up quickly. He picked up the coiled rope, and with the same hand grasped the net at a point four feet below the iron collar. He raised the skirt to his mouth, gripped it strongly with his teeth. He slid his free hand as far as it would go down the circumference of the net, so that he had three points of contact with the mass of cordage and metal. He made sure his feet were planted solidly. Then he waited, feeling the tension that is older than the human race, the fierce exhilaration of the hunter at the moment of ambush, the atavistic desire[7] to capture and kill and ultimately consume.

A mullet swirled, ahead and to the left. The man swung the heavy net back, twisting his body and bending his knees so as to get more upward thrust. He shot it forward, letting go simultaneously with rope hand and with teeth, holding a fraction of a second longer with the other hand so as to give the net the necessary spin, impart the centrifugal force[8] that would make it flare into a circle. The skiff ducked sideways, but he kept his balance. The net fell with a splash.

The man waited for five seconds. Then he began to retrieve it, pulling in a series of sharp jerks so that the drawstrings would gather the net inward, like a giant fist closing on this segment of the teeming sea. He felt the net quiver, and he knew it was not empty. He swung it, dripping, over the gunwale,[9] saw the broad silver side of the mullet quivering, saw too the gleam of a smaller fish. He looked closely to make sure no stingray[10] was hidden in the mesh, then raised the iron collar and shook the net out. The mullet fell with a thud and flapped wildly. The other victim was an angelfish, beautifully marked, but too small to keep. The man picked it up gently and dropped it overboard. He coiled the rope, took up the paddle. He would cast no more until he came to the dock.

The skiff moved on. At last, ten feet apart, a

---

6. **phosphorescence** (fos'fə-rĕs'əns): glowing light.

7. **atavistic** (ăt'ə-vĭs'tĭk) **desire:** a desire that his earliest ancestors would have had.

8. **centrifugal** (sĕn-trĭf'yə-gəl) **force:** the force that makes an object moving in a circle (here, the net) move away from the center of the circle (here, the man).

9. **gunwale** (gŭn'əl): the upper edge of the side of the boat.

10. **stingray:** a fish with a long, whiplike tail, which has one or more dangerous spines.

pair of stakes rose up gauntly out of the night. Barnacle-encrusted, they once had marked the approach from the main channel. The man guided the skiff between them, then put the paddle down softly. He stood up, reached for the net, tightened the noose around his wrist. From here he could drift down upon the dock. He could see it now, a ruined skeleton in the starshine. Beyond it a mullet jumped and fell back with a flat, liquid sound. The man raised the edge of the net, put it between his teeth. He would not cast at a single swirl, he decided; he would wait until he saw two or three close together. The skiff was barely moving. He felt his muscles tense themselves, awaiting the signal from the brain.

Behind him in the channel he heard the porpoise blow again, nearer now. He frowned in the darkness. If the porpoise chose to fish this area, the mullet would scatter and vanish. There was no time to lose.

A school of sardines surfaced suddenly, skittering along like drops of mercury. Something, perhaps the shadow of the skiff, had frightened them. The old dock loomed very close. A mullet broke water just too far away; then another, nearer. The man marked[11] the spreading ripples and decided to wait no longer.

He swung back the net, heavier now that it was wet. He had to turn his head, but out of the corner of his eye he saw two swirls in the black water just off the starboard bow.[12] They were about eight feet apart, and they had the sluggish oily look that marks the presence of something big just below the surface. His conscious mind had no time to function, but instinct told him that the net was wide enough to cover both swirls if he could alter

the direction of his cast. He could not halt the swing, but he shifted his feet slightly and made the cast off balance. He saw the net shoot forward, flare into an oval, and drop just where he wanted it.

Then the sea exploded in his face. In a frenzy of spray, a great horned thing shot like a huge bat out of the water. The man saw the mesh of his net etched against the mottled blackness of its body and he knew, in the split second in which thought was still possible, that those twin swirls had been made not by two mullet, but by the wing tips of the giant ray of the Gulf Coast, *Manta birostris*, also known as clam cracker, devil ray, sea devil.

The man gave a hoarse cry. He tried to claw the slipknot off his wrist, but there was no time. The quarter-inch line snapped taut. He shot over the side of the skiff as if he had roped a runaway locomotive. He hit the water head first and seemed to bounce once. He plowed a blinding furrow for perhaps ten yards. Then the line went slack as the sea devil jumped again. It was not the full-grown

---

11. **marked:** here, noticed.
12. **starboard bow:** the right-hand side of the front of the boat.

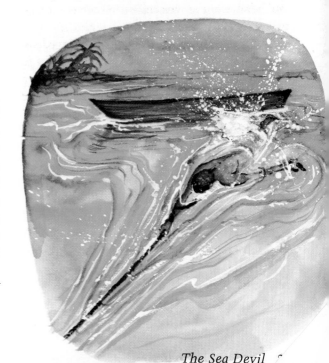

manta of the deep Gulf, but it was close to nine feet from tip to tip and it weighed over a thousand pounds. Up into the air it went, pearl-colored underbelly gleaming as it twisted in a frantic effort to dislodge the clinging thing that had fallen upon it. Up into the starlight, a monstrous survival from the dawn of time.

The water was less than four feet deep. Sobbing and choking, the man struggled for a foothold on the slimy bottom. Sucking in great gulps of air, he fought to free himself from the rope. But the slipknot was jammed deep into his wrist; he might as well have tried to loosen a circle of steel.

The ray came down with a thunderous splash and drove forward again. The flexible net followed every movement, impeding it hardly at all. The man weighed a hundred seventy-five pounds, and he was braced for the shock, and he had the desperate strength that comes from looking into the blank eyes of death. It was useless. His arm straightened out with a jerk that seemed to dislocate his shoulder; his feet shot out from under him; his head went under again. Now at last he knew how the fish must feel when the line tightens and drags him toward the alien element that is his doom. Now he knew.

Desperately he dug the fingers of his free hand into the ooze, felt them dredge a futile channel through broken shells and the ribbonlike sea grasses. He tried to raise his head, but could not get it clear. Torrents of spray choked him as the ray plunged toward deep water.

His eyes were of no use to him in the foam-streaked blackness. He closed them tight, and at once an insane sequence of pictures flashed through his mind. He saw his wife sitting in their living room, reading, waiting calmly for his return. He saw the mullet he had just caught, gasping its life away on the floorboards of the skiff. He saw the cigarette he had flung from the sea wall touch the water and expire with a tiny hiss. He saw all these things and many others simultaneously in his mind as his body fought silently and tenaciously for its existence. His hand touched something hard and closed on it in a death grip, but it was only the sharp-edged helmet of a horseshoe crab, and after an instant he let it go.

He had been underwater perhaps fifteen seconds now, and something in his brain told him quite calmly that he could last another forty or fifty and then the red flashes behind his eyes would merge into darkness, and the water would pour into his lungs in one sharp painful shock, and he would be finished.

This thought spurred him to a desperate effort. He reached up and caught his pinioned wrist with his free hand. He doubled up his knees to create more drag. He thrashed his body madly, like a fighting fish, from side to side. This did not disturb the ray, but now one of the great wings tore through the mesh, and the net slipped lower over the fins projecting like horns from below the nightmare head, and the sea devil jumped again.

And once more the man was able to get his feet on the bottom and his head above water, and he saw ahead of him the pair of ancient stakes that marked the approach to the channel. He knew that if he was dragged much beyond those stakes he would be in eight feet of water, and the ray would go down to hug the bottom as rays always do, and then no power on earth could save him. So in the moment of respite[13] that was granted him, he flung himself toward them.

For a moment he thought his captor yielded a bit. Then the ray moved off again, but more slowly now, and for a few yards the man was able to keep his feet on the bottom. Twice he

---

13. **respite** (rĕs′pĭt): relief.

hurled himself back against the rope with all his strength, hoping that something would break. But nothing broke. The mesh of the net was ripped and torn, but the draw lines were strong, and the stout perimeter cord threaded through the sinkers was even stronger.

The man could feel nothing now in his trapped hand, it was numb; but the ray could feel the powerful lunges of the unknown thing that was trying to restrain it. It drove its great wings against the unyielding water and forged ahead, dragging the man and pushing a sullen wave in front of it.

The man had swung as far as he could toward the stakes. He plunged toward one and missed it by inches. His feet slipped and he went down on his knees. Then the ray swerved sharply and the second stake came right at him. He reached out with his free hand and caught it.

He caught it just above the surface, six or eight inches below high-water mark. He felt the razor-sharp barnacles bite into his hand, collapse under the pressure, drive their tiny slime-covered shell splinters deep into his flesh. He felt the pain, and he welcomed it, and he made his fingers into an iron claw that would hold until the tendons were severed or the skin was shredded from the bone. The ray felt the pressure increase with a jerk that stopped it dead in the water. For a moment all was still as the tremendous forces came into equilibrium.[14]

Then the net slipped again, and the perimeter cord came down over the sea devil's eyes, blinding it momentarily. The great ray settled to the bottom and braced its wings against the mud and hurled itself forward and upward.

The stake was only a four-by-four of creosoted[15] pine, and it was old. Ten thousand tides

---

14. **equilibrium** (ē′kwə-lĭb′rē-əm): balance.
15. **creosoted** (krē′ə-sōt′ĭd): treated with creosote, a preservative.

had swirled around it. Worms had bored; parasites had clung. Under the crust of barnacles it still had some heart left, but not enough. The man's grip was five feet above the floor of the bay; the leverage was too great. The stake snapped off at its base.

The ray lunged upward, dragging the man and the useless timber. The man had his lungs full of air, but when the stake snapped he thought of expelling the air and inhaling the water so as to have it finished quickly. He thought of this, but he did not do it. And then, just at the channel's edge, the ray met the porpoise, coming in.

The porpoise had fed well this night and was in no hurry, but it was a methodical creature and it intended to make a sweep around the old dock before the tide dropped too low. It had no quarrel with any ray, but it feared no fish in the sea, and when the great black shadow came rushing blindly and unavoidably, it rolled fast and struck once with its massive horizontal tail.

The blow descended on the ray's flat body with a sound like a pistol shot. It would have broken a buffalo's back, and even the sea devil was half stunned. It veered wildly and turned back toward shallow water. It passed within ten feet of the man, face down in the water. It slowed and almost stopped, wing tips moving faintly, gathering strength for another rush.

The man had heard the tremendous slap of the great mammal's tail and the snorting gasp as it plunged away. He felt the line go slack again, and he raised his dripping face, and he reached for the bottom with his feet. He found it, but now the water was up to his neck. He plucked at the noose once more with his lacerated hand, but there was no strength in his fingers. He felt the tension come back into the line as the ray began to move again, and for half a second he was tempted to throw himself backward and fight

as he had been doing, pitting his strength against the vastly superior strength of the brute.

But the acceptance of imminent death had done something to his brain. It had driven out the fear, and with the fear had gone the panic. He could think now, and he knew with absolute certainty that if he was to make any use of this last chance that had been given him, it would have to be based on the one faculty that had carried man to his preeminence above all beasts, the faculty of reason. Only by using his brain could he possibly survive, and he called on his brain for a solution, and his brain responded. It offered him one.

He did not know whether his body still had the strength to carry out the brain's commands, but he began to swim forward, toward the ray that was still moving hesitantly away from the channel. He swam forward, feeling the rope go slack as he gained on the creature.

Ahead of him he saw the one remaining stake, and he made himself swim faster until he was parallel with the ray and the rope trailed behind both of them in a deep U. He swam with a surge of desperate energy that came from nowhere, so that he was slightly in the lead as they came to the stake. He passed on one side of it; the ray was on the other.

Then the man took one last deep breath, and he went down under the black water until he was sitting on the bottom of the bay. He put one foot over the line so that it passed under his bent knee. He drove both his heels into the mud, and he clutched the slimy grass with his bleeding hand, and he waited for the tension to come again.

The ray passed on the other side of the stake, moving faster now. The rope grew taut again, and it began to drag the man back toward the stake. He held his prisoned wrist close to the bottom, under his knee, and he prayed that the stake would not break. He felt the rope vibrate as the barnacles bit into it. He did not know whether the rope would crush the barnacles, or whether the barnacles would cut the rope. All he knew was that in five seconds or less he would be dragged into the stake and cut to ribbons if he tried to hold on, or drowned if he didn't.

He felt himself sliding slowly, and then faster, and suddenly the ray made a great leap forward, and the rope burned around the base of the stake, and the man's foot hit it hard. He kicked himself backward with his remaining strength, and the rope parted, and he was free.

He came slowly to the surface. Thirty feet away the sea devil made one tremendous leap and disappeared into the darkness. The man raised his wrist and looked at the frayed length of rope dangling from it. Twenty inches, perhaps. He lifted his other hand and felt the hot blood start instantly, but he didn't care. He put his hand on the stake above the barnacles and held on to the good, rough, honest wood. He heard a strange noise, and realized that it was himself, sobbing.

High above, there was a droning sound, and looking up he saw the nightly plane from New Orleans inbound for Tampa. Calm and serene, it sailed, symbol of man's proud mastery over nature. Its lights winked red and green for a moment; then it was gone.

Slowly, painfully, the man began to move through the placid water. He came to the skiff at last and climbed into it. The mullet, still alive, slapped convulsively with its tail. The man reached down with his torn hand, picked up the mullet, let it go.

He began to work on the slipknot doggedly with his teeth. His mind was almost a blank, but not quite. He knew one thing. He knew he would do no more casting alone at night. Not in the dark of the moon. No, not he.

SEEKING MEANING

1. The man in this story doesn't need to fish for a living, or even for food. Why does he go casting alone at night?

2. This story is about a fisherman who becomes the "fish." How does the man become trapped by the sea devil?

3. Like a fighting fish, the man at first uses his strength to try to save himself. Why is his strength useless against the monster?

4. The porpoise plays a part in saving the man. How does the man feel about porpoises? How does the porpoise give the man one last chance?

5. The man finally realizes that only his intelligence can save him. What solution does his reason offer him?

6. After his struggle is over, the man looks up at the sky and sees a plane, which is described in this way: "Calm and serene, it sailed, symbol of man's proud mastery over nature." What is the man's condition as he looks up at the plane from the water? Is he calm and serene? Do you think this man believes that human beings have complete "mastery over nature"? Explain your answer.

7. Why do you think the man releases the mullet after his ordeal?

DEVELOPING SKILLS IN READING

Finding the Main Idea of the Story

"The Sea Devil" is an exciting story written for entertainment. But there are clues that the author also wants to share a serious idea with us.

Here is a key passage from "The Sea Devil." Which sentence or phrase in this paragraph would you say states the main idea of this story? Try to restate this idea in your own words.

But the acceptance of imminent death had done something to his brain. It had driven out the fear, and with the fear had gone the panic. He could think now, and he knew with absolute certainty that if he was to make any use of this last chance that had been given him, it would have to be based on the one faculty that had carried man to his preeminence above all beasts, the faculty of reason. Only by using his brain could he possibly survive, and he called on his brain for a solution, and his brain responded. It offered him one.

DEVELOPING VOCABULARY

Finding the Meanings of Prefixes and Suffixes

You can figure out the meanings of many unfamiliar words if you know the meanings of some common prefixes and suffixes. A prefix is a word element added at the beginning of a word to change its meaning. The prefix *un-*, for example, means "not." When the author of this story says that the water is *unyielding*, what does he mean?

A suffix is a word element added at the end of a word to change its meaning. The suffix *-less* means "without." When the author says that the man stood *motionless*, what does he mean?

In the following lists of words from the story, the prefixes and suffixes are italicized. What meaning does each prefix or suffix add to the rest of the word? Use your dictionary to find out.

breath*less*	*in*sane	ribbon*like*
cheer*ful*	mast*ery*	slugg*ish*
*dis*locate	*re*woven	thunder*ous*

DEVELOPING SKILLS OF EXPRESSION

Using Specific Details in Description

Here is how the sea devil in this story is described:

In a frenzy of spray, a great horned thing shot like a huge bat out of the water. The man saw the mesh of his net etched against the mottled blackness of its body and he knew, in the split second in which thought was still possible, that those twin swirls had been made not by two mullet, but by the wing tips of the giant ray of the Gulf Coast, *Manta birostris,* also known as clam cracker, devil ray, sea devil. . . . It was not the full-grown manta of the deep Gulf, but it was close to nine feet from tip to tip and it weighed over a thousand pounds. Up into the air it went, pearl-colored underbelly gleaming as it twisted in a frantic effort to dislodge the clinging thing that had fallen upon it. Up into the starlight, a monstrous survival from the dawn of time.

What is the ray compared to? What are its colors? What is its scientific name? What are its "popular" names? How big is it?

Using this passage as a model, write several sentences describing an animal, either a "monstrous" animal or a domestic animal. Give the reader specific details about its appearance and about its movements. Does it have distinctive colors or sounds? Tell what names it is known by, both its scientific names and its "popular" names.

Born into slavery in Dorchester County, Maryland, she was first called by her baby name, Minty. When she showed her courage at the age of thirteen by helping a man escape, they called her by her proper name, Harriet. After this young woman made the perilous journey out of slavery herself, she returned to conduct others along the Underground Railroad to freedom. She proved her right to another name. Now they called her Moses.

  This account is from the biography called Harriet Tubman: Conductor on the Underground Railroad.

They Called Her Moses

Ann Petry

Along the Eastern Shore of Maryland, in Dorchester County, in Caroline County, the masters kept hearing whispers about the man named Moses, who was running off slaves. At first they did not believe in his existence. The stories about him were fantastic, unbelievable. Yet they watched for him. They offered rewards for his capture.

They never saw him. Now and then they heard whispered rumors to the effect that he was in the neighborhood. The woods were searched. The roads were watched. There was never anything to indicate his whereabouts. But a few days afterward, a goodly number of slaves would be gone from the plantation. Neither the master nor the overseer had heard or seen anything unusual in the quarter. Sometimes one or the other would vaguely remember having heard a whippoorwill call somewhere in the woods, close by, late at night. Though it was the wrong season for whippoorwills.

Sometimes the masters thought they had heard the cry of a hoot owl, repeated, and would remember having thought that the intervals between the low moaning cry were wrong, that it had been repeated four times in succession instead of three. There was never anything more than that to suggest that all was not well in the quarter. Yet when morning came, they invariably discovered that a group of the finest slaves had taken to their heels.

Unfortunately, the discovery was almost always made on a Sunday. Thus a whole day was lost before the machinery of pursuit could be set in motion. The posters offering rewards for the fugitives could not be printed until Monday. The men who made a living hunting for runaway slaves were out of reach, off in the woods with their dogs and their guns, in pursuit of four-footed game, or they were in camp meetings saying their prayers with their wives and families beside them.

Harriet Tubman could have told them that there was far more involved in this matter of running off slaves than signaling the would-be runaways by imitating the call of a whippoorwill, or a hoot owl, far more involved than a matter of waiting for a clear night when the North Star was visible.

In December, 1851, when she started out with the band of fugitives that she planned to take to Canada, she had been in the vicinity of the plantation for days, planning the trip, carefully selecting the slaves that she would take with her.

She had announced her arrival in the quarter by singing the forbidden spiritual[1]— "Go down, Moses, way down to Egypt Land" — singing it softly outside the door of a slave cabin, late at night. The husky voice was beautiful even when it was barely more than a murmur borne on the wind.

Once she had made her presence known, word of her coming spread from cabin to cabin. The slaves whispered to each other, ear to mouth, mouth to ear, "Moses is here." "Moses has come." "Get ready. Moses is back again." The ones who had agreed to go North with her put ashcake and salt herring in an old bandanna, hastily tied it into a bundle, and then waited patiently for the signal that meant it was time to start.

There were eleven in this party, including one of her brothers and his wife. It was the largest group that she had ever conducted, but she was determined that more and more slaves should know what freedom was like.

She had to take them all the way to Canada.

The Fugitive Slave Law[2] was no longer a great many incomprehensible words written down on the country's lawbooks. The new law had become a reality. It was Thomas Sims, a boy, picked up on the streets of Boston at night and shipped back to Georgia. It was Jerry and Shadrach, arrested and jailed with no warning.

She had never been in Canada. The route beyond Philadelphia was strange to her. But she could not let the runaways who accompanied her know this. As they walked along she told them stories of her own first flight, she kept painting vivid word pictures of what it would be like to be free.

But there were so many of them this time. She knew moments of doubt when she was half afraid, and kept looking back over her shoulder, imagining that she heard the sound of pursuit. They would certainly be pursued. Eleven of them. Eleven thousand dollars' worth of flesh and bone and muscle that belonged to Maryland planters. If they were caught, the eleven runaways would be whipped and sold South, but she — she would probably be hanged.

They tried to sleep during the day but they never could wholly relax into sleep. She could tell by the positions they assumed, by their restless movements. And they walked at night. Their progress was slow. It took them three nights of walking to reach the first stop. She had told them about the place where they would stay, promising warmth and good food, holding these things out to them as an incentive to keep going.

---

1. **forbidden spiritual:** In 1831, a slave named Nat Turner led an unsuccessful uprising in Virginia. Turner used the Biblical account of the Israelites' escape from Egypt to encourage the rebellion. After this, slaves were forbidden to sing certain spirituals. It was feared that the songs about the Israelites' march to freedom would encourage more uprisings.

2. **Fugitive Slave Law:** part of the Compromise of 1850. According to this law, escaped slaves, even if found in free states, could be forced to return to their masters. Thus, the fugitives were not really safe until they reached Canada. Anyone caught aiding a fugitive slave could be punished with six months in prison and a thousand-dollar fine.

When she knocked on the door of a farm-house, a place where she and her parties of runaways had always been welcome, always been given shelter and plenty to eat, there was no answer. She knocked again, softly. A voice from within said, "Who is it?" There was fear in the voice.

She knew instantly from the sound of the voice that there was something wrong. She said, "A friend with friends," the password on the Underground Railroad.

The door opened, slowly. The man who stood in the doorway looked at her coldly, looked with unconcealed astonishment and fear at the eleven disheveled runaways who were standing near her. Then he shouted, "Too many, too many. It's not safe. My place was searched last week. It's not safe!" and slammed the door in her face.

She turned away from the house, frowning. She had promised her passengers food and rest and warmth, and instead of that there would be hunger and cold and more walking over the frozen ground. Somehow she would have to instill courage into these eleven people, most of them strangers, would have to feed them on hope and bright dreams of freedom instead of the fried pork and corn bread and milk she had promised them.

They stumbled along behind her, half dead for sleep, and she urged them on, though she was as tired and as discouraged as they were. She had never been in Canada, but she kept painting wondrous word pictures of what it would be like. She managed to dispel their fear of pursuit, so that they would not become hysterical, panic-stricken. Then she had to bring some of the fear back, so that they would stay awake and keep walking though they drooped with sleep.

Yet during the day, when they lay down deep in a thicket, they never really slept, because if a twig snapped or the wind sighed in the branches of a pine tree, they jumped to their feet, afraid of their own shadows, shivering and shaking. It was very cold, but they dared not make fires because someone would see the smoke and wonder about it.

She kept thinking, eleven of them. Eleven thousand dollars' worth of slaves. And she had to take them all the way to Canada. Sometimes she told them about Thomas Garrett, in Wilmington. She said he was their friend even though he did not know them. He was the friend of all fugitives. He called them God's poor. He was a Quaker and his speech was a little different from that of other people. His clothing was different, too. He wore the wide-brimmed hat that the Quakers wear.

She said that he had thick white hair, soft, almost like a baby's, and the kindest eyes she had ever seen. He was a big man and strong, but he had never used his strength to harm anyone, always to help people. He would give all of them a new pair of shoes. Everybody. He always did. Once they reached his house in Wilmington, they would be safe. He would see to it that they were.

She described the house where he lived, told them about the store where he sold shoes. She said he kept a pail of milk and a loaf of bread in the drawer of his desk so that he would have food ready at hand for any of God's poor who should suddenly appear before him, fainting with hunger. There was a hidden room in the store. A whole wall swung open, and behind it was a room where he could hide fugitives. On the wall there were shelves filled with small boxes—boxes of shoes—so that you would never guess that the wall actually opened.

While she talked, she kept watching them. They did not believe her. She could tell by their expressions. They were thinking, New shoes, Thomas Garrett, Quaker, Wilmington —what foolishness was this? Who knew if she

told the truth? Where was she taking them anyway?

That night they reached the next stop—a farm that belonged to a German. She made the runaways take shelter behind trees at the edge of the fields before she knocked at the door. She hesitated before she approached the door, thinking, suppose that he, too, should refuse shelter, suppose—— Then she thought, Lord, I'm going to hold steady on to You and You've got to see me through—and knocked softly.

She heard the familiar guttural[3] voice say, "Who's there?"

She answered quickly, "A friend with friends."

He opened the door and greeted her warmly. "How many this time?" he asked.

"Eleven," she said and waited, doubting, wondering.

He said, "Good. Bring them in."

He and his wife fed them in the lamplit kitchen, their faces glowing, as they offered food and more food, urging them to eat, saying there was plenty for everybody, have more milk, have more bread, have more meat.

They spent the night in the warm kitchen. They really slept, all that night and until dusk the next day. When they left, it was with reluctance. They had all been warm and safe and well-fed. It was hard to exchange the security offered by that clean, warm kitchen for the darkness and the cold of a December night.

Harriet had found it hard to leave the warmth and friendliness, too. But she urged them on. For a while, as they walked, they seemed to carry in them a measure of contentment; some of the serenity and the cleanliness of that big, warm kitchen lingered on inside them. But as they walked farther and farther away from the warmth and light, the cold and the darkness entered into them. They fell silent, sullen, suspicious. She waited for the moment when some one of them would turn mutinous. It did not happen that night.

Two nights later she was aware that the feet behind her were moving slower and slower. She heard the irritability in their voices, knew that soon someone would refuse to go on.

She started talking about William Still and the Philadelphia Vigilance Committee.[4] No one commented. No one asked any questions. She told them the story of William and Ellen Craft and how they escaped from Georgia. Ellen was so fair that she looked as though she were white, and so she dressed up in a man's clothing and she looked like a wealthy young planter. Her husband, William, who was dark, played the role of her slave. Thus they traveled from Macon, Georgia, to Philadelphia, riding on the trains, staying at the finest hotels. Ellen pretended to be very ill— her right arm was in a sling, and her right hand was bandaged, because she was supposed to have rheumatism. Thus she avoided having to sign the register at the hotels, for she could not read or write. They finally arrived safely in Philadelphia, and then went on to Boston.

No one said anything. Not one of them seemed to have heard her.

She told them about Frederick Douglass, the most famous of the escaped slaves, of his

---

3. **guttural** (gŭt′ər-əl): a reference to the man's German language, which uses many guttural sounds—that is, sounds produced in the back of the throat.

4. **Philadelphia Vigilance Committee:** a committee of citizens who offered assistance to slaves who had escaped. William Still, a free black man, was secretary of the Committee.

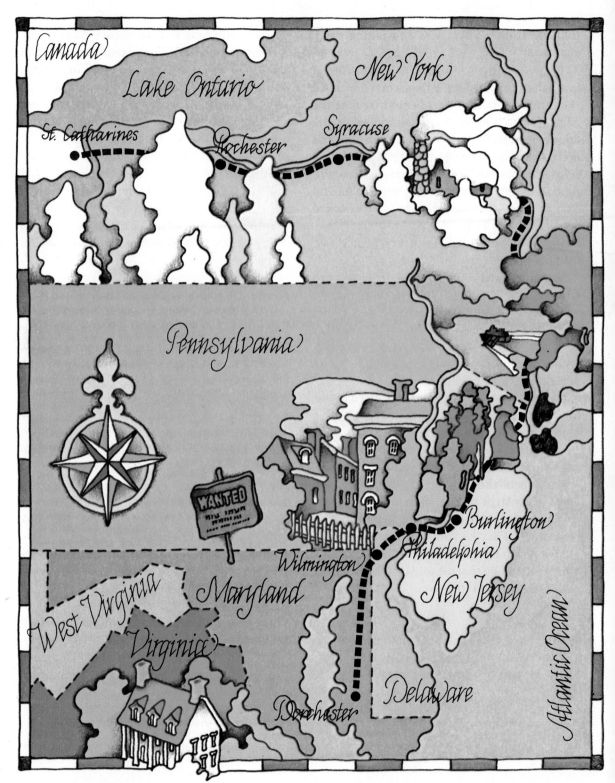

eloquence, of his magnificent appearance. Then she told them of her own first vain effort at running away, evoking the memory of that miserable life she had led as a child, reliving it for a moment in the telling.

But they had been tired too long, hungry too long, afraid too long, footsore too long. One of them suddenly cried out in despair, "Let me go back. It is better to be a slave than to suffer like this in order to be free."

She carried a gun with her on these trips. She had never used it—except as a threat. Now as she aimed it, she experienced a feeling of guilt, remembering that time, years ago, when she had prayed for the death of Edward Brodas, the Master, and then not too long afterward had heard that great wailing cry that came from the throats of the field hands, and knew from the sound that the Master was dead.

One of the runaways said, again, "Let me go back. Let me go back," and stood still, and then turned around and said, over his shoulder, "I am going back."

She lifted the gun, aimed it at the despairing slave. She said, "Go on with us or die." The husky low-pitched voice was grim.

He hesitated for a moment and then he joined the others. They started walking again. She tried to explain to them why none of them could go back to the plantation. If a runaway returned, he would turn traitor, the master and the overseer would force him to turn traitor. The returned slave would disclose the stopping places, the hiding places, the cornstacks they had used with the full knowledge of the owner of the farm, the name of the German farmer who had fed them and sheltered them. These people who had risked their own security to help runaways would be ruined, fined, imprisoned.

She said, "We got to go free or die. And freedom's not bought with dust."

This time she told them about the long agony of the Middle Passage on the old slave ships, about the black horror of the holds, about the chains and the whips. They too knew these stories. But she wanted to remind them of the long, hard way they had come, about the long hard way they had yet to go. She told them about Thomas Sims, the boy picked up on the streets of Boston and sent back to Georgia. She said when they got him back to Savannah, got him in prison there, they whipped him until a doctor who was standing by watching said, "You will kill him if you strike him again!" His master said, "Let him die!"

Thus she forced them to go on. Sometimes she thought she had become nothing but a voice speaking in the darkness, cajoling, urging, threatening. Sometimes she told them things to make them laugh, sometimes she sang to them, and heard the eleven voices behind her blending softly with hers, and then she knew that for the moment all was well with them.

She gave the impression of being a short, muscular, indomitable woman who could never be defeated. Yet at any moment she was liable to be seized by one of those curious fits of sleep, which might last for a few minutes or for hours.[5]

Even on this trip, she suddenly fell asleep in the woods. The runaways, ragged, dirty, hungry, cold, did not steal the gun, as they might have, and set off by themselves, or turn back. They sat on the ground near her and waited patiently until she awakened. They had come

---

5. **sleep . . . hours:** When Harriet was about thirteen, she accidentally received a severe blow on the head from a two-pound weight that an overseer was hurling at a man trying to escape. After the accident, Harriet frequently lost consciousness. When this happened, she could not be roused until the episode passed of its own accord.

to trust her implicitly, totally. They, too, had come to believe her repeated statement, "We got to go free or die." She was leading them into freedom, and so they waited until she was ready to go on.

Finally, they reached Thomas Garrett's house in Wilmington, Delaware. Just as Harriet had promised, Garrett gave them all new shoes, and provided carriages to take them on to the next stop.

By slow stages they reached Philadelphia, where William Still hastily recorded their names, and the plantations whence they had come, and something of the life they had led in slavery. Then he carefully hid what he had written, for fear it might be discovered. In 1872 he published this record in book form and called it *The Underground Railroad*. In the foreword to his book he said: "While I knew the danger of keeping strict records, and while I did not then dream that in my day slavery would be blotted out, or that the time would come when I could publish these records, it used to afford me great satisfaction to take them down, fresh from the lips of fugitives on the way to freedom, and to preserve them as they had given them."

William Still, who was familiar with all the station stops on the Underground Railroad, supplied Harriet with money and sent her and her eleven fugitives on to Burlington, New Jersey.

Harriet felt safer now, though there were danger spots ahead. But the biggest part of her job was over. As they went farther and farther north, it grew colder; she was aware of the wind on the Jersey ferry and aware of the cold damp in New York. From New York they went on to Syracuse, where the temperature was even lower.

In Syracuse she met the Reverend J. W. Loguen, known as "Jarm" Loguen. This was the beginning of a lifelong friendship. Both Harriet and Jarm Loguen were to become friends and supporters of Old John Brown.[6]

From Syracuse they went north again, into a colder, snowier city—Rochester. Here they almost certainly stayed with Frederick Douglass, for he wrote in his autobiography: "On one occasion I had eleven fugitives at the same time under my roof, and it was necessary for them to remain with me until I could collect sufficient money to get them to Canada. It was the largest number I ever had at any one time, and I had some difficulty in providing so many with food and shelter, but, as may well be imagined, they were not very fastidious in either direction, and were well content with very plain food, and a strip of carpet on the floor for a bed, or a place on the straw in the barnloft."

Late in December, 1851, Harriet arrived in St. Catharines, Canada West (now Ontario), with the eleven fugitives. It had taken almost a month to complete this journey; most of the time had been spent getting out of Maryland.

That first winter in St. Catharines was a terrible one. Canada was a strange, frozen land, snow everywhere, ice everywhere, and a bone-biting cold the like of which none of them had ever experienced before. Harriet rented a small frame house in the town and set to work to make a home. The fugitives boarded with her. They worked in the forests, felling trees, and so did she. Sometimes she took other jobs, cooking or cleaning house for people in the town. She cheered on these newly arrived fugitives, working herself, finding work for them, finding food for them, praying for them, sometimes begging for them.

Often she found herself thinking of the

---

6. **John Brown:** a famous white abolitionist (1800–1859). He was hanged for leading an attack on the federal arsenal at Harper's Ferry, Virginia, in order to get arms to start a slave uprising.

beauty of Maryland, the mellowness of the soil, the richness of the plant life there. The climate itself made for an ease of living that could never be duplicated in this bleak, barren countryside.

In spite of the severe cold, the hard work, she came to love St. Catharines, and the other towns and cities in Canada where black men lived. She discovered that freedom meant more than the right to change jobs at will, more than the right to keep the money that one earned. It was the right to vote and to sit on juries. It was the right to be elected to office. In Canada there were black men who were country officials and members of school boards. St. Catharines had a large colony of ex-slaves, and they owned their own homes. They lived in whatever part of town they chose and sent their children to the schools.

When spring came she decided that she would make this small Canadian city her home—as much as any place could be said to be home to a woman who traveled from Canada to the Eastern Shore of Maryland as often as she did.

In the spring of 1852, she went back to Cape May, New Jersey. She spent the summer there, cooking in a hotel. That fall she returned, as usual, to Dorchester County, and brought out nine more slaves, conducting them all the way to St. Catharines, in Canada West, to the bone-biting cold, the snow-covered forests—and freedom.

She continued to live in this fashion, spending the winter in Canada, and the spring and summer working in Cape May, New Jersey, or in Philadelphia. She made two trips a year into slave territory, one in the fall and another in the spring. She now had a definite crystallized purpose, and in carrying it out, her life fell into a pattern which remained unchanged for the next six years.

SEEKING MEANING

1. Moses was the great Biblical hero who led the Israelites out of slavery in Egypt. Moses took his people on a long, perilous journey and brought them to the "Promised Land." How was Harriet Tubman another Moses?

2. The forbidden spiritual "Go Down, Moses" was a code song used by Harriet to announce her presence. What other signals did Harriet use to announce that she had returned?

3. In what ways did Harriet keep hope alive in her group and instill courage in them? Why did she have to tell them, "Go on with us or die"?

4. The Underground Railroad, of course, was really not a railroad at all, and it was not literally "underground." Railroad terminology was part of the code. From what you've read here, tell what a "station" on the railroad was. In what sense was Harriet a "conductor" on the railroad?

5. "Freedom's not bought with dust," Harriet told her band of fugitives. What price did all these people, including Harriet, pay in order to purchase freedom?

DEVELOPING SKILLS OF EXPRESSION

Using Specific Details in Description

The account you have just read is a selection from a book about Harriet Tubman's life. Earlier in that book, Harriet is described in this way:

> She worked from dawn to dusk, worked in the rain, in the heat of the sun. Her muscles hardened. She sang when she was in the fields or working in the nearby woods. Her voice was unusual because of the faint huskiness. Once having heard it,

people remembered it. The low notes were rich and deep. The high notes were sweet and true. . . .

In 1831, Harriet started wearing a bandanna. It was made from a piece of brilliantly colored cotton cloth. She wound it around her head, deftly, smoothly, and then tied it in place, pulling the knots tight and hard. This new headgear was an indication that she was no longer regarded as a child. These colorful bandannas were worn by young women: they were a symbol of maturity. . . .

Sometimes this short, straight-backed young girl hummed under her breath, or sang, while she hoed the corn or tugged on the reins when a refractory mule refused to budge. True, work in the fields had calloused her hands, but it had given her a strong, erect body. She carried her head proudly as she sang.

One characteristic emphasized here is Harriet's beautiful voice. What specific details help you picture what Harriet looked like, and what she wore?

Write a paragraph or two describing a person you know well. Try to include a few specific details that will give your reader a picture of what this person looks like, and perhaps of the clothing he or she usually wears.

Everything her parents preached to her about responsibility rubbed her the wrong way. Then one day she found herself in her parents' position. Something she loved was in danger.

The Apprentice

Dorothy Canfield

The day had been one of those unbearable ones, when every sound had set her teeth on edge like chalk creaking on a blackboard, when every word her father or mother said to her or did not say to her seemed an intentional injustice. And of course it would happen, as the end to such a day, that just as the sun went down back of the mountain and the long twilight began, she noticed that Rollie was not around.

Tense with exasperation—she would simply explode if Mother got going—she began to call him in a carefully casual tone: "Here, Rollie! He-ere, boy! Want to go for a walk, Rollie?" Whistling to him cheerfully, her heart full of wrath at the way the world treated her, she made the rounds of his haunts; the corner of the woodshed, where he liked to curl up on the wool of Father's discarded old windbreaker; the hay barn, the cow barn, the sunny spot on the side porch—no Rollie.

Perhaps he had sneaked upstairs to lie on her bed where he was not supposed to go—not that *she* would have minded! That rule was a part of Mother's fussiness, part too of Mother's bossiness. It was *her* bed, wasn't it? But was she allowed the say-so about it? Not on your life. They told her she could have things the way she wanted in her own room, now she was in her teens, but—her heart raged against unfairness as she took the stairs stormily, two steps at a time, her pigtails flopping up and down on her back. If Rollie was on her bed, she was just going to let him stay right there, and Mother could shake her head and frown all she wanted to.

But he was not there. The bedspread and pillow were crumpled, but not from his weight. She had flung herself down to cry there that afternoon. And then she couldn't. Every nerve in her had been twanging, but she couldn't cry. She could only lie there, her hands doubled up hard, furious that she had nothing to cry about. Not really. She was too big to cry just over Father's having said to her, severely, "I told you if I let you take the chess set you were to put it away when you got through with it. One of the pawns was on the floor of our bedroom this morning. I stepped on it. If I'd had my shoes on, I'd have broken it."

Well, he *had* told her to be sure to put them away. And although she had forgotten and left them, he hadn't forbidden her ever to take the set again. No, the instant she thought about that, she knew she couldn't cry about it. She could be, and she was, in a rage about the way Father kept on talking, long after she'd got his point, "It's not that I care so much about the chess set," he said, just leaning with all his weight on being right, "it's because if you don't learn how to take care of things, you yourself will suffer for it, later. You'll forget or neglect something that will be really important, for *you*. We *have* to try to teach you to be responsible for what you've said you'll take care of. If we . . ." on and on, preaching and preaching.

She heard her mother coming down the hall, and hastily shut her door. She had a right to shut the door to her own room, hadn't she?

She had *some* rights, she supposed, even if she was only thirteen and the youngest child. If her mother opened it to ask, smiling, "What are you doing in here that you don't want me to see?" she'd say—she'd just say—

She stood there, dry-eyed, by the bed that Rollie had not crumpled, and thought, "I hope Mother sees the spread and says something about Rollie—I just hope she does."

But her mother did not open the door. Her feet went steadily on along the hall, and then, carefully, slowly, down the stairs. She probably had an armful of winter things she was bringing down from the attic. She was probably thinking that a tall, thirteen-year-old daughter was big enough to help with a chore like that. But she wouldn't *say* anything. She would just get out that insulting look of a grown-up silently putting up with a crazy, unreasonable kid. She had worn that expression all day; it was too much to be endured.

Up in her bedroom behind her closed door the thirteen-year-old stamped her foot in a rage, none the less savage and heart-shaking because it was mysterious to her.

But she had not located Rollie. Before she would let her father and mother know she had lost sight of him, forgotten about him, she would be cut into little pieces. They would not scold her, she knew. They would do worse. They would look at her. And in their silence she would hear droning on reproachfully what they had repeated and repeated when the sweet, woolly collie puppy had first been in her arms and she had been begging to keep him for her own.

How warm he had felt! Astonishing how warm and alive a puppy was compared to a doll! She had never liked her dolls much, after she had held Rollie, feeling him warm against her breast, warm and wriggling, bursting with

life, reaching up to lick her face—he had loved her from that first instant. As he felt her arms around him, his beautiful eyes had melted in trusting sweetness. And they did now, whenever he looked at her. "My dog is the only one in the whole world who *really* loves me," she thought passionately.

Even then, at the very minute when as a darling baby dog he was beginning to love her, her father and mother were saying, so cold, so reasonable—gosh! how she *hated* reasonableness!—"Now, Peg, remember that, living where we do, with sheep on the farms around us, it is a serious responsibility to have a collie dog. If you keep him, you've got to be the one to take care of him. You'll have to be the one to train him to stay at home. We're too busy with you children to start bringing up a puppy too." Rollie, nestling in her arms, let one hind leg drop awkwardly. It must be uncomfortable. She looked down at him tenderly, tucked his dangling leg up under him and gave him a hug. He laughed up in her face—he really did laugh, his mouth stretched wide in a cheerful grin.

All the time her parents kept hammering away: "If you want him, you can have him. But you must be responsible for him. If he gets to running sheep, he'll just have to be shot, you know that."

They had not said, aloud, "Like the Wilsons' collie." They never mentioned that awfulness—her racing unsuspectingly down across the fields just at the horrible moment when Mr. Wilson shot his collie caught in the very act of killing sheep. They probably thought that if they never spoke about it, she would forget it—*forget* the crack of that rifle, and the collapse of the great beautiful dog! Forget the red, red blood spurting from the hole in his head. She hadn't forgotten. She never would. She knew as well as they did how important it was to train a collie puppy about sheep. They didn't need to rub it in like that. They always rubbed everything in. She had told them, fervently, indignantly, that of *course* she would take care of him, be responsible for him, teach him to stay at home. Of course, of course. *She* understood!

And now, this afternoon, when he was six months old, tall, rangy,[1] powerful, standing up far above her knee, nearly to her waist, she didn't know where he was. But of course he must be somewhere around. He always was. She composed her face to look natural and went downstairs to search the house. He was probably asleep somewhere. She looked every room over carefully. Her mother was nowhere visible. It was safe to call him again, to give the special piercing whistle which always brought him racing to her, the white-feathered plume of his tail waving in elation that she wanted him.

But he did not answer. She stood still on the front porch to think.

Could he have gone up to their special place in the edge of the field where the three young pines, their branches growing close to the ground, made a triangular, walled-in space, completely hidden from the world? Sometimes he went up there with her. When she lay down on the dried grass to dream, he too lay down quietly, his head on his paws, his beautiful eyes fixed adoringly on her. He entered into her every mood. If she wanted to be quiet, all right, he did too.

It didn't seem as though he would have gone alone there. Still— She loped up the steep slope of the field rather fast, beginning to be anxious.

No, he was not there. She stood, irresolutely,[2] in the roofless, green-walled triangular hideout, wondering what to do next.

Then, before she knew what thought had come into her mind, its emotional impact knocked her down. At least her knees crumpled under her. Last Wednesday the Wilsons had brought their sheep down to the home farm from the upper pasture! She herself had seen them on the way to school, and like an idiot had not thought of Rollie. She had seen them grazing on the river meadow.

She was off like a racer at the crack of the starting pistol, her long, strong legs stretched in great leaps, her pigtails flying. She took the shortcut down to the upper edge of the meadow, regardless of the brambles. Their thorn-spiked, wiry stems tore at her flesh, but she did not care. She welcomed the pain. It was something she was doing for Rollie, for her Rollie.

She was tearing through the pine woods now, rushing down the steep, stony path, tripping over roots, half falling, catching herself just in time, not slackening her speed. She burst out on the open knoll above the river meadow, calling wildly, "Rollie, here, Rollie, here, boy! here! here!" She tried to whistle, but she was crying too hard to pucker her lips. She had not, till then, known she was crying.

There was nobody to see or hear her. Twilight was falling over the bare knoll. The sunless evening wind slid down the mountain like an invisible river, engulfing her in cold. Her teeth began to chatter. "Here, Rollie, here, boy, here!" She strained her eyes to look down into the meadow to see if the sheep were there. She could not be sure. She stopped calling him as if he were a dog, and called out his name despairingly, as if he were her child, "Rollie! oh, *Rollie*, where are you!"

The tears ran down her cheeks in streams. She sobbed loudly, terribly. Since there was no one to hear, she did not try to control herself. "Hou! hou! hou!" she sobbed, her face contorted grotesquely. "Oh, Rollie! Rollie!

---

1. **rangy** (rān′jē): thin and long-limbed.
2. **irresolutely** (ĭ-rĕz′ə-lōōt′lē): in an undecided way.

Rollie!" She had wanted something to cry about. Oh, how terribly now she had something to cry about.

She saw him as clearly as if he were there beside her, his muzzle and gaping mouth all smeared with the betraying blood (like the Wilsons' collie). "But he didn't *know* it was wrong!" she screamed like a wild creature. "Nobody *told* him it was wrong. It was my fault. I should have taken better care of him. I will now. I will!"

But no matter how she screamed, she could not make herself heard. In the cold gathering darkness, she saw him stand, poor, guiltless victim of his ignorance, who should have been protected from his own nature, his soft eyes looking at her with love, his splendid plumed tail waving gently. "It was my fault. I promised I would bring him up. I should have *made* him stay at home. I was responsible for him. It was my fault."

But she could not make his executioners hear her. The shot rang out, Rollie sank down, his beautiful liquid eyes glazed, the blood spurting from the hole in his head—like the Wilsons' collie. She gave a wild shriek, long, soul-satisfying, frantic. It was the scream at sudden, unendurable tragedy of a mature, full-blooded woman. It drained dry the girl of thirteen. She came to herself. She was standing on the knoll, trembling and quaking with cold, the darkness closing in on her.

Her breath had given out. For once in her life she had wept all the tears there were in her body. Her hands were so stiff with cold she could scarcely close them. How her nose was running! Simply streaming down her upper lip. And she had no handkerchief. She lifted her skirt, fumbled for her slip, stooped, blew her nose on it, wiped her eyes, drew a long quavering breath—and heard something! Far off in the distance, a faint sound, like a dog's muffled bark.

She whirled on her heels and bent her head to listen. The sound did not come from the meadow below the knoll. It came from back of her higher up, from the Wilsons' maple grove. She held her breath. Yes, it came from there.

She began to run again, but now she was not sobbing. She was silent, absorbed in her effort to cover ground. If she could only live to get there, to see if it really were Rollie. She ran steadily till she came to the fence and went over this in a great plunge. Her skirt caught on a nail. She impatiently pulled at it, not hearing or not heeding the long sibilant[3] tear as it came loose. She was in the dusky maple woods, stumbling over the rocks as she ran. As she tore on up the slope, she heard the bark again, and knew it was Rollie's.

She stopped short and leaned weakly against a tree. She was sick with the breathlessness of her straining lungs, sick in the reaction of relief, sick with anger at Rollie, who had been here having a wonderful time while she had been dying, just dying in terror about him.

For she could now not only hear that it was Rollie's bark. She could hear, in the dog language she knew as well as he, what he was saying in those excited yips—that he had run a woodchuck into a hole in the tumbled stone wall, that he had almost had him, that the intoxicating wild-animal smell was as close to him—almost—as if he had his jaws on his quarry. Yip! Woof! Yip! Yip!

The wildly joyful quality of the dog-talk enraged the girl. She had been trembling in exhaustion. Now it was indignation. So that was where he had been—when *she* was *killing* herself trying to take care of him. Plenty near enough if he had paid attention to

---

3. **sibilant** (sĭb′ə-lənt): making a hissing sound.

hear her calling and whistling to him. Just so set on having his foolish good time, he never thought to listen for her call.

She stooped to pick up a stout stick. She would teach him. She was hot with anger. It was time he had something to make him remember to listen. She started forward on a run.

But after a few steps she stopped, stood thinking. One of the things to remember about collies, everybody knew that, was that a collie who had been beaten was never "right" again. His spirit was broken. "Anything but a broken-spirited collie"—she had often heard a farmer say that. They were no good after that.

She threw down her stick. Anyhow, she thought, he was really too young to know that he had done wrong. He was still only a puppy. Like all puppies, he got perfectly crazy over wild-animal smells. Probably he truly hadn't heard her calling and whistling.

All the same, all the same—she stood stock-still, staring intently into the twilight—you couldn't let a puppy grow up just as he wanted to. It wouldn't be safe—for *him*. Somehow she would have to make him understand that he mustn't go off this way, by himself. He must be trained to know how to do what a good dog does—not because *she* wanted it, but for his own sake.

She walked on now, steady, purposeful, gathering her inner strength together, Olympian[4] in her understanding of the full meaning of the event.

When he heard his own special young god approaching, he turned delightedly and ran to

meet her, panting, his tongue hanging out. His eyes shone. He jumped up on her in an ecstasy of welcome and licked her face.

She pushed him away. Her face and voice were grave. "No, Rollie, *no!*" she said severely. "You're *bad*. You know you're not to go off in the woods without me! You are—a—bad—dog."

He was horrified. Stricken into misery. He stood facing her, frozen. The gladness went out of his eyes, the waving plume of his tail slowly lowered to slinking, guilty dejection.

"I know you were all wrapped up in that woodchuck. But that's no excuse. You *could* have heard me, calling you, whistling for you, if you'd paid attention," she went on. "You've got to learn, and I've got to teach you."

With a shudder of misery he lay down, his tail stretched out limp on the ground, his head flat on his paws, his ears drooping—ears

4. **Olympian** (ō-lǐm′pē-ən): godlike. The ancient Greek gods were believed to live on Mount Olympus in northeastern Greece.

him, "I *do* love you. I do. But I *have* to bring you up. I'm responsible for you, don't you see."

He did not see. Hearing sternness, or something else he did not recognize, in the beloved voice, he shut his eyes tight in sorrow, and made a little whimpering lament in his throat.

She had never heard him cry before. It was too much. She sat down by him and drew his head to her, rocking him in her arms, soothing him with inarticulate small murmurs.

He leaped into her arms and wriggled happily as he had when he was a baby; he reached up to lick her face as he had then. But he was no baby now. He was half as big as she, a great, warm, pulsing, living armful of love. She clasped him closely. Her heart was brimming full, but calmed, quiet. The blood flowed strongly, steadily, all through her body. She was deliciously warm. Her nose was still running, a little. She sniffed and wiped it on her sleeve.

It was almost dark now. "We'll be late to supper, Rollie," she said, responsibly. Pushing him gently off she stood up. "Home, Rollie, home."

Here was a command he could understand. At once he trotted along the path towards home. His tail, held high, waved plumelike. His short dog-memory had forgotten the suffering just back of him.

Her human memory was longer. His prancing gait was as carefree as a young child's. She plodded behind him like a serious adult. Her very shoulders seemed bowed by what she had lived through. She felt, she thought, like an old woman of thirty. But it was all right now, she knew she had made an impression on him.

When they came out into the open pasture, Rollie ran back to get her to play with him. He leaped around her in circles, barking in

ringing with the doomsday awfulness of the voice he loved and revered. To have it speak so to him, he must have been utterly wicked. He trembled, he turned his head away from her august[5] look of blame, he groveled in remorse for whatever mysterious sin he had committed.

As miserable as he, she sat down by him. "I don't *want* to scold you. But I have to! I have to bring you up right, or you'll get shot, Rollie. You mustn't go away from the house without me, do you hear, *never*."

His sharp ears, yearning for her approval, caught a faint overtone of relenting affection in her voice. He lifted his eyes to her, humbly, soft in imploring fondness.

"Oh, Rollie!" she said, stooping low over

---

5. **august** (ô-gŭst′): dignified; inspiring respect.

cheerful yawps, jumping up on her, inviting her to run a race with him, to throw him a stick, to come alive.

His high spirits were ridiculous. But infectious. She gave one little leap to match his. Rollie took this as a threat, a pretend play-threat. He planted his forepaws low and barked loudly at her, laughing between yips. He was so funny, she thought, when he grinned that way. She laughed back, and gave another mock-threatening leap at him. Radiant that his sky was once more clear, he sprang high on his steel-spring muscles in an explosion of happiness, and bounded in circles around her.

Following him, not noting in the dusk where she was going, she felt the grassy slope drop steeply. Oh, yes, she knew where she was. They had come to the rolling-down hill just back of the house. All the kids rolled down there, even the little ones, because it was soft grass without a stone. She had rolled down that slope a million times—years and years before, when she was a kid herself, six or seven years ago. It was fun. She remembered well the whirling dizziness of the descent, all the world turning crazily over and over. And the delicious giddy staggering when you first stood up, the earth still spinning under your feet.

"All right, Rollie, let's go," she cried, and flung herself down in the rolling position, her arms straight up over her head.

Rollie had never seen this skylarking before. It threw him into almost hysterical amusement. He capered around the rapidly rolling figure, half scared, mystified, enchanted.

His wild frolicsome barking might have come from her own throat, so accurately did it sound the way she felt—crazy, foolish—like a little kid, no more than five years old, the age she had been when she had last rolled down that hill.

At the bottom she sprang up, on muscles as steel-strong as Rollie's. She staggered a little, and laughed aloud.

The living-room windows were just before them. How yellow the lighted windows looked when you were in the darkness going home. How nice and yellow. Maybe Mother had waffles for supper. She was a swell cook, Mother was, and she certainly gave her family all the breaks, when it came to meals.

"Home, Rollie, home!" She burst open the door to the living room. "Hi, Mom, what'you got for supper?"

From the kitchen her mother announced coolly, "I hate to break the news to you, but it's waffles."

"Oh, *Mom!*" she shouted in ecstasy.

Her mother could not see her. She did not need to. "For goodness' sakes, go and wash," she called.

In the long mirror across the room she saw herself, her hair hanging wild, her long bare legs scratched, her broadly smiling face dirt-streaked, her torn skirt dangling, her dog laughing up at her. Gosh, was it a relief to feel your own age, just exactly thirteen years old!

SEEKING MEANING

1. At the beginning of the story, Peg is angry with her parents because they have been trying to teach her to take care of the things entrusted to her. What words spoken by her father on page 38 predict what actually does happen to Peg later that day?

2. How does the author describe Peg's scream on page 41? What does this statement tell about the change that has taken place in Peg?

3. Peg is enraged at Rollie when she finds him. In what ways do Peg's actions become just like those she had resented in her parents? How is Rollie like Peg herself?

4. Look back at the passage describing Peg and Rollie's return home. What details indicate that Peg feels she is a different person? Do you think Peg has changed her attitude toward her mother? Why?

5. By the end of the story, why do you think Peg is relieved to feel thirteen again?

DEVELOPING SKILLS IN READING

Understanding the Title of a Story

One clue to the main idea of a story may be in its title. This story, for example, is called "The Apprentice." Yet no one in the story is an apprentice in the strict sense of the word. No one is really bound to some experienced person for a period of time in order to learn a trade or business.

But if we think of an apprentice as a learner, or beginner, we can understand why the story was given this title. Why can Peg be called an "apprentice"? Who are her teachers?

Often a story expresses some truth about life or people. Think about how the apprentice in this story learns her lesson. What idea do you think the story expresses about the way young people learn to be adults?

DEVELOPING SKILLS OF EXPRESSION

Writing from Another Point of View

"The Apprentice" is not told by Peg herself, but the author does tell you everything that Peg is thinking. You are *not* told what the other characters are thinking.

Here is how the author tells you what happens as Peg's mother goes past her bedroom door. Notice that you do not know what her mother is thinking. But you do know what is going on inside Peg's mind.

> But her mother did not open the door. Her feet went steadily on along the hall, and then, carefully, slowly, down the stairs. She probably had an armful of winter things she was bringing down from the attic. She was probably thinking that a tall, thirteen-year-old daughter was big enough to help with a chore like that. But she wouldn't *say* anything. She would just get out that insulting look of a grown-up silently putting up with a crazy, unreasonable kid. She had worn that expression all day; it was too much to be endured.

If this scene were told from the mother's point of view, it might begin in this way:

> She didn't knock on the door because she didn't want to irritate Peg. She went on along the hall, and then down the stairs. She walked slowly because she was trying to figure out what to do, trying not to let the closed door bother her. . . .

Using this beginning or one of your own, rewrite this scene from the mother's point of view. Write as if you know the mother's thoughts. What does she think is causing Peg's unhappiness? What does her expression really mean?

*"Certain things are right and certain things are wrong,
And nothing ain't gonna ever change that. When you learn
that, then you're fit'n to be a man."*

Weep No More, My Lady

James Street

The moonlight symphony of swamp creatures hushed abruptly, and the dismal bog was as peaceful as unborn time and seemed to brood in its silence. The gaunt man glanced back at the boy and motioned for him to be quiet, but it was too late. Their presence was discovered. A jumbo frog rumbled a warning, and the swamp squirmed into life as its denizens scuttled to safety.

Fox fire[1] was glowing to the west and the bayou was slapping the cypress trees when suddenly a haunting laugh echoed through the wilderness, a strange chuckling yodel ending in a weird "gro-o-o."

---

1. **Fox fire:** glowing light given off by wood that has been rotted by fungus.

The boy's eyes were wide and staring. "That's it, Uncle Jess. Come on! Let's catch it!"

"Uh, oh." The man gripped his shotgun. "That ain't no animal. That's a thing."

They hurried noiselessly in the direction of the sound that Skeeter had been hearing for several nights. Swamp born and reared, they feared nothing they could shoot or outwit, so they slipped out of the morass and to the side of a ridge. Suddenly, Jesse put out his hand and stopped the child; then he pointed up the slope. The animal, clearly visible in the moonlight, was sitting on its haunches, its head cocked sideways as it chuckled. It was a merry and rather melodious little chuckle.

Skeeter grinned in spite of his surprise, then said, "Sh-h-h. It'll smell us."

Jesse said, "Can't nothing smell that far. Wonder what the durn thing is?" He peered up the ridge, studying the creature. He had no intention of shooting unless attacked, for Jesse Tolliver and his nephew never killed wantonly.

The animal, however, did smell them and whipped her nose into the wind, crouched, and braced. She was about sixteen inches high and weighed about twenty-two pounds. Her coat was red and silky, and there was a blaze of white down her chest and a circle of white around her throat. Her face was wrinkled and sad, like a wise old man's.

Jesse shook his head. "Looks som'n like a mixture of bloodhound and terrier from here," he whispered. "It beats me——"

"It's a dog, all right," Skeeter said.

"Can't no dog laugh."

"That dog can." The boy began walking toward the animal, his right hand outstretched. "Heah, heah. I ain't gonna hurt you."

The dog, for she was a dog, cocked her head from one side to the other and watched Skeeter. She was trembling, but she didn't run. And when Skeeter knelt by her, she stopped trembling, for the ways of a boy with a dog are mysterious. He stroked her, and the trim little creature looked up at him and blinked her big hazel eyes. Then she turned over, and Skeeter scratched her. She closed her eyes, stretched, and chuckled, a happy mixture of chortle and yodel. Jesse ambled up, and the dog leaped to her feet and sprang between the boy and the man.

Skeeter calmed her. "That's just Uncle Jess."

Jesse, still bewildered, shook his head again. "I still say that ain't no dog. She don't smell and she don't bark. Ain't natural. And look at her! Licking herself like a cat."

"Well, I'll be a catty wampus," Skeeter said. "Never saw a dog do that before." However, he was quick to defend any mannerism of his friend and said, "She likes to keep herself clean. She's a lady, and I'm gonna name her that, and she's mine 'cause I found her."

"Lady, huh?"

"No, sir. My Lady. If I name her just plain Lady, how folks gonna know she's mine?" He began stroking his dog again. "Gee m'netty, Uncle Jess, I ain't never had nothing like this before."

"It still don't make sense to me," Jesse said. But he didn't care, for he was happy because the child was happy.

Like most mysteries, there was no mystery at all about My Lady. She was a lady, all right, an aristocratic basenji,[2] one of those strange barkless dogs of Africa. Her ancestors were pets of the Pharaohs, and her line was well established when the now-proud races of men were wandering about Europe, begging handouts from nature. A bundle of nerves and muscles, she would fight anything and could scent game up to eighty yards. She had the gait of an antelope and was odorless, washing herself before and after meals. However, the only noises she could make were a piercing cry that sounded almost human and that chuckling little chortle. She could chuckle only when happy, and she had been happy in the woods. Now she was happy again.

As most men judge values, she was worth more than all the possessions of Jesse and his nephew. Several of the dogs had been shipped to New Orleans to avoid the dangerous upper route, thence by motor to a northern kennel. While crossing Mississippi, My Lady had escaped from the station wagon. Her keeper had advertised in several papers, but Jesse and Skeeter never saw papers.

Skeeter said, "Come on, M'Lady. Let's go home."

The dog didn't hesitate, but walked proudly at the boy's side to a cabin on the bank of the bayou. Skeeter crumbled corn bread, wet it with potlikker,[3] and put it before her. She sniffed the food disdainfully at first, eating it only when she saw the boy fix a bowl for his uncle. She licked herself clean and explored the cabin, sniffing the brush brooms, the piles of wild pecans and hickory nuts, and then the cots. Satisfied at last, she jumped on Skeeter's bed, tucked her nose under her paws, and went to sleep.

"Acts like she owns the place," Jesse said.

"Where you reckon she came from?" The boy slipped his overall straps from his shoulders, flexed his stringy muscles, and yawned.

"Lord knows. Circus maybe." He looked at M'Lady quickly. "Say, maybe she's freak and run off from some show. Bet they'd give us two dollars for her."

Skeeter's face got long. "You don't aim to get rid of her?"

The old man put his shotgun over the mantel and lit his pipe. "Skeets, if you want that thing, I wouldn't get shed of her for a piece of bottom land a mile long. Already plowed and planted."

"I reckoned you wouldn't, 'cause you like me so much. And I know how you like dogs, 'cause I saw you cry when yours got killed. But you can have part of mine."

---

2. **basenji** (bə-sĕn′jē).

3. **potlikker:** liquid left in a pot after greens and meat are cooked together.

Jesse sat down and leaned back, blowing smoke into the air to drive away mosquitoes. The boy got a brick and hammer and began cracking nuts, pounding the meat to pulp so his uncle could chew it. Skeeter's yellow hair hadn't been cut for months and was tangled. He had freckles, too. And his real name was Jonathan. His mother was Jesse's only sister and died when the child was born. No one thereabouts ever knew what happened to his father. Jesse, a leathery, toothless old man with faded blue eyes, took him to bring up and called him Skeeter because he was so little.

In the village, where Jesse seldom visited, folks wondered if he were fit'n to rear a little boy. They considered him shiftless and no-count. Jesse had lived all of his sixty years in

the swamp, and his way of life was a torment to folks who believed life must be lived by rules. He earned a few dollars selling jumbo frogs and pelts, but mostly he just paddled around the swamp, watching things and teaching Skeeter about life.

The villagers might have tried to send Skeeter to an orphanage, but for Joe (Cash) Watson, the storekeeper. Cash was a hard man, but fair. He often hunted with Jesse, and the old man had trained Cash's dogs. When there was talk of sending Skeeter away, Cash said, "You ain't gonna do it. You just don't take young'uns away from their folks." And that's all there was to it.

Jesse never coveted the "frills and furbelows[4] of durn-fool folks," and he yearned for only two things—a twenty-gauge shotgun for Skeeter and a set of Roebuckers for himself, as he called store-bought teeth. Cash had promised him the gun and the best false teeth in the catalog for forty-six dollars. Jesse had saved nine dollars and thirty-seven cents.

"Someday I'm gonna get them Roebuckers," he often told Skeeter. "Then I'm gonna eat me enough roastin' ears to kill a goat. Maybe I can get a set with a couple of gold teeth in 'em. I seen a man once with six gold teeth."

Once Skeeter asked him, "Why don't you get a job and make enough money to buy them Roebuckers?"

"I don't want 'em that bad," Jesse said.

So he was happy for Skeeter to have M'Lady, thinking the dog would sort of make up for the shotgun.

The boy cracked as many nuts as his uncle wanted, then put the hammer away. He was undressing when he glanced over at his dog. "Gosh, Uncle Jess. I'm scared somebody'll come get her."

---

4. **furbelows** (fûr'bə-lōz): fussy trimmings.

"I ain't heard of nobody losing no things around here. If'n they had, they'd been to me 'fo' now, being's I know all about dogs and the swamp."

"That's so," Skeeter said. "But you don't reckon she belonged to another fellow like me, do you? I know how I'd feel if I had a dog like her and she got lost."

Jesse said, "She didn't belong to another fellow like you. If'n she had, she wouldn't be so happy here."

Skeeter fed M'Lady biscuits and molasses for breakfast, and although the basenji ate it, she still was hungry when she went into the swamp with the boy. He was hoping he could find a bee tree or signs of wild hogs. They were at the edge of a clearing when M'Lady's chokebore[5] nose suddenly tilted and she froze to a flash point,[6] pausing only long enough to get set. Then she darted to the bayou, at least sixty yards away, dived into a clump of reeds, and snatched a water rat. She was eating it when Skeeter ran up.

"Don't do that," he scolded. "Ain't you got no more sense than to run into water after things? A snake or a gator might snatch you."

The basenji dropped the rat and tucked her head. She knew the boy was displeased, and when she looked up at him, her eyes were filled, and a woebegone expression was on her face.

Skeeter tried to explain, "I didn't mean to hurt your feelings. Don't cry." He stepped back quickly and stared at her, at the tears in her eyes. "She *is* crying! By John Brown!" Skeeter called her and ran toward the cabin, where Jesse was cutting splinters.

---

5. **chokebore:** tapered at the tip.
6. **flash point:** Huntings dogs are trained to show where game is hiding by holding a position, with body and head pointed toward the game. A flash point is such a position held briefly.

"Uncle Jess! Guess what else my dog can do!"

"Whistle," the old man laughed.

"She can cry! I declare to goodness! Not out loud, but she can cry just the same."

Jesse knew that most dogs will get watery-eyed on occasion, but, not wanting to ridicule M'Lady's accomplishments, asked, "What made her cry?"

"Well, sir, we were walking along and all of a sudden she got a scent and flash-pointed and then . . ." Skeeter remembered something.

"Then what?"

Skeeter sat on the steps. "Uncle Jess," he said slowly, "we must have been fifty or sixty yards from that rat when she smelled it."

"What rat? What's eating you?"

The child told him the story, and Jesse couldn't believe it. For a dog to pick up the scent of a water rat at sixty yards simply isn't credible. Jesse reckoned Skeeter's love for M'Lady had led him to exaggerate.

Skeeter knew Jesse didn't believe the story, so he said, "Come on. I'll show you." He whistled for M'Lady.

The dog came up. "Hey," Jesse said. "That thing knows what a whistle means. Shows she's been around folks." He caught the dog's eye and commanded, "Heel!"

But M'Lady cocked her head quizzically. Then she turned to the boy and chuckled softly. She'd never heard the order before. That was obvious. Her nose came up into the breeze and she wheeled.

Her curved tail suddenly was still and her head was poised.

"Flash-pointing," Jesse said. "Well, I'll be a monkey's uncle!"

M'Lady held the strange point only for a second, though, then dashed toward a corn patch about eighty yards from the cabin.

Halfway to the patch, she broke her gait and began creeping. A whir of feathered lightning sounded in the corn, and a covey[7] of quail exploded almost under her nose. She sprang and snatched a bird.

"Partridges!" Jesse's jaw dropped.

The child was as motionless as stone, his face white and his eyes wide in amazement. Finally he found his voice, "She was right here when she smelled them birds. A good eighty yards."

"I know she ain't no dog now," Jesse said. "Can't no dog do that."

"She's fast as greased lightning and ain't scared of nothing." Skeeter still was under the spell of the adventure. "She's a hunting dog from way back."

"She ain't no dog a-tall, I'm telling you. It ain't human." Jesse walked toward M'Lady and told her to fetch the bird, but the dog didn't understand. Instead, she pawed it. "Well," Jesse said. "One thing's certain. She ain't no bird hunter."

"She can do anything," Skeeter said. "Even hunt birds. Maybe I can make a bird dog out'n her. Wouldn't that be som'n?"

"You're batty. Maybe a coon dog, but not a bird dog. I know 'bout dogs."

"Me too," said Skeeter. And he did. He'd seen Jesse train many dogs, even pointers, and had helped him train Big Boy, Cash Watson's prize gun dog.

Jesse eyed Skeeter and read his mind.

"It can't be done, Skeets."

"Maybe not, but I aim to try. Any dog can run coons and rabbits, but it takes a pure-D humdinger to hunt birds. Ain't no sin in trying, is it?"

"Naw," Jesse said slowly. "But she'll flush[8] birds."

"I'll learn her not to."

"She won't hold no point. Any dog'll flash-point. And she'll hunt rats."

"I'm gonna learn her just to hunt birds. And I'm starting right now," Skeeter said. He started walking away, then turned. "I seen a man once train a razorback hawg to point birds. You know as good as me that if a dog's got pure-D hoss sense and a fellow's got bat brains, he can train the dog to hunt birds."

"Wanta bet?" Jesse issued the challenge in an effort to keep Skeeter's enthusiasm and determination at the high-water mark.

"Yes, sir. If I don't train my dog, then I'll cut all the splinters for a year. If I do, you cut 'em."

"It's a go," Jesse said.

Skeeter ran to the bayou and recovered the rat M'Lady had killed. He tied it round the dog's neck. The basenji was indignant and tried to claw off the hateful burden. Failing, she ran into the house and under a bed, but Skeeter made her come out . M'Lady filled up then, and her face assumed that don't-nobody-love-me look. The boy steeled himself, tapped M'Lady's nose with the rat, and left it around her neck.

"You done whittled out a job for yourself," Jesse said. "If'n you get her trained, you'll lose her in the brush. She's too fast and too little to keep up with."

"I'll bell her," Skeeter said. "I'm gonna learn her ever'thing. I got us a gun dog, Uncle Jess."

The old man sat on the porch and propped against the wall. "Bud, I don't know what that thing is. But you're a thoroughbred. John dog my hide!"

If Skeeter had loved M'Lady one bit less, his patience would have exploded during the ordeal of training the basenji. It takes judgment and infinite patience to train a bird dog properly, but to train a basenji, that'll hunt any-

---

7. **covey** (kŭv'ē): a small flock.
8. **flush:** drive out of cover.

thing, to concentrate only on quail took something more than discipline and patience. It never could have been done except for that strange affinity between a boy and a dog, and the blind faith of a child.

M'Lady's devotion to Skeeter was so complete that she was anxious to do anything to earn a pat. It wasn't difficult to teach her to heel and follow at Skeeter's feet regardless of the urge to dash away and chase rabbits. The boy used a clothesline as a guide rope and made M'Lady follow him. The first time the dog tried to chase an animal, Skeeter pinched the rope around her neck just a bit and commanded "Heel!" And when she obeyed, Skeeter released the noose. It took M'Lady only a few hours to associate disobedience with disfavor.

The dog learned that when she chased and killed a rat or rabbit, the thing would be tied around her neck. The only things she could hunt without being disciplined were quail. Of course, she often mistook the scent of game chickens for quail and hunted them, but Skeeter punished her by scolding. He never switched his dog, but to M'Lady a harsh word from the boy hurt more than a hickory limb.

Jesse watched the dog's progress and pretended not to be impressed. He never volunteered suggestions. M'Lady learned quickly, but the task of teaching her to point birds seemed hopeless. Skeeter knew she'd never point as pointers do, so he worked with his own system. He taught her to stand motionless when he shouted "Hup!" One day she got a scent of birds, paused and pointed for a moment as most animals will, and was ready to spring away when Skeeter said "Hup!"

M'Lady was confused. Every instinct urged her to chase the birds, but her master had said stand still. She broke, however, and Skeeter scolded her. She pouted at first, then filled up, but the boy ignored her until she obeyed the next command, then he patted her and she chuckled.

The lessons continued for days and weeks, and slowly and surely M'Lady learned her chores. She learned that the second she smelled birds she must stop and stand still until Skeeter flushed them; that she must not quiver when he shot.

Teaching her to fetch was easy, but teaching her to retrieve dead birds without damaging them was another matter. M'Lady had a hard mouth—that is, she sank her teeth into the birds. Skeeter used one of the oldest hunting tricks of the backwoods to break her.

He got a stick and wrapped it with wire and taught his dog to fetch it. Only once did M'Lady bite hard on the stick, and then the wire hurt her sensitive mouth. Soon she developed a habit of carrying the stick on her tongue and supporting it lightly with her teeth. Skeeter tied quail feathers on the stick, and soon M'Lady's education was complete.

Skeeter led Jesse into a field one day and turned his dog loose. She flashed to a point almost immediately. It was a funny point, and Jesse almost laughed. The dog's curved tail poked up over her back, she spraddled her front legs and sort of squatted, her nose pointing the birds, more than forty yards away. She remained rigid until the boy flushed and shot, then she leaped away, seeking and fetching dead birds.

Jesse was mighty proud. "Well, Skeets, looks like you got yourself a bird hunter."

"Yes, sir," Skeeter said. "And you got yourself a job." He pointed toward the kindling pile.

The swamp was dressing for winter when Cash Watson drove down that day to give his Big Boy a workout in the wild brush.

He fetched Jesse a couple of cans of smoking tobacco and Skeeter a bag of peppermint jawbreakers. He locked his fine pointer in the corncrib for the night and was warming himself in the cabin when he noticed M'Lady for the first time. She was sleeping in front of the fire.

"What's that?" he asked.

"My dog," said Skeeter. "Ain't she a beaut?"

"She sure is," Cash grinned at Jesse. Skeeter went out to the well, and Cash asked his old friend, "What the devil kind of mutt is that?"

"Search me," said Jesse. "Skeets found her in the swamp. I reckon she's got a trace of bloodhound in her and some terrier and a heap of just plain dog."

M'Lady cocked one ear and got up and stretched; then, apparently, not liking the company, she turned her tail toward Cash and strutted out, looking for Skeeter.

The men laughed. "Som'n wrong with her throat," Jesse said. "She can't bark. When she tries, she makes a funny sound, sort of a cackling, chuckling yodel. Sounds like she's laughing."

"Well," Cash said, "trust a young'un to love the orner'st dog he can find."

"Wait a minute," Jesse said. "She ain't nocount. She's a bird-hunting fool."

Just then Skeeter entered and Cash jestingly said, "Hear you got yourself a bird dog, son."

The boy clasped his hands behind him and rocked on the balls of his feet as he had seen the men do. "Well, now, I'll tell you, Mr. Cash. M'Lady does ever'thing except tote the gun."

"She must be fair to middling. Why not take her out with Big Boy tomorrow? Do my dog good to hunt in a brace."[9]

"Me and my dog don't want to show Big Boy up. He's a pretty good ol' dog."

"Whoa!" Cash was every inch a bird-dog man and nobody could challenge him without a showdown. Besides, Skeeter was shooting up and should be learning a few things about life. "Any old boiler can pop off steam." Cash winked at Jesse.

"Well, now, sir, if you're itching for a run, I'll just double-dog dare you to run your dog against mine. And anybody who'll take a dare will pull up young cotton and push a widow woman's ducks in the water."

Cash admired the boy's confidence. "All right, son, it's a deal. What are the stakes?"

Skeeter started to mention the twenty-gauge gun he wanted, but changed his mind quickly. He reached down and patted M'Lady, then looked up. "If my dog beats yours, then you get them Roebuckers for Uncle Jess."

Jesse's chest was suddenly tight. Cash glanced from the boy to the man, and he, too, was proud of Skeeter. "I wasn't aiming to go that high. But all right. What do I get if I win?"

"I'll cut you ten cords of stovewood."

"And a stack of splinters?"

"Yes, sir."

Cash offered his hand, and Skeeter took it. "It's a race," Cash said. "Jesse will be the judge."

The wind was rustling the sage and there was a nip in the early-morning air when they took the dogs to a clearing and set them down. Skeeter snapped a belt around M'Lady's neck, and, at a word from Jesse, the dogs were released.

Big Boy bounded away and began circling, ranging into the brush. M'Lady tilted her nose into the wind and ripped away toward the sage, her bell tinkling. Cash said, "She sure covers ground." Skeeter made no effort to keep up with her, but waited until he couldn't hear the bell, then ran for a clearing where he

---

9. **brace:** here, a couple or pair.

had last heard it. And there was M'Lady on a point.

Cash laughed out loud. "That ain't no point, son. That's a squat."

"She's got birds."

"Where?"

Jesse leaned against a tree and watched the fun.

Skeeter pointed toward a clump of sage. "She's pointing birds in that sage."

Cash couldn't restrain his mirth. "Boy, now that's what I call some pointing. Why, Skeeter, it's sixty or seventy yards to that sage."

Just then Big Boy flashed by M'Lady, his head high. He raced to the edge of the sage, caught the wind, then whipped around, freezing to a point. Cash called Jesse's attention to the point.

"That's M'Lady's point," Skeeter said. "She's got the same birds Big Boy has."

Jesse sauntered up. "The boy's right, Cash. I aimed to keep my mouth out'n this race, but M'Lady is pointing them birds. She can catch scents up to eighty yards."

Cash said, "Aw, go on. You're crazy." He walked over and flushed the birds.

Skeeter picked one off and ordered M'Lady to fetch. When she returned with the bird, the boy patted her, and she began chuckling.

When did Cash realize she was a basenji

Cash really studied her then for the first time. "Hey!" he said suddenly. "A basenji! That's a basenji!"

"A what?" Jesse asked.

"I should have known." Cash was very excited. "That's the dog that was lost by them rich Yankees. I saw about it in the paper." He happened to look at Skeeter then and wished he had cut out his tongue.

The boy's lips were compressed and his face was drawn and white. Jesse had closed his eyes and was rubbing his forehead.

Cash, trying to dismiss the subject, said, "Just 'cause it was in the paper don't make it so. I don't believe that's the same dog, come to think of it."

"Do you aim to tell 'em where the dog is?" Skeeter asked.

Cash looked at Jesse, then at the ground. "It ain't none of my business."

"How 'bout you, Uncle Jess?"

"I ain't telling nobody nothin'."

"I know she's the same dog," Skeeter said. "On account of I just know it. But she's mine now." His voice rose and trembled. "And ain't nobody gonna take her away from me." He ran into the swamp. M'Lady was at his heels.

Cash said, "Durn my lip. I'm sorry, Jesse. If I'd kept my big mouth shut he'd never known the difference."

"It can't be helped, now," Jesse said.

" 'Course she beat Big Boy. Them's the best hunting dogs in the world. And she's worth a mint of money."

They didn't feel up to hunting and returned to the cabin and sat on the porch. Neither had much to say, but kept glancing toward the swamp where Skeeter and M'Lady were walking along the bayou. "Don't you worry," he said tenderly, "ain't nobody gonna bother you."

He sat on a stump and M'Lady put her head on his knee. She wasn't worrying. Nothing could have been more contented than she was.

"I don't care if the sheriff comes down." Skeeter pulled her onto his lap and held her. "I don't give a whoop if the Governor comes down. Even the President of the United States! The whole shebang can come, but ain't nobody gonna mess with you."

His words gave him courage, and he felt better, but only for a minute. Then the tug of war between him and his conscience started.

"Once I found a Barlow knife and kept it, and it was all right," he mumbled.

"But this is different."

"Finders, keepers; losers, weepers."

"No, Skeeter."

"Well, I don't care. She's mine."

"Remember what your Uncle Jess said."

"He said a heap of things."

"Yes, but you remember one thing more than the rest. He said, 'Certain things are right and certain things are wrong. And nothing ain't gonna ever change that. When you learn that, then you're fit'n to be a man.' Remember, Skeeter?"

A feeling of despair and loneliness almost overwhelmed him. He fought off the tears as long as he could, but finally he gave in, and his sobs caused M'Lady to peer into his face and wonder why he was acting that way when she was so happy. He put his arms around her neck and pulled her to him. "My li'l old puppy dog. Poor li'l old puppy dog. But I got to do it."

He sniffed back his tears and got up and walked to the cabin. M'Lady curled up by the fire, and the boy sat down, watching the logs splutter for several minutes. Then he said, almost in a whisper, "Uncle Jess, if you keep som'n that ain't yours, it's the same as stealing, ain't it?"

Cash leaned against the mantel and stared into the fire.

Jesse puffed his pipe slowly. "Son, that's som'n you got to settle with yourself."

Skeeter stood and turned his back to the flames, warming his hands. "Mr. Cash," he said slowly, "when you get back to your store, please let them folks know their dog is here."

"If that's how it is——"

"That's how it is," Skeeter said.

The firelight dancing on Jesse's face revealed the old man's dejection, and Skeeter, seeing it, said quickly, "It's best for M'Lady. She's too good for the swamp. They'll give her a good home."

Jesse flinched, and Cash, catching the hurt look in his friend's eyes, said, "Your dog outhunted mine, Skeets. You win them Roebuckers for your uncle."

"I don't want 'em," Jesse said, rather childishly. "I don't care if'n I never eat no roastin' ears." He got up quickly and hurried outside. Cash reckoned he'd better be going and left Skeeter by the fire, rubbing his dog.

Jesse came back in directly and pulled up a chair. Skeeter started to speak, but Jesse spoke first. "I been doing a heap of thinking lately. You're sprouting up. The swamp ain't no place for you."

Skeeter forgot about his dog and faced his uncle, bewildered.

"I reckon you're too good for the swamp too," Jesse said. "I'm aiming to send you into town for a spell. I can make enough to keep you in fit'n clothes and all." He dared not look at the boy.

"Uncle Jess!" Skeeter said reproachfully. "You don't mean that. You're just saying that on account of what I said about M'Lady. I said it just to keep you from feeling so bad about our dog going away. Gee m'netty, Uncle Jess. I ain't ever gonna leave you." He buried his face in his uncle's shoulder. M'Lady put her head on Jesse's knee, and he patted the boy and rubbed the dog.

"Reckon I'll take them Roebuckers," he said at last. "I been wanting some for a long, long time."

Several days later Cash drove down and told them the man from the kennels was at his store. Skeeter didn't say a word, but called M'Lady and they got in Cash's car. All the way to town, the boy was silent. He held his dog's head in his lap.

The keeper took just one look at M'Lady and said, "That's she, all right. Miss Congo III." He turned to speak to Skeeter, but the boy was walking away. He got a glance at Skeeter's face, however. "I wish you fellows hadn't told me," he muttered. "I hate to take a dog away from a kid."

"He wanted you to know," Cash said.

"Mister"—Jesse closed his left eye and struck his swapping pose—"I'd like to swap you out'n that hound. Now, 'course she ain't much 'count. . . ."

The keeper smiled in spite of himself. "If she was mine, I'd give her to the kid. But she's not for sale. The owner wants to breed her and establish her line in this country. And if she was for sale, she'd cost more money than any of us will ever see." He called Skeeter and offered his hand. Skeeter shook it.

"You're a good kid. There's a reward for this dog."

"I don't want no reward." The boy's words tumbled out. "I don't want nothing, except to be left alone. You've got your dog, mister.

Take her and go on. Please." He walked away again, fearing he would cry.

Cash said, "I'll take the reward and keep it for him. Someday he'll want it."

Jesse went out to the store porch to be with Skeeter. The keeper handed Cash the money. "It's tough, but the kid'll get over it. The dog never will."

"Is that a fact?"

"Yep. I know the breed. They never forget. That dog'll never laugh again. They never laugh unless they're happy."

He walked to the post where Skeeter had tied M'Lady. He untied the leash and started toward his station wagon. M'Lady braced her front feet and looked around for the boy. Seeing him on the porch, she jerked away from the keeper and ran to her master.

She rubbed against his legs. Skeeter tried to ignore her. The keeper reached for the leash again, and M'Lady crouched, baring her fangs.

The keeper shrugged, a helpless gesture.

"Wild elephants couldn't pull that dog away from that boy," he said.

"That's all right, mister." Skeeter unsnapped the leash and tossed it to the keeper. Then he walked to the station wagon, opened the door of the cage, and called, "Heah, M'Lady!" She bounded to him. "Up!" he commanded. She didn't hesitate, but leaped into the cage. The keeper locked the door.

M'Lady, having obeyed a command, poked her nose between the bars, expecting a pat. The boy rubbed her head. She tried to move closer to him, but the bars held her. She looked quizzically at the bars, then tried to nudge them aside. Then she clawed them. A look of fear suddenly came to her eyes, and she fastened them on Skeeter, wistfully at first, then pleadingly. She couldn't make a sound, for her unhappiness had sealed her throat. Slowly her eyes filled up.

"Don't cry no more, M'Lady. Ever'thing's gonna be all right." He reached out to pat her, but the station wagon moved off, leaving him standing there in the dust.

Back on the porch, Jesse lit his pipe and said to his friend, "Cash, the boy has lost his dog, and I've lost a boy."

"Aw, Jesse, Skeeter wouldn't leave you."

"That ain't what I mean. He's growed up, Cash. He don't look no older, but he is. He growed up that day in the swamp."

Skeeter walked into the store and Cash followed him. "I've got that reward for you, Jonathan."

It was the first time anyone ever had called him that, and it sounded like man talk.

"And that twenty-gauge is waiting for you," Cash said. "I'm gonna give it to you."

"Thank you, Mr. Cash." The boy bit his lower lip. "But I don't aim to do no more hunting. I don't never want no more dogs."

"Know how you feel. But if you change your mind, the gun's here for you."

Skeeter looked back toward the porch where Jesse was waiting, and said, "Tell you what, though. When you get them Roebuckers, get some with a couple of gold teeth in 'em. Take it out of the reward money."

"Sure, Jonathan."

Jesse joined them, and Skeeter said, "We better be getting back toward the house."

"I'll drive you down," Cash said. "But first I aim to treat you to some lemon pop and sardines."

"That's mighty nice of you," Jesse said, "but we better be gettin' on."

"What's the hurry?" Cash opened the pop.

"It's my time to cut splinters," Jesse said. "That's what I get for betting with a good man."

SEEKING MEANING

1. Stories like "Weep No More, My Lady" and "The Apprentice" (page 37) are sometimes called "coming of age" stories. The phrase "coming of age" means that a young person has earned the right to be called an adult. Such stories usually involve a conflict, or struggle, of some kind. What conflict is part of Skeeter's "coming of age"?

2. The passage on page 55 beginning "Once I found a Barlow knife . . ." records Skeeter's mental tug of war. What voice is arguing with him there?

3. On page 49 the author says that Uncle Jesse's life "was a torment to folks who believed life must be lived by rules." However, what important "rules" has Skeeter learned from Uncle Jesse?

4. At the end of the story, why does Cash call Skeeter by his proper name, Jonathan?

5. "Weep No More, My Lady" is the refrain of a sad song, written by Stephen Foster, about people who are leaving their loved ones and their home forever. Do you think the title is a good one for this story? Why or why not?

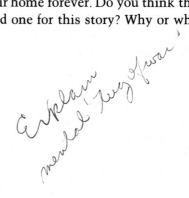

DEVELOPING SKILLS IN LANGUAGE

Understanding Regional Dialect

A *dialect* is a variety of speech used by a particular group of people. Everyone speaks in at least one dialect, though some people speak several. A dialect may be spoken in a certain region of a country, or it may be spoken by a particular social group.

The most interesting and picturesque dialects in the United States are regional dialects. Usually these are ways of speaking that have been preserved by a small group of people who have lived in one area for a long time.

A writer who wants to establish the feeling of a locale often has characters speak in a regional dialect. We are all familiar with the regional dialect of the old West from movies and television.

The author of "Weep No More, My Lady" has his characters speak in the regional dialect of the Mississippi bayou country. Sometimes they use words in ways that reflect very old meanings. For example, most people today probably use *reckon* to mean "count up" or "face up to." However, one of the word's original meanings was also "suppose" or "understand." What does Skeeter mean by it in this sentence: "Where you *reckon* she come from?"

What earlier meaning of *shed* is contained in Jesse's words: "I wouldn't get *shed* of her for a piece of bottom land a mile long"?

The author says that people thought Jesse was "no-*count*." This use of *count* goes back many centuries to a time when the word *count* was used to mean "esteem" or "regard." What does *no-count* mean in this story?

DEVELOPING SKILLS OF EXPRESSION

Using Sensory Details in Description

The setting of "Weep No More, My Lady" is very important. The reader needs to have a sense of the isolated bayou country where Jesse and Skeeter make their home.

The author begins immediately with a description of the place:

Cajun
Louisiana The moonlight symphony of swamp creatures hushed abruptly, and the dismal bog was as peaceful as unborn time and seemed to brood in its silence. The gaunt man glanced back at the boy and motioned for him to be quiet, but it was too late. Their presence was discovered. A jumbo frog rumbled a warning, and the swamp squirmed into life as its denizens scuttled to safety.

Fox fire was glowing to the west and the bayou was slapping the cypress trees when suddenly a haunting laugh echoed through the wilderness, a strange chuckling yodel ending in a weird *"gro-o-o."*

This description appeals to the senses of sight and hearing. What do you see and hear in the first two paragraphs?

Write a paragraph describing a place that you know well. Tell your readers what they would see or hear in this setting. Since there are five senses, you may also want to add what can be touched, tasted, or smelled in this place. Concentrate on only two or three senses.

Shane

Jack Schaefer

This selection is a chapter from the novel **Shane**. *In this story, Shane, a stranger with a mysterious past, has been working as a farmhand for Joe Starrett, the leader of a group of homesteaders in Wyoming. Luke Fletcher, a vicious cattle rancher, has been trying to force the homesteaders off their land.*

As the chapter opens, Fletcher has given Starrett an ultimatum: join forces with him, or else. Fletcher and his hired gunman, Stark Wilson, are waiting in town for Starrett's answer. But instead of Starrett, it is Shane, the gunfighter, who rides off for the showdown.

Joe Starrett's son, Bob, tells the story.

Nothing could have kept me there in the house that night. My mind held nothing but the driving desire to follow Shane. I waited, hardly daring to breathe, while Mother watched him go. I waited until she turned to Father, bending over him, then I slipped around the doorpost out to the porch. I thought for a moment she had noticed me, but I could not be sure and she did not call to me. I went softly down the steps and into the freedom of the night.

Shane was nowhere in sight. I stayed in the darker shadows, looking about, and at last I saw him emerging once more from the barn. The moon was rising low over the mountains, a clean, bright crescent. Its light was enough for me to see him plainly in outline. He was carrying his saddle and a sudden pain stabbed through me as I saw that with it was his saddle roll. He went toward the pasture gate not slow, not fast, just firm and steady. There was a catlike certainty in his every movement, a silent, inevitable[1] deadliness. I heard him, there by the gate, give his low whistle and the horse came out of the shadows at the far end of the pasture, its hooves making no noise in the deep grass, a dark and powerful shape etched in the moonlight drifting across the field straight to the man.

I knew what I would have to do. I crept

---

1. **inevitable** (ĭn-ĕv′ə-tə-bəl): unable to be avoided.

along the corral fence, keeping tight to it, until I reached the road. As soon as I was around the corner of the corral with it and the barn between me and the pasture, I started to run as rapidly as I could toward town, my feet plumping softly in the thick dust of the road. I walked this every school day and it had never seemed long before. Now the distance stretched ahead, lengthening in my mind as if to mock me.

I could not let him see me. I kept looking back over my shoulder as I ran. When I saw him swinging into the road, I was well past Johnson's, almost past Shipstead's, striking into the last open stretch to the edge of town. I scurried to the side of the road and behind a clump of bullberry bushes. Panting to get my breath, I crouched there and waited for him to pass. The hoofbeats swelled in my ears, mingled with the pounding beat of my own blood. In my imagination he was galloping furiously and I was positive he was already rushing past me. But when I parted the bushes and pushed forward to peer out, he was moving at a moderate pace and was only almost abreast of me.

He was tall and terrible there in the road, looming up gigantic in the mystic half-light. He was the man I saw that first day, a stranger, dark and forbidding, forging his lone way out of an unknown past in the utter loneliness of his own immovable and instinctive defiance. He was the symbol of all the dim, formless imaginings of danger and terror in the untested realm of human potentialities beyond my understanding. The impact of the menace that marked him was like a physical blow.

I could not help it. I cried out and stumbled and fell. He was off his horse and over me before I could right myself, picking me up, his grasp strong and reassuring. I looked at him, tearful and afraid, and the fear faded from me. He was no stranger. That was some trick of the shadows. He was Shane. He was shaking me gently and smiling at me.

"Bobby boy, this is no time for you to be out. Skip along home and help your mother. I told you everything would be all right."

He let go of me and turned slowly, gazing out across the far sweep of the valley silvered in the moon's glow. "Look at it, Bob. Hold it in your mind like this. It's a lovely land, Bob. A good place to be a boy and grow straight inside as a man should."

My gaze followed his, and I saw our valley as though for the first time and the emotion in me was more than I could stand. I choked and reached out for him and he was not there.

He was rising into the saddle and the two shapes, the man and the horse, became one and moved down the road toward the yellow squares that were the patches of light from the windows of Grafton's building a quarter of a mile away. I wavered a moment, but the call was too strong. I started after him, running frantically in the middle of the road.

Whether he heard me or not, he kept right on. There were several men on the long porch of the building by the saloon doors. Red Marlin's hair made him easy to spot. They were scanning the road intently. As Shane hit the panel of light from the near big front window, the store window, they stiffened to attention. Red Marlin, a startled expression on his face, dived quickly through the doors.

Shane stopped, not by the rail but by the steps on the store side. When he dismounted, he did not slip the reins over the horse's head as the cowboys always did. He left them looped over the pommel of the saddle and the horse seemed to know what this meant. It stood motionless, close by the steps, head up, waiting, ready for whatever swift need.

Shane went along the porch and halted briefly, fronting the two men still there.

"Where's Fletcher?"

They looked at each other and at Shane. One of them started to speak. "He doesn't want——" Shane's voice stopped him. It slapped at them, low and with an edge that cut right into your mind. "Where's Fletcher?"

One of them jerked a hand toward the doors and then, as they moved to shift out of his way, his voice caught them.

"Get inside. Go clear to the bar before you turn."

They stared at him and stirred uneasily and swung together to push through the doors. As the doors came back, Shane grabbed them, one with each hand, and pulled them out and wide open and he disappeared between them.

Clumsy and tripping in my haste, I scrambled up the steps and into the store. Sam Grafton and Mr. Weir were the only persons there and they were both hurrying to the entrance to the saloon, so intent that they failed to notice me. They stopped in the opening. I crept behind them to my familiar perch on my box where I could see past them.

The big room was crowded. Almost everyone who could be seen regularly around town was there, everyone but our homestead neighbors. There were many others who were new to me. They were lined up elbow to elbow nearly the entire length of the bar. The tables were full and more men were lounging along the far wall. The big round poker table at the back between the stairway to the little balcony and the door to Grafton's office was littered with glasses and chips. It seemed strange, for all the men standing, that there should be an empty chair at the far curve of the table. Someone must have been in that chair, because chips were at the place and a half-smoked cigar, a wisp of smoke curling up from it, was by them on the table.

Red Marlin was leaning against the back wall, behind the chair. As I looked, he saw the smoke and appeared to start a little. With a careful show of casualness he slid into the chair and picked up the cigar.

A haze of thinning smoke was by the ceiling over them all, floating in involved streamers around the hanging lamps. This was Grafton's saloon in the flush of a banner evening's business. But something was wrong, was missing. The hum of activity, the whirr of voices, that should have risen from the scene, been part of it, was stilled in a hush more impressive than any noise could be. The attention of everyone in the room, like a single sense, was centered on that dark figure just inside the swinging doors, back to them and touching them.

This was the Shane of the adventures I had dreamed for him, cool and competent, facing that room full of men in the simple solitude of his own invincible[2] completeness.

His eyes searched the room. They halted on a man sitting at a small table in the front corner with his hat on low over his forehead. With a thump of surprise I recognized it was Stark Wilson and he was studying Shane with

2. **invincible** (ĭn-vĭns′ə-bəl): unable to be conquered.

a puzzled look on his face. Shane's eyes swept on, checking off each person. They stopped again on a figure over by the wall and the beginnings of a smile showed in them and he nodded almost imperceptibly.[3] It was Chris,[4] tall and lanky, his arm in a sling, and as he caught the nod he flushed a little and shifted his weight from one foot to the other. Then he straightened his shoulders and over his face came a slow smile, warm and friendly, the smile of a man who knows his own mind at last.

But Shane's eyes were already moving on. They narrowed as they rested on Red Marlin. Then they jumped to Will Atkey trying to make himself small behind the bar.

"Where's Fletcher?"

Will fumbled with the cloth in his hands. "I—I don't know. He was here a while ago." Frightened at the sound of his own voice in the stillness, Will dropped the cloth, started to stoop for it, and checked himself, putting his hands to the inside rim of the bar to hold himself steady.

Shane tilted his head slightly so his eyes could clear his hatbrim. He was scanning the balcony across the rear of the room. It was empty and the doors there were closed. He stepped forward, disregarding the men by the bar, and walked quietly past them the long length of the room. He went through the doorway to Grafton's office and into the semi-darkness beyond.

And still the hush held. Then he was in the office doorway again and his eyes bored toward Red Marlin.

"Where's Fletcher?"

The silence was taut[5] and unendurable. It had to break. The sound was that of Stark Wilson coming to his feet in the far front corner. His voice, lazy and insolent,[6] floated down the room.

"Where's Starrett?"

While the words yet seemed to hang in the air, Shane was moving toward the front of the room. But Wilson was moving, too. He was crossing toward the swinging doors and he took his stand just to the left of them, a few feet out from the wall. The position gave him command of the wide aisle running back between the bar and the tables and Shane coming forward in it.

Shane stopped about three quarters of the way forward, about five yards from Wilson. He cocked his head for one quick sidewise glance again at the balcony and then he was looking only at Wilson. He did not like the setup. Wilson had the front wall and he was left in the open of the room. He understood the fact, assessed it, accepted it.

They faced each other in the aisle and the men along the bar jostled one another in their hurry to get to the opposite side of the room. A reckless arrogance was on Wilson, certain of himself and his control of the situation. He was not one to miss the significance of the slim deadliness that was Shane. But even now, I think, he did not believe that anyone in our valley would deliberately stand up to him.

"Where's Starrett?" he said once more, still mocking Shane but making it this time a real question.

The words went past Shane as if they had not been spoken. "I had a few things to say to

---

3. **imperceptibly** (ĭm'pər-sĕp'tĭ-blē): in a way that is not noticeable.
4. **Chris:** one of Fletcher's men who is recovering from a fight he had with Shane. Chris had decided to quit Fletcher and go to work with Starrett.

5. **taut:** here, tense.
6. **insolent** (ĭn'sə-lənt): rude; insulting.

Fletcher," he said gently. "That can wait. You're a pushing man, Wilson, so I reckon I had better accommodate you."

Wilson's face sobered and his eyes glinted coldly. "I've no quarrel with you," he said flatly, "even if you are Starrett's man. Walk out of here without any fuss and I'll let you go. It's Starrett I want."

"What you want, Wilson, and what you'll get are two different things. Your killing days are done."

Wilson had it now. You could see him grasp the meaning. This quiet man was pushing him just as he had pushed Ernie Wright.[7] As he measured Shane, it was not to his liking. Something that was not fear but a kind of wondering and baffled reluctance showed in his face. And then there was no escape, for that gentle voice was pegging him to the immediate and implacable[8] moment.

"I'm waiting, Wilson. Do I have to crowd you into slapping leather?"

Time stopped and there was nothing in all the world but two men looking into eternity in each other's eyes. And the room rocked in the sudden blur of action indistinct in its incredible swiftness and the roar of their guns was a single sustained blast. And Shane stood, solid on his feet as a rooted oak, and Wilson swayed, his right arm hanging useless, blood beginning to show in a small stream from under the sleeve over the hand, the gun slipping from the numbing fingers.

He backed against the wall, a bitter dis-

---

7. **Ernie Wright:** a homesteader who was forced into a fatal gunfight with Stark Wilson.

8. **implacable** (ĭm-plăʹkə-bəl): unable to be stopped or changed.

belief twisting his features. His left arm hooked and the second gun was showing and Shane's bullet smashed into his chest and his knees buckled, sliding him slowly down the wall till the lifeless weight of the body toppled it sideways to the floor.

Shane gazed across the space between and he seemed to have forgotten all else as he let his gun ease into the holster. "I gave him his chance," he murmured out of the depths of a great sadness. But the words had no meaning for me, because I noticed on the dark brown of his shirt, low and just above the belt to one side of the buckle, the darker spot gradually widening. Then others noticed, too, and there was a stir in the air and the room was coming to life.

Voices were starting, but no one focused on them. They were snapped short by the roar of a shot from the rear of the room. A wind seemed to whip Shane's shirt at the shoulder and the glass of the front window beyond shattered near the bottom.

Then I saw it.

It was mine alone. The others were turning to stare at the back of the room. My eyes were fixed on Shane and I saw it. I saw the whole man move, all of him, in the single flashing instant. I saw the head lead and the body swing and the driving power of the legs beneath. I saw the arm leap and the hand take the gun in the lightning sweep. I saw the barrel line up like—like a finger pointing—and the flame spurt even as the man himself was still in motion.

And there on the balcony Fletcher, impaled[9] in the act of aiming for a second shot, rocked on his heels and fell back into the open doorway behind him. He clawed at the jambs and pulled himself forward. He staggered to the rail and tried to raise the gun. But the strength was draining out of him and he collapsed over the rail, jarring it loose and falling with it.

Across the stunned and barren silence of the room Shane's voice seemed to come from a great distance. "I expect that finishes it," he said. Unconsciously, without looking down, he broke out the cylinder of his gun and reloaded it. The stain on his shirt was bigger now, spreading fanlike above the belt, but he did not appear to know or care. Only his movements were slow, retarded by an unutterable weariness. The hands were sure and steady, but they moved slowly and the gun dropped into the holster of its own weight.

He backed with dragging steps toward the swinging doors until his shoulders touched them. The light in his eyes was unsteady like the flickering of a candle guttering toward darkness. And then, as he stood there, a strange thing happened.

How could one describe it, the change that came over him? Out of the mysterious resources of his will the vitality came. It came creeping, a tide of strength that crept through him and fought and shook off the weakness. It shone in his eyes and they were alive again and alert. It welled up in him, sending that familiar power surging through him again until it was singing again in every vibrant line of him.

He faced that room full of men and read them all with the one sweeping glance and spoke to them in that gentle voice with that quiet, inflexible quality.

"I'll be riding on now. And there's not a one of you that will follow."

He turned his back on them in the indifference of absolute knowledge they would do as he said. Straight and superb, he was silhouetted against the doors and the patch of night

---

9. **impaled** (ĭm-pāld´): caught helplessly, as if pierced through by a stake.

above them. The next moment they were closing with a soft swish of sound.

The room was crowded with action now. Men were clustering around the bodies of Wilson and Fletcher, pressing to the bar, talking excitedly. Not a one of them, though, approached too close to the doors. There was a cleared space by the doorway as if someone had drawn a line marking it off.

I did not care what they were doing or what they were saying. I had to get to Shane. I had to get to him in time. I had to know, and he was the only one who could ever tell me.

I dashed out the store door and I was in time. He was on his horse, already starting away from the steps.

"Shane," I whispered desperately, loud as I dared without the men inside hearing me. "Oh, Shane!"

He heard me and reined around and I hurried to him, standing by a stirrup and looking up.

"Bobby! Bobby boy! What are you doing here?"

"I've been here all along," I blurted out. "You've got to tell me. Was that Wilson —"

He knew what was troubling me. He always knew. "Wilson," he said, "was mighty fast. As fast as I've ever seen."

"I don't care," I said, the tears starting. "I don't care if he was the fastest that ever was. He'd never have been able to shoot you, would he? You'd have got him straight, wouldn't you—if you had been in practice?"

He hesitated a moment. He gazed down at me and into me and he knew. He knew what goes on in a boy's mind and what can help him stay clean inside through the muddled, dirtied years of growing up.

"Sure. Sure, Bob. He'd never even have cleared the holster."

He started to bend down toward me, his hand reaching for my head. But the pain struck him like a whiplash and the hand jumped to his shirt front by the belt, pressing hard, and he reeled a little in the saddle.

The ache in me was more than I could bear. I stared dumbly at him, and because I was just

a boy and helpless I turned away and hid my face against the firm, warm flank of the horse.

"Bob."

"Yes, Shane."

"A man is what he is, Bob, and there's no breaking the mold. I tried that and I've lost. But I reckon it was in the cards from the moment I saw a freckled kid on a rail up the road there and a real man behind him, the kind that could back him for the chance another kid never had."

"But—but, Shane, you—"

"There's no going back from a killing, Bob. Right or wrong, the brand sticks and there's no going back. It's up to you now. Go home to your mother and father. Grow strong and straight and take care of them. Both of them."

"Yes, Shane."

"There's only one thing more I can do for them now."

I felt the horse move away from me. Shane was looking down the road and on to the open plain and the horse was obeying the silent command of the reins. He was riding away and I knew that no word or thought could hold him. The big horse, patient and powerful, was already settling into the steady pace that had brought him into our valley, and the two, the man and the horse, were a single dark shape in the road as they passed beyond the reach of the light from the windows.

I strained my eyes after him, and then in the moonlight I could make out the inalienable outline of his figure[10] receding into the distance. Lost in my loneliness, I watched him go, out of town, far down the road where it curved out to the level country beyond the valley. There were men on the porch behind me, but I was aware only of that dark shape growing small and indistinct along the far reach of the road. A cloud passed over the moon and he merged into the general shadow and I could not see him and the cloud passed on and the road was a plain thin ribbon to the horizon and he was gone.

I stumbled back to fall on the steps, my head in my arms to hide the tears. The voices of the men around me were meaningless noises in a bleak and empty world. It was Mr. Weir who took me home.

---

10. **inalienable** (ĭn-āl′yə-nə-bəl) **outline of his figure:** In other words, the figure clearly belongs to Shane and to no one else.

SEEKING MEANING

1. One of the most popular types of American fiction is the Western. In setting and conflict, *Shane* contains many familiar features of Westerns. *Shane* takes place in the lawless Wyoming territory during the summer of 1889. The basic conflict in the story is between a group of struggling homesteaders and a greedy, ruthless cattle rancher. How does Shane finally settle the conflict?

2. Through the admiring eyes of young Bob Starrett, who narrates the story, you see Shane as a noble, heroic figure dealing out violent justice. Which passages in the story describe Shane in such a way that he seems to take on extraordinary or superhuman characteristics?

3. Shane is a tragic figure. Although he risks death and suffers wounds, he is unable to stay and enjoy the peace and safety he provides for the homesteaders. Reread Shane's speeches on page 67, beginning "A man is what he is, Bob, and there's no breaking the mold." How do Shane's words to Bob help explain why he must now leave the town?

4. Shane knows that Bob admires him and his ability to handle a gun, but he doesn't want Bob to imitate him. Why does Shane think it would be wrong for Bob to become a gunfighter? What kind of person does Shane want Bob to become?

5. What reasons can you give for the popularity of Western books, movies, and television shows?

DEVELOPING SKILLS IN READING

Drawing Inferences

In *Shane*, Bob Starrett, the narrator, usually describes scenes directly, leaving little for the reader to guess about. But in some scenes, you must draw inferences, or conclusions, about what is happening, based on clues that you are given. For example, just after Shane has entered Grafton's crowded saloon looking for Fletcher, Bob gives you this description:

It seemed strange, for all the men standing, that there should be an empty chair at the far curve of the table. Someone must have been in that chair, because chips were at the place and a half-smoked cigar, a wisp of smoke curling up from it, was by them on the table.

Red Marlin was leaning against the back wall, behind the chair. As I looked, he saw the smoke and appeared to start a little. With a careful show of casualness he slid into the chair and picked up the cigar.

Bob does not say that Fletcher has been sitting in the chair, that he has left to hide, and that Red Marlin is trying to cover up for him. Did you realize that this is what has happened? What evidence can you find to support this inference?

In an earlier scene, Bob sees Shane going for his horse and says:

He was carrying his saddle and a sudden pain stabbed through me as I saw that with it was his saddle roll.

Bob does not say directly that he realizes that Shane is going to leave them after the showdown with Fletcher. What clue in this sentence tells you that Shane will be taking off on a journey? (You have to know what a saddle roll is.)

In an important scene after the gunfight, Shane says to Bob:

". . . But I reckon it was in the cards from the moment I saw a freckled kid on a rail up the road there and a real man behind him, the kind that could back him for the chance another kid never had."

Who do you think this "other kid" is? What inference about Shane's past can you draw from this statement?

Kennie never seemed to do anything right. "If I could have a colt all for my own," he said, "I might do better."

My Friend Flicka   *Mary O'Hara*

Report cards for the second semester were sent out soon after school closed in mid-June.

Kennie's was a shock to the whole family.

"If I could have a colt all for my own," said Kennie, "I might do better."

Rob McLaughlin glared at his son. "Just as a matter of curiosity," he said, "how do you go about it to get a *zero* in an examination? Forty in arithmetic; seventeen in history! But a *zero*? Just as one man to another, what goes on in your head?"

"Yes, tell us how you do it, Ken," chirped Howard.

"Eat your breakfast, Howard," snapped his mother.

Kennie's blond head bent over his plate until his face was almost hidden. His cheeks burned.

McLaughlin finished his coffee and pushed his chair back. "You'll do an hour a day on your lessons all through the summer."

Nell McLaughlin saw Kennie wince as if something had actually hurt him.

Lessons and study in the summertime, when the long winter was just over and there weren't hours enough in the day for all the things he wanted to do!

Kennie took things hard. His eyes turned to the wide-open window with a look almost of despair.

The hill opposite the house, covered with arrow-straight jack pines, was sharply etched in the thin air of the eight-thousand-foot altitude. Where it fell away, vivid green grass ran up to meet it; and over range and upland poured the strong Wyoming sunlight that stung everything into burning color. A big jack rabbit sat under one of the pines, waving his long ears back and forth.

Ken had to look at his plate and blink back tears before he could turn to his father and say carelessly, "Can I help you in the corral with the horses this morning, Dad?"

"You'll do your study every morning before you do anything else." And McLaughlin's scarred boots and heavy spurs clattered across the kitchen floor. "I'm disgusted with you. Come, Howard."

Howard strode after his father, nobly refraining from looking at Kennie.

"Help me with the dishes, Kennie," said Nell McLaughlin as she rose, tied on a big apron, and began to clear the table.

Kennie looked at her in despair. She poured steaming water into the dishpan and sent him for the soap powder.

"If I could have a colt," he muttered again.

"Now get busy with that dish towel, Ken. It's eight o'clock. You can study till nine and then go up to the corral. They'll still be there."

At supper that night, Kennie said, "But Dad, Howard had a colt all of his own when he was only eight. And he trained it and schooled it all himself; and now he's eleven and Highboy is three, and he's riding him. I'm nine now, and even if you did give me a colt now, I couldn't catch up to Howard because I couldn't ride it till it was a three-year-old and then I'd be twelve."

Nell laughed, "Nothing wrong with that arithmetic."

But Rob said, "Howard never gets less than

seventy-five average at school, and hasn't disgraced himself and his family by getting more demerits than any other boy in his class."

Kennie didn't answer. He couldn't figure it out. He tried hard; he spent hours poring over his books. That was supposed to get you good marks, but it never did. Everyone said he was bright; why was it that when he studied he didn't learn? He had a vague feeling that perhaps he looked out the window too much, or looked through the walls to see clouds and sky and hills and wonder what was happening out there. Sometimes it wasn't even a wonder but just a pleasant drifting feeling of nothing at all, as if nothing mattered, as if there was always plenty of time, as if the lessons would get done of themselves. And then the bell would ring and study period was over.

If he had a colt . . .

When the boys had gone to bed that night, Nell McLaughlin sat down with her overflowing mending basket and glanced at her husband.

He was at his desk as usual, working on account books and inventories.

Nell threaded a darning needle and thought, "It's either that whacking big bill from the vet for the mare that died or the last half of the tax bill."

It didn't seem just the auspicious moment to plead Kennie's cause. But then, these days, there was always a line between Rob's eyes and a harsh note in his voice.

"Rob," she began.

He flung down his pencil and turned around.

"That law!" he exclaimed.

"What law?"

"The state law that puts high taxes on pedigreed stock. I'll have to do as the rest of 'em do—drop the papers."

"Drop the papers! But you'll never get de-

cent prices if you don't have registered horses."

"I don't get decent prices now."

"But you will someday, if you don't drop the papers."

"Maybe." He bent again over the desk.

Rob, thought Nell, was a lot like Kennie himself. He set his heart. Oh, how stubbornly he set his heart on just some one thing he wanted above everything else. He had set his heart on horses and ranching way back when he had been a crack rider at West Point; and he had resigned and thrown away his army career just for the horses. Well, he'd got what he wanted. . . .

She drew a deep breath, snipped her thread, laid down the sock, and again looked across at her husband as she unrolled another length of darning cotton.

To get what you want is one thing, she was thinking. The three-thousand-acre ranch and the hundred head of horses. But to make it pay—for a dozen or more years they had been trying to make it pay. People said ranching hadn't paid since the beef barons ran their herds on public land; people said the only prosperous ranchers in Wyoming were the dude ranchers; people said . . .

But suddenly she gave her head a little rebellious, gallant shake. Rob would always be fighting and struggling against something, like Kennie, perhaps like herself too. Even those first years when there was no water piped into the house, when every day brought a new difficulty or danger, how she had loved it! How she still loved it!

She ran the darning ball into the toe of a sock, Kennie's sock. The length of it gave her a shock. Yes, the boys were growing up fast, and now Kennie—Kennie and the colt . . .

After a while she said, "Give Kennie a colt, Rob."

"He doesn't deserve it." The answer was

short. Rob pushed away his papers and took out his pipe.

"Howard's too far ahead of him; older and bigger and quicker and his wits about him, and . . ."

"Ken doesn't half try, doesn't stick at anything."

She put down her sewing. "He's crazy for a colt of his own. He hasn't had another idea in his head since you gave Highboy to Howard."

"I don't believe in bribing children to do their duty."

"Not a bribe." She hesitated.

"No? What would you call it?"

She tried to think it out. "I just have a feeling Ken isn't going to pull anything off, and" —her eyes sought Rob's—"it's time he did. It isn't the school marks alone, but I just don't want things to go on any longer with Ken never coming out at the right end of anything."

"I'm beginning to think he's just dumb."

"He's not dumb. Maybe a little thing like this—if he had a colt of his own, trained him, rode him . . ."

Rob interrupted. "But it isn't a little thing, nor an easy thing, to break and school a colt the way Howard has schooled Highboy. I'm not going to have a good horse spoiled by Ken's careless ways. He goes woolgathering. He never knows what he's doing."

"But he'd *love* a colt of his own, Rob. If he could do it, it might make a big difference in him."

"*If* he could do it! But that's a big if."

At breakfast next morning, Kennie's father said to him, "When you've done your study, come out to the barn. I'm going in the car up to section twenty-one this morning to look over the brood mares.[1] You can go with me."

"Can I go too, Dad?" cried Howard.

McLaughlin frowned at Howard. "You turned Highboy out last evening with dirty legs."

Howard wriggled. "I groomed him. . . ."

"Yes, down to his knees."

"He kicks."

"And whose fault is that? You don't get on his back again until I see his legs clean."

The two boys eyed each other, Kennie secretly triumphant and Howard chagrined.[2] McLaughlin turned at the door, "And, Ken, a week from today I'll give you a colt. Between now and then you can decide what one you want."

Kennie shot out of his chair and stared at his father. "A—a—spring colt, Dad, or a yearling?"

McLaughlin was somewhat taken aback, but his wife concealed a smile. If Kennie got a yearling colt, he would be even up with Howard.

"A yearling colt, your father means, Ken," she said smoothly. "Now hurry with your lessons. Howard will wipe."

Kennie found himself the most important personage on the ranch. Prestige lifted his head, gave him an inch more of height and a bold stare, and made him feel different all the way through. Even Gus and Tim Murphy, the ranch hands, were more interested in Kennie's choice of a colt than anything else.

Howard was fidgety with suspense. "Who'll you pick, Ken? Say—pick Doughboy, why don't you? Then when he grows up, he'll be sort of twins with mine, in his name anyway. Doughboy, Highboy, see?"

The boys were sitting on the worn wooden step of the door which led from the tack room into the corral, busy with rags and polish, shining their bridles.

---

1. **brood mares:** female horses kept for breeding.

2. **chagrined** (shə-grĩnd′): embarrassed.

Ken looked at his brother with scorn. Doughboy would never have half of Highboy's speed.

"Lassie, then," suggested Howard. "She's black as ink, like mine. And she'll be fast. . . ."

"Dad says Lassie'll never go over fifteen hands."[3]

Nell McLaughlin saw the change in Kennie and her hopes rose. He went to his books in the morning with determination and really studied. A new alertness took the place of the daydreaming. Examples in arithmetic were neatly written out, and, as she passed his door before breakfast, she often heard the monotonous drone of his voice as he read his American history aloud.

Each night, when he kissed her, he flung his arms around her and held her fiercely for a moment, then, with a winsome and blissful smile into her eyes, turned away to bed.

He spent days inspecting the different bands of horses and colts. He sat for hours on the corral fence, very important, chewing straws. He rode off on one of the ponies for half the day, wandering through the mile-square pastures that ran down toward the Colorado border.

And when the week was up, he announced his decision. "I'll take that yearling filly of Rocket's. The sorrel[4] with the cream tail and mane.

His father looked at him in surprise. "The one that got tangled in the barbed wire?— that's never been named?"

In a second all Kennie's new pride was gone. He hung his head defensively. "Yes."

"You've made a bad choice, Son. You couldn't have picked a worse."

"She's fast, Dad. And Rocket's fast. . . ."

"It's the worst line of horses I've got. There's never one among them with real sense. The mares are hellions[5] and the stal-

---

3. **fifteen hands:** 60 inches (about 150 centimeters) in height.

4. **sorrel:** a horse of reddish-brown color.
5. **hellions:** troublemakers.

lions outlaws; they're untamable.

"I'll tame her."

Rob guffawed. "Not I, nor anyone, has ever really been able to tame any one of them."

Kennie's chest heaved.

"Better change your mind, Ken. You want a horse that'll be a real friend to you, don't you?"

"Yes"—Kennie's voice was unsteady.

"Well, you'll never make a friend of that filly. She's all cut and scarred up already with tearing through barbed wire after that no-good mother of hers. No fence'll hold 'em. . . ."

"I know," said Kennie, still more faintly.

"Change your mind?" asked Howard briskly.

"No."

Rob was grim and put out. He couldn't go back on his word. The boy had to have a reasonable amount of help in breaking and taming the filly, and he could envision precious hours, whole days, wasted in the struggle.

Nell McLaughlin despaired. Once again Ken seemed to have taken the wrong turn and was back where he had begun, stoical, silent, defensive.

But there was a difference that only Ken could know. The way he felt about his colt. The way his heart sang. The pride and joy that filled him so full that sometimes he hung his head so they wouldn't see it shining out of his eyes.

He had known from the very first that he would choose that particular yearling because he was in love with her.

The year before, he had been out working with Gus, the big Swedish ranch hand, on the irrigation ditch, when they had noticed Rocket standing in a gully on the hillside, quiet for once and eyeing them cautiously.

"Ay bet she got a colt," said Gus, and they walked carefully up the draw.[6] Rocket gave a wild snort, thrust her feet out, shook her head wickedly, then fled away. And as they reached the spot, they saw standing there the wavering, pinkish colt, barely able to keep its

6. **draw:** gully.

feet. It gave a little squeak and started after its mother on crooked, wobbling legs.

"Yee whiz! Luk at de little *flicka!*" said Gus.

"What does *flicka* mean, Gus?"

"Swedish for 'little gurl,' Ken. . . ."

Ken announced at supper, "You said she'd never been named. I've named her. Her name is Flicka."

The first thing to do was to get her in. She was running with a band of yearlings on the saddleback,[7] cut with ravines and gullies, on section twenty.

They all went out after her, Ken, as owner, on old Rob Roy, the wisest horse on the ranch.

Ken was entranced to watch Flicka when the wild band of youngsters discovered that they were being pursued and took off across

---

7. **saddleback:** a hill or ridge with a depression at the top, like the back of a horse that has worn a saddle too long.

the mountain. Footing made no difference to her. She floated across the ravines, always two lengths ahead of the others. Her pink mane and tail whipped in the wind. Her long, delicate legs had only to aim, it seemed, at a particular spot for her to reach it and sail on. She seemed to Ken a fairy horse.

He sat motionless, just watching and holding Rob Roy in, when his father thundered past on Sultan and shouted, "Well, what's the matter? Why didn't you turn 'em?"

Kennie woke up and galloped after.

Rob Roy brought in the whole band. The corral gates were closed, and an hour was spent shunting the ponies in and out through the chutes, until Flicka was left alone in the small round corral in which the baby colts were branded. Gus drove the others away, out of the gate, and up the saddleback.

But Flicka did not intend to be left. She hurled herself against the poles which walled the corral. She tried to jump them. They were

seven feet high. She caught her front feet over the top rung, clung, scrambled, while Kennie held his breath for fear the slender legs would be caught between the bars and snapped. Her hold broke; she fell over backward, rolled, screamed, tore around the corral. Kennie had a sick feeling in the pit of his stomach, and his father looked disgusted.

One of the bars broke. She hurled herself again. Another went. She saw the opening and, as neatly as a dog crawls through a fence, inserted her head and forefeet, scrambled through, and fled away, bleeding in a dozen places.

As Gus was coming back, just about to close the gate to the upper range, the sorrel whipped through it, sailed across the road and ditch with her inimitable floating leap, and went up the side of the saddleback like a jack rabbit.

From way up the mountain, Gus heard excited whinnies, as she joined the band he had just driven up, and the last he saw of them they were strung out along the crest running like deer.

"Yee whiz!" said Gus, and stood motionless and staring until the ponies had disappeared over the ridge. Then he closed the gate, remounted Rob Roy, and rode back to the corral.

Rob McLaughlin gave Kennie one more chance to change his mind. "Last chance, Son. Better pick a horse that you have some hope of riding one day. I'd have got rid of this whole line of stock if they weren't so fast that I've had the fool idea that some day there might turn out one gentle one in the lot—and I'd have a racehorse. But there's never been one so far, and it's not going to be Flicka."

"It's not going to be Flicka," chanted Howard.

"Perhaps she *might* be gentled," said Kennie; and Nell, watching, saw that although his lips quivered, there was fanatical determination in his eye.

"Ken," said Rob, "it's up to you. If you say you want her, we'll get her. But she wouldn't be the first of that line to die rather than give in. They're beautiful and they're fast, but let me tell you this, young man, they're *loco!*"[8]

Kennie flinched under his father's direct glance.

"If I go after her again, I'll not give up whatever comes, understand what I mean by that?"

"Yes."

"What do you say?"

"I want her."

They brought her in again. They had better luck this time. She jumped over the Dutch half door of the stable and crashed inside. The men slammed the upper half of the door shut and she was caught.

The rest of the band were driven away, and Kennie stood outside the stable, listening to the wild hoofs beating, the screams, the crashes. His Flicka inside there! He was drenched with perspiration.

"We'll leave her to think it over," said Rob when dinnertime came. "Afterward, we'll go up and feed and water her."

But when they went up afterward there was no Flicka in the barn. One of the windows, higher than the mangers, was broken.

The window opened into a pasture an eighth of a mile square, fenced in barbed wire six feet high. Near the stable stood a wagonload of hay. When they went around the back of the stable to see where Flicka had hidden herself, they found her between the stable and the hay wagon, eating.

At their approach she leaped away, then headed east across the pasture.

---

8. *loco:* the Spanish word for "crazy."

"If she's like her mother," said Rob, "she'll go right through the wire."

"Ay bet she'll go over," said Gus. "She yumps like a deer."

"No horse can jump that," said McLaughlin.

Kennie said nothing because he could not speak. It was, perhaps, the most terrible moment of his life. He watched Flicka racing toward the eastern wire.

A few yards from it, she swerved, turned, and raced diagonally south.

"It turned her! It turned her!" cried Kennie, almost sobbing. It was the first sign of hope for Flicka. "Oh, Dad! She has got sense. She has! She has!"

Flicka turned again as she met the southern boundary of the pasture; again at the northern; she avoided the barn. Without abating anything of her whirlwind speed, following a precise, accurate calculation and turning each time on a dime, she investigated every possibility. Then, seeing that there was no hope, she raced south toward the range where she had spent her life, gathered herself, and shot into the air.

Each of the three men watching had the impulse to cover his eyes, and Kennie gave a sort of howl of despair.

Twenty yards of fence came down with her as she hurled herself through. Caught on the upper strands, she turned a complete somersault, landing on her back, her four legs dragging the wires down on top of her, and tangling herself in them beyond hope of escape.

"Blasted wire!" said McLaughlin. "If I could afford decent fences . . ."

Kennie followed the men miserably as they walked to the filly. They stood in a circle, watching while she kicked and fought and thrashed until the wire was tightly wound and knotted about her, cutting, piercing, and tearing great three-cornered pieces of flesh

and hide. At last she was unconscious, streams of blood running on her golden coat, and pools of crimson widening and spreading on the grass beneath her.

With the wire cutter which Gus always carried in the hip pocket of his overalls, he cut all the wire away, and they drew her into the pasture, repaired the fence, placed hay, a box of oats, and a tub of water near her, and called it a day.

"I don't think she'll pull out of it," said McLaughlin.

Next morning Kennie was up at five, doing his lessons. At six he went out to Flicka.

She had not moved. Food and water were untouched. She was no longer bleeding, but the wounds were swollen and caked over.

Kennie got a bucket of fresh water and poured it over her mouth. Then he leaped away, for Flicka came to life, scrambled up, got her balance, and stood swaying.

Kennie went a few feet away and sat down to watch her. When he went in to breakfast, she had drunk deeply of the water and was mouthing the oats.

There began, then, a sort of recovery. She ate, drank, limped about the pasture; stood for hours with hanging head and weakly splayed-out[9] legs, under the clump of cottonwood trees. The swollen wounds scabbed and began to heal.

Kennie lived in the pasture, too. He followed her around; he talked to her. He too lay snoozing or sat under the cottonwoods; and often, coaxing her with hand outstretched, he walked very quietly toward her. But she would not let him come near her.

Often she stood with her head at the south fence, looking off to the mountain. It made the tears come to Kennie's eyes to see the way she longed to get away.

---

9. **splayed-out:** spread outward.

Still Rob said she wouldn't pull out of it. There was no use putting a halter on her. She had no strength.

One morning, as Ken came out of the house, Gus met him and said, "De filly's down."

Kennie ran to the pasture, Howard close behind him. The right hind leg, which had been badly swollen at the knee joint, had opened in a festering wound, and Flicka lay flat and motionless, with staring eyes.

"Don't you wish now you'd chosen Dough-boy?" asked Howard.

"Go away!" shouted Ken.

Howard stood watching while Kennie sat down on the ground and took Flicka's head on his lap. Though she was conscious and moved a little, she did not struggle or seem fright-ened. Tears rolled down Kennie's cheeks as he talked to her and petted her. After a few moments, Howard walked away.

"Mother, what do you do for an infection when it's a horse?" asked Kennie.

"Just what you'd do if it was a person. Wet dressings. I'll help you, Ken. We mustn't let those wounds close or scab over until they're clean. I'll make a poultice[10] for that hind leg and help you put it on. Now that she'll let us get close to her, we can help her a lot."

"The thing to do is see that she eats," said Rob. "Keep up her strength."

But he himself would not go near her. "She won't pull out of it," he said. "I don't want to see her or think about her."

Kennie and his mother nursed the filly. The big poultice was bandaged on the hind leg. It drew out much poisoned matter, and Flicka felt better and was able to stand again.

She watched for Kennie now and followed him like a dog, hopping on three legs, holding up the right hind leg with its huge knob of a bandage in comical fashion.

"Dad, Flicka's my friend now; she likes me," said Ken.

His father looked at him. "I'm glad of that, Son. It's a fine thing to have a horse for a friend."

Kennie found a nicer place for her. In the lower pasture the brook ran over cool stones. There was a grassy bank, the size of a corral, almost on a level with the water. Here she could lie softly, eat grass, drink fresh running water. From the grass, a twenty-foot hill sloped up, crested with overhanging trees. She was enclosed, as it were, in a green, open-air nursery.

Kennie carried her oats, morning and eve-ning. She would watch for him to come, eyes and ears pointed to the hill. And one evening, Ken, still some distance off, came to a stop and a wide grin spread over his face. He had heard her nicker.[11] She had caught sight of him coming and was calling to him!

He placed the box of oats under her nose, and she ate while he stood beside her, his hand smoothing the satin-soft skin under her mane. It had a nap as deep as plush. He played with her long, cream-colored tresses, arranged her forelock neatly between her eyes. She was a bit dish-faced, like an Arab, with eyes set far apart. He lightly groomed and brushed her while she stood turning her head to him whichever way he went.

He spoiled her. Soon she would not step to the stream to drink but he must hold a bucket for her. And she would drink, then lift her dripping muzzle, rest it on the shoulder of his blue chambray shirt, her golden eyes dream-ing off into the distance, then daintily dip her

---

10. **poultice** (pōl′tĭs): a warm, moist dressing for a wound.

11. **nicker:** whinny.

mouth to drink again.

When she turned her head to the south and pricked her ears and stood tense and listening, Ken knew she heard the other colts galloping on the upland.

"You'll go back there someday, Flicka," he whispered. "You'll be three and I'll be eleven. You'll be so strong you won't know I'm on your back, and we'll fly like the wind. We'll stand on the very top where we can look over the whole world and smell the snow from the Never-Summer Range. Maybe we'll see antelope. . . ."

This was the happiest month of Kennie's life.

With the morning, Flicka always had new strength and would hop three-legged up the hill to stand broadside to the early sun, as horses love to do.

The moment Ken woke, he'd go to the window and see her there; and when he was dressed and at his table studying, he sat so that he could raise his head and see Flicka.

After breakfast, she would be waiting for him and the box of oats at the gate, and for Nell McLaughlin with fresh bandages and buckets of disinfectant; and all three would go together to the brook, Flicka hopping along ahead of them, as if she were leading the way.

But Rob McLaughlin would not look at her.

One day all the wounds were swollen again. Presently they opened, one by one; and Kennie and his mother made more poultices.

Still the little filly climbed the hill in the early morning and ran about on three legs. Then she began to go down in flesh and almost overnight wasted away to nothing. Every rib showed; the glossy hide was dull and brittle, and was pulled over the skeleton as if she were a dead horse.

Gus said, "It's de fever. It burns up her flesh. If you could stop de fever she might get vell."

McLaughlin was standing in his window one morning and saw the little skeleton hopping about three-legged in the sunshine, and he said, "That's the end. I won't have a thing like that on my place."

Kennie had to understand that Flicka had not been getting well all this time; she had been slowly dying.

"She still eats her oats," he said mechanically.

They were all sorry for Ken. Nell McLaughlin stopped disinfecting and dressing the wounds. "It's no use, Ken," she said gently. "You know Flicka's going to die, don't you?"

"Yes, Mother."

Ken stopped eating. Howard said, "Ken doesn't eat anything any more. Don't he have to eat his dinner, Mother?"

But Nell answered, "Leave him alone."

Because the shooting of wounded animals

When Kennie saw that, he stopped walking. He felt dizzy. He kept staring at the gun rack, telling himself that it surely was there—he counted again and again—he couldn't see clearly. . . .

Then he felt an arm across his shoulder and heard his father's voice.

"I know, Son. Some things are awful hard to take. We just have to take 'em. I have to, too."

Kennie got hold of his father's hand and held on. It helped steady him.

Finally he looked up. Rob looked down and smiled at him and gave him a little shake and squeeze. Ken managed a smile too.

"All right now?"

"All right, Dad."

They walked in to supper together.

Ken even ate a little. But Nell looked thoughtfully at the ashen color of his face, and at the little pulse that was beating in the side of his neck.

After supper he carried Flicka her oats, but he had to coax her and she would only eat a little. She stood with her head hanging, but when he stroked it and talked to her, she pressed her face into his chest and was content. He could feel the burning heat of her body. It didn't seem possible that anything so thin could be alive.

Presently Kennie saw Gus come into the pasture, carrying the Marlin. When he saw Ken, he changed his direction and sauntered along as if he were out to shoot some cottontails.

Ken ran to him. "When are you going to do it, Gus?"

"Ay was goin' down soon now, before it got dark. . . ."

"Gus, don't do it tonight. Wait till morning. Just one more night, Gus."

"Vell, in de morning, den, but it got to be done, Ken. Yer fader gives de order."

"I know. I won't say anything more."

is all in the day's work on the Western plains, and sickening to everyone, Rob's voice, when he gave the order to have Flicka shot, was as flat as if he had been telling Gus to kill a chicken for dinner.

"Here's the Marlin, Gus. Pick out a time when Ken's not around and put the filly out of her misery."

Gus took the rifle. "*Ja,* Boss. . . ."

Ever since Ken had known that Flicka was to be shot, he had kept his eye on the rack which held the firearms. His father allowed no firearms in the bunkhouse. The gun rack was in the dining room of the ranch house; and, going through it to the kitchen three times a day for meals, Ken's eye scanned the weapons to make sure that they were all there.

That night they were not all there. The Marlin rifle was missing.

An hour after the family had gone to bed, Ken got up and put on his clothes. It was a warm moonlit night. He ran down to the brook, calling softly, "Flicka! Flicka!"

But Flicka did not answer with a little nicker, and she was not in the nursery nor hopping about the pasture. Ken hunted for an hour.

At last he found her down the creek, lying in the water. Her head had been on the bank, but as she lay there, the current of the stream had sucked and pulled at her, and she had had no strength to resist; and little by little her head had slipped down until when Ken got there only the muzzle was resting on the bank, and the body and legs were swinging in the stream.

Kennie slid into the water, sitting on the bank, and he hauled at her head. But she was heavy, and the current dragged like a weight; and he began to sob because he had no strength to draw her out.

Then he found a leverage for his heels against some rocks in the bed of the stream, and he braced himself against these and pulled with all his might; and her head came up onto his knees, and he held it cradled in his arms.

He was glad that she had died of her own accord, in the cool water, under the moon, instead of being shot by Gus. Then, putting his face close to hers and looking searchingly into her eyes, he saw that she was alive and looking back at him.

And then he burst out crying and hugged her and said, "Oh, my little Flicka, my little Flicka."

The long night passed.

The moon slid slowly across the heavens.

The water rippled over Kennie's legs and over Flicka's body. And gradually the heat and fever went out of her. And the cool running water washed and washed her wounds.

When Gus went down in the morning with the rifle, they hadn't moved. There they were, Kennie sitting in water over his thighs and hips, with Flicka's head in his arms.

Gus seized Flicka by the head and hauled her out on the grassy bank, and then, seeing that Kennie couldn't move, cold and stiff and half paralyzed as he was, lifted him in his arms and carried him to the house.

"Gus," said Ken through chattering teeth, "don't shoot her, Gus."

"It ain't fur me to say, Ken. You know dat."

"But the fever's left her, Gus."

"Ay wait a little, Ken. . . ."

Rob McLaughlin drove to Laramie to get the doctor, for Ken was in violent chills that would not stop. His mother had him in bed, wrapped in hot blankets, when they got back.

He looked at his father imploringly as the doctor shook down the thermometer.

"She might get well now, Dad. The fever's left her. It went out of her when the moon went down."

"All right, Son. Don't worry. Gus'll feed her, morning and night, as long as she's . . ."

"As long as I can't do it," finished Ken happily.

The doctor put the thermometer in his mouth and told him to keep it shut.

All day Gus went about his work, thinking of Flicka. He had not been back to look at her. He had been given no more orders. If she was alive, the order to shoot her was still in effect. But Kennie was ill; McLaughlin, making his second trip to town, taking the doctor home, would not be back till long after dark.

After their supper in the bunkhouse, Gus and Tim walked down to the brook. They did not speak as they approached the filly, lying stretched out flat on the grassy bank, but their eyes were straining at her to see if she was dead or alive.

She raised her head as they reached her.

"By the powers!" exclaimed Tim; "there she is!"

She dropped her head, raised it again, and moved her legs and became tense as if struggling to rise. But to do so she must use her right hind leg to brace herself against the earth. That was the damaged leg, and at the first bit of pressure with it, she gave up and fell back.

"We'll swing her onto the other side," said Tim. "Then she can help herself."

"Ja. . . ."

Standing behind her, they leaned over, grabbed hold of her left legs, front and back, and gently hauled her over. Flicka was as lax and willing as a puppy. But the moment she found herself lying on her right side, she began to scramble, braced herself with her good left leg, and tried to rise.

"Yee whiz!" said Gus. "She got plenty strength yet."

"Hi!" cheered Tim. "She's up!"

But Flicka wavered, slid down again, and lay flat. This time she gave notice that she would not try again by heaving a deep sigh and closing her eyes.

Gus took his pipe out of his mouth and thought it over. Orders or no orders, he would try to save the filly. Ken had gone too far to be let down.

"Ay'm goin' to rig a blanket sling fur her, Tim, and get her on her feet and keep her up."

There was bright moonlight to work by. They brought down the posthole digger and set two aspen poles deep into the ground on either side of the filly, then, with ropes attached to the blanket, hoisted her by a pulley.

Not at all disconcerted, she rested comfortably in the blanket under her belly, touched her feet on the ground, and reached for the bucket of water Gus held for her.

Kennie was sick a long time. He nearly died. But Flicka picked up. Every day Gus passed the word to Nell, who carried it to Ken. "She's cleaning up her oats. . . . She's out of the sling. . . . She bears a little weight on the bad leg."

Tim declared it was a real miracle. They argued about it, eating their supper.

"Na," said Gus. "It was de cold water, washin' de fever outa her. And more dan dot—it was Ken—you tink it don't count? All night dot boy sits dere and says, 'Hold on, Flicka, Ay'm here wid you. Ay'm standin' by, two of us togedder.' . . ."

Tim stared at Gus without answering, while he thought it over. In the silence, a coyote yapped far off on the plains, and the wind made a rushing sound high up in the jack pines on the hill.

Gus filled his pipe.

"Sure," said Tim finally. "Sure, that's it."

Then came the day when Rob McLaughlin stood smiling at the foot of Kennie's bed and said, "Listen! Hear your friend?"

Ken listened and heard Flicka's high, eager whinny.

"She don't spend much time by the brook any more. She's up at the gate of the corral half the time, nickering for you."

"For me!"

Rob wrapped a blanket around the boy and carried him out to the corral gate.

Kennie gazed at Flicka. There was a look of marveling in his eyes. He felt as if he had been living in a world where everything was dreadful and hurting but awfully real; and *this* couldn't be real; this was all soft and happy, nothing to struggle over or worry about or fight for any more. Even his father was proud of him! He could feel it in the way Rob's big arms held him. It was all like a dream and far away. He couldn't, yet, get close to anything.

But Flicka—Flicka—alive, well, pressing up to him, recognizing him, nickering . . .

Kennie put out a hand—weak and white— and laid it on her face. His thin little fingers straightened her forelock the way he used to do, while Rob looked at the two with a strange expression about his mouth and a glow in his eyes that was not often there.

"She's still poor, Dad, but she's on four legs now."

"She's picking up."

Ken turned his face up, suddenly remembering. "Dad! She did get gentled, didn't she?"

"Gentle—as—a kitten. . . ."

They put a cot down by the brook for Ken, and boy and filly got well together.

SEEKING MEANING

1. In this story, both Kennie and Flicka have to go through long and painful ordeals before they prove themselves to the people around them. Give examples to show how both the boy and the filly are considered "misfits" or "losers" when we first meet them.

2. Kennie's father tries to get his son to change his mind about Flicka. Why does Kennie insist on his choice?

3. In what way is Kennie like his father?

4. What was perhaps "the most terrible moment" in Kennie's life (page 78)? What happens to Flicka in her leap for freedom?

5. On page 80 you are told: "This was the happiest month of Kennie's life." What makes this time so special for Kennie?

6. What does Kennie do on the night before the filly is to be shot that proves his love for his "friend" Flicka? According to Gus, what saved Flicka?

7. How do we know by the end of the story that Rob McLaughlin has changed his mind about Kennie and Flicka? How have Kennie and Flicka changed by the end of the story?

DEVELOPING VOCABULARY

Using Context Clues

Often you can guess the meaning of an unfamiliar word by using clues provided by the *context,* or the rest of the words in the sentence or paragraph.

For example, if you did not know the meaning of *thrashed,* you could figure out its meaning from clues in this sentence: ". . . she kicked and fought and *thrashed* until the wire was tightly wound and knotted about her . . . ." From the context you could guess that *thrash* refers to some kind of wild, violent movement. How does a dictionary define

thrash?

What context clues in the following sentences help you define the italicized words? Check your answers in a dictionary.

> Nell McLaughlin saw Kennie *wince* as if something had actually hurt him.
>
> "I'm not going to have a good horse spoiled by Ken's careless ways. He goes *wool-gathering.* He never knows what he's doing."
>
> . . . she often heard the monotonous *drone* of his voice as he read his American history aloud.

DEVELOPING SKILLS OF EXPRESSION

Creating a Strong Impression

In this paragraph from "My Friend Flicka," the author creates a vivid impression of the filly's enchanted lightness and speed. Notice how the words in italics help to suggest this impression:

> Ken was entranced to watch Flicka when the wild band of youngsters discovered that they were being pursued and took off across the mountain. Footing made no difference to her. She *floated* across the ravines, always two lengths ahead of the others. Her pink mane and tail *whipped in the wind.* Her long, *delicate* legs had only to aim, it seemed, at a particular spot for her to reach it and *sail* on. She seemed to Ken a *fairy* horse.

Write a short paragraph describing a person, an animal, or a place. Select specific words that will create a single strong impression. Before you write, decide the impression you want to create—for example, power, playfulness, or beauty.

Practice in Reading and Writing

DESCRIPTION

Reading Description

Description is the kind of writing that creates a picture of something—of a person, a scene, an object, or an action. This passage of description is from Arthur Gordon's story "The Sea Devil" (page 18). It helps you picture a setting.

> The man came out of the house and stood quite still, listening. Behind him, the lights glowed in the cheerful room, the books were neat and orderly in their cases, the radio talked importantly to itself. In front of him, the bay stretched dark and silent, one of the countless lagoons that border the coast where Florida thrusts its green thumb deep into the tropics.
>
> It was late in September. The night was breathless; summer's dead hand still lay heavy on the land. The man moved forward six paces and stood on the sea wall. He dropped his cigarette and noted where the tiny spark hissed and went out. The tide was beginning to ebb.

Here are some points to remember when you read descriptive passages:

1. *Look for specific details that help you imagine how something looks, sounds, smells, tastes, or feels.*

What specific sights and sounds does Gordon help you experience?

2. *Be aware of the general impression that the writer is trying to create.*

How does Gordon give you the impression that the house represents the comfort and security of civilization? What words give the impression that the natural world outside is mysterious?

3. *Interpret the figurative language.*

Gordon uses figurative language in the second paragraph when he says that "summer's dead hand still lay heavy on the land." We know, of course, that summer does not have hands, but this figure of speech helps us imagine the land being suffocated by oppressive heat even though summer is "dying." Where does Gordon use figurative language in the first paragraph? How would you explain this figure of speech? What does he mean by saying the night is "breathless"?

Writing Description

Here are some suggestions for writing effective description:

1. *Choose a few specific details that help your reader imagine how something looks, sounds, smells, tastes, or feels.*

Comic-book writers communicate sounds with words like *pow, wham,* and *ugh.* Kurt Vonnegut, in his story "The No-Talent Kid" (page 2), helps us hear a sound when he says that the music director "*clattered* his stick against the music stand." Arthur Gordon helps us share the fisherman's sensations when he says, "he felt the *hot* blood start instantly . . . ." In "My Friend Flicka" (page 70), Mary O'Hara helps us see and hear a newborn colt as Kennie saw and heard it: "It gave a little *squeak* and started after its mother on *crooked, wobbling* legs."

2. *Use precise nouns, verbs, and modifiers.*

In her story "The Apprentice" (page 37), Dorothy Canfield does not say that the girl "went" up the hill. She says the girl "loped." The verb *loped* helps us picture exactly how the girl ran—in long, swinging strides. In "They Called Her Moses" (page 27), Ann Petry does not simply say that Harriet Tubman promised her people "food." She says that she promised them "fried pork and corn bread and milk."

3. *Before you write, decide on the impression you want to create.*

You might want to state your impression in an opening sentence. Jack Schaefer does this when he begins his description of Shane (page 61) with the statement: "He was tall and *terrible.*"

Write a paragraph describing one of the following people, places, or things, or choose a subject of your own. Tell what your subject looks like. If you want to, tell also how it smells, sounds, tastes, or feels, or what it reminds you of. You might want to open with a statement giving your impression of the subject.

> An unusual person you see often
> A fried egg
> A crowd
> Running (or jumping, swimming, diving, etc.)
> An amusement park

For Further Reading

Baker, Rachel, *First Woman Doctor: The Story of Elizabeth Blackwell, M.D.* (Messner, 1944)
In the 1840's, Elizabeth Blackwell struggled against the idea of what a woman could *not* be—and became the first woman doctor in the United States.

Bolton, Carole, *Never Jam Today* (Atheneum, 1971; paperback, Atheneum)
In this novel, which is set in the early 1900's, seventeen-year-old Maddy Franklin joins the movement to give women the right to vote.

Gannon, Robert, editor, *Great Survival Adventures* (Random House, 1973)
This collection includes nine first-person accounts of struggles to survive fearful disasters.

Holman, Felice, *Slake's Limbo* (Scribner, 1974)
Thirteen-year-old Slake spends 121 days underground in the New York City subway system as a refuge from his unhappiness.

Morris, Jeannie, *Brian Piccolo: A Short Season* (Rand McNally, 1971; paperback, Dell)
This biography covers Brian Piccolo's life from his high school years, through his career as a running back with the Chicago Bears, to his battle with cancer at the age of twenty-six.

Gibson, Althea, *I Always Wanted to Be Somebody* (Harper & Row, 1958; paperback, Noble & Noble)
This famous athlete's autobiography tells of her childhood in Harlem, and of how she became one of America's great tennis players.

Gunther, John, *Death Be Not Proud: A Memoir* (Harper & Row, 1949; paperback, Harper)
A father tells of his seventeen-year-old son's battle against cancer. This true story is painful to read, but it reveals the grace and strength that people are capable of.

Portis, Charles, *True Grit* (Simon & Schuster, 1968; paperback, New American Library)
Fourteen-year-old Mattie, who has "true grit," hires Rooster G. Cogburn, an old U.S. marshal, to help her track down her father's murderer.

Schaefer, Jack, *Shane* (Houghton Mifflin, 1954; paperback, Amsco)
This famous Western novel is about a gunfighter who tries to reform and who changes the life of a fourteen-year-old boy.

Taylor, Theodore, *The Cay* (Doubleday, 1969; paperback, Avon)
The young man and the old man in this novel must survive together on a small coral island after their ship is torpedoed.

Viereck, Phillip, *The Summer I Was Lost* (John Day, 1965; paperback titled *Terror on the Mountain*, Starline)
A boy discovers that it takes more than muscle to survive when he gets lost in the woods.

White, Robb, *Deathwatch* (Doubleday, 1972; paperback, Dell)
In this suspenseful novel, a young man finds himself pursued in the desert by a vicious killer.

Two people can see the same situation, or the same event, in different ways. In this unit, you will find clashes that result from people thinking, "But that's not the way *I* see it." In some stories, young people clash with adults. In other stories, young people come into conflict with each other.

One of the values of literature is that it can expand our experience. Perhaps in some of these selections you will recognize your own point of view. But you might also discover the pleasure of seeing some aspect of life through another person's eyes.

THE VIEW
FROM HERE

Siri. A tempera painting by Andrew Wyeth (1917-   ).
Collection of the Brandywine Museum.
© Brandywine Conservancy

This true story is from a book of the same title. The narrator, who became a famous naturalist, was ten when this adventure took place. Even at that age, he was fascinated by all forms of life — including a community of scorpions he found one day in a plaster wall.

My Family and Other Animals

Gerald Durrell

I grew very fond of these scorpions. I found them to be pleasant, unassuming creatures with, on the whole, the most charming habits. Provided you did nothing silly or clumsy (like putting your hand on one) the scorpions treated you with respect, their one desire being to get away and hide as quickly as possible. They must have found me rather a trial, for I was always ripping sections of the plaster away so that I could watch them, or capturing them and making them walk about in jam jars so that I could see the way their feet moved. By means of my sudden and unexpected assaults on the wall I discovered quite a bit about scorpions. I found that they would eat bluebottles[1] (though how they caught them was a mystery I never solved), grasshoppers, moths, and lacewing flies. Several times I found one of them eating another, a habit I found most distressing in a creature otherwise so impeccable.[2]

By crouching under the wall at night with a torch,[3] I managed to catch some brief glimpses of the scorpions' wonderful courtship dances. I saw them standing, claws clasped, their bodies raised to the skies, their tails lovingly entwined; I saw them waltzing slowly in circles among the moss cushions, claw in claw. But my view of these performances was all too short, for almost as soon as I switched on the torch the partners would stop, pause for a moment, and then, seeing that I was not going to extinguish the light, would turn round and walk firmly away, claw in claw, side by side. They were definitely beasts that believed in keeping themselves *to* themselves. If I could have kept a colony in captivity I would probably have been able to see the whole of the courtship, but the family had forbidden scorpions in the house, despite my arguments in favor of them.

Then one day I found a fat female scorpion

---

1. **bluebottles:** bluish flies.
2. **impeccable** (ĭm-pĕk′ə-bəl): faultless; perfect.

3. **torch:** here, a flashlight.

in the wall, wearing what at first glance appeared to be a pale fawn fur coat. Closer inspection proved that this strange garment was made up of a mass of tiny babies clinging to the mother's back. I was enraptured by this family, and I made up my mind to smuggle them into the house and up to my bedroom so that I might keep them and watch them grow up. With infinite care I maneuvered the mother and family into a matchbox, and then hurried to the villa. It was rather unfortunate that just as I entered the door lunch should be served; however, I placed the matchbox carefully on the mantelpiece in the drawing room, so that the scorpions should get plenty of air, and made my way to the dining room and joined the family for the meal. Dawdling over my food, feeding Roger[4] surreptitiously under the table, and listening to the family arguing, I completely forgot about my exciting new captures. At last, Larry,[5] having finished, fetched the cigarettes from the drawing room, and lying back in his chair he put one in his mouth and picked up the matchbox he had brought. Oblivious of my impending doom I watched him interestedly as, still talking glibly, he opened the matchbox.

Now I maintain to this day that the female scorpion meant no harm. She was agitated and a trifle annoyed at being shut up in a matchbox for so long, and so she seized the first opportunity to escape. She hoisted herself out of the box with great rapidity, her babies clinging on desperately, and scuttled onto the back of Larry's hand. There, not quite certain what to do next, she paused, her sting curved up at the ready. Larry, feeling the movement of her claws, glanced down to see

what it was, and from that moment things got increasingly confused.

He uttered a roar of fright that made Lugaretzia[6] drop a plate and brought Roger out from beneath the table, barking wildly. With a flick of his hand he sent the unfortunate scorpion flying down the table, and she landed midway between Margo and Leslie,[7] scattering babies like confetti as she thumped onto the cloth. Thoroughly enraged at this treatment, the creature sped towards Leslie, her sting quivering with emotion. Leslie leaped to his feet, overturning his chair, and flicked out desperately with his napkin, sending the scorpion rolling across the cloth towards Margo, who promptly let out a scream that any railway engine would have been proud to produce. Mother, completely bewildered by this sudden and rapid change from peace to chaos, put on her glasses and peered down the table to see what was causing the pandemonium, and at that moment Margo, in a vain attempt to stop the scorpion's advance, hurled a glass of water at it. The shower missed the animal completely, but successfully drenched Mother, who, not being able to stand cold water, promptly lost her breath and sat gasping at the end of the table, unable even to protest. The scorpion had now gone to ground under Leslie's plate, while her babies swarmed wildly all over the table. Roger, mystified by the panic, but determined to do his share, ran round and round the room, barking hysterically.

"It's that bloody boy again . . ." bellowed Larry.

"Look out! Look out! They're coming!" screamed Margo.

---

4. **Roger:** the narrator's big, black, woolly dog.
5. **Larry:** the narrator's twenty-three-year-old brother, who tends to be very dramatic.

6. **Lugaretzia** (loo′gə-rĕt′sē-ə): the family's Greek maid, who is always worried about her health.
7. **Margo and Leslie:** Margo is the eighteen-year-old sister, and Leslie the nineteen-year-old brother.

"All we need is a book," roared Leslie; "don't panic, hit 'em with a book."

"What on earth's the *matter* with you all?" Mother kept imploring, mopping her glasses.

"It's that bloody boy . . . he'll kill the lot of us. . . . Look at the table . . . knee-deep in scorpions. . . ."

"Quick . . . quick . . . do something. . . . Look out, look out!"

"Stop screeching and get a book. . . . You're worse than the dog. . . . Shut *up*, Roger. . . ."

"By the grace of God I wasn't bitten. . . ."

"Look out . . . there's another one. . . . Quick . . . quick . . ."

"Oh, shut up and get me a book or something. . . ."

"But *how* did the scorpions get on the table, dear?"

"That bloody boy. . . . Every matchbox in the house is a deathtrap. . . ."

"Look out, it's coming towards me. . . . Quick, quick, do something. . . ."

"Hit it with your knife . . . *your knife*. . . . Go on, hit it. . . ."

Since no one had bothered to explain things to him, Roger was under the mistaken impression that the family were being attacked, and that it was his duty to defend them. As Lugaretzia was the only stranger in the room, he came to the logical conclusion that she must be the responsible party, so he bit her in the ankle. This did not help matters very much.

By the time a certain amount of order had been restored, all the baby scorpions had hidden themselves under various plates and bits of cutlery.[8] Eventually, after impassioned pleas on my part, backed up by Mother, Leslie's suggestion that the whole lot be slaughtered was quashed. While the family, still simmering with rage and fright, retired to the drawing room, I spent half an hour rounding up the babies, picking them up in a teaspoon, and returning them to their mother's back. Then I carried them outside on a saucer and, with the utmost reluctance, released them on

___

8. **cutlery:** knives, forks, and spoons.

the garden wall. Roger and I went and spent the afternoon on the hillside, for I felt it would be prudent to allow the family to have a siesta before seeing them again.

The results of this incident were numerous. Larry developed a phobia about matchboxes and opened them with the utmost caution, a handkerchief wrapped round his hand. Lugaretzia limped around the house, her ankle enveloped in yards of bandage, for weeks after the bite had healed, and came round every morning, with the tea, to show us how the scabs were getting on. But, from my point of view, the worst repercussion of the whole affair was that Mother decided I was running wild again, and that it was high time I received a little more education.

SEEKING MEANING

1. Living with the Durrells was like being in a comic movie. This part of the comedy began when Gerald found the scorpions. How did Gerald feel about the scorpions? Why were his feelings rather unusual?
2. The rest of the family didn't share Gerald's fascination with the scorpions. In a comic sequence, we are told about their reactions. The first one to react was Larry. What did he do?
3. What did each of the other family members do? How did Lugaretzia get bitten in the ankle?
4. From the family's point of view, the scorpion invasion was bad enough. But from Gerald's point of view, what was the worst result of the whole affair?
5. What did Mother fail to realize about the kind of education Gerald was getting on his own?

DEVELOPING SKILLS IN EXPRESSION

Narrating a Series of Events

After Larry felt the movement of the scorpion's claws and saw what was crawling on the back of his hand, things reached a peak of comic confusion. Look at the paragraph on page 91, beginning "He uttered a roar of fright." As if he were shooting a film, Durrell moves from character to character, showing how each action produces a reaction.

The scene is full of frenzy because Durrell uses many lively verbs. Notice all the action he makes us see: *drop, barking, flying, scattering, thumped, sped, quivering, leaped, overturning, flicked, rolling, peered, hurled, drenched, gasping, swarmed, ran.*

Using this scene as a model, write a paragraph in which you narrate a series of related events. Use verbs that will help your reader see lively movement. Choose a series of humorous events, if you like. Perhaps you can think of a scene that involves an animal, or a family, or a sports event. Your subject can be entirely imaginary.

ABOUT THE AUTHOR

Gerald Durrell (1925–   ) has never lost his fascination with animals. He and his wife founded a zoo on the isle of Jersey in the English Channel, which they devote to the conservation of endangered species. But Durrell is as skilled a writer as he is a zoologist. *My Family and Other Animals,* from which this story of the scorpions is taken, was made into a motion picture. Two of his other books are *The Overloaded Ark* and *A Zoo in My Luggage.*

At home, all her son talked about was the terrible Charles. Why couldn't she find Charles's mother at the P.T.A. meeting?

Charles   *Shirley Jackson*

The day my son Laurie started kindergarten he renounced[1] corduroy overalls with bibs and began wearing blue jeans with a belt; I watched him go off the first morning with the older girl next door, seeing clearly that an era of my life was ended, my sweet-voiced nursery-school tot replaced by a long-trousered, swaggering character who forgot to stop at the corner and wave goodbye to me.

He came home the same way, the front door slamming open, his cap on the floor, and the voice suddenly become raucous[2] shouting, "Isn't anybody *here?*"

At lunch he spoke insolently to his father, spilled his baby sister's milk, and remarked that his teacher said we were not to take the name of the Lord in vain.

"How *was* school today?" I asked, elaborately casual.

"All right," he said.

"Did you learn anything?" his father asked.

Laurie regarded his father coldly. "I didn't learn nothing," he said.

"Anything," I said. "Didn't learn anything."

"The teacher spanked a boy, though," Laurie said, addressing his bread and butter. "For being fresh," he added, with his mouth full.

"What did he do?" I asked. "Who was it?"

Laurie thought. "It was Charles," he said. "He was fresh. The teacher spanked him and made him stand in a corner. He was awfully fresh."

"What did he do?" I asked again, but Laurie slid off his chair, took a cookie, and left, while his father was still saying, "See here, young man."

---

1. **renounced** (rĭ-nounst′): gave up utterly.
2. **raucous** (rô′kəs): harsh and rough.

The next day Laurie remarked at lunch, as soon as he sat down, "Well, Charles was bad again today." He grinned enormously and said, "Today Charles hit the teacher."

"Good heavens," I said, mindful of the Lord's name, "I suppose he got spanked again?"

"He sure did," Laurie said. "Look up," he said to his father.

"What?" his father said, looking up.

"Look down," Laurie said. "Look at my thumb. Gee, you're dumb." He began to laugh insanely.

"Why did Charles hit the teacher?" I asked quickly.

"Because she tried to make him color with red crayons," Laurie said. "Charles wanted to color with green crayons so he hit the teacher and she spanked him and said nobody play with Charles but everybody did."

The third day—it was Wednesday of the first week—Charles bounced a seesaw onto the head of a little girl and made her bleed, and the teacher made him stay inside all during recess. Thursday Charles had to stand in a corner during story time because he kept pounding his feet on the floor. Friday Charles was deprived of blackboard privileges because he threw chalk.

On Saturday I remarked to my husband, "Do you think kindergarten is too unsettling for Laurie? All this toughness, and bad grammar, and this Charles boy sounds like such a bad influence."

"It'll be all right," my husband said reassuringly. "Bound to be people like Charles in the world. Might as well meet them now as later."

On Monday Laurie came home late, full of news, "Charles," he shouted as he came up the hill; I was waiting anxiously on the front steps. "Charles," Laurie yelled all the way up the hill, "Charles was bad again."

"Come right in," I said, as soon as he came close enough. "Lunch is waiting."

"You know what Charles did?" he demanded, following me through the door. "Charles yelled so in school they sent a boy in from first grade to tell the teacher she had to make Charles keep quiet, and so Charles had to stay after school. And so all the children stayed to watch him."

"What did he do?" I asked.

"He just sat there," Laurie said, climbing into his chair at the table. "Hi, Pop, y'old dust mop."

"Charles had to stay after school today," I told my husband. "Everyone stayed with him."

"What does this Charles look like?" my husband asked Laurie. "What's his other name?"

"He's bigger than me," Laurie said. "And he doesn't have any rubbers and he doesn't ever wear a jacket."

Monday night was the first Parent-Teachers meeting, and only the fact that the baby had a cold kept me from going; I wanted passionately to meet Charles's mother. On Tuesday Laurie remarked suddenly, "Our teacher had a friend come to see her in school today."

"Charles's mother?" my husband and I asked simultaneously.[3]

"Naaah," Laurie said scornfully. "It was a man who came and made us do exercises, we had to touch our toes. Look." He climbed down from his chair and squatted down and touched his toes. "Like this," he said. He got solemnly back into his chair and said, picking up his fork, "Charles didn't even *do* exercises."

"That's fine," I said heartily. "Didn't Charles want to do exercises?"

---

3. **simultaneously** (sī'məl-tā'nē-əs-lē): at the same time.

"Naaah," Laurie said. "Charles was so fresh to the teacher's friend he wasn't *let* do exercises."

"Fresh again?" I said.

"He kicked the teacher's friend," Laurie said. "The teacher's friend told Charles to touch his toes like I just did and Charles kicked him."

"What are they going to do about Charles, do you suppose?" Laurie's father asked him.

Laurie shrugged elaborately. "Throw him out of school, I guess," he said.

Wednesday and Thursday were routine; Charles yelled during story hour and hit a boy in the stomach and made him cry. On Friday Charles stayed after school again and so did all the other children.

With the third week of kindergarten Charles was an institution in our family; the baby was being a Charles when she cried all afternoon; Laurie did a Charles when he filled his wagon full of mud and pulled it through

the kitchen; even my husband, when he caught his elbow in the telephone cord and pulled telephone, ashtray, and a bowl of flowers off the table, said, after the first minute, "Looks like Charles."

During the third and fourth weeks it looked like a reformation in Charles; Laurie reported grimly at lunch on Thursday of the third week, "Charles was so good today the teacher gave him an apple."

"What?" I said, and my husband added warily,[4] "You mean Charles?"

"Charles," Laurie said. "He gave the crayons around and he picked up the books afterward and the teacher said he was her helper."

"What happened?" I asked incredulously.[5]

"He was her helper, that's all," Laurie said, and shrugged.

"Can this be true, about Charles?" I asked my husband that night. "Can something like this happen?"

"Wait and see," my husband said cynically.[6] "When you've got a Charles to deal with, this may mean he's only plotting."

He seemed to be wrong. For over a week Charles was the teacher's helper; each day he handed things out and he picked things up; no one had to stay after school.

"The P.T.A. meeting's next week again," I told my husband one evening. "I'm going to find Charles's mother there."

"Ask her what happened to Charles," my husband said. "I'd like to know."

"I'd like to know myself," I said.

On Friday of that week things were back to normal. "You know what Charles did today?" Laurie demanded at the lunch table, in a voice

---

4. **warily** (wâr′ĭ-lē): cautiously.
5. **incredulously** (ĭn-krej′ə-ləs-lē): in an unbelieving way.
6. **cynically** (sĭn′ĭk-lē): in a way showing distrust.

slightly awed. "He told a little girl to say a word and she said it and the teacher washed her mouth out with soap and Charles laughed.

"What word?" his father asked unwisely, and Laurie said, "I'll have to whisper it to you, it's so bad." He got down off his chair and went around to his father. His father bent his head down and Laurie whispered joyfully. His father's eyes widened.

"Did Charles tell the little girl to say *that?*" he asked respectfully.

"She said it *twice,*" Laurie said. "Charles told her to say it *twice.*"

"What happened to Charles?" my husband asked.

"Nothing," Laurie said. "He was passing out the crayons."

Monday morning Charles abandoned the little girl and said the evil word himself three or four times, getting his mouth washed out with soap each time. He also threw chalk.

My husband came to the door with me that evening as I set out for the P.T.A. meeting. "Invite her over for a cup of tea after the meeting," he said. "I want to get a look at her."

"If only she's there," I said prayerfully.

"She'll be there," my husband said. "I don't see how they could hold a P.T.A. meeting without Charles's mother."

At the meeting I sat restlessly, scanning each comfortable matronly face, trying to determine which one hid the secret of Charles. None of them looked to me haggard[7] enough. No one stood up in the meeting and apologized for the way her son had been acting. No one mentioned Charles.

After the meeting I identified and sought out Laurie's kindergarten teacher. She had a plate with a cup of tea and a piece of chocolate cake; I had a plate with a cup of tea and a piece of marshmallow cake. We maneuvered up to one another cautiously, and smiled.

"I've been so anxious to meet you," I said. "I'm Laurie's mother."

"We're all so interested in Laurie," she said.

"Well, he certainly likes kindergarten," I said. "He talks about it all the time."

"We had a little trouble adjusting, the first week or so," she said primly, "but now he's a fine little helper. With occasional lapses,[8] of course."

"Laurie usually adjusts very quickly," I said. "I suppose this time it's Charles's influence."

"Charles?"

"Yes," I said, laughing, "you must have your hands full in that kindergarten, with Charles."

"Charles?" she said. "We don't have any Charles in the kindergarten."

---

7. **haggard:** tired and worn-out.
8. **lapses:** slips or failures.

SEEKING MEANING

1. "Charles" is about a child's conflict, or struggle, with his teacher. What are some of the ways in which Charles opposes his teacher? Why do you suppose he behaves in this way?

2. By the end of the story, what have you learned about the character known as "Charles"? When did you begin to suspect who Charles was?

3. According to the narrator (Laurie's mother), how does Laurie show he is influenced by the terrible Charles?

4. The narrator's husband urges her to invite Charles's mother to tea: "I want to get a look at her." Once you realize who Charles is, why do comments like this one become so humorous? What other comments made by Laurie's parents become humorous once the surprise is revealed?

5. Why do you suppose Laurie's parents never questioned his explanation of what went on in kindergarten? Which passages show that Laurie enjoyed telling his shocking stories about Charles?

DEVELOPING VOCABULARY

Recognizing Suffixes

Suffixes can be used to change a word from one part of speech to another. For example, *warily* is an adverb meaning "cautiously." It is formed by adding the suffix -*ly* to the adjective *wary*. (The final *y* is changed to *i* when the suffix is added.)

Here are some other common suffixes that can be added to a word to change it from one part of speech to another:

-al	-ed	-ment
-ation *or* -tion	-er *or* -or	-ness

It is helpful to recognize suffixes like these. Often a dictionary defines only the root word, not the word with a suffix. Look in your dictionary to see if it defines the word *warily*, or just the word *wary*.

Here are some words from the story that contain suffixes. What is the root word? What suffix is added to each root word? Does your dictionary define the word with the suffix, or does it define just the root word?

awed	passionately
cynically	reformation
heartily	teacher
matronly	toughness

ABOUT THE AUTHOR

Shirley Jackson (1919–1965) is known chiefly for her horror stories. Like "Charles," these stories often end with surprising twists. She also wrote humorous stories based on her life at home with her four children and her husband, a college professor. More stories about this zany family are in *Life Among the Savages* and *Raising Demons*—the titles themselves suggesting Shirley Jackson's humorous view of her children. Another Jackson story that frequently appears in schoolbooks is "The Sneaker Crisis," in which Laurie is about thirteen years old. Her most famous horror story is "The Lottery," which is based on the old idea of ritual sacrifice.

*Steve ought to have known
the value of money. It had
been ground into him. But
the boy was crazy about
baseball.*

A Cap for Steve   *Morley Callaghan*

Dave Diamond, a poor man, a carpenter's assistant, was a small, wiry, quick-tempered individual who had learned how to make every dollar count in his home. His wife, Anna, had been sick a lot, and his twelve-year-old son, Steve, had to be kept in school. Steve, a big-eyed, shy kid, ought to have known the value of money as well as Dave did. It had been ground into him.

But the boy was crazy about baseball, and after school, when he could have been working as a delivery boy or selling papers, he played ball with the kids. His failure to appreciate that the family needed a few extra dollars disgusted Dave. Around the house he wouldn't let Steve talk about baseball, and he scowled when he saw him hurrying off with his glove after dinner.

When the Phillies came to town to play an exhibition game with the home team and Steve pleaded to be taken to the ballpark, Dave, of course, was outraged. Steve knew they couldn't afford it. But he had got his mother on his side. Finally Dave made a bargain with them. He said that if Steve came home after school and worked hard helping to make some kitchen shelves, he would take him that night to the ballpark.

Steve worked hard, but Dave was still resentful. They had to coax him to put on his good suit. When they started out, Steve held aloof, feeling guilty, and they walked down the street like strangers; then Dave glanced at Steve's face and, half ashamed, took his arm more cheerfully.

As the game went on, Dave had to listen to Steve's recitation of the batting average of every Philly that stepped up to the plate; the time the boy must have wasted learning these averages began to appall him. He showed it so plainly that Steve felt guilty again and was silent.

After the game Dave let Steve drag him onto the field to keep him company while he tried to get some autographs from the Philly players, who were being hemmed in by gangs of kids blocking the way to the clubhouse. But Steve, who was shy, let the other kids block him off from the players. Steve would push his way in, get blocked out, and come back to stand mournfully beside Dave. And Dave grew impatient. He was wasting valuable time. He wanted to get home; Steve knew it and was worried.

Then the big, blond Philly outfielder, Eddie Condon, who had been held up by a gang of

kids tugging at his arm and thrusting their score cards at him, broke loose and made a run for the clubhouse. He was jostled, and his blue cap with the red peak, tilted far back on his head, fell off. It fell at Steve's feet, and Steve stooped quickly and grabbed it. "Okay, son," the outfielder called, turning back. But Steve, holding the hat in both hands, only stared at him.

"Give him his cap, Steve," Dave said, smiling apologetically at the big outfielder, who towered over them. But Steve drew the hat closer to his chest. In an awed trance he looked up at big Eddie Condon. It was an embarrassing moment. All the other kids were watching. Some shouted, "Give him his cap."

"My cap, son," Eddie Condon said, his hand out.

"Hey, Steve," Dave said, and he gave him a shake. But he had to jerk the cap out of Steve's hands.

"Here you are," he said.

The outfielder, noticing Steve's white, worshiping face and pleading eyes, grinned and then shrugged. "Aw, let him keep it," he said.

"No, Mister Condon, you don't need to do that," Steve protested.

"It's happened before. Forget it," Eddie Condon said, and he trotted away to the clubhouse.

Dave handed the cap to Steve; envious kids circled around them and Steve said, "He said I could keep it, Dad. You heard him, didn't you?"

"Yeah, I heard him," Dave admitted. The wonder in Steve's face made him smile. He took the boy by the arm and they hurried off the field.

On the way home Dave couldn't get him to talk about the game; he couldn't get him to take his eyes off the cap. Steve could hardly believe in his own happiness. "See," he said

suddenly, and he showed Dave that Eddie Condon's name was printed on the sweatband. Then he went on dreaming. Finally he put the cap on his head and turned to Dave with a slow, proud smile. The cap was away too big for him; it fell down over his ears. "Never mind," Dave said. "You can get your mother to take a tuck in the back."

When they got home, Dave was tired and his wife didn't understand the cap's importance, and they couldn't get Steve to go to bed. He swaggered around wearing the cap and looking in the mirror every ten minutes. He took the cap to bed with him.

Dave and his wife had a cup of coffee in the kitchen, and Dave told her again how they had got the cap. They agreed that their boy must have an attractive quality that showed in his face, and that Eddie Condon must have been drawn to him—why else would he have singled Steve out from all the kids?

But Dave got tired of the fuss Steve made over that cap and of the way he wore it from the time he got up in the morning until the time he went to bed. Some kid was always coming in, wanting to try on the cap. It was childish, Dave said, for Steve to go around assuming that the cap made him important in the neighborhood, and to keep telling them how he had become a leader in the park a few blocks away where he played ball in the evenings. And Dave wouldn't stand for Steve's keeping the cap on while he was eating. He was always scolding his wife for accepting Steve's explanation that he'd forgotten he had it on. Just the same, it was remarkable what a little thing like a ball cap could do for a kid, Dave admitted to his wife as he smiled to himself.

One night Steve was late coming home from the park. Dave didn't realize how late it was until he put down his newspaper and watched his wife at the window. Her restlessness got on his nerves. "See what comes from encouraging the boy to hang around with those park loafers," he said. "I don't encourage him," she protested. "You do," he insisted irritably, for he was really worried now. A gang hung around the park until midnight. It was a bad park. It was true that on one side there was a good district with fine, expensive apartment houses, but the kids from that neighborhood left the park to the kids from the poorer homes. When his wife went out and walked down to the corner, it was his turn to wait and worry and watch at the open window. Each waiting moment tortured him. At last he heard his wife's voice and Steve's voice, and he relaxed and sighed; then he remembered his duty and rushed angrily to meet them.

"I'll fix you, Steve, once and for all," he said. "I'll show you you can't start coming into the house at midnight."

"Hold your horses, Dave," his wife said. "Can't you see the state he's in?" Steve looked utterly exhausted and beaten.

"What's the matter?" Dave asked quickly.

"I lost my cap," Steve whispered; he walked past his father and threw himself on the couch in the living room and lay with his face hidden.

"Now, don't scold him, Dave," his wife said.

"Scold him. Who's scolding him?" Dave asked, indignantly. "It's his cap, not mine. If it's not worth his while to hang on to it, why should I scold him?" But he was implying resentfully that he alone recognized the cap's value.

"So you are scolding him," his wife said. "It's his cap. Not yours. What happened, Steve?"

Steve told them he had been playing ball and he found that when he ran the bases the cap fell off; it was still too big despite the tuck his mother had taken in the band. So the next time he came to bat he tucked the cap in his hip pocket. Someone had lifted it, he was sure.

"And he didn't even know whether it was still in his pocket," Dave said sarcastically.

"I wasn't careless, Dad," Steve said. For the last three hours he had been wandering around to the homes of the kids who had been in the park at the time; he wanted to go on, but he was too tired. Dave knew the boy was apologizing to him, but he didn't know why it made him angry.

"If he didn't hang on to it, it's not worth worrying about now," he said, and he sounded offended.

After that night they knew that Steve didn't go to the park to play ball; he went to look for the cap. It irritated Dave to see him sit around listlessly, or walk in circles, trying to force his memory to find a particular incident which would suddenly recall to him the moment when the cap had been taken. It was no attitude for a growing, healthy boy to take, Dave complained. He told Steve firmly once and for all that he didn't want to hear any more about the cap.

One night, two weeks later, Dave was walking home with Steve from the shoemaker's. It was a hot night. When they passed an ice-cream parlor, Steve slowed down. "I guess I couldn't have a soda, could I?" Steve said. "Nothing doing," Dave said firmly. "Come on now," he added as Steve hung back, looking in the window.

"Dad, look!" Steve cried suddenly, pointing at the window. "My cap! There's my cap! He's coming out!"

A well-dressed boy was leaving the ice-cream parlor; he had on a blue ball cap with a red peak, just like Steve's cap. "Hey, you!" Steve cried, and he rushed at the boy, his small face fierce and his eyes wild. Before the boy could back away, Steve had snatched the cap from his head. "That's my cap!" he shouted.

"What's this?" the bigger boy said. "Hey, give me my cap or I'll give you a poke on the nose."

Dave was surprised that his own shy boy did not back away. He watched him clutch the cap in his left hand, half crying with excitement as he put his head down and drew back his right fist: he was willing to fight. And Dave was proud of him.

"Wait, now," Dave said. "Take it easy, son," he said to the other boy, who refused to back away.

"My boy says it's his cap," Dave said.

"Well, he's crazy. It's my cap."

"I was with him when he got this cap. When the Phillies played here. It's a Philly cap."

"Eddie Condon gave it to me," Steve said.

"And you stole it from me, you jerk."

"Don't call me a jerk, you little squirt. I never saw you before in my life."

"Look," Steve said, pointing to the printing on the cap's sweatband. "It's Eddie Condon's cap. See? See, Dad?"

"Yeah. You're right, Son. Ever see this boy before, Steve?"

"No," Steve said reluctantly.

The other boy realized he might lose the cap. "I bought it from a guy," he said. "I paid him. My father knows I paid him." He said he got the cap at the ballpark. He groped for some magically impressive words and suddenly found them. "You'll have to speak to my father," he said.

"Sure, I'll speak to your father," Dave said. "What's your name? Where do you live?"

"My name's Hudson. I live about ten minutes away on the other side of the park." The boy appraised Dave, who wasn't much bigger than he was and who wore a faded blue windbreaker and no tie. "My father is a lawyer," he said boldly. "He wouldn't let me keep the cap if he didn't think I should."

"Is that a fact?" Dave asked belligerently. "Well, we'll see. Come on. Let's go." And he got between the two boys and they walked along the street. They didn't talk to each other. Dave knew the Hudson boy was waiting to get to the protection of his home, and Steve knew it, too, and he looked up apprehensively at Dave. And Dave, reaching for his hand, squeezed it encouragingly and strode along, cocky and belligerent, knowing that Steve relied on him.

The Hudson boy lived in that row of fine apartment houses on the other side of the park. At the entrance to one of these houses, Dave tried not to hang back and show he was impressed, because he could feel Steve hanging back. When they got into the small elevator, Dave didn't know why he took off his hat.

In the carpeted hall on the fourth floor, the Hudson boy said, "Just a minute," and entered his own apartment. Dave and Steve were left alone in the corridor, knowing that the other boy was preparing his father for the encounter. Steve looked anxiously at his father, and Dave said, "Don't worry, Son," and he added resolutely, "No one's putting anything over on us."

A tall, balding man in a brown velvet smoking jacket suddenly opened the door. Dave had never seen a man wearing one of those jackets, although he had seen them in department store windows. "Good evening," he said, making a deprecatory[1] gesture at the cap Steve clutched tightly in his hand. "My boy didn't get your name. My name is Hudson."

"Mine's Diamond."

"Come on in," Mr. Hudson said, putting out his hand and laughing good-naturedly. He led Dave and Steve into his living room. "What's this about that cap?" he asked. "The way kids can get excited about a cap. Well, it's understandable, isn't it?"

"So it is," Dave said, moving closer to Steve, who was awed by the broadloom rug and the fine furniture. He wanted to show Steve he was at ease himself, and he wished Mr. Hudson wouldn't be so polite. That meant Dave had to be polite and affable, too, and it was hard to manage when he was standing in the middle of the floor in his old windbreaker.

"Sit down, Mr. Diamond," Mr. Hudson said. Dave took Steve's arm and sat him down beside him on the chesterfield.[2] The Hudson boy watched his father. And Dave looked at Steve and saw that he wouldn't face Mr. Hudson or the other boy; he kept looking up at Dave, putting all his faith in him.

---

1. **deprecatory** (dĕp'rə-kə-tôr'ē): apologetic.
2. **chesterfield** (chĕs'tər-fēld): a kind of sofa.

"Well, Mr. Diamond, from what I gathered from my boy, you're able to prove this cap belonged to your boy."

"That's a fact," Dave said.

"Mr. Diamond, you'll have to believe my boy bought that cap from some kid in good faith."

"I don't doubt it," Dave said. "But no kid can sell something that doesn't belong to him. You know that's a fact, Mr. Hudson."

"Yes, that's a fact," Mr. Hudson agreed. "But that cap means a lot to my boy, Mr. Diamond."

"It means a lot to my boy, too, Mr. Hudson."

"Sure it does. But supposing we called in a policeman. You know what he'd say? He'd ask you if you were willing to pay my boy what he paid for the cap. That's usually the way it works out," Mr. Hudson said, friendly and smiling, as he eyed Dave shrewdly.

"But that's not right. It's not justice," Dave protested. "Not when it's my boy's cap."

"I know it isn't right. But that's what they do."

"All right. What did you say your boy paid for the cap?" Dave said reluctantly.

"Two dollars."

"Two dollars!" Dave repeated. Mr. Hudson's smile was still kindly, but his eyes were shrewd, and Dave knew the lawyer was counting on his not having the two dollars;

Mr. Hudson thought he had Dave sized up; he had looked at him and decided he was broke. Dave's pride was hurt, and he turned to Steve. What he saw in Steve's face was more powerful than the hurt to his pride: it was the memory of how difficult it had been to get an extra nickel, the talk he heard about the cost of food, the worry in his mother's face as she tried to make ends meet, and the bewildered embarrassment that he was here in a rich man's home, forcing his father to confess that he couldn't afford to spend two dollars. Then Dave grew angry and reckless. "I'll give you the two dollars," he said.

Steve looked at the Hudson boy and grinned brightly. The Hudson boy watched his father.

"I suppose that's fair enough," Mr. Hudson said. "A cap like this can be worth a lot to a kid. You know how it is. Your boy might want to sell—I mean be satisfied. Would he take five dollars for it?"

"Five dollars?" Dave repeated. "Is it worth five dollars, Steve?" he asked uncertainly.

Steve shook his head and looked frightened.

"No, thanks, Mr. Hudson," Dave said firmly.

"I'll tell you what I'll do," Mr. Hudson said. "I'll give you ten dollars. The cap has a sentimental value for my boy, a Philly cap, a big-leaguer's cap. It's only worth about a buck and a half really," he added. But Dave shook his head again. Mr. Hudson frowned. He looked at his own boy with indulgent concern, but now he was embarrassed. "I'll tell you what I'll do," he said. "This cap—well, it's worth as much as a day at the circus to my boy. Your boy should be recompensed.[3] I want to be fair. Here's twenty dollars," and he held out two ten-dollar bills to Dave.

That much money for a cap, Dave thought, and his eyes brightened. But he knew what the cap had meant to Steve; to deprive him of it now that it was within his reach would be unbearable. All the things he needed in his life gathered around him; his wife was there, saying he couldn't afford to reject the offer, he had no right to do it; and he turned to Steve to see if Steve thought it wonderful that the cap could bring them twenty dollars.

"What do you say, Steve?" he asked uneasily.

"I don't know," Steve said. He was in a trance. When Dave smiled, Steve smiled too, and Dave believed that Steve was as impressed as he was, only more bewildered, and maybe even more aware that they could not possibly turn away that much money for a ball cap.

"Well, here you are," Mr. Hudson said, and he put the two bills in Steve's hand. "It's a lot of money. But I guess you had a right to expect as much."

With a dazed, fixed smile Steve handed the money slowly to his father, and his face was white.

Laughing jovially, Mr. Hudson led them to the door. His own boy followed a few paces behind.

In the elevator Dave took the bills out of his pocket. "See, Stevie," he whispered eagerly. "That windbreaker you wanted! And ten dollars for your bank! Won't Mother be surprised?"

"Yeah," Steve whispered, the little smile still on his face. But Dave had to turn away quickly so their eyes wouldn't meet, for he saw that it was a scared smile.

Outside, Dave said, "Here, you carry the money home, Steve. You show it to your mother."

"No, you keep it," Steve said, and then there was nothing to say. They walked in silence.

"It's a lot of money," Dave said finally.

---

3. **recompensed** (rĕk′əm-pĕnst′): paid.

When Steve didn't answer him, he added angrily, "I turned to you, Steve. I asked you, didn't I?"

"That man knew how much his boy wanted that cap," Steve said.

"Sure. But he recognized how much it was worth to us."

"No, you let him take it away from us," Steve blurted.

"That's unfair," Dave said. "Don't dare say that to me."

"I don't want to be like you," Steve muttered, and he darted across the road and walked along on the other side of the street.

"It's unfair," Dave said angrily, only now he didn't mean that Steve was unfair. He meant that what had happened in the prosperous Hudson home was unfair, and he didn't know quite why. He had been trapped, not just by Mr. Hudson, but by his own life.

Across the road Steve was hurrying along with his head down, wanting to be alone. They walked most of the way home on opposite sides of the street, until Dave could stand it no longer. "Steve," he called, crossing the street. "It was very unfair. I mean, for you to say . . ." but Steve started to run. Dave walked as fast as he could and Steve was getting beyond him, and he felt enraged and suddenly he yelled, "Steve!" and he started to chase his son. He wanted to get hold of Steve and pound him, and he didn't know why. He gained on him, he gasped for breath and he almost got him by the shoulder. Turning, Steve saw his father's face in the streetlight and was terrified; he circled away, got to the house, and rushed in, yelling, "Mother!"

"Son, Son!" she cried, rushing from the kitchen. As soon as she threw her arms around Steve, shielding him, Dave's anger left him and he felt stupid. He walked past them into the kitchen.

"What happened?" she asked anxiously.

"Have you both gone crazy? What did you do, Steve?"

"Nothing," he said sullenly.

"What did your father do?"

"We found the boy with my ball cap, and he let the boy's father take it from us."

"No, no," Dave protested. "Nobody pushed us around. The man didn't put anything over on us." He felt tired and his face was burning. He told what had happened; then he slowly took the two ten-dollar bills out of his wallet and tossed them on the table and looked up guiltily at his wife.

It hurt him that she didn't pick up the money and that she didn't rebuke him. "It is a lot of money, Son," she said slowly. "Your father was only trying to do what he knew was right, and it'll work out, and you'll understand." She was soothing Steve, but Dave knew she felt that she needed to be gentle with him, too, and he was ashamed.

When she went with Steve to his bedroom, Dave sat by himself. His son had contempt for him, he thought. His son, for the first time, had seen how easy it was for another man to handle him, and he had judged him and had wanted to walk alone on the other side of the street. He looked at the money and he hated the sight of it.

His wife returned to the kitchen, made a cup of tea, talked soothingly, and said it was incredible that he had forced the Hudson man to pay him twenty dollars for the cap, but all Dave could think of was Steve was scared of me.

Finally, he got up and went into Steve's room. The room was in darkness, but he could see the outline of Steve's body on the bed, and he sat down beside him and whispered, "Look, Son, it was a mistake. I know why. People like us — in circumstances where money can scare us. No, no," he said, feeling ashamed and shaking his head apologetically;

he was taking the wrong way of showing the boy they were together; he was covering up his own failure. The failure had been his, and it had come out of being so separated from his son that he had been blind to what was beyond the price in a boy's life. He longed now to show Steve he could be with him from day to day. His hand went out hesitantly to Steve's shoulder. "Steve, look," he said eagerly. "The trouble was I didn't realize how much I enjoyed it that night at the ballpark. If I had watched you playing for your own team — the kids around here say you could be a great pitcher. We could take that money and buy a new pitcher's glove for you, and a catcher's mitt. Steve, Steve, are you listening? I could catch you, work with you in the lane. Maybe I could be your coach . . . watch you become a great pitcher." In the half-darkness he could see the boy's pale face turn to him.

Steve, who had never heard his father talk like this, was shy and wondering. All he knew was that his father, for the first time, wanted to be with him in his hopes and adventures. He said, "I guess you do know how important that cap was." His hand went out to his father's arm. "With that man the cap was — well, it was just something he could buy, eh, Dad?" Dave gripped his son's hand hard. The wonderful generosity of childhood — the price a boy was willing to pay to be able to count on his father's admiration and approval — made him feel humble, then strangely exalted.

SEEKING MEANING

1. In this story, Dave Diamond and his son, Steve, are divided and then brought closer together because of a conflict over money. What does the first paragraph tell about the father's attitude toward money? According to the second paragraph, how has money caused hard feelings between father and son?

2. The baseball cap has a meaning for Steve that his father does not understand. Why does the cap mean so much to Steve? What does Dave think of Steve's attachment to the cap at first?

3. The bargaining for the cap that takes place at the Hudson apartment becomes a kind of test for the two fathers. Mr. Hudson "passes" the test because he has enough money to pay any price for the cap. Why does Dave "fail" the bargaining test? What should Dave have done in order to "pass" the test in his son's eyes?

4. Later, Dave looks at the money he has accepted for the cap and hates the sight of it. What has Dave realized is more important than money?

5. What does Dave finally say to make Steve see that he does know what is "beyond the price" in his son's life?

6. This story begins with a conflict. Do you think it ends with peace? Explain your answer.

DEVELOPING SKILLS IN READING

Recognizing the Causes of a Character's Actions

An important moment in this story occurs when the two fathers bargain for the baseball cap. At first, Dave offers to pay two dollars for the cap. But by the end of the scene, he has decided to give up the cap entirely.

What causes Dave to change his mind and take the money instead of the cap? The answer is in this paragraph.

> That much money for a cap, Dave thought, and his eyes brightened. But he knew what the cap had meant to Steve; to deprive him of it now that it was within his reach would be unbearable. All the things he needed in his life gathered around him; his wife was there, saying he couldn't afford to reject the offer, he had no right to do it; and he turned to Steve to see if Steve thought it wonderful that the cap could bring them twenty dollars.

The turning point of the story occurs when Dave goes into Steve's bedroom and tries to explain why he gave up the cap. Steve is angry with his father. He has already said, "I don't want to be like you." According to the last paragraph of the story, what causes Steve to forgive his father and to forget about the cap?

DEVELOPING VOCABULARY

Recognizing Multiple Meanings of Words

The meaning of a word is usually clear from its *context*—that is, from the other words in the sentence or paragraph. On page 101, Dave says, "See what comes from encouraging the boy to hang around with those park *loafers*." Clearly, *loafers* in this sentence doesn't mean a pair of shoes; it means a group of lazy people. How do you know?

What does each italicized word or phrase mean in the following quotations from the story? Write a sentence using each word or phrase in another context, to indicate a different meaning. Do some words have more than two meanings? Your dictionary will help.

> Steve . . . ought to have known the value of money as well as Dave did. It had been *ground* into him.
>
> . . . Eddie Condon must have been *drawn* to him . . . .
>
> . . . Mr. Hudson thought he had Dave *sized* up; he had looked at him and decided he was *broke*.
>
> ". . . the kids around here say you could be a great *pitcher*."

DEVELOPING SKILLS OF EXPRESSION

Writing a Dialogue

In a story or play, what the characters say to each other is called *dialogue*. Characters can address each other and respond to what other characters say, just as people do in a conversation. What each character says is enclosed in quotation marks.

Dialogue makes a character come alive. It can also add excitement to a story. For example, the scene in which Steve returns home after losing the cap could have been written in this way:

Dave was angry at Steve and yelled at him. His wife told Dave to stop, because Steve was exhausted. When Dave asked Steve what was wrong, Steve said that he'd lost his cap.

Instead, the author wrote a dialogue:

"I'll fix you, Steve, once and for all," he said. "I'll show you you can't start coming into the house at midnight."

"Hold your horses, Dave," his wife said. "Can't you see the state he's in?" Steve looked utterly exhausted and beaten.

"What's the matter?" Dave asked quickly.

"I lost my cap," Steve whispered . . . .

Write a dialogue that could have taken place between Mr. Hudson and his son while Steve and Dave were waiting outside their apartment (page 103). What do you think the Hudson boy said to his father about how he got the cap? How did he explain who the Diamonds were and what they wanted? What do you think Mr. Hudson said to his son just before he let the Diamonds in?

ABOUT THE AUTHOR

Morley Callaghan (1903–   ) is a Canadian short-story writer and novelist. He was a member of the "lost generation"—a group of writers and artists of the 1920's who gathered mostly in Paris, searching for new ways to express their ideas. In his stories, Callaghan tries to show that events which seem unimportant to others are often very important to the people involved. His stories are written in a plain and straightforward style, like those of the writer he most admires, Ernest Hemingway. Other stories by Callaghan that often appear in schoolbooks are "All the Years of Her Life," "The Snob," and "Luke Baldwin's Vow."

Squeaky had a roomful of ribbons and medals and awards. But what did her brother Raymond have to call his own?

Raymond's Run

Toni Cade Bambara

I don't have much work to do around the house like some girls. My mother does that. And I don't have to earn my pocket money. George runs errands for the big boys and sells Christmas cards. And anything else that's got to get done, my father does. All I have to do in life is mind my brother Raymond, which is enough.

Sometimes I slip and say my little brother Raymond. But as any fool can see, he's much bigger and he's older too. But a lot of people call him my little brother cause he needs looking after cause he's not quite right. And a lot of smart mouths got lots to say about that too, especially when George was minding him. But now, if anybody has anything to say to Raymond, anything to say about his big head, they have to come by me. And I don't play the dozens[1] or believe in standing around with somebody in my face doing a lot of talking. I much rather just knock you down and take my chances even if I am a little girl with skinny arms and a squeaky voice, which is

how I got the name Squeaky. And if things get too rough, I run. And as anybody can tell you, I'm the fastest thing on two feet.

There is no track meet that I don't win the first-place medal. I used to win the twenty-yard dash when I was a little kid in kindergarten. Nowadays, it's the fifty-yard dash. And tomorrow I'm subject to run the quarter-meter relay all by myself and come in first, second, and third. The big kids call me Mercury[2] cause I'm the swiftest thing in the neighborhood. Everybody knows that—except two people who know better, my father and me. He can beat me to Amsterdam Avenue with me having a two-fire-hydrant head start and him running with his hands in his pockets and whistling. But that's private information. Cause can you imagine some thirty-five-year-old man stuffing himself into PAL[3] shorts to race little kids? So as far as everyone's concerned, I'm the fastest and that goes for Gretchen, too, who has put out the tale that she is going to win the first-place

---

1. **the dozens:** a game in which players trade insults. The first person who shows anger is the loser.

2. **Mercury:** the ancient Roman messenger god, known for his speed.
3. **PAL:** Police Athletic League.

medal this year. Ridiculous. In the second place, she's got short legs. In the third place, she's got freckles. In the first place, no one can beat me and that's all there is to it.

I'm standing on the corner admiring the weather and about to take a stroll down Broadway so I can practice my breathing exercises, and I've got Raymond walking on the inside close to the buildings, cause he's subject to fits of fantasy and starts thinking he's a circus performer and that the curb is a tightrope strung high in the air. And sometimes after a rain he likes to step down off his tightrope right into the gutter and slosh around getting his shoes and cuffs wet. Then I get hit when I get home. Or sometimes if you don't watch him he'll dash across traffic to the island in the middle of Broadway and give the pigeons a fit. Then I have to go behind him apologizing to all the old people sitting around trying to get some sun and getting all upset with the pigeons fluttering around them, scattering their newspapers and upsetting the wax-paper lunches in their laps. So I keep Raymond on the inside of me, and he plays like he's driving a stagecoach, which is OK by me so long as he doesn't run me over or interrupt my breathing exercises, which I have to do on account of I'm serious about my running, and I don't care who knows it.

Now some people like to act like things come easy to them, won't let on that they practice. Not me. I'll high-prance down 34th Street like a rodeo pony to keep my knees strong even if it does get my mother uptight so that she walks ahead like she's not with me, don't know me, is all by herself on a shopping trip, and I am somebody else's crazy child. Now you take Cynthia Procter for instance. She's just the opposite. If there's a test tomorrow, she'll say something like, "Oh, I guess I'll play handball this afternoon and watch television tonight," just to let you know she ain't thinking about the test. Or like last week when she won the spelling bee for the millionth time, "A good thing you got *receive*, Squeaky, cause I would have got it wrong. I completely forgot about the spelling bee." And she'll clutch the lace on her blouse like it was a narrow escape. Oh, brother. But of course when I pass her house on my early morning trots around the block, she is practicing the scales on the piano over and over and over and over. Then in music class she always lets herself get bumped around so she falls accidentally on purpose onto the piano stool and is so surprised to find herself sitting there that she decides just for fun to try out the ole keys. And what do you know— Chopin's[4] waltzes just spring out of her fingertips and she's the most surprised thing in the world. A regular prodigy. I could kill people like that. I stay up all night studying the words for the spelling bee. And you can see me any time of day practicing running. I never walk if I can trot, and shame on Raymond if he can't keep up. But of course he does, cause if he hangs back someone's liable to walk up to him and get smart, or take his allowance from him, or ask him where he got that great big pumpkin head. People are so stupid sometimes.

So I'm strolling down Broadway breathing out and breathing in on counts of seven, which is my lucky number, and here comes Gretchen and her sidekicks: Mary Louise, who used to be a friend of mine when she first moved to Harlem from Baltimore and got beat up by everybody till I took up for her on account of her mother and my mother used to sing in the same choir when they were young girls, but people ain't grateful, so now she hangs out with the new girl Gretchen and

---

4. **Chopin** (shō′păn′): Frédéric François Chopin (1810– 1849), a Polish composer and pianist.

talks about me like a dog; and Rosie, who is as fat as I am skinny and has a big mouth where Raymond is concerned and is too stupid to know that there is not a big deal of difference between herself and Raymond and that she can't afford to throw stones. So they are steady coming up Broadway and I see right away that it's going to be one of those Dodge City[5] scenes cause the street ain't that big and they're close to the buildings just as we are. First I think I'll step into the candy store and look over the new comics and let them pass. But that's chicken and I've got a reputation to consider. So then I think I'll just walk straight on through them or even over them if necessary. But as they get to me, they slow down. I'm ready to fight, cause like I said I don't feature a whole lot of chitchat, I much prefer to just knock you down right from the jump and save everybody a lotta precious time.

"You signing up for the May Day races?" smiles Mary Louise, only it's not a smile at all. A dumb question like that doesn't deserve an answer. Besides, there's just me and Gretchen standing there really, so no use wasting my breath talking to shadows.

"I don't think you're going to win this time," says Rosie, trying to signify with her hands on her hips all salty, completely forgetting that I have whupped her many times for less salt than that.

"I always win cause I'm the best," I say straight at Gretchen, who is, as far as I'm concerned, the only one talking in this ventriloquist-dummy routine. Gretchen smiles, but it's not a smile, and I'm thinking that girls never really smile at each other because they don't know how and don't want to know how and there's probably no one to teach us how,

cause grown-up girls don't know either. Then they all look at Raymond, who has just brought his mule team to a standstill. And they're about to see what trouble they can get into through him.

"What grade you in now, Raymond?"

"You got anything to say to my brother, you say it to me, Mary Louise Williams of Raggedy Town, Baltimore."

"What are you, his mother?" sasses Rosie.

"That's right, Fatso. And the next word out of anybody and I'll be *their* mother too." So they just stand there and Gretchen shifts from one leg to the other and so do they. Then Gretchen puts her hands on her hips and is about to say something with her freckle-face self but doesn't. Then she walks around me looking me up and down but keeps walking up Broadway, and her sidekicks follow her. So me and Raymond smile at each other and he says, "Gidyap" to his team and I continue with my breathing exercises, strolling down Broadway toward the ice man on 145th with not a care in the world cause I am Miss Quicksilver herself.

I take my time getting to the park on May Day because the track meet is the last thing on the program. The biggest thing on the program is the Maypole dancing, which I can do without, thank you, even if my mother thinks it's a shame I don't take part and act like a girl for a change. You'd think my mother'd be grateful not to have to make me a white organdy dress with a big satin sash and buy me new white baby-doll shoes that can't be taken out of the box till the big day. You'd think she'd be glad her daughter ain't out there prancing around a Maypole getting the new clothes all dirty and sweaty and trying to act like a fairy or a flower or whatever you're supposed to be when you should be trying to be yourself, whatever that is, which is, as far as I am concerned, a poor black girl who really

---

5. **Dodge City:** the setting of the old television series "Gunsmoke," which often featured a showdown between the marshal and a gunfighter.

can't afford to buy shoes and a new dress you only wear once a lifetime cause it won't fit next year.

I was once a strawberry in a Hansel and Gretel pageant when I was in nursery school and didn't have no better sense than to dance on tiptoe with my arms in a circle over my head doing umbrella steps and being a perfect fool just so my mother and father could come dressed up and clap. You'd think they'd know better than to encourage that kind of nonsense. I am not a strawberry. I do not dance on my toes. I run. That is what I am all about. So I always come late to the May Day program, just in time to get my number pinned on and lay in the grass till they announce the fifty-yard dash.

I put Raymond in the little swings, which is a tight squeeze this year and will be impossible next year. Then I look around for Mr. Pearson, who pins the numbers on. I'm really looking for Gretchen if you want to know the truth, but she's not around. The park is jam-packed. Parents in hats and corsages and breast-pocket handkerchiefs peeking up. Kids in white dresses and light-blue suits. The parkees unfolding chairs and chasing the rowdy kids from Lenox as if they had no right to be there. The big guys with their caps on backwards, leaning against the fence swirling the basketballs on the tips of their fingers, waiting for all these crazy people to clear out the park so they can play. Most of the kids in my class are carrying bass drums and glockenspiels[6] and flutes. You'd think they'd put in a few bongos or something for real like that.

Then here comes Mr. Pearson with his clipboard and his cards and pencils and whistles and safety pins and fifty million other things

he's always dropping all over the place with his clumsy self. He sticks out in a crowd because he's on stilts. We used to call him Jack and the Beanstalk to get him mad. But I'm the only one that can outrun him and get away, and I'm too grown for that silliness now.

"Well, Squeaky," he says, checking my name off the list and handing me number seven and two pins. And I'm thinking he's got no right to call me Squeaky, if I can't call him Beanstalk.

"Hazel Elizabeth Deborah Parker," I correct him and tell him to write it down on his board.

"Well, Hazel Elizabeth Deborah Parker, going to give someone else a break this year?" I squint at him real hard to see if he is seriously thinking I should lose the race on purpose just to give someone else a break. "Only six girls running this time," he continues, shaking his head sadly like it's my fault all of New York didn't turn out in sneakers. "That new girl should give you a run for your money." He looks around the park for Gretchen like a periscope in a submarine movie. "Wouldn't it be a nice gesture if you were . . . to ahhh . . ."

I give him such a look he couldn't finish putting that idea into words. Grown-ups got a lot of nerve sometimes. I pin number seven to myself and stomp away, I'm so burnt. And I go straight for the track and stretch out on the grass while the band winds up with "Oh, the Monkey Wrapped His Tail Around the Flagpole," which my teacher calls by some other name. The man on the loudspeaker is calling everyone over to the track and I'm on my back looking at the sky, trying to pretend I'm in the country, but I can't, because even grass in the city feels hard as sidewalk, and there's just no pretending you are anywhere but in a "concrete jungle" as my grandfather says.

---

6. **glockenspiels** (glŏk′ən-spēlz′): musical instruments, something like xylophones, often used in marching bands.

The twenty-yard dash takes all of two minutes cause most of the little kids don't know no better than to run off the track or run the wrong way or run smack into the fence and fall down and cry. One little kid, though, has got the good sense to run straight for the white ribbon up ahead so he wins. Then the second-graders line up for the thirty-yard dash and I don't even bother to turn my head to watch cause Raphael Perez always wins. He wins before he even begins by psyching the runners, telling them they're going to trip on their shoelaces and fall on their faces or lose their shorts or something, which he doesn't really have to do since he is very fast, almost as fast as I am. After that is the forty-yard dash, which I used to run when I was in first grade. Raymond is hollering from the swings cause he knows I'm about to do my thing cause the man on the loudspeaker has just announced the fifty-yard dash, although he might just as well be giving a recipe for angel food cake cause you can hardly make out what he's saying for the static. I get up and slip off my sweat pants and then I see Gretchen standing at the starting line, kicking her legs out like a pro. Then as I get into place I see that ole Raymond is on line on the other side of the fence, bending down with his fingers on the ground just like he knew what he was doing. I was going to yell at him but then I didn't. It burns up your energy to holler.

Every time, just before I take off in a race, I always feel like I'm in a dream, the kind of dream you have when you're sick with fever and feel all hot and weightless. I dream I'm flying over a sandy beach in the early morning sun, kissing the leaves of the trees as I fly by. And there's always the smell of apples, just like in the country when I was little and used to think I was a choo-choo train, running through the fields of corn and chugging up the hill to the orchard. And all the time I'm dreaming this, I get lighter and lighter until I'm flying over the beach again, getting blown through the sky like a feather that weighs nothing at all. But once I spread my fingers in the dirt and crouch over the Get on Your Mark, the dream goes and I am solid again and am telling myself, Squeaky you must win, you must win, you are the fastest thing in the world, you can even beat your father up Amsterdam if you really try. And then I feel my weight coming back just behind my knees then down to my feet then into the earth and the pistol shot explodes in my blood and I am off and weightless again, flying past the other runners, my arms pumping up and down and the whole world is quiet except for the crunch as I zoom over the gravel in the track. I glance to my left and there is no one. To the right, a blurred Gretchen, who's got her chin jutting out as if it would win the race all by itself. And on the other side of the fence is Raymond with his arms down to his side and the palms tucked up behind him, running in his very own style, and it's the first time I ever saw that and I almost stop to watch my brother Raymond on his first run. But the white ribbon is bouncing toward me and I tear past it, racing into the distance till my feet with a mind of their own start digging up footfuls of dirt and brake me short. Then all the kids standing on the side pile on me, banging me on the back and slapping my head with their May Day programs, for I have won again and everybody on 151st Street can walk tall for another year.

"In first place . . ." the man on the loudspeaker is clear as a bell now. But then he pauses and the loudspeaker starts to whine. Then static. And I lean down to catch my breath and here comes Gretchen walking back, for she's overshot the finish line too, huffing and puffing with her hands on her hips taking it slow, breathing in steady time

like a real pro and I sort of like her a little for the first time. "In first place . . ." and then three or four voices get all mixed up on the loudspeaker and I dig my sneaker into the grass and stare at Gretchen, who's staring back, we both wondering just who did win. I can hear old Beanstalk arguing with the man on the loudspeaker and then a few others running their mouths about what the stopwatches say. Then I hear Raymond yanking at the fence to call me and I wave to shush him, but he keeps rattling the fence like a gorilla in a cage like in them gorilla movies, but then like a dancer or something he starts climbing up nice and easy but very fast. And it occurs to me, watching how smoothly he climbs hand over hand and remembering how he looked running with his arms down to his side and with the wind pulling his mouth back and his teeth showing and all, it occurred to me that Raymond would make a very fine runner. Doesn't he always keep up with me on my trots? And he surely knows how to breathe in counts of seven cause he's always doing it at the dinner table, which drives my brother George up the wall. And I'm smiling to beat the band cause if I've lost this race, or if me and Gretchen tied, or even if I've won, I can always retire as a runner and begin a whole new career as a coach with Raymond as my champion. After all, with a little more study I can beat Cynthia and her phony self at the spelling bee. And if I bugged my mother, I could get piano lessons and become a star. And I have a big rep as the baddest thing around. And I've got a roomful of ribbons and medals and awards. But what has Raymond got to call his own?

So I stand there with my new plans, laughing out loud by this time as Raymond jumps down from the fence and runs over with his teeth showing and his arms down to the side, which no one before him has quite mastered as a running style. And by the time he comes over I'm jumping up and down so glad to see him—my brother Raymond, a great runner in the family tradition. But of course everyone thinks I'm jumping up and down because the men on the loudspeaker have finally gotten themselves together and compared notes and are announcing "In first place—Miss Hazel Elizabeth Deborah Parker." (Dig that.) "In second place—Miss Gretchen P. Lewis." And I look over at Gretchen wondering what the *P* stands for. And I smile. Cause she's good, no doubt about it. Maybe she'd like to help me coach Raymond; she obviously is serious about running, as any fool can see. And she nods to congratulate me and then she smiles. And I smile. We stand there with this big smile of respect between us. It's about as real a smile as girls can do for each other, considering we don't practice real smiling every day, you know, cause maybe we too busy being flowers or fairies or strawberries instead of something honest and worthy of respect . . . you know . . . like being people.

SEEKING MEANING

1. In "Raymond's Run," a girl who believes in herself discovers the joy of believing in other people as well. What does Squeaky believe about her own abilities?

2. Squeaky believes in being honest. What actions of Cynthia Procter's irritate her?

3. Some people in the story think Squeaky should be a different kind of person. What would Squeaky's mother like her to do? What would Mr. Pearson like her to do?

4. Squeaky knows that she can win medals and "become a star." But she asks herself, "What has Raymond got to call his own?" After Raymond's run, what does Squeaky plan to do for her brother?

5. Squeaky also discovers something about her rival, Gretchen. Why do she and Gretchen smile at each other after the race?

6. Why do you think the author called this story "Raymond's Run"?

DEVELOPING SKILLS IN READING

Drawing Conclusions About a Character

In some stories, the writer may tell you directly that a character is loyal, or courageous, or mean, or dishonest. But in most stories, the writer lets you draw your own conclusions about a character's personal qualities.

In "Raymond's Run," for example, you learn a great deal about Squeaky from what she says and does, and even from what she thinks. But you are not told directly what her personal qualities are.

One way to learn about Squeaky's personal qualities is to notice how she acts toward Raymond. It would be easy to be cruel to Raymond, as some of the characters are. Name at least two of Squeaky's actions that reveal that she is loyal and kind to Raymond.

What personal qualities does Squeaky reveal by each of the following actions?

Squeaky admits that she needs to practice her running and her spelling.

Squeaky does not hide from the girls she meets on the street.

Squeaky smiles at Gretchen and admits that her rival is a good runner.

DEVELOPING SKILLS OF EXPRESSION

Writing from Another Point of View

With Squeaky as narrator, you cannot know what the other characters in "Raymond's Run" are thinking. You know only what they say and what Squeaky sees them doing.

Reread the paragraph beginning "Every time, just before I take off in a race. . . ." (page 114). Imagine that this same scene is being narrated by Gretchen. What is Gretchen thinking about as she prepares for the race? What is she thinking about during the race? What does she think about Squeaky?

Write a paragraph telling about the race, using Gretchen as the narrator. Begin with the words: "Every time, just before I take off in a race . . . ."

ABOUT THE AUTHOR

Toni Cade took the name Bambara from a signature on a sketchbook she found in her great-grandmother's trunk. (Bambara is the name of a people of northwest Africa, who are famous for their delicate woodcarvings.) Like her character Squeaky, she grew up in New York City. She says that she has been a writer since childhood, though she also "planned to be a doctor, lawyer, artist, musician, and everything else."

Many of E. E. Cummings' poems look like puzzles. Often he does not begin his sentences with capital letters or end them with periods. Sometimes he stretches words out across a line, or squeezes them together, or divides them up in unusual ways.

This poem is made up of three sentences, each beginning with the words old age. *The first part of each sentence, in parentheses, tells what old age does to youth. The second part, the part not in parentheses, tells how youth responds.*

old age sticks   *E. E. Cummings*

old age sticks
up Keep
Off
signs)&

youth yanks them   5
down(old
age
cries No

Tres)&(pas)
youth laughs   10
(sing
old age

scolds Forbid
den Stop
Must   15
n't Don't

&)youth goes
right on
gr
owing old   20

SEEKING MEANING

1. In this poem about the differences between generations, old age sticks up "Keep Off" signs. How does youth respond?

2. "No Trespassing" and "Keep Off" signs warn outsiders to keep off private property. However, in this poem, "No Trespassing" probably means more than this kind of warning. What else do you think old age is warning youth not to interfere with? How does youth respond to this cry of "No Trespassing"?

3. Which lines in the poem suggest that the difference between generations will go on and on forever? Why will this happen?

DEVELOPING SKILLS IN READING

Understanding the Poet's Technique

Notice how Cummings divides the word *growing* in lines 19–20. By stretching out the word in such a way, he suggests that growing old is a long, slow process. How would you read these lines aloud?

The words *No Trespassing* are spread out over lines 8, 9, and 11. They are interrupted by & and *youth laughs*. Shifting back and forth from *No Trespassing* to & *youth laughs* creates the same effect as that of a motion-picture camera focusing first on one character and then on another. We see what both characters are doing at the same time. How would you read these lines aloud?

ABOUT THE AUTHOR

By nature E. E. Cummings (1894–1962), whose full name was Edward Estlin Cummings, was shy and sensitive. A painter as well as a poet, he created many new ways of presenting a poem on a page. Some of his poems looked so unusual that they baffled typesetters and threw some readers into confusion.

Before the United States entered World War I, Cummings went to France as an ambulance driver. Because of a censor's error, he was placed in a French prison camp. There he gathered material for his book *The Enormous Room*, which has been called one of the best direct-observation books to come out of that war.

Cummings, however, is best known for his lyric poems, which are witty, emotional, and filled with striking images. He can make us look at the tiniest words and symbols in new ways. One of his books of poetry is called &
[*and*].

Then He Goes Free

Jessamyn West

While her mother and father awaited the arrival of Mr. and Mrs. Kibbler, who had called asking to speak to them "about Cress and Edwin, Jr.," Mr. Delahanty reminded his wife how wrong she had been about Cress.

"Not two months ago," he said, "in this very room you told me you were worried because Cress wasn't as interested in the boys as a girl her age should be. In this very room. And now look what's happened."

Mrs. Delahanty, worried now by Mrs. Kibbler's message, spoke more sharply than she had intended. "Don't keep repeating, 'in this very room,'" she said, "as if it would have been different if I'd said it in the back porch or out of doors. Besides, what has happened?"

Mr. Delahanty took off his hat, which he'd had on when Mrs. Kibbler phoned, and sailed it out of the living room toward the hall table, which he missed. "Don't ask me what's happened," he said. "I'm not the girl's mother."

Mrs. Delahanty took off her own hat and jabbed the hatpins back into it. "What do you mean, you're not the girl's mother? Of course you're not. No one ever said you were."

Mr. Delahanty picked up his fallen hat, put it on the chair beside the hall table and came back into the living room. "A girl confides in her mother," he told his wife.

"A girl confides in her mother!" Mrs. Delahanty was very scornful. "Who tells you these things, John Delahanty? Not *your* mother. She didn't have any daughter. Not me. Cress doesn't confide in anyone. How do you know these things, anyway, about mothers and daughters?"

John Delahanty seated himself upon the sofa, legs extended, head back, as straight and unrelaxed as a plank.

"Don't catch me up that way, Gertrude," he said. "You know I don't know them." Without giving his wife any opportunity to crow over this victory he went on quickly: "What I'd like to know is, why did the Kibblers have to pick a Saturday night for this call? Didn't they know we'd be going into town?"

Like most ranchers, John Delahanty stopped work early on Saturdays so that, after a quick cleanup and supper, he and his wife could drive into town. There they did nothing very important: bought groceries, saw a show, browsed around in hardware stores, visited friends. But after a week of seeing only themselves—the Delahanty ranch was off the main highway—it was pleasant simply to saunter along the sidewalks looking at the cars, the merchandise, the people in their town clothes. This Saturday trip to town was a jaunt they both looked forward to during the week, and tonight's trip, because of February's warmer air and suddenly, it seemed, longer twilight, would have been particularly pleasant.

"Five minutes more," said Mr. Delahanty, "and we'd have been on our way."

"Why didn't you tell Mrs. Kibbler we were just leaving?"

"I did. And she said for anything less important she wouldn't think of keeping us."

Mrs. Delahanty came over to the sofa and stood looking anxiously down at her husband. "John, exactly what did Mrs. Kibbler say?"

"The gist of it," said Mr. Delahanty, "was that . . ."

"I don't care about the gist of it. That's just what you think she said. I want to know what she really said."

Mr. Delahanty let his head fall forward, though he still kept his legs stiffly extended. "What she really said was, 'Is this Mr. John Delahanty?' And I said, 'Yes.' Then she said, 'This is Mrs. Edwin Kibbler, I guess you remember me.' "

"Remember her?" Mrs. Delahanty exclaimed. "I didn't know you even knew her."

"I don't," said Mr. Delahanty, "but I remember her all right. She came before the school board about a month ago to tell us we ought to take those two ollas[1] off the school grounds. She said it was old-fashioned to cool water that way, that the ollas looked messy and were unhygienic."

"Did you take them off?" Mrs. Delahanty asked, without thinking. As a private person

John Delahanty was reasonable and untalkative. As clerk of the school board he inclined toward dogmatism[2] and long-windedness. Now he began a defense of the ollas and the school board's action in retaining them.

"Look, John," said Mrs. Delahanty, "I'm not interested in the school board or its water coolers. What I want to know is, what did Mrs. Kibbler say about Cress?"

"Well, she said she wanted to have a little talk with us about Cress—and Edwin, Jr."

"I know that." Impatience made Mrs. Delahanty's voice sharp. "But what about them?"

Mr. Delahanty drew his feet up toward the sofa, then bent down and retied a shoelace. "About what Cress did to him—Edwin, Jr."

"*Did* to him!" said Mrs. Delahanty aghast.

"That's what his mother said."

Mrs. Delahanty sat down on the hassock at her husband's feet. "Did to him," she repeated again. "Why, what could Cress do to him? He's two or three years older than Cress, fifteen or sixteen anyway. What could she do to him?"

Mr. Delahanty straightened up. "She could hit him, I guess," he ventured.

"Hit him? What would she want to hit him for?"

"I don't know," said Mr. Delahanty. "I don't know that she did hit him. Maybe she kicked him. Anyway, his mother seems to think the boy's been damaged in some way."

"Damaged," repeated Mrs. Delahanty angrily. "Damaged! Why, Cress is too tenderhearted to hurt a fly. She shoos them outside instead of killing them. And you sit there talking of hitting and kicking."

"Well," said Mr. Delahanty mildly, "Edwin's got teeth out. I don't know how else she could get them out, do you?"

---

1. **ollas:** large earthenware jars.

2. **dogmatism** (dôg'mə-tĭz'əm): the insistence that his opinions are dogma, or unquestionable truth.

"I'm going to call Cress," said Mrs. Delahanty, "and ask her about this. I don't believe it for a minute."

"I don't think calling her will do any good. She left while I was talking to Mrs. Kibbler."

"What do you mean, left?"

"Went for a walk, she said."

"Well, teeth out," repeated Mrs. Delahanty unbelievingly. "Teeth out! I didn't know you could get teeth out except with pliers or a chisel."

"Maybe Edwin's teeth are weak."

"Don't joke about this, John Delahanty. It isn't any joking matter. And I don't believe it. I don't believe Cress did it or that that boy's teeth are out. Anyway I'd have to see them to believe it."

"You're going to," Mr. Delahanty said. "Mrs. Kibbler's bringing Edwin especially so you can."

Mrs. Delahanty sat for some time without saying anything at all. Then she got up and walked back and forth in front of her husband, turning her hat, which she still held, round and round on one finger. "Well, what does Mrs. Kibbler expect us to do now?" she asked. "If they really are out, that is?"

"For one thing," replied Mr. Delahanty, "she expects us to pay for some new ones. And for another . . ." Mr. Delahanty paused to listen. Faintly, in the distance a car could be heard. "Here she is now," he said.

Mrs. Delahanty stopped her pacing. "Do you think I should make some cocoa for them, John? And maybe some marguerites?"[3]

"No, I don't," said Mr. Delahanty. "I don't think Mrs. Kibbler considers this a social visit."

As the car turned into the long driveway which led between the orange grove on one side and the lemon grove on the other to the Delahanty house, Mrs. Delahanty said, "I still don't see why you think this proves I'm wrong."

Mr. Delahanty had forgotten about his wife's wrongness. "How do you mean wrong?" he asked.

"About Cress's not being interested in the boys."

"Oh," he said. "Well, you've got to be pretty interested in a person—one way or another—before you hit him."

"That's a perfectly silly notion," began Mrs. Delahanty, but before she could finish, the Kibblers had arrived.

Mr. Delahanty went to the door while Mrs. Delahanty stood in the back of the room by the fireplace unwilling to take one step toward meeting her visitors.

Mrs. Kibbler was a small woman with a large, determined nose, prominent blue eyes and almost no chin. Her naturally curly hair —she didn't wear a hat—sprang away from her head in a great cage-shaped pompadour[4] which dwarfed her face.

Behind Mrs. Kibbler was Mr. Kibbler, short, dusty, soft-looking, bald, except for a fringe of hair about his ears so thick that the top of his head, by contrast, seemed more naked than mere lack of hair could make it.

Behind Mr. Kibbler was Edwin, Jr. He was as thin as his mother, as mild and soft-looking as his father; and to these qualities he added an unhappiness all of his own. He gave one quick look at the room and the Delahantys through his thick-lensed spectacles, after which he kept his eyes on the floor.

Mr. Delahanty closed the door behind the callers, then introduced his wife to Mrs.

---

3. **marguerites:** cookies or crackers frosted with an egg-white mixture.

4. **pompadour:** a hairdo in which the hair is swept high up away from the forehead.

Kibbler. Mrs. Kibbler in turn introduced her family to the Delahantys. While the Kibblers were seating themselves — Mrs. Kibbler and Edwin, Jr., on the sofa, Mr. Kibbler on a straight-backed chair in the room's darkest corner — Mrs. Delahanty, out of nervousness, bent and lit the fire, which was laid in the fireplace, though the evening was not cold enough for it. Then she and Mr. Delahanty seated themselves in the chairs on each side of the fireplace.

Mrs. Kibbler looked at the fire with some surprise. "Do you find it cold this evening, Mrs. Delahanty?" she asked.

"No," said Mrs. Delahanty, "I don't. I don't know why I lit the fire."

To this Mrs. Kibbler made no reply. Instead, without preliminaries, she turned to her son. "Edwin," she said, "show the Delahantys what their daughter did to your teeth."

Mrs. Delahanty wanted to close her eyes, look into the fire, or find, as Edwin, Jr., had done, a spot of her own on the floor to examine. There was an almost imperceptible ripple along the length of the boy's face as if he had tried to open his mouth but found he lacked the strength. He momentarily lifted his eyes from the floor to dart a glance into the dark corner where his father sat. But Mr. Kibbler continued to sit in expressionless silence.

"Edwin," said Mrs. Kibbler, "speak to your son."

"Do what your mother says, Son," said Mr. Kibbler.

Very slowly, as if it hurt him, Edwin opened his mouth.

His teeth were white, and in his thin face they seemed very large, as well. The two middle teeth, above, had been broken across in a slanting line. The lower incisor appeared to be missing entirely.

"Wider, Edwin," Mrs. Kibbler urged. "I want the Delahantys to see exactly what their daughter is responsible for."

But before Edwin could make any further effort Mrs. Delahanty cried, "No, that's enough."

"I didn't want you to take our word for anything," Mrs. Kibbler said reasonably. "I wanted you to see."

"Oh, we see, all right," said Mrs. Delahanty earnestly.

Mr. Delahanty leaned forward and spoke to Mrs. Kibbler. "While we see the teeth, Mrs. Kibbler, it just isn't a thing we think Crescent would do. Or in fact how she *could* do it. We think Edwin must be mistaken."

"You mean lying?" asked Mrs. Kibbler flatly.

"Mistaken," repeated Mr. Delahanty.

"Tell them, Edwin," said Mrs. Kibbler.

"She knocked me down," said Edwin, very low.

Mrs. Delahanty, although she was already uncomfortably warm, held her hands nearer the fire, even rubbed them together a time or two.

"I simply can't believe that," she said.

"You mean hit you with her fist and knocked you down?" asked Mr. Delahanty.

"No," said Edwin even lower than before. "Ran into me."

"But not on purpose," said Mrs. Delahanty.

Edwin nodded. "Yes," he said. "On purpose."

"But why?" asked Mr. Delahanty. "Why? Cress wouldn't do such a thing, I know—without some cause. Why?"

"Tell them why, Edwin," said his mother.

Edwin's head went even nearer the floor—as if the spot he was watching had diminished or retreated.

"For fun," he said.

It was impossible not to believe the boy as he sat there hunched, head bent, one eyelid visibly twitching. "But Cress would never do such a thing," said Mrs. Delahanty.

Mrs. Kibbler disregarded this. "It would not have been so bad, Mr. Delahanty, except that Edwin was standing by one of those ollas. When your daughter shoved Edwin over she shoved the olla over, too. That's probably what broke his teeth. Heavy as cement and falling down on top of him and breaking up in a thousand pieces. To say nothing of his being doused with water on a cold day. And Providence alone can explain why his glasses weren't broken."

"What had you done, Edwin?" asked Mrs. Delahanty again.

"Nothing," whispered Edwin.

"All we want," said Mrs. Kibbler, "is what's perfectly fair. Pay the dentist's bill.

And have that girl of yours apologize to Edwin."

Mrs. Delahanty got up suddenly and walked over to Edwin. She put one hand on his thin shoulder and felt him twitch under her touch like a frightened colt.

"Go on, Edwin," she said. "Tell me the truth. Tell me why."

Edwin slowly lifted his head. "Go on, Edwin," Mrs. Delahanty encouraged him.

"He told you once," said Mrs. Kibbler. "Fun. That girl of yours is a big, boisterous thing from all I hear. She owes my boy an apology."

Edwin's face continued to lift until he was looking directly at Mrs. Delahanty.

He started to speak—but had said only three words, "Nobody ever wants," when Cress walked in from the hall. She had evidently been there for some time, for she went directly to Edwin.

"I apologize for hurting you, Edwin," she said.

Then she turned to Mrs. Kibbler. "I've got twelve seventy-five saved for a bicycle. That can go to help pay for his teeth."

After the Kibblers left, the three Delahantys sat for some time without saying a word. The fire had about died down and outside an owl, hunting finished, flew back toward the hills, softly hooting.

"I guess if we hurried we could just about catch the second show," Mr. Delahanty said.

"I won't be going to shows for a while," said Cress.

The room was very quiet. Mrs. Delahanty traced the outline of one of the bricks in the fireplace.

"I can save twenty-five cents a week that way. Toward his teeth," she explained.

Mrs. Delahanty took the poker and stirred the coals so that for a second there was an upward drift of sparks; but the fire was too far gone to blaze. Because it had not yet been completely dark when the Kibblers came, only one lamp had been turned on. Now that night had arrived the room was only partially lighted; but no one seemed to care. Mr. Delahanty, in Mr. Kibbler's dark corner, was almost invisible. Mrs. Delahanty stood by the fireplace. Cress sat where Edwin had sat,

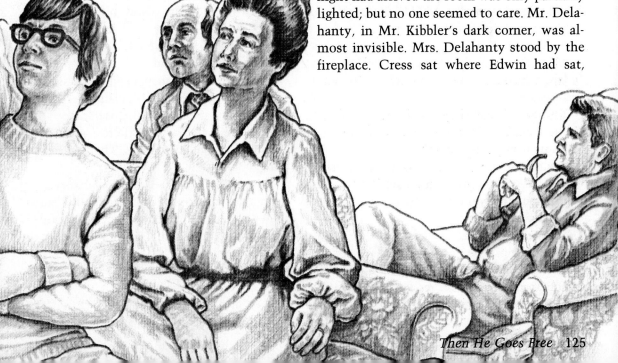

looking downward, perhaps at the same spot at which he had looked.

"One day at school," she said, "Edwin went out in the fields at noon and gathered wildflower bouquets for everyone. A lupine, a poppy, two barley heads, four yellow violets. He tied them together with blades of grass. They were sweet little bouquets. He went without his lunch to get them fixed, and when we came back from eating there was a bouquet on every desk in the study hall. It looked like a flower field when we came in and Edwin did it to surprise us."

After a while Mr. Delahanty asked, "Did the kids like that?"

"Yes, they liked it. They tore their bouquets apart," said Cress, "and used the barley beards to tickle each other. Miss Ingols made Edwin gather up every single flower and throw it in the wastepaper basket."

After a while Cress said, "Edwin has a collection of bird feathers. The biggest is from a buzzard, the littlest from a hummingbird. They're all different colors. The brightest is from a woodpecker."

"Does he kill birds," Mr. Delahanty asked, "just to get a feather?"

"Oh, no!" said Cress. "He just keeps his eyes open to where a bird might drop a feather. It would spoil his collection to get a feather he didn't find that way."

Mr. Delahanty sighed and stirred in his wooden chair so that it creaked a little.

"Edwin would like to be a missionary to China," said Cress. Some particle in the fireplace, as yet unburned, blazed up in a sudden spurt of blue flame. "Not a preaching missionary," she explained.

"A medical missionary?" asked Mr. Delahanty.

"Oh, no! Edwin says he's had to take too much medicine to ever be willing to make other people take it."

There was another long silence in the room. Mrs. Delahanty sat down in the chair her husband had vacated and once more held a hand toward the fire. There was just enough life left in the coals to make the tips of her fingers rosy. She didn't turn toward Cress at all or ask a single question. Back in the dusk Cress's voice went on.

"He would like to teach them how to play baseball."

Mr. Delahanty's voice was matter-of-fact. "Edwin doesn't look to me like he would be much of a baseball player."

"Oh he isn't," Cress agreed. "He isn't even any of a baseball player. But he could be a baseball authority. Know everything and teach by diagram. That's what he'd have to do. And learn from them how they paint. He says some of their pictures look like they had been painted with one kind of bird feather and some with another. He knows they don't really paint with bird feathers," she explained. "That's just a fancy[5] of his."

The night wind moving in off the Pacific began to stir the eucalyptus trees in the windbreak. Whether the wind blew off sea or desert didn't matter; the long eucalyptus leaves always lifted and fell with the same watery, surflike sound.

"I'm sorry Edwin happened to be standing by that olla," said Mr. Delahanty. "That's what did the damage, I suppose."

"Oh, he had to stand there," said Cress. "He didn't have any choice. That's the mush pot."

"Mush pot," repeated Mr. Delahanty.

"It's a circle round the box the olla stands on," said Crescent. "Edwin spends about his whole time there. While we're waiting for the bus anyway."

---

5. **fancy:** an imaginary idea.

"Crescent," asked Mr. Delahanty, "what is this mush pot?"

"It's prison," said Cress, surprise in her voice. "It's where the prisoners are kept. Only at school we always call it the mush pot."

"Is this a game?" asked Mr. Delahanty.

"It's dare base," said Crescent. "Didn't you ever play it? You choose up sides. You draw two lines and one side stands in the middle and tries to catch the other side as they run by. Nobody ever chooses Edwin. The last captain to choose just gets him. Because he can't help himself. They call him the handicap. He gets caught first thing and spends the whole game in the mush pot because nobody will waste any time trying to rescue him. He'd just get caught again, they say, and the whole game would be nothing but rescue Edwin."

"How do you rescue anyone, Cress?" asked her father.

"Run from home base to the mush pot without being caught. Then take the prisoner's hand. Then he goes free."

"Were you trying to rescue Edwin, Cress?"

Cress didn't answer her father at once. Finally she said, "It was my duty. I chose him for our side. I chose him first of all and didn't wait just to get him. So it was my duty to rescue him. Only I ran too hard and couldn't stop. And the olla fell down on top of him and knocked his teeth out. And humiliated him. But he was free," she said. "I got there without being caught."

Mrs. Delahanty spoke with a great surge of warmth and anger. "Humiliated him! When you were only trying to help him. Trying to rescue him. And you were black-and-blue for days yourself! What gratitude."

Cress said, "But he didn't want to be rescued, Mother. Not by me anyway. He said he liked being in the mush pot. He said . . . he got there on purpose . . . to observe. He gave me back the feathers I'd found for him. One was a road-runner feather. The only one he had."

"Well, you can start a feather collection of your own," said Mrs. Delahanty with energy. "I often see feathers when I'm walking through the orchard. After this I'll save them for you."

"I'm not interested in feathers," said Cress. Then she added, "I can get two bits an hour anytime suckering trees[6] for Mr. Hudson or cleaning blackboards at school. That would be two fifty a week at least. Plus the twelve seventy-five. How much do you suppose his teeth will be?"

"Cress," said her father, "you surely aren't going to let the Kibblers go on thinking you knocked their son down on purpose, are you? Do you want Edwin to think that?"

"Edwin doesn't really think that," Cress said. "He knows I was rescuing him. But now I've apologized—and if we pay for the new teeth and everything, maybe after a while he'll believe it."

She stood up and walked to the hall doorway. "I'm awfully tired," she said. "I guess I'll go to bed."

"But Cress," asked Mrs. Delahanty, "why do you want him to believe it? When it isn't true?"

Cress was already through the door, but she turned back to explain. "You don't knock people down you are sorry for," she said.

After Cress had gone upstairs Mrs. Delahanty said, "Well, John, you were right, of course."

"Right?" asked Mr. Delahanty, again forgetful.

"About Cress's being interested in the boys."

"Yes," said Mr. Delahanty. "Yes, I'm afraid I was."

---

6. **suckering trees:** removing the suckers, or shoots, from trees.

SEEKING MEANING

As this story unfolds, you gradually come to understand why Cress lets everyone believe that she knocked Edwin down on purpose.

1. The Kibblers aren't really interested in *why* Cress ran into Edwin and broke his teeth. What does Mrs. Kibbler want that's "perfectly fair"?

2. Cress's parents *do* want to know exactly what happened between Cress and Edwin. What do they finally discover?

3. According to what Cress tells her parents, how do the other students treat Edwin? Why would Edwin feel humiliated if he knew that Cress tried to rescue him?

4. Cress wants Edwin to believe that she knocked him down on purpose. Why? What does her explanation tell you about her feelings for Edwin?

5. You get two different views of Edwin from this story. At first, he is shown with his parents. What do you think Edwin is feeling in this scene? Does your view of Edwin change after Cress describes him to her parents? Explain your answer.

6. At the beginning of the story, Mrs. Delahanty is concerned that Cress isn't "as interested in boys as a girl her age should be." By the end of the story, how does Cress show that her mother's view of her was wrong?

DEVELOPING VOCABULARY

Using Synonyms

Synonyms are words that are close in meaning. They rarely mean precisely the same thing.

In this story, Cress remarks that Edwin was *humiliated.* The words *humiliate, degrade,* and *debase* are synonyms, but they do not have exactly the same meaning. *Humili-ate* specifically means "to embarrass a person in public, so that he or she loses self-respect." *Degrade* means "to lower someone's rank or moral character," and *debase* means "to lower the value of someone or something." Edwin was *humiliated,* but he wasn't *degraded* or *debased.* Use the words *humiliate, degrade,* and *debase* in sentences to illustrate their exact meanings.

In a dictionary, find how the synonyms *neglect, overlook,* and *ignore* vary in meaning. Use each word in a sentence to illustrate its exact meaning.

ABOUT THE AUTHOR

Jessamyn West (1907–1984) moved with her family from Indiana to California when she was six. Like Cress Delahanty's father, her own father was a rancher. As soon as he and his family landed in California, they began to take trips in the latest novelty – the car. Her parents were both Quakers. In her best-known book, *The Friendly Persuasion,* Jessamyn West drew on the legends she had heard about her Irish Quaker ancestors who had formed a community in Indiana. This book was later made into a successful movie. *Cress Delahanty* is the title of a collection of stories that trace a young girl's growing up, from age twelve to age sixteen. There is much of the author in the character of Cress. For example, Jessamyn West said that as a young girl she was "constantly in love." However, as with Cress in the story here, "it was never noted by my parents, teachers or school friends. The clue was that I never looked at, spoke to, or touched the one I was in love with."

*It was the first time John
had ever bought anything
for a girl. He wanted so
much for everything to be
right.*

The Valentine

James Jones

John Slade had not meant for it to become such a big operation, such a production. But from the moment he had first stepped into Woolworth's with his mind made up and had gone up to the candy counter and picked out the box, that was what it seemed to become. And now, the last day before Valentine's Day, with Woolworth's ready to close in just a few minutes, everything couldn't have been worse.

In the first place, there were two other paperboys from the newsstand standing there at the candy counter. And the man behind the counter was a man he knew. He was sort of the assistant manager. He had squinchy eyes and liked to needle the kids. And the two other paperboys from the newsstand were both freshmen, while he was still only an eighth-grader. It couldn't have been a much worse situation to try and buy the box in.

And this time he couldn't go away and come back another time, as he had already done three other times during the past week when he had come in and found other people standing at the candy counter. Either he had to do it now or not do it. Unless he went somewhere else, like the drugstore, and he didn't want to do that, because he knew the box he wanted, had in fact picked it out as

long as two weeks ago. It was, for the money, which was $6.95, the best box in town—all hearts that interlocked with each other within the big heart that was the box itself, and with two small paper cupids in the center of the white paper lace in the middle of that striking, eye-stopping, deep, deep red. A really beautiful box. And if he didn't take it now, after having promised himself that he would, he felt quite strongly that there would be no way out of having to face the fact that he was afraid and a liar to himself, and a coward.

It was the first time in his life that John Slade had ever really bought anything for a girl, and he wanted so bad for it to be right, as if he had done it a thousand times. Especially since the girl herself, whose lovely beautiful name was Margaret Simpson, didn't know anything about it at all yet, and wouldn't until he handed the box to her tomorrow. He wanted it to be a surprise. And he wanted it to be a secret. As far as that went, he was forced to admit, he didn't have nerve enough to do it any other way. Because he couldn't just go up to her and mention it. She might refuse. And now —

Some secret this would be! he thought. And he stood irresolute just inside the door in his corduroy, sheepskin-collared Mackinaw, despairing.

What did those guys have to be there for? And why did that sort of assistant manager have to be behind the counter? Any clerk in the store would have been better. He would have been better off if he'd gone ahead and bought it one of those other times when he'd chickened out. He didn't want it to be a big operation. But everybody made it that.

There wasn't any possibility of waiting those two guys out. They obviously weren't leaving, and there was less than five minutes left till closing. And he knew that Woolworth's wasn't going to stay open one minute after five for any thirteen-year-old kid. Unless he could succeed in covering it up from the two big kids some way—and how could he do that with that loudmouth needler behind the counter?—it would mean he would take an awful lot of razzing at the newsstand for the next month or so.

The newsstand was a good place to work, the best of the several possible paper-carrying jobs in town, and it was not, in this town, at any rate, the kind of poor-people, low-class idea of a job that most people had of paper boys in a city, for instance. The boys who worked at the newsstand were a cross section of the whole town, from the very poorest, like Otis Cole, to the most well-off; one of the boys at the counter was a doctor's son and the other a lawyer's, and he himself was the son of a dentist. But that, just the same, did not mean they weren't capable of inflicting the most roasting kind of humiliating razzing, especially when it came to anything like girls. You were liable to get yourself laughed and razzed right out of the back room of the newsstand in the predawn early mornings when everybody folded their papers before taking off. And if they found out about anybody buying a girl a great big heart-shaped box of candy for Valentine's Day!

In his case it would be even worse, since Margaret Simpson (gee, what a lovely, beautiful name that was) was not his girlfriend and never had been, and had never had any dates with him (he had never had any dates with anyone, in fact). Margaret was known to have dated freshmen in high school and even a few sophomores this past year; but he was going to ask her for a date as soon as he gave her the box tomorrow. Still, nobody knew now that he had fallen in love with her. That would make terrific news at the newsstand, after tomorrow, and it wouldn't do him any good to deny it, although he would. It wouldn't even matter if the whole thing wasn't even true, for that matter, once the guys got the idea in their heads.

For a moment, as the seconds ticked agonizingly on toward five o'clock and the hanging moment of ultimate decision, John seriously considered the luxury of just abandoning the whole project, of just turning around and going off and forgetting the whole thing and just buying her a cheap little box someplace else. Nobody would even notice a small, cheap box. Just the idea of it was an enormous relief. But he knew he could never do it. Not after having exacted of himself a solemn, faithful promise that he would go through with it. He would never be able to trust his promises again. That was the very reason he had made himself promise. So he couldn't back out.

With a feeling of acute desolation,[1] he took hold of himself mentally, so to speak, and placed both hands in the center of his own thin back and shoved himself slowly over to the counter as if he were shoving a friend on roller skates, and mumbled.

"What is it, boy? What is it? Speak up."

Louder, John said, "I said I want that six-ninety-five one there. How much is it?" His hand was in his pocket, nervously fingering his money, and he knew his mistake immediately and cursed himself for it. Old squinch-eye was staring down at him from across the counter with the beginning of his evil grin.

"How much is it!" the assistant manager said loudly, laughing. "You just told me yourself. It's six ninety-five. What do you mean how much is it?"

"I'll take it," John said nervously, fighting to keep his eyes looking straight at the squinchy ones. "Wrap it up." Down the counter he could see the two guys from the newsstand nudging each other.

"Yes, *sir*, Mr. Slade!" the Woolworth man grinned, his eyes squinching up even further. "Right *away*, sir!" He grinned down the counter at the other two guys. "Will there be anything else, sir?"

John tried to make it sound offhand, but he could tell his voice was shaky: "Nope. I guess that'll be all."

"Got yourself a new girlfriend, hunh?" the assistant manager said loudly, as he began to wrap the box. "Man, you really must be stuck on her. Six ninety-five for a box of candy." He lowered his voice. "Want to tell me who she is?" he said slyly. The other two guys from the newsstand were sidling down the counter, grinning in that way John knew so well, since he himself had done it so many times with other guys, when they knew they had some guy in a corner. The Woolworth man winked at them.

Inspired by embarrassment, John came up with an idea. "It's not for a girl," he lied; "it's for my mother." He managed to look at old squinch-eye steadily, but his voice gave him away and he knew it. Just the same, he knew that not even these guys would dare make fun about anything as sacred as a guy's mother, so it was a good lie.

The Woolworth man seemed to be a little nonplused.[2] There was a short pause as everybody stopped riding him and thought solemnly of their own mothers. Then old squinch-eye, having paused respectfully, winked at the two guys and said, "Aw, come on, Johnny. You can tell us. Who is she? Really."

"Yeah, come on and tell us," one of the guys, Ted Wright, said.

"Yeah. We'll find out anyway, Slade," the other one, Hank Lewis, said, grinning.

"I told you," John said as stoutly as he could. "I ain't got a girl. This is for my mom." The box was wrapped now, but old squinch-eye was reluctant to let go of it and spoil the fun. John took the folded bills, seven dollars in all, that he had been saving out of his route (he had even made a special trip around, when he wasn't carrying, to collect some of the back bills, so he would have enough) from his pocket and extended them, and at the same time held out his other hand.

The Woolworth man passed over the pack-

---

1. **desolation** (dĕs′ə-lā′shən): misery; hopelessness.

2. **nonplused** (nŏn-plust′): confused; unable to respond.

age with his right hand and took the money with his left, but then he would not quite let go. His hand clung to the box of candy teasingly.

"Is she in your room?" he asked. "Is she in 8A? Come on, you can tell *us*."

"Maybe she's in 8B," one of the guys said. "Maybe she's from down in Sacktown."

"Yeah. Maybe it's one of the Linder girls," the other one grinned. "Is it one of the Linder girls, Johnny?"

"I told you," John said. "Can I have my change, please?"

Finally, reluctantly, old squinch-eye let go of the box. "Your change? A whole nickel? I'm not sure I've got that much on hand." But he turned around to the register, and then finally the ordeal was over. How could any guy get to be so mean, in just thirty years or so?

Trying hard not to walk too fast, aware of his chest rising and falling fast and his arms and legs trembling, and hoping none of it showed, John went to the door with as much dignity as he could muster up.

"We'll find out anyway, Slade," one of the guys called after him. "We'll find out anyway, tomorrow."

And they would, too. It was a threatening promise of what he could expect.

Outside, he laid the wrapped package carefully in the basket of his bike, kicked up the stand and pushed off, swinging his leg over the rear wheel. Well, to heck with them. Let them find out. Let them find out he was in love with (oh, sweet, lovely name!) Margaret Simpson. He didn't care. He was proud of it. So let them find out. They would anyway.

At home, he went straight upstairs to his own room and put the wrapped box carefully away in a drawer of his dresser, and he did not tell anybody, neither his parents nor his kid sister, about it. But that night, after supper and the radio and homework and some read-ing, when he went to bed, he lay with his arms behind his head and thought about it. Finally he got up and took it out and unwrapped it (he could put it in a paper bag tomorrow to keep it clean — and hidden) and looked at it. He was both excited and scared about tomorrow. He wished there *was* somebody he could talk to about it. He hoped it would be all right, and he *thought* it would. Certainly it would be the best, the most expensive valentine any girl in the class would get. That was for sure. But you couldn't be sure with Margaret. She was a pretty sophisticated girl. Love for her welled up in him at the silent pronunciation of her name, and he put the box carefully away and climbed back into bed.

Actually, he had never spoken to Margaret about his feeling for her. Maybe he should have. His *love* for her, he corrected himself. His *love*, he said again. Actually, she was easily the most popular girl in the class, and had been elected most popular girl last year in seventh grade, and undoubtedly would again this year in eighth grade, as well as being the best-looking. She wore lots of skirts and sweaters, with the sleeves pushed up. Actually, she came from a very poor family, and lived in a very poor little house on the far side of town. Her mother was dead and she kept house for her father and those of her five big brothers who still lived at home, which were two. Actually, she was really much better-off than that sounded, because old Mrs. Carter, who was rich and had a sort of estate right next door to Margaret's home, had taken her under her wing and paid for all her clothes and things and was going to send her to college. Also, all her five brothers were musical, as she was herself, and played instruments and had played in bands around town, and so Margaret herself had been singing with a band that one of her brothers ran, at places like the Elks Club and the Country Club, ever since she had been in sixth grade. That, right there, probably accounted for a lot of her sophistication. Everybody said she was really very talented as a singer and might have a chance to go a long way someday. Also she made excellent grades, always.

Well, he bet she had never had as expensive, or as big, a valentine as this before, even from a sophomore; and thinking about her in the warmth of the bed, under the warm covers, John rolled over and, still worried, curled himself up and went to sleep.

. . .

The alarm clock was still ringing, its luminous hands showing four thirty in the dark, and he shut it off and switched on the light. It was always exciting. Nowhere in the silent, dark house did anything move or stir, nor were there any lights, any movement in any of the houses he could see through his windows as he dressed. Savoring the excitement he felt every morning, he dressed himself warmly — flannel shirt, two sweaters under his Mackinaw, warm socks inside his boots, knit cap down over his ears, heavy scarf — then picked up his heavy fleece-lined leather mittens and tiptoed down the stairs to the front door.

Outside it was steely cold, and the handlebars and sprocket and chain of his bike creaked when he moved them. The air burned his nose like dry ice, and when he tucked the scarf up over it and put on his goggles, his eyes were already watering. The freezing cold air flushing the last threads of sleepiness and reluctance out of his mind, he took off on his bike, giving himself joyously up to, and embracing happily, the discomfort which always made him feel important and as though he were accomplishing something, riding the bike downtown along deserted streets of darkened houses where nothing moved and peo-

ple slept except for a few boys like himself, scattered across town, converging on the newsstand, where the city papers would already have been picked up off the train by the owner.

Actually, nothing disastrous happened at the newsstand that morning. He was razzed unmercifully by the two who had seen him buy the box the night before, and of course their ridicule was immediately taken up by all the others as they stood at the benches folding their papers and stuffing their paper bags under the bare bulbs in the back room,

but he kept his mouth shut and did not get mad. It was easy to do because he kept a mental picture of Margaret Simpson happily opening the box in the front of his mind, as a shield. Nobody could touch him when he thought of that. Anyway, folding the papers and stacking them took only ten or fifteen minutes, and then the paperboys were outside and separated, spreading out across the town, and he was by himself again, free to enjoy again the physical discomfort that he suffered not only because of the money it made him but because it made him feel he was strong and had willpower, and also free to dwell upon, and to worry in nervous excitement over, the valentine and his happy picture of Margaret, as he made his route. Then it was back home for breakfast and to change for school.

As he was dressing, and as his excitement mounted to almost unbearably unpleasant heights as the time slid away, he almost decided to drop the whole thing. He could leave the box right here in his drawer and gradually eat the candy up himself. But once again his ironbound promise to himself, which it was against his private rules to break, would not let him, and sustained him;

that and his happy picture of Margaret Simpson's face, warm and loving as she opened up his box, and the natural sequence which automatically followed: of him telling her how much he adored her, and always had, and her warm understanding of his adoration, and then his hands touching hers. When he took the box downstairs, hidden in the paper bag, and his mother asked him what it was, he told her it was only a couple of books he was taking back.

On the way to school, as the other kids converged, it was harder to say that. He knew, of course, that the moment would come (it seemed to be rushing down on him swiftly, in fact, like a freight train) when it would have to be made public, when there would be no avoiding saying what it was, or who it was for. So, gradually he was forced back to saying simply, "Aw, nothing," or "Nothing that would interest *you*." Everybody, of course, knew by now that it was a valentine.

There were several valentines on his own desk in the 8A room when he got there, two of them from girls in the back of the room who thought they were stuck on him but whom he didn't like. These valentines he opened and looked at, in a kind of daze, hardly even seeing them, and then put them down. Then, painfully aware that he was being watched, he carefully pulled the big box out of its paper bag and laid it on his desk. Big — it was huge! It looked monstrous to him. He had attached a little card which said: *To Margaret, with love, John Slade.* He stared at that awhile. It had cost him deeply in pride and fear to even dare to write it. That word. But he couldn't stare at the envelope forever. Margaret Simpson had not yet come into the room, and the bell wouldn't ring for three and half minutes. Abruptly, suddenly, he knew he couldn't stand it, just could not wait any longer; he hadn't made a promise to himself he would *hand* it to her, had he? And besides, if he waited to give it to her himself, the way he was now he wouldn't be able to say a word, not a single solitary word. Panic had enveloped him. He wanted only to be out of sight of everyone. The valentines on his own desk had given him an idea. Jerkily, cursing himself for looking so foolish, he picked up the box and walked across the room with it and laid it on Margaret Simpson's desk, and then went out into the cloakroom pretending that he had forgotten something in his overcoat.

There was a little buzz, sort of, that he could hear from the cloakroom, and when he peeked around the door there were several kids standing around her desk looking at it, admiring it maybe. He stayed in the cloakroom. How he could manage to stay three whole minutes in the cloakroom he didn't know, and once, as a subterfuge,[3] he went back in to his desk and got some things out of it, pretending he wanted to put them in his coat to take home.

Then, finally, one minute before the bell would ring, Margaret Simpson came into the cloakroom with two boys who were on the grade-school varsity basketball team, and they hung up their coats and went inside. He pretended to be busy with his own coat and did not look at them. Completely demoralized[4] now, no longer able to control what he did, he sneaked to the door and stuck the top half of his head around it, grinning foolishly. Margaret Simpson was just showing the card, his card, to the two boys. She said something he could not hear, and then laughed and gestured with her head toward the cloakroom where he was hiding, and the two boys laughed. Then she looked down at the big red box with amusement.

He had seen enough and he jerked his head back and crept back to his own coat, pretending to himself he had to get something out of the pocket. But then he leaned his face against his coat sickly and shut his eyes, trying to shut out not only the light but his own existence too. He put his hand in the pocket of the coat so that it would look like he was hunting for something in case anybody came in. When the bell rang, how could he ever go back in there? How could he possibly? Sickness ran all through him, all over him, in long waves. And everybody had seen him peeking around the doorjamb like a silly idiot. He had ruined it. He'd messed it all up. He should have made himself stay and hand it to her. Then it would have been all right. He stood that way, clenching and unclenching his fists, knowing the bell would ring, listening for it.

When the bell rang, he forced himself to walk to the door and to his desk. He sat down, trying hard not to look at anybody. Before the bell rang again, he would have to sit at that desk for fifty whole minutes of his life.

---

3. **subterfuge** (sŭb′tər-fyo͞oj′): something done to cover up a person's true feelings or intentions.

4. **demoralized** (dĭ-môr′əl-īzd′): having lost confidence.

SEEKING MEANING

1. "The Valentine" is a story about the difference between a dream and a bitter reality. Find the passage on page 134 that describes what John imagines will happen when he gives the valentine to Margaret. What facts about Margaret make it unlikely that John's dream will come true?

2. Buying the candy and giving it to Margaret becomes more of a "big operation" than John had thought it would be. Why doesn't he abandon the whole project?

3. John knows he will be ridiculed by the other newsstand boys. What "shield" does he use to protect himself from their remarks?

4. John himself receives several valentines. How is his reaction to them like Margaret's reaction to his gift?

5. At the end of the story, John thinks that things would have turned out differently if he had handed the gift to Margaret instead of hiding in the cloakroom. He blames himself for her indifference. What has he still not realized about Margaret?

DEVELOPING SKILLS IN LANGUAGE

Recognizing Informal Language and Slang

Although John is not the narrator in "The Valentine," the story is told from his point of view. Sometimes John even seems to be thinking out loud. To make John seem real, the author used the kind of informal language and slang that an eighth-grade boy might use.

On page 129 there is this description of the man behind the news counter:

He had squinchy eyes and liked to needle the kids.

This sentence sounds like John thinking or speaking. Someone writing more formally might put the idea this way:

He had small eyes that squinted and gave his face a pinched look, and he liked to tease the children.

Some other slang and informal expressions from the story are italicized below. What does each italicized expression mean?

. . . one of these other times when he'd *chickened out.*

There was a short pause as everybody stopped *riding* him.

. . . girls in the back of the room who thought they were *stuck on* him . . . .

He'd *messed it all up.*

Rewrite these quotations, substituting more formal words for the italicized ones. Do they still sound like John thinking?

Practice in Reading and Writing

NARRATION

Reading Narration

The kind of writing that tells a story is *narration*. When you read a narrative, keep the following points in mind:

1. *Note the main events of the story.*
The first main event of "My Family and Other Animals" (page 90) occurs when the boy puts the scorpions in the matchbox. Name at least six main events that happen next.

2. *Note the relationship of events.*
Do you remember *why* the boy put the scorpions in the matchbox in the first place?

Writing Narration

Here are some suggestions for writing good narratives:

1. *Decide on the best point of view to use in telling your story.*
Suppose you are telling a story about a soccer game. Will you have the story told by an all-knowing narrator, who can tell everyone's thoughts? Or will you choose a limited point of view and have a player, a spectator, or the coach tell the story? You might even tell the story from the soccer ball's point of view. Who is narrating "My Family and Other Animals"?

2. *Open your story in an interesting way.*
Which stories in this unit open with sentences that arouse your interest? Which opening sentences do not interest you, and why?

3. *Include only events that create interest or that are needed to move your story along.*

4. *Arrange your events in logical order.*
Most narratives, such as "My Family and Other Animals," are written in *chronological order*—that is, in the order in which the events occur.

Write a narrative of your own, using one of these topics or one of your own.

What happened to a pet
What happened during the game
What happens during the life cycle of a frog
What happened on that journey
What happened to make everyone laugh

For Further Reading

Behn, Henry, *The Faraway Lurs* (World Publishing, 1963; paperback, Avon)

Two young people from warring tribes meet and fall in love in this novel set in ancient Denmark.

Bell, Margaret, *The Totem Casts a Shadow* (Morrow, 1949)

White and Indian cultures clash in this novel set in Alaska in the 1890's.

Borland, Hal, *When the Legends Die* (Lippincott, 1963; paperback, Bantam)

The Ute boy in this novel flees into the wilderness. Thomas Black Bull is a character you are not likely to forget.

Bradbury, Ray, *The Martian Chronicles* (Doubleday, 1950; paperback, Bantam)

The first colonists came to Mars for many reasons, but none of them realized they were destroying a magnificent civilization.

Landon, Margaret, *Anna and the King of Siam* (John Day, 1944; paperback, Pocket Books)

This true story of an English governess' experiences at the court of Siam was the basis for the musical *The King and I*.

Mather, Melissa, *One Summer in Between* (Harper & Row, 1967)

A black college student from the South keeps a diary during the summer she spends in Vermont.

Miller, Helen, *Kirsti* (Doubleday, 1964)

In this novel, set in Idaho in 1901, a Finnish girl falls in love with an American and tries to reconcile two cultures and two generations.

Papashvily, George, and Helen Papashvily, *Anything Can Happen* (Harper & Row, 1945)

A young Russian who arrives in America with no money and high hopes tells his own humorous story.

Richter, Conrad, *The Light in the Forest* (Knopf, 1966; paperback, Bantam)

The boy in this novel is raised by Delawares, but when he is fifteen he finds himself suddenly returned to his white family.

Saroyan, William, *The Human Comedy* (Harcourt Brace Jovanovich, 1944; paperback, Dell)

This is a short novel about a family in southern California who try to make sense out of things that baffle all of us: love, work, war, loneliness, death. Many people read right through this little novel in one sitting, but the characters remain in one's memory for a long time.

Sone, Monica, *Nisei Daughter* (Little Brown, 1953)

This true story tells of a Japanese-American girl's experiences in a "relocation center" during World War II.

Speare, Elizabeth, *The Witch of Blackbird Pond* (Houghton Mifflin, 1958; paperback, Dell)

A girl rebels against the narrow-mindedness of the witch-hunters in Puritan New England, and finds herself suspected of witchcraft.

Wojciechowska, Maia, *Shadow of a Bull* (Atheneum, 1964; paperback, Atheneum)

Everyone else in this novel expects Manolo to follow in his dead father's footsteps and become a bullfighter, but Manolo wants something else.

The literature in this unit reveals something about how Americans—past and present—have seen themselves and their society. An *image* is a word or phrase that brings a picture to the reader's mind. The unit opens with images of astronauts in outer space, and it ends with Martin Luther King, Jr.'s, vision of the future here on earth. In between are images of heroes, of national ordeals, of the frontier, and of that important American institution, the school.

IMAGES OF AMERICA

Certain beliefs expressed in these selections have been part of America's heritage for centuries. These are beliefs in independence, tolerance, and personal freedom.

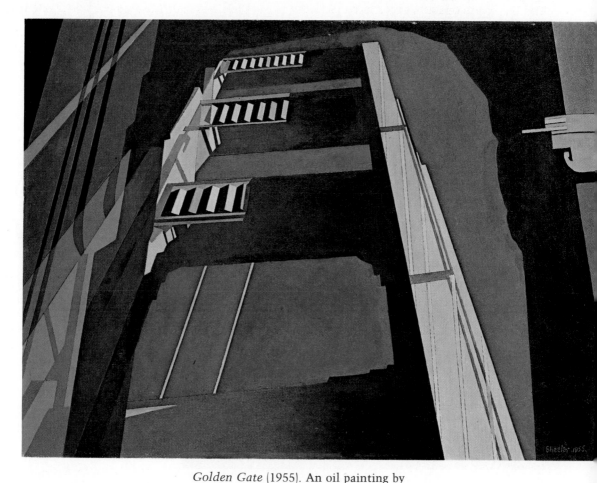

Golden Gate (1955). An oil painting by
Charles Sheeler (1883–1965).
The Metropolitan Museum of Art, New York. George A. Hearn Fund, 1955.

Snap the Whip (1872). An oil painting by Winslow Homer (1836–1910). The Butler Institute of American Art, Youngstown, Ohio.

Election Night in Herald Square (1907). An oil painting by John Sloan (1871–1955). Memorial Art Gallery of the University of Rochester, Marion Stratton Gould Fund.

The Unveiling of the Statue of Liberty
(October 28, 1886). An oil painting
by Edward Moran (1829–1901).
Transparency by Francis G. Mayer,
Art Color Slides, Inc., N.Y.C.

A woman of the coastal Salish people.
Photograph by Edward S. Curtis
(1868–1952).
Philadelphia Museum of Art: The American Museum of Photography.

A duck hunter, one of the
Kutenai people. Photograph by
Edward S. Curtis (1868–1952).
Philadelphia Museum of Art: The Ameri-
can Museum of Photography.

James Baldwin, American writer (1924–   ).
Photograph © Richard Kalvar/ Magnum Photos, Inc.

Bronco Buster (1901). A bronze sculpture by Frederic Remington (1861–1909).
The Thomas Gilcrease Institute of American History and Art, Tulsa, Oklahoma.

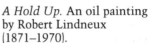

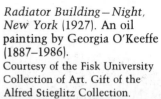

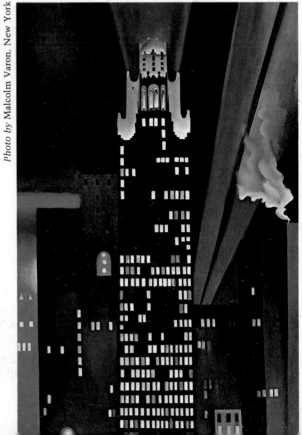

In December 1968, three young American astronauts helped us see ourselves from space for the first time. Anne Morrow Lindbergh and her husband were at the launching site in Florida to witness the historic flight of Apollo 8 to the moon. This is her record of the events following take-off.

Dialogue — Earth and Moon

Anne Morrow Lindbergh

In the days that followed, Christmas week, along with the rest of the world, we watched through television and radio the progress of the spacecraft on its 500,000-mile journey around the moon and back to earth. The voices of the control station at Houston and the voices of the astronauts bounced back and forth from spacecraft to earth, an incredible dialogue, almost without interruption over six days and nights. The terse technical space language, made up of astronomical calculations, star sightings, and computerized system checks — as vital as the heartbeats on a stethoscope — was interspersed with the very human comments, impressions, questions, hopes, fears, and prayers of three mortals in lunar space:

Control Houston. You're on your way, you're really on your way now. . . .

· · ·

Apollo 8. We see the earth now, almost as a disk. . . . We have a beautiful view of Florida . . . we can see the Cape, just the point . . . at the same time we can see Africa.

I'm looking out of my center window, which is the round window, and the window is bigger than the earth right now. . . .

The earth is very bright. . . .

It is a beautiful, beautiful view with predominantly blue background and just huge covers of clouds. . . . It is very, very beautiful. . . .

Waters are all sort of a royal blue, clouds, of course, are bright white, the reflection off the earth is much greater than the moon. The land areas are . . . sort of dark brownish to light brown in texture. . . .

At a hundred and eighty thousand miles out

in space . . . what I keep imagining is if I am some lonely traveler from another planet, what would I think about the earth at this altitude, whether I think it would be inhabited or not. . . .

The earth is now passing through my window. It's about as big as the end of my thumb. . . .

. . .

Control Houston. This is Houston . . . you are go for L.O.I. [lunar orbit insertion].
Apollo 8. Okay. Apollo 8 is go. . . .
Control Houston. You are riding the best bird we can find. . . . All systems go. . . . Safe journey. . . .

We are standing by . . . we've got it, we've got it! Apollo 8 is now in lunar orbit. . . .

. . .

Control Houston. What does the old moon look like from sixty miles?
Apollo 8. The moon is essentially gray, no color. Looks like plaster of Paris — or a grayish deep sand. . . .

The moon is a different thing to each one of us . . . a vast, lonely, forbidding-type existence, great expanse of nothing . . . clouds and clouds of pumice stone — not . . . a very inviting place to live or work. . . .

The vast loneliness up here of the moon is awe-inspiring . . . it makes you realize just what you have back there on earth. The earth from here is a grand oasis in the big vastness of space. . . .

The sky is pitch-black . . . the moon is quite light . . . a vastness of black and white, absolutely no color . . . forbidding, foreboding extents of blackness. . . .

. . .

Apollo 8 (*Christmas Eve*). We are now approaching the lunar sunrise, and for all the people back on earth, the crew of Apollo 8 has a message that we would like to send you:

In the beginning, God created the heaven and the earth.
And the earth was without form, and void; and darkness was upon the face of the deep . . . .
And God said, Let there be light . . . .
And God said, Let there be a firmament in the midst of the waters . . . .
And God said, Let the waters be gathered together and the dry land appear . . . .
And God called the dry land Earth; . . . and God saw that it was good.

And from the crew of Apollo 8, we pause with good night . . . and God bless all of you — all of you on the good earth. . . .

. . .

Control Houston. We're coming up on that trans-earth injection maneuver. . . . All systems are go, Apollo 8.
Apollo 8. Roger, thank you. This is Apollo 8.

. . .

Apollo 8. As we come back the earth looks pretty small from here [97,000 miles].

. . .

Apollo 8. How's the weather down there?
Control Houston. Beautiful. . . . They told us there is a beautiful moon out there.
Apollo 8. Now we were just saying that there's a beautiful earth out there.
Control Houston. It depends on your point of view.

. . .

Apollo 8. I think I must have the feeling that the travelers in the old sailing ships used to have. Going on a very long voyage away from home and now we're headed back and I have the feeling of being proud of the trip, but still happy to be going back home. . . . And that's . . . richer than being right here. . . .

. . .

Apollo 8. So, until then, I guess this is the Apollo 8 crew signing off and we'll see you back on that good earth very soon. . . .

Until finally, on the beginning of the seventh day, the spacecraft pierced through the narrow reentry corridor, that tiny keyhole in space, into the earth's atmosphere, trailing a hundred-mile-long tail of light as it reached for home and splashdown, under blossoming parachutes, into a welcoming Pacific and a cheering world.

DEVELOPING VOCABULARY

Recognizing Words from Greek Roots

When scientists or technologists need a new descriptive word, they often turn to the Greek language for a suitable word root. The word *astronaut*, for example, was coined by combining two Greek roots: *astro-*, meaning "star"; and *naut-*, meaning "sailor." The people who coined this word saw the astronauts as "sailors to the stars." In which passage does the astronaut speaking from Apollo 8 indicate that he sees himself as a sailor on a ship?

The following list contains other English words that come from *astro-* or *naut-*. What does each word mean or refer to? If you are not sure, look up the word in the dictionary. Which words contain Greek roots other than *astro-* and *naut-?*

aeronautics   cosmonaut
Astrodome   Nautilus

SEEKING MEANING

1. How does the author describe the two kinds of language used in this dialogue?
2. The astronauts speak as poets, not as scientists, when they describe the earth and the moon. What different things do they compare these heavenly bodies to? How do they feel about the earth?
3. Why do you suppose the astronauts chose to read the Biblical passage from Genesis as they looked at the earth from space?
4. An unmanned machine can send technical data back to scientists on the earth. Does this dialogue help you understand why we send people into space? Explain your answer.

ABOUT THE AUTHOR

After her graduation from Smith College, Anne Morrow (1906–   ) married Charles A. Lindbergh, who was at that time probably the most famous man in the world. The young pilot had won universal admiration in 1927, when he made the first solo nonstop flight across the Atlantic in a little one-engine plane, the *Spirit of St. Louis*. Anne Lindbergh's life has spanned three worlds—home and family, aviation, and literature. One of her books, *North to the Orient*, describes a flight she and her husband made over the North Pole in a small plane. On that trip Mrs. Lindbergh acted as radio operator and copilot.

Some say "the United States" began on the night of April 18, 1775. On that night, British soldiers went to raid the Massachusetts towns of Lexington and Concord. But the colonists had been warned that the soldiers were coming. Fully armed, they met the British in battle the next morning. About eighty years after this first battle of the American Revolution, Longfellow wrote the following poem.

Paul Revere's Ride   *Henry Wadsworth Longfellow*

Listen, my children, and you shall hear
Of the midnight ride of Paul Revere,
On the eighteenth of April, in seventy-five;
Hardly a man is now alive
Who remembers that famous day and year.   5

He said to his friend, "If the British march
By land or sea from the town tonight,
Hang a lantern aloft in the belfry arch
Of the North Church tower, as a signal light—
One, if by land, and two, if by sea;   10
And I on the opposite shore will be,
Ready to ride and spread the alarm
Through every Middlesex° village and farm,
For the country folk to be up and to arm."

Then he said "Good night!" and with muffled oar   15
Silently rowed to the Charlestown° shore,
Just as the moon rose over the bay,
Where, swinging wide at her moorings, lay
The *Somerset,* British man-of-war:
A phantom ship, with each mast and spar   20
Across the moon, like a prison bar,
And a huge black hulk, that was magnified
By its own reflection in the tide.

13. **Middlesex:** a county in Massachusetts.

16. **Charlestown:** a former city on Boston Harbor, now a part of Boston.

Meanwhile, his friend, through alley and street,
Wanders and watches with eager ears,
Till in the silence around him he hears   25
The muster of men at the barrack door,
The sound of arms, and the tramp of feet,
And the measured tread of the grenadiers
Marching down to their boats on the shore.   30

Then he climbed the tower of the Old North Church
By the wooden stairs, with stealthy tread,
To the belfry chamber overhead,
And startled the pigeons from their perch
On the somber rafters, that round him made   35
Masses and moving shapes of shade —
By the trembling ladder, steep and tall,
To the highest window in the wall,
Where he paused to listen and look down
A moment on the roofs of the town,   40
And the moonlight flowing over all.

Beneath, in the churchyard, lay the dead,
In their night encampment on the hill,
Wrapped in silence so deep and still
That he could hear, like a sentinel's tread,   45
The watchful night wind, as it went
Creeping along from tent to tent,
And seeming to whisper, "All is well!"
A moment only he feels the spell
Of the place and the hour, the secret dread   50
Of the lonely belfry and the dead;
For suddenly all his thoughts are bent
On a shadowy something far away,
Where the river widens to meet the bay —
A line of black, that bends and floats   55
On the rising tide, like a bridge of boats.

Meanwhile, impatient to mount and ride,
Booted and spurred, with a heavy stride
On the opposite shore walked Paul Revere.
Now he patted his horse's side,   60
Now gazed at the landscape far and near,
Then, impetuous, stamped the earth,
And turned and tightened his saddle girth;
But mostly he watched with eager search
The belfry tower of the Old North Church,   65
As it rose above the graves on the hill,
Lonely and spectral and somber and still.
And lo! as he looks, on the belfry's height
A glimmer, and then a gleam of light.
He springs to the saddle, the bridle he turns,   70
But lingers and gazes, till full on his sight
A second lamp in the belfry burns!

A hurry of hoofs in a village street,
A shape in the moonlight, a bulk in the dark,
And beneath, from the pebbles, in passing, a spark   75
Struck out by a steed flying fearless and fleet:
That was all! And yet, through the gloom and the light,
The fate of a nation was riding that night;
And the spark struck out by that steed, in his flight,
Kindled the land into flame with its heat.   80

He has left the village and mounted the steep,
And beneath him, tranquil and broad and deep,
Is the Mystic, meeting the ocean tides;
And under the alders that skirt its edge,
Now soft on the sand, now loud on the ledge,   85
Is heard the tramp of his steed as he rides.

It was twelve by the village clock,
When he crossed the bridge into Medford town.
He heard the crowing of the cock,
And the barking of the farmer's dog,   90
And felt the damp of the river fog
That rises after the sun goes down.

It was one by the village clock,
When he galloped into Lexington.
He saw the gilded weathercock   95
Swim in the moonlight as he passed,
And the meetinghouse windows, blank and bare,
Gaze at him with a spectral glare,
As if they already stood aghast
At the bloody work they would look upon.   100

It was two by the village clock,
When he came to the bridge in Concord town.
He heard the bleating of the flock,
And the twitter of birds among the trees,
And felt the breath of the morning breeze   105
Blowing over the meadows brown.
And one was safe and asleep in his bed,
Who at the bridge would be first to fall,
Who that day would be lying dead,
Pierced by a British musket ball.   110

You know the rest. In the books you have read
How the British Regulars fired and fled —
How the farmers gave them ball for ball,
From behind each fence and farmyard wall,
Chasing the redcoats down the lane,   115
Then crossing the fields to emerge again
Under the trees at the turn of the road,
And only pausing to fire and load.

So through the night rode Paul Revere;
And so through the night went his cry of alarm   120
To every Middlesex village and farm —
A cry of defiance and not of fear —
A voice in the darkness, a knock at the door,
And a word that shall echo forevermore!
For, borne on the night wind of the past,   125
Through all our history, to the last,
In the hour of darkness and peril and need,
The people will waken and listen to hear
The hurrying hoofbeats of that steed,
And the midnight message of Paul Revere.   130

SEEKING MEANING

1. The poet says in line 78: "The fate of a nation was riding that night." What do you think this line means? What does it suggest *might* have happened if Paul Revere had not been successful?

2. In lines 79–80, the poet says that "the spark struck out" by Paul Revere's horse "kindled the land into flame with its heat." You know that the horse's iron horseshoes did not actually set the land on fire. What event in American history is the poet comparing to a fire? How is this a good comparison?

3. In the last six lines of the poem, the poet says that Paul Revere's message will be heard by people throughout our history. What do you think this "message" is? Try to express it in your own words.

DEVELOPING SKILLS IN READING

Responding to a Narrative Poem

A *narrative poem* is a poem that tells a story. Like all good storytellers, Longfellow wants to hold your attention and keep you in suspense. In fact, the first word of his poem is a direction: "Listen."

Beginning with line 15, the poet gives details that help you experience the tension felt by Revere and his friend as they wait for the British to reveal their plans. Which details in lines 24–56 help you see and hear what Revere's friend sees and hears as he walks the streets, climbs the tower, and waits?

Once the British plans are known, the famous ride begins. Which details in lines 87–110 help you hear the country sounds that Revere hears as he gallops through the sleeping villages?

This poem has a strong, galloping rhythm. Does the rhythm help hold your attention? Why or why not?

DEVELOPING SKILLS IN RESEARCH

Finding the Historical Facts

If Longfellow had not written this poem, Paul Revere might be a footnote in history books. In fact, his companions that night are little known because Longfellow decided not to name them.

In a history book or an encyclopedia, look up the historical facts about all the riders who warned the farmers to arm and meet the British. In a paragraph, tell how the details in the poem differ from the details in history. What were the names of the other riders? Did Paul Revere ever reach Concord?

Why do you think people have remembered the poem long after they have forgotten the historical facts?

ABOUT THE AUTHOR

Henry Wadsworth Longfellow (1807–1882) was the most popular poet America has ever had. During his lifetime, people eagerly awaited each new poem, and his works were translated into twenty-four languages. In addition to writing, Longfellow taught at Harvard University for eighteen years. He then retired to lead a quiet life, devoting himself fully to writing poetry for his admiring public. But a catastrophe almost destroyed his desire to create. His wife died as a result of a fire in their home, and the poet needed great courage and patience to overcome his grief and begin writing again.

Longfellow was inspired by the American past. His long poems, *The Courtship of Miles Standish, Evangeline,* and *The Song of Hiawatha* show Longfellow's talent for using history as a background for poems of action and romance.

"Prisoner, hear the sentence of the court! The court decides, subject to the approval of the President, that you never hear the name of the United States again."

The Man Without a Country

Edward Everett Hale

Detail from *Seascape* (1906). An oil painting by Thomas Moran (1837–1926).
The Brooklyn Museum. Gift of the Executors, Estate of Colonel Michael Friedsam.

I suppose that very few readers of the New York *Herald* of August 13, 1863, observed in an obscure corner, among the "Deaths," the announcement:

NOLAN. Died on board the U.S. Corvette *Levant*, Lat. 2° 11' S., Long. 131° W., on May 11, PHILIP NOLAN.

Hundreds of readers would have paused at that announcement, if it had read thus: "DIED, MAY 11, THE MAN WITHOUT A COUNTRY." For it was as "The Man Without a Country" that poor Philip Nolan had generally been known by the officers who had him in charge during some fifty years, as, indeed, by all the men who sailed under them.

There can now be no possible harm in telling this poor creature's story. Reason enough there has been till now for very strict secrecy, the secrecy of honor itself, among the gentlemen of the navy who have had Nolan in charge. And certainly it speaks well for the profession and the personal honor of its members that to the press this man's story has been wholly unknown—and, I think, to the country at large also. This I do know, that no naval officer has mentioned Nolan in his report of a cruise.

But there is no need for secrecy any longer.

Now the poor creature is dead, it seems to me worthwhile to tell a little of his story, by way of showing young Americans of today what it is to be "A Man Without a Country."

Nolan's Fatal Wish

Philip Nolan was as fine a young officer as there was in the "Legion of the West," as the Western division of our army was then called. When Aaron Burr[1] made his first dashing expedition down to New Orleans in 1805, he met this gay, bright, young fellow. Burr marked[2] him, talked to him, walked with him, took him a day or two's voyage in his flatboat, and, in short, fascinated him. For the next year, barrack life was very tame to poor Nolan. He occasionally availed himself of the permission the great man had given him to write to him. Long, stilted letters the poor boy wrote and rewrote and copied. But never a line did he have in reply. The other boys in the garrison sneered at him, because he lost the fun which they found in shooting or rowing while he was working away on these grand letters to his grand friend. But before long, the young fellow had his revenge. For this time His Excellency, Honorable Aaron Burr, appeared again under a very different aspect. There were rumors that he had an army behind him and an empire before him. At that time the youngsters all envied him. Burr had not been talking twenty minutes with the commander before he asked him to send for Lieutenant Nolan. Then, after a little talk, he asked Nolan if he could show him something of the great river and the plans for the new

post. He asked Nolan to take him out in his skiff to show him a canebrake[3] or a cottonwood tree, as he said—really to win him over; and by the time the sail was over, Nolan was enlisted body and soul. From that time, though he did not yet know it, he lived as a man without a country.

What Burr meant to do I know no more than you. It is none of our business just now. Only, when the grand catastrophe came, Burr's treason trial at Richmond, Fort Adams[4] got up a string of courts-martial on the officers there. One and another of the colonels and majors were tried, and, to fill out the list, little Nolan, against whom there was evidence enough that he was sick of the service, had been willing to be false to it, and would have obeyed any order to march anywhere had the order been signed, "By command of his Exc. A. Burr." The courts dragged on. The big flies[5] escaped—rightly for all I know. Nolan was proved guilty enough, yet you and I would never have heard of him but that, when the president of the court asked him at the close whether he wished to say anything to show that he had always been faithful to the United States, he cried out in a fit of frenzy: "Damn the United States! I wish I may never hear of the United States again!"

Nolan's Punishment

I suppose he did not know how the words shocked old Colonel Morgan, who was holding the court. Half the officers who sat in it had served through the Revolution, and their lives had been risked for the very idea which

---

1. **Aaron Burr:** a controversial American political figure (1756–1836). Burr was Vice-President of the United States from 1801 to 1805. He killed Alexander Hamilton in a duel in 1804. At one time he was suspected of plotting to set up an empire in the Southwest.
2. **marked:** here, noticed.

3. **canebrake:** a dense growth of cane plant.
4. **Fort Adams:** the fort where Nolan was stationed.
5. **the big flies:** Burr and the other important men who may have plotted with him.

he cursed in his madness. He, on his part, had grown up in the West of those days. He had been educated on a plantation where the finest company was a Spanish officer or a French merchant from Orleans. His education had been perfected in commercial expeditions to Veracruz,[6] and I think he told me his father once hired an Englishman to be a private tutor for a winter on the plantation. He had spent half his youth with an older brother, hunting horses in Texas; and to him *United States* was scarcely a reality. I do not excuse Nolan; I only explain to the reader why he damned his country and wished he might never hear her name again.

From that moment, September 23, 1807, till the day he died, May 11, 1863, he never heard her name again. For that half-century and more, he was a man without a country.

Old Morgan, as I said, was terribly shocked. If Nolan had compared George Washington to Benedict Arnold, or had cried, "God save King George," Morgan would not have felt worse. He called the court into his private room and returned in fifteen minutes, with a face like a sheet, to say: "Prisoner, hear the sentence of the court! The court decides, subject to the approval of the President, that you never hear the name of the United States again."

Nolan laughed. But nobody else laughed. Old Morgan was too solemn, and the whole room was hushed dead as night for a minute. Even Nolan lost his swagger in a moment. Then Morgan added: "Mr. Marshal, take the prisoner to Orleans, in an armed boat, and deliver him to the naval commander there."

The marshal gave his orders and the prisoner was taken out of court.

"Mr. Marshal," continued old Morgan, "see that no one mentions the United States to the prisoner. Mr. Marshal, make my respects to Lieutenant Mitchell at Orleans, and request him to order that no one shall mention the United States to the prisoner while he is on board ship. You will receive your written orders from the officer on duty here this evening. The court is adjourned."

Before the *Nautilus*[7] got round from New Orleans to the northern Atlantic coast with the prisoner on board, the sentence had been approved by the President, and he was a man without a country.

The plan then adopted was substantially the same which was necessarily followed ever after. The Secretary of the Navy was requested to put Nolan on board a government vessel bound on a long cruise, and to direct that he should be only so far confined there as to make it certain that he never saw or heard of the country. We had few long cruises then, and I do not know certainly what his first cruise was. But the commander to whom he was entrusted regulated the etiquette and the precautions of the affair, and according to his scheme they were carried out till Nolan died.

When I was second officer of the *Intrepid*, some thirty years after, I saw the original paper of instructions. I have been sorry ever since that I did not copy the whole of it. It ran, however, much in this way:

> Washington [with a date, which must have been late in 1807]

Sir:

You will receive from Lieutenant Neale the person of Philip Nolan, late a lieutenant in the United States Army.

---

6. **Veracruz** (vĕr'ə-krōōz'): a seaport in Mexico.

7. *Nautilus:* the naval ship to which Nolan was delivered.

This person on trial by court-martial expressed, with an oath, the wish that he might "never hear of the United States again."

The court sentenced him to have his wish fulfilled.

For the present, the execution of the order is entrusted by the President to this department.

You will take the prisoner on board your ship, and keep him there with such precautions as shall prevent his escape.

You will provide him with such quarters, rations, and clothing as would be proper for an officer of his late rank, if he were a passenger on your vessel on the business of his government.

The gentlemen on board will make any arrangements agreeable to themselves regarding his society. He is to be exposed to no indignity of any kind, nor is he ever unnecessarily to be reminded that he is a prisoner.

But under no circumstances is he ever to hear of his country or to see any information regarding it; and you will especially caution all the officers under your command to take care that this rule, in which his punishment is involved, shall not be broken.

It is the intention of the government that he shall never again see the country which he has disowned. Before the end of your cruise, you will receive orders which will give effect to this intention.

> Respectfully yours,
> W. Southard,
> for the Secretary of the Navy

The rule adopted on board the ships on which I have met "The Man Without a Country" was, I think, transmitted from the beginning. No mess[8] liked to have him permanently, because his presence cut off all talk of home or of the prospect of return, of politics or letters, of peace or of war—cut off more than half the talk men liked to have at sea. But it was always thought too hard that he should never meet the rest of us, except to touch hats, and we finally sank into one system. He was not permitted to talk with the men unless an officer was by. With officers he had unrestrained intercourse, as far as they and he chose. But he grew shy, though he had favorites: I was one. Then the captain always asked him to dinner on Monday. Every mess in succession took up the invitation in its turn. According to the size of the ship, you had him at your mess more or less often at dinner. His breakfast he ate in his own stateroom. Whatever else he ate or drank, he ate or drank alone. Sometimes, when the marines or sailors had any special jollification,[9] they were permitted to invite Plain Buttons, as they called him. Then Nolan was sent with some officer, and the men were forbidden to speak of home while he was there. I believe the theory was that the sight of his punishment did them good. They called him Plain Buttons, because, while he always chose to wear a regulation army uniform, he was not permitted to wear the army button, for the reason that it bore either the initials or the insignia of the country he had disowned.

The Reading

I remember, soon after I joined the navy, I was on shore with some of the older officers from our ship, and some of the gentlemen fell to talking about Nolan, and someone told the

---

8. **mess:** here, a group of people who eat their meals together.
9. **jollification:** merrymaking.

system which was adopted from the first about his books and other reading. As he was almost never permitted to go on shore, even though the vessel lay in port for months, his time at the best hung heavy. Everybody was permitted to lend him books, if they were not published in America and made no allusion to it. These were common enough in the old days. He had almost all the foreign papers that came into the ship, sooner or later; only somebody must go over them first, and cut out any advertisement or stray paragraph that referred to America. This was a little cruel sometimes, when the back of what was cut out might be innocent. Right in the midst of one of Napoleon's battles poor Nolan would find a great hole, because on the back of the page of that paper there had been an advertisement of a packet[10] for New York, or a scrap from the President's message. This was the first time I ever heard of this plan. I remember it, because poor Phillips, who was of the party, told a story of something which happened at the Cape of Good Hope[11] on Nolan's first voyage. They had touched at the Cape, paid their respects to the English admiral and the fleet, and then Phillips had borrowed a lot of English books from an officer. Among them was *The Lay of the Last Minstrel*,[12] which they had all of them heard of, but which most of them had never seen. I think it could not have been published long. Well, nobody thought there could be any risk of anything national in that. So Nolan was permitted to join the circle one afternoon when a lot of them sat on deck smoking and reading aloud. In his turn, Nolan took the book and read to the others; and he read very well, as I know. Nobody in the circle knew a line of the poem, only it was all magic and chivalry, and was ten thousand years ago. Poor Nolan read steadily through the fifth canto,[13] stopped a minute and drank something, and then began, without a thought of what was coming:

Breathes there the man with soul so dead,
Who never to himself hath said . . .

It seems impossible to us that anybody ever heard this for the first time; but all these fellows did then, and poor Nolan himself went on, still unconsciously or mechanically:

This is my own, my native land!

Then they all saw that something was to pay; but he expected to get through, I suppose, turned a little pale, but plunged on:

Whose heart hath ne'er within him burned,
As home his footsteps he hath turned
From wandering on a foreign strand!
If such there breathe, go, mark him well . . .

By this time, the men were all beside themselves, wishing there was any way to make him turn over two pages; but he had not quite presence of mind for that; he gagged a little, colored crimson, and staggered on:

For him no minstrel raptures swell;
High though his titles, proud his name,
Boundless his wealth as wish can claim;
Despite these titles, power, and pelf.[14]
The wretch, concentered all in self . . .

---

10. **packet:** a boat that travels a regular route, carrying passengers, freight, and mail.
11. **Cape of Good Hope:** a projection of land on the southwestern coast of Africa.
12. *The Lay of the Last Minstrel:* a long narrative poem by Sir Walter Scott (1771–1832).

13. **canto:** a main division of certain long poems.
14. **pelf:** wealth.

Here the poor fellow choked, could not go on, but started up, swung the book into the sea, vanished into his stateroom, "And by Jove," said Phillips, "we did not see him for two months again. And I had to make up some story to that English surgeon why I did not return his Walter Scott to him."

That story shows about the time when Nolan's braggadocio[15] must have broken down. At first, they said, he took a very high tone, considered his imprisonment a mere farce, affected to enjoy the voyage, and all that; but Phillips said that after he came out of his stateroom he never was the same man again. He never read aloud again, unless it was the Bible or Shakespeare, or something else he was sure of. But it was not that merely. He never entered in with the other young men exactly as a companion again. He was always shy afterward, when I knew him —very seldom spoke unless he was spoken to, except to a very few friends. He lighted up occasionally, but generally he had the nervous, tired look of a heart-wounded man.

The Ball

When Captain Shaw was coming home, rather to the surprise of everybody they made one of the Windward Islands,[16] and lay off and on for nearly a week. The boys said the officers were sick of salt junk,[17] and meant to have turtle soup before they came home. But after several days, the *Warren* came to the same rendezvous; they exchanged signals; she told them she was outward bound, perhaps to the Mediterranean, and took poor Nolan and

Photograph by Mark W. Sexton

The ship *John* of Salem, Massachusetts, 1803. A watercolor by Michel Corne.
Peabody Museum of Salem, Massachusetts.

his traps[18] on the boat to try his second cruise. He looked very blank when he was told to get ready to join her. He had known enough of the signs of the sky to know that till that moment he was going "home." But this was a distinct evidence of something he had not thought of, perhaps—that there was no going home for him, even to a prison. And this was the first of some twenty such transfers, which brought him sooner or later into half our best vessels, but which kept him all his life at least some hundred miles from the country he had hoped he might never hear of again.

It may have been on that second cruise—it was once when he was up the Mediterranean—that Mrs. Graff, the celebrated Southern beauty of those days, danced with him.

---

15. **braggadocio** (brăg′ə-dō′shē-ō): pretended courage; in this case, Nolan's pretense that he does not mind his punishment.
16. **Windward Islands:** a group of islands in the West Indies.
17. **salt junk:** dried beef salted for preservation.

18. **traps:** here, luggage.

The ship had been lying a long time in the Bay of Naples, and the officers were very intimate in the English fleet, and there had been great festivities, and our men thought they must give a great ball on board the ship. They wanted to use Nolan's stateroom for something, and they hated to do it without asking him to the ball; so the captain said they might ask him, if they would be responsible that he did not talk with the wrong people, "who would give him intelligence."[19] So the dance went on. For ladies they had the family of the American consul, one or two travelers who had adventured so far, and a nice bevy of English girls and matrons.

Well, different officers relieved each other in standing and talking with Nolan in a friendly way, so as to be sure that nobody else spoke to him. The dancing went on with spirit, and after a while even the fellows who took this honorary guard of Nolan ceased to fear any trouble.

As the dancing went on, Nolan and our fellows all got at ease, as I said—so much that it seemed quite natural for him to bow to that splendid Mrs. Graff, and say, "I hope you have not forgotten me, Miss Rutledge. Shall I have the honor of dancing?"

He did it so quickly that Fellows, who was with him, could not hinder him. She laughed and said, "I am not Miss Rutledge any longer, Mr. Nolan; but I will dance all the same." She nodded to Fellows, as if to say he must leave Mr. Nolan to her, and led Nolan off to the place where the dance was forming.

Nolan thought he had got his chance. He had known her at Philadelphia. He said boldly

—a little pale, she said, as she told me the story years after—"And what do you hear from home, Mrs. Graff?"

And that splendid creature looked *through* him. Jove! How she *must* have looked through him!

"Home! Mr. Nolan! I thought you were the man who never wanted to hear of home again!"—and she walked directly up the deck to her husband and left poor Nolan alone. He did not dance again.

The Battle

A happier story than either of these I have told is of the war.[20] That came along soon after. I have heard this affair told in three or four ways—and, indeed, it may have happened more than once. In one of the great frigate[21] duels with the English, in which the navy was really baptized, it happened that a round shot[22] from the enemy entered one of our ports[23] square, and took right down the officer of the gun himself and almost every man of the gun's crew. Now you may say what you choose about courage, but that is not a nice thing to see. But, as the men who were not killed picked themselves up, and as they and the surgeon's people were carrying off the bodies, there appeared Nolan, in his shirtsleeves, with the rammer in his hand, and, just as if he had been the officer, told them off with authority—who should go to the cockpit with the wounded men, who should stay with him—perfectly cheery, and with that way which makes men feel sure all is right and is going to be right. And he

---

19. **intelligence:** here, information about his country.

20. **the war:** the War of 1812, between the United States and Great Britain.
21. **frigate** (frĭg′ĭt): a sailing ship equipped with war guns.
22. **round shot:** a cannonball.
23. **ports:** here, portholes for cannons.

finished loading the gun with his own hands, aimed it, and bade the men fire. And there he stayed, captain of that gun, keeping those fellows in spirits, till the enemy struck[24] — sitting on the carriage while the gun was cooling, though he was exposed all the time, showing them easier ways to handle heavy shot, making the raw hands laugh at their own blunders, and when the gun cooled again, getting it loaded and fired twice as often as any other gun on the ship. The captain walked forward by way of encouraging the men, and Nolan touched his hat and said, "I am showing them how we do this in the artillery, sir."

And this is the part of the story where all the legends agree; the commodore said, "I see you are, and I thank you, sir; and I shall never forget this day, sir, and you never shall, sir."

After the whole thing was over, and the commodore had the Englishman's sword,[25] in the midst of the state and ceremony of the quarter-deck, he said, "Where is Mr. Nolan? Ask Mr. Nolan to come here."

And when Nolan came, he said, "Mr. Nolan, we are all very grateful to you today; you are one of us today; you will be named in the dispatches."

And then the old man took off his own sword of ceremony, gave it to Nolan, and made him put it on. The man who told me this saw it. Nolan cried like a baby, and well he might. He had not worn a sword since that infernal day at Fort Adams. But always afterward on occasions of ceremony he wore that quaint old sword of the commodore.

The captain did mention him in the dispatches. It was always said he asked that Nolan might be pardoned. He wrote a special letter to the Secretary of War, but nothing ever came of it.

All that was nearly fifty years ago. If Nolan was thirty then, he must have been near eighty when he died. He looked sixty when he was forty. But he never seemed to me to change a hair afterward. As I imagine his life, from what I have seen and heard of it, he must have been in every sea, and yet almost never on land. Till he grew very old, he went aloft a great deal. He always kept up his exercise, and I never heard that he was ill. If any other man was ill, he was the kindest nurse in the world; and he knew more than half the surgeons do. Then if anybody was sick or died, or if the captain wanted him to, or on any other occassion, he was always ready to read prayers. I have said that he read beautifully.

The Slaves

My own acquaintance with Philip Nolan began six or eight years after the English war, on my first voyage after I was appointed a midshipman. From the time I joined, I believe I thought Nolan was a sort of lay chaplain — a chaplain with a blue coat. I never asked about him. Everything in the ship was strange to me. I knew it was green to ask questions, and I suppose I thought there was a Plain Buttons on every ship. We had him to dine in our mess once a week, and the caution was given that on that day nothing was to be said about home. But if they had told us not to say anything about the planet Mars or the Book of Deuteronomy,[26] I should not have asked why; there were a great many things which seemed

---

24. **struck:** struck their colors, or lowered their flag to admit defeat.
25. **the Englishman's sword:** A defeated commander used to give up his sword to the victor.

26. **Book of Deuteronomy** (doo'tə-rŏn'ə-mē): the fifth book of the Bible.

to me to have as little reason. I first came to understand anything about "The Man Without a Country" one day when we overhauled a dirty little schooner which had slaves[27] on board. An officer named Vaughan was sent to take charge of her, and, after a few minutes, he sent back his boat to ask that someone might be sent who could speak Portuguese. None of the officers did; and just as the captain was sending forward to ask if any of the people could, Nolan stepped out and said he should be glad to interpret, if the captain wished, as he understood the language. The captain thanked him, fitted out another boat with him, and in this boat it was my luck to go.

When we got there, it was such a scene as you seldom see—and never want to. Nastiness beyond account, and chaos ran loose in the midst of the nastiness. There were not a great many of the Negroes. By way of making what there were understand that they were free, Vaughan had had their handcuffs and anklecuffs knocked off. The Negroes were, most of them, out of the hold and swarming all around the dirty deck, with a central throng surrounding Vaughan and addressing him in every dialect.

As we came on deck, Vaughan looked down from a hogshead,[28] which he had mounted in desperation, and said, "Is there anybody who can make these wretches understand something?"

Nolan said he could speak Portuguese, and one or two fine-looking Krumen[29] who had worked for the Portuguese on the coast were dragged out.

"Tell them they are free," said Vaughan.

Nolan explained it in such Portuguese as the Krumen could understand, and they in turn to such of the Negroes as could understand them. Then there was a yell of delight, clenching of fists, leaping and dancing, and kissing of Nolan's feet by way of spontaneous celebration of the occasion.

"Tell them," said Vaughan, well pleased, "that I will take them all to Cape Palmas."[30]

This did not answer so well. Cape Palmas was practically as far from the homes of most of them as New Orleans or Rio de Janeiro was; that is, they would be eternally separated from home there. And their interpreters, as we could understand, instantly said, "*Ah, non Palmas*" and began to protest loudly. Vaughan was rather disappointed at this result of his liberality, and he asked Nolan eagerly what they said. The drops stood on poor Nolan's white forehead, as he hushed the men down, and said, "He says, 'Not Palmas.' He says, 'Take us home; take us to our own country; take us to our own house; take us to our own children and our own women.' He says he has an old father and mother who will die if they do not see him. And this one says that he left his people all sick, and paddled down to Fernando to beg the white doctor to come and help them, and that these devils caught him in the bay just in sight of home, and that he has never seen anybody from home since then. And this one says," choked out Nolan,

---

27. **slaves:** In 1808 the United States made it illegal to bring slaves into the country. In 1842 America and Great Britain agreed to patrol the African coast with ships to prevent any more people from being shipped off as slaves.
28. **hogshead** (hôgz'hĕd'): a large cask.
29. **Krumen** (kroo'mĕn): members of a tribe in northern Africa.

30. **Cape Palmas** (päl'məs): a point on the southern border of Liberia, on the western coast of Africa—about 2,000 miles (about 3,200 kilometers) from the home of these Africans.

"that he has not heard a word from his home in six months."

Vaughan always said Nolan grew gray himself while he struggled through this interpretation. I, who did not understand anything of the passion involved in it, saw that the very elements were melting with fervent heat and that something was to pay somewhere. Even the Negroes themselves stopped howling as they saw Nolan's agony and Vaughan's almost equal agony of sympathy. As quick as he could get words, Vaughan said, "Tell them yes, yes, yes; tell them they shall go to the Mountains of the Moon,[31] if they will. If I sail the schooner through the Great White Desert,[32] they shall go home!"

And after some fashion, Nolan said so. And then they all fell to kissing him again and wanted to rub his nose with theirs.

But he could not stand it long; and getting Vaughan to say he might go back, he beckoned me down into our boat. As we started back he said to me: "Youngster, let that show you what it is to be without a family, without a home, and without a country. If you are ever tempted to say a word or to do a thing that shall put a bar between you and your family, your home, and your country, pray God in His mercy to take you that instant home to His own heaven. Think of your home, boy; write and send and talk about it. Let it be nearer and nearer to your thought the farther you have to travel from it, and rush back to it when you are free, as that poor slave is doing now. And for your country, boy," and the words rattled in his throat, "and for that flag," and he pointed to the ship, "never dream a dream but of serving her as she bids you, though the service carry you through a thousand hells. No matter what happens to you, no matter who flatters you or who abuses you, never look at another flag, never let a night pass but you pray God to bless the flag. Remember, boy, that behind all these men you have to do with, behind officers, and government, and people even, there is the Country herself, your Country, and that you belong to her as you belong to your own mother. Stand by her, boy, as you would stand by your mother!"

I was frightened to death by his calm, hard passion; but I blundered out that I would, by all that was holy, and that I had never thought of doing anything else. He hardly seemed to hear me; but he did, almost in a whisper, say, "Oh, if anybody had said so to me when I was of your age!"

I think it was this half-confidence of his, which I never abused, that afterward made us great friends. He was very kind to me. Often he sat up, or even got up, at night, to walk the deck with me when it was my watch. He explained to me a great deal of my mathematics, and I owe him my taste for mathematics. He lent me books and helped me about my reading. He never referred so directly to his story again; but from one and another officer, I have learned, in thirty years, what I am telling.

Nolan's Repentance

After that cruise I never saw Nolan again. The other men tell me that in those fifteen years he aged very fast, but he was still the same gentle, uncomplaining, silent sufferer that he ever was, bearing as best he could his self-appointed punishment. And now it seems that the dear old fellow is dead. He has found a home at last, and a country.

Since writing this, and while considering whether or not I would print it, as a warning

---

31. **Mountains of the Moon:** a mountain range in East Central Africa.
32. **Great White Desert:** probably the Great Salt Desert in Iran.

to the young Nolans of today of what it is to throw away a country, I have received from Danforth, who is on board the *Levant*, a letter which gives an account of Nolan's last hours. It removes all my doubts about telling this story.

Here is the letter:

Dear Fred,

I try to find heart and life to tell you that it is all over with dear old Nolan. I have been with him on this voyage more than I ever was, and I can understand wholly now the way in which you used to speak of the dear old fellow. I could see that he was not strong, but I had no idea the end was so near. The doctor has been watching him very carefully, and yesterday morning he came to me and told me that Nolan was not so well and had not left his stateroom—a thing I never remember before. He had let the doctor come and see him as he lay there —the first time the doctor had been in the stateroom—and he said he should like to see me. Do you remember the mysteries we boys used to invent about his room in the old *Intrepid* days? Well, I went in, and there, to be sure, the poor fellow lay in his berth, smiling pleasantly as he gave me his hand but looking very frail. I could not help a glance round, which showed me what a little shrine he had made of the box he was lying in. The Stars and Stripes were draped up above and around a picture of Washington, and he had painted a majestic eagle, with lightnings blazing from his beak and his foot just clasping the whole globe, which his wings overshadowed. The dear old boy saw my glance, and said, with a sad smile, "Here, you see, I have a country!" Then he pointed to the foot of his bed, where I had not seen before a great map of the United States, as he had drawn it from memory, and which he had there to look upon as he lay. Quaint, queer old names were on it, in large letters: "Indiana Territory," "Mississippi Territory," and "Louisiana Territory," as I suppose our fathers learned such things: but the old fellow had patched in Texas, too; he had carried his western boundary all the way to the Pacific, but on that shore he had defined nothing.

"O Captain," he said, "I know I am dying. I cannot get home. Surely you will tell me something now? . . . Stop! Stop! . . . Do not speak till I say what I am sure you know, that there is not in this ship, that there is not in America—God bless her!—a more loyal man than I. There cannot be a man who loves the old flag as I do, or prays for it as I do, or hopes for it as I do. There are thirty-four stars in it now, Danforth. I thank God for that, though I do not know what their names are. There has never been one taken away; I thank God for that. I know by that that there has never been any successful Burr. O Danforth, Danforth," he sighed out, "how like a wretched night's dream a boy's idea of personal fame or of separate sovereignty seems, when one looks back on it after such a life as mine! But tell me—tell me something—tell me everything, Danforth, before I die!"

I swear to you that I felt like a monster because I had not told him everything before. "Mr. Nolan," said I, "I will tell you everything you ask about. Only, where shall I begin?"

Oh, the blessed smile that crept over his white face! He pressed my hand and said, "God bless you! Tell me their names," and he pointed to the stars on the flag. "The last I know is Ohio. My father lived in Kentucky. But I have guessed Michigan, and Indiana, and Mississippi—that is where Fort

A seaman's burial.
Harper's Weekly, June 12, 1869.

Adams was—they make twenty. But where are your other fourteen? You have not cut up any of the old ones, I hope?"

Well, that was not a bad text, and I told him the names in as good order as I could, and he bade me take down his beautiful map and draw them in as I best could with my pencil. He was wild with delight about Texas, told me how his cousin died there; he had marked a gold cross near where he supposed his grave was; and he had guessed at Texas. Then he was delighted as he saw California and Oregon—that, he said, he had suspected partly, because he had never been permitted to land on that shore, though the ships were there so much. Then he asked about the old war—told me the story of his serving the gun the day we took the *Java.* Then he settled down more quietly, and very happily, to hear me tell in an hour the history of fifty years.

How I wish it had been somebody who knew something! But I did as well as I could. I told him of the English war. I told

him of Fulton[33] and the steamboat beginning. I told him about old Scott,[34] and Jackson,[35] told him all I could think of about the Mississippi, and New Orleans, and Texas, and his own old Kentucky.

I tell you, it was a hard thing to condense the history of half a century into that talk with a sick man. And I do not now know what I told him—of emigration and the means of it—of steamboats, and railroads, and telegraphs—of inventions and books, and literature—of the colleges, and West Point, and the Naval School, but with the queerest interruptions that ever you heard. You see it was Robinson Crusoe asking all the accumulated questions of fifty-six years!

33. **Fulton:** Robert Fulton (1765–1815), the inventor of the steamboat.
34. **Scott:** General Winfield Scott (1786–1866), a commander in the War of 1812 and in the Mexican War.
35. **Jackson:** Andrew Jackson (1767–1845), a general in the War of 1812 and the seventh President of the United States (1829–1837).

I remember he asked, all of a sudden, who was President now; and when I told him, he asked if Old Abe was General Benjamin Lincoln's son. He said he met old General Lincoln, when he was quite a boy himself, at some Indian treaty. I said no, that Old Abe was a Kentuckian like himself, but I could not tell him of what family; he had worked up from the ranks. "Good for him!" cried Nolan; "I am glad of that." Then I got talking about my visit to Washington. I told him everything I could think of that would show the grandeur of his country and its prosperity.

And he drank it in and enjoyed it as I cannot tell you. He grew more and more silent, yet I never thought he was tired or faint. I gave him a glass of water, but he just wet his lips, and told me not to go away. Then he asked me to bring the Presbyterian Book of Public Prayer which lay there, and said, with a smile, that it would open at the right place—and so it did. There was his double red mark down the page; and I knelt down and read, and he repeated with me:

For ourselves and our country, O gracious God, we thank Thee, that, notwithstanding our manifold transgressions of Thy Holy laws, Thou hast continued to us Thy marvelous kindness . . .

and so to the end of that thanksgiving. Then he turned to the end of the same book, and I read the words more familiar to me:

Most heartily we beseech Thee with Thy favor to behold and bless Thy servant, the President of the United States, and all others in authority.

"Danforth," said he, "I have repeated those prayers night and morning—it is now fifty-five years." And then he said he would go to sleep. He bent me down over him and kissed me; and he said, "Look in my Bible, Captain, when I am gone." And I went away.

But I had no thought it was the end. I thought he was tired and would sleep. I knew he was happy, and I wanted him to be alone.

But in an hour, when the doctor went in gently, he found Nolan had breathed his life away with a smile.

We looked in his Bible, and there was a slip of paper at the place where he had marked the text:

They desire a country, even a heavenly: where God is not ashamed to be called their God: for he hath prepared for them a city.[36]

On this slip of paper he had written this:

Bury me in the sea; it has been my home, and I love it. But will not someone set up a stone for my memory, that my disgrace may not be more than I ought to bear? Say on it:

In Memory of
PHILIP NOLAN
Lieutenant in the Army
of the United States

HE LOVED HIS COUNTRY
AS NO OTHER MAN HAS LOVED HER;
BUT NO MAN DESERVED LESS
AT HER HANDS.

---

36. **They desire . . . a city:** The passage is from Hebrews 11:16.

SEEKING MEANING

1. Who is telling this story? Why does he believe the story of Philip Nolan should be told?

2. What facts does the narrator give about Nolan's early life that might explain why he joined Aaron Burr and why he later renounced the United States?

3. What was Nolan's punishment? How was the punishment carried out?

4. How did Nolan change during his years at sea?

5. After Nolan dies, the narrator tells you on page 163: "He has found a home at last, and a country." What do you think the narrator means by "home" and "country" here?

6. This story was written in 1863, when the United States was in danger of being destroyed by the Civil War. Which passages in the story show that the author wants to impress upon the reader the importance of national unity?

7. Look back at the passage from *The Lay of the Last Minstrel* on page 158. Which lines from this poem could be used to express the main idea of this story?

DEVELOPING SKILLS IN READING

Noting Details That Suggest Authenticity

"The Man Without a Country" is not a true story. However, the author uses certain techniques to make the reader think it is true, or to give it the appearance of *authenticity*. For example, the story opens with a quotation from the "Deaths" column of a real newspaper, a source most people trust. The author cites the date of the newspaper and even the name and the exact position of the ship. What real people and historical events does the author use to suggest authenticity?

DEVELOPING SKILLS OF EXPRESSION

Supporting an Opinion

A statement of your opinion is always more forceful when you present clear, logical reasons for holding it.

Do you think Philip Nolan deserved his punishment? Answer this question in a paragraph. Give at least two reasons explaining why you hold the opinion you do. Be sure to state your opinion in your opening sentence.

ABOUT THE AUTHOR

Edward Everett Hale (1822–1909), a grandnephew of the famous Nathan Hale of the American Revolution, was a highly respected clergyman, journalist, and teacher. Hale worked for many social reforms in his lifetime, including education, housing, and world peace. In 1863 he published "The Man Without a Country" to try to inspire greater patriotism during the Civil War. The story became very popular as a blend of fiction and history. In 1903 Hale was named chaplain of the United States Senate.

On November 19, 1863, President Abraham Lincoln delivered this speech at a ceremony to dedicate the Soldiers' National Cemetery at Gettysburg, Pennsylvania. Gettysburg had been the scene of one of the most terrible battles of the Civil War. Edward Everett, who spoke before Lincoln, said that the President came closer to expressing the importance of the occasion in two minutes than Everett himself had done in two hours.

The Gettysburg Address

Abraham Lincoln

Four score and seven years ago our fathers brought forth on this continent a new nation, conceived in liberty, and dedicated to the proposition that all men are created equal.

Now we are engaged in a great civil war, testing whether that nation, or any nation so conceived and so dedicated, can long endure. We are met on a great battlefield of that war. We have come to dedicate a portion of that field as a final resting place for those who here gave their lives that that nation might live. It is altogether fitting and proper that we should do this.

But, in a larger sense, we cannot dedicate — we cannot consecrate — we cannot hallow — this ground. The brave men, living and dead, who struggled here, have consecrated it far above our poor power to add or detract. The world will little note nor long remember what we say here, but it can never forget what they did here. It is for us the living, rather, to be dedicated here to the unfinished work which they who fought here have thus far so nobly advanced. It is rather for us to be here dedicated to the great task remaining before us — that from these honored dead we take increased devotion to that cause for which they gave the last full measure of devotion — that we here highly resolve that these dead shall not have died in vain — that this nation, under God, shall have a new birth of freedom — and that government of the people, by the people, for the people, shall not perish from the earth.

SEEKING MEANING

1. In the Gettysburg Address, Abraham Lincoln presents three images of America—one from the past, one of the present, one for the future. In the first paragraph how does he describe the nation that was created "four score and seven years ago"?

2. In the second and third paragraphs, Lincoln speaks of the present time. Why can't the people at the ceremony make the battleground any more sacred than it already is?

3. The last part of the third paragraph focuses on the future. What national purpose does the President set for the people?

4. Where does President Lincoln present an image of the nation as something alive?

Walt Whitman wrote this poem during a tragic time in America's history. In 1865 the American people were relieved that the Civil War was ending. But the relief turned to sadness again when the news came that President Abraham Lincoln had been assassinated.

O Captain! My Captain! *Walt Whitman*

O Captain! my Captain! our fearful trip is done,
The ship has weathered every rack,° the prize we sought
    is won,
The port is near, the bells I hear, the people all exulting,
While follow eyes the steady keel, the vessel grim and
    daring;
  But O heart! heart! heart!   5
    O the bleeding drops of red,
      Where on the deck my Captain lies,
        Fallen cold and dead.

O Captain! my Captain! rise up and hear the bells;
Rise up—for you the flag is flung—for you the bugle trills,   10
For you bouquets and ribboned wreaths—for you the
    shores a-crowding,
For you they call, the swaying mass, their eager faces
    turning;
  Here Captain! dear father!
    This arm beneath your head!
      It is some dream that on the deck   15
        You've fallen cold and dead.

My Captain does not answer, his lips are pale and still,
My father does not feel my arm, he has no pulse nor will,
The ship is anchored safe and sound, its voyage closed and
    done,
From fearful trip the victor ship comes in with object
    won;   20
  Exult O shores! and ring O bells!
    But I with mournful tread
      Walk the deck my Captain lies,
        Fallen cold and dead.

2. **rack:** here, an upheaval caused by a storm.

President Lincoln's burial service in Springfield, Illinois.
A pen-and-ink sketch by W. Waud.
Culver Pictures, Inc.

SEEKING MEANING

1. Whitman does not tell you directly who the "Captain" is. However, the readers of his day knew that the "Captain" was President Lincoln, and that the "ship" was the country. In what ways are a President and a ship's captain alike? In what ways is a nation like a ship? What else does Whitman call Lincoln?

2. This ship has been through a "fearful trip." What does this "fearful trip" stand for?

3. The ship is coming into "port." The "port" is the peace that the country has finally found. Is "port" a good way to describe peace? Why or why not?

ABOUT THE AUTHOR

Walt Whitman (1819–1892) was born on Long Island, New York. For several years he worked as a newspaperman, but he was fired from his job for his strong antislavery views. Trips to Chicago and New Orleans intensified his appreciation of his country, and he soon began to write poetry. In 1855 Whitman published a collection of his own poems called *Leaves of Grass*. It was an extraordinary work, unlike any poetry that had appeared before. The public was astonished by the driving rhythms, the enthusiastic statements, and the frank language. Throughout his life Whitman continued to revise and add poems to *Leaves of Grass*. The book has had a tremendous influence on later poets.

During the Civil War, Whitman served as a volunteer nurse, caring for the wounded who filled the military hospitals. A great lover of America, Whitman was deeply affected by the assassination of Abraham Lincoln. His greatest poem about Lincoln's death is "When Lilacs Last in the Dooryard Bloomed."

*Exactly at noon on April 22, 1889, two million acres of
Oklahoma territory were opened for settlement. On the
border, some 50,000 land-seekers massed for the biggest
stampede in the history of the West. This was the
Oklahoma Land Run, a historical event that Edna Ferber
used in her famous novel* Cimarron.

    *The following selection is a scene from that novel. The
Venables, a wealthy Kansas family, are listening to Yancey
Cravat, a son-in-law, as he relates his adventures in
the Land Run.*

The Oklahoma Land Run

Edna Ferber

"I had planned to try and get a place on the Santa Fe train that was standing, steam up, ready to run into the Nation.[1] But you couldn't get on. There wasn't room for a flea. They were hanging on the cowcatcher[2] and swarming all over the engine, and sitting on top of the cars. It was keyed down to make no more speed than a horse. It turned out they didn't even do that. They went twenty miles in ninety minutes. I decided I'd use my Indian pony. I knew I'd get endurance, anyway, if not speed. And that's what counted in the end.

"There we stood, by the thousands, all night. Morning, and we began to line up at the Border, as near as they'd let us go. Militia all along to keep us back. They had burned the prairie ahead for miles into the Nation, so as to keep the grass down and make the way clearer. To smoke out the Sooners,[3] too, who had sneaked in and were hiding in the scrub oaks, in the draws,[4] wherever they could. Most of the killing was due to them. They had crawled in and staked the land and stood ready to shoot those of us who came in, fair and square, in the Run. I knew the piece I wanted. An old freighters' trail, out of use, but still marked with deep ruts, led almost straight to it, once you found the trail, all overgrown as it was. A little creek ran through the land, and the prairie rolled a little there, too. Nothing but blackjacks[5] for miles around it, but on that section, because of the water, I suppose, there were elms and persimmons and cottonwoods and even a grove of pecans. I had noticed it many a time, riding the range. . . .

"Ten o'clock, and the crowd was nervous and restless. Hundreds of us had been followers of Payne and had gone as Boomers[6] in the old Payne colonies, and had been driven out, and had come back again. Thousands from all parts of the country had waited ten years for this day when the land-hungry would be fed. They were like people starving. I've seen the same look exactly on the faces of men who were ravenous for food.

"Well, eleven o'clock, and they were crowding and cursing and fighting for places near the Line. They shouted and sang and yelled and argued, and the sound they made wasn't human at all, but like thousands of wild animals penned up. The sun blazed down. It was cruel. The dust hung over everything in a thick cloud, blinding you and choking you. The black dust of the burned prairie was over everything. We were like a horde of fiends with our red eyes and our cracked lips and our blackened faces. Eleven thirty. It was a picture straight out of hell. The roar grew louder. People fought for an inch of gain on the Border. Just next to me was a girl who looked about eighteen—she turned out to be twenty-five—and a beauty she was, too—on a coal-black thoroughbred. . . .

"On the other side was an old fellow with a long gray beard—a plainsman, he was—a six-shooter in his belt, one wooden leg, and a flask of whiskey. He took a pull out of that

---

1. **the Nation:** the territory formerly occupied by five American Indian nations—the Cherokees, Creeks, Choctaws, Chickasaws, and Seminoles.
2. **cowcatcher:** a metal frame set on the front of a locomotive to remove obstructions, such as cows, from the tracks.
3. **Sooners:** people who occupied homestead land "sooner" than the authorized time for doing so.
4. **draws:** gullies or ravines.
5. **blackjacks:** short oaks with black bark.

6. **Payne . . . Boomers:** David L. Payne was one of the leaders of the Boomers, people who settled illegally on the Unassigned Lands of central Oklahoma, but who were evicted by United States soldiers.

every minute or two. He was mounted on an Indian pony like mine. Every now and then he'd throw back his head and let out a yell that would curdle your blood, even in that chorus of fiends. As we waited we fell to talking, the three of us, though you couldn't hear much in that uproar. The girl said she had trained her thoroughbred for the race. He was from Kentucky, and so was she. She was bound to get her hundred and sixty acres, she said. She had to have it. She didn't say why, and I didn't ask her. We were all too keyed up, anyway, to make sense. Oh, I forgot. She had on a get-up that took the attention of anyone that saw her, even in that crazy mob. The better to cut the wind, she had shortened sail and wore a short skirt, black tights, and a skull-cap. . . .

"It turned out that the three of us, there in the front line, were headed down the old freighters' trail toward the creek land. I said, 'I'll be the first in the Run to reach Little Bear.' That was the name of the creek on the section. The girl pulled her cap down tight over her ears. 'Follow me,' she laughed. 'I'll show you the way.' Then the old fellow with the wooden leg and the whiskers yelled out, 'Whoop-ee! I'll tell 'em along the Little Bear you're both a-comin'.'

"There we were, the girl on my left, the old plainsman on my right. Eleven forty-five. Along the Border were the soldiers, their guns in one hand, their watches in the other. Those last five minutes seemed years long; and funny, they'd quieted till there wasn't a sound. Listening. The last minute was an eternity. Twelve o'clock. There went up a roar that drowned the crack of the soldiers' musketry as they fired in the air as the signal of noon and the start of the Run. You could see the puffs of smoke from their guns, but you couldn't hear a sound. The thousands surged over the Line. It was like water going over a broken dam. The rush had started, and it was devil take the hindmost. We swept across the prairie in a cloud of black and red dust that covered our faces and hands in a minute, so that we looked like black demons from hell. Off we went, down the old freight trail that was two wheel ruts, a foot wide each, worn into the prairie soil. The old man on his pony kept in one rut, the girl on her thoroughbred in the other, and I on my White-foot on the raised place in the middle. That first half mile was almost a neck-and-neck race. The old fellow was yelling and waving one arm and hanging on somehow. He was beating his pony with the flask on his flanks. Then he began to drop behind. Next thing I heard a terrible scream and a great shouting behind me. I threw a quick glance over my shoulder. The old plainsman's pony had stumbled and fallen. His bottle smashed into bits, his six-shooter flew in another direction, and he lay sprawling full length in the rut of the trail. The next instant he was hidden in a welter[7] of pounding hoofs and flying dirt and cinders and wagon wheels."

A dramatic pause. . . . The faces around the table were balloons pulled by a single string. They swung this way and that with Yancey Cravat's pace as he strode the room, his Prince Albert[8] coattails billowing. This way—the faces turned toward the sideboard. That way—they turned toward the windows. Yancey held the little moment of silence like a jewel in the circlet of faces. Sabra Cravat's voice, high and sharp with suspense, cut the stillness.

"What happened? What happened to the old man?"

Yancey's pliant hands flew up in a gesture of inevitability. "Oh, he was trampled to

---

7. **welter:** great confusion or turmoil.
8. **Prince Albert:** a long, double-breasted coat.

death in the mad mob that charged over him. Crazy. They couldn't stop for a one-legged old whiskers with a quart flask. . . .

"The girl and I—funny, I never did learn her name—were in the lead because we had stuck to the old trail, rutted though it was, rather than strike out across the prairie that by this time was beyond the burned area and was covered with a heavy growth of blue stem grass almost six feet high in places. A horse could only be forced through that at a slow pace. That jungle of grass kept many a racer from winning his section that day.

"The girl followed close behind me. That thoroughbred she rode was built for speed, not distance. A racehorse, blooded. I could hear him blowing. He was trained to short bursts. My Indian pony was just getting his second wind as her horse slackened into a trot. We had come nearly sixteen miles. I was well in the lead by that time, with the girl following. She was crouched low over his neck, like a jockey, and I could hear her talking to him, low and sweet and eager, as if he were a human being. We were far in the lead now. We had left the others behind, hundreds going this way, hundreds that, scattering for miles over the prairie. Then I saw that the prairie ahead was afire. The tall grass was blazing. Only the narrow trail down which we were galloping was open. On either side of it was a wall of flame. Some skunk of a Sooner, sneaking in ahead of the Run, had set the blaze to keep the Boomers off, saving the land for himself. The dry grass burned like oiled paper. I turned around. The girl was there, her racer stumbling, breaking and going on, his head lolling now. I saw her motion with her hand. She was coming. I whipped off my hat and clapped it over Whitefoot's eyes, gave him the spurs, crouched down low and tight, shut my own eyes, and down the trail we went into the furnace. Hot! It was hell! The crackling and

snapping on either side was like a fusillade.[9] I could smell the singed hair on the flanks of the mustang. My own hair was singeing. I could feel the flames licking my legs and back. Another hundred yards and neither the horse nor I could have come through it. But we broke out into the open choking and blinded and half suffocated. I looked down the lane of flame. The girl hung on her horse's neck. Her skullcap was pulled down over her eyes. She was coming through, game. I knew that my land—the piece that I had come through hell for—was not more than a mile ahead. I knew that hanging around here would probably get me a shot through the head, for the Sooner that started that fire must be lurking somewhere in the high grass ready to kill anybody that tried to lay claim to his land. I began to wonder, too, if that girl wasn't headed for the same section that I was bound for. I made up my mind that, woman or no woman, this was a race, and devil take the hindmost. My poor little pony was coughing and sneezing and trembling. Her racer must have been ready to drop. I wheeled and went on. I kept thinking how, when I came to Little Bear Creek, I'd bathe my little mustang's nose and face and his poor heaving flanks, and how I mustn't let him drink too much, once he got his muzzle in the water.

"Just before I reached the land I was riding for I had to leave the trail and cut across the prairie. I could see a clump of elms ahead. I knew the creek was nearby. But just before I got to it I came to one of those deep gullies you find in the plains country. Drought does it—a crack in the dry earth to begin with, widening with every rain until it becomes a small canyon. Almost ten feet across this one was, and deep. No way around it that I could

---

9. **fusillade** (fyo͞o′sə-lād′): a burst of firearms.

see, and no time to look for one. I put Whitefoot to the leap and . . . he took it, landing on the other side with hardly an inch to spare. I heard a wild scream behind me. I turned. The girl on her spent racer had tried to make the gulch. He had actually taken it—a thoroughbred and a gentleman, that animal—but he came down on his knees just on the farther edge, rolled, and slid down the gully side into the ditch. The girl had flung herself free. My claim was fifty yards away. So was the girl, with her dying horse. She lay there on the prairie. As I raced toward her—my own poor little mount was nearly gone by this time—she scrambled to her knees. I can see her face now, black with cinders and soot and dirt, her hair all over her shoulders, her cheek bleeding where she had struck a stone in her fall, her black tights torn, her little short skirt sagging. She sort of sat up and looked around her, and stood there swaying, and pushing her hair out of her eyes like someone who'd been asleep. She pointed down the gully. The black of her face was streaked with tears.

" 'Shoot him!' she said. 'I can't. His two forelegs are broken. I heard them crack. Shoot him!' . . .

"So I off my horse and down to the gully's edge. There the animal lay, his eyes all whites, his poor legs doubled under him, his flanks black and sticky with sweat and dirt. He was done for, all right. I took out my six-shooter and aimed right between his eyes. He kicked once, sort of leaped—or tried to, and then lay still. I stood there a minute, to see if he had to have another. He was so game that, some way, I didn't want to give him more than he needed.

"Then something made me turn around. The girl had mounted my mustang. She was off toward the creek section. Before I had moved ten paces she had reached the very piece I had marked in my mind for my own. She leaped from the horse, ripped off her skirt, tied it to her riding whip that she still held tight in her hand, dug the whip butt into the soil of the prairie—planted her flag—and the land was hers by right of claim."

SEEKING MEANING

1. This realistic description of the Oklahoma Land Run shows how desperate people were for the new, free land. What does Yancey say the land-hungry people were like, in the third and fourth paragraphs?

2. Which details in the fourth paragraph make you picture the scene as something from hell? How do you think the author wants you to feel about the Land Run?

3. The girl next to Yancey turns out to be his chief competitor in the race. What does Yancey tell you about the girl?

4. How does the girl manage to stake her claim ahead of Yancey? What personal qualities cause Yancey's failure? What qualities make the girl the winner?

5. What do you think of the girl's actions?

DEVELOPING VOCABULARY

Recognizing Americanisms

Each region of the United States has contributed words to the national vocabulary. For example, this story of the Oklahoma Land Run contains the words *range* and *gulch*. These are examples of *Americanisms*—that is, words that originated in America or that came to have distinctive meanings in American English. Use a dictionary to find the origins and meanings of these Americanisms:

aggie	moccasin
Annie Oakley	OK
billboard	shoofly pie
French fry	tin lizzie

ABOUT THE AUTHOR

Edna Ferber (1885–1968), one of the most popular novelists in America, at first wanted to be an actress. She abandoned this ambition after her father became blind and she had to take a job as a newspaper reporter for three dollars a week. She threw her first novel away, but her mother rescued the manuscript and sent it to a publisher. Edna Ferber later admitted that she had never written a book she was fully satisfied with. Her first best seller, *Show Boat,* was made into a stage musical and three movies. She won the Pulitzer Prize for *So Big,* a novel about a woman whose rugged individualism helps her triumph over disaster. *Cimarron* was a big hit as a movie, as was *Giant,* a novel about modern life in Texas. Though she had never intended to be a writer, Edna Ferber loved her profession. She once remarked that "life can't ever defeat a writer who is in love with writing."

The narrator of this story recalls a Navajo celebration that took place when he was a boy in New Mexico. For their sacred ceremonies, the Navajos journeyed out of their reservation to a holy place many miles away. This selection is from a book called The Names, *Momaday's book of memories about the Southwest.*

It Will Not Be Seen Again

N. Scott Momaday

The activity in the pueblo reached a peak on the day before the Feast of San Diego, November twelfth. It was on that day, an especially brilliant day in which the winter held off and the sun shone like a flare, that Jemez[1] became one of the fabulous cities of the world. In the preceding days the women had plastered the houses, many of them, and they were clean and beautiful like bone in the high light; the strings of chilies at the vigas[2] had darkened a little and taken on a deeper, softer sheen; ears of colored corn were strung at the doors, and fresh cedar boughs were laid about, setting a whole, wild fragrance on the air. The women were baking bread in the outdoor ovens. Here and there men and women were at the woodpiles, chopping, taking up loads of firewood for their kitchens, for the coming feast. Even the children were at work:

the little boys looked after the stock, and the little girls carried babies about. There were gleaming antlers on the rooftops, and smoke arose from all the chimneys.

About midday the Navajos began to arrive. And they seemed *all* to come, as a whole people, as if it was their racial destiny to find at last the center of the world, the place of origin, older than *tsegi*,[3] among the rocks. From the yard of the day school I looked southward, along the road to San Ysidro,[4] and there was a train of covered wagons, extending as far as I could see. All afternoon the caravan passed by, shimmering in the winter light, its numberless facets gleaming, the hundreds of wagon wheels turning in the dust, in slow and endless motion. Never have the Navajos seemed a more beautiful people to me, for

---

1. **Jemez** (hā'mĕs): the name of this pueblo.
2. **vigas** (vē'gəz): heavy beams or rafters.

3. **tsegi:** literally, "the place among the rocks," sacred ground to the Navajos.
4. **San Ysidro** (sän ē-sēd'rō).

they bore about them the cherished memories of my childhood. This old man, had he not once told us the way to Klagetoh? That beautiful woman, had she not been a schoolgirl at Chinle? They were resplendent. The old people and the children peered out from beneath the canopies, dark-skinned and black-eyed, nearly tentative in the shadows, beautiful in the way that certain photographic negatives are beautiful, dimly traced with light. The outriders were men and women and youths on handsome horses in glossy leather trappings and rich saddle blankets, the men in big hats and fine boots and bright silk and satin shirts, the women in velveteen blouses, long, pleated skirts, and red moccasins. They all wore silver and turquoise and coral—concha belts,[5] necklaces, bracelets, and rings which flashed and glinted and gleamed in the sun. And their voices, as I hear them even now— the singing and the laughter—carried along the train like a long, rising and falling woodwind music; it is a sound that I have heard among bristlecones,[6] or upon the walls of the old ruin of Giusewa. A dog or two followed after each of the wagons, keeping closely in place. The Navajo dogs are solitary creatures. I believe that they assume very early the reserve and nobility of the people with whom they live and they consist in that assumption. They are shepherds, and they know their sheep in the way that an eagle knows its nest; and when they have not their sheep they concentrate themselves in the shadows of the wagons.

Some of the men of Jemez rode out to meet the Navajos. John Cajero was one of them.

A Navajo man. A photograph by Carl Moon. Library of Congress.

He was then a man in his prime, a Tanoan[7] man, agile and strong in his mind and body, and he was a first-rate horseman. He was mounted on a good-looking gray quarter horse, which he handled closely and well, and he cut a fine figure upon it in his blue shirt

---

5. **concha** (kôn′chä) **belts:** belts lined with shell-shaped metal disks.
6. **bristlecones:** very old pine trees.

7. **Tanoan:** Tano is the name of a family of four North American Indian languages.

and red headband, his manner easy and confident. He singled out old friends among the Navajos, and soon there was a cluster of riders holding up on the side of the road, convened in a high mood of fellowship and good humor — and a certain rivalry. Then John Cajero was holding the coils of a rope in his hands, shaking out a loop. Suddenly he leaned forward and his horse bolted into the road between two of the wagons, nearly trampling over a dog; the dog lunged away with a yelp and ran at full speed, but the horse was right upon it, bunched in motion, and the rope flashed down and caught the dog up around its hips and set it rolling and twisting in the sand, jerking it up then into the air and slamming it down hard, as the horse squatted, jamming its hooves in the earth, its whole weight cracking against the bit. And John Cajero played out a little of the rope from his saddle, and the dog slithered out of the noose and ran ahead, its tail between its legs, and went crouching and wary under its wagon. John Cajero laughed, and the others, too, though their laughter was brittle, I thought, and the Navajos watched evenly the performance, the enactment of a hard joke, and considered precisely what it was worth. There was a kind of trade in this, a bartering of nerve and arrogance and skill, of elemental pride. Then, getting down from his horse, John Cajero drew a dollar bill from his pocket, folded it once lengthwise, and stuck it down in the sand. He gestured to the others; it was a beckoning, an invitation, but I did not understand at first what he meant them to do. He swung himself up into the saddle and gestured again, pointing down to the money on the ground. No one moved; only they were watchful, and he urged his horse away, prancing, a little distance. Then he turned the horse around and set it running — or loping, rather, not fast, but easily, evenly — and reached down from the saddle for the dollar bill. It

seemed that his fingers brushed it, but he could not take hold of it, for the stride of the horse was broken slightly at the crucial moment. It was the barest miss — and a beautiful, thrilling thing to see — and he was upright in the saddle again, his motion and the motion of the horse all of a piece. I was watching him so intently that I did not at first see the girl. She came from nowhere, a lithe, lovely Navajo girl on a black horse. She was coming up fast in John Cajero's dust, faster than he had come, and her horse was holding steady in a long, loping stride, level and low. When I saw her she was already hanging down nearly the whole length of her arm from the saddle horn, her knee cocked and her long back curved like a bow, her shoulders close against the deep chest of the horse; she swung her left arm down like a scythe, and up, holding the dollar bill with the tips of her fingers until it was high over her head, and she was standing straight in the stirrups, and her horse did not break stride. And in that way she rode on, past John Cajero, along the wagon train and into the village, having stolen the show and the money, too, going in beauty, trailing laughter. Later I looked for her among the camps, but I did not find her. I imagined that her name was Desbah Yazzie and that she looked out for me from the shadows.

. . .

And the next year there were fewer covered wagons, fewer men and women on horseback. And the next there was relatively little to see on the old wagon road, but the people came in on the high road in cars and trucks. And I think often and with great longing of that first Feast of San Diego in my life at Jemez, that pageant that happened upon me like a dream: say that it was good to see, that it will not be seen again.

SEEKING MEANING

1. Find and read aloud the passages that describe the appearance of the Navajo caravan. Which words or phrases help you to imagine this fabulous scene?

2. John Cajero was a skilled horseman and proud of his ability. What feat did he first perform to impress the visiting Navajos? What details tell you how the Navajos felt about his performance with the dog?

3. John Cajero then challenged the Navajos. What happened that surprised Cajero and delighted the onlookers? How did this incident affect Momaday?

4. Momaday says that the pageant that took place on this Feast of San Diego will not be seen again. What changes took place the following year and the year after that? How do you think Momaday feels about these changes?

DEVELOPING SKILLS OF EXPRESSION

Supporting a Statement with Details

In the first paragraph of this story, Momaday says: "The activity in the pueblo reached a peak on the day before the Feast of San Diego, November twelfth." In the sentences that follow, Momaday names some of these activities:

The houses were being plastered.
Ears of corn were being strung at the door.
Fresh cedar boughs were being laid out.
The women were baking bread.
Men and women were chopping wood.
The little boys were looking after the stock.
The little girls were carrying babies.

Perhaps you also know of a special occasion that you would like to write about so that it will not be forgotten. Open your paragraph with a statement of your topic. Then, in three or four sentences, give your reader specific details that explain your topic. Here are some ideas for opening sentences.

At holiday time, our town (city) is filled with people doing things.
At holiday time in our home, everyone is busy.
At holiday time, I eat too much.

ABOUT THE AUTHOR

Navarre Scott Momaday (1934–   ) was born in Oklahoma. His father was a full-blooded Kiowa, and his mother had English, French, and Cherokee ancestors. His "young and free and beautiful" parents came to Jemez Pueblo when Momaday was twelve. For twenty-five years they taught in the Jemez Day School. Momaday left the pueblo to continue his own education. Today he lives in California and is a professor of English at Stanford University.

All of Momaday's writings tell about the ways of his people. In his novel *House Made of Dawn,* which won the Pulitzer Prize, Momaday tells the story of a young man caught between the conflicting claims of the Indian and white worlds. In *The Way to Rainy Mountain* he retraces the past of the Kiowas — their myths and legends and their long journey from Montana into the Southern Plains. Memories of his youth are the substance of *The Names.*

"The melting pot" is an expression often used to describe the United States. In "the melting pot," all nationalities are mixed together, so that they assimilate, or absorb, one another's ways. Ernesto Galarza says that his public school was not a melting pot. He thinks of it as a griddle, where knowledge was warmed into students and racial hatreds roasted out of them.

In this excerpt from Barrio° Boy, *his autobiography, Ernesto and his mother have just arrived in Sacramento, California, from their native Mexico. They are on their way to enroll Ernesto in public school.*

Barrio Boy   *Ernesto Galarza*

The two of us walked south on Fifth Street one morning to the corner of Q Street and turned right. Half of the block was occupied by the Lincoln School. It was a three-story wooden building, with two wings that gave it the shape of a double-T connected by a central hall. It was a new building, painted yellow, with a shingled roof that was not like the red tile of the school in Mazatlán.[1] I noticed other differences, none of them very reassuring.

We walked up the wide staircase hand in hand and through the door, which closed by itself. A mechanical contraption screwed to the top shut it behind us quietly.

Up to this point the adventure of enrolling me in the school had been carefully rehearsed. Mrs. Dodson[2] had told us how to find it and

we had circled it several times on our walks. Friends in the barrio explained that the *director* was called a principal, and that it was a lady and not a man. They assured us that there was always a person at the school who could speak Spanish.

Exactly as we had been told, there was a sign on the door in both Spanish and English: "Principal." We crossed the hall and entered the office of Miss Nettie Hopley.

Miss Hopley was at a roll-top desk to one side, sitting in a swivel chair that moved on wheels. There was a sofa against the opposite wall, flanked by two windows and a door that opened on a small balcony. Chairs were set around a table and framed pictures hung on the walls of a man with long white hair and another with a sad face and a black beard.

The principal half turned in the swivel chair to look at us over the pinch glasses crossed on the ridge of her nose. To do this she had to duck her head slightly as if she were about to step through a low doorway.

° **Barrio:** the neighborhood or district of a city where Spanish-speaking people live.
1. **Mazatlán** (mä'sät-län'): a city in Mexico, where Ernesto lived before coming to the United States.
2. **Mrs. Dodson:** the landlady of the boarding house in which the Galarzas lived.

A painting of a rural schoolroom, around 1900.
National Gallery of Art, Washington, D.C. Index of American Design.

What Miss Hopley said to us we did not know but we saw in her eyes a warm welcome and when she took off her glasses and straightened up she smiled wholeheartedly, like Mrs. Dodson. We were, of course, saying nothing, only catching the friendliness of her voice and the sparkle in her eyes while she said words we did not understand. She signaled us to the table. Almost tiptoeing across the office, I maneuvered myself to keep my mother between me and the gringo[3] lady. In a

matter of seconds I had to decide whether she was a possible friend or a menace. We sat down.

Then Miss Hopley did a formidable thing. She stood up. Had she been standing when we entered she would have seemed tall. But rising from her chair she soared. And what she carried up and up with her were firm shoulders, a straight sharp nose, full cheeks slightly molded by a curved line along the nostrils, thin lips that moved like steel springs, and a high forehead topped by hair gathered in a bun. Miss Hopley was not a giant in body but

---

3. **gringo:** a Spanish-American term for a foreigner.

when she mobilized it to a standing position she seemed a match for giants. I decided I liked her.

She strode to a door in the far corner of the office, opened it and called a name. A boy of about ten years appeared in the doorway. He sat down at one end of the table. He was brown like us, a plump kid with shiny black hair combed straight back, neat, cool, and faintly obnoxious.

Miss Hopley joined us with a large book and some papers in her hand. She, too, sat down and the questions and answers began by way of our interpreter. My name was Ernesto. My mother's name was Henriqueta. My birth certificate was in San Blas. Here was my last report card from the Escuela Municipal Número 3 para Varones of Mazatlán, and so forth. Miss Hopley put things down in the book and my mother signed a card.

As long as the questions continued, Doña Henriqueta could stay and I was secure. Now that they were over, Miss Hopley saw her to the door, dismissed our interpreter and without further ado took me by the hand and strode down the hall to Miss Ryan's first grade.

Miss Ryan took me to a seat at the front of the room, into which I shrank—the better to survey her. She was, to skinny, somewhat runty me, of a withering height when she patrolled the class. And when I least expected it, there she was, crouching by my desk, her blond, radiant face level with mine, her voice patiently maneuvering me over the awful idiocies of the English language.

During the next few weeks Miss Ryan overcame my fears of tall, energetic teachers as she bent over my desk to help me with a word in the preprimer. Step by step, she loosened me and my classmates from the safe anchorage of the desks for recitations at the blackboard and consultations at her desk. Fre-

quently she burst into happy announcements to the whole class. "Ito can read a sentence," and small Japanese Ito slowly read aloud while the class listened in wonder: "Come, Skipper, come. Come and run." The Korean, Portuguese, Italian, and Polish first-graders had similar moments of glory, no less shining than mine the day I conquered *butterfly,* which I had been persistently pronouncing in standard Spanish as "boo-ter-flee." "Children," Miss Ryan called for attention. "Ernesto has learned how to pronounce *butterfly!"* And I proved it with a perfect imitation of Miss Ryan. From that celebrated success, I was soon able to match Ito's progress as a sentence reader with "Come, butterfly, come fly with me."

Like Ito and several other first-graders who did not know English, I received private lessons from Miss Ryan in the closet, a narrow hall off the classroom with a door at each end. Next to one of these doors Miss Ryan placed a large chair for herself and a small one for me. Keeping an eye on the class through the open door she read with me about sheep in the meadow and a frightened chicken going to see the king, coaching me out of my phonetic ruts in words like *pasture, bow-wow-wow, hay,* and *pretty,* which to my Mexican ear and eye had so many unnecessary sounds and letters. She made me watch her lips and then close my eyes as she repeated words I found hard to read. When we came to know each other better, I tried interrupting to tell Miss Ryan how we said it in Spanish. It didn't work. She only said "oh" and went on with *pasture, bow-wow-wow,* and *pretty.* It was as if in that closet we were both discovering together the secrets of the English language and grieving together over the tragedies of Bo-Peep. The main reason I was graduated with honors from the first grade was that I had fallen in love with Miss Ryan. Her radiant, no-nonsense character made us either afraid not to love her or love her so we would not be afraid, I am not sure which. It was not only that we sensed she was with it, but also that she was with us.

Like the first grade, the rest of the Lincoln School was a sampling of the lower part of town where many races made their home. My pals in the second grade were Kazushi, whose parents spoke only Japanese; Matti, a skinny Italian boy; and Manuel, a fat Portuguese who would never get into a fight but wrestled you to the ground and just sat on you. Our assortment of nationalities included Koreans, Yugoslavs, Poles, Irish, and home-grown Americans.

Miss Hopley and her teachers never let us forget why we were at Lincoln: for those who were alien, to become good Americans; for those who were so born, to accept the rest of us. Off the school grounds we traded the same insults we heard from our elders. On the playground we were sure to be marched up to the principal's office for calling someone an insulting name. The school was not so much a melting pot as a griddle where Miss Hopley and her helpers warmed knowledge into us and roasted racial hatreds out of us.

At Lincoln, making us into Americans did not mean scrubbing away what made us originally foreign. The teachers called us as our parents did, or as close as they could pronounce our names in Spanish or Japanese. No one was ever scolded or punished for speaking in his native tongue on the playground. Matti told the class about his mother's down quilt, which she had made in Italy with the fine feathers of a thousand geese. Encarnación acted out how boys learned to fish in the Philippines. I astounded the third grade with the story of my travels on a stagecoach, which nobody else in the class had seen except in the museum at Sutter's Fort. After a visit to the Crocker Art Gallery and its collection of heroic paintings of the golden age of California, someone showed a silk scroll with a Chinese painting. Miss Hopley herself had a way of expressing wonder over these matters before a class, her eyes wide open until they popped slightly. It was easy for me to feel that becoming a proud American, as she said we should, did not mean feeling ashamed of being a Mexican.

The Americanization of Mexican me was no smooth matter. I had to fight one lout[4] who made fun of my travels on the *diligencia*,[5] and my barbaric translation of the word into "diligence." He doubled up with laughter over the word until I straightened him out with a kick. In class I made points explaining that in Mexico roosters said *"qui-qui-ri-qui"* and not "cock-a-doodle-doo," but after school I had to put up with the taunts of a big Yugoslav who said Mexican roosters were crazy.

But it was Homer who gave me the most lasting lesson for a future American.

Homer was a chunky Irishman who dressed as if every day was Sunday. He slicked his hair between a crew cut and a pompadour.[6] And Homer was smart, as he clearly showed when he and I ran for president of the third grade.

Everyone understood that this was to be a demonstration of how the American people vote for president. In an election, the teacher explained, the candidates could be generous and vote for each other. We cast our ballots in a shoebox and Homer won by two votes. I polled my supporters and came to the conclusion that I had voted for Homer and so had he.

---

4. **lout:** a clumsy, stupid person.
5. *diligencia* (dē´lē-hĕn´syä): a Spanish word meaning "a fast coach." At one time, the English word *diligence* meant "speed" or "haste." Now *diligence* means "careful effort" or "hard work."
6. **pompadour:** a hair style in which the hair is combed or brushed up high away from the forehead.

After class he didn't deny it, reminding me of what the teacher had said — we could vote for each other but didn't have to.

The lower part of town was a collage[7] of nationalities in the middle of which Miss Nettie Hopley kept school with discipline and compassion. She called assemblies in the upper hall to introduce celebrities like the police sergeant or the fire chief, to lay down the law of the school, to present awards to our athletic champions, and to make important announcements. One of these was that I had been proposed by my school and accepted as a member of the newly formed Sacramento Boys Band. "Now, isn't that a wonderful thing?" Miss Hopley asked the assembled school, all eyes on me. And everyone answered in a chorus, including myself, "Yes, Miss Hopley."

It was not only the parents who were summoned to her office and boys and girls who served sentences there who knew that Nettie Hopley meant business. The entire school witnessed her sizzling Americanism in its awful majesty one morning at flag salute.

All the grades, as usual, were lined up in the courtyard between the wings of the build-

---

7. **collage** (kō-läzh′): a collection of bits and pieces.

ing, ready to march to classes after the opening bell. Miss Shand was on the balcony of the second floor off Miss Hopley's office, conducting us in our lusty singing of "My Country tiz-a-thee." Our principal, as always, stood there like us, at attention, her right hand over her heart, joining in the song.

Halfway through the second stanza she stepped forward, held up her arm in a sign of command, and called loud and clear: "Stop the singing." Miss Shand looked flabbergasted. We were frozen with shock.

Miss Hopley was now standing at the rail of the balcony, her eyes sparking, her voice low and resonant, the words coming down to us distinctly and loaded with indignation.

"There are two gentlemen walking on the school grounds with their hats on while we are singing," she said, sweeping our ranks with her eyes. "We will remain silent until the gentlemen come to attention and remove their hats." A minute of awful silence ended when Miss Hopley, her gaze fixed on something behind us, signaled Miss Shand and we began once more the familiar hymn. That afternoon, when school was out, the word spread. The two gentlemen were the Superintendent of Schools and an important guest on an inspection.

SEEKING MEANING

1. When Ernesto came to school in the United States, he did not understand English. How did Miss Hopley, the principal, make him feel at ease?

2. Miss Ryan was a patient and encouraging teacher with a "blond, radiant face." What did she do to make Ernesto and the other first-graders enjoy learning English?

3. The teachers at the Lincoln School never let the students forget why they were there. According to the teachers, what was the purpose of school? In your own words, explain what you think the teachers meant by "good Americans" (page 185).

4. Ernesto and his classmates also kept their pride in their own backgrounds. How did the teachers encourage the students to remember their own cultures?

5. What lesson in "sizzling Americanism" did Miss Hopley give to the Superintendent of Schools and his important guest? How would you describe what Ernesto and his classmates learned from this "lesson"?

DEVELOPING SKILLS IN LANGUAGE

Comparing Words That Imitate Sounds

Ernesto discovered something about language when he realized that a Mexican rooster and an American rooster make different sounds. An American rooster is supposed to say "cock-a-doodle-doo." What does a Mexican rooster say? If there were Norwegians in Ernesto's class, they could have told him that Norwegian roosters go "*kykkeliky.*"

Here are some other words that are supposed to echo natural sounds. Notice that people in different lands seem to "hear" the sounds in different ways.

bow-wow: *oua-oua* (French); *wan-wan* (Japanese); *bu-bu* (Italian)
bang: *pum* (Spanish)
knock-knock: *pom-pom* (French)
purr: *ron-ron* (French); *schnurr* (German)

The English words *hiss, rustle,* and *tap* are supposed to echo or imitate natural sounds. Do any of your classmates know the words for these sounds in another language?

ABOUT THE AUTHOR

Ernesto Galarza's popular autobiography *Barrio Boy* began as stories he told his own children about Jalcocotán, the remote mountain village in Mexico where he was born in 1905. The Galarza family suffered great hardship during the Mexican revolution, and some of them finally made their way to Sacramento, California. There young Ernesto had his first experience with American education. Galarza went on to receive a Ph.D. from Columbia University and become a teacher and writer. His other books include several textbooks on the Mexican-American heritage.

On August 28, 1963, a quarter of a million Americans marched peacefully to Washington, D.C., to urge Congress to pass civil rights legislation. This is part of the speech delivered by Dr. King on that summer day.

I Have a Dream

Martin Luther King, Jr.

I say to you today, my friends, that in spite of the difficulties and frustrations of the moment, I still have a dream. It is a dream deeply rooted in the American dream.

I have a dream that one day this nation will rise up and live out the true meaning of its creed: "We hold these truths to be self-evident: that all men are created equal."

I have a dream that one day on the red hills of Georgia the sons of former slaves and the sons of former slave owners will be able to sit down together at the table of brotherhood.

I have a dream that my four little children will one day live in a nation where they will not be judged by the color of their skin but the content of their character.

I have a dream today.

I have a dream that one day every valley shall be exalted, every hill and mountain shall be made low, the rough places will be made plains, and the crooked places will be made straight, and the glory of the Lord shall be revealed, and all flesh shall see it together.

This is our hope. This is the faith with which I return to the South. With this faith we will be able to hew out of the mountains of despair a stone of hope. With this faith we will be able to transform the jangling discords of our nation into a beautiful symphony of brotherhood. With this faith we will be able to work together, to pray together, to struggle together, to go to jail together, to stand up for freedom together, knowing that we will be free one day.

This will be the day when all of God's children will be able to sing with new meaning, "My country, 'tis of thee, sweet land of liberty, of thee I sing. Land where my fathers died, land of the Pilgrim's pride, from every mountainside, let freedom ring."

And if America is to be a great nation, this must become true. So let freedom ring from the prodigious hilltops of New Hampshire. Let freedom ring from the mighty mountains of New York. Let freedom ring from the heightening Alleghenies of Pennsylvania.

Let freedom ring from the snow-capped Rockies of Colorado.

Let freedom ring from the curvaceous peaks of California!

Let freedom ring from Stone Mountain of Georgia!

Let freedom ring from every hill and molehill of Mississippi. From every mountainside, let freedom ring.

When we let freedom ring, when we let it ring from every village and every hamlet, from every state and every city, we will be able to speed up that day when all of God's children, black men and white men, Jews and Gentiles, Protestants and Catholics, will be able to join hands and sing in the words of that old Negro spiritual, "Free at last! Free at last! Thank God almighty, we are free at last!"

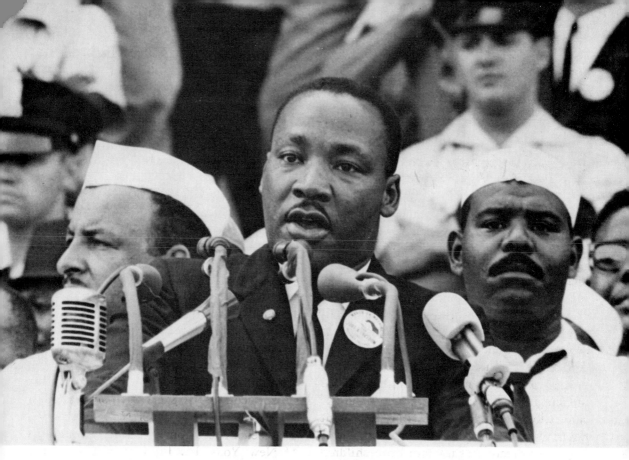

SEEKING MEANING

1. Martin Luther King, Jr., uses several images, or pictures, to express his dream. What are some of the pictures that he sees when he dreams of the perfect America?

2. King repeats "Let freedom ring!" What song is this line from? How do you think King's use of this line would affect an audience?

3. In paragraph 6, King quotes from the Biblical prophet Isaiah. Isaiah looked forward to the time when the Israelites would be led out of exile and bondage, back to their own home. Isaiah imagined that for his people's triumphant march home, mountains would be lowered, rocky places would be made into plains, and so on. What connection do you think King saw between his dream and Isaiah's?

ABOUT THE AUTHOR

Martin Luther King, Jr., (1929–1968) was a Baptist minister with a doctorate in theology from Boston University. During his graduate studies, he read from the works of the American writer Henry David Thoreau and the Indian leader Mahatma Gandhi. Both of these men advocated using nonviolent resistance to bring about social and political change. Their writings convinced King that these principles could be used to win civil rights for black people in America. Dr. King worked tirelessly for his goals. In 1957 alone, he traveled 700,000 miles and delivered 200 speeches. He spent time in jail. He preached, he marched, he wrote. In 1964 Dr. King was awarded the Nobel Prize for Peace. In 1968 he was killed by an assassin's bullet.

Practice in Reading and Writing

EXPOSITION

Reading Exposition

Exposition comes from a word meaning "to state in detail" or "to explain." Exposition is the kind of writing that presents information — that is, it "explains" something. Science books, history books, and news articles all use exposition.

This paragraph from the true story "Barrio Boy" (page 182) is a good example of effective exposition. In it, the author gives specific examples to illustrate how, at his school, making students into "Americans" did not scrub away what made them originally "foreign."

At Lincoln, making us into Americans did not mean scrubbing away what made us originally foreign. The teachers called on us as our parents did, or as close as they could pronounce our names in Spanish or Japanese. No one was ever scolded or punished for speaking in his native tongue on the playground. Matti told the class about his mother's down quilt, which she had made in Italy with the fine feathers of a thousand geese. Encarnación acted out how boys learned to fish in the Philippines. I astounded the third grade with the story of my travels on a stagecoach, which nobody else in the class had seen except in the museum at Sutter's Fort. After a visit to the Crocker Art Gallery and its collection of heroic paintings of the golden age of California, someone showed a silk scroll with a Chinese painting. Miss Hopley herself had a way of expressing wonder over these matters before a class, her eyes wide open until they popped slightly. It was easy for me to feel that becoming a proud American, as she said we should, did not mean feeling ashamed of being a Mexican.

1. *When you read exposition, look for a* topic sentence—*that is, a sentence that states the main idea.*

Not all paragraphs have topic sentences, but there is one here. Which sentence in this paragraph states the main idea?

2. *Note the reasons, examples, or other details used to support the main idea.*

Find seven examples used to support the main idea of this paragraph.

Writing Exposition

Here are some points to remember as you write exposition:

1. *Decide on the main idea of each paragraph.*

State your main idea in a topic sentence. This sentence can be placed anywhere in the paragraph, though it is usually the first or the last sentence.

2. *Provide specific details, examples, or reasons to support your main idea.*

3. *Organize your details logically.*

If you are giving directions on how to make fried chicken, you will have to organize your details in *chronological order*—the order in which the preparations take place. If you are giving examples to support an opinion, you might want to begin or end your essay with your most forceful statement.

4. *Weed out details that do not relate to your main idea.*

Write an expository paragraph on one of these topics or on a topic of your own:

What I like about where I live
How to make a perfect sandwich
Where Levis came from
Houdini's most famous escapes

For Further Reading

Cather, Willa, *My Ántonia* (Houghton Mifflin, 1918; paperback, Houghton)

This novel of pioneer days in Nebraska centers around the struggles of a poor immigrant family from Bohemia. Ántonia is the family's lively, beautiful daughter.

Clapp, Patricia, *Constance: A Story of Early Plymouth* (Lothrop, Lee & Shepard, 1968; paperback, Dell)

A fifteen-year-old girl begins her journal when the *Mayflower* arrives in the New World.

Collins, Michael, *Carrying the Fire: An Astronaut's Journeys* (Farrar, Straus & Giroux, 1974; paperback, Ballantine Books)

When the first astronaut stepped on the moon, Michael Collins was in the command module, completely alone in space. Here is his personal account of the moon adventures.

Edmonds, Walter, *Bert Breen's Barn* (Little Brown, 1975)

This suspenseful novel centers around a poor boy who acquires a barn that may have a treasure hidden in it.

Freedman, Benedict, and Nancy Freedman, *Mrs. Mike* (Coward-McCann, 1947; paperback, Medallion)

A young Boston woman, Kathie O'Fallon, goes with her husband, a Canadian mountie, to live in a cabin near the Arctic Circle.

Hunt, Irene, *Across Five Aprils* (Follett Publishing, 1964; paperback, Grosset & Dunlap)

The five Aprils are the years of the Civil War, which profoundly affect young Jethro Creighton and his family, who live on a farm in Illinois.

Johnson, Annabel, and Edgar Johnson, *Wilderness Bride* (Harper & Row, 1962)

In 1846 a fifteen-year-old girl journeys west with a large Mormon family to meet her husband.

Keith, Harold, *Rifles for Watie* (Thomas Y. Crowell, 1957)

Young Jeff Bussey longs to be a Union soldier, but he soon learns that war is not glamorous and that enemies are human.

Lane, Rose Wilder, *Let the Hurricane Roar* (Longmans, Green, 1933)

This novel tells about a young homesteading couple in the Dakotas who must face the grim realities of pioneer life. The story is told by the daughter of Laura, one of the sisters in the *Little House on the Prairie* books.

Preston, Edward, *Martin Luther King: Fighter for Freedom* (Doubleday, 1970)

This illustrated biography traces the life of the man who led the nonviolent resistance to segregation in the United States.

Sandburg, Carl, *Abe Lincoln Grows Up* (Harcourt Brace Jovanovich, 1940; paperback, Voyager)

The greatest biographer of Lincoln tells the story, with illustrations, of Lincoln's boyhood years on the prairie.

Underwood, Betty, *The Tamarack Tree* (Houghton Mifflin, 1971)

A courageous woman opens a school for young black women in Canterbury, Connecticut, in the 1830's.

Wibberley, Leonard, *John Treegate's Musket* (Ariel Books, 1959)

In this first of a series of four novels about the Treegate family, young Peter becomes involved in murder and shipwreck in the years preceding the Revolutionary War.

Wyatt, Edgar, *Cochise, Apache Warrior and Statesman* (McGraw-Hill, 1953)

This biography tells of the Apache chief who tried to live in peace with the white culture, but who was led to war by treachery and lies.

A short story is like a little piece of life. A short-story writer creates characters and places them in a setting. The characters are then involved in a conflict, or struggle of some kind. The plot of the story tells you how their conflict is worked out. In a good story, you keep on reading because you are eager to find out what happens to the characters. You have become interested in them as if they were living people.

Some stories are told purely for fun. "The Rule of Names" in this unit is an example of a story that is told just to entertain you. But most stories also have a theme—a serious idea about life and people that the writers want you to think about. "Flowers for Algernon" is a story with a theme. It is also, like other stories in this unit, one you will probably find hard to forget.

SHORT STORIES

Scene at Houghton Farm. A watercolor by Winslow Homer (1836–1910).
The Hirshhorn Museum and Sculpture Garden, The Smithsonian Institution, Washington, D. C.

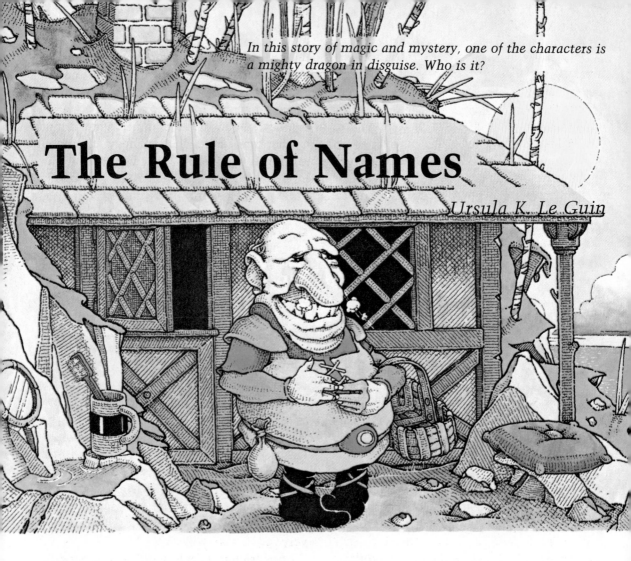

*In this story of magic and mystery, one of the characters is
a mighty dragon in disguise. Who is it?*

The Rule of Names

Ursula K. Le Guin

Mr. Underhill came out from under his hill, smiling and breathing hard. Each breath shot out of his nostrils as a double puff of steam, snow-white in the morning sunshine. Mr. Underhill looked up at the bright December sky and smiled wider than ever, showing snow-white teeth. Then he went down to the village.

"Morning, Mr. Underhill," said the villagers as he passed them in the narrow street between houses with conical, overhanging roofs like the fat red caps of toadstools. "Morning, morning!" he replied to each. (It

was of course bad luck to wish anyone a *good* morning; a simple statement of the time of day was quite enough, in a place so permeated with Influences as Sattins Island, where a careless adjective might change the weather for a week.) All of them spoke to him, some with affection, some with affectionate disdain. He was all the little island had in the way of a wizard, and so deserved respect—but how could you respect a little fat man of fifty who waddled along with his toes turned in, breathing steam and smiling? He was no great shakes as a workman either. His fireworks were fairly elaborate but his elixirs[1] were weak. Warts he charmed off frequently reappeared after three days; tomatoes he enchanted grew no bigger than canteloupes; and those rare times when a strange ship stopped at Sattins Harbor, Mr. Underhill always stayed under his hill—for fear, he explained, of the evil eye. He was, in other words, a wizard the way walleyed[2] Gan was a carpenter: by default. The villagers made do with badly-hung doors and inefficient spells, for this generation, and relieved their annoyance by treating Mr. Underhill quite familiarly, as a mere fellow villager. They even asked him to dinner. Once he asked some of them to dinner, and served a splendid repast, with silver, crystal, damask,[3] roast goose, sparkling Andrades '639,[4] and plum pudding with hard sauce; but he was so nervous all through the meal that it took the joy out of it, and besides, everybody was hungry again half an hour afterward. He did not like anyone to visit his cave, not even the anteroom, beyond which in fact nobody had ever got. When he saw people approaching the hill he always came trotting out to meet them. "Let's sit out here under the pine trees!" he would say, smiling and waving towards the fir grove, or if it was raining, "Let's go have a drink at the inn, eh?" though everybody knew he drank nothing stronger than well-water.

Some of the village children, teased by that locked cave, poked and pried and made raids while Mr. Underhill was away; but the small door that led into the inner chamber was spell-shut, and it seemed for once to be an effective spell. Once a couple of boys, thinking the wizard was over on the West Shore curing Mrs. Ruuna's sick donkey, brought a crowbar and a hatchet up there, but at the first whack of the hatchet on the door there came a roar of wrath from inside, and a cloud of purple steam. Mr. Underhill had got home early. The boys fled. He did not come out, and the boys came to no harm, though they said you couldn't believe what a huge hooting howling hissing horrible bellow that little fat man could make unless you'd heard it.

His business in town this day was three dozen fresh eggs and a pound of liver; also a stop at Seacaptain Fogeno's cottage to renew the seeing-charm on the old man's eyes (quite useless when applied to a case of detached retina,[5] but Mr. Underhill kept trying), and finally a chat with old Goody[6] Guld, the concertina[7]-maker's widow. Mr. Underhill's friends were mostly old people. He was timid with the strong young men of the village, and the girls were shy of him. "He makes me nervous, he smiles so much," they all said, pouting, twisting silky ringlets round a finger. *Nervous* was a newfangled word, and their mothers all replied grimly, "Nervous my foot, *silliness* is the word for it. Mr. Underhill is a very respectable wizard!"

After leaving Goody Guld, Mr. Underhill passed by the school, which was being held this day out on the common. Since no one on Sattins Island was literate, there were no books to learn to read from and no desks to carve initials on and no blackboards to erase, and in fact no schoolhouse. On rainy days the

---

1. **elixirs** (ĭ-lĭk′sərz): magic remedies.
2. **walleyed** (wôl′īd′): having eyes that turn outward.
3. **damask** (dăm′əsk): a fine fabric, which has a design woven into it. Here, the word refers to a tablecloth and napkins made from this fabric.
4. **Andrades '639**: a vintage of wine. The number '639 indicates the year.

5. **detached retina** (rĕt′n-ə): a serious visual disorder caused by damaged nerve tissue at the back of the eyeball.
6. **Goody**: a shortened form of *goodwife,* a title once used for married women of low social status.
7. **concertina**: a musical instrument similar to a small accordion.

children met in the loft of the Communal Barn, and got hay in their pants; on sunny days the schoolteacher, Palani, took them anywhere she felt like. Today, surrounded by thirty interested children under twelve and forty uninterested sheep under five, she was teaching an important item on the curriculum: the Rules of Names. Mr. Underhill, smiling shyly, paused to listen and watch. Palani, a plump, pretty girl of twenty, made a charming picture there in the wintry sunlight, sheep and children around her, a leafless oak above her, and behind her the dunes and sea and clear, pale sky. She spoke earnestly, her face flushed pink by wind and words. "Now you know the Rules of Names already, children. There are two, and they're the same on every island in the world. What's one of them?"

"It ain't polite to ask anybody what his name is," shouted a fat, quick boy, interrupted by a little girl shrieking, "You can't never tell your own name to nobody, my ma says!"

"Yes, Suba. Yes, Popi dear, don't screech. That's right. You never ask anybody his name. You never tell your own. Now think about that a minute and then tell me why we call our wizard Mr. Underhill." She smiled across the curly heads and the woolly backs at Mr. Underhill, who beamed, and nervously clutched his sack of eggs.

" 'Cause he lives under a hill!" said half the children.

"But is it his truename?"

"No!" said the fat boy, echoed by little Popi shrieking, "No!"

"How do you know it's not?"

" 'Cause he came here all alone and so there wasn't anybody knew his truename so they couldn't tell, and *he* couldn't—"

"Very good, Suba. Popi, don't shout. That's right. Even a wizard can't tell his truename.

When you children are through school and go through the Passage, you'll leave your childnames behind and keep only your truenames, which you must never ask for and never give away. Why is that the rule?"

The children were silent. The sheep bleated gently. Mr. Underhill answered the question: "Because the name is the thing," he said in his shy, soft, husky voice, "and the truename is the true thing. To speak the name is to control the thing. Am I right, Schoolmistress?"

She smiled and curtsied, evidently a little embarrassed by his participation. And he trotted off towards his hill, clutching his eggs to his bosom. Somehow the minute spent watching Palani and the children had made him very hungry. He locked his inner door behind him with a hasty incantation,[8] but there must have been a leak or two in the spell, for soon the bare anteroom of the cave was rich with the smell of frying eggs and sizzling liver.

The wind that day was light and fresh out of the west, and on it at noon a little boat came skimming the bright waves into Sattins Harbor. Even as it rounded the point a sharp-eyed boy spotted it, and knowing, like every child on the island, every sail and spar of the forty boats of the fishing fleet, he ran down the street calling out, "A foreign boat, a foreign boat!" Very seldom was the lonely isle visited by a boat from some equally lonely isle of the East Reach, or an adventurous trader from the Archipelago.[9] By the time the boat was at the pier half the village was there to greet it, and fishermen were following it homewards, and cowherds and clam-diggers and herb-hunters were puffing up and down all the rocky hills, heading towards the harbor.

---

8. **incantation:** a series of magic words used to cast a spell.
9. **Archipelago** (är′kə-pĕl′ə-gō′): a large group of islands.

But Mr. Underhill's door stayed shut.

There was only one man aboard the boat. Old Seacaptain Fogeno, when they told him that, drew down a bristle of white brows over his unseeing eyes. "There's only one kind of man," he said, "that sails the Outer Reach alone. A wizard, or a warlock, or a Mage. . . ."

So the villagers were breathless hoping to see for once in their lives a Mage, one of the mighty White Magicians of the rich, towered, crowded inner islands of the Archipelago. They were disappointed, for the voyager was quite young, a handsome black-bearded fellow who hailed them cheerfully from his boat, and leaped ashore like any sailor glad to have made port. He introduced himself at once as a sea-peddler. But when they told Seacaptain Fogeno that he carried an oaken walking-stick around with him, the old man nodded. "Two wizards in one town," he said. "Bad!" And his mouth snapped shut like an old carp's.

As the stranger could not give them his name, they gave him one right away: Blackbeard. And they gave him plenty of attention. He had a small mixed cargo of cloth and sandals and piswi feathers for trimming cloaks and cheap incense and levity stones and fine herbs and great glass beads from Venway—the usual peddler's lot. Everyone on Sattins Island came to look, to chat with the voyager, and perhaps to buy something—"Just to remember him by!" cackled Goody Guld, who like all the women and girls of the village was smitten with Blackbeard's bold good looks. All the boys hung round him too, to hear him tell of his voyages to far, strange islands of the Reach or describe the great rich islands of the Archipelago, the Inner Lanes, the roadsteads white with ships, and the golden roofs of Havnor. The men willingly listened to his tales; but some of them wondered why a trader should sail alone, and kept their eyes thoughtfully upon his oaken staff.

But all this time Mr. Underhill stayed under his hill.

"This is the first island I've ever seen that had no wizard," said Blackbeard one evening to Goody Guld, who had invited him and her nephew and Palani in for a cup of rushwash tea. "What do you do when you get a toothache, or the cow goes dry?"

"Why, we've got Mr. Underhill!" said the old woman.

"For what that's worth," muttered her nephew Birt, and then blushed purple and spilled his tea. Birt was a fisherman, a large, brave, wordless young man. He loved the schoolmistress, but the nearest he had come to telling her of his love was to give baskets of fresh mackerel to her father's cook.

"Oh, you do have a wizard?" Blackbeard asked. "Is he invisible?"

"No, he's just very shy," said Palani. "You've only been here a week, you know, and we see so few strangers here. . . ." She also blushed a little, but did not spill her tea.

Blackbeard smiled at her. "He's a good Sattinsman, then, eh?"

"No," said Goody Guld, "no more than you are. Another cup, nevvy?[10]—keep it in the cup this time. No, my dear, he came in a little bit of a boat, four years ago was it?—just a day after the end of the shad-run, I recall, for they was taking up the nets over in East Creek, and Pondi Cowherd broke his leg that very morning—five years ago it must be. No, four. No, five it is, 'twas the year the garlic didn't sprout. So he sails in on a bit of a sloop loaded full up with great chests and boxes and says to Seacaptain Fogeno, who wasn't blind then, though old enough goodness knows to be blind twice over, 'I hear tell,' he says, 'you've got no wizard nor warlock at all, might you be

---

10. **nevvy:** a dialectal form of *nephew*.

wanting one?' 'Indeed, if the magic's white!' says the Captain, and before you could say 'cuttlefish' Mr. Underhill had settled down in the cave under the hill and was charming the mange off Goody Beltow's cat. Though the fur grew in gray, and 'twas an orange cat. Queer-looking thing it was after that. It died last winter in the cold spell. Goody Beltow took on so at that cat's death, poor thing, worse than when her man was drowned on the Long Banks, the year of the long herring-runs, when nevvy Birt here was but a babe in petticoats." Here Birt spilled his tea again, and Blackbeard grinned, but Goody Guld proceeded undismayed, and talked on till nightfall.

Next day Blackbeard was down at the pier, seeing after the sprung board in his boat which he seemed to take a long time fixing, and as usual drawing the taciturn[11] Sattinsmen into talk. "Now which of these is your wizard's craft?" he asked. "Or has he got one of those the Mages fold up into a walnut shell when they're not using it?"

"Nay," said a stolid fisherman. "She's oop in his cave, under hill."

"He carried the boat he came in up to his cave?"

"Aye. Clear oop. I helped. Heavier as lead she was. Full oop with great boxes, and they full oop with books o' spells, he says. Heavier as lead she was." And the stolid fisherman turned his back, sighing stolidly. Goody Guld's nephew, mending a net nearby, looked up from his work and asked with equal stolidity. "Would ye like to meet Mr. Underhill, maybe?"

Blackbeard returned Birt's look. Clever black eyes met candid blue ones for a long moment; then Blackbeard smiled and said, "Yes. Will you take me up to the hill, Birt?"

"Aye, when I'm done with this," said the

---

11. **taciturn** (tăs'ə-tərn): quiet; having little to say.

fisherman. And when the net was mended, he and the Archipelagan set off up the village street towards the high green hill above it. But as they crossed the common Blackbeard said, "Hold on awhile, friend Birt. I have a tale to tell you, before we meet your wizard."

"Tell away," says Birt, sitting down in the shade of a live oak.

"It's a story that started a hundred years ago, and isn't finished yet—though it soon will be, very soon. . . . In the very heart of the Archipelago, where the islands crowd thick as flies on honey, there's a little isle called Pendor. The sealords of Pendor were mighty men, in the old days of war before the League. Loot and ransom and tribute came pouring into Pendor, and they gathered a great treasure there, long ago. Then from somewhere away out in the West Reach, where dragons breed on the lava isles, came one day a very mighty dragon. Not one of those overgrown lizards most of you Outer Reach folk call dragons, but a big, black, winged, wise, cunning monster, full of strength and subtlety, and like all dragons loving gold and precious stones above all things. He killed the Sealord and his soldiers, and the people of Pendor fled in their ships by night. They all fled away and left the dragon coiled up in Pendor Towers. And there he stayed for a hundred years, dragging his scaly belly over the emeralds and sapphires and coins of gold, coming forth only once in a year or two when he must eat. He'd raid nearby islands for his food. You know what dragons eat?"

Birt nodded and said in a whisper, "Maidens."

"Right," said Blackbeard. "Well, that couldn't be endured forever, nor the thought of his sitting on all that treasure. So after the League grew strong, and the Archipelago wasn't so busy with wars and piracy, it was decided to attack Pendor, drive out the dragon, and get the gold and jewels for the treasury of the League. They're forever wanting money, the League is. So a huge fleet gathered from fifty islands, and seven Mages stood in the prows of the seven strongest ships, and they sailed towards Pendor. . . . They got there. They landed. Nothing stirred. The houses all stood empty, the dishes on the tables full of a hundred years' dust. The bones of the old Sealord and his men lay about in the castle courts and on the stairs. And the Tower rooms reeked of dragon. But there was no dragon. And no treasure, not a diamond the size of a poppyseed, not a single silver bead. . . . Knowing that he couldn't stand up to seven Mages, the dragon had skipped out. They tracked him, and found he'd flown to a deserted island up north called Udrath; they followed his trail there, and what did they find? Bones again. His bones—the dragon's. But no treasure. A wizard, some unknown wizard from somewhere, must have met him singlehanded, and defeated him—and then made off with the treasure, right under the League's nose!"

The fisherman listened, attentive and expressionless.

"Now that must have been a powerful wizard and a clever one, first to kill a dragon, and second to get off without leaving a trace. The lords and Mages of the Archipelago couldn't track him at all, neither where he'd come from nor where he'd made off to. They were about to give up. That was last spring; I'd been off on a three-year voyage up in the North Reach, and got back about that time. And they asked me to help them find the unknown wizard. That was clever of them. Because I'm not only a wizard myself, as I think some of the oafs here have guessed, but I am also a descendant of the Lords of Pendor. That treasure is mine. It's mine, and knows that it's mine. Those fools of the League couldn't

find it, because it's not theirs. It belongs to the House of Pendor, and the great emerald, the star of the hoard, Inalkil the Greenstone, knows its master. Behold!" Blackbeard raised his oaken staff and cried aloud, "Inalkil!" The tip of the staff began to glow green, a fiery green radiance, a dazzling haze the color of April grass, and at the same moment the staff tipped in the wizard's hand, leaning, slanting till it pointed straight at the side of the hill above them.

"It wasn't so bright a glow, far away in Havnor," Blackbeard murmured, "but the staff pointed true. Inalkil answered when I called. The jewel knows its master. And I know the thief, and I shall conquer him. He's a mighty wizard, who could overcome a dragon. But I am mightier. Do you want to know why, oaf? Because I know his name!"

As Blackbeard's tone got more arrogant, Birt had looked duller and duller, blanker and blanker; but at this he gave a twitch, shut his mouth, and stared at the Archipelagan. "How did you . . . learn it?" he asked very slowly.

Blackbeard grinned, and did not answer.

"Black magic?"

"How else?"

Birt looked pale, and said nothing.

"I am the Sealord of Pendor, oaf, and I will have the gold my fathers won, and the jewels my mothers wore, and the Greenstone! For they are mine. Now, you can tell your village boobies the whole story after I have defeated this wizard and gone. Wait here. Or you can come and watch, if you're not afraid. You'll never get the chance again to see a great wizard in all his power." Blackbeard turned, and without a backward glance strode off up the hill towards the entrance to the cave.

Very slowly, Birt followed. A good distance from the cave he stopped, sat down under a hawthorn tree, and watched. The Archipelagan had stopped; a stiff, dark figure alone on the green swell of the hill before the gaping cave-mouth, he stood perfectly still. All at once he swung his staff up over his head, and the emerald radiance shone about him as he shouted, "Thief, thief of the Hoard of Pendor, come forth!"

There was a crash, as of dropped crockery, from inside the cave, and a lot of dust came spewing out. Scared, Birt ducked. When he looked again he saw Blackbeard still standing motionless, and at the mouth of the cave, dusty and disheveled, stood Mr. Underhill. He looked small and pitiful, with his toes turned in as usual, and his little bowlegs in black tights, and no staff—he never had had one, Birt suddenly thought. Mr. Underhill spoke. "Who are you?" he said in his husky little voice.

"I am the Sealord of Pendor, thief, come to claim my treasure!"

At that, Mr. Underhill slowly turned pink, as he always did when people were rude to him. But he then turned something else. He turned yellow. His hair bristled out, he gave a coughing roar—and was a yellow lion leaping down the hill at Blackbeard, white fangs gleaming.

But Blackbeard no longer stood there. A gigantic tiger, color of night and lightning, bounded to meet the lion. . . .

The lion was gone. Below the cave all of a sudden stood a high grove of trees, black in the winter sunshine. The tiger, checking himself in mid-leap just before he entered the shadow of the trees, caught fire in the air, became a tongue of flame lashing out at the dry black branches. . . .

But where the trees had stood a sudden cataract[12] leaped from the hillside, an arch of silvery crashing water, thundering down upon the fire. But the fire was gone. . . .

For just a moment before the fisherman's staring eyes two hills rose—the green one he knew, and a new one, a bare, brown hillock ready to drink up the rushing waterfall. That passed so quickly it made Birt blink, and after blinking he blinked again, and moaned, for what he saw now was a great deal worse. Where the cataract had been there hovered a dragon. Black wings darkened all the hill, steel claws reached groping, and from the dark, scaly, gaping lips fire and steam shot out.

Beneath the monstrous creature stood Blackbeard, laughing.

"Take any shape you please, little Mr. Underhill!" he taunted. "I can match you. But the game grows tiresome. I want to look upon my treasure, upon Inalkil. Now, big dragon, little wizard, take your true shape. I command you by the power of your truename—Yevaud!"

Birt could not move at all, not even to blink. He cowered, staring whether he would or not. He saw the black dragon hang there in the air above Blackbeard. He saw the fire lick like many tongues from the scaly mouth, the steam jet from the red nostrils. He saw Blackbeard's face grow white, white as chalk, and the beard-fringed lips trembling.

"Your name is Yevaud!"

"Yes," said a great, husky, hissing voice. "My truename is Yevaud, and my true shape is this shape."

"But the dragon was killed—they found dragon bones on Udrath Island——"

"That was another dragon," said the dragon, and then stooped like a hawk, talons outstretched. And Birt shut his eyes.

When he opened them the sky was clear, the hillside empty, except for a reddish-blackish trampled spot, and a few talon-marks in the grass.

Birt the fisherman got to his feet and ran. He

---

12. **cataract** (kăt′ə-răkt′): a waterfall.

ran across the common, scattering sheep to right and left, and straight down to the village street to Palani's father's house. Palani was out in the garden weeding the nasturtiums. "Come with me!" Birt gasped. She stared. He grabbed her wrist and dragged her with him. She screeched a little, but did not resist. He ran with her straight to the pier, pushed her into his fishing sloop the *Queenie*, untied the painter,[13] took up the oars and set off rowing like a demon. The last that Sattins Island saw of him and Palani was the *Queenie*'s sail vanishing in the direction of the nearest island westward.

The villagers thought they would never stop talking about it, how Goody Guld's nephew Birt had lost his mind and sailed off with the schoolmistress on the very same day that the peddler Blackbeard disappeared without a trace, leaving all his feathers and beads behind. But they did stop talking about it, three days later. They had other things to talk about, when Mr. Underhill finally came out of his cave.

Mr. Underhill had decided that since his truename was no longer a secret, he might as well drop his disguise. Walking was a lot harder than flying, and besides, it was a long, long time since he had had a real meal.

---

13. **painter:** here, a rope attached to a boat.

SEEKING MEANING

1. By the end of this story we know that Yevaud, the powerful dragon, came to Sattins Island disguised as Mr. Underhill. What does Mr. Underhill keep hidden in his cave? Why does Blackbeard, the Sealord of Pendor, come to Sattins Island?

2. Mr. Underhill does not seem to be much of an opponent for Blackbeard. How do they differ in appearance?

3. According to the magical Rule of Names, if you say someone's "truename," you can gain control over that person. How does Blackbeard plan to conquer Mr. Underhill? Why doesn't his plan work?

4. The author doesn't tell you directly what happened to Blackbeard. Find the passage toward the end of the story that reveals what became of the handsome stranger.

5. According to Blackbeard, what do dragons eat? At the end of the story, Birt runs away with Palani, the schoolteacher. Why do you think he does this?

6. After destroying Blackbeard, why does Mr. Underhill decide to drop his disguise? What do you think this decision will mean for the people living on Sattins Island?

7. Perhaps you've heard the saying: "There's an exception to every rule." How does this saying apply to the story?

DEVELOPING SKILLS IN READING

Noting Techniques That Create Suspense

Ursula Le Guin gains interest and creates suspense by dropping clues about what is going to happen. This technique is called *foreshadowing*.

For example, the opening paragraph of this story describes Mr. Underhill breathing a "double puff of steam" and showing "snow-white teeth." These clues hint that he is a dragon. You get another hint of his true nature when you are told that "the minute spent watching Palani and the children had made him very hungry." Later you learn that a dragon eats maidens. Can you find other clues that foreshadow Mr. Underhill's identity?

Sometimes this author drops false clues to put you off balance and to keep you in suspense. For example, from Blackbeard's story, you are led to think that a great wizard killed the dragon, stole its treasure, and fled to Sattins Island. What actually happened?

DEVELOPING VOCABULARY

Looking Up Word Histories

In this story of fantasy, Seacaptain Fogeno knows that the mysterious Blackbeard is a wizard when he hears that the stranger carries an *"oaken* walking-stick." Thousands of years ago in Europe, many people considered the oak to be a sacred tree with magical properties. In ancient Greece, the oak was the special tree of Zeus, the chief god.

Using a dictionary or an encyclopedia, find the meaning and history of these words:

dragon	mage	warlock
incantation	magic	wizard

ABOUT THE AUTHOR

Writer of science fiction and fantasy, Ursula K. Le Guin (1929–   ) is the author of such award-winning novels as *The Earthsea Trilogy, The Left Hand of Darkness,* and *The Dispossessed.* "The Rule of Names" is from her short-story collection *The Wind's Twelve Quarters.* She says the story was one of her first "explorations" of the imaginary planet of Earthsea.

" 'What are you looking
for; what do you want?'
I held my breath, then
said it. 'Escape.' "

Of Missing Persons

Jack Finney

*Walk in as though it were an ordinary travel
bureau,* the stranger I'd met at a bar had told
me. *Ask a few ordinary questions—about a
trip you're planning, a vacation, anything
like that. Then hint about The Folder a little,
but whatever you do, don't mention it directly; wait till he brings it up himself. And if
he doesn't, you might as well forget it. If you
can. Because you'll never see it; you're not
the type, that's all. And if you ask about it,
he'll just look at you as though he doesn't
know what you're talking about.*

I rehearsed it all in my mind, over and over,
but what seems possible at night over a beer
isn't easy to believe on a raw, rainy day, and I
felt like a fool, searching the storefronts for
the street number I'd memorized. It was noon
hour, West 42nd Street, New York, rainy and
windy; and like half the men around me, I
walked with a hand on my hatbrim, wearing
an old trench coat, head bent into the slanting
rain, and the world was real and drab, and this
was hopeless.

Anyway, I couldn't help thinking, who am I
to see The Folder, even if there is one? Name?
I said to myself, as though I were already
being asked. It's Charley Ewell, and I'm a
young guy who works in a bank; a teller. I
don't like the job; I don't make much money,
and I never will. I've lived in New York for

over three years and haven't many friends. What the heck, there's really nothing to say—I see more movies than I want to, read too many books, and I'm sick of meals alone in restaurants. I have ordinary abilities, looks, and thoughts. Does that suit you; do I qualify?

Now I spotted it, the address in the 200 block, an old, pseudo-modernized office building, tired, outdated, refusing to admit it but unable to hide it. New York is full of them, west of Fifth.

I pushed through the brass-framed glass doors into the tiny lobby, paved with freshly mopped, permanently dirty tile. The green-painted walls were lumpy from old plaster repairs; in a chrome frame hung a little wall directory—white-celluloid, easily changed letters on a black-felt background. There were some twenty-odd names, and I found "Acme Travel Bureau" second on the list, between "A-1 Mimeo" and "Ajax Magic Supplies." I pressed the bell beside the old-style, open-grille elevator door; it rang high up in the shaft. There was a long pause, then a thump, and the heavy chains began rattling slowly down toward me, and I almost turned and left —this was insane.

But upstairs the Acme office had divorced itself from the atmosphere of the building. I pushed open the pebble-glass door, walked in, and the big square room was bright and clean, fluorescent-lighted. Beside the wide double windows, behind a counter, stood a tall, gray-haired, grave-looking man, a telephone at his ear. He glanced up, nodded to beckon me in, and I felt my heart pumping—he fitted the description exactly. "Yes, United Air Lines," he was saying into the phone. "Flight"—he glanced at a paper on the glass-topped counter —"seven-oh-three, and I suggest you check in forty minutes early."

Standing before him now, I waited, leaning on the counter, glancing around; he was the man, all right, and yet this was just an ordinary travel agency: big bright posters on the walls, metal floor racks full of folders, printed schedules under the glass on the counter. This is just what it looks like and nothing else, I thought, and again I felt like a fool.

"Can I help you?" Behind the counter the tall gray-haired man was smiling at me, replacing the phone, and suddenly I was terribly nervous.

"Yes." I stalled for time, unbuttoning my raincoat. Then I looked up at him again and said, "I'd like to—get away." You fool, that's too fast, I told myself. Don't rush it! I watched in a kind of panic to see what effect my answer had had, but he didn't flick an eyelash.

"Well, there are a lot of places to go," he said politely. From under the counter he brought out a long, slim folder and laid it on the glass, turning it right side up for me. "Fly to Buenos Aires—Another World!" it said in a double row of pale-green letters across the top.

I looked at it long enough to be polite. It showed a big silvery plane banking over a harbor at night, a moon shining on the water, mountains in the background. Then I just shook my head; I was afraid to talk, afraid I'd say the wrong thing.

"Something quieter, maybe?" He brought out another folder: thick old tree trunks, rising way up out of sight, sunbeams slanting down through them—"The Virgin Forests of Maine, via Boston and Maine Railroad." "Or"—he laid a third folder on the glass— "Bermuda is nice just now." This one said, "Bermuda, Old World in the New."

I decided to risk it. "No," I said, and shook my head. "What I'm really looking for is a permanent place. A new place to live and settle down in." I stared directly into his eyes. "For the rest of my life." Then my nerve failed me, and I tried to think of a way to backtrack.

But he only smiled pleasantly and said, "I don't know why we can't advise you on that." He leaned forward on the counter, resting on his forearms, hands clasped; he had all the time in the world for me, his posture conveyed. "What are you looking for; what do you want?"

I held my breath, then said it. "Escape."

"From what?"

"Well——" Now I hesitated; I'd never put it into words before. "From New York, I'd say. And cities in general. From worry. And fear. And the things I read in my newspapers. From loneliness." And then I couldn't stop, though I knew I was talking too much, the words spilling out. "From never doing what I really want to do or having much fun. From selling my days just to stay alive. From life itself— the way it is today, at least." I looked straight at him and said softly, "From the world."

Now he was frankly staring, his eyes studying my face intently with no pretense of doing anything else, and I knew that in a moment he'd shake his head and say, "Mister, you better get to a doctor." But he didn't. He continued to stare, his eyes examining my forehead now. He was a big man, his gray hair crisp and curling, his lined face very intelligent, very kind; he looked the way ministers should look; he looked the way all fathers should look.

He lowered his gaze to look into my eyes and beyond them; he studied my mouth, my chin, the line of my jaw, and I had the sudden conviction that without any difficulty he was learning a great deal about me, more than I knew myself. Suddenly he smiled and placed both elbows on the counter, one hand grasping the other fist and gently massaging it. "Do you like people? Tell the truth, because I'll know if you aren't."

"Yes. It isn't easy for me to relax, though, and be myself, and make friends."

He nodded gravely, accepting that. "Would you say you're a reasonably decent kind of man?"

"I guess so; I think so." I shrugged.

"Why?"

I smiled wryly; this was hard to answer. "Well—at least when I'm not, I'm usually sorry about it."

He grinned at that, and considered it for a moment or so. Then he smiled—deprecatingly,[1] as though he were about to tell a little joke that wasn't too good. "You know," he said casually, "we occasionally get people in here who seem to be looking for pretty much what you are. So just as a sort of little joke——"

I couldn't breathe. This was what I'd been told he would say if he thought I might do.

"——we've worked up a little folder. We've even had it printed. Simply for our own amusement, you understand. And for occasional clients like you. So I'll have to ask you to look at it here if you're interested. It's not the sort of thing we'd care to have generally known."

I could barely whisper, "I'm interested."

He fumbled under the counter, then brought out a long thin folder, the same size and shape as the others, and slid it over the glass toward me.

I looked at it, pulling it closer with a fingertip, almost afraid to touch it. The cover was dark blue, the shade of a night sky, and across the top in white letters it said, "Visit Enchanting Verna!" The blue cover was sprinkled with white dots—stars—and in the lower left corner was a globe, the world, half surrounded by clouds. At the upper right, just under the word *Verna*, was a star larger and brighter than the others; rays shot out from it,

---

1. **deprecatingly** (dĕp′rĭ-kāt′ĭng-lē): with regret or embarrassment.

like from a star on a Christmas card. Across the bottom of the cover it said, "Romantic Verna, where life is the way it *should* be." There was a little arrow beside the legend,[2] meaning turn the page.

I turned, and the folder was like most travel folders inside—there were pictures and text, only these were about "Verna" instead of Paris, or Rome, or the Bahamas. And it was beautifully printed; the pictures looked real. What I mean is, you've seen color stereopticon[3] pictures? Well, that's what these were like, only better, far better. In one picture you could see dew glistening on the grass, and it looked wet. In another, a tree trunk seemed to curve out of the page, in perfect detail, and it was a shock to touch it and feel smooth paper instead of the rough actuality of bark. Miniature human faces, in a third picture, seemed about to speak, the lips moist and alive, the eyeballs shining, the actual texture of skin right there on paper; and it seemed impossible, as you stared, that the people wouldn't move and speak.

I studied a large picture spreading across the tops of two open pages. It seemed to have been taken from the top of a hill; you saw the land dropping away at your feet far down into a valley, then rising up again, way over on the other side. The slopes of both hills were covered with forest, and the color was beautiful, perfect; there were miles of green, majestic trees, and you knew as you looked that this forest was virgin, almost untouched. Curving through the floor of the valley, far below, ran a stream, blue from the sky in most places; here and there, where the current broke around massive boulders, the water was foam-

ing white; and again it seemed that if you'd only look closely enough you'd be certain to see that stream move and shine in the sun. In clearings beside the stream there were shake-roofed[4] cabins, some of logs, some of brick or adobe. The caption under the picture simply said, "The Colony."

"Fun fooling around with a thing like that," the man behind the counter murmured, nodding at the folder in my hands. "Relieves the monotony. Attractive-looking place, isn't it?"

I could only nod dumbly, lowering my eyes to the picture again because that picture told you even more than just what you saw. I don't know how you knew this, but you realized, staring at that forest-covered valley, that this was very much the way America once looked when it was new. And you knew this was only a part of a whole land of unspoiled, unharmed forests, where every stream ran pure; you were seeing what people, the last of them dead over a century ago, had once looked at in Kentucky and Wisconsin and the old Northwest. And you knew that if you could breathe in that air you'd feel it flow into your lungs sweeter than it's been anywhere on Earth for a hundred and fifty years.

Under that picture was another, of six or eight people on a beach—the shore of a lake, maybe, or the river in the picture above. Two children were squatting on their haunches, dabbling in the water's edge, and in the foreground a half circle of adults were sitting, kneeling, or squatting in comfortable balance on the yellow sand. They were talking, several were smoking, and most of them held half-filled coffee cups; the sun was bright, you knew the air was balmy and that it was morn-

---

2. **legend:** here, a caption, or explanation of a picture or chart.

3. **stereopticon:** (stĕr′ē-ŏp′tĭ-kŏn′): slide projector that can fade from one picture into another; also called a *magic lantern*.

4. **shake-roofed:** shingle-roofed.

ing, just after breakfast. They were smiling, one woman talking, the others listening. One man had half risen from his squatting position to skip a stone out onto the surface of the water.

You knew this; that they were spending twenty minutes or so down on that beach after breakfast before going to work, and you knew they were friends and that they did this every day. You knew—I tell you, you *knew*—that they liked their work, all of them, whatever it was; that there was no forced hurry or pressure about it. And that—well, that's all, I guess; you just knew that every day after breakfast these families spent a leisurely half-hour sitting and talking, there in the morning sun, down on that wonderful beach.

I'd never seen anything like their faces before. They were ordinary enough in looks, the people in that picture—pleasant, more or less familiar types. Some were young, in their twenties; others were in their thirties; one

man and woman seemed around fifty. But the faces of the youngest couple were completely unlined, and it occurred to me then that they had been born there, and that it was a place where no one worried or was ever afraid. The others, the older ones, there were lines in their foreheads, grooves around their mouths, but you felt that the lines were no longer deepening, that they were healed and untroubled scars. And in the faces of the oldest couple was a look of—I'd say it was a look of permanent *relief*. Not one of those faces bore a trace of malice; these people were *happy*. But even more than that, you knew they'd *been* happy, day after day after day for a long, long time, and that they always would be, and they knew it.

I wanted to join them. The most desperate longing roared up in me from the bottom of my soul to *be* there—on that beach, after breakfast, with those people in the sunny morning—and I could hardly stand it. I looked up at the man behind the counter and managed to smile. "This is—very interesting."

"Yes." He smiled back, then shook his head in amusement. "We've had customers so interested, so carried away, that they didn't want to talk about anything else." He laughed. "They actually wanted to know rates, details, everything."

I nodded to show I understood and agreed with them. "And I suppose you've worked out a whole story to go with this?" I glanced at the folder in my hands.

"Oh, yes. What would you like to know?"

"These people," I said softly, and touched the picture of the group on the beach. "What do they do?"

"They work; everyone does." He took a pipe from his pocket. "They simply live their lives doing what they like. Some study. We have, according to our little story," he added, and smiled, "a very fine library. Some of our people farm, some write, some make things with their hands. Most of them raise children, and—well, they work at whatever it is they really want to do."

"And if there isn't anything they really want to do?"

He shook his head. "There is always something, for everyone, that he really wants to do. It's just that here there is so rarely time to find out what it is." He brought out a tobacco pouch and, leaning on the counter, began filling his pipe, his eyes level with mine, looking at me gravely. "Life is simple there, and it's serene. In some ways, the good ways, it's like the early pioneering communities here in your country, but without the drudgery that killed people young. There is electricity. There are washing machines, vacuum cleaners, plumbing, modern bathrooms, and modern medicine, very modern. But there are no radios, television, telephones, or automobiles. Distances are small, and people live and work in small communities. They raise or make most of the things they use. Every man builds his own house, with all the help he needs from his neighbors. Their recreation is their own, and there is a great deal of it, but there is no recreation for sale, nothing you buy a ticket to. They have dances, card parties, weddings, christenings, birthday celebrations, harvest parties. There are swimming and sports of all kinds. There is conversation, a lot of it, plenty of joking and laughter. There is a great deal of visiting and sharing of meals, and each day is well filled and well spent. There are no pressures, economic or social, and life holds few threats. Every man, woman, and child is a happy person." After a moment he smiled. "I'm repeating the text, of course, in our little joke"—he nodded at the folder.

"Of course," I murmured, and looked down at the folder again, turning a page. "Homes in The Colony," said a caption, and there, true and real, were a dozen or so pictures of the interiors of what must have been the cabins I'd seen in the first photograph, or others like them. There were living rooms, kitchens, dens, patios. Many of the homes seemed to be furnished in a kind of Early American style, except that it looked—authentic, as though those rocking chairs, cupboards, and tables, and hooked rugs had been made by the people themselves, taking their time and making them well and beautifully. Others of the interiors seemed modern in style; one showed a definite Oriental influence.

All of them had, plainly and unmistakably, one quality in common: you knew as you looked at them that these rooms were *home*, really home, to the people who lived in them. On the wall of one living room, over the stone fireplace, hung a hand-stitched motto; it said, "There Is No Place Like Home," but the words didn't seem quaint or amusing, they didn't seem old-fashioned, resurrected or copied from a past that was gone. They seemed real; they belonged; those words were nothing more or less than a simple expression of true feeling and fact.

"Who are you?" I lifted my head from the folder to stare into the man's eyes.

He lighted his pipe, taking his time, sucking the match flame down into the bowl, eyes glancing up at me. "It's in the text," he said then, "on the back page. We—that is to say, the people of Verna, the original inhabitants—are people like yourself. Verna is a planet of air, sun, land, and sea, like this one. And of the same approximate temperature. So life evolved there, of course, just about as it has here, though rather earlier; and we are people like you. There are trivial anatomical differences, but nothing important. We read and enjoy your James Thurber, John Clayton, Rabelais, Allen Marple, Hemingway, Grimm, Mark Twain, Alan Nelson.[5] We like your chocolate, which we didn't have, and a great deal of your music, and you'd like many of the things we have. Our thoughts, though, and the great aims and directions of our history and development have been—drastically different from yours." He smiled and blew out a puff of smoke. "Amusing fantasy, isn't it?"

"Yes." I knew I sounded abrupt, and I hadn't stopped to smile; the words were spilling out. "And where is Verna?"

"Light-years away, by your measurements."

I was suddenly irritated, I didn't know why. "A little hard to get to, then, wouldn't it be?"

For a moment he looked at me; then he turned to the window beside him. "Come here," he said, and I walked around the counter to stand beside him. "There, off to the left"—he put a hand on my shoulder and pointed with his pipe stem—"are two apartment buildings, built back to back. The entrance to one is on Fifth Avenue, the entrance to the other on Sixth. See them? In the middle of the block; you can just see their roofs."

I nodded, and he said, "A man and his wife live on the fourteenth floor of one of those buildings. A wall of their living room is the back wall of the building. They have friends on the fourteenth floor of the other building, and a wall of *their* living room is the back wall of *their* building. These two couples live, in other words, within two feet of one another, since the back walls actually touch."

The big man smiled. "But when the Robinsons want to visit the Bradens, they walk from their living room to the front door. Then they walk down a long hall to the elevators. They ride fourteen floors down; then, in the street, they must walk around to the next block. And the city blocks there are long; in bad weather they have sometimes actually taken a cab. They walk into the other building, then go on through the lobby, ride up fourteen floors, walk down a hall, ring a bell, and are finally admitted into their friends' living room—only two feet from their own."

The big man turned back to the counter, and I walked around it to the other side again. "All I can tell you," he said then, "is that the way the Robinsons travel is like space travel, the actual physical crossing of those enormous distances." He shrugged. "But if they could only step through those two feet of wall without harming themselves or the wall—well, that is how we 'travel.' We don't cross space, we avoid it." He smiled. "Draw a breath here—and exhale it on Verna."

I said softly, "And that's how they arrived, isn't·it? The people in the picture. You took

5. **James Thurber . . . Alan Nelson:** writers. Rabelais, Grimm, and Twain were dead at the time this story was written. The others were popular authors of the day.

them there." He nodded, and I said, "Why?"

He shrugged. "If you saw a neighbor's house on fire, would you rescue his family if you could? As many as you could, at least?"

"Yes."

"Well—so would we."

"You think it's that bad, then? With us?"

"How does it look to you?"

I thought about the headlines in my morning paper, that morning and every morning. "Not so good."

He just nodded and said, "We can't take you all, can't even take very many. So we've been selecting a few."

"For how long?"

"A long time." He smiled. "One of us was a member of Lincoln's cabinet. But it was not until just before your First World War that we felt we could see what was coming; until then we'd been merely observers. We opened our first agency in Mexico City in nineteen thirteen. Now we have branches in every major city."

"Nineteen thirteen," I murmured, as something caught at my memory. "Mexico. Listen! Did—"

"Yes." He smiled anticipating my question. "Ambrose Bierce[6] joined us that year, or the next. He lived until nineteen thirty-one, a very old man, and wrote four more books, which we have." He turned back a page in the folder and pointed to a cabin in the first large photograph. "That was his home."

"And what about Judge Crater?"[7]

"Crater?"

---

6. **Ambrose Bierce:** a famous American writer, born in 1842, who was last heard from in a letter from Mexico dated December 26, 1913. He was thought to have been killed in the Mexican Revolution, but his body was never found.

7. **Judge Crater:** On August 6, 1930, Joseph Crater, a justice of the New York State Supreme Court, stepped into a taxicab in New York City and was never seen again.

"Another famous disappearance; he was a New York judge who simply disappeared some years ago."

"I don't know. We had a judge, I remember, from New York City, some twenty-odd years ago, but I can't recall his name."

I leaned across the counter toward him, my face very close to his, and I nodded. "I like your little joke," I said. "I like it very much, more than I can possibly tell you." Very softly I added, "When does it stop being a joke?"

For a moment he studied me; then he spoke. "Now. If you want it to."

You've got to decide on the spot, the middle-aged man at the Lexington Avenue bar had told me, *because you'll never get another chance. I know; I've tried.* Now I stood there thinking; there were people I'd hate never to see again, and a girl I was just getting to know, and this was the world I'd been born in. Then I thought about leaving that room, going back to my job, then back to my room at night. And finally I thought of the deep-green valley in the picture and the little yellow beach in the morning sun. "I'll go," I whispered. "If you'll have me."

He studied my face. "Be sure," he said sharply. "Be certain. We want no one there who won't be happy, and if you have any least doubt, we'd prefer that—"

"I'm sure," I said.

After a moment the gray-haired man slid open a drawer under the counter and brought out a little rectangle of yellow cardboard. One side was printed, and through the printing ran a band of light green; it looked like a railroad ticket to White Plains or somewhere. The printing said, "Good, when validated, for ONE TRIP TO VERNA. Nontransferable. One-way only."

"Ah—how much?" I said, reaching for my wallet, wondering if he wanted me to pay.

He glanced at my hand on my hip pocket.

"All you've got. Including your small change." He smiled. "You won't need it any more, and we can use your currency for operating expenses. Light bills, rent, and so on."

"I don't have much."

"That doesn't matter." From under the counter he brought out a heavy stamping machine, the kind you see in railroad-ticket offices. "We once sold a ticket for thirty-seven hundred dollars. And we sold another just like it for six cents." He slid the ticket into the machine, struck the lever with his fist, then handed the ticket to me. On the back, now, was a freshly printed rectangle of purple ink, and within it the words, "Good this day only," followed by the date. I put two five-dollar bills, a one, and seventeen cents in change on the counter. "Take the ticket to the Acme Depot," the gray-haired man said, and, leaning across the counter, began giving me directions for getting there.

It's a tiny hole in the wall, the Acme Depot; you may have seen it—just a little storefront on one of the narrow streets west of Broadway. On the window is painted, not very well, "Acme." Inside, the walls and ceiling, under layers of old paint, are covered with the kind of stamped tin you see in the old buildings. There's a worn wooden counter and a few battered chrome-and-imitation-red-leather chairs. There are scores of places like the Acme Depot in that area—little theater-ticket agencies, obscure bus-line offices, employment agencies. You could pass this one a thousand times and never really see it; and if you live in New York, you probably have.

Behind the counter, when I arrived, a shirt-sleeved man smoking a cigar stump stood working on some papers; four or five people silently waited in the chairs. The man at the counter glanced up as I stepped in, looked down at my hand for my ticket, and when I showed it, nodded at the last vacant chair, and I sat down.

There was a girl beside me, hands folded on her purse. She was pleasant-looking, rather pretty; I thought she might have been a stenographer. Across the narrow little office sat a young man in work clothes, his wife beside him holding their little girl in her lap. And there was a man of around fifty, his face averted from the rest of us, staring out into the rain at passing pedestrians. He was expensively dressed and wore a gray homburg hat; he could have been the vice president of a large bank, I thought, and wondered what his ticket had cost.

Maybe twenty minutes passed, the man behind the counter working on some papers; then a small, battered old bus pulled up at the curb outside, and I heard the hand brake set. The bus was a shabby thing, bought third- or fourth-hand and painted red and white over the old paint, the fenders lumpy from countless pounded-out dents, the tire treads worn almost smooth. On the side, in red letters, it said "Acme," and the driver wore a leather jacket and the kind of worn cloth cap that cab drivers wear. It was precisely the sort of obscure little bus you see around there, ridden always by shabby, tired, silent people, going no one knows where.

It took nearly two hours for the little bus to work south through the traffic, toward the tip of Manhattan, and we all sat, each wrapped in his own silence and thoughts, staring out the rain-spattered windows; the little girl was asleep. Through the streaking glass beside me I watched drenched people huddled at city bus stops, and saw them rap angrily on the closed doors of buses jammed to capacity, and saw the strained, harassed faces of the drivers. At 14th Street I saw a speeding cab splash a sheet of street-dirty water on a man at the curb, and saw the man's mouth writhe as he cursed.

Often our bus stood motionless, the traffic light red, as throngs flowed out into the street from the curb, threading their way around us and the other waiting cars. I saw hundreds of faces, and not once did I see anyone smile.

I dozed; then we were on a glistening black highway somewhere on Long Island, I slept again, and awakened in darkness as we jolted off the highway onto a muddy double-rut road, and I caught a glimpse of a farmhouse, the windows dark. Then the bus slowed, lurched once, and stopped. The hand brake set, the motor died, and we were parked beside what looked like a barn.

It *was* a barn—the driver walked up to it, pulled the big sliding wood door open, its wheels creaking on the rusted old trolley overhead, and stood holding it open as we filed in. Then he released it, stepping inside with us, and the big door slid closed of its own weight. The barn was damp, old, the walls no longer plumb,[8] and it smelled of cattle; there was nothing inside on the packed-dirt floor but a bench of unpainted pine, and the driver indicated it with a beam of a flashlight. "Sit here, please," he said quietly. "Get your tickets ready." Then he moved down the line, punching each of our tickets, and on the floor I caught a momentary glimpse, in the shifting beam of his light, of tiny mounds of countless more round bits of cardboard, like little drifts of yellow confetti. Then he was at the door again, sliding it open just enough to pass through, and for a moment we saw him silhouetted against the night sky. "Good luck," he said. "Just wait where you are." He released the door; it slid closed, snipping off the wavering beam of his flashlight; and a moment later we heard the motor start and the bus lumber away in low gear.

---

8. **plumb:** straight.

The dark barn was silent now, except for our breathing. Time ticked away, and I felt an urge, presently, to speak to whoever was next to me. But I didn't quite know what to say, and I began to feel embarrassed, a little foolish, and very aware that I was simply sitting in an old and deserted barn. The seconds passed and I moved my feet restlessly; presently I realized that I was getting cold and chilled. Then suddenly I knew—and my face flushed in violent anger and a terrible shame. We'd been tricked!—bilked out of our money by our pathetic will to believe an absurd and fantastic fable and left, now, to sit there as long as we pleased, until we came to our senses finally, like countless others before us, and made our way home as best we could. It was suddenly impossible to understand or even remember how I could have been so gullible, and I was on my feet, stumbling through the dark across the uneven floor, with some notion of getting to a phone and the police. The big barn door was heavier than I'd thought, but I slid it back, took a running step through it, then turned to shout back to the others to come along.

You perhaps have seen how very much you can observe in the fractional instant of a lightning flash—an entire landscape sometimes, every detail etched on your memory, to be seen and studied in your mind for long moments afterwards. As I turned back toward the opened door the inside of that barn came alight. Through every wide crack of its walls and ceiling and through the big dust-coated windows in its side streamed the light of an intensely brilliant blue and sunny sky, and the air pulling into my lungs as I opened my mouth to shout was sweeter than any I had ever tasted in my life. Dimly, through a wide, dust-smeared window of that barn, I looked—for less than the blink of an eye—down into a deep majestic V of forest-covered slope, and I

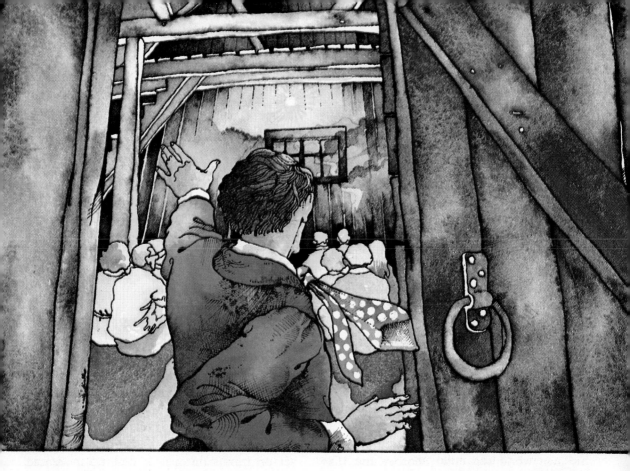

saw, tumbling through it, far below, a tiny stream, blue from the sky, and at that stream's edge between two low roofs a yellow patch of sun-drenched beach. And then, that picture engraved on my mind forever, the heavy door slid shut, my fingernails rasping along the splintery wood in a desperate effort to stop it — and I was standing alone in a cold and rain-swept night.

It took four or five seconds, no longer, fumbling at that door, to heave it open again. But it was four or five seconds too long. The barn was empty, dark. There was nothing inside but a worn pine bench — and, in the flicker of the lighted match in my hand, tiny drifts of what looked like damp confetti on the floor. As my mind had known even as my hands scratched at the outside of that door, there was no one inside now; and I knew

where they were — knew they were walking, laughing aloud in a sudden wonderful and eager ecstasy, down into that forest-green valley, toward home.

I work in a bank, in a job I don't like; and I ride to and from it in the subway, reading the daily papers, the news they contain. I live in a rented room, and in the battered dresser under a pile of my folded handkerchiefs is a little rectangle of yellow cardboard. Printed on its face are the words "Good, when validated for ONE TRIP TO VERNA," and stamped on the back is a date. But the date is gone, long since, the ticket void, punched in a pattern of tiny holes.

I've been back to the Acme Travel Bureau. The first time the tall gray-haired man walked up to me and laid two five-dollar bills, a one, and seventeen cents in change before me. "You left this on the counter the last time you were here," he said gravely. Looking me squarely in the eyes, he added blankly, "I don't know why." Then some customers came in, he turned to greet them, and there was nothing for me to do but leave.

Walk in as though it were the ordinary agency it seems — you can find it, somewhere, in any city you try! Ask a few ordinary questions — about a trip you're planning, a vacation, anything you like. Then hint about The Folder a little, but don't mention it directly. Give him time to size you up and offer it himself. And if he does, if you're the type, if you can believe — then make up your mind and stick to it! Because you won't ever get a second chance. I know, because I've tried. And tried. And tried.

SEEKING MEANING

1. This story is about a man's wish to leave his own world and enter another one. The man's own world is New York City, and the other world is Verna, a world supposed to exist far away in space. How does the narrator, Charley Ewell, describe the New York City he knows?

2. Describe Charley's personal life in the city. Why is he unhappy?

3. Find the passages of the story that describe Verna. How does Verna contrast with New York City? Why are the people on Verna happy?

4. When he arranges the trip to Verna, the travel agent tells Charley, "Be sure. . . . Be certain. We want no one there who won't be happy, and if you have any least doubt, we'd prefer that — " What suspicions and doubts does Charley have while he waits in the barn? Why does Charley fail to reach Verna?

5. Think about Charley Ewell's character.

What do you think keeps him from being happy on Earth? If you could give Charley some advice, what would you tell him to do?

6. What does the title of the story mean? (According to the story, what happened to the real people mentioned in the footnotes on page 210?)

7. There are many stories about people searching for ideal worlds that offer perfect happiness. How would you account for the popularity of this kind of story? Can you name other perfect worlds from movies or books?

DEVELOPING SKILLS IN READING

Recognizing the Importance of Setting

The time and place in which the action of a story occurs is called the *setting*. Writers may place their characters in the past, present, or future. The characters may live in actual places or imaginary ones. Stories have been set on mountaintops, in deserts, in rented rooms, on the surface of the moon, and in Stone Age caves. How far do you have to read in this story before the New York City setting is revealed? When is "romantic Verna" introduced?

Sometimes setting is not an important element of a story. In "Of Missing Persons," however, the setting is very important.

Why do you suppose the author chooses a large city as one setting of this story, instead of some blue-skied, unpolluted, green section of Earth?

Look up *vernal* in a dictionary, and tell why Verna is a good name for this ideal world.

You may feel that this writer is deliberately describing only the unpleasant side of city life. Can you imagine how a city setting might be desirable to someone other than Charley Ewell?

Jimmy Valentine was not a bad fellow at heart, but he refused to stop cracking safes. What could force a fellow like Jimmy to go straight?

A Retrieved Reformation

O. Henry

A guard came to the prison shoeshop, where Jimmy Valentine was assiduously[1] stitching uppers, and escorted him to the front office. There the warden handed Jimmy his pardon, which had been signed that morning by the Governor. Jimmy took it in a tired kind of way. He had served nearly ten months of a four-year sentence. He had expected to stay only about three months, at the longest. When a man with as many friends on the outside as Jimmy Valentine had is received in the "stir," it is hardly worthwhile to cut his hair.

"Now, Valentine," said the warden, "you'll go out in the morning. Brace up, and make a man of yourself. You're not a bad fellow at heart. Stop cracking safes, and live straight."

"Me?" said Jimmy, in surprise. "Why, I never cracked a safe in my life."

"Oh, no," laughed the warden. "Of course not. Let's see, now. How was it you happened to get sent up on that Springfield job? Was it because you wouldn't prove an alibi for fear of compromising somebody in extremely high-toned society? Or was it simply a case of a mean old jury that had it in for you? It's always one or the other with you innocent victims."

"Me?" said Jimmy, still blankly virtuous. "Why, Warden, I never was in Springfield in my life!"

"Take him back, Cronin," smiled the warden, "and fix him with outgoing clothes. Unlock him at seven in the morning, and let him come to the bullpen.[2] Better think over my advice, Valentine."

At a quarter past seven on the next morning Jimmy stood in the warden's outer office. He had on a suit of the villainously fitting, ready-made clothes and a pair of the stiff, squeaky shoes that the state furnishes to its discharged compulsory guests.

The clerk handed him a railroad ticket and the five-dollar bill with which the law expected him to rehabilitate himself into good

---

1. **assiduously** (ə-sĭj′ōō-əs-lē): steadily and busily.

2. **bullpen:** a barred room where prisoners are held temporarily.

citizenship and prosperity. The warden gave him a cigar, and shook hands. Valentine, 9762, was chronicled on the books "Pardoned by Governor," and Mr. James Valentine walked out into the sunshine.

Disregarding the song of the birds, the waving green trees, and the smell of the flowers, Jimmy headed straight for a restaurant. There he tasted the first sweet joys of liberty in the shape of a broiled chicken and a bottle of white wine—followed by a cigar a grade better than the one the warden had given him. From there he proceeded leisurely to the depot. He tossed a quarter into the hat of a blind man sitting by the door and boarded his train. Three hours set him down in a little town near the state line. He went to the café of one Mike Dolan and shook hands with Mike, who was alone behind the bar.

"Sorry we couldn't make it sooner, Jimmy, me boy," said Mike. "But we had that protest from Springfield to buck against, and the Governor nearly balked. Feeling all right?"

"Fine," said Jimmy. "Got my key?"

He got his key and went upstairs, unlocking the door of a room at the rear. Everything was just as he had left it. There on the floor was still Ben Price's collar button that had been torn from that eminent detective's shirt band when they had overpowered Jimmy to arrest him.

Pulling out from the wall a folding bed, Jimmy slid back a panel in the wall and dragged out a dust-covered suitcase. He opened this and gazed fondly at the finest set of burglar's tools in the East. It was a complete set, made of specially tempered steel, the latest designs in drills, punches, braces and bits, jimmies, clamps, and augers,[3] with two or three novelties invented by Jimmy

himself, in which he took pride. Over nine hundred dollars they had cost him to have made at ——, a place where they make such things for the profession.

In half an hour Jimmy went downstairs and through the café. He was now dressed in tasteful and well-fitting clothes and carried his dusted and cleaned suitcase in his hand.

"Got anything on?" asked Mike Dolan genially.

"Me?" said Jimmy, in a puzzled tone. "I don't understand. I'm representing the New York Amalgamated Short Snap Biscuit Cracker and Frazzled Wheat Company."

This statement delighted Mike to such an extent that Jimmy had to take a seltzer and milk on the spot. He never touched "hard" drinks.

A week after the release of Valentine, 9762, there was a neat job of safe burglary done in Richmond, Indiana, with no clue to the author. A scant eight hundred dollars was all that was secured. Two weeks after that a patented, improved, burglarproof safe in Logansport was opened like a cheese to the tune of fifteen hundred dollars, currency; securities and silver untouched. That began to interest the rogue-catchers.[4] Then an old-fashioned bank safe in Jefferson City became active and threw out of its crater an eruption of bank notes amounting to five thousand dollars. The losses were now high enough to bring the matter up into Ben Price's class of work. By comparing notes, a remarkable similarity in the methods of the burglaries was noticed. Ben Price investigated the scenes of the robberies and was heard to remark:

"That's Dandy Jim Valentine's autograph. He's resumed business. Look at that combination knob—jerked out as easy as pulling up a

---

3. **drills . . . augers** (ô′gərz): tools for working with metal.

4. **rogue-catchers:** an elaborate way of describing the police.

radish in wet weather. He's got the only clamps that can do it. And look how clean those tumblers were punched out! Jimmy never has to drill but one hole. Yes, I guess I want Mr. Valentine. He'll do his bit next time without any short-time or clemency foolishness."

Ben Price knew Jimmy's habits. He had learned them while working up the Springfield case. Long jumps, quick getaways, no confederates,[5] and a taste for good society—these ways had helped Mr. Valentine to become noted as a successful dodger of retribution.[6] It was given out that Ben Price had taken up the trail of the elusive cracksman, and other people with burglarproof safes felt more at ease.

One afternoon Jimmy Valentine and his suitcase climbed out of the mail hack[7] in Elmore, a little town five miles off the railroad down in the blackjack country of Arkansas. Jimmy, looking like an athletic young senior just home from college, went down the board sidewalk toward the hotel.

A young lady crossed the street, passed him at the corner, and entered a door over which was the sign "The Elmore Bank." Jimmy Valentine looked into her eyes, forgot what he was, and became another man. She lowered her eyes and colored slightly. Young men of Jimmy's style and looks were scarce in Elmore.

Jimmy collared a boy that was loafing on the steps of the bank as if he were one of the stockholders, and began to ask him questions about the town, feeding him dimes at intervals. By and by the young lady came out, looking royally unconscious of the young man with the suitcase, and went her way.

"Isn't that young lady Miss Polly Simpson?" asked Jimmy, with specious guile.[8]

"Naw," said the boy. "She's Annabel Adams. Her pa owns this bank. What'd you come to Elmore for? Is that a gold watch chain? I'm going to get a bulldog. Got any more dimes?"

Jimmy went to Planters' Hotel, registered as Ralph D. Spencer, and engaged a room. He leaned on the desk and declared his platform[9] to the clerk. He said he had come to Elmore to look for a location to go into business. How was the shoe business, now, in the town? He had thought of the shoe business. Was there an opening?

The clerk was impressed by the clothes and manner of Jimmy. He, himself, was something of a pattern of fashion to the thinly gilded[10] youth of Elmore, but he now perceived his shortcomings. While trying to figure out Jimmy's manner of tying his four-in-hand,[11] he cordially gave information.

Yes, there ought to be a good opening in the shoe line. There wasn't an exclusive shoe store in the place. The dry goods and general stores handled them. Business in all lines was fairly good. Hoped Mr. Spencer would decide to locate in Elmore. He would find it a pleasant town to live in, and the people very sociable.

Mr. Spencer thought he would stop over in the town a few days and look over the situation. No, the clerk needn't call the boy. He would carry up his suitcase, himself; it was rather heavy.

---

5. **confederates:** accomplices.
6. **retribution** (rĕt'rə-byoo'shən): punishment.
7. **mail hack:** a horse-drawn carriage used to carry mail from one town to another.

8. **with specious** (spē'shəs) **guile** (gīl): in a tricky way that appears to be innocent.
9. **platform:** here, intentions; plans.
10. **thinly gilded:** only seeming to be well-dressed. To be *gilded* is to be covered with a layer of gold.
11. **four-in-hand:** a necktie.

Mr. Ralph Spencer, the phoenix[12] that arose from Jimmy Valentine's ashes—ashes left by the flame of a sudden and alterative[13] attack of love—remained in Elmore and prospered. He opened a shoe store and secured a good run of trade.

Socially he was also a success and made many friends. And he accomplished the wish of his heart. He met Miss Annabel Adams and became more and more captivated by her charms.

At the end of a year the situation of Mr. Ralph Spencer was this: he had won the respect of the community, his shoe store was flourishing, and he and Annabel were engaged to be married in two weeks. Mr. Adams, the typical, plodding country banker, approved of Spencer. Annabel's pride in him almost equaled her affection. He was as much at home in the family of Mr. Adams and that of Annabel's married sister as if he were already a member.

One day Jimmy sat down in his room and wrote this letter, which he mailed to the safe address of one of his old friends in St. Louis:

Dear Old Pal:

I want you to be at Sullivan's place in Little Rock, next Wednesday night, at nine o'clock. I want you to wind up some little matters for me. And, also, I want to make you a present of my kit of tools. I know you'll be glad to get them—you couldn't duplicate the lot for a thousand dollars. Say, Billy, I've quit the old business—a year ago. I've got a nice store. I'm making an honest living, and I'm going to marry the finest girl on earth two weeks from now. It's the only life, Billy—the straight one. I wouldn't touch a dollar of another man's money now for a million. After I get married I'm going to sell out and go West, where there won't be so much danger of having old scores brought up against me. I tell you, Billy, she's an angel. She believes in me; and I wouldn't do another crooked thing for the whole world. Be sure to be at Sully's, for I must see you. I'll bring along the tools with me.

Your old friend,
Jimmy

On the Monday night after Jimmy wrote this letter, Ben Price jogged unobtrusively[14] into Elmore in a livery buggy.[15] He lounged about town in his quiet way until he found out what he wanted to know. From the drugstore across the street from Spencer's shoe store, he got a good look at Ralph D. Spencer.

"Going to marry the banker's daughter, are you, Jimmy?" said Ben to himself softly. "Well, I don't know!"

The next morning Jimmy took breakfast at the Adamses'. He was going to Little Rock that day to order his wedding suit and buy something nice for Annabel. That would be the first time he had left town since he came to Elmore. It had been more than a year now since those last professional "jobs," and he thought he could safely venture out.

After breakfast quite a family party went downtown together—Mr. Adams, Annabel, Jimmy, and Annabel's married sister with her two little girls, aged five and nine. They came

---

12. **phoenix** (fē′nĭks): a bird in ancient Egyptian mythology. It was believed that the phoenix burned itself up and that from its ashes a new bird arose.
13. **alterative** (ôl′tə-rā′tĭv): causing an alteration, or change. Jimmy's love changed him.

14. **unobtrusively** (ŭn′əb-trōō′sĭv-lē): without attracting attention.
15. **livery buggy:** a hired horse and carriage.

by the hotel where Jimmy still boarded, and he ran up to his room and brought along his suitcase. Then they went on to the bank. There stood Jimmy's horse and buggy and Dolph Gibson, who was going to drive him over to the railroad station.

All went inside the high, carved oak railings into the banking room — Jimmy included, for Mr. Adams' future son-in-law was welcome anywhere. The clerks were pleased to be greeted by the good-looking, agreeable young man who was going to marry Miss Annabel. Jimmy set his suitcase down. Annabel, whose heart was bubbling with happiness and lively youth, put on Jimmy's hat and picked up the suitcase. "Wouldn't I make a nice drummer?"[16] asked Annabel. "My! Ralph, how heavy it is! Feels like it was full of gold bricks."

"Lot of nickel-plated shoehorns in there," said Jimmy coolly, "that I'm going to return. Thought I'd save express charges by taking them up. I'm getting awfully economical."

The Elmore Bank had just put in a new safe and vault. Mr. Adams was very proud of it and insisted on an inspection by everyone. The vault was a small one, but it had a new patented door. It fastened with three solid steel bolts thrown simultaneously with a single handle, and had a time lock. Mr. Adams beamingly explained its workings to Mr. Spencer, who showed a courteous but not too intelligent interest. The two children, May and Agatha, were delighted by the shining metal and funny clock and knobs.

While they were thus engaged, Ben Price sauntered in and leaned on his elbow, looking casually inside between the railings. He told the teller that he didn't want anything; he was just waiting for a man he knew.

---

16. **drummer:** here, a traveling salesman.

Suddenly there was a scream or two from the women and a commotion. Unperceived by the elders, May, the nine-year-old girl, in a spirit of play had shut Agatha in the vault. She had then shot the bolts and turned the knob of the combination as she had seen Mr. Adams do.

The old banker sprang to the handle and tugged at it for a moment. "The door can't be opened," he groaned. "The clock hasn't been wound nor the combination set."

Agatha's mother screamed again, hysterically.

"Hush!" said Mr. Adams, raising his trembling hand. "All be quiet for a moment. Agatha!" he called as loudly as he could. "Listen to me." During the following silence they could just hear the faint sound of the child wildly shrieking in the dark vault in a panic of terror.

"My precious darling!" wailed the mother. "She will die of fright! Open the door! Oh, break it open! Can't you men do something?"

"There isn't a man nearer than Little Rock who can open that door," said Mr. Adams, in a shaky voice. "Spencer, what shall we do? That child — she can't stand it long in there. There isn't enough air, and, besides, she'll go into convulsions from fright."

Agatha's mother, frantic now, beat the door of the vault with her hands. Somebody wildly suggested dynamite. Annabel turned to Jimmy, her large eyes full of anguish, but not yet despairing. To a woman nothing seems quite impossible to the powers of the man she worships.

"Can't you do something, Ralph — *try*, won't you?"

He looked at her with a queer, soft smile on his lips and in his keen eyes.

"Annabel," he said, "give me that rose you are wearing, will you?"

Hardly believing that she heard him aright,

she unpinned the bud from the bosom of her dress, and placed it in his hand. Jimmy stuffed it into his vest pocket, threw off his coat, and pulled up his shirt sleeves. With that act Ralph D. Spencer passed away, and Jimmy Valentine took his place.

"Get away from the door, all of you," he commanded, shortly.

He set his suitcase on the table, and opened it out flat. From that time on he seemed to be unconscious of the presence of anyone else. He laid out the shining, queer implements swiftly and orderly, whistling softly to himself as he always did when at work. In a deep silence and immovable, the others watched him as if under a spell.

In a minute Jimmy's pet drill was biting smoothly into the steel door. In ten minutes —breaking his own burglarious record—he threw back the bolts and opened the door.

Agatha, almost collapsed, but safe, was gathered into her mother's arms.

Jimmy Valentine put on his coat, and walked outside the railings toward the front door. As he went he thought he heard a far-away voice that he once knew call "Ralph!" But he never hesitated.

At the door a big man stood somewhat in his way.

"Hello, Ben!" said Jimmy, still with his strange smile. "Got around at last, have you? Well, let's go. I don't know that it makes much difference, now."

And then Ben Price acted rather strangely.

"Guess you're mistaken, Mr. Spencer," he said. "Don't believe I recognize you. Your buggy's waiting for you, ain't it?"

And Ben Price turned and strolled down the street.

SEEKING MEANING

1. At the beginning of the story, the prison warden tells Jimmy Valentine to stop cracking safes and reform. What does Jimmy do after his release that shows he plans to ignore the warden's advice?

2. How does the power of love make Jimmy decide to "go straight"? Describe the new life that Jimmy has created for himself at the end of a year in Elmore.

3. The reader knows that Ben Price, the great detective, is on Jimmy's trail. But Jimmy himself is unaware of this danger. How do you think Ben Price finds out that Jimmy is in Elmore?

4. When he opens the safe to free Agatha, Jimmy believes he is destroying his chances for a new life. However, opening the safe actually *saves* Jimmy's happiness. Why doesn't Ben Price arrest Jimmy?

5. *Retrieved* means "brought back" or "recaptured." A *reformation* is a "change" or "improvement." How was Jimmy's reformation endangered? How was it "retrieved"?

6. What other stories, films, or television shows do you know that feature a good-hearted detective like Ben Price, or a tough character like Jimmy Valentine transformed by the power of love?

DEVELOPING SKILLS IN READING

Following the Plot

At the beginning of this story, you meet Jimmy Valentine in jail, where he has already spent ten months for breaking the law. At the end of the story, Jimmy is a reformed character. The series of events in the story, or the *plot*, tells you how this change occurs in the hero. In other words, plot is "what happens" in a story.

At the heart of every plot there is a *conflict*, or struggle. Often a character wants something that pits him or her in a struggle against someone or something else.

Conflicts with another person, an animal, or a force of nature, such as a hurricane, are called *external conflicts*. What is Jimmy's external conflict? Many stories also include *internal conflicts*. These are struggles that take place within a character's mind or feelings. Internal conflicts often involve decisions. How does Agatha's imprisonment in the vault force Jimmy into a difficult internal conflict?

In most stories there is a *climax*, or turning point. At this point you know whether the story will end happily or unhappily. The climax is a time of great suspense or emotion. It is usually the most exciting and tense part of the story. Which scene in this story would you say is the climax? What were your feelings at that point?

One of Jimmy's conflicts is finally resolved when he meets Ben Price after the safecracking scene. Were you surprised at Ben's actions at the end of the story? Did this ending satisfy you? Why or why not?

Recognizing Irony

If you were to say "That's just great!" when you really mean that something is terrible, you would be using *irony*. When people speak ironically, they are saying just the opposite of what they mean, or the opposite of what is true. Can you explain the irony in O. Henry's description of prisoners as "compulsory guests"?

Often an entire situation is ironic. In other words, it turns out to be exactly the opposite of what should happen, or the opposite of what we would expect to happen. O. Henry is famous for the humorously ironic situations in his stories.

Why is it ironic that Jimmy Valentine, the notorious safecracker, should win the hand of the banker's daughter, with the banker's approval?

Why is it ironic that Jimmy thought that opening the safe to free Agatha would ruin his chances for happiness? (Would Ben Price have let Jimmy go if he hadn't observed what Jimmy did to save Agatha?)

ABOUT THE AUTHOR

O. Henry (1862–1910) wrote "A Retrieved Reformation" while he was a prisoner in the Ohio federal penitentiary, serving time for embezzling funds from a Texas bank. The character of Jimmy Valentine—the criminal with a heart—was based on a safecracker that O. Henry knew in prison. As *Alias Jimmy Valentine*, O. Henry's story became a successful Broadway play.

O. Henry was the pen name of William Sydney Porter, who grew up in Greensboro, North Carolina, and became an apprentice to a pharmacist. He moved to Texas to work on an uncle's ranch. Later he was a bookkeeper, a bank teller, a newspaper writer, and owner of a weekly newspaper called *The Rolling Stone*. When he was summoned for trial on the embezzlement charge, he jumped bail and fled to Honduras. A year and half later, when he returned to Texas to visit his dying wife, he was arrested and spent the next three years in jail. By 1903 he was in New York City, where he roamed the parks, streets, and restaurants, talking to people and collecting story material. His stories—more than two hundred fifty in all—became immensely popular.

You can almost count on an O. Henry story to have a surprise ending. Two of his other stories that you might enjoy are "The Gift of the Magi" and "The Ransom of Red Chief."

"The door was open. He could make a dash for it down the hall. He could run, run, run, run, run!"

Thank You, M'am

Langston Hughes

She was a large woman with a large purse that had everything in it but hammer and nails. It had a long strap and she carried it slung across her shoulder. It was about eleven o'clock at night, and she was walking alone, when a boy ran up behind her and tried to snatch her purse. The strap broke with the single tug the boy gave it from behind. But the boy's weight, and the weight of the purse combined, caused him to lose his balance so, instead of taking off full blast as he had hoped, the boy fell on his back on the sidewalk, and his legs flew up. The large woman simply turned around and kicked him right square in his blue-jeaned sitter. Then she reached down, picked the boy up by his shirt front, and shook him until his teeth rattled.

After that the woman said, "Pick up my pocketbook, boy, and give it here."

She still held him. But she bent down enough to permit him to stoop and pick up her purse. Then she said, "Now ain't you ashamed of yourself.?"

Firmly gripped by his shirt front, the boy said, "Yes'm."

The woman said, "What did you want to do it for?"

The boy said, "I didn't aim to."

She said, "You a lie!"

By that time two or three people passed, stopped, turned to look, and some stood watching.

"If I turn you loose, will you run?" asked the woman.

"Yes'm," said the boy.

"Then I won't turn you loose," said the woman. She did not release him.

"I'm very sorry, lady, I'm sorry," whispered the boy.

"Um-hum! And your face is dirty. I got a great mind to wash your face for you. Ain't you got nobody home to tell you to wash your face?"

"No'm," said the boy.

"Then it will get washed this evening," said the large woman starting up the street, dragging the frightened boy behind her.

He looked as if he were fourteen or fifteen, frail and willow-wild, in tennis shoes and blue jeans.

The woman said, "You ought to be my son. I would teach you right from wrong. Least I can do right now is to wash your face. Are you hungry?"

"No'm," said the being-dragged boy. "I just want you to turn me loose."

"Was I bothering *you* when I turned that corner?" asked the woman.

"No'm."

"But you put yourself in contact with *me*," said the woman. "If you think that that contact is not going to last awhile, you got another thought coming. When I get through with you, sir, you are going to remember Mrs. Luella Bates Washington Jones."

Sweat popped out on the boy's face and he began to struggle. Mrs. Jones stopped, jerked him around in front of her, put a half nelson[1] about his neck, and continued to drag him up the street. When she got to her door, she dragged the boy inside, down a hall, and into a large kitchenette-furnished room at the rear of the house. She switched on the light and left the door open. The boy could hear other roomers laughing and talking in the large house. Some of their doors were opened, too, so he knew he and the woman were not alone. The woman still had him by the neck in the middle of her room.

She said, "What is your name?"

"Roger," answered the boy.

"Then, Roger, you go to that sink and wash your face," said the woman, whereupon she turned him loose—at last. Roger looked at the door—looked at the woman—looked at the door—*and went to the sink.*

"Let the water run until it gets warm," she said. "Here's a clean towel."

"You gonna take me to jail?" asked the boy, bending over the sink.

"Not with that face, I would not take you nowhere," said the woman. "Here I am trying to get home to cook me a bite to eat and you snatch my pocketbook! Maybe you ain't been to your supper either, late as it be. Have you?"

"There's nobody home at my house," said the boy.

"Then we'll eat," said the woman. "I believe you're hungry—or been hungry—to try to snatch my pocketbook."

"I wanted a pair of blue suede shoes," said the boy.

"Well, you didn't have to snatch *my* pocketbook to get some suede shoes," said Mrs. Luella Bates Washington Jones. "You could of asked me."

"M'am?"

The water dripping from his face, the boy looked at her. There was a long pause. A very long pause. After he had dried his face and not knowing what else to do dried it again, the boy turned around, wondering what next. The door was open. He could make a dash for it down the hall. He could run, run, run, run, *run!*

The woman was sitting on the daybed. After a while she said, "I were young once and I wanted things I could not get."

There was another long pause. The boy's mouth opened. Then he frowned, but not knowing he frowned.

The woman said, "Um-hum! You thought I was going to say *but,* didn't you? You thought I was going to say, *but I didn't snatch people's pocketbooks.* Well, I wasn't going to say that." Pause. Silence. "I have done things, too, which I would not tell you, son—neither tell God, if he didn't already know. So you set down while I fix us something to eat. You might run that comb through your hair so you will look presentable."

In another corner of the room behind a screen was a gas plate and an icebox. Mrs. Jones got up and went behind the screen. The woman did not watch the boy to see if he was going to run now, nor did she watch her purse which she left behind her on the daybed. But the boy took care to sit on the far side of the

---

1. **half nelson:** a wrestling hold made with one arm.

room where he thought she could easily see him out of the corner of her eye, if she wanted to. He did not trust the woman *not* to trust him. And he did not want to be mistrusted now.

"Do you need somebody to go to the store," asked the boy, "maybe to get some milk or something?"

"Don't believe I do," said the woman, "unless you just want sweet milk yourself. I was going to make cocoa out of this canned milk I got here."

"That will be fine," said the boy.

She heated some lima beans and ham she had in the icebox, made the cocoa, and set the table. The woman did not ask the boy anything about where he lived, or his folks, or anything else that would embarrass him. Instead, as they ate, she told him about her job in a hotel beauty shop that stayed open late, what the work was like, and how all kinds of women came in and out, blondes, redheads, and Spanish. Then she cut him a half of her ten-cent cake.

"Eat some more, son," she said.

When they were finished eating she got up and said, "Now, here, take this ten dollars and buy yourself some blue suede shoes. And next time, do not make the mistake of latching on to *my* pocketbook *nor nobody else's—* because shoes come by devilish like that will burn your feet. I got to get my rest now. But I wish you would behave yourself, son, from here on in."

She led him down the hall to the front door and opened it. "Good night! Behave yourself, boy!" she said, looking out into the street.

The boy wanted to say something else other than, "Thank you, m'am," to Mrs. Luella Bates Washington Jones, but he couldn't do so as he turned at the barren stoop and looked back at the large woman in the door. He barely managed to say, "Thank you," before she shut the door. And he never saw her again.

SEEKING MEANING

1. In this story, the characters do not act in the way you might expect them to act. For example, many people who are robbed would call for help or call the police. What does Mrs. Jones do instead?

2. Most people in Roger's situation would run when they had a chance. Why do you think Roger decides not to run away when he can?

3. What does Mrs. Jones reveal about her past when she and Roger are in her home? How do you think this information makes Roger feel?

4. During the time that Roger is in her apartment, how does Mrs. Jones show that she does not want to embarrass him or hurt his feelings? What does this concern reveal about her character?

5. What do Mrs. Jones's home and the meal she serves reveal about her own financial situation?

6. In your opinion, why does Mrs. Jones give Roger the ten dollars? What do you think he learns from her warmth and generosity?

7. Why do you suppose Roger cannot say more than "Thank you, m'am"?

DEVELOPING SKILLS IN READING

Recognizing Techniques of Characterization
Characterization is the means an author uses to reveal the characters in a story. When writers *tell* what characters are like through description, they are using *direct characterization*. For example, in the first sentence of this story, Langston Hughes describes Mrs. Jones as "a large woman with a large purse that had everything in it but hammer and nails." Later he also describes Roger, saying, "He looked as if he were about fourteen or fifteen, frail and willow-wild, in tennis shoes

and blue jeans." These are examples of direct characterization. They are the only direct statements made about the two characters in the story.

Yet you know much more about these two characters because you have watched their actions and listened to their conversations and thoughts. When writers let you know characters in this way—by having you watch what they do and by letting you know what they say and think—they are using *indirect characterization*. What incident in the story lets you know, for example, that Mrs. Jones is physically strong? What does she say or do that shows she is generous and kind?

ABOUT THE AUTHOR

"Mightily did he use the street," poet Gwendolyn Brooks has written about her friend Langston Hughes (1902–1967). "He found its multiple heart, its tastes, smells, alarms, formulas, flowers, garbage, and convulsions. He brought them all to his tabletop . . . ." During his long and diverse career, Hughes wrote poems, short stories, novels, plays, songs, and essays, though he is best known for his poems. He attended Columbia University in New York City for a year, but left to write and travel. He worked as a seaman on transatlantic ships and as a cook in Paris. In 1925 he took a job as a busboy in a Washington, D.C., hotel, where the poet Vachel Lindsay was staying. Hughes left three of his poems next to Lindsay's plate one day. Lindsay, recognizing their merit, read them to his audience that night and introduced a new young poet to the world of literature. One critic has said that Hughes has written "some of the saddest, most humorous, and beautiful insights ever given into the heart of a race." One of his famous poems is "Mother to Son."

*"I heard a slight groan, and
I knew that it was the
groan of mortal terror."*

The Tell-Tale Heart

Edgar Allan Poe

True!—nervous—very, very dreadfully nervous I had been and am; but why *will* you say that I am mad? The disease had sharpened my senses—not destroyed—not dulled them. Above all was the sense of hearing acute. I heard all things in the heaven and in the earth. I heard many things in hell. How, then, am I mad? Hearken! and observe how healthily—how calmly I can tell you the whole story.

It is impossible to say how first the idea entered my brain; but once conceived, it haunted me day and night. Object there was none. Passion there was none. I loved the old man. He had never wronged me. He had never given me insult. For his gold I had no desire. I think it was his eye! yes, it was this! He had the eye of a vulture—a pale blue eye, with a film over it. Whenever it fell upon me, my blood ran cold; and so by degrees—very gradually—I made up my mind to take the life of the old man, and thus rid myself of the eye forever.

Now this is the point. You fancy[1] me mad. Madmen know nothing. But you should have seen *me*. You should have seen how wisely I proceeded—with what caution—with what foresight—with what dissimulation[2] I went to work! I was never kinder to the old man than during the whole week before I killed him. And every night, about midnight, I turned the latch of his door and opened it—oh, so gently! And then, when I had made an opening sufficient for my head, I put in a dark lantern,[3] all closed, closed, so that no light shone out, and then I thrust in my head. Oh, you would have laughed to see how cunningly I thrust it in! I moved it slowly—very, very slowly, so that I might not disturb the old man's sleep. It took me an hour to place my whole head within the opening so far that I could see him as he lay upon his bed. Ha!—would a madman have been so wise as this? And then, when my head was well in the room, I undid the lantern cautiously—oh, so cautiously—cautiously (for the hinges creaked)—I undid it just so much that a single thin ray fell upon the vulture eye. And this I did for seven long nights—every night just at midnight—but I found the eye always closed; and so it was impossible to do the work; for it was not the old man who vexed me, but his Evil Eye. And every morning, when the day broke, I went boldly into the chamber, and spoke courageously to him, calling him by name in a hearty tone, and in-

1. **fancy:** imagine.
2. **dissimulation** (dĭ-sĭm′yə-lā′shən): concealment of plans or intentions.

3. **dark lantern:** a lantern with a shutter that can conceal its light.

quiring how he had passed the night. So you see he would have been a very profound old man, indeed, to suspect that every night, just at twelve, I looked in upon him while he slept.

Upon the eighth night I was more than usually cautious in opening the door. A watch's minute hand moves more quickly than did mine. Never before that night had I *felt* the extent of my own powers—of my sagacity.[4] I could scarcely contain my feelings of triumph. To think that there I was, opening the door, little by little, and he not even to dream of my secret deeds or thoughts. I fairly chuckled at the idea; and perhaps he heard me; for he moved on the bed suddenly, as if startled. Now you may think that I drew back —but no. His room was as black as pitch with the thick darkness (for the shutters were close fastened, through fear of robbers), and so I knew that he could not see the opening of the door, and I kept pushing it on steadily, steadily.

I had my head in, and was about to open the lantern, when my thumb slipped upon the tin fastening, and the old man sprang up in bed, crying out—"Who's there?"

I kept quite still and said nothing. For a whole hour I did not move a muscle, and in the meantime I did not hear him lie down. He was still sitting up in the bed listening—just as I have done, night after night, hearkening to the deathwatches[5] in the wall.

Presently I heard a slight groan, and I knew it was the groan of mortal terror. It was not a groan of pain or of grief—oh, no!—it was the low stifled sound that arises from the bottom of the soul when overcharged with awe. I knew the sound well. Many a night, just at midnight, when all the world slept, it has welled up from my own bosom, deepening, with its dreadful echo, the terrors that distracted me. I say I knew it well. I knew what the old man felt, and pitied him, although I chuckled at heart. I knew that he had been lying awake ever since the first slight noise, when he had turned in the bed. His fears had been ever since growing upon him. He had been trying to fancy them causeless, but could not. He had been saying to himself, "It is nothing but the wind in the chimney—it is only a mouse crossing the floor," or "It is merely a cricket which has made a single chirp." Yes, he had been trying to comfort himself with these suppositions: but he had found all in vain. *All in vain*; because Death, in approaching him, had stalked with his black shadow before him, and enveloped the victim. And it was the mournful influence of the unperceived shadow that caused him to feel—although he neither saw nor heard—to *feel* the presence of my head within the room.

When I had waited a long time, very patiently, without hearing him lie down, I resolved to open a little—a very, very little crevice[6] in the lantern. So I opened it—you cannot imagine how stealthily, stealthily—until, at length, a simple dim ray, like the thread of the spider, shot from out the crevice and fell full upon the vulture eye.

It was open—wide, wide open—and I grew furious as I gazed upon it. I saw it with perfect distinctness—all a dull blue, with a hideous veil over it that chilled the very marrow in my bones; but I could see nothing else of the old man's face or person: for I had directed the

---

4. **sagacity** (sə-găs'ə-tē): keen intelligence and good judgment.
5. **deathwatches**: small insects which make a ticking sound, believed by superstitious people to be a forewarning of death.

6. **crevice**: an opening. The shutter opens to let the light shine out.

ray as if by instinct, precisely upon the damned spot.

And have I not told you that what you mistake for madness is but overacuteness of the senses?—now, I say, there came to my ears a low, dull, quick sound, such as a watch makes when enveloped in cotton. I knew *that* sound well, too. It was the beating of the old man's heart. It increased my fury, as the beating of a drum stimulates the soldier into courage.

But even yet I refrained and kept still. I scarcely breathed. I held the lantern motionless. I tried how steadily I could maintain the ray upon the eye. Meantime the hellish tattoo[7] of the heart increased. It grew quicker and quicker, and louder and louder every instant. The old man's terror *must* have been

extreme! It grew louder, I say, louder every moment!—do you mark[8] me well? I have told you that I am nervous: so I am. And now at the dead hour of the night, amid the dreadful silence of that old house, so strange a noise as this excited me to uncontrollable terror. Yet, for some minutes longer I refrained and stood still. But the beating grew louder, louder! I thought the heart must burst. And now a new anxiety seized me—the sound would be heard by a neighbor! The old man's hour had come! With a loud yell, I threw open the lantern and leaped into the room. He shrieked once—once only. In an instant I dragged him to the floor, and pulled the heavy bed over him. I then smiled gaily, to find the deed so far done. But, for many minutes, the heart beat on with a

---

7. **tattoo:** here, a rhythmic beating.

8. **mark:** here, pay attention to.

muffled sound. This, however, did not vex me; it would not be heard through the wall. At length it ceased. The old man was dead. I removed the bed and examined the corpse. Yes, he was stone, stone dead. I placed my hand upon the heart and held it there many minutes. There was no pulsation. He was stone dead. His eye would trouble me no more.

If still you think me mad, you will think so no longer when I describe the wise precautions I took for the concealment of the body. The night waned,[9] and I worked hastily, but in silence. First of all I dismembered the corpse. I cut off the head and the arms and the legs.

I then took up three planks from the flooring of the chamber, and deposited all between the scantlings.[10] I then replaced the boards so cleverly, so cunningly, that no human eye—not even *his*—could have detected anything wrong. There was nothing to wash out—no stain of any kind—no blood spot whatever. I had been too wary for that. A tub had caught all—ha! ha!

When I had made an end of these labors, it was four o'clock—still dark as midnight. As the bell sounded the hour, there came a knocking at the street door. I went down to open it with a light heart, for what had I *now* to fear? There entered three men, who introduced themselves, with perfect suavity,[11] as officers of the police. A shriek had been heard by a neighbor during the night; suspicion of foul play had been aroused; information had been lodged at the police office, and they (the officers) had been deputed to search the premises.

I smiled, for *what* had I to fear? I bade the gentlemen welcome. The shriek, I said, was my own in a dream. The old man, I mentioned, was absent in the country. I took my visitors all over the house. I bade them search—search *well*. I led them, at length, to *his* chamber. I showed them his treasures, secure, undisturbed. In the enthusiasm of my confidence, I brought chairs into the room, and desired them *here* to rest from their fatigues, while I myself, in the wild audacity[12] of my perfect triumph, placed my own seat upon the very spot beneath which reposed the corpse of the victim.

The officers were satisfied. My *manner* had convinced them. I was singularly at ease. They sat, and while I answered cheerily, they chatted of familiar things. But, ere long, I felt myself getting pale and wished them gone. My head ached, and I fancied a ringing in my ears; but still they sat and still chatted. The ringing became more distinct—it continued and became more distinct; I talked more freely to get rid of the feeling; but it continued and gained definiteness—until, at length, I found that the noise was *not* within my ears.

No doubt, I now grew *very* pale—but I talked more fluently, and with a heightened voice. Yet the sound increased—and what could I do? It was *a low, dull, quick sound—much such a sound as a watch makes when enveloped in cotton.* I gasped for breath—and yet the officers heard it not. I talked more quickly—more vehemently; but the noise steadily increased. I arose and argued about trifles, in a high key and with violent gesticulations;[13] but the noise steadily increased. Why *would* they not be gone? I paced the floor to and fro with heavy strides, as if excited to fury by the observations of the men—but the noise

---

9. **waned** (wānd): drew to a close.
10. **scantlings:** crosspieces of wood.
11. **suavity** (swäv′ə-tē): politeness.

12. **audacity** (ô-dăs′ə-tē): daring.
13. **gesticulations** (jĕ-stĭk′yə-lā′shənz): gestures; movements of the arms and legs.

steadily increased. Oh what *could* I do? I foamed—I raved—I swore! I swung the chair upon which I had been sitting, and grated it upon the boards, but the noise arose over all and continually increased. It grew louder—louder—*louder!* And still the men chatted pleasantly, and smiled. Was it possible they heard not? No, no! They heard!—they suspected—they *knew!*—they were making a *mockery* of my horror—this I thought, and this I think. But anything was better than this agony! Anything was more tolerable than this derision![14] I could bear those hypocritical smiles no longer! I felt that I must scream or die!—and now—again!—hark! louder! louder! louder! *louder!*—

"Villains!" I shrieked, "dissemble[15] no more! I admit the deed!—tear up the planks!—here, here!—it is the beating of his hideous heart!"

---

14. **derision** (dĭ-rĭzh'ən): mockery.
15. **dissemble** (dĭ-sĕm'bəl): pretend.

SEEKING MEANING

1. In the first sentence of this horror story, the narrator asks a question: ". . . but why *will* you say that I am mad?" How does the narrator try to convince you that he is sane?
2. What does the narrator claim is his motive for killing the old man?
3. The narrator tells how he opens the old man's door every night for seven nights. Why doesn't he kill the man until the eighth night?
4. Find the passage in which the narrator first describes hearing the sound of the old man's heart (page 229). How does this sound affect him?
5. At first, the narrator is able to convince the three police officers that nothing is wrong. What do you think makes him reveal where the old man's body is hidden?

DEVELOPING SKILLS IN READING

Responding to Atmosphere

Poe once said that he wanted to give the readers of his stories a "single overwhelming impression." In other words, he wanted to create a certain *atmosphere,* or emotional effect. Poe uses several techniques to create the atmosphere in this unusual story.

The very first word of the first sentence is set off with an exclamation point: "True!" In what other ways does the first sentence emphasize the narrator's nervousness?

Sometimes Poe uses short, jerky sentences and dashes to create an effect of nervousness and tension. Look back at the passage on page 230 beginning "No doubt, I now grew *very* pale . . . ." Which details in this passage make you feel the narrator's excitement and increasing nervousness?

A single word can help create atmosphere. For example, Poe compares the old man's eye to the eye of a *vulture*. What kind of bird is a vulture? Suppose Poe had compared the eye to the eye of a robin, or the eye of a kitten. How would the effect be different?

If you had to identify the "single overwhelming impression" that this story created for you, what would you say it was: horror, pity, sadness, fear, or something entirely different?

DEVELOPING SKILLS OF EXPRESSION

Reading a Story Aloud

Read "The Tell-Tale Heart" aloud. Make your voice sound the way you imagine the narrator would sound. At different points in the story, he sounds nervous, calm, excited, frightened, pleased with himself, or almost hysterical.

Be sure to notice the punctuation marks as you read. The dashes signal places where the narrator interrupts his thoughts, and the exclamation marks signal strong feeling or excitement. Notice especially the last paragraphs of the story. How would you read these sentences to suggest the narrator's panic?

ABOUT THE AUTHOR

Edgar Allan Poe (1809–1849) — poet, short-story writer, and literary critic — is one of the most important American writers of the nineteenth century. He is called "the father of the American short story" and "the inventor of the detective story."

Poe was the son of professional actors. He was orphaned by the age of three and was raised and educated by a wealthy couple in Richmond, Virginia, named Allan. As Poe grew older, he came into conflict with his foster father, who disapproved of his literary ambitions. Poe attended the University of Virginia briefly and then enlisted in the army. Hoping to win back the favor of his foster father, he served for a short time as a West Point cadet. But he purposely got himself dismissed when he realized that reconciliation with the Allan family was impossible.

Marriage to his young cousin Virginia Clemm provided Poe with some affection and family life. He eked out a meager living by writing for newspapers and literary magazines. Though he was a good editor, Poe was unable to hold a job for long. His temper was erratic, and he always seemed to be exhausted and underfed. In 1847 his young wife died of tuberculosis. Poe, grief-stricken and ill, survived her by only two years.

One of Poe's most famous poems is "The Raven." Some of Poe's other famous horror stories are "The Fall of the House of Usher," "The Pit and the Pendulum," "The Cask of Amontillado," and "The Masque of the Red Death."

"And I got to thinking that something might come out of the water. It didn't have a name or a shape. But it was there."

The Land and the Water

Shirley Ann Grau

From the open Atlantic beyond Timbalier Head[1] a few scattered foghorns grunted, muffled and faint. That bank[2] had been hanging offshore for days. We'd been watching the big draggers[3] chug up to it, get dimmer and dimmer, and finally disappear in its grayness, leaving only the stifled sounds of their horns behind. It had been there so long we got used to it, and came to think of it as always being there, like another piece of land, maybe.

The particular day I'm thinking about started out clear and hot with a tiny breeze — a perfect day for a snipe or a sailfish.[4] There were a few of them moving on the big bay, not many. And they stayed close to shore, for the barometer was drifting slowly down in its tube and the wind was shifting slowly backward around the compass.[5]

Larger sailboats never came into the bay — it was too shallow for them — and these small ones, motorless, moving with the smallest stir of air, could sail for home, if the fog came in, by following the shore — or if there was really no wind at all, they could be paddled in and beached. Then their crews could walk to the nearest phone and call to be picked up. You had to do it that way, because the fog always came in so quick. As it did that morning.

My sister and I were working by our dock, scraping and painting the little dinghy.[6] Because the spring tides washed over this stretch, there were no trees, no bushes even, just snail grass and beach lettuce and pink flowering sea lavender, things that liked salt. All morning it had been bright and blue and shining. Then all at once it turned gray and wet, like an unfalling rain, moveless and still. We went right on sanding and from being sweaty hot we turned sweaty cold, the fog chilling and dripping off our faces.

"It isn't worth the money," my sister said.

---

1. **Timbalier** (tăm′bəl-yā′) **Head:** the part of Louisiana that juts into Timbalier Bay.
2. **bank:** a mass of fog.
3. **draggers:** trawlers, or fishing boats that use huge nets to catch fish.
4. **snipe . . . sailfish:** sailboats.
5. **the barometer . . . compass:** A drop in atmospheric pressure and a change in wind direction are signs that a storm is approaching.

6. **dinghy** (dĭng′ē): a small rowboat.

She is ten and that is her favorite sentence. This time it wasn't even true. She was the one who'd talked my father into giving us the job.

I wouldn't give her the satisfaction of an answer, though I didn't like the wet any more than she did. It was sure to make my hair roll up in tight little curls all over my head and I would have to wash it again and sleep on the hard metal curlers to get it back in shape.

Finally my sister said, "Let's go get a Coke."

When we turned around to go back up to the house, we found that it had disappeared. It was only a couple of hundred yards away, right behind us and up a little grade, a long slope of beach plum and poison ivy, salt-burned and scrubby. You couldn't see a thing now, except gray. The land and the water all looked the same; the fog was that thick.

There weren't any Cokes. Just some bottles of Dr. Pepper and a lot of empties waiting in cases on the back porch. "Well," my sister said, "let's go tell her."

She meant my mother, of course, and we didn't have to look for her very hard. The house wasn't big, and being a summer house, it had very thin walls: we could hear her playing cards with my father in the living room.

They were sitting by the front window. On a clear day there was really something to see out there: the sweep of the bay and the pattern of the inlets and, beyond it all, the dark blue of the Atlantic. Today there was nothing, not even a bird, if you didn't count the occasional yelp of a sea gull off high overhead somewhere.

"There's no Cokes," my sister said. "Not a single one."

"Tomorrow's grocery day," my mother said. "Go make a lemonade."

"Look," my father said, "why not go back to work on the dinghy? You'll get your money faster."

So we went, only stopping first to get our oilskin hats. And pretty soon, fog was dripping from the brims like a kind of gentle rain.

But we didn't go back to work on the dinghy. For a while we sat on the edge of the dock and looked at the minnow-flecked water, and then we got out the crab nets and went over to the tumbled heap of rocks to see if we could catch anything. We spent a couple of hours out there, skinning our knees against the rough barnacled[7] surfaces. Once a sea gull swooped down so low he practically touched the tops of our hats. Almost but not quite. I don't think we even saw a crab, though we dragged our nets around in the water just for the fun of it. Finally we dug a dozen or so clams, ate them, and tried to skip the shells along the water. That was how the afternoon passed, with one thing or the other, and us not hurrying, not having anything we'd rather be doing.

We didn't have a watch with us, but it must have been late afternoon when they all came down from the house. We heard them before we saw them, heard the brush of their feet on the grass path.

It was my mother and my father and Robert, my biggest brother, the one who is eighteen. My father had the round black compass and a coil of new line. Robert had a couple of gas lanterns and a big battery one. My mother had the life jackets and a little wicker basket and a thermos bottle. They all went out along the narrow rickety dock and began to load the gear into my father's *Sea Skiff*. It wasn't a big boat and my father had to take a couple of minutes to pack it, stowing the basket way up forward under the cowling[8] and wedging the thermos bottle on top of that. Robert, who'd

---

7. **barnacled** (bär′nə-kəld): covered with barnacles, tiny shellfish that cling to rocks and wood.
8. **cowling**: a metal lid that covers an engine.

left his lanterns on the ground to help him, came back to fetch them.

"I thought you were at the McKays'," I said. "How'd you get over here?"

"Dad called me." He lifted one eyebrow. "Remember about something called the telephone?" And he picked up his gear and walked away.

"Well," my sister said.

They cast off; the big outboard sputtered gently, throttled way down. They would have to move very slowly in the fog. As they swung away, Robert at the tiller, we saw my father set out his compass and take a bearing off it.

My mother watched them out of sight, which didn't take more than a half-minute. Then she stood watching the fog for a while and, I guess, following the sound of the steady put-put. It seemed to me, listening to it move off and blend with the sounds of the bay—the sounds of a lot of water, of tiny waves and fish feeding—that I could pick out two or three other motors.

Finally my mother got tired of standing on the end of the dock and she turned around and walked up to us. I expected her to pass right by and go on up to the house. But she didn't. We could hear her stop and stand looking at us. My sister and I just scraped a little harder, pretending we hadn't noticed.

"I guess you're wondering what that was all about?" she said finally.

"I don't care," my sister said. She was lying. She was just as curious as I was.

My mother didn't seem to have heard her. "It's Linda Holloway and Stan Mitchell and Butch Rodgers."

We knew them. They were sailing people, a little older than I, a little younger than my brother Robert. They lived in three houses lined up one by the other on the north shore of Marshall's Inlet. They were all-right kids, nothing special either way, sort of a gang, living as close as they did. This year they had turned up with a new sailboat, a twelve-foot fiberglass job that somebody had designed and built for Stan Mitchell as a birthday present.

"What about them?" my sister asked, forgetting that she wasn't interested.

"They haven't come home."

"Oh," I said.

"They were sailing," my mother said. "The Brewers think they saw them off their place just before the fog. They were sort of far out."

"You mean Dad's gone to look for them?" She nodded.

"Is that all?" my sister said. "Just somebody going to have to sit in their boat and wait until the fog lifts."

My mother looked at us. Her curly red hair was dripping with the damp of the fog and her face was smeared with dust. "The Lord save me from children," she said quietly. "The glass is twenty-nine eighty and it's still going down fast."

We went back up to the house with her, to help fix supper—a quiet nervous kind of supper. The thick luminous fish-colored fog turned into deep solid night fog. Just after supper, while we were drying the dishes, the wind sprang up. It shook the whole line of windows in the kitchen and knocked over every single pot of geraniums on the back porch.

"Well," my mother said, "it's square into the east now."

A low barometer and a wind that had gone backwards into the east—there wasn't one of us didn't know what that meant. And it wasn't more than half an hour before there was a grumble of approaching thunder and the fog began to swirl around the windows, streaming like torn cotton as the wind increased.

"Dad'll come back now, huh?" my sister asked.

Detail from *Approaching Storm: Beach Near Newport.* An oil painting by
Martin Johnson Heade (1819-1904).
Museum of Fine Arts, Boston. Fund—M. and M. Karolik Collection.

"Yes," my mother said. "All the boats'll have to come back now."

We settled down to television, half watching it and half listening to the storm outside. In a little while, an hour or so, my mother said, "Turn off that thing."

"What?"

"Turn it off, quick." She hurried on the porch, saying over her shoulder: "I hear something."

The boards of the wide platform were wet and slippery under our feet, and the eaves of the house poured water in steady small streams that the wind grabbed and tore away. Between the crashes of thunder, we heard it too. There was a boat coming into our cove. By the sound of it, it would be my father and Robert.

"Is that the motor?" my mother asked.

"Sure," I said. It had a little tick and it was higher pitched than any of the others. You couldn't miss it.

Without another word to us she went scuttling across the porch and down the stairs toward the cove. We followed and stood close by, off the path and a little to one side. It was tide marsh there, and salt mud oozed over the tops of our sneakers. The cove itself was sheltered—it was in the lee[9] of Cedar Tree Neck—but even so it was pretty choppy. Whitecaps were beginning to run high and broken, wind against tide, and the spume from them stung as it hit your face and your eyes. You could hear the real stuff blowing overhead, with the peculiar sound wind has when it gets past half a gale.

My father's boat was sidling up to the dock now, pitching and rolling in the broken water. Its motor sputtered into reverse and then the hull rubbed gently against the pilings. They had had a bad time. In the quick lightning

9. **lee:** the side away from the wind; the protected side.

flashes you could see every scupper[10] pouring water. You could see the slow weary way they made the lines fast.

"There wasn't anything else to do," my father was saying as they came up the path, beating their arms for warmth; "with it blowing straight out the east, we had to come in."

Robert stopped a moment to pull off his oilskins. Under them his shirt was as drenched as if he hadn't had any protection at all.

"We came the long way around," my father said, "hugging the lee as much as we could."

"We almost swamped," Robert said.

Then we were at the house and they went off to dry their clothes, and that was that. They told us later that everybody had come in, except only for the big Coast Guard launch. And with only one boat it was no wonder they didn't find them.

The next morning was bright and clear and a lot cooler. The big stretch of bay was still shaken and tousled-looking, spotted with whitecaps. Soon as it was light, my father went to the front porch and looked and looked with his glasses. He checked the anemometer[11] dial and shook his head. "It's still too rough for us." In a bit the Coast Guard boats —two of them—appeared, and a helicopter began its chopping noisy circling.

It was marketing day too, so my mother, my sister, and I went off, as we always did. We stopped at the laundromat and the hardware, and then my mother had to get some pine trees for the slope behind the house. It was maybe four o'clock before we got home.

The wind had dropped; the bay was almost quiet again. Robert and my father were gone, and so was the boat. "I thought they'd go out again," my mother said. She got a cup of coffee and the three of us sat watching the fleet of boats work their way back and forth across the bay, searching.

Just before dark—just when the sky was beginning to take its twilight color—my father and Robert appeared. They were burned lobster-red with great white circles around their eyes where their glasses had been.

"Did you find anything?" my sister asked.

My father looked at my mother, who was opening a can of beer for him.

"You might as well tell them," she said. "They'll know anyway."

"Well," my father said, "they found the boat."

"That's what they were expecting to find, wasn't it?" my mother asked quietly.

He nodded. "It's kind of hard to say what happened. But it looks like they got blown on East Shoal with the tide going down and the chop tearing the keel out."[12]

"Oh," my mother said.

"Oh," my sister said.

"They found the boat around noon."

My mother said: "Have they found them?"

"Not that I heard."

"You think," my mother said, "they could have got to shore way out on Gull Point or some place like that?"

"No place is more than a four-hour walk," my father said. "They'd have turned up by now."

And it was later still, after dark, ten o'clock or so, that Mr. Robinson, who lived next door, stopped by the porch on his way home. "Found one," he said wearily. "The Mitchell boy."

---

10. **scupper:** an opening in a ship's side at deck level that allows water to run off the deck.
11. **anemometer** (ăn′ə-mŏm′ə-tər): an instrument that measures wind speed.

12. **the chop tearing the keel out:** the choppy waves tearing out the keel, or supporting beam at the bottom of the boat.

"Oh," my mother said, "oh, oh."

"Where?" my father asked.

"Just off the shoal, they said, curled up in the eelgrass."

"My God," my mother said softly.

Mr. Robinson moved off without so much as a goodbye. And after a while my sister and I went to bed.

But not to sleep. We played cards for an hour or so, until we couldn't stand that any more. Then we did a couple of crossword puzzles together. Finally we just sat in our beds, in the chilly night, and listened. There were the usual sounds from outside the open windows, sounds of the land and the water. Deer moving about in the brush on their way to eat the wild watercress and wild lettuce that grew around the spring. The deep pumping sounds of an owl's wings in the air. Little splashes from the bay—the fishes and the muskrats and the otters.

"I didn't know there'd be so many things moving at night," my sister said.

"You just weren't ever awake."

"What do you reckon it's like," she said, "being on the bottom in the eelgrass?"

"Shut up," I told her.

"Well," she said, "I just asked. Because I was wondering."

"Don't."

Her talking had started a funny shaking quivering feeling from my navel right straight back to my backbone. The tips of my fingers hurt too, the way they always did.

"I thought the dogs would howl," she said.

"They can't smell anything from the water," I told her. "Now quit."

She fell asleep then and maybe I did too, because the night seemed awful short. Or maybe the summer dawns really come that quick. Not dawn, no. The quiet deep dark that means dawn is just about to come. The birds started whistling and the gulls started shriek-

ing. I got up and looked out at the dripping beach plum bushes and the twisted, salt-burned jack pines, then I slipped out the window. I'd done it before. You lifted the screen and lowered yourself down. It wasn't anything of a drop—all you had to watch was the patch of poison ivy. I circled around the house and took the old deer trail down to the bay. It was chilly, and I began to wish I had brought my robe or a coat. With just cotton pajamas my teeth would begin chattering very soon.

I don't know what I expected to see. And I didn't see anything at all. Just some morning fog in the hollows and around the spring. And the dock, with my father's boat bobbing in the run of the tide.

The day was getting close now. The sky overhead turned a sort of luminous dark blue. As it did, the water darkened to a lead-colored gray. It looked heavy and oily and impenetrable.[13] I tried to imagine what would be under it. I always thought I knew. There would be horseshoe crabs and hermit crabs and blue crabs, and scallops squirting their way along, and there'd be all the different kinds of fish, and the eels. I kept telling myself that that was all.

But this time I couldn't seem to keep my thoughts straight. I kept wondering what it must be like to be dead and cold and down in the sand and mud with the eelgrass brushing you and the crabs bumping you and the fish—I had felt their little sucking mouths sometimes when I swam.

The water was thick and heavy and the color of a mirror in a dark room. Minnows broke the surface right under the wharf. I jumped. I couldn't help it.

And I got to thinking that something might come out of the water. It didn't have a name

---

13. **impenetrable** (ĭm-pĕn′ə-trə-bəl): unable to be penetrated, or pierced; also, unable to be understood.

or a shape. But it was there.

I stood where I was for a while, trying to fight down the idea. When I found I couldn't do that, I decided to walk slowly back to the house. At least I thought I was going to walk, but the way the boards of the wharf shook under my feet I know that I must have been running. On the path up to the house my bare feet hit some of the sharp cut-off stubs of the rosa rugosa bushes, but I didn't stop. I went crashing into the kitchen because that was the closest door.

The room was thick with the odor of frying bacon, the softness of steam: my mother had gotten up early. She turned around when I came in, not seeming surprised—as if it was the most usual thing in the world for me to be wandering around before daylight in my pajamas.

"Go take those things off, honey," she said. "You're drenched."

"Yes ma'am," I told her.

I stripped off the clothes and saw that they really were soaking. I knew it was just the dew and the fog. But I couldn't help thinking it was something else. Something that had reached for me, and missed. Something that was wet, that had come from the water, something that had splashed me as it went past.

SEEKING MEANING

1. At the beginning of this story, a girl and her sister are peacefully scraping their dinghy near a dock on a bright, sunny day. At the end of the story, the girl runs in terror from the same dock in the darkness just before dawn. What tragedy has occurred to bring about this change in her feelings? What details show that she now views the water as a frightening place, a place where death lives?

2. The land and the water produce very different feelings in this story. Find passages in the story that suggest that the land is a safe and comfortable place.

3. Why do you suppose the girl goes down to the dock in the darkness before dawn?

4. A young person's first reaction to death is a common subject in stories. Do you think the girl's reactions in this story are believable? Why or why not?

DEVELOPING SKILLS IN READING

Stating the Theme

Many stories are written purely for entertainment. Detective stories, Westerns, love stories—many of these are written just to be enjoyed. But many stories are also written to illustrate some central idea or truth about human life or experience. This central idea is called the *theme* of the story. Writers do not generally state the theme in their stories. They expect the reader to derive the theme from all the events that take place in the story.

The theme of a story is different from the *plot*, which is the sequence of events that occur in the story. Plot is what happens in the story. Theme is what the story means.

Here are two statements about this story. One is a statement of the plot. The other is a statement about the theme. Which one states the theme?

1. The narrator hears that three of her young neighbors are missing on a sailboat. The fog is coming in, and a storm is expected. She waits while her father and older brother aid in the search. Late the next day she hears that the three young people have been lost. One of them is found dead in the eelgrass. Shortly before dawn the next day, she goes to the dock. There she feels some terror in the water and rushes home.

2. A girl learns for the first time that death can touch young people like her. She discovers how fragile and vulnerable human life is. Though nature can seem mild and pleasant, beneath its surface are destructive forces which can destroy without warning and without reason. She has escaped death this time, but she realizes that it can reach out for her just as it has reached out and caught her young neighbors.

This story might have suggested other meanings to you. Why do you think the author associates death with *water?* Do you know of any other stories where something evil and fearful is associated with the sea?

DEVELOPING VOCABULARY

Analyzing Words with Greek and Latin Roots

At one point in this story, the father checks the *anemometer* dial. As the footnote on page 237 indicates, an *anemometer* is a device for measuring the speed of wind. It comes from *anemos,* a Greek root word meaning "wind," and *metron,* a Greek root word meaning "a measure."

What Latin and Greek roots are used to form these words? A dictionary will help.

anemone	meter	thermometer
barometer	pedometer	thermos

ABOUT THE AUTHOR

Shirley Ann Grau (1929–   ) lives in a suburb of New Orleans, where she was born. She has planned novels while cooking, corrected manuscript in the pediatrician's waiting room and written in a house filled with the babble of children, the slamming of doors, and the barks of dogs. Under these hectic conditions, she has produced two volumes of short stories and several novels. Her third novel, *The Keepers of the House,* won the 1964 Pulitzer Prize for fiction. She says that the goal of all her fiction is to make more understandable, more bearable, the muddle of human life.

The doctors told Charlie that if he volunteered for this experiment he might "get smart." If the operation worked, Charlie would be the first of a new breed of intellectual supermen. If it failed . . . ?

Flowers for Algernon

Daniel Keyes

progris riport—martch 5 1965

Dr. Strauss says I shud rite down what I think and evrey thing that happins to me from now on. I dont know why but he says its importint so they will see if they will use me. I hope they use me. Miss Kinnian says maybe they can make me smart. I want to be smart. My name is Charlie Gordon. I am 37 years old and 2 weeks ago was my brithday. I have nuthing more to rite now so I will close for today.

progris riport 2—martch 6

I had a test today. I think I faled it. and I think that maybe now they wont use me. What happind is a nice young man was in the room and he had some white cards with ink spillled all over them. He sed Charlie what do you see on this card. I was very skared even tho I had my rabits foot in my pockit because when I was a kid I always faled tests in school and I spilled ink to.

I told him I saw an inkblot. He said yes and it made me feel good. I thot that was all but when I got up to go he stopped me. He said now sit down Charlie we are not thru yet. Then I dont remember so good but he wantid me to say what was in the ink. I dint see

nuthing in the ink but he said there was picturs there other pepul saw some picturs. I coudnt see any picturs. I reely tried to see. I held the card close up and then far away. Then I said if I had my glases I coud see better I usally only ware my glases in the movies or TV but I said they are in the closit in the hall. I got them. Then I said let me see that card agen I bet Ill find it now.

I tryed hard but I still coudnt find the picturs I only saw the ink. I told him maybe I need new glases. He rote somthing down on a paper and I got skared of faling the test. I told him it was a very nice inkblot with littel points all around the eges. He looked very sad so that wasnt it. I said please let me try agen. Ill get it in a few minits becaus Im not so fast somtimes. Im a slow reeder too in Miss Kinnians class for slow adults but I'm trying very hard.

He gave me a chance with another card that had 2 kinds of ink spillled on it red and blue.

He was very nice and talked slow like Miss Kinnian does and he explaned to me that it was a *raw shok*.[1] He said pepul see things in the ink. I said show me where. He said think.

---

1. **raw shok:** Charlie means the *Rorschach* (rôr′shäk) test, a personality test in which people tell what is suggested to them by a series of inkblot designs.

I told him I think a inkblot but that wasnt rite eather. He said what does it remind you – pretend something. I closd my eyes for a long time to pretend. I told him I pretned a fowntan pen with ink leeking all over a table cloth. Then he got up and went out.

I dont think I passd the *raw shok* test.

progris report 3 – martch 7

Dr Strauss and Dr Nemur say it dont matter about the inkblots. I told them I dint spill the ink on the cards and I coudnt see anything in the ink. They said that maybe they will still use me. I said Miss Kinnian never gave me tests like that one only spelling and reading. They said Miss Kinnian told that I was her bestist pupil in the adult nite scool becaus I tryed the hardist and I reely wantid to lern. They said how come you went to the adult nite scool all by yourself Charlie. How did you find it. I said I askd pepul and sumbody told me where I shud go to lern to read and spell good. They said why did you want to. I told them becaus all my life I wantid to be smart and not dumb. But its very hard to be smart. They said you know it will probly be tempirery. I said yes. Miss Kinnian told me. I dont care if it herts.

Later I had more crazy tests today. The nice lady who gave it me told me the name and I asked her how do you spellit so I can rite it in my progris riport. THEMATIC APPERCEPTION TEST. I dont know the frist 2 words but I know what *test* means. You got to pass it or you get bad marks. This test lookd easy becaus I coud see the picturs. Only this time she dint want me to tell her the picturs. That mixd me up. I said the man yesterday said I shoud tell him what I saw in the ink she said that dont make no difrence. She said make up storys about the pepul in the picturs.

I told her how can you tell storys about

pepul you never met. I said why shud I make up lies. I never tell lies any more becaus I always get caut.

She told me this test and the other one the raw-shok was for getting personalty. I laffed so hard. I said how can you get that thing from inkblots and fotos. She got sore and put her picturs away. I dont care. It was sily. I gess I faled that test too.

Later some men in white coats took me to a difernt part of the hospitil and gave me a game to play. It was like a race with a white mouse. They called the mouse Algernon. Algernon was in a box with a lot of twists and turns like all kinds of walls and they gave me a pencil and a paper with lines and lots of boxes. On one side it said START and on the other end it said FINISH. They said it was *amazed*[2] and that Algernon and me had the same *amazed* to do. I dint see how we could have the same *amazed* if Algernon had a box and I had a paper but I dint say nothing. Anyway there wasnt time because the race started.

One of the men had a watch he was trying to hide so I woudnt see it so I tryed not to look and that made me nervus.

Anyway that test made me feel worser than all the others because they did it over 10 times with difernt *amazeds* and Algernon won every time. I dint know that mice were so smart. Maybe thats because Algernon is a white mouse. Maybe white mice are smarter then other mice.

progris riport 4 – Mar 8

Their going to use me! Im so exited I can hardly write. Dr Nemur and Dr Strauss had a

---

2. **amazed:** Charlie means *a maze,* a series of winding paths with one exit and many dead ends. The intelligence of laboratory animals is measured by the amount of time it takes them to find the exit.

argament about it first. Dr Nemur was in the office when Dr Strauss brot me in. Dr Nemur was worryed about using me but Dr Strauss told him Miss Kinnian rekemmended me the best from all the people who she was teaching. I like Miss Kinnian becaus shes a very smart teacher. And she said Charlie your going to have a second chance. If you volenteer for this experament you mite get smart. They dont know if it will be perminint but theirs a chance. Thats why I said ok even when I was scared because she said it was an operashun. She said dont be scared Charlie you done so much with so little I think you deserv it most of all.

So I got scaird when Dr Nemur and Dr Strauss argud about it. Dr Strauss said I had something that was very good. He said I had a good motor-vation.[3] I never even knew I had that. I felt proud when he said that not every body with an eye-q of 68 had that thing. I dont know what it is or where I got it but he said Algernon had it too. Algernons motor-vation is the cheese they put in his box. But it cant be that because I didnt eat any cheese this week.

Then he told Dr Nemur something I dint understand so while they were talking I wrote down some of the words.

He said Dr Nemur I know Charlie is not what you had in mind as the first of your new brede of intelek** (coudnt get the word) superman. But most people of his low ment** are host** and uncoop** they are usualy dull

---

3. **motor-vation:** Charlie means *motivation* (mō′tə-vā′shən), the inner drive to work hard at something.

apath** and hard to reach. He has a good natcher hes intristed and eager to please.

Dr Nemur said remember he will be the first human beeng ever to have his intelijence trippled by surgicle meens.

Dr Strauss said exakly. Look at how well hes lerned to read and write for his low mentel age its as grate an acheve** as you and I lerning einstines therey of **vity without help. That shows the intenss motor-vation. Its comparat** a tremen** achev** I say we use Charlie.

I dint get all the words and they were talking to fast but it sounded like Dr Strauss was on my side and like the other one wasnt.

Then Dr Nemur nodded he said all right maybe your right. We will use Charlie. When he said that I got so exited I jumped up and shook his hand for being so good to me. I told him thank you doc you wont be sorry for giving me a second chance. And I mean it like I told him. After the operashun Im gonna try to be smart. Im gonna try awful hard.

progris ript 5 — Mar 10

Im skared. Lots of people who work here and the nurses and the people who gave me the tests came to bring me candy and wish me luck. I hope I have luck. I got my rabits foot and my lucky penny and my horse shoe. Only a black cat crossed me when I was comming to the hospitil. Dr Strauss says dont be supersitis Charlie this is sience. Anyway Im keeping my rabits foot with me.

I asked Dr Strauss if Ill beat Algernon in the race after the operashun and he said maybe. If the operashun works Ill show that mouse I can be as smart as he is. Maybe smarter. Then Ill be abel to read better and spell the words good and know lots of things and be like other people. I want to be smart like other people. If it works perminint they will make everybody smart all over the wurld.

They dint give me anything to eat this morning. I dont know what that eating has to do with getting smart. Im very hungry and Dr Nemur took away my box of candy. That Dr Nemur is a grouch. Dr Strauss says I can have it back after the operashun. You cant eat befor a operashun . . .

Progress Report 6 — Mar 15

The operashun dint hurt. He did it while I was sleeping. They took off the bandijis from my eyes and my head today so I can make a PROGRESS REPORT. Dr Nemur who looked at some of my other ones says I spell PROGRESS wrong and he told me how to spell it and REPORT too. I got to try and remember that.

I have a very bad memary for spelling. Dr Strauss says its ok to tell about all the things that happin to me but he says I shoud tell more about what I feel and what I think. When I told him I dont know how to think he said try. All the time when the bandijis were on my eyes I tryed to think. Nothing happened. I dont know what to think about. Maybe if I ask him he will tell me how I can think now that Im suppose to get smart. What do smart people think about. Fancy things I suppose. I wish I knew some fancy things alredy.

Progress Report 7 — mar 19

Nothing is happining. I had lots of tests and different kinds of races with Algernon. I hate that mouse. He always beats me. Dr Strauss said I got to play those games. And he said some time I got to take those tests over again. Those inkblots are stupid. And those pictures are stupid too. I like to draw a picture of a man and a woman but I wont make up lies about people.

I got a headache from trying to think so much. I thot Dr Strauss was my frend but he dont help me. He dont tell me what to think or when Ill get smart. Miss Kinnian dint come to see me. I think writing these progress reports are stupid too.

Progress Report 8 — Mar 23

Im going back to work at the factery. They said it was better I shud go back to work but I cant tell anyone what the operashun was for and I have come to the hospitil for an hour evry night after work. They are gonna pay me mony every month for lerning to be smart.

Im glad Im going back to work because I miss my job and all my frends and all the fun we have there.

Dr Strauss says I shud keep writing things down but I dont have to do it every day just when I think of something or something speshul happins. He says dont get discoridged because it takes time and it happins slow. He says it took a long time with Algernon before he got 3 times smarter than he was before. Thats why Algernon beats me all the time because he had that operashun too. That makes me feel better. I coud probly do that *amazed* faster than a reglar mouse. Maybe some day Ill beat Algernon. Boy that would be something. So far Algernon looks like he mite be smart perminent.

Mar 25 (I dont have to write PROGRESS RE-PORT on top any more just when I hand it in once a week for Dr Nemur to read. I just have to put the date on. That saves time)

We had a lot of fun at the factery today. Joe Carp said hey look where Charlie had his operashun what did they do Charlie put some brains in. I was going to tell him but I remembered Dr Strauss said no. Then Frank Reilly said what did you do Charlie forget your key

and open your door the hard way. That made me laff. Their really my friends and they like me.

Sometimes somebody will say hey look at Joe or Frank or George he really pulled a Charlie Gordon. I dont know why they say that but they always laff. This morning Amos Borg who is the 4 man at Donnegans used my name when he shouted at Ernie the office boy. Ernie lost a packige. He said Ernie what are you trying to be a Charlie Gordon. I dont understand why he said that. I never lost any packiges.

Mar 28 Dr Strauss came to my room to-night to see why I dint come in like I was suppose to. I told him I dont like to race with Algernon any more. He said I dont have to for a while but I shud come in. He had a present for me only it wasnt a present but just for lend. I thot it was a little television but it wasnt. He said I got to turn it on when I go to sleep. I said your kidding why shud I turn it on when Im going to sleep. Who ever herd of a thing like that. But he said if I want to get smart I got to do what he says. I told him I dint think I was going to get smart and he put his hand on my sholder and said Charlie you dont know it yet but your getting smarter all the time. You wont notice for a while. I think he was just being nice to make me feel good because I dont look any smarter.

Oh yes I almost forgot. I asked him when I can go back to the class at Miss Kinnians school. He said I wont go their. He said that soon Miss Kinnian will come to the hospitil to start and teach me speshul. I was mad at her for not comming to see me when I got the operashun but I like her so maybe we will be frends again.

Mar 29 That crazy TV kept me up all night. How can I sleep with something yelling crazy things all night in my ears. And the nutty pictures. Wow. I dont know what it says when Im up so how am I going to know when Im sleeping.

Dr Strauss says its ok. He says my brains are lerning when I sleep and that will help me when Miss Kinnian starts my lessons in the hospitl (only I found out it isnt a hospitil its a labatory). I think its all crazy. If you can get smart when your sleeping why do people go to school. That thing I dont think will work. I use to watch the late show and the late late show on TV all the time and it never made me smart. Maybe you have to sleep while you watch it.

Dr Strauss showed me how to keep the TV turned low so now I can sleep. I dont hear a thing. And I still dont understand what it says. A few times I play it over in the morning to find out what I lerned when I was sleeping and I dont think so. Miss Kinnian says Maybe its another langwidge or something. But most times it sounds american. It talks so fast faster than even Miss Gold who was my teacher in 6 grade and I remember she talked so fast I coudnt understand her.

I told Dr Strauss what good is it to get smart

in my sleep. I want to be smart when Im awake. He says its the same thing and I have two minds. Theres the *subconscious* and the *conscious* (thats how you spell it). And one dont tell the other one what its doing. They dont even talk to each other. Thats why I dream. And boy have I been having crazy dreams. Wow. Ever since that night TV. The late late late late late show.

I forgot to ask him if it was only me or if everybody had those two minds.

(I just looked up the word in the dictionary Dr Strauss gave me. The word is *subconscious. adj. Of the nature of mental operations yet not present in consciousness; as, subconscious conflict of desires.*) Theres more but I still don't know what it means. This isnt a very good dictionary for dumb people like me.

Anyway the headache is from the party. My frends from the factery Joe Carp and Frank Reilly invited me to go with them to Muggsys Saloon for some drinks. I dont like to drink but they said we will have lots of fun. I had a good time.

Joe Carp said I shoud show the girls how I mop out the toilet in the factory and he got me a mop. I showed them and everyone laffed when I told that Mr Donnegan said I was the best janiter he ever had because I like my job and do it good and never come late or miss a day except for my operashun.

I said Miss Kinnian always said Charlie be proud of your job because you do it good.

Everybody laffed and we had a good time and they gave me lots of drinks and Joe said Charlie is a card. I dont know what that means but everybody likes me and we have fun. I cant wait to be smart like my best friends Joe Carp and Frank Reilly.

I dont remember how the party was over but I think I went out to buy a newspaper and coffe for Joe and Frank and when I came back there was no one their. I looked for them all over till late. Then I dont remember so good but I think I got sleepy or sick. A nice cop brot me back home. Thats what my landlady Mrs Flynn says.

But I got a headache and a big lump on my head and black and blue all over. I think maybe I fell. Anyway I got a bad headache and Im sick and hurt all over. I dont think Ill drink anymore.

April 6 I beat Algernon! I dint even know I beat him until Burt the tester told me. Then the second time I lost because I got so exited I fell off the chair before I finished. But after that I beat him 8 more times. I must be getting smart to beat a smart mouse like Algernon. But I dont *feel* smarter.

I wanted to race Algernon some more but Burt said thats enough for one day. They let me hold him for a minit. Hes not so bad. Hes soft like a ball of cotton. He blinks and when he opens his eyes their black and pink on the eges.

I said can I feed him because I felt bad to beat him and I wanted to be nice and make frends. Burt said no Algernon is a very specshul mouse with an operashun like mine, and he was the first of all the animals to stay smart so long. He told me Algernon is so smart that every day he has to solve a test to get his food. Its a thing like a lock on a door that changes every time Algernon goes in to eat so he has to lern something new to get his food. That made me sad because if he couldnt lern he woud be hungry.

I dont think its right to make you pass a test to eat. How woud Dr Nemur like it to have to pass a test every time he wants to eat. I think Ill be frends with Algernon.

April 9 Tonight after work Miss Kinnian was at the laboratory. She looked like she was glad to see me but scared. I told her dont worry Miss Kinnian Im not smart yet and she laffed. She said I have confidence in you Charlie the way you struggled so hard to read and right better than all the others. At werst you will have it for a littel wile and your doing somthing for sience.

We are reading a very hard book. I never read such a hard book before. Its called *Robinson Crusoe* about a man who gets merooned on a dessert Iland. Hes smart and figers out all kinds of things so he can have a house and food and hes a good swimmer. Only I feel sorry because hes all alone and has no frends. But I think their must be somebody else on the iland because theres a picture with his funny umbrella looking at footprints. I hope he gets a frend and not be lonly.

April 10 Miss Kinnian teaches me to spell better. She says look at a word and close your eyes and say it over and over until you remember. I have lots of truble with *through* that you say *threw* and *enough* and *tough* that you dont say *enew* and *tew*. You got to say *enuff* and *tuff*. Thats how I use to write it before I started to get smart. Im confused but Miss Kinnian says theres no reason in spelling.

Apr 14 Finished *Robinson Crusoe*. I want to find out more about what happens to him but Miss Kinnian says thats all there is. *Why*

Apr 15 Miss Kinnian says Im lerning fast. She read some of the Progress Reports and she looked at me kind of funny. She says Im a fine person and Ill show them all. I asked her why. She said never mind but I shouldnt feel bad if I find out that everybody isnt nice like I think. She said for a person who god gave so little to you done more then a lot of people with brains they never even used. I said all my frends are smart people but there good. They

like me and they never did anything that wasnt nice. Then she got something in her eye and she had to run out to the ladys room.

Apr 16 Today, I lerned, the *comma,* this is a comma (,) a period, with a tail, Miss Kinnian, says its important, because it makes writing, better, she said, somebody, coud lose, a lot of money, if a comma, isnt, in the, right place, I dont have, any money, and I dont see, how a comma, keeps you, from losing it,

But she says, everybody, uses commas, so Ill use, them too,

Apr 17 I used the comma wrong. Its punctuation. Miss Kinnian told me to look up long words in the dictionary to lern to spell them. I said whats the difference if you can read it anyway. She said its part of your education so now on Ill look up all the words Im not sure how to spell. It takes a long time to write that way but I think Im remembering. I only have to look up once and after that I get it right. Anyway thats how come I got the word *punctuation* right. (Its that way in the dictionary). Miss Kinnian says a period is punctuation too, and there are lots of other marks to lern. I told her I thot all the periods had to have tails but she said no.

You got to mix them up, she showed? me" how, to mix! them(up,, and now; I can! mix up all kinds" of punctuation, in! my writing? There, are lots! of rules? to lern; but Im gettin'g them in my head.

One thing I? like about, Dear Miss Kinnian: (thats the way it goes in a business letter if I ever go into business) is she, always gives me' a reason" when—I ask. She's a gen'ius! I wish! I cou'd be smart" like, her;

(Punctuation, is; fun!)

Apr 18 What a dope I am! I didn't even understand what she was talking about. I read the grammar book last night and it explanes the whole thing. Then I saw it was the same way as Miss Kinnian was trying to tell me, but I didn't get it. I got up in the middle of the night, and the whole thing straightened out in my mind.

Miss Kinnian said that the TV working in my sleep helped out. She said I reached a plateau. Thats like the flat top of a hill.

After I figgered out how punctuation worked, I read over all my old Progress Reports from the beginning. Boy, did I have crazy spelling and punctuation! I told Miss Kinnian I ought to go over the pages and fix all the mistakes but she said, "No, Charlie, Dr. Nemur wants them just as they are. That's why he let you keep them after they were photostated, to see your own progress. You're coming along fast, Charlie."

That made me feel good. After the lesson I went down and played with Algernon. We don't race any more.

April 20 I feel sick inside. Not sick like for a doctor, but inside my chest it feels empty like getting punched and a heartburn at the same time.

I wasn't going to write about it, but I guess I got to, because it's important. Today was the first time I ever stayed home from work.

Last night Joe Carp and Frank Reilly invited me to a party. There were lots of girls and some men from the factory. I remembered how sick I got last time I drank too much, so I told Joe I didn't want anything to drink. He gave me a plain Coke instead. It tasted funny, but I thought it was just a bad taste in my mouth.

We had a lot of fun for a while. Joe said I should dance with Ellen and she would teach me the steps. I fell a few times and I couldn't understand why because no one else was dancing besides Ellen and me. And all the time I was tripping because somebody's foot was always sticking out.

Then when I got up I saw the look on Joe's face and it gave me a funny feeling in my stomack. "He's a scream," one of the girls said. Everybody was laughing.

Frank said, "I ain't laughed so much since we sent him off for the newspaper that night at Muggsy's and ditched him."

"Look at him. His face is red."

"He's blushing. Charlie is blushing."

"Hey, Ellen, what'd you do to Charlie? I never saw him act like that before."

I didn't know what to do or where to turn. Everyone was looking at me and laughing and I felt naked. I wanted to hide myself. I ran out into the street and I threw up. Then I walked home. It's a funny thing I never knew that Joe and Frank and the others liked to have me around all the time to make fun of me.

Now I know what it means when they say "to pull a Charlie Gordon."

I'm ashamed.

PROGRESS REPORT 10

April 21 Still didn't go into the factory. I told Mrs. Flynn my landlady to call and tell Mr. Donnegan I was sick. Mrs. Flynn looks at me very funny lately like she's scared of me.

I think it's a good thing about finding out how everybody laughs at me. I thought about it a lot. It's because I'm so dumb and I don't even know when I'm doing something dumb. People think it's funny when a dumb person can't do things the same way they can.

Anyway, now I know I'm getting smarter every day. I know punctuation and I can spell good. I like to look up all the hard words in the dictionary and I remember them. I'm reading a lot now, and Miss Kinnian says I read very fast. Sometimes I even understand what I'm reading about, and it stays in my mind. There are times when I can close my eyes and think of a page and it all comes back like a picture.

Besides history, geography, and arithmetic, Miss Kinnian said I should start to learn a few foreign languages. Dr. Strauss gave me some more tapes to play while I sleep. I still don't understand how that conscious and unconscious mind works, but Dr. Strauss says not to worry yet. He asked me to promise that when I start learning college subjects next week I wouldn't read any books on psychology—that is, until he gives me permission.

I feel a lot better today, but I guess I'm still a little angry that all the time people were laughing and making fun of me because I wasn't so smart. When I become intelligent like Dr. Strauss says, with three times my I.Q. of 68, then maybe I'll be like everyone else and people will like me and be friendly.

I'm not sure what an I.Q. is. Dr. Nemur said it was something that measured how intelligent you were—like a scale in the drugstore weighs pounds. But Dr. Strauss had a big argument with him and said an I.Q. didn't weigh intelligence at all. He said an I.Q. showed how much intelligence you could get, like the numbers on the outside of a measuring cup. You still had to fill the cup up with stuff.

Then when I asked Burt, who gives me my intelligence tests and works with Algernon, he said that both of them were wrong (only I had to promise not to tell them he said so). Burt says that the I.Q. measures a lot of different things including some of the things you learned already, and it really isn't any good at all.

So I still don't know what I.Q. is except that mine is going to be over 200 soon. I didn't want to say anything, but I don't see how if they don't know *what* it is, or *where* it is—I don't see how they know *how much* of it you've got.

Dr. Nemur says I have to take a *Rorschach Test* tomorrow. I wonder what *that* is.

April 22 I found out what a *Rorschach* is. It's the test I took before the operation—the one with the inkblots on the pieces of cardboard. The man who gave me the test was the same one.

I was scared to death of those inkblots. I knew he was going to ask me to find the pictures and I knew I wouldn't be able to. I was thinking to myself, if only there was some way of knowing what kind of pictures were hidden there. Maybe there weren't any pictures at all. Maybe it was just a trick to see if I was dumb enough to look for something that wasn't there. Just thinking about that made me sore at him.

"All right, Charlie," he said, "you've seen these cards before, remember?"

"Of course I remember."

The way I said it, he knew I was angry, and he looked surprised. "Yes, of course. Now I want you to look at this one. What might this be? What do you see on this card? People see all sorts of things in these inkblots. Tell me what it might be for you—what it makes you think of."

I was shocked. That wasn't what I had expected him to say at all. "You mean there are no pictures hidden in those inkblots?"

He frowned and took off his glasses. "What?"

"Pictures. Hidden in the inkblots. Last time you told me that everyone could see them and you wanted me to find them too."

He explained to me that the last time he had used almost the exact same words he was using now. I didn't believe it, and I still have the suspicion that he misled me at the time just for the fun of it. Unless—I don't know any more—could I have been *that* feeble-minded?

We went through the cards slowly. One of

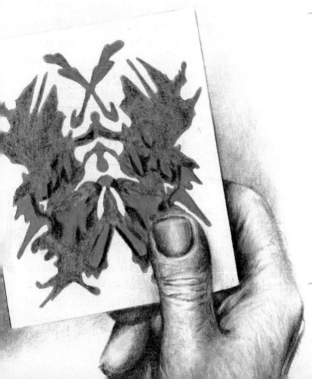

them looked like a pair of bats tugging at something. Another one looked like two men fencing with swords. I imagined all sorts of things. I guess I got carried away. But I didn't trust him any more, and I kept turning them around and even looking on the back to see if there was anything there I was supposed to catch. While he was making his notes, I peeked out of the corner of my eye to read it. But it was all in code that looked like this:

WF+A   DdF—Ad orig.   WF—A   SF+obj

The test still doesn't make sense to me. It seems to me that anyone could make up lies about things that they didn't really see. How could he know I wasn't making a fool of him by mentioning things that I didn't really imagine? Maybe I'll understand it when Dr. Strauss lets me read up on psychology.

April 25   I figured out a new way to line up the machines in the factory, and Mr. Donnegan says it will save him ten thousand dollars a year in labor and increased production. He gave me a twenty-five-dollar bonus.

I wanted to take Joe Carp and Frank Reilly out to lunch to celebrate, but Joe said he had to buy some things for his wife, and Frank said he was meeting his cousin for lunch. I guess it'll take a little time for them to get used to the changes in me. Everybody seems to be frightened of me. When I went over to Amos Borg and tapped him on the shoulder, he jumped up in the air.

People don't talk to me much any more or kid around the way they used to. It makes the job kind of lonely.

April 27   I got up the nerve today to ask Miss Kinnian to have dinner with me tomorrow night to celebrate my bonus.

At first she wasn't sure it was right, but I

asked Dr. Strauss and he said it was okay. Dr. Strauss and Dr. Nemur don't seem to be getting along so well. They're arguing all the time. This evening when I came in to ask Dr. Strauss about having dinner with Miss Kinnian, I heard them shouting. Dr. Nemur was saying that it was *his* experiment and *his* research, and Dr. Strauss was shouting back that he contributed just as much, because he found me through Miss Kinnian and he performed the operation. Dr. Strauss said that someday thousands of neurosurgeons might be using his technique all over the world.

Dr. Nemur wanted to publish the results of the experiment at the end of this month. Dr. Strauss wanted to wait a while longer to be sure. Dr. Strauss said that Dr. Nemur was more interested in the Chair[4] of Psychology at Princeton than he was in the experiment. Dr. Nemur said that Dr. Strauss was nothing but an opportunist who was trying to ride to glory on *his* coattails.

When I left afterwards, I found myself trembling. I don't know why for sure, but it was as if I'd seen both men clearly for the first time. I remember hearing Burt say that Dr. Nemur had a shrew of a wife who was pushing him all the time to get things published so that he could become famous. Burt said that the dream of her life was to have a big-shot husband.

Was Dr. Strauss really trying to ride on his coattails?

April 28 I don't understand why I never noticed how beautiful Miss Kinnian really is. She has brown eyes and feathery brown hair that comes to the top of her neck. She's only thirty-four! I think from the beginning I had the feeling that she was an unreachable

---

4. **Chair:** here, a professorship.

genius—and very, very old. Now, every time I see her she grows younger and more lovely.

We had dinner and a long talk. When she said that I was coming along so fast that soon I'd be leaving her behind, I laughed.

"It's true, Charlie. You're already a better reader than I am. You can read a whole page at a glance while I can take in only a few lines at a time. And you remember every single thing you read. I'm lucky if I can recall the main thoughts and the general meaning."

"I don't feel intelligent. There are so many things I don't understand."

She took out a cigarette and I lit it for her. "You've got to be a *little* patient. You're accomplishing in days and weeks what it takes normal people to do in half a lifetime. That's what makes it so amazing. You're like a giant sponge now, soaking things in. Facts, figures, general knowledge. And soon you'll begin to connect them, too. You'll see how the different branches of learning are related. There are many levels, Charlie, like steps on a giant ladder that take you up higher and higher to see more and more of the world around you."

"I can see only a little bit of that, Charlie, and I won't go much higher than I am now, but you'll keep climbing up and up, and see more and more, and each step will open new worlds that you never even knew existed." She frowned. "I hope . . . I just hope to God—"

"What?"

"Never mind, Charles. I just hope I wasn't wrong to advise you to go into this in the first place."

I laughed. "How could that be? It worked, didn't it? Even Algernon is still smart."

We sat there silently for a while and I knew what she was thinking about as she watched me toying with the chain of my rabbit's foot and my keys. I didn't want to think of that possibility any more than elderly people want

to think of death. I *knew* that this was only the beginning. I knew what she meant about levels because I'd seen some of them already. The thought of leaving her behind made me sad.

I'm in love with Miss Kinnian.

PROGRESS REPORT 11

April 30 — I've quit my job with Donnegan's Plastic Box Company. Mr. Donnegan insisted that it would be better for all concerned if I left. What did I do to make them hate me so?

The first I knew of it was when Mr. Donnegan showed me the petition. Eight hundred and forty names, everyone connected with the factory, except Fanny Girden. Scanning the list quickly, I saw at once that hers was the only missing name. All the rest demanded that I be fired.

Joe Carp and Frank Reilly wouldn't talk to me about it. No one else would either, except Fanny. She was one of the few people I'd known who set her mind to something and believed it no matter what the rest of the world proved, said, or did — and Fanny did not believe that I should have been fired. She had been against the petition on principle and despite the pressure and threats she'd held out.

"Which don't mean to say," she remarked, "that I don't think there's something mighty strange about you, Charlie. Them changes. I don't know. You used to be a good, dependable, ordinary man — not too bright maybe, but honest. Who knows what you done to yourself to get so smart all of a sudden. Like everybody around here's been saying, Charlie, it's not right."

"But how can you say that, Fanny? What's wrong with a man becoming intelligent and wanting to acquire knowledge and understanding of the world around him?"

She stared down at her work and I turned to leave. Without looking at me, she said: "It was evil when Eve[5] listened to the snake and ate from the tree of knowledge. It was evil when she saw that she was naked. If not for that none of us would ever have to grow old and sick, and die."

Once again now I have the feeling of shame burning inside me. This intelligence has driven a wedge between me and all the people I once knew and loved. Before, they laughed at me and despised me for my ignorance and dullness; now, they hate me for my knowledge and understanding. What do they want of me?

They've driven me out of the factory. Now I'm more alone than ever before. . . .

May 15 Dr. Strauss is very angry at me for not having written any progress reports in two weeks. He's justified because the lab is now paying me a regular salary. I told him I was too busy thinking and reading. When I pointed out that writing was such a slow process that it made me impatient with my poor handwriting, he suggested that I learn to type. It's much easier to write now because I can type nearly seventy-five words a minute. Dr. Strauss continually reminds me of the need to speak and write simply so that people will be able to understand me.

I'll try to review all the things that happened to me during the last two weeks. Algernon and I were presented to the American Psychological Association sitting in convention with the World Psychological Association last Tuesday. We created quite a sensation. Dr. Nemur and Dr. Strauss were proud of us.

I suspect that Dr. Nemur, who is sixty — ten years older than Dr. Strauss — finds it necessary to see tangible results of his work. Undoubtedly the result of pressure by Mrs. Nemur.

Contrary to my earlier impressions of him, I realize that Dr. Nemur is not at all a genius. He has a very good mind, but it struggles under the specter of self-doubt. He wants people to take him for a genius. Therefore, it is important for him to feel that his work is accepted by the world. I believe that Dr. Nemur was afraid of further delay because he worried that someone else might make a discovery along these lines and take the credit from him.

5. **Eve:** The story of Adam and Eve is told in Genesis 2–3.

Dr. Strauss on the other hand might be called a genius, although I feel that his areas of knowledge are too limited. He was educated in the tradition of narrow specialization; the broader aspects of background were neglected far more than necessary — even for a neurosurgeon.

I was shocked to learn that the only ancient languages he could read were Latin, Greek, and Hebrew, and that he knows almost nothing of mathematics beyond the elementary levels of the calculus of variations. When he admitted this to me, I found myself almost annoyed. It was as if he'd hidden this part of himself in order to deceive me, pretending — as do many people I've discovered — to be what he is not. No one I've ever known is what he appears to be on the surface.

Dr. Nemur appears to be uncomfortable around me. Sometimes when I try to talk to him, he just looks at me strangely and turns away. I was angry at first when Dr. Strauss told me I was giving Dr. Nemur an inferiority complex. I thought he was mocking me and I'm oversensitive at being made fun of.

How was I to know that a highly respected psychoexperimentalist like Nemur was unacquainted with Hindustani and Chinese? It's absurd when you consider the work that is being done in India and China today in the very field of his study.

I asked Dr. Strauss how Nemur could refute Rahajamati's attack on his method and results if Nemur couldn't even read it in the first place. That strange look on Dr. Strauss's face can mean only one of two things. Either he doesn't want to tell Nemur what they're saying in India, or else — and this worries me — Dr. Strauss doesn't know either. I must be careful to speak and write clearly and simply so that people won't laugh.

May 18 I am very disturbed. I saw Miss Kinnian last night for the first time in over a week. I tried to avoid all discussions of intellectual concepts and to keep the conversation on a simple, everyday level, but she just stared at me blankly and asked me what I meant about the mathematical variance equivalent in Dobermann's Fifth Concerto.

When I tried to explain she stopped me and laughed. I guess I got angry, but I suspect I'm approaching her on the wrong level. No matter what I try to discuss with her, I am unable to communicate. I must review Vrostadt's equations on *Levels of Semantic Progression*. I find that I don't communicate with people much any more. Thank God for books and music and things I can think about. I am alone in my apartment at Mrs. Flynn's boardinghouse most of the time and seldom speak to anyone.

May 20 I would not have noticed the new dishwasher, a boy of about sixteen, at the corner diner where I take my evening meals if not for the incident of the broken dishes.

They crashed to the floor, shattering and sending bits of white china under the tables. The boy stood there, dazed and frightened, holding the empty tray in his hand. The whistles and catcalls from the customers (the cries of "Hey, there go the profits!" . . . "Mazel tov!"[6] . . . and "Well, *he* didn't work here very long. . . ." which invariably seem to follow the breaking of glass or dishware in a public restaurant) all seemed to confuse him.

When the owner came to see what the excitement was about, the boy cowered as if he expected to be struck and threw up his arms as if to ward off the blow.

"All right! All right, you dope," shouted the owner, "don't just stand there! Get the broom

6. *Mazel tov!* (mä′zəl tôf): Hebrew for "Congratulations!"

and sweep that mess up. A broom . . . a broom, you idiot! It's in the kitchen. Sweep up all the pieces.''

The boy saw that he was not going to be punished. His frightened expression disappeared and he smiled and hummed as he came back with the broom to sweep the floor. A few of the rowdier customers kept up the remarks, amusing themselves at his expense.

"Here, sonny, over here there's a nice piece behind you. . . .''

"C'mon, do it again. . . .''

"He's not so dumb. It's easier to break 'em than to wash 'em. . . .''

As his vacant eyes moved across the crowd of amused onlookers, he slowly mirrored their smiles and finally broke into an uncertain grin at the joke which he obviously did not understand.

I felt sick inside as I looked at his dull, vacuous smile, the wide, bright eyes of a child, uncertain but eager to please. They were laughing at him because he was mentally retarded.

And I had been laughing at him too.

Suddenly, I was furious at myself and all those who were smirking at him. I jumped up and shouted, "Shut up! Leave him alone! It's not his fault he can't understand! He can't help what he is! But . . . he's still a human being!''

The room grew silent. I cursed myself for losing control and creating a scene. I tried not to look at the boy as I paid my check and walked out without touching my food. I felt ashamed for both of us.

How strange it is that people of honest feelings and sensibility, who would not take advantage of a man born without arms or legs or eyes—how such people think nothing of abusing a man born with low intelligence. It infuriated me to think that not too long ago, I, like this boy, had foolishly played the clown.

And I had almost forgotten.

I'd hidden the picture of the old Charlie Gordon from myself because now that I was intelligent it was something that had to be pushed out of my mind. But today in looking at that boy, for the first time I saw what I had been. *I was just like him!*

Only a short time ago, I learned that people laughed at me. Now I can see that unknowingly I joined with them in laughing at myself. That hurts most of all.

I have often reread my progress reports and seen the illiteracy, the childish naiveté, the mind of low intelligence peering from a dark room, through the keyhole, at the dazzling light outside. I see that even in my dullness I knew that I was inferior, and that other people had something I lacked—something denied me. In my mental blindness, I thought that it was somehow connected with the ability to read and write, and I was sure that if I could get those skills I would automatically have intelligence too.

Even a feebleminded man wants to be like other men.

A child may not know how to feed itself, or what to eat, yet it knows of hunger.

This then is what I was like; I never knew. Even with my gift of intellectual awareness, I never really knew.

This day was good for me. Seeing the past more clearly, I have decided to use my knowledge and skills to work in the field of increasing human intelligence levels. Who is better equipped for this work? Who else has lived in both worlds? These are my people. Let me use my gift to do something for them.

Tomorrow, I will discuss with Dr. Strauss the manner in which I can work in this area. I may be able to help him work out the problems of widespread use of the technique which was used on me. I have several good ideas of my own.

There is so much that might be done with this technique. If I could be made into a genius, what about thousands of others like myself? What fantastic levels might be achieved by using this technique on normal people? On *geniuses?*

There are so many doors to open. I am impatient to begin.

PROGRESS REPORT 12

May 23 It happened today. Algernon bit me. I visited the lab to see him as I do occasionally, and when I took him out of his cage, he snapped at my hand. I put him back and watched him for a while. He was unusually disturbed and vicious.

May 24 Burt, who is in charge of the experimental animals, tells me that Algernon is changing. He is less cooperative; he refuses to run the maze any more; general motivation has decreased. And he hasn't been eating. Everyone is upset about what this may mean.

May 25 They've been feeding Algernon, who now refuses to work the shifting-lock problem. Everyone identifies me with Algernon. In a way we're both the first of our kind. They're all pretending that Algernon's behavior is not necessarily significant for me. But it's hard to hide the fact that some of the other animals who were used in the experiment are showing strange behavior.

Dr. Strauss and Dr. Nemur have asked me not to come to the lab any more. I know what they're thinking but I can't accept it. I am going ahead with my plans to carry their research forward. With all due respect to both of these fine scientists, I am well aware of their limitations. If there is an answer, I'll have to find it out for myself. Suddenly, time has become very important to me.

May 29 I have been given a lab of my own and permission to go ahead with the research. I'm on to something. Working day and night. I've had a cot moved into the lab. Most of my writing time is spent on the notes which I keep in a separate folder, but from time to time I feel it necessary to put down my moods and my thoughts out of sheer habit.

I find the *calculus of intelligence* to be a fascinating study. Here is the place for the application of all the knowledge I have acquired. In a sense it's the problem I've been concerned with all my life.

May 31 Dr. Strauss thinks I'm working too hard. Dr. Nemur says I'm trying to cram a lifetime of research and thought into a few weeks. I know I should rest, but I'm driven on by something inside that won't let me stop. I've got to find the reason for the sharp regression in Algernon. I've got to know *if* and *when* it will happen to me.

June 4
LETTER TO DR. STRAUSS (*copy*)

Dear Dr. Strauss:

Under separate cover I am sending you a copy of my report entitled "The Algernon-Gordon Effect: A Study of Structure and Function of Increased Intelligence," which I would like to have you read and have published.

As you see, my experiments are completed. I have included in my report all of my formulae, as well as mathematical analysis in the appendix. Of course, these should be verified.

Because of its importance to both you and Dr. Nemur (and need I say to myself, too?) I have checked and rechecked my results a dozen times in the hope of finding an error.

I am sorry to say the results must stand. Yet for the sake of science, I am grateful for the little bit that I here add to the knowledge of the function of the human mind and of the laws governing the artificial increase of human intelligence.

I recall your once saying to me that an experimental *failure* or the *disproving* of a theory was as important to the advancement of learning as a success would be. I know now that this is true. I am sorry, however, that my own contribution to the field must rest upon the ashes of the work of two men I regard so highly.

Yours truly,
Charles Gordon

June 5 I must not become emotional. The facts and the results of my experiments are clear, and the more sensational aspects of my own rapid climb cannot obscure the fact that the tripling of intelligence by the surgical technique developed by Drs. Strauss and Nemur must be viewed as having little or no practical applicability (at the present time) to the increase of human intelligence.

As I review the records and data on Algernon, I see that although he is still in his physical infancy, he has regressed mentally. Motor activity[7] is impaired; there is a general reduction of glandular activity; there is an accelerated loss of coordination.

There are also strong indications of progressive amnesia.

As will be seen by my report, these and other physical and mental deterioration syndromes can be predicted with statistically significant results by the application of my formula.

---

7. **Motor activity:** movement.

The surgical stimulus to which we were both subjected has resulted in an intensification and acceleration of all mental processes. The unforeseen development, which I have taken the liberty of calling the "Algernon-Gordon Effect," is the logical extension of the entire intelligence speedup. The hypothesis here proven may be described simply in the following terms: Artificially increased intelligence deteriorates at a rate of time directly proportional to the quantity of the increase.

I feel that this, in itself, is an important discovery.

As long as I am able to write, I will continue to record my thoughts in these progress reports. It is one of my few pleasures. However, by all indications, my own mental deterioration will be very rapid.

I have already begun to notice signs of emotional instability and forgetfulness, the first symptoms of the burnout.

June 10 Deterioration progressing. I have become absent-minded. Algernon died two days ago. Dissection shows my predictions were right. His brain had decreased in weight and there was a general smoothing out of cerebral convolutions[8] as well as a deepening and broadening of brain fissures.[9]

I guess the same thing is or will soon be happening to me. Now that's it's definite, I don't want it to happen.

I put Algernon's body in a cheese box and buried him in the backyard. I cried.

June 15 Dr. Strauss came to see me again. I wouldn't open the door and I told him to go away. I want to be left to myself. I have become touchy and irritable. I feel the darkness closing in. It's hard to throw off thoughts of suicide. I keep telling myself how important this introspective journal will be.

It's a strange sensation to pick up a book that you've read and enjoyed just a few months ago and discover that you don't remember it. I remembered how great I thought John Milton was, but when I picked up *Paradise Lost* I couldn't understand it at all. I got so angry I threw the book across the room.

I've got to try to hold on to some of it. Some of the things I've learned. Oh, God, please don't take it all away.

June 19 Sometimes, at night, I go out for a walk. Last night I couldn't remember where I lived. A policeman took me home. I have the strange feeling that this has all happened to me before—a long time ago. I keep telling myself I'm the only person in the world who can describe what's happening to me.

June 21 Why can't I remember? I've got to fight. I lie in bed for days and I don't know who or where I am. Then it all comes back to me in a flash. Fugues of amnesia.[10] Symptoms of senility—second childhood. I can watch them coming on. It's so cruelly logical. I learned so much and so fast. Now my mind is deteriorating rapidly. I won't let it happen. I'll fight it. I can't help thinking of the boy in the restaurant, the blank expression, the silly smile, the people laughing at him. No—please —not that again . . .

June 22 I'm forgetting things that I learned recently. It seems to be following the classic

---

8. **cerebral** (sə-rē'brəl) **convolutions** (kŏn'və-loo'shənz): irregular folds in the cerebrum, the part of the brain where thinking takes place.
9. **fissures** (fĭsh'ərz): deep cracks or grooves.

10. **Fugues** (fyoōgz) **of amnesia** (ăm-nē'zhə): periods of time in which a person behaves normally but later has no memory of what has happened.

pattern — the last things learned are the first things forgotten. Or is that the pattern? I'd better look it up again. . . .

I reread my paper on the "Algernon-Gordon Effect" and I get the strange feeling that it was written by someone else. There are parts I don't even understand.

Motor activity impaired. I keep tripping over things, and it becomes increasingly difficult to type.

June 23 I've given up using the typewriter completely. My coordination is bad. I feel that I'm moving slower and slower. Had a terrible shock today. I picked up a copy of an article I used in my research, Krueger's "Über psychische Ganzheit," to see if it would help me understand what I had done. First I thought there was something wrong with my eyes. Then I realized I could no longer read German. I tested myself in other languages. All gone.

June 30 A week since I dared to write again. It's slipping away like sand through my fingers. Most of the books I have are too hard for me now. I get angry with them because I know that I read and understood them just a few weeks ago.

I keep telling myself I must keep writing these reports so that somebody will know what is happening to me. But it gets harder to form the words and remember spellings. I have to look up even simple words in the dictionary now and it makes me impatient with myself.

Dr. Strauss comes around almost every day, but I told him I wouldn't see or speak to anybody. He feels guilty. They all do. But I don't blame anyone. I knew what might happen. But how it hurts.

July 7 I don't know where the week went.

Todays Sunday I know becuase I can see through my window people going to church. I think I stayed in bed all week but I remember Mrs. Flynn bringing food to me a few times. I keep saying over and over I've got to do something but then I forget or maybe its just easier not to do what I say Im going to do.

I think of my mother and father a lot these days. I found a picture of them with me taken at a beach. My father has a big ball under his arm and my mother is holding me by the hand. I dont remember them the way they are in the picture. All I remember is my father arguing with mom about money. He never shaved much and he used to scratch my face when he hugged me. He said he was going to take me to see cows on a farm once but he never did. He never kept his promises . . .

July 10 My landlady Mrs Flynn is very worried about me. She said she doesnt like loafers. If Im sick its one thing, but if Im a loafer thats another thing and she wont have it. I told her I think Im sick.

I try to read a little bit every day, mostly stories, but sometimes I have to read the same thing over and over again because I dont know what it means. And its hard to write. I know I should look up all the words in the dictionary but its so hard and Im so tired all the time.

Then I got the idea that I would only use the easy words instead of the long hard ones. That saves time. I put flowers on Algernons grave about once a week. Mrs Flynn thinks Im crazy to put flowers on a mouses grave but I told her that Algernon was special.

July 14 Its sunday again. I dont have anything to do to keep me busy now because my television set is broke and I dont have any money to get it fixed. (I think I lost this months check from the lab. I don't remember)

I get awful headaches and asperin doesnt

help me much. Mrs Flynn knows Im really sick and she feels very sorry for me. Shes a wonderful woman whenever someone is sick.

July 22 Mrs Flynn called a strange doctor to see me. She was afraid I was going to die. I told the doctor I wasnt too sick and that I only forget sometimes. He asked me did I have any friends or relatives and I said no I dont have any. I told him I had a friend called Algernon once but he was a mouse and we used to run races together. He looked at me kind of funny like he thought I was crazy.

He smiled when I told him I used to be a genius. He talked to me like I was a baby and he winked at Mrs Flynn. I got mad and chased him out because he was making fun of me the way they all used to.

July 24 I have no money and Mrs Flynn says I got to go to work somewhere and pay the rent because I havent paid for over two months. I dont know any work but the job I used to have at Donnegans Plastic Box Company. I dont want to go back there because they all knew me when I was smart and maybe theyll laugh at me. But I dont know what else to do to get money.

July 25 I was looking at some of my old progress reports and its very funny but I cant read what I wrote. I can make out some of the words but they dont make sense.

Miss Kinnian came to the door but I said go away I dont want to see you. She cried and I cried too but I wouldnt let her in because I didnt want her to laugh at me. I told her I didn't like her any more. I told her I didnt want to be smart any more. Thats not true. I still love her and I still want to be smart but I had to say that so shed go away. She gave Mrs Flynn money to pay the rent. I dont want that. I got to get a job.

Please . . . please let me not forget how to read and write . . .

July 27 Mr Donnegan was very nice when I came back and asked him for my old job of janitor. First he was very suspicious but I told him what happened to me then he looked very sad and put his hand on my shoulder and said Charlie Gordon you got guts.

Everybody looked at me when I came downstairs and started working in the toilet sweeping it out like I used to. I told myself Charlie if they make fun of you dont get sore because you remember their not so smart as you once thot they were. And besides they were once your friends and if they laughed at you that doesnt mean anything because they liked you too.

One of the new men who came to work there after I went away made a nasty crack he said hey Charlie I hear your a very smart fella a real quiz kid. Say something intelligent. I felt bad but Joe Carp came over and grabbed him by the shirt and said leave him alone or Ill break your neck. I didnt expect Joe to take my part so I guess hes really my friend.

Later Frank Reilly came over and said Charlie if anybody bothers you or trys to take advantage you call me or Joe and we will set em straight. I said thanks Frank and I got choked up so I had to turn around and go into the supply room so he wouldnt see me cry. Its good to have friends.

July 28 I did a dumb thing today I forgot I wasnt in Miss Kinnians class at the adult center any more like I use to be. I went in and sat down in my old seat in the back of the room and she looked at me funny and she said Charles. I dint remember she ever called me that before only Charlie so I said hello Miss Kinnian Im redy for my lesin today only I lost my reader that we was using. She startid to cry and run out of the room and everybody looked at me and I saw they wasnt the same pepul who used to be in my class.

Then all of a suddin I rememberd some things about the operashun and me getting smart and I said holy smoke I reely pulled a Charlie Gordon that time. I went away before she come back to the room.

Thats why Im going away from New York for good. I dont want to do nothing like that agen. I dont want Miss Kinnian to feel sorry for me. Evry body feels sorry at the factery and I dont want that eather so Im going someplace where nobody knows that Charlie Gordon was once a genus and now he cant even reed a book or rite good.

Im taking a cuple of books along and even if I cant reed them Ill practise hard and maybe I wont forget every thing I lerned. If I try reel hard maybe Ill be a littel bit smarter then I was before the operashun. I got my rabits foot and my luky penny and maybe they will help me.

If you ever reed this Miss Kinnian dont be sorry for me Im glad I got a second chanse to be smart becaus I lerned a lot of things that I never even new were in this world and Im grateful that I saw it all for a littel bit. I dont know why Im dumb agen or what I did wrong maybe its becaus I dint try hard enuff. But if I try and practis very hard maybe Ill get a littl smarter and know what all the words are. I remember a littel bit how nice I had a feeling with the blue book that has the torn cover when I red it. Thats why Im gonna keep trying to get smart so I can have that feeling agen. Its a good feeling to know things and be smart. I wish I had it rite now if I did I would sit down and reed all the time. Anyway I bet Im the first dumb person in the world who ever found out somthing importent for sience. I remember I did somthing but I dont remember what. So I gess its like I did it for all the dumb pepul like me.

Good-by Miss Kinnian and Dr Strauss and evreybody. And P.S. please tell Dr Nemur not to be such a grouch when pepul laff at him and he woud have more frends. Its easy to make frends if you let pepul laff at you. Im going to have lots of frends where I go. P.P.S. Please if you get a chanse put some flowrs on Algernons grave in the bak yard . . .

SEEKING MEANING

1. "Flowers for Algernon" is a story about a young man who undergoes a remarkable transformation, or change, through surgery. According to the Progress Report dated March 8, what are the doctors planning to do with their daring techniques?

2. What evidence in the entries of March 10 through April 18 shows Charlie's increase in intelligence?

3. In the entry of April 20, Charlie's feelings change. What happens to make him feel ashamed?

4. As Charlie becomes *more* intelligent, how do his relations with other people change? How do the doctors, Miss Kinnian, and the people at the factory treat him when he *loses* his intelligence?

5. Charlie feels shame again in the entry of May 20. What does Charlie learn about himself in the scene with the dishwasher? What resolution does he make at the end of this entry?

6. The entry of May 23 opens with the dramatic words: "It happened today." What happened, and why does Charlie see such significance in it?

7. In his P.S., Charlie says, "Its easy to make frends if you let pepul laff at you. Im going to have a lot of frends where I go." Why is this statement sad?

8. In the entry of April 30, one of Charlie's co-workers, Fanny, says that it was evil when Eve listened to the snake and ate from the tree of knowledge. Why do you think she reminds Charlie of the temptation of Adam and Eve? How does Charlie, like Adam and Eve, have to pay a terrible price for his decision?

9. What is going to happen to Charlie? How do you know?

10. Why is Algernon so important to Charlie?

11. If Charlie had understood what would happen to him, do you think he would still have chosen to be intelligent, or to be limited mentally, as he is at the beginning and the end of this story? What evidence from his own reports can you find to support your answer?

DEVELOPING SKILLS IN READING

Understanding Point of View

"Flowers for Algernon" is written from the point of view of Charlie Gordon, the narrator. You learn about the characters and events in the story only through what Charlie writes in his reports. A story told by one of its characters is written in the *first-person point of view*. (The first-person pronoun is *I,* and it is an *I* who tells the story.)

The first-person point of view enables you to learn the narrator's thoughts and feelings, but it limits your understanding of other characters. First-person narrators can report only conversations and events they are aware of. Charlie's limited understanding of the people around him is clear at the beginning of his story. For example, what is really happening to Miss Kinnian in this entry of April 15?

> I said all my frends are smart people but there good. They like me and they never did anything that wasnt nice. Then she got something in her eye and she had to run out to the ladys room.

A writer may choose any of the characters in the story to be the narrator. Why do you think Daniel Keyes made Charlie Gordon the narrator, instead of Miss Kinnian or one of the doctors? Why do you think he chose to write the story in the form of personal reports, which are like diary entries?

DEVELOPING SKILLS IN LANGUAGE

Identifying Levels of Usage

As Charlie Gordon's intelligence changes, his use of language also changes. Notice the dramatic contrast in the following sentences.

> I dint see nuthing in the ink but he said there was picturs there other pepul saw some picturs.

> I am sorry, however, that my own contribution to the field must rest upon the ashes of the work of two men I regard so highly.

What mistakes can you find in the first sentence? This type of language, or level of usage, is called *nonstandard English* because it does not follow the generally accepted rules of English usage and English spelling.

The second sentence is an example of *standard English,* the level of usage most widely accepted by English-speaking people. When Charlie Gordon begins to write in standard English, what do you realize is happening to him mentally?

Charlie's command of vocabulary also changes in this story. His intelligence is probably at its peak on June 4 and 5. How do the reports written on these two days show that he has acquired an extensive scientific vocabulary? Contrast these reports with the one written on March 8.

Despite the different levels of usage in his Progress Reports, Charlie Gordon retains the same human feelings. Did your own feelings for Charlie change after his writing improved? Why or why not?

DEVELOPING SKILLS OF EXPRESSION

Writing from a Different Point of View
Choose an incident from this story, and retell it from the point of view of a character other than Charlie Gordon. Have your new narrator write a diary entry telling what happened, what was said, and how he or she felt about the incident. You may choose any episode in the story. Here are some suggestions:

April 20. Joe Carp gets Charlie to dance with Ellen. (Use Ellen as the narrator.)

April 28. Miss Kinnian and Charlie have dinner together and talk about how Charlie has changed. (Use Miss Kinnian as the narrator.)

May 15. Dr. Nemur is uncomfortable around Charlie. (Use Dr. Nemur as the narrator.)

July 27. Joe Carp comes to Charlie's rescue when a new man makes a nasty crack about Charlie's former intelligence. (Use Joe Carp as the narrator.)

ABOUT THE AUTHOR

Daniel Keyes (1927–   ) was born in New York City, and graduated from Brooklyn College. He has worked as a merchant seaman, a fiction editor, a photographer, and an English teacher. His story "Flowers for Algernon" won the Hugo Award given by the Science Fiction Writers of America in 1959, and it has been translated into many languages. Keyes expanded the story into a novel, which won the Nebula Award for science fiction in 1966. The story was also successful as a television play called *The Two Worlds of Charlie Gordon*, and as a movie called *Charly*.

Practice in Reading and Writing

STORIES

Stories do not need to be lengthy. This action story, told to writer Claude Brown by one of his teachers, takes only a single paragraph.

There were two frogs sitting on a milk vat one time. The frogs fell into the milk vat. It was very deep. They kept swimming and swimming around, and they couldn't get out. They couldn't climb out because they were too far down. One frog said, "Oh, I can't make it, and I'm going to give up." And the other frog kept swimming and swimming. His arms became more and more tired, and it was harder and harder and harder for him to swim. Then he couldn't do another stroke. He couldn't throw one more arm into the milk. He kept trying and trying; it seemed as if the milk was getting hard and heavy. He kept trying; he knew that he was going to die, but as long as he had that little bit of life in him, he was going to keep on swimming. On his last stroke, it seemed as though he had to pull a whole ocean back, but he did it and found himself sitting on a vat of butter.

Reading Stories

There are four questions you can ask yourself about almost any story ever written or told:

1. *Who are the characters and what do they want?*

These two frogs want something very much. What is it?

2. *What is the conflict in the story?*

Why can't the frogs get what they want?

3. *What happens?*

In other words, what is the story's *plot*?

What does each frog finally do to solve his conflict?

4. *What does the story mean?*

Does the story express a *theme*, or an idea about life and people? Clearly, this little story about the swimming frogs has a point to it. In a sentence or two, explain the meaning you find in this story.

Writing Stories

Professional novelists and short-story writers usually tell young writers to write about what they know best. Many writers' first stories are about their own childhoods or about characters or events they know from their own towns.

Here are some points to keep in mind as you write a story:

1. *Think about the characters in your story.*
   Who will the main characters be? What will they want?
2. *What will the conflict be?*
   What will your characters have to struggle against in order to get what they want?

3. *Outline the main events that will make up your plot.*
   What event will open your story? What will happen in the middle? Will the characters get what they want at the end?

Perhaps you can get an idea for a story from one of the following situations. Your story can be based on a true event, or it can be something that takes place only in your imagination.

A child's first experience with a bully
A dream that became a nightmare (or vice versa)
How a young person discovered adult responsibility
How a person did something that seemed impossible

For Further Reading

Buck, Pearl S., *Fourteen Stories* (John Day, 1961; paperback, Pocket Books)

 The winner of the Nobel Prize for literature tells moving stories about people in peace and at war in China, Japan, and America.

Daly, Maureen, editor, *My Favorite Suspense Stories* (Dodd, Mead, 1968)

 These eighteen exciting stories will keep you wondering what happens next.

Doyle, Sir Arthur Conan, *Adventures of Sherlock Holmes* (Harper & Row, 1930; paperback, many editions)

 Here are a dozen stories of Sherlock Holmes's most famous cases of crime.

Du Maurier, Daphne, *Don't Look Now* (Doubleday, 1971; paperback, Avon)

 A famous writer's tales about strange and supernatural events.

Henry, O., *The Gift of the Magi and Five Other Stories* (Franklin Watts, 1967)

 These stories with surprise endings include "The Ransom of Red Chief," about two kidnappers who are tormented by a ten-year-old boy.

Manley, Seon, editor, *Ladies of Horror* (Lothrop, Lee & Shepard, 1971)

 Among the thirteen horror stories in this book are Daphne Du Maurier's "The Birds" and Shirley Jackson's "The Lovely House."

Norton, Andre, editor, *Gate to Tomorrow: An Introduction to Science Fiction* (Atheneum, 1973)

 These twelve short stories are about alien invasion, robots, spaceships, and time travel.

Poe, Edgar Allan, *Tales of Terror and Fantasy* (Dutton, 1972)

 Ten of Poe's most suspenseful stories are included in this anthology.

Schaefer, Jack, *The Plainsman* (Houghton Mifflin, 1963)

 This anthology of humorous Western stories includes one about how Cooter James cured his nervousness.

Schulman, L. M., editor, *Winners and Losers: An Anthology of Great Sports Fiction* (Macmillan, 1968)

 Here are twelve action narratives about sports by such writers as Ring Lardner, Jack London, Ernest Hemingway, and William Faulkner.

Sohn, David A., editor, *Ten Top Stories* (paperback, Bantam, 1964)

 Students selected these stories as their favorites. All of them are about young adults.

Stolz, Mary, *The Beautiful Friend and Other Stories* (Harper & Row, 1960)

 In these stories, young people face turning points in their lives and make important decisions.

Sutcliff, Rosemary, *Heather, Oak, and Olive* (Dutton, 1972)

 Prehistoric times are relived in three tales by a skillful storyteller.

Wells, H. G., *The Complete Short Stories of H. G. Wells* (St. Martin's, 1971)

 Included in this collection are strange, fantastic, and humorous stories, such as "The Door in the Wall" and "The Country of the Blind."

DRAMA

The word *drama* comes from a Greek word meaning "to do" or "to act." A drama is a story that is "acted" out, as if it were real life. If you have ever seen a live play, you know that the theater darkens, and that when the curtain rises, only the stage area is lit. This means that you are supposed to forget where you are sitting and think of the stage as a new world.

When you read a play, of course, you must let your imagination go to work. You must picture the stage in your mind. You must imagine how the actors and actresses speak their lines. If your imagination is allowed to do its job, this will be no problem. You will find that the story will easily come "alive" in your own mind.

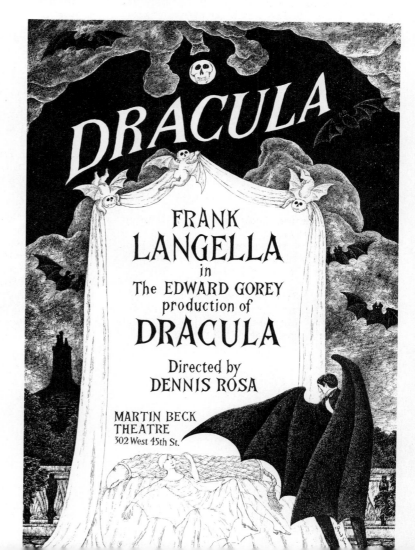

DRACULA

FRANK
LANGELLA
in
The EDWARD GOREY
production of
DRACULA

Directed by
DENNIS ROSA

MARTIN BECK
THEATRE
302 West 45th St.

The Hitchhiker *is a radio play. It is meant to be read
aloud before microphones and accompanied by sound
effects that create a particular mood. The mood of this
play is one of terror and panic, as the narrator gradually
comes to realize the horrible truth about the hitchhiker.*

As you read The Hitchhiker, *you must use your
imagination even more than if you were hearing the play
broadcast over the radio. Pay close attention to the
directions printed in italics. They describe the sounds you
must try to hear. They will also help you picture what the
characters are doing.*

The Hitchhiker   Lucille Fletcher

Characters

Ronald Adams
His Mother
The Gray Man
A Mechanic
Henry
Henry's Wife
A Girl
A Telephone Operator
A Long-Distance Operator
An Albuquerque Operator
A New York Operator
Mrs. Whitney

The time of the play is the early 1940's.

[Sound: *Automobile wheels humming over concrete road.* Music: *Something weird and shuddery.*]

Adams. I am in an auto camp on Route Sixty-six just west of Gallup, New Mexico. If I tell it, perhaps it will help me. It will keep me from going mad. But I must tell this quickly. I am not mad now. I feel perfectly well, except that I am running a slight temperature. My name is Ronald Adams. I am thirty-six years of age, unmarried, tall, dark, with a black mustache. I drive a 1940 Ford V-8, license number 6V-7989. I was born in Brooklyn. All this I know. I know that I am at this moment perfectly sane. That it is not I who have gone mad—but something else—something utterly beyond my control. But I must speak quickly. At any moment the link with life may break. This may be the last thing I ever tell on earth . . . the last night I ever see the stars. . . .

[Music: *In.*]

Adams. Six days ago I left Brooklyn, to drive to California. . . .
Mother. Goodbye, Son. Good luck to you, my boy. . . .
Adams. Goodbye, Mother. Here—give me a kiss, and then I'll go. . . .
Mother. I'll come out with you to the car.
Adams. No. It's raining. Stay here at the door. Hey—what is this? Tears? I thought you promised me you wouldn't cry.
Mother. I know, dear. I'm sorry. But I—do hate to see you go.
Adams. I'll be back. I'll only be on the Coast three months.
Mother. Oh, it isn't that. It's just—the trip. Ronald—I wish you weren't driving.
Adams. Oh—Mother. There you go again. People do it every day.
Mother. I know. But you'll be careful, won't you? Promise me you'll be extra careful. Don't fall asleep—or drive fast—or pick up any strangers on the road. . . .
Adams. Lord, no. You'd think I was still seventeen to hear you talk—
Mother. And wire me as soon as you get to Hollywood, won't you, Son?
Adams. Of course I will. Now don't you worry. There isn't anything going to happen. It's just eight days of perfectly simple driving on smooth, decent, civilized roads, with a hot dog or a hamburger stand every ten miles. . . . *(Fade)*

[Sound: *Auto hum.* Music: *In.*]

Adams. I was in excellent spirits. The drive ahead of me, even the loneliness, seemed like a lark. But I reckoned without *him.*

[Music: *Changes to something weird and empty.*]

Adams. Crossing Brooklyn Bridge that morning in the rain, I saw a man leaning against the cables. He seemed to be waiting for a lift. There were spots of fresh rain on his shoulders. He was carrying a cheap overnight bag in one hand. He was thin, nondescript, with a cap pulled down over his eyes. He stepped off the walk and if I hadn't swerved, I'd have hit him.

[Sound: *Terrific skidding.* Music: *In.*]

Adams. I would have forgotten him completely, except that just an hour later, while crossing the Pulaski Skyway over the Jersey flats, I saw him again. At least, he looked like the same person. He was standing now, with one thumb pointing west. I couldn't figure out how he'd got there, but I thought probably one of those fast trucks had picked him up, beaten me to the Skyway, and let him off. I didn't stop for him. Then—late that night, I saw him again.

[Music: *Changing.*]

Adams. It was on the new Pennsylvania Turnpike between Harrisburg and Pittsburgh. It's two hundred and sixty-five miles long, with a very high speed limit. I was just slowing down for one of the tunnels—when I saw him—standing under an arc light by the side of the road. I could see him quite distinctly. The bag, the cap, even the spots of fresh rain spattered over his shoulders. He hailed me this time. . . .

Voice (*very spooky and faint*). Hall-ooo. . . . (*Echo as through tunnel*) Hall-ooo . . . !

Adams. I stepped on the gas like a shot. That's lonely country through the Alleghenies, and I had no intention of stopping. Besides, the coincidence, or whatever it was, gave me the willies. I stopped at the next gas station.

[Sound: *Auto tires screeching to stop . . . horn honk.*]

Mechanic. Yes, sir.
Adams. Fill her up.
Mechanic. Certainly, sir. Check your oil, sir?
Adams. No, thanks.

[Sound: *Gas being put into car . . . bell tinkle, etc.*]

Mechanic. Nice night, isn't it?
Adams. Yes. It—hasn't been raining here recently, has it?
Mechanic. Not a drop of rain all week.
Adams. Hm. I suppose that hasn't done your business any harm.
Mechanic. Oh—people drive through here all kinds of weather. Mostly business, you know. There aren't many pleasure cars out on the Turnpike this season of the year.
Adams. I suppose not. (*Casually*) What about hitchhikers?
Mechanic (*half laughing*). Hitchhikers *here*?
Adams. What's the matter? Don't you ever see any?
Mechanic. Not much. If we did, it'd be a sight for sore eyes.
Adams. Why?
Mechanic: A guy'd be a fool who started out to hitch rides on this road. Look at it. It's two hundred and sixty-five miles long, there's practically no speed limit, and it's a straightaway. Now what car is going to stop to pick up a guy under those conditions? Would you stop?
Adams. No. (*Slowly, with puzzled emphasis*) Then you've never seen anybody?
Mechanic. Nope. Mebbe they get the lift before the Turnpike starts—I mean, you know—just before the tollhouse—but then it'd be a mighty long ride. Most cars wouldn't want to pick up a guy for that long a ride. And you

know—this is pretty lonesome country here—mountains, and woods. . . . You ain't seen anybody like that, have you?

Adams. No. (*Quickly*) Oh no, not at all. It was—just a—technical question.

Mechanic. I see. Well—that'll be just a dollar forty-nine—with the tax. . . . (*Fade*)

[Sound: *Auto hum up. Music: Changing.*]

Adams. The thing gradually passed from my mind, as sheer coincidence. I had a good night's sleep in Pittsburgh. I did not think about the man all next day—until just outside Zanesville, Ohio, I saw him again.

[Music: *Dark, ominous note.*]

Adams. It was a bright sunshiny afternoon. The peaceful Ohio fields, brown with the autumn stubble, lay dreaming in the golden light. I was driving slowly, drinking it in, when the road suddenly ended in a detour. In front of the barrier, *he* was standing.

[Music: *In.*]

Adams. Let me explain about his appearance before I go on. I repeat. There was nothing sinister about him. He was as drab as a mud fence. Nor was his attitude menacing. He merely stood there, waiting, almost drooping a little, the cheap, overnight bag in his hand. He looked as though he had been waiting there for hours. Then he looked up. He hailed me. He started to walk forward.

Voice (*far-off*). Hall-ooo . . . Hall-ooo. . . .

Adams. I had stopped the car, of course, for the detour. And for a few moments, I couldn't seem to find the new road. I knew he must be thinking that I had stopped for him.

Voice (*closer*). Hall-ooo . . . Hallll . . . ooo . . . .

[Sound: *Gears jamming . . . sound of motor turning over hard . . . nervous accelerator.*]

Voice (*closer*). Halll . . . . oooo. . . . .

Adams (*panicky*). No. Not just now. Sorry. . . .

Voice (*closer*) Going to California?

[Sound: *Starter starting . . . gears jamming.*]

Adams (*as though sweating blood*). No. Not today. The other way. Going to New York. Sorry . . . sorry. . . .

[Sound: *Car starts with squeal of wheels on dirt . . . into auto hum. Music: In.*]

Adams. After I got the car back onto the road again, I felt like a fool. Yet the thought of picking him up, of having him sit beside me, was somehow unbearable. Yet, at the same time, I felt, more than ever, unspeakably alone.

[Sound: *Auto hum up.*]

Adams. Hour after hour went by. The fields, the towns ticked off, one by one. The lights changed. I knew now that I was going to see him again. And though I dreaded the sight, I caught myself searching the side of the road, waiting for him to appear.

[Sound: *Auto hum up . . . car screeches to a halt . . . impatient honk two or three times . . . door being unbolted.*]

Sleepy Man's Voice. Yep? What is it? What do you want?

Adams (*breathless*). You sell sandwiches and pop here, don't you?

Voice (*cranky*). Yep. We do. In the daytime. But we're closed up now for the night.

The Hitchhiker 273

Adams. I know. But—I was wondering if you could possibly let me have a cup of coffee—black coffee.

Voice. Not at this time of night, mister. My wife's the cook and she's in bed. Mebbe further down the road—at the Honeysuckle Rest. . . .

[Sound: *Door squeaking on hinges as though being closed.*]

Adams. No-no. Don't shut the door. (*Shakily*) Listen—just a minute ago, there was a man standing here—right beside this stand—a suspicious-looking man. . . .

Woman's Voice (*from distance*). Hen-ry? Who is it, Hen-ry?

Henry. It's nobuddy, Mother. Just a feller thinks he wants a cup of coffee. Go back to bed.

Adams. I don't mean to disturb you. But you see, I was driving along—when I just happened to look—and there he was. . . .

Henry. What was he doing?

Adams. Nothing. He ran off—when I stopped the car.

Henry. Then what of it? That's nothing to wake a man in the middle of his sleep about. (*Sternly*) Young man, I've got a good mind to turn you over to the sheriff.

Adams. But—I——

Henry. You've been taking a nip, that's what you've been doing. And you haven't got anything better to do than to wake decent folk out of their hard-earned sleep. Get going. Go on.

Adams. But—he looked as though he were going to rob you.

Henry. I ain't got nothin' in this stand to lose. Now—on your way before I call out Sheriff Oakes. (*Fade*)

[Sound: *Auto hum up.*]

Adams. I got into the car again, and drove on slowly. I was beginning to hate the car. If I could have found a place to stop . . . to rest a little. But I was in the Ozark Mountains of Missouri now. The few resort places there were closed. Only an occasional log cabin, seemingly deserted, broke the monotony of the wild wooded landscape. I *had* seen him at that roadside stand: I knew I would see him again—perhaps at the next turn of the road. I knew that when I saw him next, I would run him down. . . .

[Sound: *Auto hum up.*]

Adams. But I did not see him again until late next afternoon. . . .

[Sound: *Of railroad warning signal at crossroads.*]

Adams. I had stopped the car at a sleepy little junction just across the border into Oklahoma—to let a train pass by—when he appeared, across the tracks, leaning against a telephone pole.

[Sound: *Distant sound of train chugging . . . bell ringing steadily.*]

Adams (*very tense*). It was a perfectly airless, dry day. The red clay of Oklahoma was baking under the southwestern sun. Yet there were spots of fresh rain on his shoulders. I couldn't stand that. Without thinking, blindly, I started the car across the tracks.

[Sound: *Train chugging closer.*]

Adams. He didn't even look up at me. He was staring at the ground. I stepped on the gas hard, veering the wheel sharply toward him. I could hear the train in the distance now, but I

didn't care. Then something went wrong with the car. It stalled right on the tracks.

[Sound: *Train chugging closer. Above this, sound of car stalling.*]

Adams. The train was coming closer. I could hear its bell ringing, and the cry of its whistle. Still he stood there. And now—I knew that he was beckoning—beckoning me to my death.

[Sound: *Train chugging close. Whistle blows wildly. Then train rushes up and by with pistons going, etc.*]

Adams. Well—I frustrated him that time. The starter had worked at last. I managed to back up. But when the train passed, he was gone. I was all alone in the hot, dry afternoon.

[Sound: *Train retreating. Crickets begin to sing. Music: In.*]

Adams. After that, I knew I had to do something. I didn't know who this man was or what he wanted of me. I only knew that from now on, I must not let myself be alone on the road for one moment.

[Sound: *Auto hum up. Slow down. Stop. Door opening.*]

Adams. Hello, there. Like a ride?
Girl. What do you think? How far you going?
Adams. Amarillo . . . I'll take you to Amarillo.
Girl. Amarillo, Texas?
Adams. I'll drive you there.
Girl. Gee!

[Sound: *Door closed—car starts.* Music: *In.*]

Girl. Mind if I take off my shoes? My dogs are killing me.

Adams. Go right ahead.

Girl. Gee, what a break this is. A swell car, a decent guy, and driving all the way to Amarillo. All I been getting so far is trucks.

Adams. Hitchhike much?

Girl. Sure. Only it's tough sometimes, in these great open spaces, to get the breaks.

Adams. I should think it would be. Though I'll bet if you get a good pickup in a fast car, you can get to places faster than—say, another person, in another car.

Girl. I don't get you.

Adams. Well, take me, for instance. Suppose I'm driving across the country, say, at a nice steady clip of about forty-five miles an hour. Couldn't a girl like you, just standing beside the road, waiting for lifts, beat me to town after town—provided she got picked up every time in a car doing from sixty-five to seventy miles an hour?

Girl. I dunno. Maybe she could and maybe she couldn't. What difference does it make?

Adams. Oh—no difference. It's just a—crazy idea I had sitting here in the car.

Girl (*laughing*). Imagine spending your time in a swell car thinking of things like that!

Adams. What would you do instead?

Girl (*admiringly*). What would I do? If I was a good-looking fellow like yourself? Why—I'd just *enjoy* myself—every minute of the time. I'd sit back, and relax, and if I saw a good-looking girl along the side of the road . . . (*Sharply*) Hey! Look out!

Adams (*breathlessly*). Did you see him too?

Girl. See who?

Adams. That man. Standing beside the barbed-wire fence.

Girl. I didn't see—anybody. There wasn't nothing but a bunch of steers—and the barbed-wire fence. What did you think you was doing? Trying to run into the barbed-wire fence?

Adams. There was a man there, I tell you . . . a thin, gray man, with an overnight bag in his hand. And I was trying to—run him down.

Girl. Run him down? You mean—kill him?

Adams. He's a sort of—phantom. I'm trying to get rid of him—or else prove that he's real. But (*desperately*) you say you didn't see him back there? You're sure?

Girl (*queerly*). I didn't see a soul. And as far as that's concerned, mister . . .

Adams. Watch for him the next time, then. Keep watching. Keep your eyes peeled on the road. He'll turn up again—maybe any minute now. (*Excitedly*) There. Look there—

[Sound: *Auto sharply veering and skidding.* Girl *screams.* Sound: *Crash of car going into barbed-wire fence Frightened lowing of steer.*]

Girl. How does this door work? I—I'm gettin' outta here.

Adams. Did you see him that time?

Girl (*sharply*). No. I didn't see him that time. And personally, mister, I don't expect never to see him. All I want to do is to go on living— and I don't see how I will very long driving with you—

Adams. I'm sorry. I—I don't know what came over me. (*Frightened*) Please—don't go. . . .

Girl. So if you'll excuse me, mister—

Adams. You can't go. Listen, how would you like to go to California? I'll drive you to California.

Girl. Seeing pink elephants all the way? No thanks.

Adams (*desperately*). I could get you a job there. You wouldn't have to be a waitress. I have friends there—my name is Ronald Adams—You can check up.

[Sound: *Door opening.*]

Girl. Uhn-hunh. Thanks just the same.

Adams. Listen. Please. For just one minute. Maybe you think I am half cracked. But this man. You see, I've been seeing this man all the way across the country. He's been following me. And if you could only help me—stay with me—until I reach the Coast——

Girl. You know what I think you need, big boy? Not a girl friend. Just a good dose of sleep. . . . There, I got it now.

[Sound: *Door opens . . . slams.*]

Adams. No. You can't go.

Girl (*screams*). Leave your hands offa me, do you hear! Leave your——

Adams. Come back here, please, come back.

[Sound: *Struggle . . . slap . . . footsteps running away on gravel . . . lowing of steer.*]

Adams. She ran from me, as though I were a monster. A few minutes later, I saw a passing truck pick her up. I knew then that I was utterly alone.

[Sound: *Lowing of steer up.*]

Adams. I was in the heart of the great Texas prairies. There wasn't a car on the road after the truck went by. I tried to figure out what to do, how to get hold of myself. If I could find a place to rest. Or even, if I could sleep right here in the car for a few hours, along the side of the road. . . . I was getting my winter overcoat out of the back seat to use as a blanket (*Hall-ooo*) when I saw him coming toward me (*Hall-ooo*), emerging from the herd of moving steers. . . .

Voice. Hall-ooo . . . Hall-ooo. . . .

[Sound: *Auto starting violently . . . up to steady hum.* Music: *In.*]

Adams. I didn't wait for him to come any closer. Perhaps I should have spoken to him then, fought it out then and there. For now he began to be everywhere. Whenever I stopped, even for a moment—for gas, or oil, for a drink of pop, a cup of coffee, a sandwich—he was there.

[Music: *Faster.*]

Adams. I saw him standing outside the auto camp in Amarillo that night, when I dared to slow down. He was sitting near the drinking fountain in a little camping spot just inside the border of New Mexico.

[Music: *Faster.*]

Adams. He was waiting for me outside the Navajo reservation, where I stopped to check my tires. I saw him in Albuquerque, where I bought twelve gallons of gas. . . . I was afraid now, afraid to stop. I began to drive faster and faster. I was in lunar landscape now—the great arid mesa country of New Mexico. I drove through it with the indifference of a fly crawling over the face of the moon.

[Music: *Faster.*]

Adams. But now he didn't even wait for me to stop. Unless I drove at eighty-five miles an hour over those endless roads—he waited for me at every other mile. I would see his figure, shadowless, flitting before me, still in its same attitude, over the cold and lifeless ground, flitting over dried-up rivers, over broken stones cast up by old glacial upheavals, flitting in the pure and cloudless air. . . .

[Music: *Strikes sinister note of finality.*]

Adams. I was beside myself when I finally reached Gallup, New Mexico, this morning. There is an auto camp here—cold, almost deserted at this time of year. I went inside, and asked if there was a telephone. I had the feeling that if only I could speak to someone familiar, someone that I loved, I could pull myself together.

[Sound: *Nickel put in slot.*]

Operator. Number, please?
Adams. Long distance.
Operator. Thank you.

[Sound: *Return of nickel; buzz.*]

Long Distance. This is long distance.
Adams. I'd like to put in a call to my home in Brooklyn, New York. I'm Ronald Adams. The number is Beechwood 2-0828.
Long Distance. Thank you. What is your number?

Adams. 312.

Albuquerque Operator. Albuquerque.

Long Distance. New York for Gallup. *(Pause)*

New York Operator. New York.

Long Distance. Gallup, New Mexico, calling Beechwood 2-0828. *(Fade)*

Adams. I had read somewhere that love could banish demons. It was the middle of the morning. I knew Mother would be home. I pictured her, tall, white-haired, in her crisp housedress, going about her tasks. It would be enough, I thought, merely to hear the even calmness of her voice. . . .

Long Distance. Will you please deposit three dollars and eighty-five cents for the first three minutes? When you have deposited a dollar and a half, will you wait until I have collected the money?

[Sound: *Clunk of six coins.*]

Long Distance. All right, deposit another dollar and a half.

[Sound: *Clunk of six coins.*]

Long Distance. Will you please deposit the remaining eighty-five cents?

[Sound: *Clunk of four coins.*]

Long Distance. Ready with Brooklyn—go ahead, please.

Adams. Hello.

Mrs. Whitney. Mrs. Adams' residence.

Adams. Hello. Hello—Mother?

Mrs. Whitney *(very flat and rather proper).* This is Mrs. Adams' residence. Who is it you wished to speak to, please?

Adams. Why—who's this?

Mrs. Whitney. This is Mrs. Whitney.

Adams. Mrs. Whitney? I don't know any Mrs. Whitney. Is this Beechwood 2-0828?

Mrs. Whitney. Yes.

Adams. Where's my mother? Where's Mrs. Adams?

Mrs. Whitney. Mrs. Adams is not at home. She is still in the hospital.

Adams. The hospital!

Mrs. Whitney. Yes. Who is this calling, please? Is it a member of the family?

Adams. What's she in the hospital for?

Mrs. Whitney. She's been prostrated[1] for five days. Nervous breakdown. But who is this calling?

Adams. Nervous breakdown? But—my mother was never nervous.

Mrs. Whitney. It's all taken place since the death of her oldest son, Ronald.

Adams. Death of her oldest son, Ronald . . . ? Hey—what is this? What number is this?

Mrs. Whitney. This is Beechwood 2-0828. It's all been very sudden. He was killed just six days ago in an automobile accident on the Brooklyn Bridge.

Operator *(breaking in).* Your three minutes are up, sir. *(Pause)* Your three minutes are up, sir. *(Pause)* Your three minutes are up, sir. *(Fade)* Sir, your three minutes are up. Your three minutes are up, sir.

Adams *(in a strange voice).* And so, I am sitting here in this deserted auto camp in Gallup, New Mexico. I am trying to think. I am trying to get hold of myself. Otherwise, I shall go mad. . . . Outside it is night—the vast, soulless night of New Mexico. A million stars are in the sky. Ahead of me stretch a thousand miles of empty mesa, mountains, prairies—desert. Somewhere among them, he is waiting for me. Somewhere I shall know who he is, and who . . . I . . . am. . . .

[Music: *Up.*]

---

1. **prostrated:** overcome by exhaustion or grief; weak and helpless.

SEEKING MEANING

1. Like all good thrillers, this play keeps you in suspense until the very end. Only then do you know why Adams, the main character, is so disturbed in his opening speech. What does Adams tell you in this speech? Which details in the speech made you want to read on?

2. After the opening speech, the play flashes back to the beginning of Adams' trip, six days earlier. What does Adams say happened to him on the Brooklyn Bridge? How do the music directions give a clue that something is strange about the gray man?

3. Adams sees the gray man again on the Pennsylvania Turnpike. The man still has fresh raindrops on his shoulders. What does the mechanic on the Pennsylvania Turnpike tell Adams about the weather that adds to the mystery about the gray man?

4. Adams nearly has an accident when he tries to run down the gray man at the railroad junction in Oklahoma. What does he believe the gray man is trying to do to him?

5. Why does Adams give a ride to the girl going to Texas? How does he discover that only he can see the gray man?

6. Why does Adams make the telephone call to Brooklyn? What do you discover really happened on the Brooklyn Bridge? Did you expect to hear this news?

7. In a way, this play doesn't end at all. Instead, Adams and the reader are kept in suspense. What do you think Adams will do after the end of the play? Who or what do you think the gray man represents?

DEVELOPING SKILLS IN READING

Reading a Radio Play

Adams' drive across the country would be difficult to portray realistically on a stage. But a radio play is not tied down by a stage or scenery. *The Hitchhiker* opens on Route 66 in New Mexico. Where else does it take place?

Sound effects help the radio audience imagine the different settings. Car sounds are important in this play. Notice the sound effects that help you picture the scene at the gas station on the Pennsylvania Turnpike: "*Auto tires screeching,*" "*horn honk,*" "*Gas being put into the car,*" "*bell tinkle,*" "*auto hum.*" What sound effects help you picture the scene at Henry's store?

The dialogue of a radio play also helps you picture characters and settings. You have an idea of what the mysterious gray man looks like because Adams describes him in detail. Look at Adams' speech on page 277, beginning "He was waiting for me outside the Navajo reservation . . . ." What details in this speech, and in the one following it, help you imagine the strange setting of this last scene?

DEVELOPING SKILLS OF EXPRESSION

Re-creating Sound Effects

Some of the tricks used to re-create sounds on radio are now famous. Does the writer call for the sound of bacon frying? Cellophane is crumpled slowly in front of the microphone. Is thunder needed? A sheet of metal is rippled in front of the mike.

The sound effects in *The Hitchhiker* are important in creating mood, suspense, and realism. If you were in charge of the sound effects for this radio thriller, you would have to decide exactly how to reproduce each sound.

List the different sound effects you would need for this play, including the different kinds of music. Explain how you would produce each sound. For example, the echoing voice of the gray man might be produced by speaking into a metal wastebasket.

Nothing in this comical fairy-tale kingdom is quite the way we expect it to be. The King is not very kingly. The Queen is very bossy. The Princess is not beautiful, and the Prince can't swim. But one thing in this play works just the way we expect it to. That one thing is love, and that's what this comedy is really all about.

The Ugly Duckling

A. A. Milne

Characters

The King
The Queen
The Princess Camilla
The Chancellor
Dulcibella
Prince Simon
Carlo
A Voice

Scene: *The Throne Room of the palace, a room of many doors, or, if preferred, curtain openings, simply furnished with three thrones for Their Majesties and Her Royal Highness the Princess Camilla—in other words, with three handsome chairs. At each side is a long seat, reserved, as it might be, for His Majesty's Council (if any), but useful, as today, for other purposes.*

The King is asleep on his throne, with a handkerchief over his face. He is a king of any country from any storybook, in whatever costume you please. But he should be wearing his crown.

A Voice (*announcing*). His Excellency, the Chancellor!

[*The* Chancellor, *an elderly man in horn-rimmed spectacles, enters bowing. The* King *wakes up with a start and removes the handkerchief from his face.*]

King (*with simple dignity*). I was thinking.
Chancellor (*bowing*). Never, Your Majesty, was greater need for thought than now.
King. That's what I was thinking. (*He struggles into a more dignified position.*) Well, what is it? More trouble?
Chancellor. What we might call the old trouble, Your Majesty.
King. It's what I was saying last night to the Queen. "Uneasy lies the head that wears a crown,"[1] was how I put it.
Chancellor. A profound and original thought, which may well go down to posterity.
King. You mean it may go down well with posterity. I hope so. Remind me to tell you some time of another little thing I said to Her Majesty: something about a fierce light beating on a throne.[2] Posterity would like that, too. Well, what is it?
Chancellor. It is in the matter of Her Royal Highness' wedding.
King. Oh . . . yes.
Chancellor. As Your Majesty is aware, the young Prince Simon arrives today to seek Her Royal Highness' hand in marriage. He has been traveling in distant lands and, as I understand, has not—er—has not——
King. You mean he hasn't heard anything.

Chancellor. It is a little difficult to put this tactfully, Your Majesty.
King. Do your best, and I will tell you afterwards how you got on.
Chancellor. Let me put it this way. The Prince Simon will naturally assume that Her Royal Highness has the customary—so customary as to be, in my own poor opinion, slightly monotonous—has what one might call the inevitable—so inevitable as to be, in my opinion again, almost mechanical—will assume, that she has the, as *I* think of it, faultily faultless, icily regular, splendidly——
King. What you are trying to say in the fewest words possible is that my daughter is not beautiful.
Chancellor. Her beauty is certainly elusive, Your Majesty.
King. It is. It has eluded you, it has eluded me, it has eluded everybody who has seen her. It even eluded the Court Painter. His last words were, "Well, I did my best." His successor is now painting the view across the water meadows from the West Turret. He says that his doctor has advised him to keep to landscape.
Chancellor. It is unfortunate, Your Majesty, but there it is. One just cannot understand how it could have occurred.
King. You don't think she takes after *me*, at all? You don't detect a likeness?
Chancellor. Most certainly not, Your majesty.
King. Good. . . . Your predecessor did.
Chancellor. I have often wondered what happened to my predecessor.
King. Well, now you know.

[*There is a short silence.*]

Chancellor. Looking at the bright side, although Her Royal Highness is not, strictly speaking, beautiful——

---

1. **"Uneasy . . . crown":** This line is a quotation from *Henry IV, Part II* by William Shakespeare. Throughout the play, the King quotes from famous poets and claims to have made up the lines himself. He probably really thinks he has.
2. **a fierce . . . throne:** These words are an approximate quotation from *Idylls of the King* by Alfred, Lord Tennyson.

King. Not, truthfully speaking, beautiful —

Chancellor. Yet she has great beauty of character.

King. My dear Chancellor, we are not considering her Royal Highness' character, but her chances of getting married. You observe that there is a distinction.

Chancellor. Yes, Your Majesty.

King. Look at it from the suitor's point of view. If a girl is beautiful, it is easy to assume that she has, tucked away inside her, an equally beautiful character. But it is impossible to assume that an unattractive girl, however elevated in character, has, tucked away inside her, an equally beautiful face. That is, so to speak, not where you want it—tucked away.

Chancellor. Quite so, Your Majesty.

King. This doesn't, of course, alter the fact that the Princess Camilla is quite the nicest person in the kingdom.

Chancellor (enthusiastically). She is indeed, Your Majesty. (Hurriedly) With the exception, I need hardly say, of Your Majesty—and Her Majesty.

King. Your exceptions are tolerated for their loyalty and condemned for their extreme fatuity.[3]

Chancellor. Thank you, Your Majesty.

King. As an adjective for your King, the word *nice* is ill-chosen. As an adjective for Her Majesty, it is—ill-chosen.

[*At which moment the* Queen *comes in. The* King *rises. The* Chancellor *puts himself at right angles.*]

Queen (briskly). Ah. Talking about Camilla? (She sits down.)

King (returning to his throne). As always, my dear, you are right.

---

3. **fatuity** (fə-tōō'ə-tē): stupidity.

Queen (to the Chancellor). This fellow, Simon—what's he like?

Chancellor. Nobody has seen him, Your Majesty.

Queen. How old is he?

Chancellor. Five-and-twenty, I understand.

Queen. In twenty-five years he must have been seen by somebody.

King (to the Chancellor). Just a fleeting glimpse?

Chancellor. I meant, Your Majesty, that no detailed report of him has reached this country, save that he has the usual personal advantages and qualities expected of a prince and has been traveling in distant and dangerous lands.

Queen. Ah! Nothing gone wrong with his eyes? Sunstroke or anything?

Chancellor. Not that I am aware of, Your Majesty. At the same time, as I was venturing to say to His Majesty, Her Royal Highness' character and disposition are so outstandingly —

Queen. Stuff and nonsense. You remember what happened when we had the Tournament of Love last year.

Chancellor. I was not myself present, Your Majesty. I had not then the honor of—I was abroad, and never heard the full story.

Queen. No, it was the other fool. They all rode up to Camilla to pay their homage—it was the first time they had seen her. The heralds blew their trumpets and announced that she would marry whichever prince was left master of the field when all but one had been unhorsed. The trumpets were blown again, they charged enthusiastically into the fight, and — (The King *looks nonchalantly at the ceiling and whistles a few bars.*) Don't do that.

King. I'm sorry, my dear.

Queen (to the Chancellor). And what happened? They all simultaneously fell off their

horses and assumed the posture of defeat.

King. One of them was not quite so quick as the others. I was very quick. I proclaimed him the victor.

Queen. At the Feast of Betrothal held that night —

King. We were all very quick.

Queen. — the Chancellor announced that by the laws of the country the successful suitor had to pass a further test. He had to give the correct answer to a riddle.

Chancellor. Such undoubtedly is the fact, Your Majesty.

King. There are times for announcing facts, and times for looking at things in a broad-minded way. Please remember that, Chancellor.

Chancellor. Yes, Your Majesty.

Queen. I invented the riddle myself. Quite an easy one. What is it that has four legs and barks like a dog? The answer is, "A dog."

King (to the Chancellor). You see that?

Chancellor. Yes, Your Majesty.

King. It isn't difficult.

Queen. He, however, seemed to find it so. He said an eagle. Then he said a serpent; a very high mountain with slippery sides; two peacocks; a moonlight night; the day after tomorrow —

King. Nobody could accuse him of not trying.

Queen. *I* did.

King. I *should* have said that nobody could fail to recognize in his attitude an appearance of doggedness.

Queen. Finally he said death. I nudged the King —

King. Accepting the word *nudge* for the moment, I rubbed my ankle with one hand, clapped him on the shoulder with the other, and congratulated him on the correct answer. He disappeared under the table, and, personally, I never saw him again.

Queen. His body was found in the moat next morning.

Chancellor. But what was he doing in the moat, Your Majesty?

King. Bobbing about. Try not to ask needless questions.

Chancellor. It all seems so strange.

Queen. What does?

Chancellor. That Her Royal Highness, alone of all the princesses one has ever heard of, should lack that invariable attribute of royalty, supreme beauty.

Queen *(to the* King*).* That was your Great-Aunt Malkin. She came to the christening. You know what she said.

King. It was cryptic.[4] Great-Aunt Malkin's besetting weakness. She came to *my* christening—she was one hundred and one then, and that was fifty-one years ago. *(To the* Chancellor*)* How old would that make her?

Chancellor. One hundred and fifty-two, your Majesty.

King *(after thought).* About that, yes. She promised me that when I grew up I should have all the happiness which my wife deserved. It struck me at the time—well, when I say "at the time," I was only a week old—but it did strike me as soon as anything could strike me—I mean of that nature—well, work it out for yourself, Chancellor. It opens up a most interesting field of speculation. Though naturally I have not liked to go into it at all deeply with Her Majesty.

Queen. I never heard anything less cryptic. She was wishing you extreme happiness.

King. I don't think she was *wishing* me anything. However.

Chancellor *(to the* Queen*).* But what, Your Majesty, did she wish Her Royal Highness?

Queen. Her other godmother—on my side—had promised her the dazzling beauty for which all the women in my family are famous.

[*She pauses, and the* King *snaps his fingers surreptitiously[5] in the direction of the* Chancellor.]

Chancellor *(hurriedly).* Indeed, yes, Your Majesty.

[*The* King *relaxes.*]

Queen. And Great-Aunt Malkin said—— *(To the* King*)* What were the words?

King. I give you with this kiss
A wedding-day surprise.
Where ignorance is bliss
'Tis folly to be wise.[6]

I thought the last two lines rather neat. But what it *meant*——

Queen. We can all see what it meant. She was given beauty—and where is it? Great-Aunt Malkin took it away from her. The wedding-day surprise is that there will never be a wedding day.

King. Young men being what they are, my dear, it would be much more surprising if there *were* a wedding day. So how——

[*The* Princess *comes in. She is young, happy, healthy, but not beautiful. Or let us say that by some trick of makeup or arrangement of hair she seems plain to us, unlike the princesses of the storybooks.*]

Princess *(to the* King*).* Hallo, darling! *(Seeing the others)* Oh, I say! Affairs of state? Sorry.

---

4. **cryptic** (krĭp′tĭk): puzzling.

5. **surreptitiously** (sûr′əp-tĭsh′əs-lē): secretly.
6. **Where . . . wise:** These lines come from a poem called "A Distant Prospect of Eton College" by Thomas Gray.

King *(holding out his hand).* Don't go, Camilla.

[*She takes his hand.*]

Chancellor. Shall I withdraw, Your Majesty?

Queen. You are aware, Camilla, that Prince Simon arrives today?

Princess. He has arrived. They're just letting down the drawbridge.

King *(jumping up).* Arrived! I must——

Princess. Darling, you know what the drawbridge is like. It takes at *least* half an hour to let it down.

King *(sitting down).* It wants oil. *(To the* Chancellor*)* Have *you* been grudging it oil?

Princess. It wants a new drawbridge, darling.

Chancellor. Have I Your Majesty's permission——

King. Yes, yes.

[*The* Chancellor *bows and goes out.*]

Queen. You've told him, of course? It's the only chance.

King. Er—no. I was just going to, when——

Queen. Then I'd better. *(She goes to the door.)* You can explain to the girl; I'll have her sent to you. You've told Camilla?

King. Er—no. I was just going to, when——

Queen. Then you'd better tell her now.

King. My dear, are you sure——

Queen. It's the only chance left. *(Dramatically, to heaven)* My daughter! *(She goes out. There is a little silence when she is gone.)*

King. Camilla, I want to talk seriously to you about marriage.

Princess. Yes, Father.

King. It is time that you learned some of the facts of life.

Princess. Yes, Father.

King. Now the great fact about marriage is that once you're married you live happy ever after. All our history books affirm this.

Princess. And your own experience too, darling.

King *(with dignity).* Let us confine ourselves to history for the moment.

Princess. Yes, Father.

King. Of course, there *may* be an exception here and there, which, as it were, proves the rule; just as—oh, well, never mind.

Princess *(smiling).* Go on, darling. You were going to say that an exception here and there proves the rule that all princesses are beautiful.

King. Well—leave that for the moment. The point is that it doesn't matter *how* you marry, or *who* you marry, as long as you *get* married. Because you'll be happy ever after in any case. Do you follow me so far?

Princess. Yes, Father.

King. Well, your mother and I have a little plan——

Princess. Was that it, going out of the door just now?

King. Er—yes. It concerns your waiting-maid.

Princess. Darling, I have several.

King. Only one that leaps to the eye, so to speak. The one with the—well, with everything.

Princess. Dulcibella?

King. That's the one. It is our little plan that at the first meeting she should pass herself off as the Princess—a harmless ruse,[7] of which you will find frequent record in the history books—and allure Prince Simon to his—that is to say, bring him up to the—— In other words, the wedding will take place immediately afterwards, and as quietly as possible— well, naturally in view of the fact that your Aunt Malkin is one hundred and fifty-two; and since you will be wearing the family

---

7. **ruse** (rōōz): trick.

bridal veil—which is no doubt how the custom arose—the surprise after the ceremony will be his. Are you following me at all? Your attention seems to be wandering.

Princess. I was wondering why you needed to tell me.

King. Just a precautionary measure, in case you happened to meet the Prince or his attendant before the ceremony; in which case, of course, you would pass yourself off as the maid——

Princess. A harmless ruse, of which, also, you will find frequent record in the history books.

King. Exactly. But the occasion need not arise.

A Voice *(announcing).* The woman Dulcibella!

King. Ah! *(To the* Princess*)* Now, Camilla, if you will just retire to your own apartments, I will come to you there when we are ready for the actual ceremony. *(He leads her out as he is talking, and as he returns calls out.)* Come in, my dear! *(Dulcibella comes in. She is beautiful, but dumb.)* Now don't be frightened, there is nothing to be frightened about. Has Her Majesty told you what you have to do?

Dulcibella. Y-yes, Your Majesty.

King. Well now, let's see how well you can do it. You are sitting here, we will say. *(He leads her to a seat.)* Now imagine that I am Prince Simon. *(He curls his mustache and puts his stomach in. She giggles.)* You are the beautiful Princess Camilla whom he has never seen. *(She giggles again.)* This is a serious moment in your life, and you will find that a giggle will not be helpful. *(He goes to the door.)* I am announced: "His Royal Highness Prince Simon!" That's me being announced. Remember what I said about giggling. You should have a faraway look upon the face. *(She does her best.)* Farther away than that.

(She tries again.) No, that's too far. You are sitting there, thinking beautiful thoughts—in maiden meditation, fancy-free,[8] as I remember saying to Her Majesty once—speaking of somebody else—fancy-free, but with the mouth definitely shut—that's better. I advance and fall upon one knee. *(He does so.)* You extend your hand graciously—graciously; you're not trying to push him in the face—that's better, and I raise it to my lips—so—and I kiss it *(He kisses it warmly)*—no, perhaps not so ardently as that, more like this *(He kisses it again)*, and I say, "Your Royal Highness, this is the most—er—— Your Royal Highness, I shall ever be—no—— Your Royal Highness, it is the proudest——" Well, the point is that *he* will say it, and it will be something complimentary, and then he will take your hand in both of his and press it to his heart. *(He does so.)* And then—what do *you* say?

Dulcibella. Coo!

King. No, *not* "Coo."

Dulcibella. Never had anyone do *that* to me before.

King. That also strikes the wrong note. What you want to say is, "Oh, Prince Simon!" . . . Say it.

Dulcibella *(loudly).* Oh, Prince Simon!

King. No, no. You don't need to shout until he has said "What?" two or three times. Always consider the possibility that he *isn't* deaf. Softly, and giving the words a dying fall, letting them play around his head like a flight of doves.

Dulcibella *(still a little overloud).* O-o-o-o-h, Prinsimon!

King. Keep the idea in your mind of a flight of *doves* rather than a flight of panic-stricken elephants, and you will be all right. Now I'm

---

8. **in . . . fancy-free:** The King is quoting from Shakespeare again—this time from *A Midsummer Night's Dream.*

going to get up, and you must, as it were, *waft*[9] me into a seat by your side. *(She starts wafting.) Not* rescuing a drowning man, that's another idea altogether, useful at times, but at the moment inappropriate. Wafting. Prince Simon will put the necessary muscles into play—all you require to do is indicate by a gracious movement of the hand the seat you require him to take. Now! *(He gets up, a little stiffly, and sits next to her.)* That was better. Well, here we are. Now, I think you give me a look: something, let us say, halfway between breathless adoration and regal dignity, touched, as it were, with good comradeship. Now try that. *(She gives him a vacant look of bewilderment.)* Frankly, that didn't quite get it. There was just a little something missing.

---

9. **waft** (wäft): carry gently, as if through the air.

An absence, as it were, of all the qualities I asked for, and in their place an odd resemblance to an unsatisfied fish. Let us try to get at it another way. Dulcibella, have you a young man of your own?

Dulcibella *(eagerly, seizing his hand).* Oo, yes, he's ever so smart, he's an archer, well, not as you might say a real archer, he works in the armory, but old Bottlenose, *you* know who I mean, the Captain of the Guard, says the very next man they ever has to shoot, my Eg shall take his place, knowing Father and how it is with Eg and me, and me being maid to Her Royal Highness and can't marry me till he's a real soldier, but ever so loving, and funny like, the things he says, I said to him once, "Eg," I said—

King *(getting up).* I rather fancy, Dulcibella, that if you think of Eg all the time, *say* as little as possible, and, when thinking of Eg, see that the mouth is not more than partially open, you will do very well. I will show you where you are to sit and wait for His Royal Highness. *(He leads her out. On the way he is saying)* Now remember—*waft—waft*—not *hoick*.[10]

[Prince Simon *wanders in from the back unannounced. He is a very ordinary-looking young man in rather dusty clothes. He gives a deep sigh of relief as he sinks into the throne of the* King. . . . Camilla, *a new and strangely beautiful* Camilla, *comes in.*]

Princess *(surprised)*. Well!
Prince. Oh, hallo!
Princess. Ought you?
Prince *(getting up)*. Do sit down, won't you?
Princess. Who are you, and how did you get here?
Prince. Well, that's rather a long story. Couldn't we sit down? You could sit here if you liked, but it isn't very comfortable.
Princess. That is the King's Throne.
Prince. Oh, is that what it is?
Princess. Thrones are not meant to be comfortable.
Prince. Well, I don't know if they're meant to be, but they certainly aren't.
Princess. Why were you sitting on the King's Throne, and who are you?
Prince. My name is Carlo.
Princess. Mine is Dulcibella.
Prince. Good. And now couldn't we sit down?
Princess *(sitting down on the long seat to the left of the throne, and, as it were, wafting him to a place next to her)*. You may sit here, if you like. Why are you so tired?

[*He sits down.*]

---

10. **hoick:** yank or pull abruptly.

Prince. I've been taking very strenuous exercise.
Princess. Is that part of the long story?
Prince. It is.
Princess *(settling herself)*. I love stories.
Prince. This isn't a story really. You see, I'm attendant on Prince Simon, who is visiting here.
Princess. Oh? I'm attendant on Her Royal Highness.
Prince. Then you know what he's here for.
Princess. Yes.
Prince. She's very beautiful, I hear.
Princess. Did you hear that? Where have you been lately?
Prince. Traveling in distant lands—with Prince Simon.
Princess. Ah! All the same, I don't understand. Is Prince Simon in the palace now? The drawbridge *can't* be down yet!
Prince. I don't suppose it is. *And* what a noise it makes coming down!
Princess. Isn't it terrible?
Prince. I couldn't stand it any more. I just had to get away. That's why I'm here.
Princess. But how?
Prince. Well, there's only one way, isn't there? That beech tree, and then a swing and a grab for the battlements, and don't ask me to remember it all—— *(He shudders.)*
Princess. You mean you came across the moat by that beech tree?
Prince. Yes. I got so tired of hanging about.
Princess. But it's terribly dangerous!
Prince. That's why I'm so exhausted. Nervous shock. *(He lies back and breathes loudly.)*
Princess. Of course, it's different for *me*.
Prince *(sitting up)*. Say that again. I must have got it wrong.
Princess. It's different for me, because I'm used to it. Besides, I'm so much lighter.
Prince. You don't mean that *you*—

Princess. Oh yes, often.

Prince. And I thought I was a brave man! At least, I didn't until five minutes ago, and now I don't again.

Princess. Oh, but you are! And I think it's wonderful to do it straight off the first time.

Prince. Well, *you* did.

Princess. Oh no, not the first time. When I was a child.

Prince. You mean that you crashed?

Princess. Well, you only fall into the moat.

Prince. Only! Can you *swim?*

Princess. Of course.

Prince. So you swam to the castle walls, and yelled for help, and they fished you out and walloped you. And next day you tried again. Well, if *that* isn't pluck—

Princess. Of course I didn't. I swam back, and did it at once; I mean I tried again at once. It wasn't until the third time that I actually did it. You see, I was afraid I might lose my nerve.

Prince. Afraid she might lose her nerve!

Princess. There's a way of getting over from this side, too; a tree grows out from the wall and you jump into another tree—I don't think it's quite so easy.

Prince. Not quite so easy. Good. You must show me.

Princess. Oh, I will.

Prince. Perhaps it might be as well if you taught me how to swim first. I've often heard about swimming, but never——

Princess. You can't swim?

Prince. No. Don't look so surprised. There are a lot of other things that I can't do. I'll tell you about them as soon as you have a couple of years to spare.

Princess. You can't swim and yet you crossed by the beech tree! And you're *ever* so much heavier than I am! Now who's brave?

Prince *(getting up).* You keep talking about how light you are. I must see if there's anything in it. Stand up! *(She stands obediently*

and he picks her up.) You're right, Dulcibella. I could hold you here forever. *(Looking at her)* You're very lovely. Do you know how lovely you are?

Princess. Yes. *(She laughs suddenly and happily.)*

Prince. Why do you laugh?

Princess. Aren't you tired of holding me?

Prince. Frankly, yes. I exaggerated when I said I could hold you forever. When you've been hanging by the arms for ten minutes over a very deep moat, wondering if it's too late to learn how to swim—— *(He puts her down.)* What I meant was that I should *like* to hold you forever. Why did you laugh?

Princess. Oh, well, it was a little private joke of mine.

Prince. If it comes to that, I've got a private joke too. Let's exchange them.

Princess. Mine's very private. One other woman in the whole world knows, and that's all.

Prince. Mine's just as private. One other man knows, and that's all.

Princess. What fun. I love secrets. . . . Well, here's mine. When I was born, one of my god-mothers promised that I should be very beautiful.

Prince. How right she was.

Princess. But the other one said this:

> I give you with this kiss
> A wedding-day surprise.
> Where ignorance is bliss
> 'Tis folly to be wise.

And nobody knew what it meant. And I grew up very plain. And then, when I was about ten, I met my godmother in the forest one day. It was my tenth birthday. Nobody knows this—except you.

Prince. Except us.

Princess. Except us. And she told me what her gift meant. It meant that I *was* beautiful—

but everybody else was to go on being ignorant and thinking me plain, until my wedding day. Because, she said, she didn't want me to grow up spoiled and willful and vain, as I should have done if everybody had always been saying how beautiful I was; and the best thing in the world, she said, was to be quite sure of yourself, but not to expect admiration from other people. So ever since then my mirror has told me I'm beautiful, and everybody else thinks me ugly, and I get a lot of fun out of it.

Prince. Well, seeing that Dulcibella is the result, I can only say that your godmother was very, very wise.

Princess. And now tell me *your* secret.

Prince. It isn't such a pretty one. You see, Prince Simon was going to woo Princess Camilla, and he'd heard that she was beautiful and haughty and imperious—all *you* would have been if your godmother hadn't been so wise. And being a very ordinary-looking fellow himself, he was afraid she wouldn't think much of him, so he suggested to one of his attendants, a man called Carlo, of extremely attractive appearance, that *he* should pretend to be the Prince and win the Princess' hand; and then at the last moment they would change places—

Princess. How would they do that?

Prince. The Prince was going to have been married in full armor—with his visor down.

Princess (*laughing happily*). Oh, what fun!

Prince. Neat, isn't it?

Princess (*laughing*). Oh, very . . . very . . . very.

Prince. Neat, but not so terribly *funny*. Why do you keep laughing?

Princess. Well, that's another secret.

Prince. If it comes to that, *I've* got another one up my sleeve. Shall we exchange again?

Princess. All right. You go first this time.

Prince. Very well. . . . I am not Carlo. *(Standing up and speaking dramatically)* I am Simon!—ow! *(He sits down and rubs his leg violently.)*

Princess *(alarmed).* What is it?

Prince. Cramp. *(In a mild voice, still rubbing)* I was saying that I was Prince Simon.

Princess. Shall I rub it for you? *(She rubs.)*

Prince *(still hopefully).* I am Simon.

Princess. Is that better?

Prince *(despairingly).* I am Simon.

Princess. I know.

Prince. How did you know?

Princess. Well, you told me.

Prince. But oughtn't you to swoon or something?

Princess. Why? History records many similar ruses.

Prince *(amazed).* Is that so? I've never read history. I thought I was being profoundly original.

Princess. Oh, no! Now I'll tell you *my* secret. For reasons very much like your own, the Princess Camilla, who is held to be extremely plain, feared to meet Prince Simon. Is the drawbridge down yet?

Prince. Do your people give a faint, surprised cheer every time it gets down?

Princess. Naturally.

Prince. Then it came down about three minutes ago.

Princess. Ah! Then at this very moment your man Carlo is declaring his passionate love for my maid, Dulcibella. That, I think, is funny. *(So does the* Prince. *He laughs heartily.)* Dulcibella, by the way, is in love with a man she calls Eg, so I hope Carlo isn't getting carried away.

Prince. Carlo is married to a girl he calls "the little woman," so Eg has nothing to fear.

Princess. By the way, I don't know if you heard, but I said, or as good as said, that I am the Princess Camilla.

Prince. I wasn't surprised. History, of which I read a great deal, records many similar ruses.

Princess *(laughing).* Simon!

Prince *(laughing).* Camilla! *(He stands up.)* May I try holding you again? *(She nods. He takes her in his arms and kisses her.)* Sweetheart!

Princess. You see, when you lifted me up before, you said, "You're very lovely," and my godmother said that the first person to whom I would seem lovely was the man I should marry; so I knew then that you were Simon and I should marry you.

Prince. I knew directly[11] I saw you that I should marry you, even if you were Dulcibella. By the way, which of you *am* I marrying?

Princess. When she lifts her veil, it will be Camilla. *(Voices are heard outside.)* Until then it will be Dulcibella.

Prince *(in a whisper).* Then goodbye, Camilla, until you lift your veil.

Princess. Goodbye, Simon, until you raise your visor.

[*The* King *and* Queen *come in arm-in-arm, followed by* Carlo *and* Dulcibella *also arm-in-arm. The* Chancellor *precedes them, walking backwards, at a loyal angle.*]

Prince *(supporting the* Chancellor *as an accident seems inevitable).* Careful!

[*The* Chancellor *turns indignantly round.*]

King. Who and what is this? More accurately who and what are all these?

---

11. **directly:** here, as soon as.

Carlo. My attendant, Carlo, Your Majesty. He will, with Your Majesty's permission, prepare me for the ceremony.

[*The* Prince *bows.*]

King. Of course, of course!

Queen *(to Dulcibella).* Your maid, Dulcibella, is it not, my love? *(Dulcibella nods violently.)* I thought so. *(To Carlo)* She will prepare Her Royal Highness.

[*The* Princess *curtsies.*]

King. Ah, yes. Yes. *Most* important.

Princess *(curtsying).* I beg your pardon, Your Majesty, if I've done wrong, but I found the gentleman wandering——

King *(crossing to her).* Quite right, my dear, quite right. *(He pinches her cheek and takes advantage of this kingly gesture to speak in a loud whisper.)* We've pulled it off!

[*They sit down: the* King *and* Queen *on their thrones,* Dulcibella *on the* Princess' *throne.* Carlo *stands behind* Dulcibella, *the* Chancellor *on the right of the* Queen, *and the* Prince *and* Princess *behind the long seat on the left.*]

Chancellor *(consulting documents).* H'r'm! Have I Your Majesty's authority to put the final test to His Royal Highness?

Queen *(whispering to the* King). Is this safe?

King *(whispering).* Perfectly, my dear. I told him the answer a minute ago. *(Over his shoulder, to* Carlo) Don't forget. "Dog." *(Aloud)* Proceed, Your Excellency. It is my desire that the affairs of my country should ever be conducted in a strictly constitutional manner.

Chancellor *(oratorically).* By the constitution of the country, a suitor to Her Royal Highness' hand cannot be deemed successful until he has given the correct answer to a riddle. *(Conversationally)* The last suitor answered incorrectly, and thus failed to win his bride.

King. By a coincidence he fell into the moat.

Chancellor *(to* Carlo). I have now to ask Your Royal Highness if you are prepared for the ordeal?

Carlo *(cheerfully).* Absolutely.

Chancellor. I may mention, as a matter possibly of some slight historical interest to our visitor, that by the constitution of the country, the same riddle is not allowed to be asked on two successive occasions.

King *(startled).* What's that?

Chancellor. This one, it is interesting to recall, was propounded exactly a century ago, and we must take it as a fortunate omen that it was well and truly solved.

King *(to the* Queen). I may want my sword directly.

Chancellor. The riddle is this: What is it that has four legs and mews like a cat?

Carlo *(promptly).* A dog.

King *(still more promptly).* Bravo, bravo! *(He claps loudly and nudges the* Queen, *who claps too.)*

Chancellor *(peering at his documents).* According to the records of the occasion to which I referred, the correct answer would seem to be——

Princess *(to the* Prince). Say something, quick!

Chancellor. ——not "dog," but——

Prince. Your Majesty, have I permission to speak? Naturally His Royal Highness could not think of justifying himself on such an occasion, but I think that with Your Majesty's gracious permission, I could——

King. Certainly, certainly.

Prince. In our country, we have an animal to which we have given the name "dog," or, in the local dialect of the more mountainous districts, "doggie." It sits by the fireside and purrs.

Carlo. That's right. It purrs like anything.

Prince. When it needs milk, which is its staple food, it mews.

Carlo *(enthusiastically).* Mews like nobody's business.

Prince. It also has four legs.

Carlo. One at each corner.

Prince. In some countries, I understand, this animal is called a "cat." In one distant country to which His Royal Highness and I penetrated, it was called by the very curious name of "hippopotamus."

Carlo. That's right. *(To the* Prince) Do you remember that ginger-colored hippopotamus which used to climb onto my shoulder and lick my ear?

Prince. I shall never forget it, sir. *(To the* King) So you see, Your Majesty —

King. Thank you. I think that makes it perfectly clear. *(Firmly, to the* Chancellor) You are about to agree?

Chancellor. Undoubtedly, Your Majesty. May I be the first to congratulate His Royal Highness on solving the riddle so accurately?

King. You may be the first to see that all is in order for an immediate wedding.

Chancellor. Thank you, Your Majesty.

[*He bows and withdraws. The* King *rises, as do the* Queen *and* Dulcibella.]

King *(to* Carlo). Doubtless, Prince Simon, you will wish to retire and prepare yourself for the ceremony.

Carlo. Thank you, sir.

Prince. Have I Your Majesty's permission to attend His Royal Highness? It is the custom of his country for princes of the royal blood to be married in full armor, a matter which requires a certain adjustment —

King. Of course, of course. *(Carlo bows to the* King *and* Queen *and goes out. As the* Prince *is about to follow, the* King *stops him.)* Young man, you have a quality of quickness which I admire. It is my pleasure to reward it in any way which commends itself to you.

Prince. Your Majesty is ever gracious. May I ask for my reward *after* the ceremony?

[*The* Prince *catches the eye of the* Princess, *and they give each other a secret smile.*]

King. Certainly. *(The* Prince *bows and goes out. To* Dulcibella) Now, young woman, make yourself scarce. You have done your work excellently, and we will see that you and your — What was his name?

Dulcibella. Eg, Your Majesty.

King. —that you and your Eg are not forgotten.

Dulcibella. Coo! *(She curtsies and goes out.)*

Princess *(calling).* Wait for me, Dulcibella!

King *(to the Queen).* Well, my dear, we may congratulate ourselves. As I remember saying to somebody once, "You have not lost a daughter, you have gained a son." How does he strike you?

Queen. Stupid.

King. They made a very handsome pair, I thought, he and Dulcibella.

Queen. Both stupid.

King. I said nothing about stupidity. What I *said* was that they were both extremely handsome. That is the important thing. *(Struck by a sudden idea)* Or isn't it?

Queen. What do *you* think of Prince Simon, Camilla?

Princess. I adore him. We shall be so happy together.

King. Well, of course you will. I told you so. Happy ever after.

Queen. Run along now and get ready.

Princess. Yes, Mother. *(She throws a kiss to them and goes out.)*

King *(anxiously).* My dear, have we been wrong about Camilla all this time? It seemed to me that she wasn't looking *quite* so plain as usual just now. Did *you* notice anything?

Queen *(carelessly).* Just the excitement of the marriage.

King *(relieved).* Ah, yes, that would account for it.

[*Curtain.*]

SEEKING MEANING

1. In the fairy tale "The Ugly Duckling" by Hans Christian Andersen, a young bird believes he is ugly until he grows into a beautiful swan. In this play, a young woman is believed to be very plain until love reveals her beauty. In the scene on page 291, what does the Princess say will happen on her wedding day?

2. Fairy tales are filled with characters such as a dignified king, a serene and ladylike queen, a beautiful princess, and a fearless and strong prince. But the characters in this humorous play are not at all what they would be in the usual fairy tale. What actions of the King show that he is undignified and a bit foolish? How does the Queen show she is bossy and quick-tempered? How do you learn that the Prince is not fearless and strong?

3. Fairy tales are also filled with trials and tests such as tournaments and riddles. But this comedy is filled with surprising twists. What humorous unexpected events occurred in the Tournament of Love that the King and Queen gave for Camilla?

4. Disguises are often used in comedies. These add to the fun, because the audience usually knows who is under the disguise, but the other characters don't. What disguises are part of the King and Queen's plan to trick Prince Simon? What disguises are part of the Prince's plan to trick the King and Queen?

5. The most important part of this story will take place after the play ends. What will happen then? What surprising discoveries will be made when all the disguises are removed?

6. Most comedies end with all problems solved and everyone living "happily ever after." Do you believe that Simon and Camilla will live "happily ever after"? What will happen to Dulcibella to help her and Eg live "happily ever after"?

DEVELOPING SKILLS IN READING

Recognizing the Elements of a Comedy

The Ugly Duckling is a comedy. In a comedy the characters often include some young lovers, the plot ends happily, and the theme often has something to do with love.

Comic Characters. One of the basic elements of humor is the unexpected. Characters like a king who is nagged by his queen and a prince who is timid are funny because they are different from what you expect them to be. Why is Dulcibella's attempt to act like a princess so funny? Why is it humorous to see a fairy-tale chancellor in horn-rimmed glasses?

Comic Plot. In every play, the characters face some struggle or conflict. The plot tells what they do to solve their problem. In a comedy, the characters solve the problem happily. In every play there is also a *climax,* or turning point, when we know whether the play will end happily or unhappily. The climax in this play comes when the Chancellor tests the fake "Prince" with the riddle (page 293). How does the real Prince win his bride and make the play end happily?

Comic Theme. Most comedies are about love or happiness. What does *The Ugly Duckling* say about the power of love? Look at the Princess' speech on page 291, in which she reveals her secret to the Prince. Which line sums up what this play says about happiness?

Understanding Stage Terms

The theater has its own technical terminology, just as baseball, medicine, and electronics do. If you ever stage a play, you'll have to know the vocabulary of the stage.

Almost every production of a play has people in charge of *sets, props, lighting,* and *costumes.* The *director* of the play supervises all aspects of the play's production.

Set: all the scenery and furniture used on the stage. Some plays use more than one set. Each time a play is produced, it usually has a different set. Describe (or draw) the set you would design for *The Ugly Duckling.* Would it be a reversal of what the audience expects a castle to be like, or would it be a typical fairy-tale castle?

Props: the properties, or objects that the characters need to use as they act out the play. Props may include a handkerchief, a glass of water, a sword, or a paper bag. Make a list of the props needed for this play. Start with the handkerchief.

Lighting: all the lights that are focused on the stage, including footlights and spotlights. Lighting must be planned to create the right mood for the play. What kind of lighting would you use for *The Ugly Duckling?*

Costumes: the clothes the characters wear. Each time a play is produced, the costumes may differ. If you were the costume designer for a production of *The Ugly Duckling,* you would need to tell exactly what each character would wear. Using words or drawings (or both), describe the costumes you would design for the characters in *The Ugly Duckling.* Would you have the King wear a business suit, a typical fairy-tale costume, or a humorous combination of both? (Notice that the stage direction at the opening of the play says, *"But he should be wearing his crown."*) How would you make Dulcibella's costume differ from Camilla's?

DEVELOPING SKILLS OF EXPRESSION

Presenting a Scene
Perhaps the funniest scene in this play is the one in which the King tries to teach the giggling Dulcibella to act like a princess (page 287). Dulcibella tries hard — too hard — but she is a hilarious flop as a princess. You might try presenting this scene in class.

Read the scene carefully to find out what props you will need.

Pay close attention to the stage directions in parentheses. They tell how the characters should say their lines, and what they should be doing. For example, one stage direction to the King reads:

(He curls his mustache and puts his stomach in.)

What does Dulcibella do in response to this action?

You will also get clues to actions from the speeches of the characters. For example, the King tells Dulcibella to be "thinking beautiful thoughts." Then he adds, "but with the mouth definitely shut." What is Dulcibella doing to look as if she is having beautiful thoughts?

ABOUT THE AUTHOR

A. A. Milne (1882–1956) was a British novelist and playwright whose stories of Winnie-the-Pooh and Christopher Robin (a character based on his own son) have overshadowed everything else he wrote. Milne worked for the British humor magazine *Punch.* He wrote his first play at the front lines during World War I. His plays were huge successes. Among them are *Mr. Pim Passes By* and a mystery called *The Perfect Alibi.*

The Diary of Anne Frank *is a play based upon a diary found at the end of World War II in a pile of rubbish in an old warehouse in Amsterdam. A young Jewish girl named Anne Frank had kept this diary for twenty-five months. In it, she had recorded the small details of domestic life and her own thoughts during the last years of one of the most terrible wars in history.*

To escape the Nazis, Anne Frank's family had moved from Germany to the Netherlands. But when the Nazis took over the Netherlands in 1940, they immediately began persecuting the Jews there.

In July 1942 Anne's family went into hiding in a secret apartment. Their hiding place was on the top floors of a building that Otto Frank, Anne's father, had used as his warehouse and business office. It was in these hidden rooms that Anne kept the diary that has since been translated into many languages. It was here that, in the midst of fear and suffering, she could write: "In spite of everything, I still believe that people are really good at heart."

The Diary of Anne Frank

Frances Goodrich and Albert Hackett

Characters

Mr. Frank	Peter Van Daan	Mr. Kraler [5]
Miep (mēp)	Mrs. Frank	Dussel [6]
Mrs. Van Daan	Margot Frank	
Mr. Van Daan	Anne Frank	

The Time: During the years of World War II and immediately thereafter.

The Place: Amsterdam.

There are two acts.

Act One

Scene 1

The scene remains the same throughout the play. It is the top floor of a warehouse and office building in Amsterdam, Holland. The sharply peaked roof of the building is outlined against a sea of other rooftops, stretching away into the distance. Nearby is the belfry of a church tower, the Westertoren, whose carillon rings out the hours. Occasionally faint sounds float up from below: the voices of children playing in the street, the tramp of marching feet, a boat whistle from the canal.

The three rooms of the top floor and a small attic space above are exposed to our view. The largest of the rooms is in the center, with two small rooms, slightly raised, on either side. On the right is a bathroom, out of sight. A narrow, steep flight of stairs at the back leads up to the attic. The rooms are sparsely furnished with a few chairs, cots, a table or two. The windows are painted over, or covered with makeshift blackout curtains. In the main room there is a sink, a gas ring for cooking, and a wood-burning stove for warmth.

The room on the left is hardly more than a closet. There is a skylight in the sloping ceiling. Directly under this room is a small steep stairwell, with steps leading down to a door. This is the only entrance from the building below. When the door is opened we see that it has been concealed on the outer side by a bookcase attached to it.

The curtain rises on an empty stage. It is late afternoon, November, 1945.

The rooms are dusty, the curtains in rags. Chairs and tables are overturned.

The door at the foot of the small stairwell swings open. Mr. Frank comes up the steps

into view. He is a gentle, cultured European in his middle years. There is still a trace of a German accent in his speech.

He stands looking slowly around, making a supreme effort at self-control. He is weak, ill. His clothes are threadbare.

After a second he drops his rucksack on the couch and moves slowly about. He opens the door to one of the smaller rooms and then abruptly closes it again, turning away. He goes to the window at the back, looking off at the Westertoren as its carillon strikes the hour of six; then he moves restlessly on.

From the street below we hear the sound of a barrel organ and children's voices at play. There is a many-colored scarf hanging from a nail. Mr. Frank *takes it, putting it around his neck. As he starts back for his rucksack, his eye is caught by something lying on the floor. It is a woman's white glove. He holds it in his hand and suddenly all of his self-control is gone. He breaks down, crying.*

We hear footsteps on the stairs. Miep Gies comes up, looking for Mr. Frank. Miep *is a Dutch girl of about twenty-two. She wears a coat and hat, ready to go home. She is pregnant. Her attitude toward* Mr. Frank *is protective, compassionate.*

Miep. Are you all right, Mr. Frank?

Mr. Frank *(quickly controlling himself)*. Yes, Miep, yes.

Miep. Everyone in the office has gone home. . . . It's after six. *(Then pleading)* Don't stay up here, Mr. Frank. What's the use of torturing yourself like this?

Mr. Frank. I've come to say goodbye. . . . I'm leaving here, Miep.

Miep. What do you mean? Where are you going? Where?

Mr. Frank. I don't know yet, I haven't decided.

Miep. Mr. Frank, you can't leave here! This is your home! Amsterdam is your home. Your business is here, waiting for you. . . . You're needed here. . . . Now that the war is over, there are things that . . .

Mr. Frank. I can't stay in Amsterdam, Miep. It has too many memories for me. Everywhere there's something . . . the house we lived in . . . the school . . . that street organ playing out there. . . . I'm not the person you used to know, Miep. I'm a bitter old man. *(Breaking off)* Forgive me. I shouldn't speak to you like this . . . after all that you did for us . . . the suffering . . .

Miep. No. No. It wasn't suffering. You can't say we suffered. *(As she speaks, she straightens a chair which is overturned.)*

Mr. Frank. I know what you went through, you and Mr. Kraler. I'll remember it as long as I live. *(He gives one last look around.)* Come, Miep. *(He starts for the steps, then remembers his rucksack, going back to get it.)*

Miep *(hurrying up to a cupboard)*. Mr. Frank, did you see? There are some of your papers here. *(She brings a bundle of papers to him.)* We found them in a heap of rubbish on the floor after . . . after you left.

Mr. Frank. Burn them. *(He opens his rucksack to put the glove in it.)*

Miep. But, Mr. Frank, there are letters, notes . . .

Mr. Frank. Burn them. All of them.

Miep. Burn *this?* *(She hands him a paperbound notebook.)*

Mr. Frank *(quietly)*. Anne's diary. *(He opens the diary and begins to read.)* "Monday, the sixth of July, nineteen forty-two." *(To* Miep) Nineteen forty-two. Is it possible, Miep? . . . Only three years ago. *(As he continues his reading, he sits down on the couch.)* "Dear Diary, since you and I are going to be great friends, I will start by telling you about myself. My name is Anne Frank. I am thirteen

[Mr. Frank's *voice dies out.* Anne's *voice continues alone. The lights dim slowly to darkness. The curtain falls on the scene.*]

Anne's Voice. You could not do this and you could not do that. They forced Father out of his business. We had to wear yellow stars. I had to turn in my bike. I couldn't go to a Dutch school any more. I couldn't go to the movies, or ride in an automobile, or even on a streetcar, and a million other things. But somehow we children still managed to have fun. Yesterday Father told me we were going into hiding. Where, he wouldn't say. At five o'clock this morning Mother woke me and told me to hurry and get dressed. I was to put on as many clothes as I could. It would look too suspicious if we walked along carrying suitcases. It wasn't until we were on our way that I learned where we were going. Our hiding place was to be upstairs in the building where Father used to have his business. Three other people were coming with us . . . the Van Daans and their son Peter. . . . Father knew the Van Daans but we had never met them. . . .

[*During the last lines the curtain rises on the scene. The lights dim on.* Anne's *voice fades out.*]

years old. I was born in Germany the twelfth of June, nineteen twenty-nine. As my family is Jewish, we emigrated to Holland when Hitler came to power."

[*As* Mr. Frank *reads on, another voice joins his, as if coming from the air. It is* Anne's *voice.*]

Mr. Frank and **Anne.** "My father started a business, importing spice and herbs. Things went well for us until nineteen forty. Then the war came, and the Dutch capitulation,[1] followed by the arrival of the Germans. Then things got very bad for the Jews."

---

1. **capitulation** (kə-pĭ'chŏŏ-lā'shən): surrender. The Netherlands was taken over by the Nazis in May 1940. The Dutch underground, however, was active in helping escaped Allied prisoners and Jewish refugees.

Scene 2

It is early morning, July, 1942. The rooms are bare, as before, but they are now clean and orderly.

Mr. Van Daan, *a tall, portly man in his late forties, is in the main room, pacing up and down, nervously smoking a cigarette. His clothes and overcoat are expensive and well cut.*

Mrs. Van Daan *sits on the couch, clutching her possessions—a hatbox, bags, etc. She is a pretty woman in her early forties. She wears a fur coat over her other clothes.*

Peter Van Daan *is standing at the window of the room on the right, looking down at the street below. He is a shy, awkward boy of sixteen. He wears a cap, a raincoat, and long Dutch trousers, like "plus fours."[2] At his feet is a black case, a carrier for his cat.*

The yellow Star of David[3] is conspicuous on all of their clothes.

Mrs. Van Daan *(rising, nervous, excited).* Something's happened to them! I know it!

Mr. Van Daan. Now, Kerli!

Mrs. Van Daan. Mr. Frank said they'd be here at seven o'clock. He said . . .

Mr. Van Daan. They have two miles to walk. You can't expect . . .

Mrs. Van Daan. They've been picked up. That's what's happened. They've been taken. . . .

[Mr. Van Daan *indicates that he hears someone coming.*]

Mr. Van Daan. You see?

[Peter *takes up his carrier and his schoolbag, etc., and goes into the main room as* Mr. Frank *comes up the stairwell from below.* Mr. Frank *looks much younger now. His movements are brisk, his manner confident. He wears an overcoat and carries his hat and a small cardboard box. He crosses to the* Van Daans, *shaking hands with each of them.*]

Mr. Frank. Mrs. Van Daan, Mr. Van Daan, Peter. *(Then, in explanation of their lateness)* There were too many of the Green Police[4] on the streets. . . . We had to take the long way around.

[*Up the steps come* Margot Frank, Mrs. Frank, Miep *(not pregnant now), and* Mr. Kraler. *All of them carry bags, packages, and so forth. The Star of David is conspicuous on all of the Franks' clothing. Margot is eighteen, beautiful, quiet, shy. Mrs. Frank is a young mother, gently bred, reserved. She, like Mr. Frank, has a slight German accent. Mr. Kraler is a Dutchman, dependable, kindly.*

As Mr. Kraler *and* Miep *go upstage to put down their parcels,* Mrs. Frank *turns back to call* Anne.]

Mrs. Frank. Anne?

[Anne *comes running up the stairs. She is thirteen, quick in her movements, interested in everything, mercurial[5] in her emotions. She wears a cape, long wool socks, and carries a schoolbag.*]

Mr. Frank *(introducing them).* My wife, Edith. Mr. and Mrs. Van Daan

[Mrs. Frank *hurries over, shaking hands with them.*]

. . . their son, Peter . . . my daughters, Margot and Anne.

---

2. **"plus fours"**: baggy trousers that are gathered in under the knee; also called *knickers.*
3. **Star of David**: a six-pointed star, an ancient symbol of Judaism. The Nazis required Jews to sew the Star of David onto all their clothing so that they would be immediately identifiable as Jews.
4. **Green Police:** the Nazi police, who wore green uniforms.
5. **mercurial** (mər-kyŏŏr'ē-əl): quickly changeable.

[Anne *gives a polite little curtsy as she shakes* Mr. Van Daan's *hand. Then she immediately starts off on a tour of investigation of her new home, going upstairs to the attic room.*

Miep and Mr. Kraler *are putting the various things they have brought on the shelves.*]

Mr. Kraler. I'm sorry there is still so much confusion.

Mr. Frank. Please. Don't think of it. After all, we'll have plenty of leisure to arrange everything ourselves.

Miep *(to* Mrs. Frank*)*. We put the stores of food you sent in here. Your drugs are here . . . soap, linen here.

Mrs. Frank. Thank you, Miep.

Miep. I made up the beds . . . the way Mr. Frank and Mr. Kraler said. *(She starts out.)* Forgive me. I have to hurry. I've got to go to the other side of town to get some ration books[6] for you.

Mrs. Van Daan. Ration books? If they see our names on ration books, they'll know we're here.

Mr. Kraler. There isn't anything . . .

Miep. Don't worry. Your names won't be on them. *(As she hurries out)* I'll be up later.

(Together)

Mr. Frank. Thank you, Miep.

Mrs. Frank *(to* Mr. Kraler*)*. It's illegal, then, the ration books? We've never done anything illegal.

Mr. Frank. We won't be living here exactly according to regulations.

[*As* Mr. Kraler *reassures* Mrs. Frank, *he takes various small things, such as matches, soap, etc., from his pockets, handing them to her.*]

Mr. Kraler. This isn't the black market,[7] Mrs. Frank. This is what we call the white market . . . helping all of the hundreds and hundreds who are hiding out in Amsterdam.

[*The carillon is heard playing the quarter-hour before eight.* Mr. Kraler *looks at his watch.* Anne *stops at the window as she comes down the stairs.*]

Anne. It's the Westertoren!

Mr. Kraler. I must go. I must be out of here and downstairs in the office before the workmen get here. *(He starts for the stairs leading out.)* Miep or I, or both of us, will be up each day to bring you food and news and find out what your needs are. Tomorrow I'll get you a better bolt for the door at the foot of the stairs. It needs a bolt that you can throw yourself and open only at our signal. *(To* Mr. Frank*)* Oh . . . You'll tell them about the noise?

Mr. Frank. I'll tell them.

Mr. Kraler. Goodbye then for the moment. I'll come up again, after the workmen leave.

Mr. Frank. Goodbye, Mr. Kraler.

Mrs. Frank *(shaking his hand)*. How can we thank you?

[*The others murmur their goodbyes.*]

Mr. Kraler. I never thought I'd live to see the day when a man like Mr. Frank would have to go into hiding. When you think —

---

6. **ration books:** books given to each citizen during wartime, containing a certain number of stamps for various items such as food, clothing, and gasoline. These items could not be purchased without the stamps. Ration books were used to make sure that scarce items would be rationed, or evenly distributed.

7. **black market:** an illegal system for buying and selling goods without ration stamps.

[*He breaks off, going out.* Mr. Frank *follows him down the steps, bolting the door after him. In the interval before he returns,* Peter *goes over to* Margot, *shaking hands with her. As* Mr. Frank *comes back up the steps,* Mrs. Frank *questions him anxiously.*]

Mrs. Frank. What did he mean, about the noise?

Mr. Frank. First let us take off some of these clothes.

[*They all start to take off garment after garment. On each of their coats, sweaters, blouses, suits, dresses, is another yellow Star of David.* Mr. *and* Mrs. Frank *are underdressed quite simply. The others wear several things—sweaters, extra dresses, bathrobes, aprons, nightgowns, etc.*]

Mr. Van Daan. It's a wonder we weren't arrested, walking along the streets . . . Petronella with a fur coat in July . . . and that cat of Peter's crying all the way.

Anne. A cat?

[*Finally, as they have all removed their surplus clothes, they look to* Mr. Frank, *waiting for him to speak.*]

Mr. Frank. Now. About the noise. While the men are in the building below, we must have complete quiet. Every sound can be heard down there, not only in the workrooms, but in the offices too. The men come at about eight thirty, and leave at about five thirty. So, to be perfectly safe, from eight in the morning

group.) . . . No trash must ever be thrown out which might reveal that someone is living up here . . . not even a potato paring. We must burn everything in the stove at night. This is the way we must live until it is over, if we are to survive.

[*There is silence for a second.*]

Mrs. Frank. Until it is over.

Mr. Frank *(reassuringly).* After six we can move about . . . we can talk and laugh and have our supper and read and play games . . . just as we would at home. *(He looks at his watch.)* And now I think it would be wise if we all went to our rooms, and were settled before eight o'clock. Mrs. Van Daan, you and your husband will be upstairs. I regret that there's no place up there for Peter. But he will be here, near us. This will be our common room, where we'll meet to talk and eat and read, like one family.

Mr. Van Daan. And where do you and Mrs. Frank sleep?

Mr. Frank. This room is also our bedroom.

Mrs. Van Daan. That isn't right. We'll sleep here and you take the room upstairs. } *(Together)*

Mr. Van Daan. It's your place.

Mr. Frank. Please. I've thought this out for weeks. It's the best arrangement. The only arrangement.

Mrs. Van Daan *(to Mr. Frank).* Never, never can we thank you. *(Then, to Mrs. Frank)* I don't know what would have happened to us, if it hadn't been for Mr. Frank.

Mr. Frank. You don't know how your husband helped me when I came to this country . . . knowing no one . . . not able to speak the language. I can never repay him for that. *(Going to Mr. Van Daan)* May I help you with your things?

until six in the evening we must move only when it is necessary, and then in stockinged feet. We must not speak above a whisper. We must not run any water. We cannot use the sink, or even, forgive me, the w.c.[8] The pipes go down through the workrooms. It would be heard. No trash . . . *(Mr. Frank stops abruptly as he hears the sound of marching feet from the street below. Everyone is motionless, paralyzed with fear. Mr. Frank goes quietly into the room on the right to look down out of the window. Anne runs after him, peering out with him. The tramping feet pass without stopping. The tension is relieved. Mr. Frank, followed by Anne, returns to the main room and resumes his instructions to the*

---

8. **w.c.:** water closet, or toilet.

Mr. Van Daan. No. No. (*To* Mrs. Van Daan) Come along, *liefje.*[9]

Mrs. Van Daan. You'll be all right, Peter? You're not afraid?

Peter (*embarrassed*). Please, Mother.

[*They start up the stairs to the attic room above.* Mr. Frank *turns to* Mrs. Frank.]

Mr. Frank. You too must have some rest, Edith. You didn't close your eyes last night. Nor you, Margot.

Anne. I slept, Father. Wasn't that funny? I knew it was the last night in my own bed, and yet I slept soundly.

Mr. Frank. I'm glad, Anne. Now you'll be able to help me straighten things in here. (*To* Mrs. Frank *and* Margot) Come with me. . . . You and Margot rest in this room for the time being. (*He picks up their clothes, starting for the room on the right.*)

Mrs. Frank. You're sure . . . ? I could help. . . . And Anne hasn't had her milk. . . .

Mr. Frank. I'll give it to her. (*To* Anne *and* Peter) Anne, Peter . . . it's best that you take off your shoes now, before you forget. (*He leads the way to the room, followed by* Margot.)

Mrs. Frank. You're sure you're not tired, Anne?

Anne. I feel fine. I'm going to help Father.

Mrs. Frank. Peter, I'm glad you are to be with us.

Peter. Yes, Mrs. Frank.

[Mrs. Frank *goes to join* Mr. Frank *and* Margot.

During the following scene Mr. Frank *helps* Margot *and* Mrs. Frank *to hang up their* clothes. *Then he persuades them both to lie down and rest. The Van Daans in their room above settle themselves. In the main room* Anne *and* Peter *remove their shoes.* Peter *takes his cat out of the carrier.*]

Anne. What's your cat's name?

Peter. Mouschi.

Anne. Mouschi! Mouschi! Mouschi! (*She picks up the cat, walking away with it. To* Peter) I love cats. I have one . . . a darling little cat. But they made me leave her behind. I left some food and a note for the neighbors to take care of her. . . . I'm going to miss her terribly. What is yours? A him or a her?

Peter. He's a tom. He doesn't like strangers. (*He takes the cat from her, putting it back in its carrier.*)

Anne (*unabashed*). Then I'll have to stop being a stranger, won't I? Where did you go to school?

Peter. Jewish Secondary.

Anne. But that's where Margot and I go! I never saw you around.

Peter. I used to see you . . . sometimes . . .

Anne. You did?

Peter. . . . in the schoolyard. You were always in the middle of a bunch of kids. (*He takes a penknife from his pocket.*)

Anne. Why didn't you ever come over?

Peter. I'm sort of a lone wolf. (*He starts to rip off his Star of David.*)

Anne. What are you doing?

Peter. Taking it off.

Anne. But you can't do that. They'll arrest you if you go out without your Star. (*He tosses his knife on the table.*)

Peter. Who's going out?

Anne. Why, of course! You're right! Of course we don't need them any more. (*She picks up his knife and starts to take her Star off.*) I wonder what our friends will think when we don't show up today?

---

9. *liefje* (lēf′hyə): Dutch for "little loved one."

Peter. I didn't have any dates with anyone.

Anne. Oh, I did. I had a date with Jopie to go and play ping-pong at her house. Do you know Jopie deWaal?

Peter. No.

Anne. Jopie's my best friend. I wonder what she'll think when she telephones and there's no answer? . . . Probably she'll go over to the house. . . . I wonder what she'll think . . . we left everything as if we'd suddenly been called away . . . breakfast dishes in the sink . . . beds not made. . . . *(As she pulls off her Star the cloth underneath shows clearly the color and form of the Star.)* Look! It's still there! *(Peter goes over to the stove with his Star.)* What're you going to do with yours?

Peter. Burn it.

Anne. *(She starts to throw hers in, and cannot.)* It's funny, I can't throw mine away. I don't know why.

Peter. You can't throw . . . ? Something they branded you with . . . ? That they made you wear so they could spit on you?

Anne. I know. I know. But after all, it *is* the Star of David, isn't it?

[*In the bedroom, right,* Margot *and* Mrs. Frank *are lying down.* Mr. Frank *starts quietly out.*]

Peter. Maybe it's different for a girl.

[Mr. Frank *comes into the main room.*]

Mr. Frank. Forgive me, Peter. Now let me see. We must find a bed for your cat. *(He goes to a cupboard.)* I'm glad you brought your cat. Anne was feeling so badly about hers. *(Getting a used small washtub)* Here we are. Will it be comfortable in that?

Peter *(gathering up his things).* Thanks.

Mr. Frank *(opening the door of the room on the left).* And here is your room. But I warn you, Peter, you can't grow any more. Not an inch, or you'll have to sleep with your feet out of the skylight. Are you hungry?

Peter. No.

Mr. Frank. We have some bread and butter.

Peter. No, thank you.

Mr. Frank. You can have it for luncheon then. And tonight we will have a real supper . . . our first supper together.

Peter. Thanks. Thanks. *(He goes into his room. During the following scene he arranges his possessions in his new room.)*

Mr. Frank. That's a nice boy, Peter.

Anne. He's awfully shy, isn't he?

Mr. Frank. You'll like him, I know.

Anne. I certainly hope so, since he's the only boy I'm likely to see for months and months.

[Mr. Frank *sits down, taking off his shoes.*]

Mr. Frank. Annele,[10] there's a box there. Will you open it?

[*He indicates a carton on the couch.* Anne *brings it to the center table. In the street below there is the sound of children playing*].

Anne *(as she opens the carton).* You know the way I'm going to think of it here? I'm going to think of it as a boardinghouse. A very peculiar summer boardinghouse, like the one that we — *(She breaks off as she pulls out some photographs.)* Father! My movie stars! I was wondering where they were! I was looking for them this morning . . . and Queen Wilhelmina![11] How wonderful!

---

10. **Annele** (än'ə-lə): an affectionate form of the name Anne in Yiddish.
11. **Queen Wilhelmina:** queen of the Netherlands from 1890 to 1948. She died in 1962.

Mr. Frank. There's something more. Go on. Look further. *(He goes over to the sink, pouring a glass of milk from a thermos bottle.)*
Anne *(pulling out a pasteboard-bound book).* A diary! *(She throws her arms around her father.)* I've never had a diary. And I've always longed for one. *(She looks around the room.)* Pencil, pencil, pencil, pencil. *(She starts down the stairs.)* I'm going down to the office to get a pencil.
Mr. Frank. Anne! No! *(He goes after her, catching her by the arm and pulling her back.)*
Anne *(startled).* But there's no one in the building now.
Mr. Frank. It doesn't matter. I don't want you ever to go beyond that door.
Anne *(sobered).* Never . . . ? Not even at nighttime, when everyone is gone? Or on Sundays? Can't I go down to listen to the radio?
Mr. Frank. Never, I am sorry, Anneke.[12] It isn't safe. No, you must never go beyond that door.

[For the first time Anne realizes what "going into hiding" means.]

Anne. I see.
Mr. Frank. It'll be hard, I know. But always remember this, Anneke. There are no walls, there are no bolts, no locks that anyone can put on your mind. Miep will bring us books. We will read history, poetry, mythology. *(He gives her the glass of milk.)* Here's your milk. *(With his arm about her, they go over to the couch, sitting down side by side.)* As a matter of fact, between us, Anne, being here has certain advantages for you. For instance, you remember the battle you had with your

---

12. **Anneke** (än'ə-kə): an affectionate form of the name Anne in German.

mother the other day on the subject of overshoes? You said you'd rather die than wear overshoes? But in the end you had to wear them? Well now, you see, for as long as we are here you will never have to wear overshoes! Isn't that good? And the coat that you inherited from Margot, you won't have to wear that any more. And the piano! You won't have to practice on the piano. I tell you, this is going to be a fine life for you!

[Anne's panic is gone. Peter appears in the doorway of his room, with a saucer in his hand. He is carrying his cat.]

Peter. I . . . I . . . I thought I'd better get some water for Mouschi before . . .
Mr. Frank. Of course.

[As he starts toward the sink the carillon begins to chime the hour of eight. He tiptoes to the window at the back and looks down at the street below. He turns to Peter, indicating in pantomime that it is too late. Peter starts back for his room. He steps on a creaking board. The three of them are frozen for a minute in fear. As Peter starts away again, Anne tiptoes over to him and pours some of the milk from her glass into the saucer for the cat. Peter squats on the floor, putting the milk before the cat. Mr. Frank gives Anne his fountain pen and then goes into the room at the right. For a second Anne watches the cat; then she goes over to the center table and opens her diary.

In the room at the right, Mrs. Frank has sat up quickly at the sound of the carillon. Mr. Frank comes in and sits down beside her on the settee, his arm comfortingly around her.

Upstairs, in the attic room, Mr. and Mrs. Van Daan have hung their clothes in the closet and are now seated on the iron bed. Mrs. Van Daan leans back exhausted. Mr.

Van Daan *fans her with a newspaper.*

Anne *starts to write in her diary. The lights dim out; the curtain falls.*

In the darkness Anne's *voice comes to us again, faintly at first, and then with growing strength.*]

Anne's Voice. I expect I should be describing what it feels like to go into hiding. But I really don't know yet myself. I only know it's funny never to be able to go outdoors . . . never to breathe fresh air . . . never to run and shout and jump. It's the silence in the nights that frightens me most. Every time I hear a creak in the house, or a step on the street outside, I'm sure they're coming for us. The days aren't so bad. At least we know that Miep and Mr. Kraler are down there below us in the office. Our protectors, we call them. I asked Father what would happen to them if the Nazis found out they were hiding us. Pim said that they would suffer the same fate that we would. . . . Imagine! They know this, and yet when they come up here, they're always cheerful and gay as if there were nothing in the world to bother them. . . . Friday, the twenty-first of August, nineteen forty-two. Today I'm going to tell you our general news. Mother is unbearable. She insists on treating me like a baby, which I loathe. Otherwise things are going better. The weather is . . .

[*As* Anne's *voice is fading out, the curtain rises on the scene.*]

Scene 3

end of october

It is a little after six o'clock in the evening, two months later.

Margot is in the bedroom at the right, studying. Mr. Van Daan is lying down in the attic room above.

The rest of the "family" is in the main room. Anne and Peter sit opposite each other at the center table, where they have been doing their lessons. Mrs. Frank is on the couch. Mrs. Van Daan is seated with her fur coat, on which she has been sewing, in her lap. None of them are wearing their shoes.

Their eyes are on Mr. Frank, waiting for him to give them the signal which will release them from their day-long quiet. Mr. Frank, his shoes in his hand, stands looking down out of the window at the back, watching to be sure that all of the workmen have left the building below.

After a few seconds of motionless silence, Mr. Frank turns from the window.

Mr. Frank *(quietly, to the group)*. It's safe now. The last workman has left.

[There is an immediate stir of relief.]

Anne *(Her pent-up energy explodes)*. WHEE!
Mrs. Frank *(startled, amused)*. Anne!
Mrs. Van Daan. I'm first for the w.c.

[She hurries off to the bathroom. Mrs. Frank puts on her shoes and starts up to the sink to prepare supper. Anne sneaks Peter's shoes from under the table and hides them behind her back. Mr. Frank goes into Margot's room.]

Mr. Frank *(to Margot)*. Six o'clock. School's over.

[Margot gets up, stretching. Mr. Frank sits down to put on his shoes. In the main room Peter tries to find his.]

Peter *(to Anne)*. Have you seen my shoes?
Anne *(innocently)*. Your shoes?
Peter. You've taken them, haven't you?
Anne. I don't know what you're talking about.
Peter. You're going to be sorry!
Anne. Am I?

[Peter goes after her. Anne, with his shoes in her hand, runs from him, dodging behind her mother.]

Mrs. Frank *(protesting)*. Anne, dear!
Peter. Wait till I get you!
Anne. I'm waiting! *(Peter makes a lunge for her. They both fall to the floor. Peter pins her down, wrestling with her to get the shoes.)* Don't! Don't! Peter, stop it. Ouch!
Mrs. Frank. Anne! . . . Peter!

[Suddenly Peter becomes self-conscious. He grabs his shoes roughly and starts for his room.]

Anne *(following him)*. Peter, where are you going? Come dance with me.
Peter. I tell you I don't know how.
Anne. I'll teach you.
Peter. I'm going to give Mouschi his dinner.
Anne. Can I watch?
Peter. He doesn't like people around while he eats.
Anne. Peter, please.
Peter. No!

[He goes into his room. Anne slams his door after him.]

Mrs. Frank. Anne, dear, I think you shouldn't play like that with Peter. It's not dignified.

Anne. Who cares if it's dignified? I don't want to be dignified.

[Mr. Frank *and* Margot *come from the room on the right.* Margot *goes to help her mother.* Mr. Frank *starts for the center table to correct* Margot's *school papers.*]

Mrs. Frank *(to Anne).* You complain that I don't treat you like a grown-up. But when I do, you resent it.

Anne. I only want some fun . . . someone to laugh and clown with. . . . After you've sat still all day and hardly moved, you've got to have some fun. I don't know what's the matter with that boy.

Mr. Frank. He isn't used to girls. Give him a little time.

Anne. Time? Isn't two months time? I could cry. *(Catching hold of* Margot*)* Come on, Margot . . . dance with me. Come on, please.

Margot. I have to help with supper.

Anne. You know we're going to forget how to dance. . . . When we get out we won't remember a thing.

[*She starts to sing and dance by herself.* Mr. Frank *takes her in his arms, waltzing with her.* Mrs. Van Daan *comes in from the bathroom.*]

Mrs. Van Daan. Next? *(She looks around as she starts putting on her shoes.)* Where's Peter?

Anne *(as they are dancing).* Where would he be!

Mrs. Van Daan. He hasn't finished his lessons, has he? His father'll kill him if he catches him in there with that cat and his work not done. *(*Mr. Frank *and* Anne *finish their dance. They bow to each other with extravagant formality.)* Anne, get him out of there, will you?

Anne *(at Peter's door).* Peter? Peter?

Peter *(opening the door a crack).* What is it?

Anne. Your mother says to come out.

Peter. I'm giving Mouschi his dinner.

Mrs. Van Daan. You know what your father says. *(She sits on the couch, sewing on the lining of her fur coat.)*

Peter. For heaven's sake, I haven't even looked at him since lunch.

Mrs. Van Daan. I'm just telling you, that's all.

Anne. I'll feed him.

Peter. I don't want you in there.

Mrs. Van Daan. Peter!

Peter *(to Anne).* Then give him his dinner and come right out, you hear?

[*He comes back to the table.* Anne *shuts the door of* Peter's *room after her and disappears behind the curtain covering his closet.*]

Mrs. Van Daan (*to* Peter). Now is that any way to talk to your little girlfriend?

Peter. Mother . . . for heaven's sake . . . will you please stop saying that?

Mrs. Van Daan. Look at him blush! Look at him!

Peter. Please! I'm not . . . anyway . . . let me alone, will you?

Mrs. Van Daan. He acts like it was something to be ashamed of. It's nothing to be ashamed of, to have a little girlfriend.

Peter. You're crazy. She's only thirteen.

Mrs. Van Daan. So what? And you're sixteen. Just perfect. Your father's ten years older than I am. (*To* Mr. Frank) I warn you, Mr. Frank, if this war lasts much longer, we're going to be related and then . . .

Mr. Frank. *Mazel tov!*[13]

Mrs. Frank (*deliberately changing the conversation*). I wonder where Miep is. She's usually so prompt.

[*Suddenly everything else is forgotten as they hear the sound of an automobile coming to a screeching stop in the street below. They are tense, motionless in their terror. The car starts away. A wave of relief sweeps over them. They pick up their occupations again.* Anne *flings open the door of* Peter's *room, making a dramatic entrance. She is dressed in* Peter's *clothes.* Peter *looks at her in fury. The others are amused.*]

Anne. Good evening, everyone. Forgive me if I don't stay. (*She jumps up on a chair.*) I have a friend waiting for me in there. My friend Tom. Tom Cat. Some people say that we look alike. But Tom has the most beautiful whiskers, and I have only a little fuzz. I am hoping . . . in time . . .

Peter. All right, Mrs. Quack Quack!

Anne (*outraged—jumping down*). Peter!

Peter. I heard about you. . . . How you talked so much in class they called you Mrs. Quack Quack. How Mr. Smitter made you write a composition . . . " 'Quack, quack,' said Mrs. Quack Quack."

Anne. Well, go on. Tell them the rest. How it was so good that he read it out loud to the class and then read it to all his other classes!

Peter. Quack! Quack! Quack . . . Quack . . . Quack . . .

[Anne *pulls off the coat and trousers.*]

Anne. You are the most intolerable, insufferable boy I've ever met!

[*She throws the clothes down the stairwell.* Peter *goes down after them.*]

Peter. Quack, quack, quack!

Mrs. Van Daan (*to* Anne). That's right, Anneke! Give it to him!

Anne. With all the boys in the world . . . Why I had to get locked up with one like you! . . .

Peter. Quack, quack, quack, and from now on stay out of my room!

[*As* Peter *passes her,* Anne *puts out her foot, tripping him. He picks himself up and goes on into his room.*]

Mrs. Frank (*quietly*). Anne, dear . . . your hair. (*She feels* Anne's *forehead.*) You're warm. Are you feeling all right?

Anne. Please, Mother. (*She goes over to the center table, slipping into her shoes.*)

Mrs. Frank (*following her*). You haven't a fever, have you?

---

13. *Mazel tov!* (mä′zəl tôf′): Hebrew for "Congratulations!"

Anne (*pulling away*). No. No.

Mrs. Frank. You know we can't call a doctor here, ever. There's only one thing to do . . . watch carefully. Prevent an illness before it comes. Let me see your tongue.

Anne. Mother, this is perfectly absurd.

Mrs. Frank. Anne, dear, don't be such a baby. Let me see your tongue. (*As* Anne *refuses,* Mrs. Frank *appeals to* Mr. Frank.) Otto . . . ?

Mr. Frank. You hear your mother, Anne.

[Anne *flicks out her tongue for a second, then turns away.*]

Mrs. Frank. Come on—open up! (*As* Anne *opens her mouth very wide*) You seem all right . . . but perhaps an aspirin . . .

Mrs. Van Daan. For heaven's sake, don't give that child any pills. I waited for fifteen minutes this morning for her to come out of the W.C.

Anne. I was washing my hair!

Mrs. Frank. I think there's nothing the matter with our Anne that a ride on her bike or a visit with her friend Jopie deWaal wouldn't cure. Isn't that so, Anne?

[Mr. Van Daan *comes down into the room. From outside we hear faint sounds of bombers going over and a burst of ack-ack.*[14]]

Mr. Van Daan. Miep not come yet?

Mrs. Van Daan. The workmen just left, a little while ago.

Mr. Van Daan. What's for dinner tonight?

Mrs. Van Daan. Beans.

Mr. Van Daan. Not again!

Mrs. Van Daan. Poor Putti! I know. But what can we do? That's all that Miep brought us.

---

14. **ack-ack:** antiaircraft fire.

[Mr. Van Daan *starts to pace, his hands behind his back.* Anne *follows behind him, imitating him.*]

Anne. We are now in what is known as the "bean cycle." Beans boiled, beans en casserole, beans with strings, beans without strings . . .

[Peter *has come out of his room. He slides into his place at the table, becoming immediately absorbed in his studies.*]

Mr. Van Daan (*to* Peter). I saw you . . . in there, playing with your cat.

Mrs. Van Daan. He just went in for a second, putting his coat away. He's been out here all the time, doing his lessons.

Mr. Frank (*looking up from the paper*). Anne, you got an excellent in your history paper today . . . and very good in Latin.

Anne (*sitting beside him*). How about algebra?

Mr. Frank. I'll have to make a confession. Up until now I've managed to stay ahead of you in algebra. Today you caught up with me. We'll leave it to Margot to correct.

Anne. Isn't algebra *vile,* Pim!

Mr. Frank. Vile!

Margot (*to* Mr. Frank). How did I do?

Anne (*getting up*). Excellent, excellent, excellent, excellent!

Mr. Frank (*to* Margot). You should have used the subjunctive here. . . .

Margot. Should I? . . . I thought . . . look here . . . I didn't use it here. . . .

[*The two become absorbed in the papers.*]

Anne. Mrs. Van Daan, may I try on your coat?

Mrs. Frank. No, Anne.

Mrs. Van Daan (*giving it to* Anne). It's all right . . . but careful with it. (Anne *puts it on* *and struts with it.)* My father gave me that the year before he died. He always bought the best that money could buy.

Anne. Mrs. Van Daan, did you have a lot of boyfriends before you were married?

Mrs. Frank. Anne, that's a personal question. It's not courteous to ask personal questions.

Mrs. Van Daan. Oh, I don't mind. *(To Anne)* Our house was always swarming with boys. When I was a girl we had . . .

Mr. Van Daan. Oh, God. Not again!

Mrs. Van Daan *(good-humored).* Shut up! *(Without a pause, to Anne. Mr. Van Daan mimics Mrs. Van Daan, speaking the first few words in unison with her.)* One summer we had a big house in Hilversum. The boys came buzzing round like bees around a jam pot. And when I was sixteen! . . . We were wearing our skirts very short those days and I had good-looking legs. *(She pulls up her skirt, going to Mr. Frank)* I still have 'em. I may not be as pretty as I used to be, but I still have my legs. How about it, Mr. Frank?

Mr. Van Daan. All right. All right. We see them.

Mrs. Van Daan. I'm not asking you. I'm asking Mr. Frank.

Peter. Mother, for heaven's sake.

Mrs. Van Daan. Oh, I embarrass you, do I? Well, I just hope the girl you marry has as good. *(Then, to Anne)* My father used to worry about me, with so many boys hanging round. He told me, if any of them gets fresh, you say to him . . . "Remember, Mr. So-and-So, remember I'm a lady."

Anne. "Remember, Mr. So-and-So, remember I'm a lady." *(She gives Mrs. Van Daan her coat.)*

Mr. Van Daan. Look at you, talking that way in front of her! Don't you know she puts it all down in that diary?

Mrs. Van Daan. So, if she does? I'm only telling the truth!

[Anne *stretches out, putting her ear to the floor, listening to what is going on below. The sound of the bombers fades away.*]

Mrs. Frank *(setting the table).* Would you mind, Peter, if I moved you over to the couch?

Anne *(listening).* Miep must have the radio on.

[Peter *picks up his papers, going over to the couch beside* Mrs. Van Daan.]

Mr. Van Daan *(accusingly, to* Peter*).* Haven't you finished yet?

Peter. No.

Mr. Van Daan. You ought to be ashamed of yourself.

Peter. All right. All right. I'm a dunce. I'm a hopeless case. Why do I go on?

Mrs. Van Daan. You're not hopeless. Don't talk that way. It's just that you haven't anyone to help you, like the girls have. *(To Mr. Frank)* Maybe you could help him, Mr. Frank?

Mr. Frank. I'm sure that his father . . . ?

Mr. Van Daan. Not me. I can't do anything with him. He won't listen to me. You go ahead . . . if you want.

Mr. Frank *(going to* Peter*).* What about it, Peter? Shall we make our school coeducational?

Mrs. Van Daan *(kissing* Mr. Frank*).* You're an angel, Mr. Frank. An angel. I don't know why I didn't meet you before I met that one there. Here, sit down, Mr. Frank. . . . *(She forces him down on the couch beside* Peter.) Now, Peter, you listen to Mr. Frank.

Mr. Frank. It might be better for us to go into Peter's room.

[Peter *jumps up eagerly, leading the way.*]

Mrs. Van Daan. That's right. You go in there, Peter. You listen to Mr. Frank. Mr. Frank is a highly educated man.

[*As* Mr. Frank *is about to follow* Peter *into his room,* Mrs. Frank *stops him and wipes the lipstick from his lips. Then she closes the door after them.*]

Anne (*on the floor, listening*). Shh! I can hear a man's voice talking.

Mr. Van Daan (*to* Anne). Isn't it bad enough here without your sprawling all over the place?

[Anne *sits up.*]

Mrs. Van Daan (*to* Mr. Van Daan). If you didn't smoke so much, you wouldn't be so bad-tempered.

Mr. Van Daan. Am I smoking? Do you see me smoking?

Mrs. Van Daan. Don't tell me you've used up all those cigarettes.

Mr. Van Daan. One package. Miep only brought me one package.

Mrs. Van Daan. It's a filthy habit anyway. It's a good time to break yourself.

Mr. Van Daan. Oh, stop it, please.

Mrs. Van Daan. You're smoking up all our money. You know that, don't you?

Mr. Van Daan. Will you shut up? (*During this,* Mrs. Frank *and* Margot *have studiously kept their eyes down. But* Anne, *seated on the floor, has been following the discussion interestedly.* Mr. Van Daan *turns to see her staring up at him.*) And what are you staring at?

Anne. I never heard grown-ups quarrel before. I thought only children quarreled.

Mr. Van Daan. This isn't a quarrel! It's a discussion. And I never heard children so rude before.

Anne (*rising, indignantly*). I, rude!

Mr. Van Daan. Yes!

Mrs. Frank (*quickly*). Anne, will you get me my knitting? (Anne *goes to get it.*) I must remember, when Miep comes, to ask her to bring me some more wool.

Margot (*going to her room*). I need some hairpins and some soap. I made a list. (*She goes into her bedroom to get the list.*)

Mrs. Frank (*to* Anne). Have you some library books for Miep when she comes?

Anne. It's a wonder that Miep has a life of her own, the way we make her run errands for us. Please, Miep, get me some starch. Please take my hair out and have it cut. Tell me all the latest news, Miep. (*She goes over, kneeling on the couch beside* Mrs. Van Daan.) Did you know she was engaged? His name is Dirk, and Miep's afraid the Nazis will ship him off to Germany to work in one of their war plants. That's what they're doing with some of the young Dutchmen . . . they pick them up off the streets——

Mr. Van Daan (*interrupting*). Don't you ever get tired of talking? Suppose you try keeping still for five minutes. Just five minutes.

[*He starts to pace again. Again* Anne *follows him, mimicking him.* Mrs. Frank *jumps up and takes her by the arm up to the sink, and gives her a glass of milk.*]

Mrs. Frank. Come here, Anne. It's time for your glass of milk.

Mr. Van Daan. Talk, talk, talk. I never heard such a child. Where is my . . . ? Every evening it's the same, talk, talk, talk. (*He looks around.*) Where is my . . . ?

Mrs. Van Daan. What're you looking for?

Mr. Van Daan. My pipe. Have you seen my pipe?

Mrs. Van Daan. What good's a pipe? You haven't got any tobacco.

Mr. Van Daan. At least I'll have something to hold in my mouth! (*Opening* Margot's *bedroom door*) Margot, have you seen my pipe?
Margot. It was on the table last night.

[Anne *puts her glass of milk on the table and picks up his pipe, hiding it behind her back.*]

Mr. Van Daan. I know. I know. Anne, did you see my pipe? . . . Anne!
Mrs. Frank. Anne, Mr. Van Daan is speaking to you.
Anne. Am I allowed to talk now?
Mr. Van Daan. You're the most aggravating . . . The trouble with you is, you've been spoiled. What you need is a good old-fashioned spanking.
Anne (*mimicking* Mrs. Van Daan). "Remember, Mr. So-and-So, remember I'm a lady." (*She thrusts the pipe into his mouth, then picks up her glass of milk.*)
Mr. Van Daan (*restraining himself with difficulty*). Why aren't you nice and quiet like your sister Margot? Why do you have to show off all the time? Let me give you a little advice, young lady. Men don't like that kind of thing in a girl. You know that? A man likes a girl who'll listen to him once in a while . . . a domestic girl, who'll keep her house shining for her husband . . . who loves to cook and sew and . . .
Anne. I'd cut my throat first! I'd open my veins! I'm going to be remarkable! I'm going to Paris . . .
Mr. Van Daan (*scoffingly*). Paris!
Anne. . . . to study music and art.
Mr. Van Daan. Yeah! Yeah!
Anne. I'm going to be a famous dancer or singer . . . or something wonderful.

[She makes a wide gesture, spilling the glass of milk on the fur coat in Mrs. Van Daan's lap. Margot rushes quickly over with a towel. Anne tries to brush the milk off with her skirt.]

Mrs. Van Daan. Now look what you've done . . . you clumsy little fool! My beautiful fur coat my father gave me . . .
Anne. I'm so sorry.
Mrs. Van Daan. What do you care? It isn't yours. . . . So go on, ruin it! Do you know what that coat cost? Do you? And now look at it! Look at it!
Anne. I'm very, very sorry.
Mrs. Van Daan. I could kill you for this. I could just kill you!

[Mrs. Van Daan *goes up the stairs, clutching the coat.* Mr. Van Daan *starts after her.*]

Mr. Van Daan. Petronella . . . *liefje! Liefje!* . . . Come back . . . the supper . . . come back!
Mrs. Frank. Anne, you must not behave in that way.
Anne. It was an accident. Anyone can have an accident.
Mrs. Frank. I don't mean that. I mean the answering back. You must not answer back. They are our guests. We must always show the greatest courtesy to them. We're all living under terrible tension. (*She stops as* Margot *indicates that* Mr. Van Daan *can hear. When he is gone, she continues.*) That's why we must control ourselves. . . . You don't hear Margot getting into arguments with them, do you? Watch Margot. She's always courteous with them. Never familiar. She keeps her distance. And they respect her for it. Try to be like Margot.
Anne. And have them walk all over me, the way they do her? No, thanks!
Mrs. Frank. I'm not afraid that anyone is going to walk all over you, Anne. I'm afraid for other people, that you'll walk on them. I

don't know what happens to you, Anne. You are wild, self-willed. If I had ever talked to my mother as you talk to me . . .

Anne. Things have changed. People aren't like that any more. "Yes, Mother." "No, Mother." "Anything you say, Mother." I've got to fight things out for myself! Make something of myself!

Mrs. Frank. It isn't necessary to fight to do it. Margot doesn't fight, and isn't she . . . ?

Anne *(violently, rebellious)*. Margot! Margot! Margot! That's all I hear from everyone . . . how wonderful Margot is . . . "Why aren't you like Margot?"

Margot *(protesting)*. Oh, come on, Anne, don't be so . . .

Anne *(paying no attention)*. Everything she does is right, and everything I do is wrong! I'm the goat around here! . . . You're all against me! . . . And you worst of all!

[*She rushes off into her room and throws herself down on the settee, stifling her sobs. Mrs. Frank sighs and starts toward the stove.*]

Mrs. Frank *(to Margot)*. Let's put the soup on the stove . . . if there's anyone who cares to eat. Margot, will you take the bread out? *(Margot gets the bread from the cupboard.)* I don't know how we can go on living this way . . . I can't say a word to Anne . . . she flies at me. . . .

Margot. You know Anne. In half an hour she'll be out here, laughing and joking.

Mrs. Frank. And . . . *(She makes a motion upwards, indicating the Van Daans.)* I told your father it wouldn't work . . . but no . . . no . . . he had to ask them, he said . . . he owed it to him, he said. Well, he knows now that I was right! These quarrels! . . . This bickering!

Margot *(with a warning look)*. Shush. Shush.

[*The buzzer for the door sounds. Mrs. Frank gasps, startled.*]

Mrs. Frank. Every time I hear that sound, my heart stops!

Margot *(starting for Peter's door)*. It's Miep. *(She knocks at the door.)* Father?

[Mr. Frank *comes quickly from* Peter's room.]

Mr. Frank. Thank you, Margot. *(As he goes down the steps to open the outer door)* Has everyone his list?

Margot. I'll get my books. *(Giving her mother a list)* Here's your list. (Margot *goes into her and* Anne's *bedroom on the right.* Anne *sits up, hiding her tears, as* Margot *comes in.)* Miep's here.

[Margot *picks up her books and goes back.* Anne *hurries over to the mirror, smoothing her hair.*]

Mr. Van Daan *(coming down the stairs)*. Is it Miep?

Margot. Yes. Father's gone down to let her in.

Mr. Van Daan. At last I'll have some cigarettes!

Mrs. Frank *(to Mr. Van Daan)*. I can't tell you how unhappy I am about Mrs. Van Daan's coat. Anne should never have touched it.

Mr. Van Daan. She'll be all right.

Mrs. Frank. Is there anything I can do?

Mr. Van Daan. Don't worry.

[*He turns to meet* Miep. *But it is not* Miep *who comes up the steps. It is* Mr. Kraler, *followed by* Mr. Frank. *Their faces are grave.* Anne *comes from the bedroom.* Peter *comes from his room.*]

Mrs. Frank. Mr. Kraler!

Mr. Van Daan. How are you, Mr. Kraler?

Margot. This is a surprise.

Mrs. Frank. When Mr. Kraler comes, the sun begins to shine.

Mr. Van Daan. Miep is coming?

Mr. Kraler. Not tonight. (Mr. Kraler *goes to* Margot *and* Mrs. Frank *and* Anne, *shaking hands with them.*)

Mrs. Frank. Wouldn't you like a cup of coffee? . . . Or, better still, will you have supper with us?

Mr. Frank. Mr. Kraler has something to talk over with us. Something has happened, he says, which demands an immediate decision.

Mrs. Frank (*fearful*). What is it?

[Mr. Kraler *sits down on the couch. As he talks he takes bread, cabbages, milk, etc., from his briefcase, giving them to* Margot *and* Anne *to put away.*]

Mr. Kraler. Usually, when I come up here, I try to bring you some bit of good news. What's the use of telling you the bad news when there's nothing that you can do about it? But today something has happened. . . . Dirk . . . Miep's Dirk, you know, came to me just now. He tells me that he has a Jewish friend living near him. A dentist. He says he's in trouble. He begged me, could I do anything for this man? Could I find him a hiding place? . . . So I've come to you. . . . I know it's a terrible thing to ask of you, living as you are, but would you take him in with you?

Mr. Frank. Of course we will.

Mr. Kraler (*rising*). It'll be just for a night or two . . . until I find some other place. This happened so suddenly that I didn't know where to turn.

Mr. Frank. Where is he?

Mr. Kraler. Downstairs in the office.

Mr. Frank. Good. Bring him up.

Mr. Kraler. His name is Dussel . . . Jan Dussel.

Mr. Frank. Dussel . . . I think I know him.

Mr. Kraler. I'll get him.

[*He goes quickly down the steps and out. Mr.* Frank *suddenly becomes conscious of the others.*]

Mr. Frank. Forgive me. I spoke without consulting you. But I knew you'd feel as I do.

Mr. Van Daan. There's no reason for you to consult anyone. This is your place. You have a right to do exactly as you please. The only thing I feel . . . there's so little food as it is . . . and to take in another person . . .

[Peter *turns away, ashamed of his father.*]

Mr. Frank. We can stretch the food a little. It's only for a few days.

Mr. Van Daan. You want to make a bet?

Mrs. Frank. I think it's fine to have him. But, Otto, where are you going to put him? Where?

Peter. He can have my bed. I can sleep on the floor. I wouldn't mind.

Mr. Frank. That's good of you, Peter. But your room's too small . . . even for *you.*

Anne. I have a much better idea. I'll come in here with you and Mother, and Margot can take Peter's room, and Peter can go in our room with Mr. Dussel.

Margot. That's right. We could do that.

Mr. Frank. No, Margot. You mustn't sleep in that room . . . neither you nor Anne. Mouschi has caught some rats in there. Peter's brave. He doesn't mind.

Anne. Then how about *this?* I'll come in here with you and Mother, and Mr. Dussel can have my bed.

Mrs. Frank. No. No. *No!* Margot will come in here with us and he can have her bed. It's the only way. Margot, bring your things in here. Help her, Anne.

[Margot *hurries into her room to get her things.*]

Anne (to her mother). Why Margot? Why can't I come in here?

Mrs. Frank. Because it wouldn't be proper . . . Please, Anne. Don't argue. Please.

[Anne *starts slowly away.*]

Mr. Frank (to Anne). You don't mind sharing your room with Mr. Dussel, do you, Anne?

Anne. No. No, of course not.

Mr. Frank. Good. (Anne *goes off into her bedroom, helping* Margot. Mr. Frank *starts to search in the cupboards.*) Where's the cognac?

Mrs. Frank. It's there. But, Otto, I was saving it in case of illness.

Mr. Frank. I think we couldn't find a better time to use it. Peter, will you get five glasses for me?

[Peter *goes for the glasses.* Margot *comes out of her bedroom, carrying her possessions, which she hangs behind a curtain in the main room.* Mr. Frank *finds the cognac and pours it into the five glasses that* Peter *brings him.* Mr. Van Daan *stands looking on sourly.* Mrs. Van Daan *comes downstairs and looks around at all of the bustle.*]

Mrs. Van Daan. What's happening? What's going on?

Mr. Van Daan. Someone's moving in with us.

Mrs. Van Daan. In here? You're joking.

Margot. It's only for a night or two . . . until Mr. Kraler finds him another place.

Mr. Van Daan. Yeah! Yeah!

[Mr. Frank *hurries over as* Mr. Kraler *and* Dussel *come up.* Dussel *is a man in his late fifties, meticulous, finicky . . . bewildered now. He wears a raincoat. He carries a briefcase, stuffed full, and a small medicine case.*]

Mr. Frank. Come in, Mr. Dussel.

Mr. Kraler. This is Mr. Frank.

Dussel. Mr. Otto Frank?

Mr. Frank. Yes. Let me take your things. (He *takes the hat and briefcase, but* Dussel *clings to his medicine case.*) This is my wife Edith . . . Mr. and Mrs. Van Daan . . . their son, Peter . . . and my daughters, Margot and Anne.

[Dussel *shakes hands with everyone.*]

Mr. Kraler. Thank you, Mr. Frank. Thank you all. Mr. Dussel, I leave you in good hands. Oh . . . Dirk's coat.

[Dussel *hurriedly takes off the raincoat, giving it to* Mr. Kraler. *Underneath is his white dentist's jacket, with a yellow Star of David on it.*]

Dussel (to Mr. Kraler). What can I say to thank you . . . ?

Mrs. Frank (to Dussel). Mr. Kraler and Miep . . . They're our lifeline. Without them we couldn't live.

Mr. Kraler. Please, please. You make us seem very heroic. It isn't that at all. We simply don't like the Nazis. (To Mr. Frank, *who offers him a drink*) No, thanks. (Then going on) We don't like their methods. We don't like . . .

Mr. Frank (smiling). I know. I know. "No one's going to tell us Dutchmen what to do with our Jews!"

Mr. Kraler (to Dussel). Pay no attention to Mr. Frank. I'll be up tomorrow to see that they're treating you right. (To Mr. Frank) Don't trouble to come down again. Peter will bolt the door after me, won't you, Peter?

Peter. Yes, sir.

Mr. Frank. Thank you, Peter. I'll do it.

Mr. Kraler. Good night. Good night.

Group. Good night, Mr. Kraler. We'll see you tomorrow, *etc. etc.*

[Mr. Kraler *goes out with* Mr. Frank. Mrs. Frank *gives each one of the "grown-ups" a glass of cognac.*]

Mrs. Frank. Please, Mr. Dussel, sit down.

[Mr. Dussel *sinks into a chair. Mrs. Frank gives him a glass of cognac.*]

Dussel. I'm dreaming. I know it. I can't believe my eyes. Mr. Otto Frank here! *(To* Mrs. Frank*)* You're not in Switzerland then? A woman told me . . . She said she'd gone to your house . . . the door was open, everything was in disorder, dishes in the sink. She said she found a piece of paper in the wastebasket with an address scribbled on it . . . an address in Zurich. She said you must have escaped to Zurich.

Anne. Father put that there purposely . . . just so people would think that very thing!

Dussel. And you've been *here* all the time?

Mrs. Frank. All the time . . . ever since July.

[Anne *speaks to her father as he comes back.*]

Anne. It worked, Pim . . . the address you left! Mr. Dussel says that people believe we escaped to Switzerland.

Mr. Frank. I'm glad. . . . And now let's have a little drink to welcome Mr. Dussel. *(Before they can drink,* Dussel *bolts his drink. Mr. Frank smiles and raises his glass.)* To Mr. Dussel. Welcome. We're very honored to have you with us.

Mrs. Frank. To Mr. Dussel, welcome.

[*The Van Daans murmur a welcome. The "grown-ups" drink.*]

Mrs. Van Daan. Um. That was good.

Mr. Van Daan. Did Mr. Kraler warn you that you won't get much to eat here? You can imagine . . . three ration books among the seven of us . . . and now you make eight.

[Peter *walks away, humiliated. Outside a street organ is heard dimly.*]

Dussel (*rising*). Mr. Van Daan, you don't realize what is happening outside that you should warn me of a thing like that. You don't realize what's going on. . . . (*As Mr. Van Daan starts his characteristic pacing, Dussel turns to speak to the others.*) Right here in Amsterdam every day hundreds of Jews disappear. . . . They surround a block and search house by house. Children come home from school to find their parents gone. Hundreds are being deported . . . people that you and I know . . . the Hallensteins . . . the Wessels . . .

Mrs. Frank (*in tears*). Oh, no. No!

Dussel. They get their call-up notice . . . come to the Jewish theater on such and such a day and hour . . . bring only what you can carry in a rucksack. And if you refuse the call-up notice, then they come and drag you from your home and ship you off to Mauthausen. The death camp!

Mrs. Frank. We didn't know that things had got so much worse.

Dussel. Forgive me for speaking so.

Anne (*coming to Dussel*). Do you know the deWaals? . . . What's become of them? Their daughter Jopie and I are in the same class. Jopie's my best friend.

Dussel. They are gone.

Anne. Gone?

Dussel. With all the others.

Anne. Oh, no. Not Jopie!

[*She turns away, in tears.* Mrs. Frank *motions to Margot to comfort her.* Margot *goes to Anne, putting her arms comfortingly around her.*]

Mrs. Van Daan. There were some people called Wagner. They lived near us . . . ?

Mr. Frank (*interrupting with a glance at Anne*). I think we should put this off until later. We all have many questions we want to ask. . . . But I'm sure that Mr. Dussel would like to get settled before supper.

Dussel. Thank you. I would. I brought very little with me.

Mr. Frank (*giving him his hat and brief-case*). I'm sorry we can't give you a room alone. But I hope you won't be too uncomfortable. We've had to make strict rules here . . . a schedule of hours. . . . We'll tell you after supper. Anne, would you like to take Mr. Dussel to his room?

Anne (*controlling her tears*). If you'll come with me, Mr. Dussel? (*She starts for her room.*)

Dussel (*shaking hands with each in turn*). Forgive me if I haven't really expressed my gratitude to all of you. This has been such a shock to me. I'd always thought of myself as Dutch. I was born in Holland. My father was born in Holland, and my grandfather. And now . . . after all these years . . . (*He breaks off.*) If you'll excuse me.

[Dussel *gives a little bow and hurries off after* Anne. Mr. Frank *and the others are subdued.*]

Anne (*turning on the light*). Well, here we are.

[Dussel *looks around the room. In the main room* Margot *speaks to her mother.*]

Margot. The news sounds pretty bad, doesn't it? It's so different from what Mr. Kraler tells us. Mr. Kraler says things are improving.

Mr. Van Daan. I like it better the way Kraler tells it.

[*They resume their occupations, quietly.* Peter *goes off into his room. In* Anne's *room,* Anne *turns to* Dussel.]

Anne. You're going to share the room with me.

Dussel. I'm a man who's always lived alone. I haven't had to adjust myself to others. I hope you'll bear with me until I learn.

Anne. Let me help you. (*She takes his briefcase.*) Do you always live all alone? Have you no family at all?

Dussel. No one. (*He opens his medicine case and spreads his bottles on the dressing table.*)

Anne. How dreadful. You must be terribly lonely.

Dussel. I'm used to it.

Anne. I don't think I could ever get used to it. Didn't you even have a pet? A cat, or a dog?

Dussel. I have an allergy for fur-bearing animals. They give me asthma.

Anne. Oh, dear. Peter has a cat.

Dussel. Here? He has it here?

Anne. Yes. But we hardly ever see it. He keeps it in his room all the time. I'm sure it will be all right.

Dussel. Let us hope so. (*He takes some pills to fortify himself.*)

Anne. That's Margot's bed, where you're going to sleep. I sleep on the sofa there. (*Indicating the clothes hooks on the wall*) We cleared these off for your things. (*She goes over to the window.*) The best part about this room. . . you can look down and see a bit of the street and the canal. There's a houseboat . . . you can see the end of it . . . a bargeman lives there with his family. . . . They have a baby and he's just beginning to walk and I'm so afraid he's going to fall into the canal some day. I watch him. . . .

Dussel (*interrupting*). Your father spoke of a schedule.

Anne (*coming away from the window*). Oh, yes. It's mostly about the times we have to be quiet. And times for the w.c. You can use it now if you like.

Dussel (*stiffly*). No, thank you.

Anne. I suppose you think it's awful, my talking about a thing like that. But you don't know how important it can get to be, especially when you're frightened. . . . About this room, the way Margot and I did . . . she had it to herself in the afternoons for studying, reading . . . lessons, you know . . . and I took the mornings. Would that be all right with you?

Dussel. I'm not at my best in the morning.

Anne. You stay in here in the mornings then. I'll take the room in the afternoons.

Dussel. Tell me, when you're in here, what happens to me? Where am I spending my time? In there, with all the people?

Anne. Yes.

Dussel. I see. I see.

Anne. We have supper at half past six.

Dussel (*going over to the sofa*). Then, if you don't mind . . . I like to lie down quietly for ten minutes before eating. I find it helps the digestion.

Anne. Of course. I hope I'm not going to be too much of a bother to you. I seem to be able to get everyone's back up.

[Dussel *lies down on the sofa, curled up, his back to her.*]

Dussel. I always get along very well with children. My patients all bring their children to me, because they know I get on well with them. So don't you worry about that.

[Anne *leans over him, taking his hand and shaking it gratefully.*]

Anne. Thank you. Thank you, Mr Dussel.

[*The lights dim to darkness. The curtain falls on the scene. Anne's voice comes to us faintly at first, and then with increasing power.*]

Anne's Voice. . . . And yesterday I finished Cissy Van Marxvelt's latest book. I think she is a first-class writer. I shall definitely let my children read her. Monday, the twenty-first of September, nineteen forty-two. Mr. Dussel and I had another battle yesterday. Yes, Mr. Dussel! According to him, nothing, I repeat . . . nothing, is right about me . . . my appearance, my character, my manners. While he was going on at me I thought . . . sometime I'll give you such a smack that you'll fly right up to the ceiling! Why is it that every grown-up thinks he knows the way to bring up children? Particularly the grown-ups that never had any. I keep wishing that Peter was a girl instead of a boy. Then I would have someone to talk to. Margot's a darling, but she takes everything too seriously. To pause for a moment on the subject of Mrs. Van Daan. I must tell you that her attempts to flirt with Father are getting her nowhere. Pim, thank goodness, won't play.

[*As she is saying the last lines, the curtain rises on the darkened scene. Anne's voice fades out.*]

Scene 4

It is the middle of the night, several months later. The stage is dark except for a little light which comes through the skylight in Peter's room.

Everyone is in bed. Mr. *and* Mrs. Frank *lie on the couch in the main room, which has been pulled out to serve as a makeshift double bed.*

Margot *is sleeping on a mattress on the floor in the main room, behind a curtain stretched across for privacy. The others are all in their accustomed rooms.*

From outside we hear two drunken soldiers singing "Lili Marlene." A girl's high giggle is heard. The sound of running feet is heard coming closer and then fading in the distance. Throughout the scene there is the distant sound of airplanes passing overhead.

A match suddenly flares up in the attic. We dimly see Mr. Van Daan. *He is getting his bearings. He comes quickly down the stairs and goes to the cupboard where the food is stored. Again the match flares up, and is as quickly blown out. The dim figure is seen to steal back up the stairs.*

There is quiet for a second or two, broken only by the sound of airplanes, and running feet on the street below.

Suddenly, out of the silence and the dark, we hear Anne *scream.*

Anne (*screaming*). No! No! Don't . . . don't take me!

[*She moans, tossing and crying in her sleep. The other people wake, terrified. Dussel sits up in bed, furious.*]

Dussel. Shush! Anne! Anne, for God's sake, shush!

Anne (*still in her nightmare*). Save me! Save me!

[*She screams and screams. Dussel gets out of bed, going over to her, trying to wake her.*]

Dussel. For God's sake! Quiet! Quiet! You want someone to hear?

[*In the main room* Mrs. Frank *grabs a shawl and pulls it around her. She rushes in to* Anne, *taking her in her arms.* Mr. Frank *hurriedly gets up, putting on his overcoat.* Margot *sits up, terrified.* Peter's *light goes on in his room.*]

Mrs. Frank (*to* Anne, *in her room*). Hush, darling, hush. It's all right. It's all right. (*Over her shoulder, to* Dussel) Will you be kind enough to turn on the light, Mr. Dussel? (*Back to* Anne) It's nothing, my darling. It was just a dream.

[Dussel *turns on the light in the bedroom.* Mrs. Frank *holds* Anne *in her arms. Gradually* Anne *comes out of her nightmare, still trembling with horror.* Mr. Frank *comes into the room and goes quickly to the window, looking out to be sure that no one outside has heard* Anne's *screams.* Mrs. Frank *holds* Anne, *talking softly to her. In the main room* Margot *stands on a chair, turning on the center hanging lamp. A light goes on in the Van Daans' room overhead.* Peter *puts his robe on, coming out of his room.*]

Dussel (*to* Mrs. Frank, *blowing his nose*). Something must be done about that child, Mrs. Frank. Yelling like that! Who knows but there's somebody on the streets? She's endangering all our lives.
Mrs. Frank. Anne, darling.
Dussel. Every night she twists and turns. I don't sleep. I spend half my night shushing her. And now it's nightmares!

[Margot *comes to the door of* Anne's *room, followed by* Peter. Mr. Frank *goes to them, indicating that everything is all right.* Peter *takes* Margot *back.*]

Mrs. Frank (*to* Anne). You're here, safe, you see? Nothing has happened. (*To* Dussel)

Please, Mr. Dussel, go back to bed. She'll be herself in a minute or two. Won't you, Anne?
Dussel (*picking up a book and a pillow*). Thank you, but I'm going to the w.c. The one place where there's peace!

[*He stalks out.* Mr. Van Daan, *in underwear and trousers, comes down the stairs.*]

Mr. Van Daan (*to* Dussel). What is it? What happened?
Dussel. A nightmare. She was having a nightmare!
Mr. Van Daan. I thought someone was murdering her.
Dussel. Unfortunately, no.

[*He goes into the bathroom.* Mr. Van Daan *goes back up the stairs.* Mr. Frank, *in the main room, sends* Peter *back to his own bedroom.*]

Mr. Frank. Thank you, Peter. Go back to bed.

[Peter *goes back to his room.* Mr. Frank *follows him, turning out the light and looking out the window. Then he goes back to the main room and gets up on a chair, turning out the center hanging lamp.*]

Mrs. Frank (*to* Anne). Would you like some water? (Anne *shakes her head.*) Was it a very bad dream? Perhaps if you told me . . . ?
Anne. I'd rather not talk about it.
Mrs. Frank. Poor darling. Try to sleep then. I'll sit right here beside you until you fall asleep. (*She brings a stool over, sitting there.*)
Anne. You don't have to.
Mrs. Frank. But I'd like to stay with you . . . very much. Really.
Anne. I'd rather you didn't.
Mrs. Frank. Good night, then. (*She leans down to kiss* Anne. Anne *throws her arm up*

over her face, turning away. Mrs. Frank, *hiding her hurt, kisses* Anne's *arm.)* You'll be all right? There's nothing that you want?

Anne. Will you please ask Father to come.

Mrs. Frank *(after a second).* Of course, Anne dear. *(She hurries out into the other room.* Mr. Frank *comes to her as she comes in.) Sie verlangt nach Dir!*[15]

Mr. Frank *(sensing her hurt).* Edith, Liebe, schau . . .[16]

Mrs. Frank. *Es macht nichts! Ich danke dem lieben Herrgott, dass sie sich wenigstens an Dich wendet, wenn sie Trost braucht! Geh hinein, Otto, sie ist ganz hysterisch vor Angst.*[17] *(As* Mr. Frank *hesitates) Geh zu ihr.*[18] *(He looks at her for a second and then goes to get a cup of water for* Anne. Mrs. Frank *sinks down on the bed, her face in her hands, trying to keep from sobbing aloud.* Margot *comes over to her, putting her arms around her.)* She wants nothing of me. She pulled away when I leaned down to kiss her.

Margot. It's a phase . . . You heard Father. . . . Most girls go through it . . . they turn to their fathers at this age . . . they give all their love to their fathers.

Mrs. Frank. You weren't like this. You didn't shut me out.

Margot. She'll get over it. . . .

[*She smooths the bed for* Mrs. Frank *and sits beside her a moment as* Mrs. Frank *lies down. In* Anne's *room* Mr. Frank *comes in, sitting down by* Anne. Anne *flings her arms around him, clinging to him. In the distance we hear the sound of ack-ack.*]

Anne. Oh, Pim. I dreamed that they came to get us! The Green Police! They broke down the door and grabbed me and started to drag me out the way they did Jopie.

Mr. Frank. I want you to take this pill.

Anne. What is it?

Mr. Frank. Something to quiet you.

[*She takes it and drinks the water. In the main room* Margot *turns out the light and goes back to her room.*]

Mr. Frank *(to* Anne*).* Do you want me to read to you for a while?

Anne. No. Just sit with me for a minute. Was I awful? Did I yell terribly loud? Do you think anyone outside could have heard?

Mr. Frank. No. No. Lie quietly now. Try to sleep.

---

15. *Sie verlangt nach Dir!:* She's asking to see you!
16. *Liebe, schau . . . .* dear, look . . .
17. *Es macht . . . Angst:* It doesn't matter. I just thank the dear Lord that at least she turns to you when she needs comfort. Go, Otto, she's utterly hysterical with fear.
18. *Geh zu ihr:* Go to her.

Anne. I'm a terrible coward. I'm so disappointed in myself. I think I've conquered my fear . . . I think I'm really grown-up . . . and then something happens . . . and I run to you like a baby. . . . I love you, Father. I don't love anyone but you.

Mr. Frank *(reproachfully)*. Annele!

Anne. It's true. I've been thinking about it for a long time. You're the only one I love.

Mr. Frank. It's fine to hear you tell me that you love me. But I'd be happier if you said you loved your mother as well. . . . She needs your help so much . . . your love . . .

Anne. We have nothing in common. She doesn't understand me. Whenever I try to explain my views on life to her she asks me if I'm constipated.

Mr. Frank. You hurt her very much now. She's crying. She's in there crying.

Anne. I can't help it. I only told the truth. I didn't want her here. . . . *(Then, with sudden change)* Oh, Pim, I was horrible, wasn't I? And the worst of it is, I can stand off and look at myself doing it and know it's cruel and yet I can't stop doing it. What's the matter with me? Tell me. Don't say it's just a phase! Help me.

Mr. Frank. There is so little that we parents can do to help our children. We can only try to set a good example . . . point the way. The rest you must do yourself. You must build your own character.

Anne. I'm trying. Really I am. Every night I think back over all of the things I did that day that were wrong . . . like putting the wet mop in Mr. Dussel's bed . . . and this thing now with Mother. I say to myself, that was wrong. I make up my mind, I'm never going to do that again. Never! Of course I may do something worse . . . but at least I'll never do *that* again! . . . I have a nicer side, Father . . . a sweeter, nicer side. But I'm scared to show it. I'm afraid that people are going to laugh at me if

I'm serious. So the mean Anne comes to the outside and the good Anne stays on the inside, and I keep on trying to switch them around and have the good Anne outside and the bad Anne inside and be what I'd like to be . . . and might be . . . if only . . . only . . .

[*She is asleep.* Mr. Frank *watches her for a moment and then turns off the light and starts out. The lights dim out. The curtain falls on the scene. Anne's voice is heard dimly at first, and then with growing strength.*]

Anne's Voice. . . . The air raids are getting worse. They come over day and night. The noise is terrifying. Pim says it should be music to our ears. The more planes, the sooner will come the end of the war. Mrs. Van Daan pretends to be a fatalist. What will be, will be. But when the planes come over, who is the most frightened? No one else but Petronella! . . . Monday, the ninth of November, nineteen forty-two. Wonderful news! The Allies have landed in Africa. Pim says that we can look for an early finish to the war. Just for fun he asked each of us what was the first thing we wanted to do when we got out of here. Mrs. Van Daan longs to be home with her own things, her needlepoint chairs, the Beckstein piano her father gave her . . . the best that money could buy. Peter would like to go to a movie. Mr. Dussel wants to get back to his dentist's drill. He's afraid he is losing his touch. For myself, there are so many things . . . to ride a bike again . . . to laugh till my belly aches . . . to have new clothes from the skin out . . . to have a hot tub filled to overflowing and wallow in it for hours . . . to be back in school with my friends . . .

[*As the last lines are being said, the curtain rises on the scene. The lights dim on as Anne's voice fades away.*]

Scene 5

It is the first night of the Hanukkah[19] celebration. Mr. Frank is standing at the head of the table, on which is the menorah.[20] He lights the shamas,[21] or servant candle, and holds it as he says the blessing. Seated listening is all of the "family," dressed in their best. The men wear hats; Peter wears his cap.

Mr. Frank *(reading from a prayer book)*. "Praised be Thou, O Lord our God, Ruler of the universe, who hast sanctified us with Thy commandments and bidden us kindle the Hanukkah lights. Praised be Thou, O Lord our God, Ruler of the universe, who hast wrought wondrous deliverances for our fathers in days of old. Praised be Thou, O Lord our God, Ruler of the universe, that Thou hast given us life and sustenance and brought us to this happy season." *(Mr. Frank lights the one candle of the menorah as he continues.)* "We kindle this Hanukkah light to celebrate the great and wonderful deeds wrought through the zeal with which God filled the hearts of the heroic Maccabees, two thousand years ago. They fought against indifference, against tyranny and oppression, and they restored our Temple to us. May these lights remind us that we should ever look to God, whence cometh our help." Amen. *(Pronounced "O-mayn")*
All. Amen.

[Mr. Frank hands Mrs. Frank the prayer book.]

Mrs. Frank *(reading)*. "I lift up mine eyes unto the mountains, from whence cometh my help. My help cometh from the Lord who made heaven and earth. He will not suffer thy foot to be moved. He that keepeth thee will not slumber. He that keepeth Israel doth neither slumber nor sleep. The Lord is thy keeper. The Lord is thy shade upon thy right hand. The sun shall not smite thee by day, nor the moon by night. The Lord shall keep thee from all evil. He shall keep thy soul. The Lord shall guard thy going out and thy coming in, from this time forth and forevermore." Amen.
All. Amen.

[Mrs. Frank puts down the prayer book and goes to get the food and wine. Margot helps her. Mr. Frank takes the men's hats and puts them aside.]

Dussel *(rising)*. That was very moving.
Anne *(pulling him back)*. It isn't over yet!
Mrs. Van Daan. Sit down! Sit down!
Anne. There's a lot more, songs and presents.
Dussel. Presents?
Mrs. Frank. Not this year, unfortunately.
Mrs. Van Daan. But always on Hanukkah everyone gives presents . . . everyone!
Dussel. Like our St. Nicholas' Day.[22]

---

19. **Hanukkah** (ᴋʜä′nŏŏ-kə): a joyful holiday lasting eight days, usually in December, which celebrates a victorious fight for religious liberty in 165 B.C. At that time, a Greek king of Syria who ruled the Jews had been forcing them to worship Greek gods. Led by a family known as the Maccabees, the Jews won their independence from Syria and restored their holy Temple, which the Syrians had used to make offerings to Zeus.
20. **menorah** (mə-nôr′ə): a ritual candleholder. The Hanukkah menorah holds nine candles.
21. **shamas** (shä′məs): the central candle in the menorah, which is used to light the others.

22. **our St. Nicholas' Day:** Christian children in the Netherlands receive gifts on St. Nicholas' Day, December 6. Mr. Dussel considers himself a Christian. However, he is one of the many people who were hunted by the Nazis because they had Jewish ancestry.

[*There is a chorus of* no's *from the group.*]

Mrs. Van Daan. No! Not like St. Nicholas! What kind of a Jew are you that you don't know Hanukkah?

Mrs. Frank (*as she brings the food*). I remember particularly the candles. . . . First one, as we have tonight. Then the second night you light two candles, the next night three . . . and so on until you have eight candles burning. When there are eight candles it is truly beautiful.

Mrs. Van Daan. And the potato pancakes.

Mr. Van Daan. Don't talk about them!

Mrs. Van Daan. I make the best *latkes* you ever tasted!

Mrs. Frank. Invite us all next year . . . in your own home.

Mr. Frank. God willing!

Mrs. Van Daan. God willing.

Margot. What I remember best is the presents we used to get when we were little . . . eight days of presents . . . and each day they got better and better.

Mrs. Frank (*sitting down*). We are all here, alive. That is present enough.

Anne. No, it isn't. I've got something. . . . (*She rushes into her room, hurriedly puts on a little hat improvised from the lampshade, grabs a satchel bulging with parcels and comes running back.*)

Mrs. Frank. What is it?

Anne. Presents!

Mrs. Van Daan. Presents!

Dussel. Look!

Mr. Van Daan. What's she got on her head?

Peter. A lampshade!

Anne (*She picks out one at random*). This is for Margot. (*She hands it to* Margot, *pulling her to her feet.*) Read it out loud.

Margot (*reading*).

"You have never lost your temper.

You never will, I fear,

You are so good.

But if you should,

Put all your cross words here."

(*She tears open the package.*) A new crossword puzzle book! Where did you get it?

Anne. It isn't new. It's one that you've done. But I rubbed it all out, and if you wait a little and forget, you can do it all over again.

Margot (*sitting*). It's wonderful, Anne. Thank you. You'd never know it wasn't new.

[*From outside we hear the sound of a street-car passing.*]

Anne (*with another gift*). Mrs. Van Daan.

Mrs. Van Daan (*taking it*). This is awful. . . . I haven't anything for anyone. . . . I never thought . . .

Mr. Frank. This is all Anne's idea.

Mrs. Van Daan (*holding up a bottle*). What is it?

Anne. It's hair shampoo. I took all the odds and ends of soap and mixed them with the last of my toilet water.

Mrs. Van Daan. Oh, Anneke!

Anne. I wanted to write a poem for all of them, but I didn't have time. (*Offering a large box to* Mr. Van Daan) Yours, Mr. Van Daan, is *really* something . . . something you want more than anything. (*As she waits for him to open it*) Look! Cigarettes!

Mr. Van Daan. Cigarettes!

Anne. Two of them! Pim found some old pipe tobacco in the pocket lining of his coat . . . and we made them . . . or rather, Pim did.

Mrs. Van Daan. Let me see. . . . Well, look at that! Light it, Putti! Light it.

[Mr. Van Daan *hesitates.*]

Anne. It's tobacco, really it is! There's a little fluff in it, but not much.

[*Everyone watches as* Mr. Van Daan *cautiously lights it. The cigarette flares up. Everyone laughs.*]

Peter. It works!

Mrs. Van Daan. Look at him.

Mr. Van Daan (*spluttering*). Thank you, Anne. Thank you.

[Anne *rushes back to her satchel for another present.*]

Anne (*handing her mother a piece of paper*). For Mother, Hanukkah greeting. (*She pulls her mother to her feet.*)

Mrs. Frank (*She reads*).

"Here's an IOU that I promise to pay.

Ten hours of doing whatever you say.

Signed, Anne Frank." (*Mrs. Frank, touched, takes* Anne *in her arms, holding her close.*)

Dussel (*to* Anne). Ten hours of doing what you're told? *Anything* you're told?

Anne. That's right.

Dussel. You wouldn't want to sell that, Mrs. Frank?

Mrs. Frank. Never! This is the most precious gift I've ever had!

[*She sits, showing her present to the others.* Anne *hurries back to the satchel and pulls out a scarf, the scarf that* Mr. Frank *found in the first scene.*]

Anne *(offering it to her father).* For Pim.

Mr. Frank. Anneke . . . I wasn't supposed to have a present! *(He takes it, unfolding it and showing it to the others.)*

Anne. It's a muffler . . . to put round your neck . . . like an ascot, you know. I made it myself out of odds and ends. . . . I knitted it in the dark each night, after I'd gone to bed. I'm afraid it looks better in the dark!

Mr. Frank *(putting it on).* It's fine. It fits me perfectly. Thank you, Annele.

[Anne *hands* Peter *a ball of paper, with a string attached to it.*]

Anne. That's for Mouschi.

Peter *(rising to bow).* On behalf of Mouschi, I thank you.

Anne *(hesitant, handing him a gift).* And . . . this is yours . . . from Mrs. Quack Quack. *(As he holds it gingerly in his hands)* Well . . . open it. . . . Aren't you going to open it?

Peter. I'm scared to. I know something's going to jump out and hit me.

Anne. No. It's nothing like that, really.

Mrs. Van Daan *(as he is opening it).* What is it, Peter? Go on. Show it.

Anne *(excitedly).* It's a safety razor!

Dussel. A what?

Anne. A razor!

Mrs. Van Daan *(looking at it).* You didn't make that out of odds and ends.

Anne *(to Peter).* Miep got it for me. It's not new. It's secondhand. But you really do need a razor now.

Dussel. For what?

Anne. Look on his upper lip . . . you can see the beginning of a mustache.

Dussel. He wants to get rid of that? Put a little milk on it and let the cat lick it off.

Peter (starting for his room). Think you're funny, don't you.

Dussel. Look! He can't wait! He's going to try it!

Peter. I'm going to give Mouschi his present! (He goes into his room, slamming the door behind him.)

Mr. Van Daan (disgustedly). Mouschi, Mouschi, Mouschi.

[In the distance we hear a dog persistently barking. Anne brings a gift to Dussel.]

Anne. And last but never least, my roommate, Mr. Dussel.

Dussel. For me? You have something for me? (He opens the small box she gives him.)

Anne. I made them myself.

Dussel (puzzled). Capsules! Two capsules!

Anne. They're earplugs!

Dussel. Earplugs?

Anne. To put in your ears so you won't hear me when I thrash around at night. I saw them advertised in a magazine. They're not real ones. . . . I made them out of cotton and candle wax. Try them. . . . See if they don't work . . . see if you can hear me talk. . . .

Dussel (putting them in his ears). Wait now until I get them in . . . so.

Anne. Are you ready?

Dussel. Huh?

Anne. Are you ready?

Dussel. Good God! They've gone inside! I can't get them out! (They laugh as Dussel jumps about, trying to shake the plugs out of his ears. Finally he gets them out. Putting them away) Thank you, Anne! Thank you!

Mr. Van Daan. A real Hanukkah!

Mrs. Van Daan. Wasn't it cute of her?

Mrs. Frank. I don't know when she did it.

Margot. I love my present.

(Together)

Anne (sitting at the table). And now let's have the song, Father . . . please. . . . (To Dussel) Have you heard the Hanukkah song, Mr. Dussel? The song is the whole thing! (She sings.)
"Oh, Hanukkah! Oh, Hanukkah!
The sweet celebration. . . ."

Mr. Frank (quieting her). I'm afraid, Anne, we shouldn't sing that song tonight. (To Dussel) It's a song of jubilation, of rejoicing. One is apt to become too enthusiastic.

Anne. Oh, please, please. Let's sing the song. I promise not to shout!

Mr. Frank. Very well. But quietly now . . . I'll keep an eye on you and when . . .

[As Anne starts to sing, she is interrupted by Dussel, who is snorting and wheezing.]

Dussel (pointing to Peter). You . . . you! (Peter is coming from his bedroom, ostentatiously holding a bulge in his coat as if he were holding his cat, and dangling Anne's present before it.) How many times . . . I told you . . . Out! Out!

Mr. Van Daan (going to Peter). What's the matter with you? Haven't you any sense? Get that cat out of here.

Peter (innocently). Cat?

Mr. Van Daan. You heard me. Get it out of here!

Peter. I have no cat.

[Delighted with his joke, he opens his coat and pulls out a bath towel. The group at the table laugh, enjoying the joke.]

Dussel (*still wheezing*). It doesn't need to be the cat . . . his clothes are enough . . . when he comes out of that room. . . .

Mr. Van Daan. Don't worry. You won't be bothered any more. We're getting rid of it.

Dussel. At last you listen to me. (*He goes off into his bedroom.*)

Mr. Van Daan (*calling after him*). I'm not doing it for you. That's all in your mind . . . all of it! (*He starts back to his place at the table.*) I'm doing it because I'm sick of seeing that cat eat all our food.

Peter. That's not true! I only give him bones . . . scraps . . .

Mr. Van Daan. Don't tell me! He gets fatter every day! Cat looks better than any of us. Out he goes tonight!

Peter. No! No!

Anne. Mr. Van Daan, you can't do that! That's Peter's cat. Peter loves that cat.

Mrs. Frank (*quietly*). Anne.

Peter (*to Mr. Van Daan*). If he goes, I go.

Mr. Van Daan. Go! Go!

Mrs. Van Daan. You're not going and the cat's not going! Now please . . . this is Hanukkah . . . Hanukkah . . . this is the time to celebrate. . . . What's the matter with all of you? Come on, Anne. Let's have the song.

Anne (*singing*).

"Oh, Hanukkah! Oh, Hanukkah!
The sweet celebration."

Mr. Frank (*rising*). I think we should first blow out the candle . . . then we'll have something for tomorrow night.

Margot. But, Father, you're supposed to let it burn itself out.

Mr. Frank. I'm sure that God understands shortages. (*Before blowing it out*) "Praised be Thou, O Lord our God, who hast sustained us and permitted us to celebrate this joyous festival."

[*He is about to blow out the candle when*

suddenly there is a crash of something falling below. They all freeze in horror, motionless. For a few seconds there is complete silence. Mr. Frank slips off his shoes. The others noiselessly follow his example. Mr. Frank turns out a light near him. He motions to Peter to turn off the center lamp. Peter tries to reach it, realizes he cannot and gets up on a chair. Just as he is touching the lamp he loses his balance. The chair goes out from under him. He falls. The iron lampshade crashes to the floor. There is a sound of feet below, running down the stairs.]

Mr. Van Daan (*under his breath*). God almighty! (*The only light left comes from the Hanukkah candle. Dussel comes from his room. Mr. Frank creeps over to the stairwell and stands listening. The dog is heard barking excitedly.*) Do you hear anything?

Mr. Frank (*in a whisper*). No. I think they've gone.

Mrs. Van Daan. It's the Green Police. They've found us.

Mr. Frank. If they had, they wouldn't have left. They'd be up here by now.

Mrs. Van Daan. I know it's the Green Police. They've gone to get help. That's all, they'll be back.

Mr. Van Daan. Or it may have been the Gestapo,[23] looking for papers. . . .

Mr. Frank (*interrupting*). Or a thief, looking for money.

Mrs. Van Daan. We've got to do something. . . . Quick! Quick! Before they come back.

Mr. Van Daan. There isn't anything to do. Just wait.

[*Mr. Frank holds up his hand for them to be quiet. He is listening intently. There is complete silence as they all strain to hear any*

---

23. **Gestapo** (gə-stä′pō): the Nazi secret police.

sound from below. Suddenly Anne *begins to sway. With a low cry she falls to the floor in a faint.* Mrs. Frank *goes to her quickly, sitting beside her on the floor and taking her in her arms.*]

Mrs. Frank. Get some water, please! Get some water!

[Margot *starts for the sink.*]

Mr. Van Daan *(grabbing* Margot*).* No! No! No one's going to run water!

Mr. Frank. If they've found us, they've found us. Get the water. *(*Margot *starts again for the sink.* Mr. Frank, *getting a flashlight)* I'm going down.

[Margot *rushes to him, clinging to him.* Anne *struggles to consciousness.*]

Margot. No, Father, no! There may be someone there, waiting. . . . It may be a trap!

Mr. Frank. This is Saturday. There is no way for us to know what has happened until Miep or Mr. Kraler comes on Monday morning. We cannot live with this uncertainty.

Margot. Don't go, Father!

Mrs. Frank. Hush, darling, hush. *(*Mr. Frank *slips quietly out, down the steps and out through the door below.)* Margot! Stay close to me.

[Margot *goes to her mother.*]

Mr. Van Daan. Shush! Shush!

[Mrs. Frank *whispers to* Margot *to get the water.* Margot *goes for it.*]

Mrs. Van Daan. Putti, where's our money?

The Diary of Anne Frank   Act One, Scene 5   333

Get our money. I hear you can buy the Green Police off, so much a head. Go upstairs quick! Get the money!

Mr. Van Daan. Keep still!

Mrs. Van Daan (*kneeling before him, pleading*). Do you want to be dragged off to a concentration camp? Are you going to stand there and wait for them to come up and get you? Do something, I tell you!

Mr. Van Daan (*pushing her aside*). Will you keep still!

[*He goes over to the stairwell to listen.* Peter *goes to his mother, helping her up onto the sofa. There is a second of silence. Then* Anne *can stand it no longer.*]

Anne. Someone go after Father! Make Father come back!

Peter (*starting for the door*). I'll go.

Mr. Van Daan. Haven't you done enough?

[*He pushes* Peter *roughly away. In his anger against his father* Peter *grabs a chair as if to hit him with it, then puts it down, burying his face in his hands.* Mrs. Frank *begins to pray softly.*]

Anne. Please, please, Mr. Van Daan. Get Father.

Mr. Van Daan. Quiet! Quiet!

[Anne *is shocked into silence.* Mrs. Frank *pulls her closer, holding her protectively in her arms.*]

Mrs. Frank (*softly, praying*). "I lift up mine eyes unto the mountains, from whence cometh my help. My help cometh from the Lord who made heaven and earth. He will not suffer thy foot to be moved. . . . He that keepeth thee will not slumber. . . .

[*She stops as she hears someone coming. They all watch the door tensely.* Mr. Frank *comes quietly in.* Anne *rushes to him, holding him tight.*]

Mr. Frank. It was a thief. That noise must have scared him away.

Mrs. Van Daan. Thank God.

Mr. Frank. He took the cashbox. And the radio. He ran away in such a hurry that he didn't stop to shut the street door. It was swinging wide open. (*A breath of relief sweeps over them.*) I think it would be good to have some light.

Margot. Are you sure it's all right?

Mr. Frank. The danger has passed. (Margot *goes to light the small lamp.*) Don't be so terrified, Anne. We're safe.

Dussel. Who says the danger has passed? Don't you realize we are in greater danger than ever?

Mr. Frank. Mr. Dussel, will you be still! (Mr. Frank *takes* Anne *back to the table, making her sit down with him, trying to calm her.*)

Dussel (*pointing to* Peter). Thanks to this clumsy fool, there's someone now who knows we're up here! Someone now knows we're up here, hiding!

Mrs. Van Daan (*going to* Dussel). Someone knows we're here, yes. But who is the someone? A thief! A thief! You think a thief is going to go to the Green Police and say . . . I was robbing a place the other night and I heard a noise up over my head? You think a thief is going to do that?

Dussel. Yes. I think he will.

Mrs. Van Daan (*hysterically*). You're crazy!

[*She stumbles back to her seat at the table.* Peter *follows protectively, pushing* Dussel *aside.*]

Dussel. I think someday he'll be caught and then he'll make a bargain with the Green

Police . . . if they'll let him off, he'll tell them where some Jews are hiding!

[*He goes off into the bedroom. There is a second of appalled silence.*]

Mr. Van Daan. He's right.
Anne. Father, let's get out of here! We can't stay here now. . . . Let's go. . . .
Mr. Van Daan. Go! Where?
Mrs. Frank (*sinking into her chair at the table*). Yes. Where?
Mr. Frank (*rising, to them all*). Have we lost all faith? All courage? A moment ago we thought that they'd come for us. We were sure it was the end. But it wasn't the end. We're alive, safe. (*Mr. Van Daan goes to the table and sits. Mr. Frank prays.*) "We thank Thee, O Lord our God, that in Thy infinite mercy Thou hast again seen fit to spare us." (*He blows out the candle, then turns to* Anne.). Come on, Anne. The song! Let's have the song!

[*He starts to sing. Anne finally starts falteringly to sing as Mr. Frank urges her on. Her voice is hardly audible at first.*]

Anne (*singing*).
"Oh, Hanukkah! Oh, Hanukkah!
The sweet . . . celebration. . . ."

[*As she goes on singing, the others gradually join in, their voices still shaking with fear.* Mrs. Van Daan *sobs as she sings.*]

Group.
"Around the feast . . . we . . . gather
In complete . . . jubilation. . . .
Happiest of sea . . . sons
Now is here.
Many are the reasons for good cheer.

(Dussel *comes from the bedroom. He comes over to the table, standing beside* Margot, *listening to them as they sing.*)
"Together
We'll weather
Whatever tomorrow may bring.
(*As they sing on with growing courage, the lights start to dim.*)
"So hear us rejoicing
And merrily voicing
The Hanukkah song that we sing.
Hoy!
(*The lights are out. The curtain starts slowly to fall.*)
"Hear us rejoicing
And merrily voicing
The Hanukkah song that we sing."

[*They are still singing as the curtain falls.*]

SEEKING MEANING

Act One

Scene 1

1. *The Diary of Anne Frank* is about a group of people who are forced to leave the outside world and to retreat into a small, secret hiding place. What details of the set indicate that this will be a realistic, or lifelike, story?

2. The play opens in November 1945. But in what year does most of this act take place? What prompts Mr. Frank's thoughts to flash back in time?

Scene 2

3. Anne's entrance is an important moment in the play. How does the stage direction on page 302, before her entrance, describe her personality? What does Anne do as soon as she comes onstage?

4. Why do you think Anne cannot destroy the Star of David, as Peter does?

5. When does Anne first realize what "going into hiding" means?

6. What does Mr. Frank say cannot be locked up? What does he suggest he and Anne can do to hold on to one kind of freedom?

Scene 3

7. After several months together in their enclosed world, the "family" members find their tempers growing shorter. What do Anne and Peter argue about in this scene? What do the Van Daans quarrel about?

8. Anne has grown lonely and frustrated in the last several months. What are Anne's dreams for her future? What does she accuse her family of feeling about her?

9. Mr. Dussel brings the group the harsh news which they have been ignorant of. What does he tell them has been happening in the outside world?

Scene 4

10. What is Anne's nightmare? How is it completely different from the dreams of her future that she expressed in Scene 3?

11. Anne says that there is a person inside her that is different from the one that people see. What kind of person remains hidden inside her? Why doesn't Anne allow this side of her nature to show?

Scene 5

12. What gifts has Anne managed to gather together for the members of her "family"? How does the celebration help unite them in the midst of their suffering?

13. The Hanukkah song gives the characters hope and courage. Yet the words of the song do not at all describe their true situation. Tell how each of the following lines from the song differs from the real condition of the singers:

Around the feast . . . we . . . gather
Many are the reasons for good cheer.
So hear us rejoicing

Knowing what you do of the actual circumstances of the characters, tell how their singing of the Hanukkah song makes you feel.

14. Act One ends with the characters (and the audience) in a state of worry and suspense. What do the characters fear caused the noise downstairs?

Act Two

Scene 1

In the darkness we hear Anne's *voice, again reading from the diary.*

Anne's Voice. Saturday, the first of January, nineteen forty-four. Another new year has begun and we find ourselves still in our hiding place. We have been here now for one year, five months and twenty-five days. It seems that our life is at a standstill.

[*The curtain rises on the scene. It is late afternoon. Everyone is bundled up against the cold. In the main room* Mrs. Frank *is taking down the laundry, which is hung across the back.* Mr. Frank *sits in the chair down left, reading.* Margot *is lying on the couch with a blanket over her and the many-colored knitted scarf around her throat.* Anne *is seated at the center table, writing in her diary.* Peter, Mr. *and* Mrs. Van Daan, *and* Dussel *are all in their own rooms, reading or lying down.*

As the lights dim on, Anne's *voice continues, without a break.*]

Anne's Voice. We are all a little thinner. The Van Daans' "discussions" are as violent as ever. Mother still does not understand me. But then I don't understand her either. There is one great change, however. A change in myself. I read somewhere that girls of my age don't feel quite certain of themselves. . . .

[*We hear the chimes and then a hymn being played on the carillon outside.*

The buzzer of the door below suddenly sounds. Everyone is startled; Mr. Frank *tiptoes cautiously to the top of the steps and listens. Again the buzzer sounds, in* Miep's *V-for-Victory signal.[1]*]

Mr. Frank. It's Miep!

[*He goes quickly down the steps to unbolt the door.* Mrs. Frank *calls upstairs to the* Van Daans *and then to* Peter.]

Mrs. Frank. Wake up, everyone! Miep is here! (Anne *quickly puts her diary away.* Margot *sits up, pulling the blanket around her shoulders.* Dussel *sits on the edge of his bed, listening, disgruntled.* Miep *comes up the steps, followed by* Mr. Kraler. *They bring flowers,*

---

1. **V-for-Victory signal:** three short rings and one long ring, the Morse code for V, used as the Allied symbol for victory.

books, newspapers, etc. Anne *rushes to* Miep, *throwing her arms affectionately around her.)* Miep . . . and Mr. Kraler . . . What a delightful surprise!

Mr. Kraler. We came to bring you New Year's greetings.

Mrs. Frank. You shouldn't . . . you should have at least one day to yourselves. *(She goes quickly to the stove and brings down teacups and tea for all of them.)*

Anne. Don't say that, it's so wonderful to see them! *(Sniffing at* Miep's *coat)* I can smell the wind and the cold on your clothes.

Miep *(giving her the flowers).* There you are. *(Then, to* Margot, *feeling her forehead)* How are you, Margot? . . . Feeling any better?

Margot. I'm all right.

Anne. We filled her full of every kind of pill so she won't cough and make a noise.

[*She runs into her room to put the flowers in water.* Mr. *and* Mrs. Van Daan *come from upstairs. Outside there is the sound of a band playing.*]

Mrs. Van Daan. Well, hello, Miep. Mr. Kraler.

Mr. Kraler *(giving a bouquet of flowers to* Mrs. Van Daan*).* With my hope for peace in the New Year.

Peter *(anxiously).* Miep, have you seen Mouschi? Have you seen him anywhere around?

Miep. I'm sorry, Peter. I asked everyone in the neighborhood had they seen a gray cat. But they said no.

[Mrs. Frank *gives* Miep *a cup of tea.* Mr. Frank *comes up the steps, carrying a small cake on a plate.*]

Mr. Frank. Look what Miep's brought for us!

Mrs. Frank *(taking it).* A cake!

Mr. Van Daan. A cake! *(He pinches* Miep's *cheeks gaily and hurries up to the cupboard.)* I'll get some plates.

[Dussel, *in his room, hastily puts a coat on and starts out to join the others.*]

Mrs. Frank. Thank you, Miepia. You shouldn't have done it. You must have used all of your sugar ration for weeks. *(Giving it to* Mrs. Van Daan*)* It's beautiful, isn't it?

Mrs. Van Daan. It's been ages since I even saw a cake. Not since you brought us one last year. *(Without looking at the cake, to* Miep*)* Remember? Don't you remember, you gave us one on New Year's Day? Just this time last year? I'll never forget it because you had "Peace in nineteen forty-three" on it. *(She looks at the cake and reads.)* "Peace in nineteen forty-four!"

Miep. Well, it has to come sometime, you know. *(As* Dussel *comes from his room)* Hello, Mr. Dussel.

Mr. Kraler. How are you?

Mr. Van Daan *(bringing plates and a knife).* Here's the knife, *liefje.* Now, how many of us are there?

Miep. None for me, thank you.

Mr. Frank. Oh, please. You must.

Miep. I couldn't.

Mr. Van Daan. Good! That leaves one . . . two . . . three . . . seven of us.

Dussel. Eight! Eight! It's the same number as it always is!

Mr. Van Daan. I left Margot out. I take it for granted Margot won't eat any.

Anne. Why wouldn't she!

Mrs. Frank. I think it won't harm her.

Mr. Van Daan. All right! All right! I just didn't want her to start coughing again, that's all.

Dussel. And please, Mrs. Frank should cut the cake.

Mr. Van Daan. What's the dif- } *(Together)*
ference?
Mrs. Van Daan. It's not Mrs.
Frank's cake, is it, Miep? It's for
all of us.

Dussel. Mrs. Frank divides things better.

Mrs. Van Daan *(going to Dus-* } *(Together)*
sel). What are you trying to say?
Mr. Van Daan. Oh, come on!
Stop wasting time!

Mrs. Van Daan *(to* Dussel*).* Don't I always give everybody exactly the same? Don't I?

Mr. Van Daan. Forget it, Kerli.

Mrs. Van Daan. No. I want an answer! Don't I?

Dussel. Yes. Yes. Everybody gets exactly the same . . . except Mr. Van Daan always gets a little bit more.

[Mr. Van Daan *advances on* Dussel, *the knife still in his hand.*]

Mr. Van Daan. That's a lie!

[Dussel *retreats before the onslaught of the Van Daans.*]

Mr. Frank. Please, please! *(Then, to* Miep*)* You see what a little sugar cake does to us? It goes right to our heads!

Mr. Van Daan *(handing* Mrs. Frank *the knife).* Here you are, Mrs. Frank.

Mrs. Frank. Thank you. *(Then, to* Miep *as she goes to the table to cut the cake)* Are you sure you won't have some?

Miep *(drinking her tea).* No, really, I have to go in a minute.

[*The sound of the band fades out in the distance.*]

Peter *(to* Miep*).* Maybe Mouschi went back to our house . . . they say that cats . . . Do you ever get over there . . . ? I mean . . . do you suppose you could . . . ?

Miep. I'll try, Peter. The first minute I get I'll try. But I'm afraid, with him gone a week . . .

Dussel. Make up your mind, already someone has had a nice big dinner from that cat!

[Peter *is furious, inarticulate. He starts toward* Dussel *as if to hit him.* Mr. Frank *stops him.* Mrs. Frank *speaks quickly to ease the situation.*]

Mrs. Frank *(to* Miep*).* This is delicious, Miep!

Mrs. Van Daan *(eating hers).* Delicious!

Mr. Van Daan *(finishing it in one gulp).* Dirk's in luck to get a girl who can bake like this!

Miep *(putting down her empty teacup).* I have to run. Dirk's taking me to a party tonight.

Anne. How heavenly! Remember now what everyone is wearing, and what you have to eat and everything, so you can tell us tomorrow.

Miep. I'll give you a full report! Goodbye, everyone!

Mr. Van Daan *(to* Miep*).* Just a minute. There's something I'd like you to do for me. *(He hurries off up the stairs to his room.)*

Mrs. Van Daan *(sharply).* Putti, where are you going? *(She rushes up the stairs after him, calling hysterically.)* What do you want? Putti, what are you going to do?

Miep *(to* Peter*).* What's wrong?

Peter *(His sympathy is with his mother).* Father says he's going to sell her fur coat. She's crazy about that old fur coat.

Dussel. Is it possible? Is it possible that anyone is so silly as to worry about a fur coat in times like this?

Peter. It's none of your darn business . . . and if you say one more thing . . . I'll, I'll take you and I'll . . . I mean it . . . I'll . . .

[*There is a piercing scream from* Mrs. Van Daan *above. She grabs at the fur coat as* Mr. Van Daan *is starting downstairs with it.*]

Mrs. Van Daan. No! No! No! Don't you dare take that! You hear? It's mine! (*Downstairs* Peter *turns away, embarrassed, miserable.*) My father gave me that! You didn't give it to me. You have no right. Let go of it . . . you hear?

[Mr. Van Daan *pulls the coat from her hands and hurries downstairs.* Mrs. Van Daan *sinks to the floor, sobbing. As* Mr. Van Daan *comes into the main room the others look away, embarrassed for him.*]

Mr. Van Daan (*to* Mr. Kraler). Just a little — discussion over the advisability of selling this coat. As I have often reminded Mrs. Van Daan, it's very selfish of her to keep it when people outside are in such desperate need of clothing. . . . (*He gives the coat to* Miep.) So if you will please to sell it for us? It should fetch a good price. And by the way, will you get me cigarettes. I don't care what kind they are . . . get all you can.

Miep. It's terribly difficult to get them, Mr. Van Daan. But I'll try. Goodbye.

[*She goes.* Mr. Frank *follows her down the steps to bolt the door after her.* Mrs. Frank *gives* Mr. Kraler *a cup of tea.*]

Mrs. Frank. Are you sure you won't have some cake, Mr. Kraler?

Mr. Kraler. I'd better not.

Mr. Van Daan. You're still feeling badly? What does your doctor say?

Mr. Kraler. I haven't been to him.

Mrs. Frank. Now, Mr. Kraler! . . .

Mr. Kraler (*sitting at the table*). Oh, I tried. But you can't get near a doctor these days . . .

they're so busy. After weeks I finally managed to get one on the telephone. I told him I'd like an appointment . . . I wasn't feeling very well. You know what he answers . . . over the telephone . . . Stick out your tongue! (*They laugh. He turns to* Mr. Frank *as* Mr. Frank *comes back.*) I have some contracts here. . . . I wonder if you'd look over them with me. . . .

Mr. Frank (*putting out his hand*). Of course.

Mr. Kraler (*He rises*). If we could go downstairs . . . (Mr. Frank *starts ahead;* Mr. Kraler *speaks to the others.*) Will you forgive us? I won't keep him but a minute. (*He starts to follow* Mr. Frank *down the steps.*)

Margot (*with sudden foreboding*). What's happened? Something's happened! Hasn't it, Mr. Kraler?

[Mr. Kraler *stops and comes back, trying to reassure* Margot *with a pretense of casualness.*]

Mr. Kraler. No, really. I want your father's advice. . . .

Margot. Something's gone wrong! I know it!

Mr. Frank (*coming back, to* Mr. Kraler). If it's something that concerns us here, it's better that we all hear it.

Mr. Kraler (*turning to him, quietly*). But . . . the children . . . ?

Mr. Frank. What they'd imagine would be worse than any reality.

[*As* Mr. Kraler *speaks, they all listen with intense apprehension.* Mrs. Van Daan *comes down the stairs and sits on the bottom step.*]

Mr. Kraler. It's a man in the storeroom. . . . I don't know whether or not you remember him . . . Carl, about fifty, heavyset, nearsighted . . . He came with us just before you left.

Mr. Frank. He was from Utrecht?

Mr. Kraler. That's the man. A couple of weeks ago, when I was in the storeroom, he closed the door and asked me . . . how's Mr. Frank? What do you hear from Mr. Frank? I told him I only knew there was a rumor that you were in Switzerland. He said he'd heard that rumor too, but he thought I might know something more. I didn't pay any attention to it . . . but then a thing happened yesterday. . . . He'd brought some invoices to the office for me to sign. As I was going through them, I looked up. He was standing staring at the bookcase . . . your bookcase. He said he thought he remembered a door there. . . . Wasn't there a door there that used to go up to the loft? Then he told me he wanted more money. Twenty guilders[2] more a week.

Mr. Van Daan. Blackmail!

Mr. Frank. Twenty guilders? Very modest blackmail.

Mr. Van Daan. That's just the beginning.

Dussel (coming to Mr. Frank). You know what I think? He was the thief who was down there that night. That's how he knows we're here.

Mr. Frank (to Mr. Kraler). How was it left? What did you tell him?

Mr. Kraler. I said I had to think about it. What shall I do? Pay him the money? . . . Take a chance on firing him . . . or what? I don't know.

Dussel (frantic). For God's sake don't fire him! Pay him what he asks . . . keep him here where you can have your eye on him.

Mr. Frank. Is it so much that he's asking? What are they paying nowadays?

Mr. Kraler. He could get it in a war plant. But this isn't a war plant. Mind you, I don't know if he really knows . . . or if he doesn't know.

Mr. Frank. Offer him half. Then we'll soon find out if it's blackmail or not.

---

2. **Twenty guilders:** about five dollars at the time.

Dussel. And if it is? We've got to pay it, haven't we? Anything he asks we've got to pay!

Mr. Frank. Let's decide that when the time comes.

Mr. Kraler. This may be all imagination. You get to a point, these days, where you suspect everyone and everything. Again and again . . . on some simple look or word, I've found myself . . .

[The telephone rings in the office below.]

Mrs. Van Daan (hurrying to Mr. Kraler). There's the telephone! What does that mean, the telephone ringing on a holiday?

Mr. Kraler. That's my wife. I told her I had to go over some papers in my office . . . to call me there when she got out of church. (He starts out.) I'll offer him half then. Goodbye . . . we'll hope for the best!

[The group call their goodbyes halfheartedly. Mr. Frank follows Mr. Kraler, to bolt the door below. During the following scene, Mr. Frank comes back up and stands listening, disturbed.]

Dussel (to Mr. Van Daan). You can thank your son for this . . . smashing the light! I tell you, it's just a question of time now. (He goes to the window at the back and stands looking out.)

Margot. Sometimes I wish the end would come . . . whatever it is.

Mrs. Frank (shocked). Margot!

[Anne goes to Margot, sitting beside her on the couch with her arms around her.]

Margot. Then at least we'd know where we were.

Mrs. Frank. You should be ashamed of yourself! Talking that way! Think how lucky we are! Think of the thousands dying in the war, every day. Think of the people in concentration camps.

Anne (*interrupting*). What's the good of that? What's the good of thinking of misery when you're already miserable? That's stupid!

Mrs. Frank. Anne!

[*As* Anne *goes on raging at her mother,* Mrs. Frank *tries to break in, in an effort to quiet her.*]

Anne. We're young. Margot and Peter and I! You grown-ups have had your chance! But look at us. . . . If we begin thinking of all the horror in the world, we're lost! We're trying to hold on to some kind of ideals . . . when everything . . . ideals, hopes . . . everything, are being destroyed! It isn't our fault that the world is in such a mess! We weren't around when all this started! So don't try to take it out on us! (*She rushes off to her room, slamming the door after her. She picks up a brush from the chest and hurls it to the floor. Then she sits on the settee, trying to control her anger.*)

Mr. Van Daan. She talks as if we started the war! Did we start the war?

[*He spots* Anne's *cake. As he starts to take it,* Peter *anticipates him.*]

Peter. She left her cake. (*He starts for* Anne's *room with the cake. There is silence in the main room.* Mrs. Van Daan *goes up to her room, followed by* Mr. Van Daan. Dussel *stays looking out the window.* Mr. Frank *brings* Mrs. Frank *her cake. She eats it slowly, without relish.* Mr. Frank *takes his cake to* Margot *and sits quietly on the sofa beside her.* Peter *stands in the doorway of* Anne's *darkened room, looking at her, then* makes *a little movement to let her know he is there.* Anne *sits up, quickly, trying to hide the signs of her tears.* Peter *holds out the cake to her.*) You left this.

Anne (*dully*). Thanks.

[Peter *starts to go out, then comes back.*]

Peter. I thought you were fine just now. You know just how to talk to them. You know just how to say it. I'm no good . . . I never can think . . . especially when I'm mad. . . . That Dussel . . . when he said that about Mouschi . . . someone eating him . . . all I could think is . . . I wanted to hit him. I wanted to give him such a . . . a . . . that he'd . . . That's what I used to do when there was an argument at school. . . . That's the way I . . . but here . . . And an old man like that . . . it wouldn't be so good.

Anne. You're making a big mistake about me. I do it all wrong. I say too much. I go too far. I hurt people's feelings. . . .

[Dussel *leaves the window, going to his room.*]

Peter. I think you're just fine. . . . What I want to say . . . if it wasn't for you around here, I don't know. What I mean . . .

[Peter *is interrupted by* Dussel's *turning on the light.* Dussel *stands in the doorway, startled to see* Peter. Peter *advances toward him forbiddingly.* Dussel *backs out of the room.* Peter *closes the door on him.*]

Anne. Do you mean it, Peter? Do you really mean it?

Peter. I said it, didn't I?

Anne. Thank you, Peter!

[*In the main room* Mr. *and* Mrs. Frank *collect the dishes and take them to the sink, washing them.* Margot *lies down again on the*

couch. Dussel, *lost, wanders into* Peter's *room and takes up a book, starting to read.*]

Peter *(looking at the photographs on the wall).* You've got quite a collection.
Anne. Wouldn't you like some in your room? I could give you some. Heaven knows you spend enough time in there . . . doing heaven knows what. . . .
Peter. It's easier. A fight starts, or an argument . . . I duck in there.
Anne. You're lucky, having a room to go to. His Lordship is always here. . . . I hardly ever get a minute alone. When they start in on me, I can't duck away. I have to stand there and take it.
Peter. You gave some of it back just now.
Anne. I get so mad. They've formed their opinions . . . about everything . . . but we . . . we're still trying to find out. . . . We have problems here that no other people our age

have ever had. And just as you think you've solved them, something comes along and bang! You have to start all over again.
Peter. At least you've got someone you can talk to.
Anne. Not really. Mother . . . I never discuss anything serious with her. She doesn't understand. Father's all right. We can talk about everything . . . everything but one thing. Mother. He simply won't talk about her. I don't think you can be really intimate with anyone if he holds something back, do you?
Peter. I think your father's fine.
Anne. Oh, he is, Peter! He is! He's the only one who's ever given me the feeling that I have any sense. But anyway, nothing can take the place of school and play and friends of your own age . . . or near your age . . . can it?
Peter. I suppose you miss your friends and all.
Anne. It isn't just . . . *(She breaks off, staring up at him for a second.)* Isn't it funny, you

and I? Here we've been seeing each other every minute for almost a year and a half, and this is the first time we've ever really talked. It helps a lot to have someone to talk to, don't you think? It helps you to let off steam.

Peter (going to the door). Well, any time you want to let off steam, you can come into my room.

Anne (following him). I can get up an awful lot of steam. You'll have to be careful how you say that.

Peter. It's all right with me.

Anne. Do you really mean it?

Peter. I said it, didn't I?

[He goes out. Anne stands in her doorway looking after him. As Peter gets to his door, he stands for a minute looking back at her. Then he goes into his room. Dussel rises as he comes in, and quickly passes him, going out. He starts across for his room. Anne sees him coming and pulls her door shut. Dussel turns back toward Peter's room. Peter pulls his door shut. Dussel stands there, bewildered, forlorn.

The scene slowly dims out. The curtain falls on the scene. Anne's voice comes over in the darkness . . . faintly at first, and then with growing strength.]

Anne's Voice. We've had bad news. The people from whom Miep got our ration books have been arrested. So we have had to cut down on our food. Our stomachs are so empty that they rumble and make strange noises, all in different keys. Mr. Van Daan's is deep and low, like a bass fiddle. Mine is high, whistling like a flute. As we all sit around waiting for supper, it's like an orchestra tuning up. It only needs Toscanini[3] to raise his baton and we'd be off in the "Ride of the Valkyries."[4] Monday, the sixth of March, nineteen forty-four. Mr. Kraler is in the hospital. It seems he has ulcers. Pim says we are his ulcers. Miep has to run the business and us too. The Americans have landed on the southern tip of Italy. Father looks for a quick finish to the war. Mr. Dussel is waiting every day for the warehouseman to demand more money. Have I been skipping too much from one subject to another? I can't help it. I feel that spring is coming. I feel it in my whole body and soul. I feel utterly confused. I am longing . . . so longing . . . for everything . . . for friends . . . for someone to talk to . . . someone who understands . . . someone young, who feels as I do. . . .

[As these last lines are being said, the curtain rises on the scene. The lights dim on. Anne's voice fades out.]

Scene 2

It is evening, after supper. From the outside we hear the sound of children playing. The "grown-ups," with the exception of Mr. Van Daan, are all in the main room. Mrs. Frank is doing some mending. Mrs. Van Daan is reading a fashion magazine. Mr. Frank is going over business accounts. Dussel, in his dentist's jacket, is pacing up and down, impatient to get into his bedroom. Mr. Van Daan is upstairs working on a piece of embroidery in an embroidery frame.

In his room Peter is sitting before the mirror, smoothing his hair. As the scene goes on, he puts on his tie, brushes his coat and puts it on, preparing himself meticulously for a visit from Anne. On his wall are now hung some of Anne's motion-picture stars.

---

3. **Toscanini** (tŏs′kə-nē′nē): Arturo Toscanini, a famous conductor.

4. **"Ride of the Valkyries"** (văl-kîr′ēz): a rousing piece of music from an opera by the German composer Richard Wagner.

In her room Anne *too is getting dressed. She stands before the mirror in her slip, trying various ways of dressing her hair.* Margot *is seated on the sofa, hemming a skirt for* Anne *to wear.*

In the main room Dussel *can stand it no longer. He comes over, rapping sharply on the door of his and* Anne's *bedroom.*

Anne *(calling to him)*. No, no, Mr. Dussel! I am not dressed yet. *(Dussel walks away, furious, sitting down and burying his head in his hands.* Anne *turns to* Margot.*) How is that? How does that look?

Margot *(glancing at her briefly)*. Fine.

Anne. You didn't even look.

Margot. Of course I did. It's fine.

Anne. Margot, tell me, am I terribly ugly?

Margot. Oh, stop fishing.

Anne. No. No. Tell me.

Margot. Of course you're not. You've got nice eyes . . . and a lot of animation, and . . .

Anne. A little vague, aren't you?

[*Outside,* Mrs. Frank, *feeling sorry for* Dussel, *comes over, knocking at the girls' door.*]

Mrs. Frank *(outside)*. May I come in?

Margot. Come in, Mother.

Mrs. Frank *(shutting the door behind her)*. Mr. Dussel's impatient to get in here.

Anne. Heavens, he takes the room for himself the entire day.

Mrs. Frank *(gently)*. Anne, dear, you're not going in again tonight to see Peter?

Anne *(dignified)*. That is my intention.

Mrs. Frank. But you've already spent a great deal of time in there today.

Anne. I was in there exactly twice. Once to get the dictionary, and then three quarters of an hour before supper.

Mrs. Frank. Aren't you afraid you're disturbing him?

Anne. Mother, I have some intuition.

Mrs. Frank. Then may I ask you this much, Anne. Please don't shut the door when you go in.

Anne. You sound like Mrs. Van Daan!

Mrs. Frank. No. No. I don't mean to suggest anything wrong. I only wish that you wouldn't expose yourself to criticism . . . that you wouldn't give Mrs. Van Daan the opportunity to be unpleasant.

Anne. Mrs. Van Daan doesn't need an opportunity to be unpleasant!

Mrs. Frank. Everyone's on edge, worried about Mr. Kraler. This is one more thing. . . .

Anne. I'm sorry, Mother. I'm going to Peter's room. I'm not going to let Petronella Van Daan spoil our friendship.

[Mrs. Frank *hesitates for a second, then goes out, closing the door after her. She gets a pack of playing cards and sits at the center table, playing solitaire. In* Anne's *room* Margot *hands the finished skirt to* Anne. *As* Anne *is putting it on,* Margot *takes off her high-heeled shoes and stuffs paper in the toes so that* Anne *can wear them.*]

Margot *(to* Anne). Why don't you two talk in the main room? It'd save a lot of trouble. It's hard on Mother, having to listen to those remarks from Mrs. Van Daan and not say a word.

Anne. Why doesn't she say a word? I think it's ridiculous to take it and take it.

Margot. You don't understand Mother at all, do you? She can't talk back. She's not like you. It's just not in her nature to fight back.

Anne. Anyway . . . the only one I worry about is you. I feel awfully guilty about you. *(She sits on the stool near* Margot, *putting on* Margot's *high-heeled shoes.)*

Margot. What about?

Anne. I mean, every time I go into Peter's room, I have a feeling I may be hurting you.

(Margot *shakes her head.*) I know if it were me, I'd be wild. I'd be desperately jealous, if it were me.

Margot. Well, I'm not.

Anne. You don't feel badly? Really? Truly? You're not jealous?

Margot. Of course I'm jealous . . . jealous that you've got something to get up in the morning for. . . . But jealous of you and Peter? No.

[Anne *goes back to the mirror.*]

Anne. Maybe there's nothing to be jealous of. Maybe he doesn't really like me. Maybe I'm just taking the place of his cat. . . . (*She picks up a pair of short, white gloves, putting them on.*) Wouldn't you like to come in with us?

Margot. I have a book.

[*The sound of the children playing outside fades out. In the main room* Dussel *can stand it no longer. He jumps up, going to the bedroom door and knocking sharply.*]

Dussel. Will you please let me in my room!

Anne. Just a minute, dear, dear Mr. Dussel. (*She picks up her mother's pink stole and adjusts it elegantly over her shoulders, then gives a last look in the mirror.*) Well, here I go . . . to run the gantlet.⁵ (*She starts out, followed by* Margot.)

Dussel (*as she appears—sarcastic*). Thank you so much.

[Dussel *goes into his room.* Anne *goes toward* Peter's *room, passing* Mrs. Van Daan *and her parents at the center table.*]

Mrs. Van Daan. My God, look at her! (Anne *pays no attention. She knocks at* Peter's

door.) I don't know what good it is to have a son. I never see him. He wouldn't care if I killed myself. (Peter *opens the door and stands aside for* Anne *to come in.*) Just a minute, Anne. (*She goes to them at the door.*) I'd like to say a few words to my son. Do you mind? (Peter *and* Anne *stand waiting.*) Peter, I don't want you staying up till all hours tonight. You've got to have your sleep. You're a growing boy. You hear?

Mrs. Frank. Anne won't stay late. She's going to bed promptly at nine. Aren't you, Anne?

Anne. Yes, Mother . . . (*to* Mrs. Van Daan) May we go now?

Mrs. Van Daan. Are you asking me? I didn't know I had anything to say about it.

Mrs. Frank. Listen for the chimes, Anne dear.

[*The two young people go off into* Peter's *room, shutting the door after them.*]

Mrs. Van Daan (*to* Mrs. Frank). In my day it was the boys who called on the girls. Not the girls on the boys.

Mrs. Frank. You know how young people like to feel that they have secrets. Peter's room is the only place where they can talk.

Mrs. Van Daan. Talk! That's not what they called it when I was young.

[Mrs. Van Daan *goes off to the bathroom.* Margot *settles down to read her book.* Mr. Frank *puts his papers away and brings a chess game to the center table. He and* Mrs. Frank *start to play. In* Peter's *room,* Anne *speaks to* Peter, *indignant, humiliated.*]

Anne. Aren't they awful? Aren't they impossible? Treating us as if we were still in the nursery.

[*She sits on the cot.* Peter *gets a bottle of pop and two glasses.*]

---

5. **run the gantlet** (gônt′lĭt): go forward under attack from both sides.

cream cones. We'd all been playing ping-pong. . . . We used to have heavenly times . . . we'd finish up with ice cream at the Delphi, or the Oasis, where Jews were allowed . . . there'd always be a lot of boys . . . we'd laugh and joke. . . . I'd like to go back to it for a few days or a week. But after that I know I'd be bored to death. I think more seriously about life now. I want to be a journalist . . . or something. I love to write. What do you want to do?

Peter. I thought I might go off someplace . . . work on a farm or something . . . some job that doesn't take much brains.

Anne. You shouldn't talk that way. You've got the most awful inferiority complex.

Peter. I know I'm not smart.

Anne. That isn't true. You're much better than I am in dozens of things . . . arithmetic and algebra and . . . well, you're a million times better than I am in algebra. *(With sudden directness)* You like Margot, don't you? Right from the start you liked her, liked her much better than me.

Peter *(uncomfortably).* Oh, I don't know.

[*In the main room* Mrs. Van Daan *comes from the bathroom and goes over to the sink, polishing a coffeepot.*]

Anne. It's all right. Everyone feels that way. Margot's so good. She's sweet and bright and beautiful and I'm not.

Peter. I wouldn't say that.

Anne. Oh, no, I'm not. I know that. I know quite well that I'm not a beauty. I never have been and never shall be.

Peter. I don't agree at all. I think you're pretty.

Anne. That's not true!

Peter. And another thing. You've changed . . . from at first, I mean.

Anne. I have?

Peter. I used to think you were awful noisy.

Peter. Don't let it bother you. It doesn't bother me.

Anne. I suppose you can't really blame them . . . they think back to what *they* were like at our age. They don't realize how much more advanced we are. . . . When you think what wonderful discussions we've had! . . . Oh, I forgot. I was going to bring you some more pictures.

Peter. Oh, these are fine, thanks.

Anne. Don't you want some more? Miep just brought me some new ones.

Peter. Maybe later. *(He gives her a glass of pop and, taking some for himself, sits down facing her.)*

Anne *(looking up at one of the photographs).* I remember when I got that. . . . I won it. I bet Jopie that I could eat five ice-

Anne. And what do you think now, Peter? How have I changed?

Peter. Well . . . er . . . you're . . . quieter.

[*In his room* Dussel *takes his pajamas and toilet articles and goes into the bathroom to change.*]

Anne. I'm glad you don't just hate me.

Peter. I never said that.

Anne. I bet when you get out of here you'll never think of me again.

Peter. That's crazy.

Anne. When you get back with all of your friends, you're going to say . . . now what did I ever see in that Mrs. Quack Quack.

Peter. I haven't got any friends.

Anne. Oh, Peter, of course you have. Everyone has friends.

Peter. Not me. I don't want any. I get along all right without them.

Anne. Does that mean you can get along without me? I think of myself as your friend.

Peter. No. If they were all like you, it'd be different.

[*He takes the glasses and the bottle and puts them away. There is a second's silence and then* Anne *speaks, hesitantly, shyly.*]

Anne. Peter, did you ever kiss a girl?

Peter. Yes. Once.

Anne (*to cover her feelings*). That picture's crooked. (Peter *goes over, straightening the photograph.*) Was she pretty?

Peter. Huh?

Anne. The girl that you kissed.

Peter. I don't know. I was blindfolded. (*He comes back and sits down again.*) It was at a party. One of those kissing games.

Anne (*relieved*). Oh, I don't suppose that really counts, does it?

Peter. It didn't with me.

Anne. I've been kissed twice. Once a man I'd never seen before kissed me on the cheek when he picked me up off the ice and I was crying. And the other was Mr. Koophuis, a friend of Father's who kissed my hand. You wouldn't say those counted, would you?

Peter. I wouldn't say so.

Anne. I know almost for certain that Margot would never kiss anyone unless she was engaged to them. And I'm sure too that Mother never touched a man before Pim. But I don't know . . . things are so different now. . . . What do you think? Do you think a girl shouldn't kiss anyone except if she's engaged or something? It's so hard to try to think what to do, when here we are with the whole world falling around our ears and you think . . . well . . . you don't know what's going to happen tomorrow and . . . What do you think?

Peter. I suppose it'd depend on the girl. Some girls, anything they do's wrong. But others . . . well . . . it wouldn't necessarily be wrong with them. (*The carillon starts to strike nine o'clock.*) I've always thought that when two people . . .

Anne. Nine o'clock. I have to go.

Peter. That's right.

Anne (*without moving*). Good night.

[*There is a second's pause; then* Peter *gets up and moves toward the door.*]

Peter. You won't let them stop you coming?

Anne. No. (*She rises and starts for the door.*) Sometime I might bring my diary. There are so many things in it that I want to talk over with you. There's a lot about you.

Peter. What kind of thing?

Anne. I wouldn't want you to see some of it. I thought you were a nothing, just the way you thought about me.

Peter. Did you change your mind, the way I changed my mind about you?

Anne. Well . . . You'll see. . . .

[*For a second* Anne *stands looking up at* Peter, *longing for him to kiss her. As he makes no move she turns away. Then suddenly* Peter *grabs her awkwardly in his arms, kissing her on the cheek.* Anne *walks out dazed. She stands for a minute, her back to the people in the main room. As she regains her poise she goes to her mother and father and* Margot, *silently kissing them. They murmur their good-nights to her. As she is about to open her bedroom door, she catches sight of* Mrs. Van Daan. *She goes quickly to her, taking her face in her hands and kissing her first on one cheek and then on the other. Then she hurries off into her room.* Mrs. Van Daan *looks after her and then looks over at* Peter's *room. Her suspicions are confirmed.*]

Mrs. Van Daan *(She knows).* Ah hah!

[*The lights dim out. The curtain falls on the scene. In the darkness* Anne's *voice comes faintly at first, and then with growing strength.*]

Anne's Voice. By this time we all know each other so well that if anyone starts to tell a story, the rest can finish it for him. We're having to cut down still further on our meals. What makes it worse, the rats have been at work again. They've carried off some of our precious food. Even Mr. Dussel wishes now that Mouschi was here. Thursday, the twentieth of April, nineteen forty-four. Invasion fever is mounting every day. Miep tells us that people outside talk of nothing else. For myself, life has become much more pleasant. I often go to Peter's room after supper. Oh, don't think I'm in love, because I'm not. But it does make life more bearable to have someone with whom you can exchange views. No

more tonight. P.S. . . . I must be honest. I must confess that I actually live for the next meeting. Is there anything lovelier than to sit under the skylight and feel the sun on your cheeks and have a darling boy in your arms? I admit now that I'm glad the Van Daans had a son and not a daughter. I've outgrown another dress. That's the third. I'm having to wear Margot's clothes after all. I'm working hard on my French and am now reading *La Belle Nivernaise.*[6]

[*As she is saying the last lines, the curtain rises on the scene. The lights dim on as* Anne's *voice fades out.*]

Scene 3

It is night, a few weeks later. Everyone is in bed. There is complete quiet. In the Van Daans' *room a match flares up for a moment and then is quickly put out.* Mr. Van Daan, *in bare feet, dressed in underwear and trousers, is dimly seen coming stealthily down the stairs and into the main room, where* Mr. *and* Mrs. Frank *and* Margot *are sleeping. He goes to the food safe and again lights a match. Then he cautiously opens the safe, taking out a half-loaf of bread. As he closes the safe, it creaks. He stands rigid.* Mrs. Frank *sits up in bed. She sees him.*

Mrs. Frank *(screaming). Otto! Otto! Komme schnell!*[7]

[*The rest of the people wake, hurriedly getting up.*]

Mr. Frank. *Was ist los? Was ist passiert?*[8]

---

6. *La Belle Nivernaise:* a novel by the French writer Alphonse Daudet.
7. *Komme schnell!:* Come quickly!
8. *Was ist los? Was ist passiert?:* What's wrong? What happened?

[Dussel, *followed by* Anne, *comes from his room.*]

Mrs. Frank *(as she rushes over to* Mr. Van Daan). *Er stiehlt das Essen!*[9]

Dussel *(grabbing* Mr. Van Daan). You! You! Give me that.

Mrs. Van Daan *(coming down the stairs).* Putti . . . Putti . . . what is it?

Dussel *(his hands on* Van Daan's neck). You dirty thief . . . stealing food . . . you good-for-nothing . . .

Mr. Frank. Mr. Dussel! For God's sake! Help me, Peter!

[Peter *comes over, trying, with* Mr. Frank, *to separate the two struggling men.*]

Peter. Let him go! Let go!

---

9. *Er stiehlt das Essen!:* He's stealing the food!

[Dussel *drops* Mr. Van Daan, *pushing him away. He shows them the end of a loaf of bread that he has taken from* Mr. Van Daan.]

Dussel. You greedy, selfish . . .

[Margot *turns on the lights.*]

Mrs. Van Daan. Putti . . . what is it?

[*All of* Mrs. Frank's *gentleness, her self-control, is gone. She is outraged, in a frenzy of indignation.*]

Mrs. Frank. The bread! He was stealing the bread!

Dussel. It was you, and all the time we thought it was the rats!

Mr. Frank. Mr. Van Daan, how could you!

Mr. Van Daan. I'm hungry.

Mrs. Frank. We're all of us hungry! I see the children getting thinner and thinner. Your own son Peter . . . I've heard him moan in his sleep, he's so hungry. And you come in the night and steal food that should go to them . . . to the children!

Mrs. Van Daan (going to Mr. Van Daan protectively). He needs more food than the rest of us. He's used to more. He's a big man.

[Mr. Van Daan breaks away, going over and sitting on the couch.]

Mrs. Frank (turning on Mrs. Van Daan). And you . . . you're worse than he is! You're a mother, and yet you sacrifice your child to this man . . . this . . . this . . .

Mr. Frank. Edith! Edith!

[Margot picks up the pink woolen stole, putting it over her mother's shoulders.]

Mrs. Frank (paying no attention, going on to Mrs. Van Daan). Don't think I haven't seen you! Always saving the choicest bits for him! I've watched you day after day and I've held my tongue. But not any longer! Not after this! Now I want him to go! I want him to get out of here!

Mr. Frank. Edith!

Mr. Van Daan. Get out of here? } (Together)

Mrs. Van Daan. What do you mean?

Mrs. Frank. Just that! Take your things and get out!

Mr. Frank (to Mrs. Frank). You're speaking in anger. You cannot mean what you are saying.

Mrs. Frank. I mean exactly that!

[Mrs. Van Daan takes a cover from the Franks' bed, pulling it about her.]

Mr. Frank. For two long years we have lived here, side by side. We have respected each other's rights . . . we have managed to live in peace. Are we now going to throw it all away? I know this will never happen again, will it, Mr. Van Daan?

Mr. Van Daan. No. No.

Mrs. Frank. He steals once! He'll steal again!

[Mr. Van Daan, holding his stomach, starts for the bathroom. Anne puts her arms around him, helping him up the step.]

Mr. Frank. Edith, please. Let us be calm. We'll all go to our rooms . . . and afterwards we'll sit down quietly and talk this out . . . we'll find some way . . .

Mrs. Frank. No! No! No more talk! I want them to leave!

Mrs. Van Daan. You'd put us out, on the streets?

Mrs. Frank. There are other hiding places.

Mrs. Van Daan. A cellar . . . a closet. I know. And we have no money left even to pay for that.

Mrs. Frank. I'll give you money. Out of my own pocket I'll give it gladly. (She gets her purse from a shelf and comes back with it.)

Mrs. Van Daan. Mr. Frank, you told Putti you'd never forget what he'd done for you when you came to Amsterdam. You said you could never repay him, that you . . .

Mrs. Frank (counting out money). If my husband had any obligation to you, he's paid it, over and over.

Mr. Frank. Edith, I've never seen you like this before. I don't know you.

Mrs. Frank. I should have spoken out long ago.

Dussel. You can't be nice to some people.

Mrs. Van Daan (turning on Dussel). There would have been plenty for all of us, if you hadn't come in here!

Mr. Frank. We don't need the Nazis to destroy us. We're destroying ourselves.

[*He sits down, with his head in his hands. Mrs. Frank goes to Mrs. Van Daan.*]

Mrs. Frank (*giving* Mrs. Van Daan *some money*). Give this to Miep. She'll find you a place.

Anne. Mother, you're not putting *Peter* out. Peter hasn't done anything.

Mrs. Frank. He'll stay, of course. When I say I must protect the children, I mean Peter too.

[*Peter rises from the steps where he has been sitting.*]

Peter. I'd have to go if Father goes.

[*Mr. Van Daan comes from the bathroom. Mrs. Van Daan hurries to him and takes him to the couch. Then she gets water from the sink to bathe his face.*]

Mrs. Frank (*while this is going on*). He's no father to you . . . that man! He doesn't know what it is to be a father!

Peter (*starting for his room*). I wouldn't feel right. I couldn't stay.

Mrs. Frank. Very well, then. I'm sorry.

Anne (*rushing over to* Peter). No, Peter! No! (*Peter goes into his room, closing the door after him. Anne turns back to her mother, crying.*) I don't care about the food. They can have mine! I don't want it! Only don't send them away. It'll be daylight soon. They'll be caught. . . .

Margot (*putting her arms comfortingly around* Anne). Please, Mother!

Mrs. Frank. They're not going now. They'll stay here until Miep finds them a place. (*To* Mrs. Van Daan) But one thing I insist on! He must never come down here again! He must never come to this room where the food is stored! We'll divide what we have . . . an equal share for each! (*Dussel hurries over to get a sack of potatoes from the food safe. Mrs. Frank goes on, to* Mrs. Van Daan.) You can cook it here and take it up to him.

[*Dussel brings the sack of potatoes back to the center table.*]

Margot. Oh, no. No. We haven't sunk so far that we're going to fight over a handful of rotten potatoes.

Dussel (*dividing the potatoes into piles*). Mrs. Frank, Mr. Frank, Margot, Anne, Peter, Mrs. Van Daan, Mr. Van Daan, myself . . . Mrs. Frank . . .

[*The buzzer sounds in Miep's signal.*]

Mr. Frank. It's Miep! (*He hurries over, getting his overcoat and putting it on.*)

Margot. At this hour?

Mrs. Frank. It is trouble.

Mr. Frank (*as he starts down to unbolt the door*). I beg you, don't let her see a thing like this!

Mr. Dussel (*counting without stopping*). . . . Anne, Peter, Mrs. Van Daan, Mr. Van Daan, myself . . .

Margot (*to* Dussel). Stop it! Stop it!

Dussel. . . . Mr. Frank, Margot, Anne, Peter, Mrs. Van Daan, Mr. Van Daan, myself, Mrs. Frank . . .

Mrs. Van Daan. You're keeping the big ones for yourself! All the big ones . . . Look at the size of that! . . . And that! . . .

[*Dussel continues on with his dividing. Peter, with his shirt and trousers on, comes from his room.*]

Margot. Stop it! Stop it!

[*We hear Miep's excited voice speaking to Mr. Frank below.*]

Miep. Mr. Frank . . . the most wonderful news! . . . The invasion has begun!

Mr. Frank. Go on, tell them! Tell them!

[Miep *comes running up the steps, ahead of* Mr. Frank. *She has a man's raincoat on over her nightclothes and a bunch of orange-colored flowers in her hand.*]

Miep. Did you hear that, everybody? Did you hear what I said? The invasion has begun! The invasion!

[*They all stare at* Miep, *unable to grasp what she is telling them.* Peter *is the first to recover his wits.*]

Peter. Where?

Mrs. Van Daan. When? When, Miep?

Miep. It began early this morning. . . .

[*As she talks on, the realization of what she has said begins to dawn on them. Everyone goes crazy. A wild demonstration takes place.* Mrs. Frank *hugs* Mr. Van Daan.]

Mrs. Frank. Oh, Mr. Van Daan, did you hear that?

[Dussel *embraces* Mrs. Van Daan. Peter *grabs a frying pan and parades around the room, beating on it, singing the Dutch national anthem.* Anne *and* Margot *follow him, singing,*

The Diary of Anne Frank   Act Two, Scene 3   353

weaving in and out among the excited grown-ups. Margot *breaks away to take the flowers from* Miep *and distribute them to everyone. While this pandemonium is going on* Mrs. Frank *tries to make herself heard above the excitement.*]

Mrs. Frank *(to* Miep*).* How do you know?
Miep. The radio . . . The B.B.C.![10] They said they landed on the coast of Normandy!
Peter. The British?
Miep. British, Americans, French, Dutch, Poles, Norwegians . . . all of them! More than four thousand ships! Churchill[11] spoke, and General Eisenhower![12] D-Day they call it!
Mr. Frank. Thank God, it's come!
Mrs. Van Daan. At last!
Miep *(starting out).* I'm going to tell Mr. Kraler. This'll be better than any blood transfusion.
Mr. Frank *(stopping her).* What part of Normandy did they land, did they say?
Miep. Normandy . . . that's all I know now. . . . I'll be up the minute I hear some more! *(She goes hurriedly out.)*
Mr. Frank *(to* Mrs. Frank*).* What did I tell you? What did I tell you?

[Mrs. Frank *indicates that he has forgotten to bolt the door after* Miep. *He hurries down the steps.* Mr. Van Daan, *sitting on the couch, suddenly breaks into a convulsive sob. Everybody looks at him, bewildered.*]

Mrs. Van Daan *(hurrying to him).* Putti! Putti! What is it? What happened?

Mr. Van Daan. Please. I'm so ashamed.

[Mr. Frank *comes back up the steps.*]

Dussel. Oh, for God's sake!
Mrs. Van Daan. Don't, Putti.
Margot. It doesn't matter now!
Mr. Frank *(going to* Mr. Van Daan*).* Didn't you hear what Miep said? The invasion has come! We're going to be liberated! This is a time to celebrate. *(He embraces* Mrs. Frank *and then hurries to the cupboard and gets the cognac and a glass.)*
Mr. Van Daan. To steal bread from children!
Mrs. Frank. We've all done things that we're ashamed of.
Anne. Look at me, the way I've treated Mother . . . so mean and horrid to her.
Mrs. Frank. No, Anneke, no.

[Anne *runs to her mother, putting her arms around her.*]

Anne. Oh, Mother, I was. I was awful.
Mr. Van Daan. Not like me. No one is as bad as me!
Dussel *(to* Mr. Van Daan*).* Stop it now! Let's be happy!
Mr. Frank *(giving* Mr. Van Daan *a glass of cognac).* Here! Here! Schnapps! L'chaim![13]

[Mr. Van Daan *takes the cognac. They all watch him. He gives them a feeble smile.* Anne *puts up her fingers in a V-for-Victory sign. As* Mr. Van Daan *gives an answering V-sign, they are startled to hear a loud sob from*

---

10. **B.B.C.:** British Broadcasting Corporation, a British radio network.
11. **Churchill:** Sir Winston Churchill (1874–1965), a British prime minister (1940–1945;1951–1955).
12. **General Eisenhower:** Dwight D. Eisenhower (1890–1969), the commander of the Allied forces in Europe during World War II, and later the thirty-fourth President of the United States (1953–1961).

13. *Schnapps!* (shnäps) *L'chaim!* (lə-kнä′yĭm): *Schnapps* means "a drink" in German. *L'chaim* is a toast in Hebrew, meaning "To life!"

behind them. It is Mrs. Frank, *stricken with remorse. She is sitting on the other side of the room.*]

Mrs. Frank *(through her sobs)*. When I think of the terrible things I said . . .

[Mr. Frank, Anne *and* Margot *hurry to her, trying to comfort her.* Mr. Van Daan *brings her his glass of cognac.*]

Mr. Van Daan. No! No! You were right!
Mrs. Frank. That I should speak that way to you! . . . Our friends! . . . Our guests! *(She starts to cry again.)*
Dussel. Stop it, you're spoiling the whole invasion!

[*As they are comforting her, the lights dim out. The curtain falls.*]

Anne's Voice *(faintly at first, and then with growing strength)*. We're all in much better spirits these days. There's still excellent news of the invasion. The best part about it is that I have a feeling that friends are coming. Who knows? Maybe I'll be back in school by fall. Ha, ha! The joke is on us! The warehouseman doesn't know a thing and we are paying him all that money! . . . Wednesday, the second of July, nineteen forty-four. The invasion seems temporarily to be bogged down. Mr. Kraler has to have an operation, which looks bad. The Gestapo have found the radio that was stolen. Mr. Dussel says they'll trace it back and back to the thief, and then, it's just a matter of time till they get to us. Everyone is low. Even poor Pim can't raise their spirits. I have often been downcast myself . . . but never in despair. I can shake off everything if I write. But . . . and that is the great question . . . will I ever be able to write well? I want to so much. I want to go on living even after my death.

Another birthday has gone by, so now I am fifteen. Already I know what I want. I have a goal, an opinion.

[*As this is being said, the curtain rises on the scene, the lights dim on, and* Anne's *voice fades out.*]

Scene 4

It is an afternoon a few weeks later. . . . Everyone but Margot *is in the main room. There is a sense of great tension.*

Both Mrs. Frank *and* Mr. Van Daan *are nervously pacing back and forth;* Dussel *is standing at the window, looking down fixedly at the street below.* Peter *is at the center table, trying to do his lessons.* Anne *sits opposite him, writing in her diary.* Mrs. Van Daan *is seated on the couch, her eyes on* Mr. Frank *as he sits reading.*

The sound of a telephone ringing comes from the office below. They all are rigid, listening tensely. Dussel *rushes down to* Mr. Frank.

Dussel. There it goes again, the telephone! Mr. Frank, do you hear?
Mr. Frank *(quietly)*. Yes. I hear.
Dussel *(pleading, insistent)*. But this is the third time, Mr. Frank! The third time in quick succession! It's a signal! I tell you it's Miep, trying to get us! For some reason she can't come to us and she's trying to warn us of something!
Mr. Frank. Please. Please.
Mr. Van Daan *(to* Dussel*)*. You're wasting your breath.
Dussel. Something has happened, Mr. Frank. For three days now Miep hasn't been to see us! And today not a man has come to work. There hasn't been a sound in the building!

Mrs. Frank. Perhaps it's Sunday. We may have lost track of the days.

Mr. Van Daan (to Anne). You with the diary there. What day is it?

Dussel (going to Mrs. Frank). I don't lose track of the days! I know exactly what day it is! It's Friday, the fourth of August. Friday, and not a man at work. (He rushes back to Mr. Frank, pleading with him, almost in tears.) I tell you Mr. Kraler's dead. That's the only explanation. He's dead and they've closed down the building, and Miep's trying to tell us!

Mr. Frank. She'd never telephone us.

Dussel (frantic). Mr. Frank, answer that! I beg you, answer it!

Mr. Frank. No.

Mr. Van Daan. Just pick it up and listen. You don't have to speak. Just listen and see if it's Miep.

Dussel (speaking at the same time). For God's sake . . . I ask you.

Mr. Frank. No. I've told you, no. I'll do nothing that might let anyone know we're in the building.

Peter. Mr. Frank's right.

Mr. Van Daan. There's no need to tell us what side you're on.

Mr. Frank. If we wait patiently, quietly, I believe that help will come.

[There is silence for a minute as they all listen to the telephone ringing.]

Dussel. I'm going down. (He rushes down the steps. Mr. Frank tries ineffectually to hold him. Dussel runs to the lower door, unbolting it. The telephone stops ringing. Dussel bolts the door and comes slowly back up the steps.) Too late.

[Mr. Frank goes to Margot in Anne's bedroom.]

Mr. Van Daan. So we just wait here until we die.

Mrs. Van Daan (hysterically). I can't stand it. I'll kill myself! I'll kill myself!

Mr. Van Daan. For God's sake, stop it!

[In the distance, a German military band is heard playing a Viennese waltz.]

Mrs. Van Daan. I think you'd be glad if I did! I think you want me to die!

Mr. Van Daan. Whose fault is it we're here? [Mrs. Van Daan starts for her room. He follows, talking at her.) We could've been safe somewhere . . . in America or Switzerland. But no! No! You wouldn't leave when I wanted to. You couldn't leave your things. You couldn't leave your precious furniture.

Mrs. Van Daan. Don't touch me!

[She hurries up the stairs, followed by Mr. Van Daan. Peter, unable to bear it, goes to his room. Anne looks after him, deeply concerned. Dussel returns to his post at the window. Mr. Frank comes back into the main room and takes a book, trying to read. Mrs. Frank sits near the sink, starting to peel some potatoes. Anne quietly goes to Peter's room, closing the door after her. Peter is lying face down on the cot. Anne leans over him, holding him in her arms, trying to bring him out of his despair.]

Anne. Look, Peter, the sky. (She looks up through the skylight.) What a lovely, lovely day! Aren't the clouds beautiful? You know what I do when it seems as if I couldn't stand being cooped up for one more minute? I think myself out. I think myself on a walk in the park where I used to go with Pim. Where the jonquils and the crocuses and violets grow down the slopes. You know the most wonderful part about thinking yourself out? You can have it any way you like. You can have roses and violets and chrysanthemums all blooming at the same time. . . . It's funny . . . I used to take it all for granted . . . and now I've gone crazy about everything to do with nature. Haven't you?

Peter. I've just gone crazy. I think if something doesn't happen soon . . . if we don't get out of here . . . I can't stand much more of it!

Anne *(softly).* I wish you had a religion, Peter.

Peter. No, thanks! Not me!

Anne. Oh, I don't mean you have to be Orthodox[14] . . . or believe in heaven and hell and purgatory and things . . . I just mean some religion . . . it doesn't matter what. Just to believe in something! When I think of all that's out there . . . the trees . . . the flowers . . . and sea gulls . . . when I think of the dearness of you, Peter . . . and the goodness of the people we know . . . Mr. Kraler, Miep, Dirk, the vegetable man, all risking their lives for us every day . . . When I think of these good things, I'm not afraid any more . . . I find myself, and God, and I . . .

[Peter *interrupts, getting up and walking away.*]

Peter. That's fine! But when I begin to think, I get mad! Look at us, hiding out for two years. Not able to move! Caught here like . . . waiting for them to come and get us . . . and all for what?

Anne. We're not the only people that've had to suffer. There've always been people that've had to . . . sometimes one race . . . sometimes another . . . and yet . . .

Peter. That doesn't make me feel any better!

_____

14. **be Orthodox:** follow the most strictly traditional branch of Judaism.

Anne *(going to him).* I know it's terrible, trying to have any faith . . . when people are doing such horrible . . . But you know what I sometimes think? I think the world may be going through a phase, the way I was with Mother. It'll pass, maybe not for hundreds of years, but someday. . . . I still believe, in spite of everything, that people are really good at heart.

Peter. I want to see something now. . . . Not a thousand years from now!

[*He goes over, sitting down again on the cot.*]

Anne. But, Peter, if you'd only look at it as part of a great pattern . . . that we're just a little minute in the life . . . *(She breaks off.)* Listen to us, going at each other like a couple of stupid grown-ups! Look at the sky now. Isn't it lovely? *(She holds out her hand to him.* Peter *takes it and rises, standing with her at the window looking out, his arms around her.)* Someday, when we're outside again, I'm going to . . .

[*She breaks off as she hears the sound of a car, its brakes squealing as it comes to a sudden stop. The people in the other rooms also become aware of the sound. They listen tensely. Another car roars up to a screeching stop.* Anne *and* Peter *come from* Peter's *room.* Mr. *and* Mrs. Van Daan *creep down the stairs.* Dussel *comes out from his room. Everyone is listening, hardly breathing. A doorbell clangs again and again in the building below.* Mr. Frank *starts quietly down the steps to the door.* Dussel *and* Peter *follow him. The others stand rigid, waiting, terrified.*

In a few seconds Dussel *comes stumbling back up the steps. He shakes off* Peter's *help and goes to his room.* Mr. Frank *bolts the door below and comes slowly back up the* steps. *Their eyes are all on him as he stands there for a minute. They realize that what they feared has happened. Mrs. Van Daan starts to whimper. Mr. Van Daan puts her gently in a chair, and then hurries off up the stairs to their room to collect their things. Peter goes to comfort his mother. There is a sound of violent pounding on a door below.*]

Mr. Frank (*quietly*). For the past two years we have lived in fear. Now we can live in hope.

[*The pounding below becomes more insistent. There are muffled sounds of voices, shouting commands.*]

Men's Voices. *Aufmachen! Da drinnen! Aufmachen! Schnell! Schnell! Schnell!* [15] etc., etc.

[*The street door below is forced open. We hear the heavy tread of footsteps coming up. Mr. Frank gets two schoolbags from the shelves and gives one to Anne and the other to Margot. He goes to get a bag for Mrs. Frank. The sound of feet coming up grows louder. Peter comes to Anne, kissing her goodbye; then he goes to his room to collect his things. The buzzer of their door starts to ring. Mr. Frank brings Mrs. Frank a bag. They stand together, waiting. We hear the thud of gun butts on the door, trying to break it down.*

Anne stands, holding her school satchel, looking over at her father and mother with a soft, reassuring smile. She is no longer a child, but a woman with courage to meet whatever lies ahead.

The lights dim out. The curtain falls on the scene. We hear a mighty crash as the door is shattered. After a second Anne's voice is heard.]

---

15. *Aufmachen!* . . . *Schnell!:* Open up! You in there! Open up! Quick! Quick! Quick!

Anne's Voice. And so it seems our stay is over. They are waiting for us now. They've allowed us five minutes to get our things. We can each take a bag and whatever it will hold of clothing. Nothing else. So, dear Diary, that means I must leave you behind. Goodbye for a while. P.S. Please, please, Miep, or Mr. Kraler, or anyone else. If you should find this diary, will you please keep it safe for me, because someday I hope . . .

[*Her voice stops abruptly. There is silence. After a second the curtain rises.*]

Scene 5

It is again the afternoon in November 1945. The rooms are as we saw them in the first scene. Mr. Kraler has joined Miep and Mr. Frank. There are coffee cups on the table. We see a great change in Mr. Frank. He is calm now. His bitterness is gone. He slowly turns a few pages of the diary. They are blank.

Mr. Frank. No more. (*He closes the diary and puts it down on the couch beside him.*)
Miep. I'd gone to the country to find food. When I got back the block was surrounded by police. . . .
Mr. Kraler. We made it our business to learn how they knew. It was the thief . . . the thief who told them.

[*Miep goes up to the gas burner, bringing back a pot of coffee.*]

Mr. Frank (*after a pause*). It seems strange to say this, that anyone could be happy in a concentration camp. But Anne was happy in the camp in Holland where they first took us. After two years of being shut up in these rooms, she could be out . . . out in the sunshine and the fresh air that she loved.

Miep (*offering the coffee to* Mr. Frank). A little more?

Mr. Frank (*holding out his cup to her*). The news of the war was good. The British and Americans were sweeping through France. We felt sure that they would get to us in time. In September we were told that we were to be shipped to Poland. . . . The men to one camp. The women to another. I was sent to Auschwitz. They went to Belsen. In January we were freed, the few of us who were left. The war wasn't yet over, so it took us a long time to get home. We'd be sent here and there behind the lines where we'd be safe. Each time our train would stop . . . at a siding, or a crossing . . . we'd all get out and go from group to group. . . . Where were you? Were you at Belsen? At Buchenwald? At Mauthausen? Is it possible that you knew my wife? Did you ever see my husband? My son? My daughter?

That's how I found out about my wife's death . . . of Margot, the Van Daans . . . Dussel. But Anne . . . I still hoped . . . Yesterday I went to Rotterdam. I'd heard of a woman there. . . . She'd been in Belsen with Anne. . . . I know now.

[*He picks up the diary again and turns the pages back to find a certain passage. As he finds it we hear* Anne's *voice.*]

Anne's Voice. In spite of everything, I still believe that people are really good at heart.

[Mr. Frank *slowly closes the diary.*]

Mr. Frank. She puts me to shame.

[*They are silent. The curtain falls.*]

Anne's actual diary ends on August 1, 1944. On August 4 the Nazis broke into the warehouse and sent all the occupants to concentration camps. Anne's father was the only one to survive. Anne died of typhus fever at Bergen-Belsen in March 1945, two months before the liberation of the Netherlands.

SEEKING MEANING

Act Two

Scene 1

1. Anne's voice reading from her diary provides basic information about the story. What facts does the diary relate at the opening of Act Two?

2. Most of the characters own a few small possessions that are very precious to them. What do you think Peter's cat means to him?

Why is Mrs. Van Daan's coat so important to her?

3. The suspense in the play is increased by a new worry. What fear does Mr. Kraler's news bring?

Scene 2

4. Love, which unites some of the characters, also divides them. How would you describe Mrs. Van Daan's reaction to the interest that Anne and Peter show in each other?

5. Peter says that Anne has changed from the

kind of girl she was when they first met. How has Anne changed? How does she explain her new relationship with Peter in her diary?

Scene 3

6. Mr. Frank says, "We don't need the Nazis to destroy us. We're destroying ourselves." The constant threat of the Nazis on the outside terrifies the characters. What human fears and weaknesses attack them from the inside?

7. In one moment the "family" realizes that their quarrels are unimportant compared to the greater evil in the outside world. What event changes their fear to hope, and their hatred to forgiveness? What is the first reaction of Mrs. Frank and Mr. Van Daan?

Scene 4

8. In spite of the great tension around her, Anne still has a way to escape to a happy and beautiful world. What does she do? Where does she go?

9. How does Anne explain the war and the world's madness? What belief, in spite of everything, gives her hope?

10. At the opening of the play, Anne is a girl just beginning to understand the world around her. How has she changed by the end of the play?

Scene 5

11. This scene returns to the first scene of the play. Mr. Frank tells Miep about the concentration camps. What does he say happened to all the other members of the "family"?

12. Mr. Frank feels ashamed because he cannot share Anne's belief in the goodness of people. Do you think any events in the play support Anne's belief?

DEVELOPING SKILLS IN READING

Recognizing the Elements of a Tragedy

The Diary of Anne Frank is a tragedy. Most tragedies end with the hero or heroine suffering death or defeat.

Tragic Characters. In tragedies, attention is focused on one or two outstanding characters. These are people whose courage, dignity, or other heroic qualities strongly distinguish them from the rest of the people in the play. Which characters in this play are you most interested in? What makes you admire them?

Tragic Plot. In tragedies, the characters face some powerful force that finally overcomes them. What terrible outside forces are seeking to destroy the characters in this play? You knew from the beginning of the play that Anne would not survive. Did you want to read on, even though you knew that the story would end sadly for her?

Tragic Theme. Tragedies need not be depressing, even though they show people facing overwhelming odds and often death. In fact, many tragedies lift up our spirits. They make us see nobility and courage and dignity in people, despite the terrible things that happen to them. What would you say is the theme, or main idea about life, that this play expresses?

In what ways is Anne victorious, despite her tragedy?

Understanding Dramatic Terms

Here are some terms that are useful in understanding *The Diary of Anne Frank* and other plays.

Subplot: a second plot or "story" within the larger main plot. In *The Diary of Anne Frank*, the main plot tells what happens as the "family" hides from the Nazis. The subplot tells what happens between Anne and Peter. Plot and subplot are often related. Anne and Peter, for instance, must hide their world of love from the grown-ups, just as the whole "family" must hide from the hostile outside world. How does this subplot involving Anne and Peter add a hopeful mood to the play?

Flashback: a way of taking the audience back in time, in order to recall events already past. Almost all of *The Diary of Anne Frank* is a flashback. Who is remembering these events?

Monologue: a long speech delivered by one character. In English, the suffix *-logue* means "words." *Monologue* means "words spoken by one person." *Dialogue* means "conversation, or words exchanged between characters." Monologues often contain ideas that are important in the play. In this play, Anne delivers several monologues. Which sentence in Anne's monologue in Act Two, Scene 3, expresses an important wish?

New York Herald Tribune
October 6, 1955

=== THEATER ===
'The Diary of Anne Frank'
=== By WALTER F. KERR ===

NEARLY all of the characters in "The Diary of Anne Frank"—they are Dutch Jews hiding out from Hitler in a dingy and overcrowded garret—are doomed to death. Yet the precise quality of the new play at the Cort is the quality of glowing, ineradicable life—life in its warmth, its wonder, its spasms of anguish, and its wild and flaring humor.

Perhaps no scene in the play is more touching than that in which a fifteen-year-old girl and a nineteen-year-old boy enter into the formalities of courtship. They have, with their families, been cooped up on the top floor of an Amsterdam office building for nearly two years. They have seen each other morning, noon and night during all this time, eaten together, squabbled together, been terrified together, simply grown up together.

When the time comes, though, for each to seek the other out in a shy, faltering, heartbreak-ing romance, they at once begin to behave like lovers who have just been introduced. In her own little corner of the densely populated living quarters, the girl piles her hair on top of her head and hopefully drapes a scarf about her shoulders; in his cubbyhole the boy puts on a jacket, straightens his tie, and trembles in expectation. The girl 'goes out' for the evening to see him—just across the room, past her chess-playing parents, past the boy's greedy father and frivolous mother—to a door that opens gently not more than twenty feet away.

• • •

The circumstances around her are the circumstances of despair and decay. In the midst of this, a fresh and shining dignity, a springtime innocence and an instinctive honor rise to fill the shabby room. Since you know that Anne Frank's life is to end in the horrors of Belsen, the play cannot help but break your heart. But along the way it

takes great care to let you know that the moments of living—short as they were—were all moments of growth and discovery and very great joy.

Frances Goodrich and Albert Hackett have fashioned a wonderfully sensitive and theatrically craftsmanlike narrative out of the real-life legacy left us by a spirited and straightforward Jewish girl. Garson Kanin has not so much staged it as orchestrated it—from the simple and homely rhythms of a silent couple doing the dinner dishes to the sudden, catlike tensions of an alarmed household listening in panic to a telephone bell that may be a warning.

Authors and director together have given us a series of vivid, utterly lifelike yet colorfully dramatic pictures: the happy new refugees stripping off layer after layer of concealed clothing, the night-time stir that responds to an adolescent's scream, the religious ritual by candlelight that turns into an antic round of gift-giving.

• • •

And Mr. Kanin has found a superb company for the purpose. A few seasons ago young Susan Strasberg suggested, in an off-Broadway performance, that she had the magic of which stars are made. That star is beginning to shine now—not with absolute authority, perhaps,

but with a puppyish effervescence that is like a promise of the world on a platter.

If Miss Strasberg has a little difficulty still with the reflective passages that come with the girl's new maturity, she has nothing but enchantment to bring the earlier scenes of tomboy fire and prankish ebullience. Clambering over the furniture, pounding her hands against her head excitedly, dancing demurely with her father, or donning oversize trousers for a flash of mimic impudence, she is breathtaking.

Joseph Schildkraut's controlled and confident father is a tower of strength to the family—and to the play—he must hold together. David Levin's boy-next-door is quietly moving, Jack Gilford's fussy dentist, Lou Jacobi's eternally hungry business man, Dennie Moore's vain and pathetic wife, and Clinton Sundberg's restrained friend of the oppressed are all crystal-clear portraits. And you aren't likely to forget Gusti Huber's drawn face across a festive table as she realizes with absolute certainty that they are all bound to be discovered.

Boris Aronson's gabled setting, from which the homeless look out on a thousand homes, is brilliantly drawn, a stunning background for a play that is—for all its pathos—as bright and shining as a banner.

Practice in
Reading and Writing

DRAMA

Reading a Drama

Many people find plays easy and fast-moving to read, because they consist almost entirely of dialogue. Dialogue as-
sumes great importance in drama, for the entire story must
be told through the characters' conversations.

When you read a drama, you must imagine how the characters are speaking and what they are doing on stage. There are
devices built right into a drama that help you. For example,
read this comic passage from *The Ugly Duckling* (page 287).
The King is teaching Dulcibella, the Princess' maid, how to
behave when Prince Simon woos her:

King. . . . and then he will take your hand in both of his and
press it to his heart. *(He does so.)* And then—what do *you*
say?

Dulcibella. Coo!

King. No, *not* "Coo."

Dulcibella. Never had anyone do *that* to me before.

King. That also strikes the wrong note. What you want to say
is, "Oh, Prince Simon!" . . . Say it.

Dulcibella *(loudly)*. Oh, Prince Simon!

King. No, no. You don't need to shout until he has said
"What?" two or three times. Always consider the possibility
that he *isn't* deaf. Softly, and giving the words a dying fall,
letting them play around his head like a flight of doves.

Dulcibella *(still a little overloud)*. O-o-o-o-h, Prinsimon!

King. Keep the idea in your mind of a flight of *doves* rather
than a flight of panic-stricken elephants, and you will be all
right. Now I'm going to get up, and you must, as it were,
waft me into a seat by your side. *(She starts wafting.)* Not
rescuing a drowning man, that's another idea altogether . . . .

1. *Note the stage directions that tell how speeches are to be spoken and what the players are to be doing.*

According to the stage directions, what does the King do in his first speech? How is Dulcibella instructed to deliver her "Oh, Prince Simon!" speeches?

2. *Note clues in the speeches themselves that tell what the players are doing, or how their speeches are to be delivered.*

For example, the King wants Dulcibella to "waft" him into a seat. How does Dulcibella actually move? (The clue is in the King's speech, when he says, *"Not* rescuing a drown-ing man . . . ."*) You will find an additional clue on how Dulcibella delivers her second "Oh, Prince Simon!" speech by reading the King's response to it. (The clue is in his remark about a flight of panic-stricken elephants.)

3. *Imagine the actions taking place that are not indicated in stage directions or in the speeches.*

What do you imagine the King is doing as he gives his speech beginning "No, no. You don't need to shout . . ."? What expressions do you think Dulcibella has on her face during this scene?

Writing Dialogue

When you write dialogue, you should suit the dialogue to the characters. For example, the King in this play usually speaks formally, in a stuffy, conceited way. Dulcibella, on the other hand, speaks rapidly and runs many of her sentences together, in a breathless way:

Oo, yes, he's ever so smart, he's an archer, well, not as you might say a real archer, he works in the armory, but old Bottlenose, *you* know who I mean . . . .

Notice how the girl in *The Hitchhiker* uses expressions like "gee," "swell," and "dunno." She says "dogs" for "feet" and she occasionally uses nonstandard English:

There wasn't nothing but a bunch of steers . . . .

Look at a few of the speeches of Adams, the main character in this play. Does he use slang and nonstandard English?

Write a dialogue that might take place between the following characters or between two characters of your own choosing. Where you think necessary, use stage directions to tell how the characters are speaking or what they are doing.

A shy boy and a shy girl
An angry boss and a fast-talking young employee
A highly educated Martian and a five-year-old Earthling
An optimist and a pessimist

For Further Reading

Gibson, William, *The Miracle Worker* (Knopf, 1957; paperback, Bantam)
This play is based on the true story of how Annie Sullivan taught Helen Keller—a deaf and blind child—that there are words and ways to communicate.

Hammerstein, Oscar, *Six Plays by Rodgers and Hammerstein* (Modern Library, 1955)
This collection contains the scripts and lyrics of some famous musical comedies: *Oklahoma, Carousel, South Pacific,* and *The King and I.*

Hansberry, Lorraine, *A Raisin in the Sun* (Random House, 1969; paperback, New American Library)
Three generations of a middle-class black family in Chicago face many troubles when Mama buys a house.

Kozelka, Paul, editor, *Fifteen American One-Act Plays* (paperback, Washington Square Press, 1961)
The outstanding plays here include comedies (*The Trysting Place* by Booth Tarkington), suspense stories (*Sorry, Wrong Number* by Lucille Fletcher), and fantasies (*The Devil and Daniel Webster* by Stephen Vincent Benét).

Laurents, Arthur, *West Side Story* (Random House, 1958; paperback, Dell)
This tragic Romeo and Juliet story, set in Spanish Harlem, tells of two opposing teen-age gangs who doom the love between Maria and Tony.

Schary, Dore, *Sunrise at Campobello* (Random House, 1958)
In this drama, Franklin D. Roosevelt is stricken by polio and struggles to regain an active life.

Sherwood, Robert, *Abe Lincoln in Illinois* (Scribner, 1937)
Lincoln comes alive as a very human figure in this play, which begins when he is a young man and ends when he becomes President.

Sills, Paul, *Story Theatre* (paperback, Samuel French, 1971)
This humorous, fast-moving dramatization of ten old folk-tales was presented on Broadway in 1970. Popular songs and funny dialogue give lively new twists to such old tales as "Henny Penny," "The Golden Goose," and "The Fisherman and His Wife."

Stone, Peter, and Sherman Edwards, *1776: A Musical Play* (Viking, 1970; paperback, Viking)
This musical gives you an unusual view of the people who shaped America's history in the struggle to adopt the Declaration of Independence.

Vidal, Gore, editor, *Visit to a Small Planet and Other Television Plays* (Little, Brown, 1957)
This collection includes Vidal's own satire about a visitor from outer space who is fascinated by life on our "primitive" planet.

Wilder, Thornton, *Our Town* (Harper & Row, 1960; paperback, Avon)
One of the most famous of American plays, this drama examines the priceless value of everyday life. The play is set in a small town called Grover's Corners, New Hampshire. Another famous Wilder play is *The Happy Journey to Trenton and Camden,* available in several collections.

The writings in this unit are *nonfiction*—that is, they are about actual people and actual events. Nonfiction can be about almost anything—sports, wars, inventions, adventures, disasters, people's lives. It can take the form of diaries, letters, biographies, magazine articles, speeches, or interviews.

Like all literature, nonfiction helps you share experiences. In this unit, you will read about a forest fire, a fight on a Mississippi steamboat, and a deadly cobra. You will learn how one writer had to fight the neighborhood bullies, and how another one learned to live with a bossy, bad-tempered dog.

NONFICTION

You will be reading nonfiction all of your life. It is a form of writing that can give you information about the world and personal pleasure as well.

"It was as if the fire had come from the bowels of the earth . . . ." This description of a forest fire is from a famous series of diaries. Anaïs Nin witnessed the disaster when she was living in Sierra Madre, a small town east of Los Angeles, in the foothills of a mountain range. The diary entry is dated "Winter, 1953–1954."

Forest Fire   *Anaïs Nin*

A man rushed in to announce he had seen smoke on Monrovia Peak. As I looked out of the window I saw the two mountains facing the house on fire. The entire rim burning wildly in the night. The flames, driven by hot Santa Ana winds from the desert, were as tall as the tallest trees, the sky already tinted coral, and the crackling noise of burning trees, the ashes and the smoke were already increasing. The fire raced along, sometimes descending behind the mountain where I could only see the glow, sometimes descending toward us. I thought of the foresters in danger. I made coffee for the weary men who came down occasionally with horses they had led out, or with old people from the isolated cabins. They were covered with soot from their battle with the flames.

At six o'clock the fire was on our left side and rushing toward Mount Wilson. Evacuees from the cabins began to arrive and had to be given blankets and hot coffee. The streets were blocked with fire engines readying to fight the fire if it touched the houses. Policemen and firemen and guards turned away the

sightseers. Some were relatives concerned over the fate of the foresters or the pack-station family. The policemen lighted flares, which gave the scene a theatrical, tragic air. The red lights on the police cars twinkled alarmingly. More fire engines arrived. Ashes fell, and the roar of the fire was now like thunder.

We were told to ready ourselves for evacuation. I packed the diaries. The saddest spectacle, besides that of the men fighting the fire as they would a war, were the animals, rabbits, coyotes, mountain lions, deer, driven by the fire to the edge of the mountain, taking a look at the crowd of people and panicking, choosing rather to rush back into the fire.

The fire was now like a ring around Sierra Madre, every mountain was burning. People living at the foot of the mountain were packing their cars. I rushed next door to the Campion children, who had been left with a baby sitter, and got them into the car. It was impossible to save all the horses. We parked the car on the field below us. I called up the Campions, who were out for the evening, and

reassured them. The baby sitter dressed the children warmly. I made more coffee. I answered frantic telephone calls.

All night the fire engines sprayed water over the houses. But the fire grew immense, angry, and rushing at a speed I could not believe. It would rush along, and suddenly leap over a road, a trail, like a monster, devouring all in its path. The firefighters cut breaks in the heavy brush, but when the wind was strong enough, the fire leaped across them. At dawn one arm of the fire reached the back of our houses but was finally contained.

But high above and all around, the fire was burning, more vivid than the sun, throwing spirals of smoke in the air like the smoke from a volcano. Thirty-three cabins burned, and twelve thousand acres of forest still burn-

ing endangered countless homes below the fire. The fire was burning to the back of us now, and a rain of ashes began to fall and continued for days. The smell of the burn in the air, acid and pungent and tenacious. The dragon tongues of flames devouring, the flames leaping, the roar of destruction and dissolution, the eyes of the panicked animals, caught between fire and human beings, between two forms of death. They chose the fire. It was as if the fire had come from the bowels of the earth, like that of a fiery volcano, it was so powerful, so swift, and so ravaging. I saw trees become skeletons in one minute, I saw trees fall, I saw bushes turned to ashes in a second, I saw weary, ash-covered men, looking like men returned from war, some with burns, others overcome by smoke.

The men were rushing from one spot to another watching for recrudescence.[1] Some started backfiring up the mountain so that the ascending flames could counteract the descending ones.

As the flames reached the cities below, hundreds of roofs burst into flame at once. There was no water pressure because all the fire hydrants were turned on at the same time, and the fire departments were helpless to save more than a few of the burning homes.

. . .

The blaring loudspeakers of passing police cars warned us to prepare to evacuate in case the wind changed and drove the fire in our direction. What did I wish to save? I thought only of the diaries. I appeared on the porch carrying a huge stack of diary volumes, preparing to pack them in the car. A reporter for the Pasadena *Star News* was taking pictures of the evacuation. He came up, very annoyed with me. "Hey, lady, next time could you bring out something more important than all those old papers? Carry some clothes on the next trip. We gotta have human interest in these pictures!"

A week later, the danger was over.

Gray ashy days.

In Sierra Madre, following the fire, the January rains brought floods. People are sandbagging their homes. At four A.M. the streets are covered with mud. The bare, burnt, naked mountains cannot hold the rains and slide down bringing rocks and mud. One of the rangers must now take photographs and movies of the disaster. He asks if I will help by holding an umbrella over the cameras. I put on my raincoat and he lends me hip boots which look to me like seven-league boots.

We drive a little way up the road. At the third curve it is impassable. A river is rushing across the road. The ranger takes pictures while I hold the umbrella over the camera. It is terrifying to see the muddied waters and rocks, the mountain disintegrating. When we are ready to return, the road before us is covered by large rocks but the ranger pushes on as if the truck were a jeep and forces it through. The edge of the road is being carried away.

I am laughing and scared too. The ranger is at ease in nature, and without fear. It is a wild moment of danger. It is easy to love nature in its peaceful and consoling moments, but one must love it in its furies too, in its despairs and wildness, especially when the damage is caused by us.

Anaïs Nin, with her diaries.

---

1. **recrudescence** (rē′krōō-dĕs′əns): a new outbreak of something that has been inactive, such as a disease or a volcano.

SEEKING MEANING

1. Diaries and journals are personal documents. What details in this entry show that Anaïs Nin wanted to record her personal thoughts and reactions to the fire and to the flood that followed it?

2. In the third and fourth paragraphs, the author tells us what she did when she was ordered to evacuate. What do you think her actions reveal about her values, or the things she considered important?

3. Anaïs Nin describes the fire as if it were a terrible destructive creature, a kind of monster. Which details in her description help you see the fire as a "monster"?

4. The Pasadena *Star News* reporter wanted a "human interest" picture of the catastrophe. In other words, he wanted a picture showing how the fire affected people, as well as property. Although he did not realize it at the time, the reporter really *had* a "human interest" picture. How would a photograph of a famous person saving her life's work contain "human interest"? What caption would you write for such a photograph?

DEVELOPING SKILLS OF EXPRESSION

Writing a Firsthand Record

One of the things that readers like about Anaïs Nin's diaries is her ability to make them see vividly what she saw.

Record a series of events that you have witnessed firsthand. Try to present the events as vividly as possible, so that your reader will "see" what you saw. You might imitate this sentence from the diary entry, with its four uses of "I saw"

I saw trees become skeletons in one minute, I saw trees fall, I saw bushes turned to ashes in a second, I saw weary, ash-covered men, looking like men returned from war, some with burns, others overcome by smoke.

You might prefer to write four separate sentences, each beginning with "I saw." Remember that Anaïs Nin doesn't say she saw trees and bushes burn. She saw "trees become skeletons" and "bushes turned to ashes."

ABOUT THE AUTHOR

Anaïs Nin (1903–1977) was born in France and spent her early years there. When she was eleven years old, she moved to New York with her mother and brother. She returned to Paris in the 1920's and became part of a circle of brilliant writers and artists. In the early 1930's, she began keeping a diary that she continued for the rest of her life. In her diary, she recorded her personal reactions to the events in her life and to the extraordinary people she knew. The entire unedited manuscript of this diary consists of about 150 volumes or 15,000 typewritten pages. The first volume was published in 1966, and four more volumes are now in print. Anaïs Nin said that she wanted in her writing to unmask the deeper self that lies hidden behind the self presented to the world.

The Coyotes

John Steinbeck

The Mojave is a big desert and a frightening one. It's as though nature tested a man for endurance and constancy to prove whether he was good enough to get to California. The shimmering dry heat made visions of water on the flat plain. And even when you drive at high speed, the hills that mark the boundaries recede before you. Charley, always a dog for water, panted asthmatically, jarring his whole body with the effort, and a good eight inches of his tongue hung out flat as a leaf and dripping. I pulled off the road into a small gulley to give him water from my thirty-gallon tank. But before I let him drink I poured water all over him and on my hair and shoulders and shirt. The air is so dry that evaporation makes you feel suddenly cold.

I opened a can of beer from my refrigerator

and sat well inside the shade of Rocinante,[1] looking out at the sun-pounded plain, dotted here and there with clumps of sagebrush.

About fifty yards away two coyotes stood watching me, their tawny coats blending with sand and sun. I knew that with any quick or suspicious movement of mine they could drift into invisibility. With the most casual slowness I reached down my new rifle from its sling over my bed—the .222 with its bitter little high-speed, long-range stings. Very slowly I brought the rifle up. Perhaps in the shade of my house I was half hidden by the blinding light outside. The little rifle has a beautiful telescope sight with a wide field. The coyotes had not moved.

I got both of them in the field of my telescope, and the glass brought them very close. Their tongues lolled out so that they seemed to smile mockingly. They were favored animals, not starved, but well furred, the golden hair tempered with black guard hairs. Their little lemon-yellow eyes were plainly visible in the glass. I moved the cross hairs to the breast of the right-hand animal, and pushed the safety. My elbows on the table steadied the gun. The cross hairs lay unmoving on the brisket.[2] And then the coyote sat down like a dog and its right rear paw came up to scratch the right shoulder.

My finger was reluctant to touch the trigger. I must be getting very old and my ancient conditioning[3] worn thin. Coyotes are vermin. They steal chickens. They thin the ranks of quail and all other game birds. They must be killed. They are the enemy. My first shot would drop the sitting beast, and the other would whirl to fade away. I might very well pull him down with a running shot because I am a good rifleman.

And I did not fire. My training said, "Shoot!" and my age replied, "There isn't a chicken within thirty miles, and if there are any they aren't my chickens. And this waterless place is not quail country. No, these boys are keeping their figures with kangaroo rats and jack rabbits, and that's vermin eat vermin. Why should I interfere?"

"Kill them," my training said. "Everyone kills them. It's a public service." My finger moved to the trigger. The cross was steady on the breast just below the panting tongue. I could imagine the splash and jar of angry steel, the leap and struggle until the torn heart failed, and then, not too long later, the shadow of a buzzard, and another. By that time I would be long gone—out of the desert and across the Colorado River. And beside the sagebrush there would be a naked, eyeless skull, a few picked bones, a spot of black dried blood and a few rags of golden fur.

I guess I'm too old and too lazy to be a good citizen. The second coyote stood sidewise to my rifle. I moved the cross hairs to his shoulder and held steady. There was no question of missing with that rifle at that range. I owned both animals. Their lives were mine. I put the safety on and laid the rifle on the table. Without the telescope they were not so intimately close. The hot blast of light tousled[4] the air to shimmering.

Then I remembered something I heard long ago that I hope is true. It was unwritten law in China, so my informant told me, that when

---

1. **Rocinante** (rō'sĭ-nän'tä): the name of Steinbeck's camper. He named it after the horse that the fictional Spanish knight Don Quixote rode on his quests.
2. **brisket:** the breast of an animal.
3. **conditioning:** training that produces an automatic response.

4. **tousled** (tou'zəld): here, disturbed in some way.

one man saved another's life he became responsible for that life to the end of its existence. For, having interfered with a course of events, the savior could not escape his responsibility. And that has always made good sense to me.

Now I had a token responsibility for two live and healthy coyotes. In the delicate world of relationships, we are tied together for all time. I opened two cans of dog food and left them as a votive.[5]

---

5. **votive:** an offering, especially one that fulfills a vow.

SEEKING MEANING

1. Which details in the fourth paragraph make the coyotes seem beautiful—more like pets than like dangerous animals?

2. The next three paragraphs describe Steinbeck's mixed feelings about killing the coyotes. What did his "training" tell him to do? What did his "age" reply? What do you think the word *age* means in this passage?

3. Steinbeck's training kept insisting that coyotes are vermin. *Vermin* are pests that carry disease; some eat chickens or other livestock. People see vermin as intruders on their territory. In what way was Steinbeck, not the coyotes, the real intruder in this desert scene?

4. Steinbeck says, "I guess I'm too old and too lazy to be a good citizen." Do you think he really means what he says? What good qualities kept him from shooting the coyotes?

5. What did an unwritten Chinese law teach Steinbeck about his responsibilities for the two animals he had nearly killed?

6. Which sentence in the last paragraph could sum up what Steinbeck finally learned from his experience? How would you state this idea in your own words?

ABOUT THE AUTHOR

John Steinbeck (1902–1968) was born in California. For more than thirty years he was one of the foremost American novelists, with an international reputation. He wrote about people he knew: local farmers, migrant fruit pickers, fishermen. He generally used settings in his native California. His writing combines social realism with an affirmation of basic human values.

Steinbeck won the Pulitzer Prize for his novel *The Grapes of Wrath*, a story about the experiences of migrant farm workers during the Depression of the 1930's. In 1962, he became the seventh American-born author to win the Nobel Prize for literature. Some of Steinbeck's stories that you might enjoy are "Flight," "The Gift," and "The Leader of the People." Many of his novels have been made into movies.

". . . I ran away. I said I would never come home again till I was a pilot . . . ." A hundred years ago many boys living along the Mississippi dreamed of becoming steamboat pilots. The reason we remember the boy who said these words is that he went on to become a famous American writer. This story is from Mark Twain's book Life on the Mississippi.

Cub Pilot on the Mississippi   *Mark Twain*

When I was a boy, there was but one permanent ambition among my comrades in our village on the west bank of the Mississippi River. That was to be a steamboatman. We had transient[1] ambitions of other sorts, but they were only transient. When a circus came and went, it left us all burning to become clowns; the first minstrel show that ever came to our section left us all suffering to try that kind of life; now and then we had a hope

that, if we lived and were good, God would permit us to be pirates. These ambitions faded out, each in its turn; but the ambition to be a steamboatman always remained.

I first wanted to be a cabin boy, so that I could come out with a white apron on and shake a tablecloth over the side, where all my old comrades could see me; later I thought I would rather be the deckhand who stood on the end of the stage plank with the coil of rope in his hand, because he was particularly conspicuous.

---

1. **transient** (trăn′shənt): temporary; passing.

Cub Pilot on the Mississippi   373

Boy after boy managed to get on the river. The minister's son became an engineer. The doctor's and the postmaster's sons became "mud clerks";[2] the wholesale liquor dealer's son became a barkeeper on a boat; four sons of the chief merchant, and two sons of the county judge, became pilots. Pilot was the grandest position of all. The pilot, even in those days of trivial wages, had a princely salary—from a hundred and fifty to two hundred and fifty dollars a month, and no board to pay. Two months of his wages would pay a preacher's salary for a year. Now some of us were left disconsolate. We could not get on the river—at least our parents would not let us.

So, by and by, I ran away. I said I would never come home again till I was a pilot and could come in glory.

During the two or two and a half years of my apprenticeship I served under many pilots, and had experience of many kinds of steamboatmen and many varieties of steamboats. I am to this day profiting somewhat by that experience; for in that brief, sharp schooling, I got personally and familiarly acquainted with about all the different types of human nature that are to be found in fiction, biography, or history.

The figure that comes before me oftenest, out of the shadows of that vanished time, is that of Brown, of the steamer *Pennsylvania*. He was a middle-aged, long, slim, bony, smooth-shaven, horsefaced, ignorant, stingy, malicious, snarling, fault-hunting, mote[3]-magnifying tyrant. I early got the habit of coming on watch with dread at my heart. No matter how good a time I might have been having with the off-watch below, and no matter how high my spirits might be when I started aloft, my soul became lead in my body the moment I approached the pilothouse.

I still remember the first time I ever entered the presence of that man. The boat had backed out from St. Louis and was "straightening down." I ascended to the pilothouse in high feather, and very proud to be semiofficially a member of the executive family of so fast and famous a boat. Brown was at the wheel. I paused in the middle of the room, all fixed to make my bow, but Brown did not look around. I thought he took a furtive glance at me out of the corner of his eye, but as not even this notice was repeated, I judged I had been mistaken. By this time he was picking his way among some dangerous "breaks" abreast the woodyards; therefore it would not be proper to interrupt him; so I stepped softly to the high bench and took a seat.

---

2. **mud clerks:** the lowest of several clerks who assisted the purser, the officer in charge of financial accounts. A mud clerk was paid very little.
3. **mote:** a small particle, such as a speck of dust.

There was silence for ten minutes; then my new boss turned and inspected me deliberately and painstakingly from head to heel for about—as it seemed to me—a quarter of an hour. After which he removed his countenance, and I saw it no more for some seconds; then it came around once more, and this question greeted me: "Are you Horace Bixby's cub?"

"Yes, sir."

After this there was a pause and another inspection. Then: "What's your name?"

I told him. He repeated it after me. It was probably the only thing he ever forgot; for although I was with him many months he never addressed himself to me in any other way than "Here!" and then his command followed.

"Where was you born?"

"In Florida, Missouri."

A pause. Then: "Dern sight better stayed there!"

By means of a dozen or so of pretty direct questions, he pumped my family history out of me.

The leads[4] were going now in the first crossing. This interrupted the inquest.

It must have been all of fifteen minutes— fifteen minutes of dull, homesick silence— before that long horseface swung round upon me again—and then what a change! It was as red as fire, and every muscle in it was working. Now came this shriek: "Here! You going to set there all day?"

I lit in the middle of the floor, shot there by the electric suddenness of the surprise. As soon as I could get my voice I said apologetically: "I have had no orders, sir."

"You've had no *orders!* My, what a fine bird we are! We must have *orders!* Our father was a *gentleman*— and *we've* been to *school.* Yes,

---

4. **leads** (lĕdz): weights lowered to test the depth of the river.

we are a gentleman, *too,* and got to have *orders!* ORDERS, is it? ORDERS is what you want! Dod dern my skin, *I'll* learn you to swell yourself up and blow around *here* about your dod-derned *orders!* G'way from the wheel!" (I had approached it without knowing it.)

I moved back a step or two and stood as in a dream, all my senses stupefied by this frantic assault.

"What you standing there for? Take that ice pitcher down to the texas tender![5] Come, move along, and don't you be all day about it!"

The moment I got back to the pilothouse Brown said:

"Here! What was you doing down there all this time?"

"I couldn't find the texas tender; I had to go all the way to the pantry."

"Derned likely story! Fill up the stove."

I proceeded to do so. He watched me like a cat. Presently he shouted: "Put down that shovel! Derndest numskull I ever saw—ain't even got sense enough to load up a stove."

All through the watch this sort of thing went on. Yes, and the subsequent watches were much like it during a stretch of months. As I have said, I soon got the habit of coming on duty with dread. The moment I was in the presence, even in the darkest night, I could feel those yellow eyes upon me and knew their owner was watching for a pretext to spit out some venom on me. Preliminarily he would say: "Here! Take the wheel."

Two minutes later: "*Where* in the nation you going to? Pull her down! Pull her down!"

After another moment: "Say! You going to hold her all day? Let her go—meet her! Meet her!"

Then he would jump from the bench, snatch the wheel from me, and meet her himself, pouring out wrath upon me all the time.

George Ritchie was the other pilot's cub. He was having good times now, for his boss, George Ealer, was as kindhearted as Brown wasn't. Ritchie had steered for Brown the season before; consequently, he knew exactly how to entertain himself and plague me, all by the one operation. Whenever I took the wheel for a moment on Ealer's watch, Ritchie would sit back on the bench and play Brown, with continual ejaculations of "Snatch her! Snatch her! Derndest mudcat I ever saw!" "Here! Where are you going *now*? Going to run over that snag?" "Pull her *down!* Don't you hear me? Pull her *down!*" "There she goes! *Just* as I expected! I told you not to cramp that reef. G'way from the wheel!"

So I always had a rough time of it, no matter whose watch it was; and sometimes it seemed to me that Ritchie's good-natured badgering was pretty nearly as aggravating as Brown's dead-earnest nagging.

I often wanted to kill Brown, but this would not answer. A cub had to take everything his boss gave, in the way of vigorous comment and criticism; and we all believed that there was a United States law making it a penitentiary offense to strike or threaten a pilot who was on duty.

Two trips later, I got into serious trouble. Brown was steering; I was "pulling down." My younger brother [Henry] appeared on the hurricane deck, and shouted to Brown to stop at some landing or other, a mile or so below. Brown gave no intimation that he had heard anything. But that was his way: he never condescended to take notice of an underclerk. The wind was blowing; Brown was deaf (al-

---

5. **texas tender:** the waiter in the officers' quarters. The rooms on Mississippi steamboats were named after the states. Since the officers' area was the largest, and since Texas was the largest state at this time, it was called the *texas.*

though he always pretended he wasn't), and I very much doubted if he had heard the order. If I had had two heads, I would have spoken; but as I had only one, it seemed judicious to take care of it; so I kept still.

Presently, sure enough, we went sailing by that plantation. Captain Klinefelter appeared on the deck, and said: "Let her come around, sir, let her come around. Didn't Henry tell you to land here?"

"*No*, sir!"

"I sent him up to do it."

"He *did* come up; and that's all the good it done, the dod-derned fool. He never said anything."

"Didn't *you* hear him?" asked the captain of me.

Of course I didn't want to be mixed up in this business, but there was no way to avoid it; so I said: "Yes, sir."

I knew what Brown's next remark would be, before he uttered it. It was: "Shut your mouth! You never heard anything of the kind."

I closed my mouth, according to instructions. An hour later Henry entered the pilot-house, unaware of what had been going on. He was a thoroughly inoffensive boy, and I was sorry to see him come for I knew Brown would have no pity on him. Brown began, straightway: "Here! Why didn't you tell me we'd got to land at that plantation?"

"I did tell you, Mr. Brown."

"It's a lie!"

I said: "You lie, yourself. He did' tell you."

Brown glared at me in unaffected surprise; and for as much as a moment he was entirely speechless; then he shouted to me: "I'll attend to your case in a half a minute!"; then to Henry, "And you leave the pilothouse; out with you!"

It was pilot law, and must be obeyed. The boy started out, and even had his foot on the upper step outside the door, when Brown, with a sudden access of fury, picked up a ten-pound lump of coal and sprang after him; but I was between, with a heavy stool, and I hit Brown a good honest blow which stretched him out.

I had committed the crime of crimes—I had lifted my hand against a pilot on duty! I supposed I was booked for the penitentiary sure, and couldn't be booked any surer if I went on and squared my long account with this person while I had the chance; consequently I stuck to him and pounded him with my fists a considerable time. I do not know how long; the pleasure of it probably made it seem longer than it really was; but in the end he struggled free and jumped up and sprang to the wheel: a very natural solicitude, for, all this time, here was this steamboat tearing down the river at the rate of fifteen miles an hour and nobody at the helm! However, Eagle Bend was two miles wide at this bank-full stage, and correspondingly long and deep; and the boat was steering herself straight down the middle and taking no chances. Still, that was only luck—a body *might* have found her charging into the woods.

Perceiving at a glance that the *Pennsylvania* was in no danger, Brown gathered up the big spyglass, war-club fashion, and ordered me out of the pilothouse with more than bluster. But I was not afraid of him now; so, instead of going, I tarried and criticized his grammar. I reformed his ferocious speeches for him and put them into good English, calling his attention to the advantages of pure English over the dialect of the Pennsylvania collieries[6] whence he was extracted. He could have done his part to admiration in a crossfire of mere vituperation,[7] of course; but he was

---

6. **collieries** (kol'yər-ēz): coal mines.
7. **vituperation** (vī-tōō'pə-rā'shən): abusive language.

not equipped for this species of controversy; so he presently laid aside his glass and took the wheel, muttering and shaking his head; and I retired to the bench. The racket had brought everybody to the hurricane deck, and I trembled when I saw the old captain looking up from amid the crowd. I said to myself, "Now I *am* done for!" for although, as a rule, he was so fatherly and indulgent toward the boat's family, and so patient of minor shortcomings, he could be stern enough when the fault was worth it.

I tried to imagine what he *would* do to a cub pilot who had been guilty of such a crime as mine, committed on a boat that was guard-deep[8] with costly freight and alive with passengers. Our watch was nearly ended. I

thought I would go and hide somewhere till I got a chance to slide ashore. So I slipped out of the pilothouse, and down the steps, and around to the texas door, and I was in the act of gliding within, when the captain confronted me! I dropped my head, and he stood over me in silence a moment or two, then said impressively: "Follow me."

I dropped into his wake; he led the way to his parlor in the forward end of the texas. We were alone now. He closed the afterdoor, then moved slowly to the forward one and closed that. He sat down; I stood before him. He looked at me some little time, then said: "So you have been fighting Mr. Brown?"

---

8. **guard-deep:** The *guard* of a ship is an extension of the deck. In this case, it refers to a wooden frame protecting the paddle wheel.

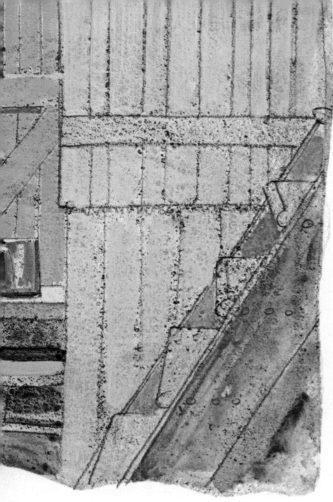

"He—he fell, sir."

"Did you follow it up? Did you do anything further?"

"Yes, sir."

"What did you do?"

"Pounded him, sir."

"Pounded him?"

"Yes, sir."

"Did you pound him much? That is, severely?"

"One might call it that, sir, maybe."

"I'm deuced glad of it! Hark ye, never mention that I said that. You have been guilty of a great crime; and don't you ever be guilty of it again, on this boat. *But*—lay for him ashore! Give him a good sound thrashing, do you hear? I'll pay the expenses. Now go—and mind you, not a word of this to anybody. Clear out with you! You've been guilty of a great crime, you whelp!"[9]

I slid out, happy with the sense of a close shave and a mighty deliverance, and I heard him laughing to himself and slapping his fat thighs after I had closed his door.

When Brown came off watch he went straight to the captain, who was talking with some passengers on the boiler deck, and demanded that I be put ashore in New Orleans —and added: "I'll never turn a wheel on this boat again while that cub stays."

The captain said: "But he needn't come round when you are on watch, Mr. Brown."

"I won't even stay on the same boat with him. *One* of us has got to go ashore."

"Very well," said the captain, "let it be yourself," and resumed his talk with the passengers.

During the brief remainder of the trip I knew how an emancipated slave feels, for I was an emancipated slave myself.

I answered meekly: "Yes, sir."

"Do you know that that is a very serious matter?"

"Yes, sir."

"Are you aware that this boat was plowing down the river fully five minutes with no one at the wheel?"

"Yes, sir."

"Did you strike him first?"

"Yes, sir."

"What with?"

"A stool, sir."

"Hard?"

"Middling, sir."

"Did it knock him down?"

---

9. **whelp:** a puppy or cub; here, a disrespectful young man.

SEEKING MEANING

1. Twain tells a story in this part of his recollections. At the heart of the story is a conflict between two very different people. What was the conflict? How did the captain settle it?

2. Brown seemed to be furious at Twain the first time they met. Why do you think the old pilot disliked the young cub so much?

3. Why did Twain finally attack Brown?

4. People seem to enjoy reading about a conflict between an underdog and a bully—when the underdog wins. Were your sympathies with the cub or with Brown? With whom did the captain sympathize?

DEVELOPING SKILLS IN READING

Recognizing the Writer's Tone

Tone is the attitude a writer takes toward a subject. Tone can be serious, humorous, sarcastic, affectionate, and so on.

The events that Twain narrates here are certainly unpleasant. Yet the overall effect is not heavy and tragic because of the tone of the writing—the attitude that Twain takes toward these events.

Twain begins by itemizing the ambitions of his childhood comrades on page 373. What details here would make a reader smile?

Brown is clearly a bully and a villain. Yet a reader has to smile at his conflict with the cub. Look again at the first description of Brown on page 374. The sentence has twelve adjectives and one noun describing Brown. The first few adjectives seem unbiased: *middle-aged, long, slim, smooth-shaven.* Even *bony* and *horsefaced* might be considered neutral. But then the list builds to a comic crescendo: *ignorant, stingy, malicious, snarling, fault-hunting, mote-magnifying.* The final noun, *tyrant,* finishes the list off perfectly. Part of the fun is the exaggeration. We are used to the term *fault-finding.* How does *fault-hunting* differ from that?

A *mote* is a tiny speck, a bit of dust. What would a *mote-magnifying* person be like?

What is unusual about the way in which the cub humiliates the bully after attacking him? (Have you ever heard of a person using grammar to win a battle?)

How would you describe this story's tone?

ABOUT THE AUTHOR

Mark Twain (1835–1910) is the pen name of Samuel Langhorne Clemens. The name came from the steamboatmen's cry: "By the mark, twain!" This cry meant that by their *mark* (measure), the river was *twain* (two) fathoms deep, which was a safe depth.

Twain was born in Missouri and lived an adventuresome boyhood, which he later made use of in his novels *The Adventures of Tom Sawyer* and *The Adventures of Huckleberry Finn.* For a while, he worked for a newspaper, but he gave up this occupation to apprentice himself to a steamboat pilot on the Mississippi. He stayed on the river until the Civil War brought the steamboats nearly to a standstill. After the war, Twain started his career as a traveler and journalistic humorist in the frontier style. He was soon one of the most popular writers and lecturers in America, perhaps because he showed typical American irreverence for stuffiness and tradition.

Financial difficulties and the deaths of his wife and two daughters caused Twain great unhappiness. This is reflected in the bitter tone of some of his later writings. But he is remembered chiefly for his earlier, comic writings—his Western tales and his two great novels of American boyhood. One of his famous Western tales is "The Celebrated Jumping Frog of Calaveras County."

The young girl in this autobiography felt lonely and unloved—until she met an unusual woman who threw her a "lifeline." In this part of her true story, Maya Angelou and her older brother Bailey lived with their grandmother in the small rural town of Stamps, Arkansas.

I Know Why the Caged Bird Sings

Maya Angelou

We lived with our grandmother and uncle in the rear of the Store (it was always spoken of with a capital *s*), which she had owned some twenty-five years.

Early in the century, Momma (we soon stopped calling her Grandmother) sold lunches to the sawmen in the lumberyard (east Stamps) and the seedmen at the cotton gin (west Stamps). Her crisp meat pies and cool lemonade, when joined to her miraculous ability to be in two places at the same time, assured her business success. From being a mobile lunch counter, she set up a stand between the two points of fiscal[1] interest and supplied the workers' needs for a few years. Then she had the Store built in the heart of the Negro area. Over the years it became the lay[2] center of activities in town. On Saturdays, barbers sat their customers in the shade on the porch of the Store, and troubadours on their ceaseless crawlings

through the South leaned across its benches and sang their sad songs of the Brazos[3] while they played juice harps[4] and cigar-box guitars.

The formal name of the Store was the Wm. Johnson General Merchandise Store. Customers could find food staples, a good variety of colored thread, mash for hogs, corn for chickens, coal oil for lamps, light bulbs for the wealthy, shoestrings, hair dressing, balloons, and flower seeds. Anything not visible had only to be ordered.

Until we became familiar enough to belong to the Store and it to us, we were locked up in a Fun House of Things where the attendant had gone home for life.

Weighing the half-pounds of flour, excluding the scoop, and depositing them dust-free into the thin paper sacks held a simple kind of adventure for me. I developed an eye for measuring how full a silver-looking ladle of flour,

---

1. **fiscal:** financial.
2. **lay:** not religious. The religious center would be the church.

3. **the Brazos** (brăz′əs): a district in central Texas around the Brazos River.
4. **juice harps:** the author's misunderstanding, as a child, of *jew's-harps*, musical instruments held in the mouth and plucked.

mash, meal, sugar or corn had to be to push the scale indicator over to eight ounces or one pound. When I was absolutely accurate our appreciative customers used to admire: "Sister Henderson sure got some smart grandchildrens." If I was off in the Store's favor, the eagle-eyed women would say, "Put some more in that sack, child. Don't you try to make your profit offa me."

Then I would quietly but persistently punish myself. For every bad judgment, the fine was no silver-wrapped kisses, the sweet chocolate drops that I loved more than anything in the world, except Bailey. And maybe canned pineapples. My obsession with pineapples nearly drove me mad. I dreamt of the days when I would be grown and able to buy a whole carton for myself alone.

Although the syrupy golden rings sat in their exotic cans on the shelves year round, we only tasted them during Christmas. Momma used the juice to make almost-black fruit cakes. Then she lined heavy soot-encrusted iron skillets with the pineapple rings for rich upside-down cakes. Bailey and I received one slice each, and I carried mine around for hours, shredding off the fruit until nothing was left except the perfume on my fingers. I'd like to think that my desire for pineapples was so sacred that I wouldn't allow myself to steal a can (which was possible) and eat it alone out in the garden, but I'm certain that I must have weighed the possibility of the scent exposing me and didn't have the nerve to attempt it.

Until I was thirteen and left Arkansas for

Store and spread itself over the family in washed life waves.

At this point in her story, Maya was about ten years old and had returned to Stamps from a visit to St. Louis with her mother. She had become very unhappy and withdrawn.

For nearly a year, I sopped around the house, the Store, the school and the church, like an old biscuit. Then I met, or rather got to know, the lady who threw me my first lifeline.

Mrs. Bertha Flowers was the aristocrat of Black Stamps. She had the grace of control to appear warm in the coldest weather, and on the Arkansas summer days it seemed she had a private breeze which swirled around, cooling her. She was thin without the taut look of wiry people, and her printed voile dresses and flowered hats were as right for her as denim overalls for a farmer.

Her skin was a rich black that would have peeled like a plum if snagged, but then no one would have thought of getting close enough to Mrs. Flowers to ruffle her dress, let alone snag her skin. She didn't encourage familiarity. She wore gloves too.

I don't think I ever saw Mrs. Flowers laugh, but she smiled often. A slow widening of her thin black lips to show even, small white teeth, then the slow effortless closing. When she chose to smile on me, I always wanted to thank her. The action was so graceful and inclusively benign.[5]

She was one of the few gentlewomen I have ever known, and has remained throughout my life the measure of what a human being can be.

One summer afternoon, sweet-milk fresh in my memory, she stopped at the Store to

good, the Store was my favorite place to be. Alone and empty in the mornings, it looked like an unopened present from a stranger. Opening the front doors was pulling the ribbon off the unexpected gift. The light would come in softly (we faced north), easing itself over the shelves of mackerel, salmon, tobacco, thread. It fell flat on the big vat of lard and by noontime during the summer the grease had softened to a thick soup. Whenever I walked into the Store in the afternoon, I sensed that it was tired. I alone could hear the slow pulse of its job half done. But just before bedtime, after numerous people had walked in and out, had argued over their bills, or joked about their neighbors, or just dropped in "to give Sister Henderson a 'Hi y'all,' " the promise of magic mornings returned to the

---

5. **benign** (bĭ-nīn′): kind.

buy provisions. Another woman of her health and age would have been expected to carry the paper sacks home in one hand, but Momma said, "Sister Flowers, I'll send Bailey up to your house with these things."

She smiled that slow dragging smile, "Thank you, Mrs. Henderson. I'd prefer Marguerite, though." My name was beautiful when she said it. "I've been meaning to talk to her, anyway." They gave each other age-group looks.

There was a little path beside the rocky road, and Mrs. Flowers walked in front swinging her arms and picking her way over the stones.

She said, without turning her head, to me, "I hear you're doing very good schoolwork, Marguerite, but that it's all written. The teachers report that they have trouble getting you to talk in class." We passed the triangular farm on our left and the path widened to allow us to walk together. I hung back in the separate unasked and unanswerable questions.

"Come and walk along with me, Marguerite." I couldn't have refused even if I wanted to. She pronounced my name so nicely. Or more correctly, she spoke each word with such clarity that I was certain a foreigner who didn't understand English could have understood her.

"Now no one is going to make you talk— possibly no one can. But bear in mind, language is man's way of communicating with his fellowman and it is language alone which separates him from the lower animals." That was a totally new idea to me, and I would need time to think about it.

"Your grandmother says you read a lot. Every chance you get. That's good, but not good enough. Words mean more than what is set down on paper. It takes the human voice to infuse them with the shades of deeper meaning."

I memorized the part about the human voice infusing words. It seemed so valid and poetic.

She said she was going to give me some books and that I not only must read them, I must read them aloud. She suggested that I try to make a sentence sound in as many different ways as possible.

"I'll accept no excuse if you return a book to me that has been badly handled." My imagination boggled at the punishment I would deserve if in fact I did abuse a book of Mrs. Flowers'. Death would be too kind and brief.

The odors in the house surprised me. Somehow I had never connected Mrs. Flowers with food or eating or any other common experience of common people. There must have been an outhouse, too, but my mind never recorded it.

The sweet scent of vanilla had met us as she opened the door.

"I made tea cookies this morning. You see, I had planned to invite you for cookies and lemonade so we could have this little chat. The lemonade is in the icebox."

It followed that Mrs. Flowers would have ice on an ordinary day, when most families in our town bought ice late on Saturdays only a few times during the summer to be used in the wooden ice cream freezers.

She took the bags from me and disappeared through the kitchen door. I looked around the room that I had never in my wildest fantasies imagined I would see. Browned photographs leered or threatened from the walls and the white, freshly done curtains pushed against themselves and against the wind. I wanted to gobble up the room entire and take it to Bailey, who would help me analyze and enjoy it.

"Have a seat, Marguerite. Over there by the table." She carried a platter covered with a tea towel. Although she warned that she hadn't tried her hand at baking sweets for some time, I was certain that like everything else about her the cookies would be perfect.

They were flat round wafers, slightly browned on the edges and butter-yellow in the center. With the cold lemonade they were sufficient for childhood's lifelong diet. Remembering my manners, I took nice little ladylike bites off the edges. She said she had made them expressly for me and that she had a few in the kitchen that I could take home to my brother. So I jammed one whole cake in my mouth and the rough crumbs scratched the insides of my jaws, and if I hadn't had to swallow, it would have been a dream come true.

As I ate she began the first of what we later called "my lessons in living." She said that I must always be intolerant of ignorance but understanding of illiteracy. That some people, unable to go to school, were more educated and even more intelligent than college professors. She encouraged me to listen carefully to what country people called mother wit. That in those homely[6] sayings was couched the collective wisdom of generations.

When I finished the cookies she brushed off the table and brought a thick, small book from the bookcase. I had read *A Tale of Two Cities* and found it up to my standards as a romantic novel. She opened the first page and I heard poetry for the first time in my life.

"It was the best of times, it was the worst of times . . . ." Her voice slid in and curved down through and over the words. She was nearly

---

6. **homely:** ordinary; everyday.

singing. I wanted to look at the pages. Were they the same that I had read? Or were there notes, music, lined on the pages, as in a hymnbook? Her sounds began cascading gently. I knew from listening to a thousand preachers that she was nearing the end of her reading, and I hadn't really heard, heard to understand, a single word.

"How do you like that?"

It occurred to me that she expected a response. The sweet vanilla flavor was still on my tongue and her reading was a wonder in my ears. I had to speak.

I said, "Yes, ma'am." It was the least I could do, but it was the most also.

"There's one more thing. Take this book of poems and memorize one for me. Next time you pay me a visit, I want you to recite."

I have tried often to search behind the sophistication of years for the enchantment I so easily found in those gifts. The essence escapes but its aura[7] remains. To be allowed, no, invited, into the private lives of strangers, and to share their joys and fears, was a chance to exchange bitter wormwood[8] for a cup of mead with Beowulf[9] or a hot cup of tea and milk with Oliver Twist. When I said aloud, "It is a far, far better thing that I do, than I have ever done . . ."[10] tears of love filled my eyes at my selflessness.

On that first day, I ran down the hill and into the road (few cars ever came along it) and had the good sense to stop running before I reached the Store.

I was liked, and what a difference it made. I was respected not as Mrs. Henderson's grandchild or Bailey's sister but for just being Marguerite Johnson.

Childhood's logic never asks to be proved (all conclusions are absolute). I didn't question why Mrs. Flowers had singled me out for attention, nor did it occur to me that Momma might have asked her to give me a little talking to. All I cared about was that she had made tea cookies for *me* and read to *me* from her favorite book. It was enough to prove that she liked me.

---

7. **aura** (ôr′ə): an atmosphere; a general feeling or quality.

8. **wormwood:** a bitter-tasting plant.

9. **Beowulf:** the hero of an old Anglo-Saxon epic. In this epic, people drink mead, a sweet drink made with honey.

10. **"It is . . . than I have ever done":** The speech is from *A Tale of Two Cities* by Charles Dickens. The narrator of this novel imagines that the hero says these words as he heroically goes to die on the guillotine so that another man can live.

SEEKING MEANING

1. In this part of her autobiography, Maya Angelou tells about a place and a person that were important in her childhood. The place was the Store. She compares the Store to a "Fun House of Things." What does she say the Store looked like in the morning? What do these descriptions tell you about her feelings for the Store?

2. The important person in Maya's childhood was Mrs. Flowers. How did Mrs. Flowers teach her to have compassion for other people in her first "lesson in living"?

3. How did Mrs. Flowers show that she "liked" and "respected" Maya?

4. Maya eventually grew up to become a well-known writer. What details in this story show that Mrs. Flowers probably awakened her love of language?

5. Maya compares herself to an old biscuit. What beautiful fruit does she compare Mrs. Flowers' skin to? What do these two comparisons tell you of Maya's feelings about herself and Mrs. Flowers?

ABOUT THE AUTHOR

Maya Angelou (1928–   ) eventually moved far away from Stamps, Arkansas. She lived in San Francisco for a while and studied to become a professional dancer and an actress. She toured Europe and Africa in a production of *Porgy and Bess* for the State Department. She worked for Dr. Martin Luther King, Jr., and wrote for newspapers in Egypt and Ghana.

She took the title *I Know Why the Caged Bird Sings* from a poem called "Sympathy" by the black poet Paul Laurence Dunbar. Like the poet, Maya Angelou identifies with the songbird that sings because it wants to be free. The writer James Baldwin has said about her autobiography: "Not since the days of my childhood, when people in books were more real than the people we saw every day, have I found myself so moved. . . ."

Maya Angelou, with her autobiography.

*Who really runs a family?
According to this essay,
James Thurber's family
was once ruled by a bad-
tempered dog who bit
everyone in sight.*

The Dog That Bit People

James Thurber

Probably no one man should have as many dogs in his life as I have had, but there was more pleasure than distress in them for me except in the case of an Airedale named Muggs. He gave me more trouble than all the other fifty-four or -five put together, although my moment of keenest embarrassment was the time a Scotch terrier named Jeannie, who had just had four puppies in the shoe closet of a fourth-floor apartment in New York, had the fifth and last at the corner of—but we shall get around to that later on. Then, too, there was the prizewinning French poodle, a great big black poodle—none of your little, untroublesome white miniatures—who got sick riding in the rumble seat[1] of a car with me on her way to the Greenwich Dog Show. She had a red rubber bib tucked around her throat and, since a rainstorm came up when we were halfway through the Bronx, I had to hold over her a small green umbrella, really more of a parasol. The rain beat down fearfully, and suddenly the driver of the car drove into a big garage, filled with mechanics. It happened so quickly that I forgot to put the umbrella down, and I shall always remember the look of incredulity[2] that came over the face of the garageman who came over to see what we wanted. "Get a load of this, Mac," he called to someone behind him.

But the Airedale, as I have said, was the worst of all my dogs. He really wasn't my dog, as a matter of fact; I came home from a vacation one summer to find that my brother Robert had bought him while I was away. A big, burly, choleric[3] dog, he always acted as if he thought I wasn't one of the family. There was a slight advantage in being one of the family, for he didn't bite the family as often as he bit strangers. Still, in the years that we had him he bit everybody but Mother, and he made a pass at her once but missed. That was during the month when we suddenly had mice, and Muggs refused to do anything about them.

---

1. **rumble seat:** an open seat in the back of some early automobiles. It could be folded shut when not in use.

2. **incredulity** (ĭn′krə-dōō′lə-tē): disbelief.
3. **choleric** (kŏl′ər-ĭk): bad-tempered.

Nobody ever had mice exactly like the mice we had that month. They acted like pet mice, almost like mice somebody had trained. They were so friendly that one night when Mother entertained at dinner the Friraliras, a club she and my father had belonged to for twenty years, she put down a lot of little dishes with food in them on the pantry floor so that the mice would be satisfied with that and wouldn't come into the dining room. Muggs stayed out in the pantry with the mice, lying on the floor, growling to himself—not at the mice, but about all the people in the next room that he would have liked to get at. Mother slipped out into the pantry once to see how everything was going. Everything was going fine. It made her so mad to see Muggs lying there, oblivious of[4] the mice—they came running up to her—that she slapped him and he slashed at her, but didn't make it. He was sorry immediately, Mother said. He was always sorry, she said, after he bit someone, but we could not understand how she figured this out. He didn't act sorry.

Mother used to send a box of candy every Christmas to the people the Airedale bit. The list finally contained forty or more names. Nobody could understand why we didn't get rid of the dog. I didn't understand it very well myself, but we didn't get rid of him. I think that one or two people tried to poison Muggs—he acted poisoned once in a while— and old Major Moberly fired at him once with his service revolver near the Seneca Hotel on East Broad Street—but Muggs lived to be almost eleven years old, and even when he could hardly get around, he bit a congressman who had called to see my father on business. My mother had never liked the congressman —she said the signs of his horoscope showed he couldn't be trusted (he was Saturn with the moon in Virgo)—but she sent him a box of candy that Christmas. He sent it right back, probably because he suspected it was trick candy. Mother persuaded herself it was all for the best that the dog had bitten him, even though Father lost an important business association because of it. "I wouldn't be associated with such a man," Mother said. "Muggs could read him like a book."

We used to take turns feeding Muggs to be on his good side, but that didn't always work. He was never in a very good humor, even after a meal. Nobody knew exactly what was the matter with him, but whatever it was it made him irascible,[5] especially in the mornings. Robert never felt very well in the morning either, especially before breakfast, and once when he came downstairs and found that Muggs had moodily chewed up the morning paper, he hit him in the face with a grapefruit and then jumped up on the dining-room table, scattering dishes and silverware and spilling the coffee. Muggs's first free leap carried him all the way across the table and into a brass fire screen in front of the gas grate, but he was back on his feet in a moment, and in the end he got Robert and gave him a pretty vicious bite in the leg. Then he was all over it; he never bit anyone more than once at a time. Mother always mentioned that as an argument in his favor; she said he had a quick temper but that he didn't hold a grudge. She was forever defending him. I think she liked him because he wasn't well. "He's not strong," she would say, pityingly, but that was inaccurate; he may not have been well, but he was terribly strong.

One time my mother went to the Chittenden Hotel to call on a woman mental healer who was lecturing in Columbus on the subject of "Harmonious Vibrations." She wanted

---

4. **oblivious of:** forgetful of; not mindful of.

5. **irascible** (ĭ-răs′ə-bəl): irritable.

to find out if it was possible to get harmonious vibrations into a dog. "He's a large, tan-colored Airedale," Mother explained. The woman said she had never treated a dog, but she advised my mother to hold the thought that he did not bite and would not bite. Mother was holding the thought the very next morning when Muggs got the iceman, but she blamed that slip-up on the iceman. "If you didn't think he would bite you, he wouldn't," Mother told him. He stomped out of the house in a terrible jangle of vibrations.

One morning when Muggs bit me slightly, more or less in passing, I reached down and grabbed his short stumpy tail and hoisted him into the air. It was a foolhardy thing to do, and the last time I saw my mother, about six months ago, she said she didn't know what possessed me. I don't either, except that I was pretty mad. As long as I held the dog off the floor by his tail he couldn't get at me, but he twisted and jerked so, snarling all the time, that I realized I couldn't hold him that way very long. I carried him to the kitchen and flung him onto the floor and shut the door on him just as he crashed against it. But I forgot about the back stairs. Muggs went up the back stairs and down the front stairs and had me cornered in the living room. I managed to get up onto the mantelpiece above the fireplace, but it gave way and came down with a tremendous crash, throwing a large marble clock, several vases, and myself heavily to the floor. Muggs was so alarmed by the racket that when I picked myself up he had disappeared. We couldn't find him anywhere, although we whistled and shouted, until old Mrs. Detweiler called after dinner that night. Muggs had bitten her once, in the leg, and she came into the living room only after we assured her that Muggs had run away. She had just seated herself when, with a great growling and scratching of claws, Muggs emerged

from under a davenport where he had been quietly hiding all the time and bit her again. Mother examined the bite and put arnica[6] on it and told Mrs. Detwwiler that it was only a bruise. "He just bumped you," she said. But Mrs. Detweiler left the house in a nasty state of mind.

Lots of people reported our Airedale to the police, but my father held a municipal office at the time and was on friendly terms with the police. Even so, the cops had been out a couple of times—once when Muggs bit Mrs. Rufus Sturtevant and again when he bit Lieutenant Governor Malloy—but Mother told them that it hadn't been Muggs's fault but the fault of the people who were bitten. "When he starts for them, they scream," she explained, "and that excites him." The cops suggested that it might be a good idea to tie the dog up, but Mother said that it mortified him to be tied up and that he wouldn't eat when he was tied up.

Muggs at his meals was an unusual sight. Because of the fact that if you reached toward the floor he would bite you, we usually put his food plate on top of an old kitchen table with a bench alongside the table. Muggs would stand on the bench and eat. I remember that my mother's Uncle Horatio, who boasted that he was the third man up Missionary Ridge,[7] was splutteringly indignant when he found out that we fed the dog on a table because we were afraid to put his plate on the floor. He said he wasn't afraid of any dog that ever lived and that he would put the dog's plate on the floor if we would give it to him. Robert said that if Uncle Horatio had fed Muggs on the ground just before the battle, he

---

6. **arnica:** a preparation for sprains and bruises made from the arnica plant.
7. **Missionary Ridge:** a ridge in Tennessee and Georgia, the site of an important Civil War battle.

would have been the first man up Missionary Ridge. Uncle Horatio was furious. "Bring him in! Bring him in now!" he shouted. "I'll feed the — on the floor!" Robert was all for giving him a chance, but my father wouldn't hear of it. He said that Muggs had already been fed. "I'll feed him again!" bawled Uncle Horatio. We had quite a time quieting him.

In his last year Muggs used to spend practically all of his time outdoors. He didn't like to stay in the house for some reason or other — perhaps it held too many unpleasant memories for him. Anyway, it was hard to get him to come in, and as a result, the garbage man, the iceman, and the laundryman wouldn't come near the house. We had to haul the garbage down to the corner, take the laundry out and bring it back, and meet the iceman a block from home. After this had gone on for some time, we hit on an ingenious arrangement for getting the dog in the house so that we could lock him up while the gas meter was read, and so on. Muggs was afraid of only one thing, an electrical storm. Thunder and lightning frightened him out of his senses (I think he thought a storm had broken the day the mantelpiece fell). He would rush into the house and hide under a bed or in a clothes closet. So we fixed up a thunder machine out of a long narrow piece of sheet iron with a wooden handle on one end. Mother would shake this vigorously when she wanted to get Muggs into the house. It made an excellent imitation of thunder, but I suppose it was the most roundabout system for running a household that was ever devised. It took a lot out of Mother.

A few months before Muggs died, he got to "seeing things." He would rise slowly from the floor, growling low, and stalk stiff-legged and menacing toward nothing at all. Sometimes the Thing would be just a little to the right or left of a visitor. Once a Fuller brush salesman got hysterics. Muggs came wandering into the room like Hamlet following his father's ghost. His eyes were fixed on a spot just to the left of the Fuller brush man, who stood it until Muggs was about three slow, creeping paces from him. Then he shouted. Muggs wavered on past him into the hallway, grumbling to himself, but the Fuller brush man went on shouting. I think Mother had to throw a pan of cold water on him before he stopped. That was the way she used to stop us boys when we got into fights.

Muggs died quite suddenly one night. Mother wanted to bury him in the family plot under a marble stone with some such inscription as "Flights of angels sing thee to thy rest,"[8] but we persuaded her it was against the law. In the end we just put up a smooth board above his grave along a lonely road. On the board I wrote with an indelible pencil "Cave Canem."[9] Mother was quite pleased with the simple, classic dignity of the old Latin epitaph.

---

8. **"Flights . . . rest"**: words spoken to the dead Hamlet in Shakespeare's play.
9. *Cave Canem* (kä′vä kän′ĕm): Latin for "Beware of the dog." In ancient Rome, this warning was often put on the doorways of homes.

SEEKING MEANING

1. This essay is made up of a series of anecdotes, or amusing stories, about a particular subject—here, a dog. Thurber pokes fun at himself and his family as he tells how they tried to keep Muggs in a good mood. How does the opening incident with the prize poodle prepare you for a story about people who would do anything for their pets?

2. Part of the fun of this story lies in the ridiculous lengths a whole family went to, in order to stay on the good side of their dog. What did the family do about Muggs's food, and about their garbage, their laundry, and the iceman? Why did they rig up the thunder machine?

3. Thurber's mother saw Muggs as having human characteristics. What were some of the excuses she made for his behavior? Do you think many people see their pets in the same way that Mother saw Muggs? Explain your answer.

ABOUT THE AUTHOR

James Thurber (1894–1961) wrote about all kinds of animals—seals, dolphins, unicorns, polar bears, fiddler crabs, wombats, wogglebugs, bowerbirds, bandicoots, and bristle worms. But he wrote enough dog stories to collect them into an entire book, called *Thurber's Dogs.* Thurber also wrote stories about the kind of person who is victimized by life and its problems. He gave this character a shape and a name in one of his most famous humorous stories, "The Secret Life of Walter Mitty."

Thurber was blinded in one eye in a childhood accident, and he became completely blind during the last years of his life. Nevertheless, he continued to write and he even appeared nightly as himself in *A Thurber Carnival,* a Broadway show based on his work. Thurber once said that humor was a serious thing, one of our greatest national resources, which must be preserved at all cost. One of his humorous twists on a familiar fairy-tale plot is called "The Princess and the Tin Box."

The boy was so full of fear he could hardly breathe. But he had an adult's responsibility now. He had to make the journey down those streets.

The Street   *Richard Wright*

Hunger stole upon me so slowly that at first I was not aware of what hunger really meant. Hunger had always been more or less at my elbow when I played, but now I began to wake up at night to find hunger standing at my bedside, staring at me gauntly. The hunger I had known before this had been no grim, hostile stranger; it had been a normal hunger that had made me beg constantly for bread, and when I ate a crust or two I was satisfied. But this new hunger baffled me, scared me, made me angry and insistent. Whenever I begged for food now my mother would pour me a cup of tea which would still the clamor[1] in my stomach for a moment or two; but a little later I would feel hunger nudging my ribs, twisting my empty guts until they ached. I would grow dizzy and my vision would dim. I became less active in my play, and for the first time in my life I had to pause and think of what was happening to me.

"Mama, I'm hungry," I complained one afternoon.

"Jump up and catch a kungry," she said, trying to make me laugh and forget.

"What's a *kungry*?"

"It's what little boys eat when they get hungry," she said.

"What does it taste like?"

"I don't know."

"Then why do you tell me to catch one?"

"Because you said that you were hungry," she said, smiling.

I sensed that she was teasing me and it made me angry.

"But I'm hungry. I want to eat."

"You'll have to wait."

"But I want to eat now."

"But there's nothing to eat," she told me.

"Why?"

"Just because there's none," she explained.

"But I want to eat," I said, beginning to cry.

"You'll just have to wait," she said again.

"But why?"

"For God to send some food."

"When is He going to send it?"

"I don't know."

"But I'm hungry!"

She was ironing and she paused and looked at me with tears in her eyes.

"Where's your father?" she asked me.

I stared in bewilderment. Yes, it was true that my father had not come home to sleep for many days now and I could make as much noise as I wanted. Though I had not known why he was absent, I had been glad that he was not there to shout his restrictions at me. But it had never occurred to me that his absence would mean that there would be no food.

---

1. **clamor:** noise.

"I don't know," I said.

"Who brings food into the house?" my mother asked me.

"Papa," I said. "He always brought food."

"Well, your father isn't here now," she said.

"Where is he?"

"I don't know," she said.

"But I'm hungry," I whimpered, stomping my feet.

"You'll have to wait until I get a job and buy food," she said.

As the days slid past, the image of my father became associated with my pangs of hunger, and whenever I felt hunger I thought of him with a deep biological bitterness.

My mother finally went to work as a cook and left me and my brother alone in the flat[2] each day with a loaf of bread and a pot of tea. When she returned at evening she would be tired and dispirited and would cry a lot. Sometimes, when she was in despair, she would call us to her and talk to us for hours, telling us that we now had no father, that our lives would be different from those of other children, that we must learn as soon as possible to take care of ourselves, to dress ourselves, to prepare our own food; that we must take upon ourselves the responsibility of the flat while she worked. Half frightened, we would promise solemnly. We did not understand what had happened between our father and our mother and the most that these long talks did to us was to make us feel a vague dread. Whenever we asked why Father had left, she would tell us that we were too young to know.

One evening my mother told me that thereafter I would have to do the shopping for food. She took me to the corner store to show me the way. I was proud; I felt like a grown-up. The next afternoon I looped the basket over

---

2. **flat:** an apartment.

my arm and went down the pavement toward the store. When I reached the corner, a gang of boys grabbed me, knocked me down, snatched the basket, took the money, and sent me running home in panic. That evening I told my mother what had happened, but she made no comment; she sat down at once, wrote another note, gave me more money, and sent me out to the grocery again. I crept down the steps and saw the same gang of boys playing down the street. I ran back into the house.

"What's the matter?" my mother asked.

"It's those same boys," I said. "They'll beat me."

"You've got to get over that," she said. "Now, go on."

"I'm scared," I said.

"Go on and don't pay any attention to them," she said.

I went out of the door and walked briskly down the sidewalk, praying that the gang would not molest me. But when I came abreast of them someone shouted.

"There he is!"

They came toward me and I broke into a wild run toward home. They overtook me and flung me to the pavement. I yelled, pleaded, kicked, but they wrenched the money out of my hand. They yanked me to my feet, gave me a few slaps, and sent me home sobbing. My mother met me at the door.

"They b-beat m-me," I gasped. "They t-t-took the m-money."

I started up the steps, seeking the shelter of the house.

"Don't you come in here," my mother warned me.

I froze in my tracks and stared at her.

"But they're coming after me," I said.

"You just stay right where you are," she said in a deadly tone. "I'm going to teach you this night to stand up and fight for yourself."

She went into the house and I waited, terrified, wondering what she was about. Presently, she returned with more money and another note; she also had a long heavy stick.

"Take this money, this note, and this stick," she said. "Go to the store and buy those groceries. If those boys bother you, then fight."

I was baffled. My mother was telling me to fight, a thing that she had never done before.

"But I'm scared," I said.

"Don't you come into this house until you've gotten those groceries," she said.

"They'll beat me; they'll beat me," I said.

"Then stay in the streets; don't come back here!"

I ran up the steps and tried to force my way past her into the house. A stinging slap came on my jaw. I stood on the sidewalk, crying.

"Please, let me wait until tomorrow," I begged.

"No," she said. "Go now! If you come back into this house without those groceries, I'll whip you!"

She slammed the door and I heard the key turn in the lock. I shook with fright. I was alone upon the dark, hostile streets and gangs were after me. I had the choice of being beaten at home or away from home. I clutched the stick, crying, trying to reason. If I were beaten at home, there was absolutely nothing that I could do about it; but if I were beaten in the streets, I had a chance to fight and defend myself. I walked slowly down the sidewalk, coming closer to the gang of boys, holding the stick tightly. I was so full of fear that I could scarcely breathe. I was almost upon them now.

"There he is again!" the cry went up.

They surrounded me quickly and began to grab for my hand.

"I'll kill you!" I threatened.

They closed in. In blind fear I let the stick fly, feeling it crack against a boy's skull. I swung again, lamming another skull, then another. Realizing that they would retaliate if I let up for but a second, I fought to lay them low, to knock them cold, to kill them so that they could not strike back at me. I flayed with tears in my eyes, teeth clenched, stark fear making me throw every ounce of my strength behind each blow. I hit again and again, dropping the money and the grocery list. The boys scattered, yelling, nursing their heads, staring at me in utter disbelief. They had never seen such frenzy. I stood panting, egging them on, taunting them to come on and fight. When they refused, I ran after them and they tore out for their homes, screaming. The parents of the boys rushed into the streets and threatened me, and for the first time in my life I shouted at grown-ups, telling them that I would give them the same if they bothered me. I finally found my grocery list and the money and went to the store. On my way back I kept my stick poised for instant use, but there was not a single boy in sight. That night I won the right to the streets of Memphis.

SEEKING MEANING

1. In this true story, a boy battled a street gang. But the boy's family faced another "enemy" at home. Look back at the opening paragraph. What enemy did the family face? How did this enemy hurt the boy?

2. When a hero in a story has to fight, it is usually for some purpose that we understand and sympathize with. Sometimes a hero is unwilling to fight. Why do you think the mother forced the boy to face the gang in the street?

3. What do you think the boy proved, to his mother and to himself, by winning the street battle?

DEVELOPING SKILLS IN READING

Responding to Figurative Language

Wright wants to impress upon the reader how hunger haunted his family. To do this, he describes hunger as if it were a person: "Hunger had always been more or less at my elbow when I played." Where does he find hunger at night? What does hunger look like to him?

Wright is using *figurative* language here. He is comparing hunger to a person. Figurative language is not literally, or factually, true. Hunger does not really have eyes, and it can't actually stand or move. But figurative language helps you see things in sharp, new ways. How did Wright's unusual description of hunger affect you?

ABOUT THE AUTHOR

This selection is taken from *Black Boy,* the autobiography of Richard Wright (1908–1960). Wright's childhood was full of heartbreak. It was disrupted by family problems and by his mother's long illness. When he was very young, Wright learned to escape through listening to stories. With his mother's help, he learned to read before he entered school. His formal schooling didn't last long. Wright was only fifteen years old when he left home and set off on his own. Later in his life he said that it had been only through books that he had managed to keep himself alive. Whenever his environment failed to support or nourish him, he clutched at books. Wright is now recognized as one of the important American writers of the twentieth century.

"As the woman slowly lowered her hand, the snake gave that most terrible of all animal noises — the unearthly hiss of a deadly snake."

A Running Brook of Horror

Daniel Mannix

It was through my interest in snakes that, while in California, Jule and I had the most terrible experience of our career.

I had first heard of Grace Wiley some years before when Dr. William Mann, then director of the National Zoological Park in Washington, D.C., handed me a picture of a tiny woman with a gigantic king cobra draped over her shoulders like a garden hose. The snake had partly spread his hood and was looking intently into the camera while his mistress stroked his head to quiet him. Dr. Mann told me: "Grace lives in a little house full of poisonous snakes, imported from all over the world. She lets them wander around like cats. There's been more nonsense written about 'snake charming' than nearly any other subject. Grace is probably the only non-Oriental who knows the real secrets of this curious business."

Looking at the picture of that deadly creature I knew what Ruskin[1] meant when he

described a snake as a "running brook of horror." Still, I like snakes and when Jule and I moved into our Malibu house, I made it a point to call on Grace Wiley.

Grace wasn't at the address Dr. Mann had given me. The neighbors had seen some of her pets in the yard and called the police. Grace finally settled outside Los Angeles near the little town of Cypress. After a phone call, I drove out to see her. She was living in a small three-room cottage, surrounded by open fields. Behind the cottage was a big, ramshackle barn where the snakes were kept. Grace was cleaning snake boxes with a hose when I arrived. She was a surprisingly little lady, scarcely over five feet, and probably weighed less than a hundred pounds. Although Grace was sixty-four years old, she was as active as a boy and worked with smooth dexterity. When she saw me, she hurriedly picked up the four-foot rattlesnake who had been sunning himself while his box was cleaned and poured him into his cage. The snake raised his head but made no attempt to strike or even to rattle. I

---

1. **Ruskin:** John Ruskin (1819–1900), an English writer.

was impressed but not astonished. In captivity, rattlers often grow sluggish and can be handled with comparative impunity.[2]

Grace came forward, drying her hands on her apron. "Oh dear, I meant to get dressed up for you," she said, trying to smooth down her thatch of brown hair. "But I haven't anybody here to help me with the snakes, except Mother — and she's eighty-four years old. Don't trip over an alligator," she added as I came forward. I noticed for the first time in the high grass a dozen or so alligators and crocodiles. They ranged from a three-foot Chinese croc to a big Florida gator more than twelve feet long. I threaded my way among them without mishap, although several opened their huge jaws to hiss at me.

"They don't mean anything by that, any more than a dog barking," Grace explained fondly. "They're very tame and most of them know their names. Now come in and meet my little family of snakes."

We entered the barn. The walls were lined with cages of all sizes and shapes containing snakes. Grace stopped at each cage, casually lifting the occupant and pointing out his fine points while she stroked and examined him. Grace unquestionably had one of the world's finest collections of reptiles. I watched her handle diamondback rattlesnakes from Texas, vipers from Italy, fer-de-lance[3] from the West Indies, a little Egyptian cobra (the "asp" that killed Cleopatra), and the deadly karait[4] from India. Then I saw Grace perform a feat I would have believed impossible.

We had stopped in front of a large, glass-fronted cage containing apparently nothing but newspaper. "These little fellows arrived only a short time ago, so they're very wild," explained Grace indulgently. She quietly lifted the paper. Instantly a forest of heads sprang up in the cage. Grace moved the paper slightly. At the movement, the heads seemed to spread and flatten. Then I saw that they were not heads but hoods. I was looking at the world's most deadly creature — the Indian cobra.

Man-eating tigers are said to kill 600 natives a year but cobras kill 25,000 people a year in India alone. Hunters have been mauled by wounded elephants and lived to tell about it, but no one survives a body bite from a big cobra. I have caught rattlesnakes with a forked stick and my bare hands, but I'm not ashamed to say I jumped back from that cage as though the devil were inside — as indeed he was.

Grace advanced her hand toward the nearest cobra. The snake swayed like a reed in the wind, feinting[5] for the strike. Grace raised her hand above the snake's head, the reptile twisting around to watch her. As the woman slowly lowered her hand, the snake gave that most terrible of all animal noises — the unearthly hiss of a deadly snake. I have seen children laugh with excitement at the roar of a lion, but I have never seen anyone who did not cringe at that cold, uncanny sound. Grace deliberately tried to touch the rigid, quivering hood. The cobra struck at her hand. He missed. Quietly, Grace presented her open palm. The cobra hesitated a split second, his reared body quivering like a plucked banjo string. Then he struck.

I felt sick as I saw his head hit Grace's hand, but the cobra did not bite. He struck with his mouth closed. As rapidly as an expert boxer drumming on a punching bag, the snake

---

2. **impunity** (ĭm-pyōō′nĭ-tē): freedom from harm.
3. **fer-de-lance** (fĕr′də-lăns′).
4. **karait** (kə-rīt′).

5. **feinting** (fānt′ĭng): moving in a deceptive way to throw an opponent off guard.

struck three times against Grace's palm, always for some incredible reason with his mouth shut. Then Grace slid her open hand over his head and stroked his hood. The snake hissed again and struggled violently under her touch. Grace continued to caress him. Suddenly the snake went limp and his hood began to close. Grace slipped her other hand under the snake's body and lifted him out of the cage. She held the reptile in her arms as though he were a baby. The cobra raised his head to look Grace in the face; his dancing tongue was less than a foot from her mouth. Grace braced her hand against the curve of his body and talked calmly to him until he folded his hood. He curled up in her arms quietly until I made a slight movement; then he instantly reared up again, threatening me.

I had never seen anything to match this performance. Later, Grace opened the cobra's mouth to show me that the fangs were still intact. The yellow venom was slowly oozing over their tips.

If Grace Wiley had wished to make a mystery out of her amazing ability I am certain she could have made a fortune by posing as a woman with supernatural power. There isn't a zoologist alive who could have debunked her.[6] But Grace was a perfectly honest person who was happy to explain in detail exactly how she could handle these terrible creatures. I spent several weeks with her studying her technique and now that I understand it I'm even more impressed than I was before.

---

6. **debunked her:** exposed her as a fraud.

Although I had kept snakes for many years, I was probably more astonished by Grace's performance than someone who knew nothing about reptiles. My mistake lay in supposing that all snakes are more or less alike. I knew rattlesnakes but I knew nothing about cobras. Although the cobra is intrinsically[7] a far more dangerous snake than the rattlesnake, Grace would never have attempted to handle a diamondback rattler in the manner she handled this cobra. To understand why, you have to know the physical and psychological differences between the two reptiles.

A rattler has two "coils." When he is resting, he lies coiled up like a length of rope with his head lying on the topmost coil and his rattle sticking up in the center of the heap. When he is angry, he rears the upper third of his body a foot or more off the ground, coiling it into an S-shaped design and sounding his rattle continuously. Snake men call this position the "business coil." The rattler is like a coiled spring. He can strike out the full length of the S, inject his venom, and return into position for another strike literally faster than the eye can follow. He cannot strike farther than the raised S, nor will he attack. To attack, he would have to come out of coil and lose his advantageous position. He is like a boxer with his bent arm drawn back for a haymaker.[8] As soon as his opponent comes close enough, he can let him have it.

A cobra, on the other hand, rears straight upward. If you put your elbow on a table, cup your hand to represent the open hood, and sway your forearm back and forth, you will have a good idea of the fighting stance of a cobra. Your index finger represents the tiny, mouselike head that does the business. You will see at once that you cannot strike out as far as you could with your arm drawn back. Your range is limited to the length of your forearm. Here is a large part of the secret in handling cobras.

Because of the deceptively coiled S, no one can tell exactly how far a rattler can strike. But with a little practice, you can tell a cobra's range to the inch. Also, the blow of a cobra is comparatively slow. A man with steady nerves can jerk away in time to avoid being bitten. This is exactly what a mongoose[9] does. The mongoose keeps just outside the cobra's range and when he does dart in for a bite, he can jump clear of the blow. A mongoose would stand no chance at all against a rattlesnake.

Another vital difference lies in the method of striking. The rattler does not bite. He stabs with his fangs. A rattler's fangs are very long, so long that they would pierce his lower jaw if he did not keep them folded back against the roof of his mouth. When he strikes, the rattler opens his mouth to its fullest extent, the fangs snap down into place, and the snake stabs. The fangs are hollow and connect directly with the poison glands in either side of the snake's head. When the snake feels his fangs go home, he instantly discharges his venom deep into the wound. The fangs operate like miniature hypodermic needles and are extremely efficient.

The cobra has no such elaborate apparatus. His fangs are short and do not fold back. Instead of stabbing like the rattler, he must actually bite. He grabs his victims and then deliberately chews while the venom runs down into the wound he is making. These apparently minor distinctions mean the dif-

---

7. **intrinsically** (ĭn-trĭn′zĭk-lē): by nature.
8. **haymaker:** a powerful punch meant to knock a person out.

9. **mongoose:** a weasellike animal known for its ability to kill snakes.

ference between life and death to anyone working with snakes.

When Grace approached a wild cobra, she moved her hand back and forth just outside the snake's range. The cobra would then strike angrily until he became tired. Then he was reluctant to strike again. Grace's next move was to raise her hand over the snake's hood and bring it down slowly. Because of his method of rearing, a cobra cannot strike directly upward (a rattler can strike up as easily as in any other direction), and Grace could actually touch the top of the snake's head. The snake became puzzled and frustrated. He felt that he was fighting an invulnerable opponent who, after all, didn't seem to mean him any harm. Then came the final touch. Grace would put her open palm toward the snake. At last the cobra was able to hit her. But he had to bite and he could not get a grip on the flat surface of the palm. If he could get a finger or a loose fold of skin he could fasten his teeth in it and start chewing. But his strike is sufficiently slow that Grace could meet each blow with the flat of her palm. At last Grace would be able to get her hand over the snake's head and stroke his hood. This seemed to relax the reptile and from then on Grace could handle him with some degree of confidence.

I don't mean to suggest that this is a cut-and-dried procedure. Grace knew snakes perfectly and could tell by tiny, subtle indications what the reptile would probably do next. She had been bitten many times—she would never tell me just how many—but never by a cobra. You're only bitten once by a cobra.

"Now I'll show you what I know you're waiting to see," said Grace as she put the snake away. "My mated pair of king cobras." Dropping her voice reverently, she added, "I call the big male 'the king of kings.'" She led the way to a large enclosure and for the first time in my life I was looking into the eyes of that dread reptile, the king cobra—or hamadryad.[10]

The common cobra is rarely more than five feet long. Even so, he has enough venom in his poison glands to kill fifty men. Grace's king cobras were more than fifteen feet long—longer than a boa constrictor. The two hamadryads contained enough venom, if injected drop by drop, to kill nearly a thousand human beings. That wasn't all. The hamadryad is the only snake known to attack without any provocation. These fearful creatures have been reported to trail a man through a jungle for the express purpose of biting him. They are so aggressive that they have closed roads in India by driving away all traffic. This is probably because the hamadryads, unlike other snakes, guard their eggs and young, and if a pair sets up housekeeping in a district, every other living thing must get out—including elephants. When a king cobra rears up, he stands higher than the head of a kneeling man. They are unquestionably the most dangerous animal in the world today.

When Grace first got these monsters, she was unable to handle them as she would ordinary cobras; so she had to devise an entirely new method of working with them. When the kings first arrived, they were completely unapproachable. They reared up more than four feet, snorting and hissing, their lower jaws open to expose the poison fangs. "A very threatening look, indeed," Grace called it. She put them in a large cage with a sliding partition. Unlike other snakes, hamadryads are knowing enough to notice that when their keeper opens the door in the side of the cage

---

10. **hamadryad** (hăm′ə-drī′əd): In Greek mythology, a hamadryad is a nymph, or nature goddess, supposed to inhabit a tree and live until the tree dies. The king cobra is also a tree-dweller.

to put in fresh water, he must expose his hand for a fraction of a second. These cobras soon learned to lie against the side of the cage and wait for Grace to open the door. She outwitted them by waiting until both of the hamadryads were on one side of the cage and then sliding in the partition before changing water pans. She did not dare to go near them with her bare hands; she used a padded stick to stroke them. Yet she was able to touch them four days after their arrival. "I petted the kings on their tails when their heads were far away." she told me. "Later in the day I had a little visit with them and told them how perfectly lovely they were, that I liked them and was sure we were going to be good friends."

A few weeks later, the king of kings began shedding his skin. Snakes are irritable and nervous while shedding and the hamadryad had trouble sloughing off[11] the thin membrane covering his eyes. Grace wrote in her diary: "I stroked his head and then pulled off the eyelids with eyebrow forceps. He flinched a little but was unafraid. He put out his tongue in such a knowing manner! I mounted the eyelids and they looked just like pearls. What a pity that there have been nothing but unfriendly, aggressive accounts about this sweet snake. Really, the intelligence of these creatures is unbelievable."

The king of kings was so heavy that Grace was unable to lift him by herself. Jule offered to help her carry the snake outside for a picture. While Jule and Grace were staggering out the door with the monster reptile between them, the king suddenly reared and rapped Jule several times on her forehead with his closed mouth. "He's trying to tell you something!" exclaimed Grace. He was indeed. I saw that the Chinese crocodile had rushed out from under a table and grabbed the hamadryad by the tail. Jule relaxed her grip and the king dropped his head and gave a single hiss. The croc promptly let go and the ladies bore the cobra out into the sunlight. I was the only person who seemed upset by the incident.

Out of curiosity, I asked Grace if she ever used music in taming her snakes. She laughed and told me what I already knew: all snakes are deaf.[12] Grace assured me that the Hindu fakir[13] uses his flute only to attract a crowd and by swaying his own body back and forth the fakir keeps the snake swaying as the cobra is feinting to strike. The man times his music to correspond to the snake's movements and

---

11. **sloughing** (slŭf'ĭng) **off:** shedding.

12. **all snakes are deaf:** Since this article was written, it has been discovered that snakes are sensitive to sounds of low frequency. However, it is not known whether they can be trained to respond to such sounds.

13. **fakir** (fə-kîr'): a Hindu holy man. Some fakirs claim to perform miracles. Many are snake charmers.

it appears to dance to the tune. The fakir naturally keeps well outside of the cobra's striking range. Years later when I was in India, I discovered that this is exactly what happens. I never saw any Oriental snake charmer even approximate Grace's marvelous powers over reptiles.

Grace's only source of income was to exhibit her snakes to tourists, although she was occasionally able to rent a snake to a studio (she always went along to make sure the reptile wasn't frightened or injured) and sometimes she bought ailing snakes from dealers, cured them, and resold them for a small profit to zoos. While I was with her, a dusty car stopped and discharged a plump couple with three noisy children who had seen her modest sign: *Grace Wiley — Reptiles*. Grace explained that she would show them her collection, handle the poisonous snakes, call over the tame alligators, and let the children play with Rocky, an eighteen-foot Indian Rock python[14] which she had raised from a baby. The charge was twenty-five cents. "That's too much," the woman said to her husband, and they went back to the car. Grace sighed. "No one seems interested in my snakes. No one really cares about them. And they're so wonderful."

One day Grace telephoned me to say that she had gotten in a new shipment of snakes, including some Indian cobras from Siam. "One of them has markings that form a complete G on the back of his hood," she told me. "Isn't it curious that the snake and I have the same initial! I call him 'my snake.' " We laughed about this, and then Jule and I went out to Cypress to take a last set of pictures of Grace and her snakes for an article I was doing about this remarkable woman.

When we arrived Grace was talking to a couple of kids who had brought a pet turtle to show her. We set up our photographic apparatus and after a while I began to grow restless. "Couldn't we go ahead with our pictures?" I hinted. Grace replied gently, "These boys have come for miles on their bicycles to show me this turtle. They really seem to love reptiles and I can't send them away." We waited for more than an hour before the boys departed with their remarkable turtle.

We took several pictures and then I asked Grace to let me get a picture of the cobra with the G on the hood. "I didn't look very well in those other pictures," said Grace anxiously. "I'll comb my hair and put on another blouse." She was back in a few minutes. Jule and I had set up our cameras in the yard behind the barn, first removing several alligators and a big monitor lizard[15] named Slinky to avoid any possibility of accidents. I wanted a shot of the cobra with spread hood, and Grace brought him out cradled in her arms. Before allowing me to take the picture, she removed her glasses, as she felt that she looked better without them. The cobra refused to spread and Grace put him down on the ground and extended her flat palm toward him to make him rear — something I had often seen her do before, but never without her glasses.

I was watching through the finder of my camera. I saw the cobra spread and strike as I clicked the shutter. As the image disappeared from the ground glass of my Graflex, I looked up and saw the snake had seized Grace by the middle finger. She said in her usual quiet voice, "Oh, he's bitten me."

I dropped the camera and ran toward her, feeling an almost paralyzing sense of shock,

---

14. **python** (pī'thŏn'): a nonpoisonous snake that crushes its prey.

15. **monitor lizard:** a large, flesh-eating lizard, so called because of the notion that it warns of the presence of crocodiles.

for I knew that Grace Wiley was a dead woman. At the same time I thought, "Good Lord, it's just like the book," for the cobra was behaving exactly as textbooks on cobras say they behave; he was deliberately chewing on the wound to make the venom run out of his glands. It was a terrible sight.

Quietly and expertly, Grace took hold of the snake on either side of his jaws and gently forced his mouth open. I knew that her only chance for life was to put a tourniquet around the finger instantly and slash open the wound to allow the venom to run out. Seconds counted. I reached out my hand to take the snake above the hood so she could immediately start squeezing out the venom, but Grace motioned me away. She stood up, still holding the cobra, and walked into the barn. Carefully, she put the snake into his cage and closed the door.

This must have taken a couple of minutes and I knew that the venom was spreading through her system each moment. "Jule," said Grace, "call Wesley Dickinson. He's a herpetologist[16] and a friend of mine. He'll know what to do." Calmly and distinctly she gave Jule the telephone number and Jule ran to the phone. Then Grace turned to me. Suddenly she said, "He didn't really bite me, did he?" It was the only emotion I saw her show. I could only say, "Grace, where's your snakebite kit?" We both knew that nothing except immediate amputation of her arm could save her, but anything was worth a chance.

She pointed to a cabinet. There was a tremendous collection of the surgical aids used for snakebite but I don't believe any of the stuff had been touched for twenty years. I pulled out a rubber tourniquet and tried to twist it around her finger. The old rubber snapped in my hands. Grace didn't seem to notice. I pulled out my handkerchief and tried that. It was too thick to go around her finger and I twisted it around her wrist. "I'll faint in a few minutes," said Grace. "I want to show you where everything is before I lose consciousness."

Cobra venom, unlike rattlesnake, affects the nervous system. In a few minutes the victim becomes paralyzed and the heart stops beating. I knew Grace was thinking of this. She said, "You must give me strychnine[17] injections to keep my heart going when I begin to pass out. I'll show you where the strychnine is kept. You may have to give me caffeine[18] also."

She walked to the other end of the room and I ran alongside trying to keep the tourniquet in place. She got out the tiny glass vials of strychnine and caffeine and also a hypodermic syringe with several needles. I saw some razor blades with the outfit and picked one up, intending to make a deep incision to let out as much of the venom as possible. Grace shook her head. "That won't do any good," she told me. Cobra venom travels along the nerves, so making the wound bleed wouldn't be very effective; but it was all I could think of to do.

Jule came back with a Mr. Tanner, Grace's cousin who lived next door. Tanner immediately got out his jackknife, intending to cut open the wound, but Grace stopped him. "Wait until Wesley comes," she said. Tanner told me afterward that he was convinced that if he had amputated the finger Grace might

---

16. **herpetologist** (hûr′pə-tŏl′ə-jĭst): one who studies reptiles.

17. **strychnine** (strĭk′nīn′): a poison. In small doses it is used as a stimulant for the heart or the nerves.
18. **caffeine** (kă-fēn′): a stimulant for the heart or the nerves.

have lived. This is doubtful. Probably nothing except amputation of her arm would have saved her then, and we had nothing but a jack-knife. She probably would have died of shock and loss of blood.

Grace lay on the floor to keep as quiet as possible and slow the absorption of the venom. "You'd better give me the strychnine now, dear," she told Jule. Jule snapped off the tip of one of the glass vials but the cylinder broke in her hands. She opened another tube and tried to fill the syringe; the needle was rusted shut. Jule selected another needle, tested it, and filled the syringe. "I'm afraid it will hurt," she told Grace. "Now don't worry, dear," said Grace comfortingly. "I know you'll do it very well."

After the injection, Grace asked Jule to put a newspaper under her head to keep her hair from getting dirty. A few minutes later, the ambulance, with Wesley Dickinson following in his own car, arrived. Wesley had telephoned the hospital and arranged for blood transfusions and an iron lung. As Grace was lifted into the ambulance, she called back to Tanner, "Remember to cut up the meat for my frogs very fine and take good care of my snakes." That was the last we ever saw of her.

Grace died in the hospital half an hour later. She lived about ninety minutes after being bitten. In the hospital, Wesley directed the doctors to drain the blood out of her arm and pump in fresh blood. When her heart began to fail she was put into the lung. She had become unconscious. Then her heart stopped. Stimulants were given. The slow beating began again but grew steadily weaker. Each time stimulants were given, the heart responded less strongly, and finally stopped forever.

We waited with Mr. and Mrs. Tanner at the snake barn, calling the hospital at intervals. When we heard that Grace was dead, Mrs. Tanner burst into tears. "Grace was such a beautiful young girl—and so talented," she moaned. "There wasn't anything she couldn't do. Why did she ever want to mess around with those awful snakes?"

"I guess that's something none of us will ever understand," said her husband sadly.

Grace was born in Kansas in 1884. She studied entomology[19] at the University of Kansas and during field trips to collect insects it was a great joke among Grace's fellow students that she was terrified of even harmless garter snakes. Later Grace turned with a passionate interest to the creatures she had so long feared. In 1923 she became curator of the Museum of Natural History at the Minneapolis Public Library but quarreled with the directors, who felt that her reckless handling of poisonous snakes endangered not only her own life but that of others. She went to the Brookfield Zoo in Chicago; here the same difficulty arose. Finally Grace moved to California where she could work with reptiles as she wished.

An attempt was made by several of Grace's friends to keep her collection together for a Grace Wiley Memorial Reptile House, but this failed. The snakes were auctioned off and the snake that had killed Grace was purchased by a roadside zoo in Arizona; huge signboards bearing an artist's conception of the incident were erected for miles along the highways. So passed one of the most remarkable people I have ever known.

---

19. **entomology** (ĕn'tə-mŏl'ə-jē): the study of insects.

SEEKING MEANING

1. What did the author see and hear about Grace Wiley that made him want to meet her? What details in the first three paragraphs make you realize that Grace Wiley was an unusual person?

2. The author gives you information on the cobra to prepare you for the crucial part of this article. He calls the cobra "the world's most deadly creature." He describes its hiss as "unearthly" and "uncanny." He says that when he saw the photograph of Grace with the king cobra, he understood why someone had called snakes "a running brook of horror." Why does he regard cobras as such monsters?

3. Grace Wiley was clearly a professional at handling snakes. Yet she made a mistake when the author wanted to photograph her with the cobra. Why did she remove her glasses? How did this seemingly unimportant act bring on the tragedy?

4. We call a situation *ironic* when it turns out to be the reverse of what we expect. For example, if a ship named the *Unsinkable* sinks, the situation is ironic. In this essay, we learn that Grace Wiley thought of her reptiles as a "little family." What other comments did Grace make about her snakes to show that she regarded them as her friends? What is ironic about her friendly feelings for the snakes?

5. Grace had given a name to the cobra that killed her. What was its name? Why is the name also ironic?

6. How did Grace Wiley react after the cobra bit her? What do you think her actions reveal about her character?

DEVELOPING SKILLS IN READING

Responding to Suspense

One device that a good storyteller uses to hold our interest is suspense. Suspense keeps us wanting to read on to find out what happens next. The good storyteller keeps us "suspended," or dangling, until the very end of the tale.

Daniel Mannix immediately captures our attention by saying that he is going to relate "the most terrible experience" of an entire career. What were your feelings when you read that statement? Did it make you want to read on?

Mannix spends some time explaining how a cobra strikes (page 401). Why do you think he does this? Which details in this explanation could make a reader feel uneasy about Grace's snakes?

At several points in the story, you might have thought that Grace was going to be bitten. When did you think this terrible event might happen? When did you know for certain how this story would end?

DEVELOPING SKILLS OF EXPRESSION

Writing a Character Sketch

Write a paragraph in which you describe someone who has made a strong impression on you. Remember that you want your readers to feel that they know this person. You can do this by describing what the person looks like. You can also do this by showing your character in action.

Try to open or close your character sketch with a statement that tells why this person made an impression on you.

The Bandanna

J. Frank Dobie

Modern cowboys seem to be giving up the bandanna handkerchief. Perhaps the moving pictures have made it tawdry.[1] Yet there was a time when this article was almost as necessary to a cowboy's equipment as a rope, and it served for purposes almost as varied. The prevailing color of the bandanna was red, but blues and blacks were common, and of course silk bandannas were prized above those made of cotton.

When the cowboy got up in the morning and went down to the water hole to wash his face he used his bandanna for a towel. Then he tied it around his neck, letting the fold

---

1. **tawdry** (tô′drē): cheap and flashy.

hang down in front, thus appearing rather nattily[2] dressed for breakfast. After he had roped out his bronc and tried to bridle him he probably found that the horse had to be blindfolded before he could do anything with him. The bandanna was what he used to blindfold the horse with. Mounted, the cowboy removed the blind from the horse and put it again around his own neck. Perhaps he rode only a short distance before he spied a big calf that should be branded. He roped the calf; then if he did not have a "piggin' string"—a short rope used for tying down animals—he tied the calf's legs together with the bandanna and thus kept the calf fast while he branded it. In the summertime the cowboy adjusted the bandanna to protect his neck from the sun. He often wore gloves too, for he liked to present neat hands and neck. If the hot sun was in his face, he adjusted the bandanna in front of him, tying it so that the fold would hang over his cheeks, nose, and mouth like a mask. If his business was with a dust-raising herd of cattle, the bandanna adjusted in the same way made a respirator; in blizzardly weather it likewise protected his face and ears. In the swift, unhalting work required in the pen the cowboy could, without losing time, grab a fold of the bandanna loosely hung about his neck and wipe away the blinding sweat. In the pen, too, the bandanna served as a rag for holding the hot handles of branding irons.

Many a cowboy has spread his bandanna, perhaps none too clean itself, over dirty, muddy water and used it as a strainer to drink through; sometimes he used it as a cup towel, which he called a "drying rag." If the bandanna was dirty, it was probably not so dirty as the other apparel of the cowboy, for when he came to a hole of water, he was wont to dismount and wash out his handkerchief, letting it dry while he rode along, holding it in his hand or spread over his hat. Often he wore it under his hat in order to help keep his head cool. At other times, in the face of a fierce gale, he used it to tie down his hat. The bandanna made a good sling for a broken arm; it made a good bandage for a blood wound. Early Irish settlers on the Nueces River[3] used to believe that a bandanna handkerchief that had been worn by a drowned man would, if cast into a stream above the sunken body, float until it came over the body and then sink, thus locating it. Many a cowboy out on the lonely plains had been buried with a clean bandanna spread over his face to keep the dirt, or the coarse blanket on which the dirt was poured, from touching it. The bandanna has been used to hang men with. Rustlers used to "wave" strangers around with it, as a warning against nearer approach, though the hat was more commonly used for signaling. Like the Mexican sombrero or the four-gallon Stetson, the bandanna could not be made too large. When the cowboys of the West make their final parade on the grassy shores of Paradise, the guidon[4] that leads them should be a bandanna handkerchief. It deserves to be called the flag of the range country.

---

3. **Nueces** (nōō-ā′səs) **River:** a river in southern Texas that flows into the Gulf of Mexico.
4. **guidon** (gī′dŏn′): a small flag or pennant.

---

2. **nattily:** attractively.

SEEKING MEANING

1. In this informative essay, Dobie makes you see how important the bandanna was in the cowhand's daily life. He does this mainly by describing the bandanna's uses. List the nouns that can name these many uses. Start with *towel.*

2. How do the two final sentences of this article help you understand how significant Dobie thinks the bandanna really was?

3. How does Dobie's article itself help keep alive the memory of an old tradition?

DEVELOPING SKILLS OF RESEARCH

Finding Out About the Cowhand's Tools

In this article, Dobie explains the many ways in which the bandanna was used on the Western range. In the following list you will find some other pieces of "equipment" that have been part of working life on the range. Choose one of the following items and write a paragraph explaining where it originated and how it has been used. Consult a dictionary for the origin of the word. Consult an encyclopedia for details telling how the item has been used. If there is a picture of the item in the encyclopedia, include a description of it in your paragraph.

chaps   sombrero
lasso   Western saddle
poncho

Where do dictionaries get their authority? This answer, written by a well-known linguist, may surprise you.

How Dictionaries Are Made
S. I. Hayakawa

It is widely believed that every word has a correct meaning, that we learn these meanings principally from teachers and grammarians (except that most of the time we don't bother to, so that we ordinarily speak "sloppy English"), and that dictionaries and grammars are the supreme authority in matters of meaning and usage. Few people ask by what authority the writers of dictionaries and grammars say what they say. I once got into a dispute with an Englishwoman over the pronunciation of a word and offered to look it up in the dictionary. The Englishwoman said firmly, "What for? I am English. I was born and brought up in England. The way I speak *is* English." Such self-assurance about one's own language is not uncommon among the English. In the United States, however, anyone who is willing to quarrel with the dictionary is regarded as either eccentric[1] or mad.

Let us see how dictionaries are made and how the editors arrive at definitions. What follows applies, incidentally, only to those dictionary offices where firsthand, original re-

search goes on — not those in which editors simply copy existing dictionaries. The task of writing a dictionary begins with reading vast amounts of the literature of the period or subject that the dictionary is to cover. As the editors read, they copy on cards every interesting or rare word, every unusual or peculiar occurrence of a common word, a large number of common words in their ordinary uses, and also the sentences in which each of these words appears, thus:

> pail
> The dairy *pails* bring home increase of milk
>
> Keats, *Endymion*
> I, 44–45

That is to say, the context of each word is collected, along with the word itself. For a really big job of dictionary writing, such as the *Oxford English Dictionary* (usually bound in about twenty-five volumes), millions of such cards are collected, and the task of editing occupies decades. As the cards are collected, they are alphabetized and sorted.

---

1. **eccentric** (ĕk-sĕn′trĭk): odd; out of the ordinary.

When the sorting is completed, there will be for each word anywhere from two or three to several hundred illustrative quotations, each on its card.

To define a word, then, the dictionary editor places before him the stack of cards illustrating that word; each of the cards represents an actual use of the word by a writer of some literary or historical importance. He reads the cards carefully, discards some, rereads the rest, and divides up the stack according to what he thinks are the several senses of the word. Finally, he writes his definitions, following the hard-and-fast rule that each definition *must* be based on what the quotations in front of him reveal about the meaning of the word. The editor cannot be influenced by what *he* thinks a given word *ought* to mean. He must work according to the cards or not at all.

The writing of a dictionary, therefore, is not a task of setting up authoritative statements about the "true meanings" of words, but a task of *recording*, to the best of one's ability, what various words *have meant* to authors in the distant or immediate past. *The writer of a dictionary is a historian, not a lawgiver.* If, for example, we had been writing a dictionary in 1890, or even as late as 1919, we could have said that the word *broadcast* means "to scatter" (seed, for example), but we could not have decreed[2] that from 1921 on, the most common meaning of the word should become "to disseminate audible messages, etc., by radio transmission." To regard the dictionary as an "authority," therefore, is to credit the dictionary writer with gifts of prophecy which neither he nor anyone else possesses. In choosing our words when we speak or write, we can be *guided* by the historical record afforded[3] us by the dictionary, but we cannot be *bound* by it, because new situations, new experiences, new inventions, new feelings are always compelling us to give new uses to old words. Looking under a *hood*, we should ordinarily have found, five hundred years ago, a monk; today, we find a motorcar engine.

---

2. **decreed:** ordered; officially decided.
3. **afforded:** provided.

SEEKING MEANING

1. The purpose of this selection is to explain where dictionaries get their authority. Hayakawa wants his readers to understand what dictionaries *are,* and what they are *not.* In his first paragraph, what does Hayakawa say most people believe about words and dictionaries?

2. In the second paragraph, Hayakawa begins to explain how dictionary editors arrive at the definitions of words. What important information about words do the editors put on their cards?

3. Hayakawa says that editors cannot be influenced by what they think a word ought to mean. What "hard-and-fast rule" do the editors follow when they write the definitions of a word?

4. Which sentences in the last paragraph summarize the main idea of this article? Try to restate this idea in your own words.

DEVELOPING VOCABULARY

Recognizing Multiple Meanings of Words
At the end of this essay, Hayakawa tells us that the word *hood* has acquired at least one new meaning in the past five hundred years.

Here are some other words that have acquired additional meanings over the years. What different meanings does your dictionary give for each word? Use each word in two sentences, to show at least two different meanings.

bear	dove	hawk	project
bug	grill	press	satellite

DEVELOPING SKILLS OF EXPRESSION

Explaining a Process
In this well-constructed essay, Hayakawa includes a brief explanation of the process of making a dictionary.

Which sentence in the second paragraph announces that the explanation is about to begin?

How many paragraphs does Hayakawa use to explain the process?

The process is explained in chronological order, or the order in which the work is done. Notice the words that help you follow the sequence of steps: *as, when, finally.*

Write a brief explanation of how something is done. Select as your topic a process that you are very familiar with, such as preparing a food, building something, training an animal, or performing an art. Use words like *first, second, when, after,* and *now* to help your reader follow the steps in the process. State your topic in the first sentence.

ABOUT THE AUTHOR

S. (for Samuel) I. (for Ichiye) Hayakawa, American educator and semantics expert, was born in British Columbia in 1906. He came to the United States to teach at the University of Wisconsin. Later he taught at San Francisco State University and became its first president. This article is from his lively and popular book *Language in Thought and Action,* which was a Book-of-the-Month-Club selection when it was first published. In 1976 Hayakawa was elected to the United States Senate.

Practice in Reading and Writing

NONFICTION

Reading Nonfiction

Fiction is "invented" or "imagined." Short stories and novels are examples of fiction.

Nonfiction is *not* invented; it is "true" or "factual." Examples of nonfiction in this unit include a diary entry, part of an autobiography, and an essay on the uses of a bandanna. Other examples of nonfiction are news articles, articles on science or history, movie reviews, how-to-do-it books, letters, and speeches.

Here is part of a paragraph from a memoir in this unit (page 388). *Memoir* comes from a French word meaning "memory." In this memoir, James Thurber remembers something about his childhood.

> Probably no one man should have as many dogs in his life as I have had, but there was more pleasure than distress in them for me except in the case of an Airedale named Muggs. He gave me more trouble than all the other fifty-four or -five put together, although my moment of keenest embarrassment was the time a Scotch terrier named Jeannie, who had just had four puppies in the shoe closet of a fourth-floor apartment in New York, had the fifth and last at the corner of—but we shall get around to that later on. Then, too, there was the prizewinning French poodle, a great big black poodle —none of your little, untroublesome white miniatures— who got sick riding in the rumble seat of a car with me on her way to the Greenwich Dog Show.

Here are some questions you should ask yourself as you read nonfiction:

1. *What is the topic?*

According to the preceeding passage, what is the topic of Thurber's memoir?

2. *What details develop the topic?*

From what you recall of Thurber's memoir, tell what details and anecdotes he uses to develop his topic.

3. *Does the writer state any conclusions about the topic?*

Not all writers state conclusions about their topics. But sometimes a writer will draw some general conclusion, or meaning, about a subject. Maya Angelou, for example, sums up her story about her experience with Mrs. Flowers (page 381) by saying, "I was liked, and what a difference it made." What general observation about the natural world concludes Anaïs Nin's diary entry (page 366)? Do you agree with her?

4. *What is the writer's purpose?*

Does the writer want to entertain you, to inform you about something, to influence the way you think about something—or a combination of these things? Thurber's purpose in "The Dog That Bit People" seems to be to entertain and amuse us. What is Hayakawa's purpose in his article on dictionaries (page 411)? What is Richard Wright's purpose in telling you the details of his childhood (page 393)?

Stating and Supporting a Topic

Here are two important points to remember when you write a science report, a profile of someone, a personal memoir, an essay of opinion, or any kind of factual prose:

1. *State your topic at the beginning or end of your composition.*

2. *Use specific details to support or illustrate your topic.*

Write a factual paragraph on one of these topics or on one of your own choosing:

How to raise a hamster
The origin of soccer
The disappearance of Pompeii
Famous monster movies
An accidental scientific discovery

For Further Reading

Anderson, Marian, *My Lord, What a Morning: An Autobiography* (Viking, 1956)

One of America's greatest singers tells her own story, including the time she delivered an unforgettable concert before 75,000 people on the steps of the Lincoln Memorial in Washington, D.C.

Barth, Edna, *I'm Nobody! Who Are You?: The Story of Emily Dickinson* (Seabury, 1971)

This easy-to-read biography of the secluded life of the New England poet includes some of her poems and passages from her letters.

Branley, Franklyn M., *The Mystery of Stonehenge* (Thomas Y. Crowell, 1969)

The author presents several theories about the origins of the mysterious ring of massive stones set up in England about 1800 B.C.

Buckmaster, Henrietta, *Women Who Shaped History* (Macmillan, 1966; paperback, Collier)

These six nineteenth-century women succeeded in changing the future.

Butler, Hal, *Sports Heroes Who Wouldn't Quit* (Messner, 1973)

Here are stories about men and women who overcame handicaps to succeed in baseball, swimming, hockey, track, golf, and other sports.

Clemens, Samuel L., *Autobiography of Mark Twain* (Harper & Row, 1959; paperback, Harper)

America's greatest humorist tells about his life. This is a big book that is worth sampling.

Day, Clarence, *Life with Father* (Knopf, 1946; paperback, Washington Square Press)

The author writes humorously about his stubborn father and their family life in New York City in the 1890's.

Hersey, John, *Hiroshima* (Knopf, 1946; paperback, Bantam)

This famous and unforgettable report follows six people who survived the atomic blast in Hiroshima, Japan, in 1945.

Lindbergh, Charles A., *The Spirit of St. Louis* (Scribner, 1953; paperback, Ballantine Books)

Lindbergh tells his own exciting story of the first nonstop solo transatlantic flight from New York to Paris.

Ogg, Oscar, *The Twenty-Six Letters* (Thomas Y. Crowell, 1971)

When did people begin to write—and why? This illustrated book traces the history of writing from ancient to present times.

Place, Marian T., *On the Track of Bigfoot* (Dodd, Mead, 1974)

Monstrous hairy creatures are said to roam the mountains of the Pacific Northwest. Do they really exist? The author presents the evidence and lets you decide.

Robertson, Dougal, *Survive the Savage Sea* (Praeger, 1973; paperback, Bantam)

This is a true account of a family's struggle to survive thirty-eight days on a raft, adrift in the Pacific Ocean, after their boat had been destroyed by killer whales. The incredible story is told by the father.

Roueché, Berton, *Eleven Blue Men* (Little, Brown, 1954; paperback, Berkley)

These are stories about health workers who investigate mysterious killer diseases.

Steinbeck, John, *Travels with Charley in Search of America* (Viking, 1962; paperback, Bantam)

Accompanied by a comical old poodle named Charley, Steinbeck travels in a camper across America in the hopes of "rediscovering" a country he has known all his life.

POETRY

Long before there was writing, there was poetry. When people wanted to commemorate a battle or a birth, they did it in the rhythmic language we call poetry. When they told the history of their society, they did it in a form of poetry. Many of their most important laws, rituals, and beliefs were passed on from generation to generation in the form of poetry.

Poetry is a rhythmic use of language that seems to come naturally to people. Children use poetry. They recite nursery rhymes and nonsense jingles. They play games to the swing of rhythmic chants. Perhaps you recall using poetry to aid your memory. Remember the rhyme about the days of the months beginning "Thirty days hath September. . ."?

Poetry packs a good deal of meaning into a small space. It can help us see the world in an entirely fresh, new way. It can make us use our emotions. Robert Frost, himself a poet, said that poetry helped him remember things he didn't know he knew. Perhaps some of the poems in this unit will have a special effect on you.

Autumn Grasses. From a Japanese screen painting, Momoyama Period (1573–1614).
The Metropolitan Museum of Art, New York. Bell, Fletcher, Wiesenberger, Seymour, and Bennett Funds.

Less Is More

Southbound on the Freeway   *May Swenson*

A tourist came in from Orbitville,
parked in the air, and said:

The creatures of this star
are made of metal and glass.

Through the transparent parts   5
you can see their guts.

Their feet are round and roll
on diagrams or long

measuring tapes, dark
with white lines.   10

They have four eyes.
The two in back are red.

Sometimes you can see a five-eyed
one, with a red eye turning

on the top of his head.   15
He must be special—

the others respect him
and go slow

when he passes, winding
among them from behind.   20

They all hiss as they glide,
like inches, down the marked

tapes. Those soft shapes,
shadowy inside

the hard bodies—are they   25
their guts or their brains?

SEEKING MEANING

1. What clues in the first four lines tell you that the tourist is from outer space?

2. The tourist describes creatures that are made of metal and glass (lines 3–4). In what other ways does this tourist describe the creatures? What are they?

3. What are the soft shapes (line 23) that the tourist sees inside the creatures? How do they puzzle the tourist?

4. This poem describes a part of our world from an unusual point of view. The poet may be suggesting that human beings have become so dependent on mechanical devices that they have lost part of their human identity. Do the tourist's conclusions force you to think about this idea? Why or why not?

5. What does the tourist fail to see on our star?

DEVELOPING SKILLS IN READING

Responding to Imagery

This poet uses several unusual *images*, or sense experiences created in words. For example, the image in lines 7–10 helps you see cars as creatures with round feet.

Images can also help you imagine how a thing sounds, tastes, or smells. They can even help you imagine how something feels — whether, for example, it is rough or smooth.

What image in line 21 helps you hear what the tourist hears? What causes the sound? Which words in the last two stanzas tell you how the tourist imagines the insides of the creatures feel?

How do you think a person traveling on this freeway would see the tourist? Create two or three images that describe how the occupants of the cars might see the tourist.

This poem describes a train. Yet the speaker never mentions the word train, and, in fact, seems to be describing an animal. She appears to be looking at this great noisy train from above, watching it as it goes through the New England mountains.

I Like to See It Lap the Miles

Emily Dickinson

I like to see it lap the miles,
And lick the valleys up,
And stop to feed itself at tanks;
And then, prodigious,° step

Around a pile of mountains,   5
And, supercilious,° peer
In shanties by the sides of roads;
And then a quarry pare°

To fit its sides, and crawl between,
Complaining all the while   10
In horrid, hooting stanza;
Then chase itself down hill

And neigh like Boanerges;°
Then, punctual as a star,
Stop—docile and omnipotent°—   15
At its own stable door.

4. **prodigious** (prə-dĭj′əs): huge.

6. **supercilious** (soo′pər-sĭl′ē-əs): proud and scornful.

8. **pare:** trim or peel away.

13. **Boanerges** (bō′ə-nûr′jēz): any loud, thunderous public speaker.

15. **omnipotent** (ŏm-nĭp′ə-tənt): all-powerful.

Manchester Valley. Oil with sand on canvas by
Joseph Pickett (1848–1918).
The Museum of Modern Art, New York. Gift of Abby Aldrich Rockefeller.

SEEKING MEANING

1. The speaker in this poem uses images that seem to describe an animal. What words and phrases help you picture this animal's activities as it moves along?
2. What words and phrases help you picture the animal as something huge and powerful?
3. What words in the last stanza identify the animal with a horse? Could it be a horse in the other stanzas? Why or why not?
4. The poet never names what she is describing. What clues in the poem reveal that its subject is a train?
5. This train is both "docile" (manageable) and "omnipotent" (all-powerful) at the same time. What other things can be both docile and omnipotent at the same time?
6. How do you think the poet feels about this train?

DEVELOPING SKILLS OF EXPRESSION

Using an Unusual Point of View •

In Swenson's poem on page 418, a speaker looks down at cars on the freeway and describes them as if they were living creatures. In Dickinson's poem, a speaker looks down at a train and describes it as if it were an animal.

Imagine that you are a visitor from outer space. How would you describe the mechanical things you see around you? A radio might be a small, rigid creature that talks and sings in different voices. A subway might be a serpent that screams. A bicycle and its rider might be a creature that moves on two round feet.

Choose an ordinary object or device. Try to think of something that moves or makes noise. In two or three sentences, describe it as though you were a tourist from another planet

ABOUT THE AUTHOR

A seventh-generation New Englander, Emily Dickinson (1830–1886) lived and died in the house in which she was born, in Amherst, Massachusetts. For most of her adult life, she traveled no farther than her own garden. She wrote her poems in the rhythms she found in her Bible and hymnbook. A few friends knew that she had written some poems, but after her death, even her sister was amazed to discover almost eighteen hundred poems tied in bundles in her bedroom. Emily Dickinson might have lacked worldly experience, but she lived an intense inner life. In her imagination, the smallest, most ordinary object or scene could be a sign of something deep and mysterious.

Child on Top of a Greenhouse

Theodore Roethke

The wind billowing out the seat of my britches,
My feet crackling splinters of glass and dried putty,
The half-grown chrysanthemums staring up like accusers,
Up through the streaked glass, flashing with sunlight,
A few white clouds all rushing eastward,
A line of elms plunging and tossing like horses,
And everyone, everyone pointing up and shouting!

SEEKING MEANING

1. Suppose the title of this poem had not been given. What clues would tell you where this speaker is standing?

2. What do you think the child is feeling? What about the people on the ground?

DEVELOPING SKILLS IN READING

Recognizing Similes

When Roethke says in line 3 that the chrysanthemums are "staring up like accusers," he is using a simile. A *simile* is a figure of speech that compares two basically unlike things by using a word such as *like* or *as.* Similes are not limited to poems. They are used all the time in ordinary conversation: "Her cheeks are like apples"; "His feet are like lead"; "She's as white as a sheet."

Poets use similes to help you see unexpected likenesses between different things. When Roethke says that chrysanthemums are "staring up like accusers," he compares the flowers to people. Their "faces" look up at the boy as he stands on his "ship" high above the ground. Like angry people, they are accusing him of doing something wrong. Perhaps he feels they are saying, "Get down from there!"

Roethke uses another simile when he describes the elm trees in line 6. What is he comparing the elms to? What does this simile make you see in your imagination?

ABOUT THE AUTHOR

Theodore Roethke (1908–1963) said that he grew up in Saginaw, Michigan, in and around a beautiful greenhouse. Later Roethke wrote several "greenhouse poems," including the poem here. In another one, called "Big Wind," Roethke imagines the glass house as a ship, this time riding out a storm, carrying her full cargo of roses. Roethke also wrote some very witty poems. The whale, the hippo, and a singing serpent are three of his humorous animal subjects.

*You **have** to read the title of this poem as its first line. Fifties refers to the 1950's.*

For My Sister Molly Who in the Fifties
Alice Walker

Once made a fairy rooster from
Mashed potatoes
Whose eyes I forget
But green onions were his tail
And his two legs were carrot sticks   5
A tomato slice his crown.
Who came home on vacation
When the sun was hot
and cooked
and cleaned   10
And minded least of all
The children's questions
A million or more
Pouring in on her
Who had been to school   15
And knew (and told us too) that certain
Words were no longer good
And taught me not to say us for we
No matter what "Sonny said" up the
road.   20

FOR MY SISTER MOLLY WHO IN THE FIFTIES
Knew Hamlet well and read into the night
And coached me in my songs of Africa
A continent I never knew
But learned to love
Because "they" she said could carry   25
A tune
And spoke in accents never heard
In Eatonton.
Who read from *Prose and Poetry*   30
And loved to read "Sam McGee from Tennessee"
On nights the fire was burning low
And Christmas wrapped in angel hair
And I for one prayed for snow.

WHO IN THE FIFTIES   35
Knew all the written things that made
Us laugh and stories by
The hour   Waking up the story buds
Like fruit. Who walked among the flowers
And brought them inside the house   40
And smelled as good as they
And looked as bright.
Who made dresses, braided
Hair. Moved chairs about
Hung things from walls   45
Ordered baths
Frowned on wasp bites
And seemed to know the endings
Of all the tales
I had forgot.   50

SEEKING MEANING

1. The speaker in this poem wants you to know her sister Molly. What details in the first part of the poem help you see what Molly created with vegetables?

2. According to the second part of the poem, what new experiences did Molly bring into the speaker's life in Eatonton?

3. The speaker uses a simile in lines 38–39 when she tells of Molly's "waking up the story buds / Like fruit." What picture does this simile put in your mind's eye?

4. In what ways was Molly like the flowers she brought into the house?

5. The speaker never states directly how she feels about her sister Molly. How would you describe her feelings for Molly?

Still Life, Number Two. A lithograph by Louis Lozowick (1892–1973).
The Museum of Modern Art, New York.   Gift of Abby Aldrich Rockefeller.

The Bean Eaters   *Gwendolyn Brooks*

They eat beans mostly, this old yellow pair.
Dinner is a casual affair.
Plain chipware on a plain and creaking wood,
Tin flatware.

Two who are Mostly Good.   5
Two who have lived their day,
But keep on putting on their clothes
And putting things away.

And remembering . . .
Remembering, with twinklings and twinges,   10
As they lean over the beans in their rented back room that
     is full of beads and receipts and dolls and cloths,
     tobacco crumbs, vases and fringes.

SEEKING MEANING

1. This poem presents a picture of two old people who live alone in a rented back room. Which images in the poem make you realize they are poor?

2. These two "have lived their day" (line 6). What do they do now?

3. The old couple remember their past "with twinklings and twinges" (line 10). What do these words tell you about the kinds of memories they have?

4. The speaker says that this old couple are "Mostly Good." How do you think she feels toward them? Is she suggesting that they deserve something better than their poverty?

5. What effect does this poem have on you? How does the effect compare with the effect created by Walker's poem on page 424?

DEVELOPING SKILLS OF EXPRESSION

Re-creating the Scene of a Poem

The famous Dutch artist Vincent van Gogh painted a picture called *The Potato Eaters*. It shows a family of peasants, sitting around a table, eating a simple meal of potatoes and tea. There are a few details in the room: one framed picture is on the wall, and a hanging lamp sheds its light on the family's faces. The mood of the picture is not cheerful, but the viewer can sense the painter's affection for the "potato eaters."

Suppose you were going to paint a picture called *The Bean Eaters*. Which details from the poem would you include in the painting? The color that dominates van Gogh's painting is gray. What color would dominate your painting *The Bean Eaters?* What mood would you strive for? Write a paragraph describing your painting of this scene. If you prefer, re-create the scene in a painting or a collage.

ABOUT THE AUTHOR

Gwendolyn Brooks (1917–   ) remembers that she was writing all the time when she was a young girl. "My mother says I began rhyming at seven—but my notebooks date back to my eleventh year only." After graduating from Wilson Junior College in Chicago, she attended a poetry-writing class given in her neighborhood. Her first volume of poetry was called *A Street in Bronzeville*. (Bronzeville was an old name for a black neighborhood in Chicago.) In 1950 she won the Pulitzer Prize for *Annie Allen*, a collection of poems about a black girl growing up in Chicago. When asked why she writes poetry, she replied: "I like the concentration, the crush; I like working with language, as others like working with paints and clay, or notes." She says that many people hated "The Bean Eaters" when it was published. They felt she was forsaking pure poetry for social commentary. She recalls, with a laugh, that she was warned, "Watch it, Miss Brooks!"

Mother to Son

Langston Hughes

Well, son, I'll tell you:
Life for me ain't been no crystal stair.
It's had tacks in it,
And splinters,
And boards torn up,   5
And places with no carpet on the floor—
Bare.
But all the time
I'se been a-climbin' on,
And reachin' landin's,   10
And turnin' corners,
And sometimes goin' in the dark
Where there ain't been no light.
So boy, don't you turn back.
Don't set you down on the steps   15
'Cause you finds it's kinder hard.
Don't you fall now—
For I'se still goin', honey,
I'se still climbin',
And life for me ain't been no crystal stair.   20

SEEKING MEANING

1. In this poem, a mother talks to her son about her life. What does she compare her life to?

2. What images does the mother use to describe the difficulties she has faced?

3. Although the mother has often been "Where there ain't been no light" (line 13), she is "still climbin' " (line 19). What advice does she give her son?

DEVELOPING SKILLS IN READING

Recognizing Metaphors

When you compare two different things by using a word such as *like* or *as*, you are using a *simile:* "Russell is like a lamb"; "Her eyes are like stars"; "The dog is like a devil." When you identify two different things, without using a word such as *like* or *as*, you are using a *metaphor:* "Russell is a lamb"; "Her eyes are stars"; "The dog is a devil."

phor, even though it is expressed negatively. What kind of stairway would you say the mother's life has been? In what ways are life and a stairway alike? What do you think the mother means when she says her stairway has had "bare" spots in it? What is "the dark"?

Can you think of another metaphor to describe life? Complete this statement to create your own metaphor about life: "Life is _____."

Emily Dickinson's poem "I Like to See It Lap the Miles" (page 420) is built around a metaphor. How would you state the metaphor in her poem?

Recognizing Conversational Rhythms
The language that we use in conversation has a rhythm and a music of its own. "Mother to Son" is an example of how plain speech can be made into poetry.

There is no rhyme in this poem. There is no regular pattern of rhythm. Instead, Langston Hughes uses the natural rhythms of everyday speech to create a poetic effect.

> It's had tacks in it,
> And splinters,
> And boards torn up,
> And places with no carpet on the floor—
> Bare.

The poet uses these ordinary speech patterns in a careful, deliberate way. How does the repetition of *and* suggest the climb up a long, winding staircase?

The poet puts the word *bare* on a line by itself. What does he want to emphasize? How would you say this line aloud?

Plain speech can be used to suggest strong emotions. Which lines of this poem do you think should be spoken softly and tenderly?

Metaphors, of course, are not literally, or factually, true. Russell is not really a lamb; her eyes are not really stars; the dog is not really a devil. However, metaphors are very powerful. Like similes, they help us use our imagination to see surprising likenesses between things that are basically different.

In its simplest form, a metaphor says directly that one thing *is* another, different thing. In this poem, the mother says, "Life for me ain't been no crystal stair." This is a meta-

The Road Not Taken   *Robert Frost*

Two roads diverged° in a yellow wood,
And sorry I could not travel both
And be one traveler, long I stood
And looked down one as far as I could
To where it bent in the undergrowth;   5

Then took the other, as just as fair,
And having perhaps the better claim,
Because it was grassy and wanted wear;
Though as for that the passing there
Had worn them really about the same,   10

And both that morning equally lay
In leaves no step had trodden black.
Oh, I kept the first for another day!
Yet knowing how way leads on to way,
I doubted if I should ever come back.   15

I shall be telling this with a sigh
Somewhere ages and ages hence:
Two roads diverged in a wood, and I—
I took the one less traveled by,
And that has made all the difference.   20

1. **diverged** (dĭ-vûrjd′): branched off.

SEEKING MEANING

1. How does this speaker feel when he has to choose one road instead of the other?

2. Why does the second road seem to be a better choice?

3. The speaker hopes to take the first road on "another day." Yet why does he doubt that he will ever be able to do this?

4. What larger choices in life do you think the poet could be talking about here? Name some choices that could "make all the difference" in a person's life.

5. How would you describe the mood, or feeling, of this poem?

DEVELOPING SKILLS IN READING

Recognizing Symbols

When you see the colors red, white, and blue together, you probably think of the United States. These colors stand for the United States, just as a dove stands for peace and a red rose stands for love or beauty. These are examples of *symbols*. A *symbol* is anything that represents, or stands for, something else.

A road is a common symbol for life. What would we mean, for example, if we said "It's the end of the road for him"? The forked road in this poem is a symbol for a choice that the speaker has to make. Why is a forked road a good symbol for choices in life?

The speaker says that "way leads on to way." How does this suggest that life is a maze of roads that cannot be retraveled?

If a road is a symbol for life, what kind of life does the speaker choose when he takes a road "less traveled by"?

The title of the poem is "The Road *Not* Taken." How do you think the speaker feels about the roads he did *not* take and can never find again?

ABOUT THE AUTHOR

After working as a country schoolteacher, a newspaper editor, and a cobbler, Robert Frost (1874–1963) tended a small chicken farm in New Hampshire. In 1912, having had little success as a farmer, he sold the farm and moved to England with his family. There he devoted all his time to writing. He soon published his first two volumes of poems. These books were so highly praised that when Frost returned to America in 1915, he was recognized as a major poet. The rest of his long and productive life was spent living quietly on a small farm in Vermont, writing poetry and occasionally lecturing and teaching. Though Robert Frost's poems reflect the quiet dignity and simplicity of the countryside, they often give us a glimpse into the tragic and puzzling sides of life.

The Secret Heart
Robert P. Tristram Coffin

Across the years he could recall
His father one way best of all.

In the stillest hour of night
The boy awakened to a light.

Half in dreams, he saw his sire°
With his great hands full of fire.

The man had struck a match to see
If his son slept peacefully.

He held his palms each side the spark
His love had kindled in the dark.

His two hands were curved apart
In the semblance° of a heart.

He wore, it seemed to his small son,
A bare heart on his hidden one,

A heart that gave out such a glow
No son awake could bear to know.

It showed a look upon a face
Too tender for the day to trace.

One instant, it lit all about,
And then the secret heart went out.

But it shone long enough for one
To know that hands held up the sun.

5   **5. sire:** father.

           10

           12. semblance: a likeness, a shape.

           15

           20

SEEKING MEANING

1. Which details tell you that the "secret heart" reveals the father's great love for his son?

2. There is a line in an old spiritual that goes: "He's got the whole world in his hands." Whose hands are these? How might this image from the spiritual be like the last one in the poem?

Sound Effects

Blue-Butterfly Day   *Robert Frost*

It is blue-butterfly day here in spring,
And with these sky-flakes down in flurry on flurry
There is more unmixed color on the wing
Than flowers will show for days unless they hurry.

But these are flowers that fly and all but sing:
And now from having ridden out desire
They lie closed over in the wind and cling
Where wheels have freshly sliced the April mire.°   8. **mire:** wet, soggy ground; mud.

SEEKING MEANING

1. The speaker in this poem is sharing the experience of a spring day with the reader. Why is this day so special?

2. The phrase "sky-flakes" in line 2 is a metaphor. A metaphor identifies one thing with another, different thing. What does the speaker identify the butterflies with, when he calls them "sky-flakes"?

3. What does the speaker identify the butterflies with in line 5? What other identification does the verb *sing* suggest?

4. Until the butterflies reach the ground in line 6, the day is described in beautiful images. Which words in the last two lines suggest that the butterflies' landing place is *not* beautiful and that it might be dangerous?

DEVELOPING SKILLS IN READING

Understanding the Uses of Rhyme

Rhyme is one of the musical devices that give pleasure in poetry. Think about some of the popular songs you happen to enjoy. Do their lyrics use rhyme? Would the songs be as pleasant to listen to without the use of rhyming words?

Sometimes rhyme is used to add to the meaning of a poem. In this poem, Robert Frost uses three rhyming sounds. One rhyme is found in the words *spring, wing, sing,* and *cling.* Another rhyme is found in the words *flurry* and *hurry.* Read these rhymes aloud. Notice how light and airy the rhymes sound. They help convey the carefree flight of the butterflies.

However, the last rhyme of the poem, *desire* and *mire,* does not have the same effect. Read this rhyme aloud. It has a slower, heavier sound. This change in rhyme sounds helps point out the change in mood. In the first stanza, the butterflies seem to float lightly and freely in the air, and the mood is happy. How has the mood changed at the end of the poem when the "sky-flakes" land on earth?

DEVELOPING SKILLS OF EXPRESSION

Using Contrast in Description

In this poem, Frost uses beautiful images to describe the flight of butterflies on a spring day. But he also uses a few images that are not so beautiful. He reminds us that nature can be threatening even on a spring day.

You can find such contrasts in nature almost anywhere you look. The sun is a brilliant star that gives heat and light. Yet when you look directly at the sun, it hurts your eyes. A rose is a beautiful flower. Yet its petals may hide a bee, and its stem is covered with thorns.

Think of an object or a scene in nature that is both beautiful and threatening in some way. Describe the contrast in a poem or in a paragraph.

One of William Shakespeare's comedies, Love's Labor's Lost, *ends with two songs—the first is Spring's song and the second is Winter's. This is the song of Winter.*

When Icicles Hang by the Wall

William Shakespeare

When icicles hang by the wall,
  And Dick the shepherd blows his nail,°
And Tom bears logs into the hall,
  And milk comes frozen home in pail,
When blood is nipped, and ways be foul,°   5
Then nightly sings the staring owl,
  Tu-whit,
Tu-who, a merry note,
While greasy Joan doth keel° the pot.

When all aloud the wind doth blow,   10
  And coughing drowns the parson's saw,°
And birds sit brooding in the snow,
  And Marian's nose looks red and raw,
When roasted crabs° hiss in the bowl,
Then nightly sings the staring owl,   15
  Tu-whit,
Tu-who, a merry note,
While greasy Joan doth keel the pot.

2. **blows his nail:** blows on his fingernails to warm his hands.

5. **ways be foul:** roads are muddy.

9. **keel:** cool by stirring.

11. **saw:** wise saying.

14. **crabs:** crab apples.

SEEKING MEANING

1. This poem uses images to help you imagine a cold winter scene in sixteenth-century England. For example, line 2 pictures a shepherd blowing on his fingernails to warm his hands. What other images in the poem help you picture this cold winter scene? What sounds do you hear?

2. Although the images in the poem emphasize the harshness of winter, some of them suggest warmth and comfort. Tom's logs (line 3) must be for a fire. What do you think Joan is stirring in the pot? Which image suggests that something tasty is being cooked?

3. Many poems about autumn or winter give the reader a sense of sadness or loneliness. How does this "Winter's song" affect you?

Detail from *Winter Landscape*. An oil painting by Pieter Bruegel (1522?–1569).
Musées Royaux des Beaux Arts, Brussels.

DEVELOPING SKILLS IN READING

Recognizing Alliteration

You may have heard some of these expressions used in everyday conversation: "hale and hearty," "rough and ready," "dribs and drabs," "now or never." All of these expressions use *alliteration* because they repeat initial consonant sounds.

Poetry written in the English language has always used alliteration. Sometimes it is used as an aid to memory (it is easy to remember "She sells sea shells by the seashore"). Sometimes it is used to emphasize certain words. Sometimes it is used for sound effects.

Where does Shakespeare use alliteration in lines 12 and 13? Can you find other uses of alliteration in this song?

ABOUT THE AUTHOR

William Shakespeare (1564–1616) was the son of a prominent merchant in the town of Stratford-on-Avon in England. When he was in his twenties, he went to London to seek his fortune. There he joined a famous acting company. For this company, he wrote thirty-seven brilliant plays, including tragedies, comedies, and history plays. Plays such as *Hamlet* and *Romeo and Juliet*, which were great successes in their own day, are still being read and performed all over the world. Shakespeare's comedies always include songs and dances. The comedy *Love's Labor's Lost*, which this song is from, was probably first presented at a Christmas house party. This might explain why it ends with Winter's song.

When Icicles Hang by the Wall 437

This story takes place in the fifteenth century, when "Border" wars raged between England and Scotland. Lochinvar had gone off to battle. But shocking news brings him home . . .

Lochinvar   *Sir Walter Scott*

Oh, young Lochinvar is come out of the west,
Through all the wide Border his steed was the best;
And, save his good broadsword, he weapons had none,
He rode all unarmed, and he rode all alone.
So faithful in love, and so dauntless in war,   5
There never was knight like the young Lochinvar.

He stayed not for brake,° and he stopped not for stone,
He swam the Eske River where ford there was none;
But ere he alighted at Netherby gate,
The bride had consented, the gallant came late: 10
For a laggard° in love, and a dastard° in war,
Was to wed the fair Ellen of brave Lochinvar.

So boldly he entered the Netherby Hall,
Among bridesmen, and kinsmen, and brothers, and all.
Then spoke the bride's father, his hand on his sword   15
(For the poor craven° bridegroom said never a word),
"Oh, come ye in peace here, or come ye in war,
Or to dance at our bridal, young Lord Lochinvar?"

"I long wooed your daughter, my suit you denied—
Love swells like the Solway,° but ebbs like its tide—   20
And now I am come, with this lost love of mine,
To lead but one measure,° drink one cup of wine.
There are maidens in Scotland more lovely by far,
That would gladly be bride to the young Lochinvar."

The bride kissed the goblet; the knight took it up;   25
He quaffed off° the wine, and he threw down the cup.
She looked down to blush, and she looked up to sigh,
With a smile on her lips, and a tear in her eye.
He took her soft hand, ere her mother could bar—
"Now tread we a measure!" said young Lochinvar.   30

7. **brake:** a clump of bushes or trees.

11. **laggard:** a slow person. **dastard:** a sneak.

16. **craven:** cowardly.

20. **Solway:** an inlet between England and Scotland.

22. **measure:** a movement of the dance.

26. **quaffed** (kwŏft) **off:** drank deeply.

So stately his form, and so lovely her face,
That never a hall such a galliard° did grace;
While her mother did fret, and her father did fume,
And the bridegroom stood dangling his bonnet and
    plume,
And the bridesmaidens whispered, "Twere better by far,   35
To have matched our fair cousin with young Lochinvar."

One touch to her hand, and one word to her ear,
When they reached the hall door, and the charger° stood
    near,
So light to the croup° the fair lady he swung,
So light to the saddle before her he sprung!   40
"She is won! we are gone, over bank, brush, and scaur;°
They'll have fleet steeds that follow," quoth young
    Lochinvar.

There was mounting 'mong Graemes of the Netherby
    clan;
Forsters, Fenwicks, and Musgraves, they rode and they
    ran.
There was racing and chasing on Cannobie Lee,°   45
But the lost bride of Netherby ne'er did they see.
So daring in love, and so dauntless in war,
Have ye e'er heard of gallant like young Lochinvar?

32. galliard (găl′yərd): a lively dance.

38. charger: a horse.

39. croup (krōōp): the horse's back, behind the saddle area.

41. scaur (skär): a rocky hillside.

45. Cannobie Lee: a meadow.

SEEKING MEANING

1. When Lochinvar arrives at Netherby Hall, Ellen is about to marry another man. How does the bridegroom contrast with Lochinvar?
2. What does Ellen's father fear when Lochinvar arrives? What answer does Lochinvar give to reassure him?
3. What are Ellen's reactions when Lochinvar drinks the goblet of wine? What do her reactions tell about her feelings for Lochinvar?
4. How do Lochinvar and Ellen trick everyone?

DEVELOPING SKILLS IN READING

Responding to Rhythm

All spoken language has rhythm. When you speak, your voice rises and falls naturally in ways that help communicate meaning. In a poem, rhythm often follows a pattern. Read the following lines from "Lochinvar" aloud, and listen to the rhythm. The symbol (´) indicates a stressed syllable. The symbol (˘) indicates an unstressed syllable.

He stayed not for brake, and he stopped not for stone,

He swam the Eske River where ford there was none;

But ere he alighted at Netherby gate,

The bride had consented, the gallant came late:

Sometimes the rhythm of a poem suggests what the poem is about. "Lochinvar" is about a knight who gallops over the countryside. Reread the lines above and tap out the rhythm gently on your desk. Does the rhythm sound like the galloping of a horse?

Recognizing Inverted Word Order

Poets, like other writers, sometimes reverse the usual order of words in their sentences. When they do, they are using *inverted* word order. For example, in line 3 Scott says, ". . . he weapons had none." A standard English sentence would use subject-verb-object order: "he had no weapons." But what happens to Scott's swinging, regular rhythm when "he had no weapons" is substituted for "he weapons had none"?

Rewrite the following inverted lines from the poem so that they reflect standard English word order:

. . . where ford there was none;   (line 8)
Now tread we a measure!   (line 30)
That never a hall such a galliard did grace;   (line 32)
So light to the croup the fair lady he swung,   (line 39)
But the lost bride of Netherby ne'er did they see.   (line 46)

ABOUT THE AUTHOR

As a boy, Walter Scott (1771–1832) was fascinated by the tales of Scotland's past that his mother and grandfather told him. When he grew older, he traveled throughout the countryside on ballad "raids," writing down the songs he heard. At the age of thirty-one, he published a collection of these old Scottish folk ballads. He then wrote three long narrative poems, of which *The Lady of the Lake* is the most famous. Scott was the best-loved poet in England when he began publishing a series of historical novels, which were filled with adventure and romance. *Ivanhoe* is one of the most famous of these novels.

The Raven *Edgar Allan Poe*

The Raven. A lithograph by Édouard Manet (1832–1883), which appeared in Stéphane Mallarmé's translation of "The Raven," 1875.

Museum of Fine Arts, Boston. Gift of W. G. Russell Allen.

Once upon a midnight dreary, while I pondered, weak and
    weary,
Over many a quaint and curious volume of forgotten
    lore°—
While I nodded, nearly napping, suddenly there came a
    tapping,
As of someone gently rapping, rapping at my chamber
    door.
" 'Tis some visitor," I muttered, "tapping at my chamber
    door—   5
               Only this and nothing more."

Ah, distinctly I remember it was in the bleak December;
And each separate dying ember wrought its ghost upon
    the floor.
Eagerly I wished the morrow—vainly I had sought to bor-
    row
From my books surcease° of sorrow—sorrow for the lost
    Lenore—   10
For the rare and radiant maiden whom the angels name
    Lenore—
               Nameless *here* forevermore.

2. **lore:** knowledge.

10. **surcease:** an end.

And the silken, sad, uncertain rustling of each purple curtain
Thrilled me—filled me with fantastic terrors never felt before;
So that now, to still the beating of my heart, I stood repeating, 15
" 'Tis some visitor entreating entrance at my chamber door—
Some late visitor entreating entrance at my chamber door—
    That it is and nothing more."

Presently my soul grew stronger; hesitating then no longer,
"Sir," said I, "or Madam, truly your forgiveness I implore; 20
But the fact is I was napping, and so gently you came rapping,
And so faintly you came tapping, tapping at my chamber door,
That I scarce was sure I heard you"—here I opened wide the door—
    Darkness there and nothing more.

Deep into that darkness peering, long I stood there won-
dering, fearing,   25
Doubting, dreaming dreams no mortal ever dared to
dream before;
But the silence was unbroken, and the stillness gave no
token,
And the only word there spoken was the whispered word,
"Lenore?"
This I whispered, and an echo murmured back the word
"Lenore!"—
                    Merely this and nothing more.   30

Back into the chamber turning, all my soul within me
burning,
Soon again I heard a tapping somewhat louder than before.
"Surely," said I, "surely that is something at my window
lattice;
Let me see, then, what thereat is, and this mystery
explore—
Let my heart be still a moment and this mystery ex-
plore—   35
                    'Tis the wind and nothing more!"

Open here I flung the shutter, when, with many a flirt and
    flutter,
In there stepped a stately Raven of the saintly days of
    yore;
Not the least obeisance° made he; not a minute stopped or
    stayed he;
But, with mien° of lord or lady, perched above my
    chamber door—   40
Perched upon a bust of Pallas° just above my chamber
    door—
                    Perched, and sat, and nothing more.

Then this ebony bird beguiling my sad fancy into smiling,
By the grave and stern decorum of the countenance it
    wore,
"Though thy crest be shorn and shaven, thou," I said, "art
    sure no craven,°   45
Ghastly, grim, and ancient Raven wandering from the
    Nightly shore—
Tell me what thy lordly name is on the Night's Plutonian
    shore!"°
                    Quoth the Raven, "Nevermore."

Much I marveled this ungainly fowl to hear discourse so
    plainly,
Though its answer little meaning—little relevancy bore;   50
For we cannot help agreeing that no living human being
Ever yet was blessed with seeing bird above his chamber
    door—
Bird or beast upon the sculptured bust above his chamber
    door,
                    With such name as "Nevermore."

But the Raven, sitting lonely on the placid bust, spoke
    only   55
That one word, as if his soul in that one word he did out-
    pour.
Nothing further then he uttered, not a feather then he
    fluttered—
Till I scarcely more than muttered, "Other friends have
    flown before—
On the morrow *he* will leave me, as my Hopes have flown
    before."
                    Then the bird said, "Nevermore."   60

39. **obeisance** (ō-bā′səns): a gesture of respect; a bow.

40. **mien** (mēn): manner.

41. **bust of Pallas:** a statue of the head of Pallas Athena, the Greek goddess of wisdom.

45. **craven:** coward.

47. **Plutonian shore:** the shore of the river leading to the underworld, ruled by Pluto.

Startled at the stillness broken by reply so aptly spoken,
"Doubtless," said I, "what it utters is its only stock and
    store
Caught from some unhappy master whom unmerciful
    Disaster
Followed fast and followed faster till his songs one bur-
    den° bore—
Till the dirges of his Hope that melancholy burden bore   65
                Of 'Never—nevermore.' "

But the Raven still beguiling all my fancy° into smiling,
Straight I wheeled a cushioned seat in front of bird and
    bust and door;
Then, upon the velvet sinking, I betook myself to linking
Fancy unto fancy, thinking what this ominous° bird of
    yore—   70
What this grim, ungainly, ghastly, gaunt, and ominous
    bird of yore
                Meant in croaking, "Nevermore."

This I sat engaged in guessing, but no syllable expressing
To the fowl, whose fiery eyes now burned into my bos-
    om's core;
This and more I sat divining, with my head at ease reclin-
    ing   75
On the cushion's velvet lining that the lamplight gloated
    o'er,
But whose velvet violet lining with the lamplight gloating
    o'er,
                She shall press, ah, nevermore!

Then, methought, the air grew denser, perfumed from an
    unseen censer°
Swung by seraphim° whose footfalls tinkled on the tufted
    floor.   80
"Wretch," I cried, "thy God hath lent thee—by these
    angels he hath sent thee
Respite°—respite and nepenthe° from thy memories of
    Lenore!
Quaff°, oh, quaff this kind nepenthe and forget this lost
    Lenore!"
                Quoth the Raven, "Nevermore."

64. **burden:** here, a repeated word or phrase in a song.

67. **fancy:** imagination.

70. **ominous** (ŏm'ə-nəs): threatening.

79. **censer:** a container for incense.

80. **seraphim** (sĕr'ə-fĭm): angels.

82. **respite** (rĕs'pĭt): relief or rest.
nepenthe (nĭ-pĕn'thē): a drug thought to banish sorrow.
83. **Quaff** (kwŏf): drink.

"Prophet!" said I, "thing of evil—prophet still, if bird or
    devil!—   85
Whether Tempter° sent, or whether tempest tossed thee
    here ashore,
Desolate yet all undaunted, on this desert land en-
    chanted—
On this home by Horror haunted—tell me truly, I im-
    plore—
Is there—*is* there balm in Gilead?°—tell me—tell me, I
    implore!"
                     Quoth the Raven, "Nevermore."   90

"Prophet!" said I, "thing of evil!—prophet still, if bird or
    devil!
By that Heaven that bends above us—by that God we
    both adore—
Tell this soul with sorrow laden if, within the distant
    Aidenn,°
It shall clasp a sainted maiden whom the angels name
    Lenore—
Clasp a rare and radiant maiden whom the angels name
    Lenore."   95
                     Quoth the Raven, "Nevermore."

86. **Tempter:** Satan.

89. **Is there . . . Gilead** (gĭl′ē-əd): This line is from the Bible, where it means "Is there any relief from pain?"

93. **Aidenn** (ā′dən): Paradise.

446 Poetry

"Be that word our sign of parting, bird or fiend!" I
    shrieked, upstarting—
"Get thee back into the tempest and the Night's Plu-
    tonian shore!
Leave no black plume as a token of that lie thy soul hath
    spoken!
Leave my loneliness unbroken!—quit the bust above my
    door!   100
Take thy beak from out my heart, and take thy form from
    off my door!"
               Quoth the Raven, "Nevermore."

And the Raven, never flitting, still is sitting, *still* is sitting
On the pallid° bust of Pallas just above my chamber door;   **104. pallid:** pale.
And his eyes have all the seeming of a demon's that is
    dreaming,   105
And the lamplight o'er him streaming throws his shadow
    on the floor;
And my soul from out that shadow that lies floating on
    the floor
               Shall be lifted—nevermore!

SEEKING MEANING

1. In this mysterious poem, a man is driven to hysteria by a Raven that enters his room and refuses to leave. What is the poem's *setting*, or the time and place of the action? How does the setting create a mood of mystery?

2. What tragic loss has the speaker suffered? How does this create a mood of loneliness?

3. The mystery increases when the Raven enters the room (line 38). Ravens are often associated with death and evil. What evidence in the poem tells you that the speaker thinks this bird is a visitor from the land of the dead?

4. What three questions does the speaker ask the Raven (see lines 47, 89, and 93–95)? How does the Raven answer?

5. What is the speaker's final, shrieking demand in the next-to-last stanza? How do you know that the Raven will never leave the speaker's chamber?

6. Some people say that this poem describes a nightmare. Others say it tells of a man going insane. What do you think?

DEVELOPING SKILLS IN READING

Responding to Sounds in a Poem

The speaker talks about a woman named Lenore. The name *Lenore* is repeated throughout the poem. Each stanza also has words that rhyme with *Lenore*. Identify these rhyming words in each stanza. How does the echoing of the dead woman's name suggest what is going on in the speaker's mind?

Rhymes are heard in every line of this poem. Poe even rhymes words within the same line. In the first line, the word *weary* rhymes with *dreary*. Find another example of this *internal rhyme* in line 3. Read aloud the first and third lines of every stanza to hear the internal rhymes.

Poe creates other musical effects by using alliteration:

> And the silken, sad, uncertain rustling of each purple curtain

Read this line aloud so that the repeated **s** sounds suggest the faint "rustling" of the curtains. If you look closely at each stanza of this poem, you will find other lines that use alliteration. Read some of these lines aloud.

In addition to alliteration and rhyme, Poe uses words that suggest or echo mysterious and frightening sounds. Here are some from the first stanza alone:

> tapping   rapping   muttered

Add words from other stanzas to this list.

Understanding Allusions

In Greek and Roman mythology, the underworld—the land of the dead—was ruled by a god known as Pluto. It was believed that the spirits of the dead reached the underworld by being ferried across the River Styx. When Poe refers to "Night's Plutonian shore" (line 47), he has in mind the shore of the river leading to the underworld. Such a reference to a place, a character, or an event is called an *allusion*.

In line 89 the speaker cries out, "Is there— is there balm in Gilead?" This line is an allusion to the Bible, in which the prophet Jeremiah, in his sorrow, asks the same question. Gilead was a region of ancient Palestine where balm, a soothing ointment, was made. You will find the source of this allusion in Jeremiah 8:22.

In Dickinson's poem "I Like to See It Lap the Miles" (page 420) there is another allusion to the Bible. Look in Mark 3:17. How does this Biblical passage explain the allusion in line 14?

Sense and Nonsense

Anonymous Limericks

There was a young man of Bengal
Who went to a fancy-dress ball.
  He went just for fun
  Dressed up as a bun,
And a dog ate him up in the hall.

There was a young fellow of Perth,
Who was born on the day of his birth;
  He was married, they say,
  On his wife's wedding day,
And he died when he quitted the earth.

I sat next the Duchess at tea.
It was just as I feared it would be:
  Her rumblings abdominal
  Were simply abominable,
And everyone thought it was me.

A gentleman dining at Crewe
Found quite a large mouse in his stew.
  Said the waiter, "Don't shout,
  And wave it about,
Or the rest will be wanting one too!"

DEVELOPING SKILLS OF EXPRESSION

Writing Limericks

No one knows who invented this funny five-line verse form. Some say limericks began in Limerick, Ireland, but most people there refuse to take responsibility for them. Wherever they came from, limericks seem here to stay. Some groups hold limerick contests. Great poets write limericks for fun. A former President of the United States wrote limericks.

After having read these limericks, you might be inspired to try a few yourself. Often limericks include the name of some town or country, or the name of a person. You could start out with a line like one of these:

There was a young lady from York
There once was a fellow named Hank

Find the rhyme pattern and rhythms of the limericks here, and try to imitate them.

Private Zoo　　*Ogden Nash*

The Octopus

Tell me, O Octopus, I begs,
Is those things arms, or is they legs?
I marvel at thee, Octopus;
If I were thou, I'd call me Us.

The Panther

The panther is like a leopard,
Except it hasn't been peppered.
Should you behold a panther crouch,
Prepare to say Ouch.
Better yet, if called by a panther,
Don't anther.

The Rhinoceros

The rhino is a homely beast,
For human eyes he's not a feast.
Farewell, farewell, you old rhinoceros.
I'll stare at something less prepocerous.

DEVELOPING SKILLS IN READING

Recognizing Humorous Rhymes

Ogden Nash often creates humorous rhymes by twisting words, or by using made-up words. How is the grammar in "The Octopus" misused so that the lines rhyme?

Which word in "The Panther" is invented to fit the rhyme? Which word in "The Rhinoceros" is also original? What familiar words do these two made-up words sound like? Substitute the familiar words for the made-up ones, and then reread the poems. What happens to the humor?

This poem is a tongue twister. Can you read it aloud quickly?

Hints on Pronunciation for Foreigners *T. S. W.*

I take it you already know
Of tough and bough and cough and dough?
Others may stumble but not you,
On hiccough, thorough, lough,° and through?   4. **lough** (lŏкн): lake.
Well done! And now you wish, perhaps,   5
To learn of less familiar traps?

Beware of heard, a dreadful word
That looks like beard and sounds like bird,
And dead: it's said like bed, not bead—
For goodness sake don't call it "deed"!   10
Watch out for meat and great and threat.
(They rhyme with suite and straight and debt.)
A moth is not a moth in mother
Nor both in bother, broth in brother,
And here is not a match for there   15
Nor dear and fear for bear and pear,
And then there's dose and rose and lose—
Just look them up—and goose and choose,
And cork and work and card and ward,
And font and front and word and sword,   20
And do and go and thwart and cart—
Come, come, I've hardly made a start!
A dreadful language? Man alive!
I'd mastered it when I was five!

SEEKING MEANING

1. The humor in this poem comes from an unlikely source: the illogical *spelling* of many English words. What are some of the words in the poem that rhyme, but look as if they shouldn't? What are some of the words that look as if they should sound alike, but don't?
2. What do you think this speaker is saying about the English language?

DEVELOPING SKILLS IN LANGUAGE

Distinguishing Homophones ,

Some of the illogical spellings of English words can be traced to Dr. Samuel Johnson, a great literary man who completed the first major dictionary of the English language in 1775. Up until that time, the same word was often spelled in different ways. Dr. Johnson tried to regulate English spellings. He made many interesting decisions, some of which still torment people learning to spell today. For example, Dr. Johnson is the one who kept the *k* in *know*, the *gh* in *light*, and the *b* in *debt*. He also made the *p* in *receipt* official, but he didn't do the same for *conceit* and *deceit*.

Many people, like the author of this poem, have fun with English words. One kind of wordplay that this poet did *not* use is the confusion of homophones. *Homophones* are words that sound exactly alike, but are spelled differently and have different meanings. Examples of homophones are *know* and *no*, and *two*, *too*, and *to*.

What is the homophone of each of the following words? Which words have more than one homophone? Perhaps you can use the words and their homophones in a humorous poem. If you can't write a verse about them, use each word and its homophone in separate sentences to illustrate their different meanings.

bear	nose	sight
made	rays	son
main	right	soul
meet	see	steak

The word vanity *in this title means "uselessness." The title has a serious ring to it, but don't let it fool you.*

On the Vanity of Earthly Greatness

Arthur Guiterman

The tusks that clashed in mighty brawls
Of mastodons, are billiard balls.

The sword of Charlemagne the Just
Is ferric oxide, known as rust.

The grizzly bear whose potent hug
Was feared by all, is now a rug.

Great Caesar's bust is on the shelf,
And I don't feel so well myself.

DEVELOPING SKILLS IN READING

Recognizing the Techniques of Comic Verse
Many writers over the ages have written seriously about the passage of time and the worthlessness of earthly success. But this poem is meant to be comical. Part of its humor comes from the way in which the poet links very mighty things with very ordinary things. For example, when he thinks of the mastodon's gigantic tusks, he thinks of billiard balls, which are all that he imagines is left of them today.

What other mighty things from the past does he think of? What does he say is left of them today? Is it any wonder that the poet doesn't feel well himself?

This verse is also comical because of its strong rhymes and rhythms. Notice how the poet never skips a beat, even though he probably had to do some thinking to match up "potent hug" with "now a rug."

Perhaps you can add to the poet's comical complaint. What other great and glorious things are now gone, remaining only as leather shoes, note paper, or old portraits?

Reflections Dental

Phyllis McGinley

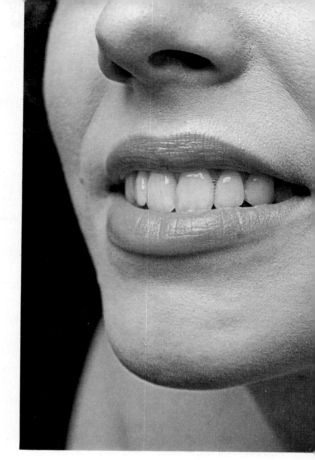

How pure, how beautiful, how fine
Do teeth on television shine!
No flutist flutes, no dancer twirls,
But comes equipped with matching pearls.
Gleeful announcers all are born   5
With sets like rows of hybrid corn.
Clowns, critics, clergy, commentators,
Ventriloquists and roller skaters,
M.C.'s who beat their palms together,
The girl who diagrams the weather,   10
The crooner crooning for his supper—
All flash white treasures, lower and upper.
With miles of smiles the airwaves teem,
And each an orthodontist's dream.

'Twould please my eye as gold a miser's—   15
One charmer with uncapped incisors.

DEVELOPING SKILLS IN READING

Recognizing Comic Exaggeration

Exaggeration is often used for comic effect. In line 6, Phyllis McGinley exaggerates when she says that television announcers' teeth are like rows of hybrid corn. What humorous image does this suggest to you? Find other examples of comic exaggeration in lines 4, 12, and 13.

How does the speaker feel about the perfect teeth she sees on television? Is she really praising them? Look at the last two lines. Why do you suppose the speaker feels so strongly about all these perfect teeth?

Casey at the Bat

Ernest Lawrence Thayer

The outlook wasn't brilliant for the Mudville nine that
    day;
The score stood four to two, with but one inning more to
    play;
And so, when Cooney died at first, and Burrows did the
    same,
A sickly silence fell upon the patrons of the game.

A straggling few got up to go in deep despair. The rest   5
Clung to the hope which springs eternal in the human
    breast;
They thought, if only Casey could but get a whack, at
    that,
They'd put up even money now, with Casey at the bat.

But Flynn preceded Casey, as did also Jimmy Blake,
And the former was a pudding, and the latter was a fake;   10
So upon that stricken multitude grim melancholy sat,
For there seemed but little chance of Casey's getting to
    the bat.

But Flynn let drive a single, to the wonderment of all,
And Blake, the much-despised, tore the cover off the ball;
And when the dust had lifted, and they saw what had oc-
    curred,   15
There was Jimmy safe on second, and Flynn a-hugging
    third.

Then from the gladdened multitude went up a joyous
    yell;
It bounded from the mountaintop, and rattled in the dell;
It struck upon the hillside, and recoiled upon the flat;
For Casey, mighty Casey, was advancing to the bat.   20

There was ease in Casey's manner as he stepped into his
  place;
There was pride in Casey's bearing, and a smile on
  Casey's face;
And when, responding to the cheers, he lightly doffed his
  hat,
No stranger in the crowd could doubt 'twas Casey at the
  bat.

Ten thousand eyes were on him as he rubbed his hands
  with dirt;   25
Five thousand tongues applauded when he wiped them on
  his shirt;
Then while the writhing pitcher ground the ball into his
  hip,
Defiance gleamed in Casey's eye, a sneer curled Casey's
  lip.

And now the leather-covered sphere came hurtling
  through the air,
And Casey stood a-watching it in haughty grandeur there;   30
Close by the sturdy batsman the ball unheeded sped.
"That ain't my style," said Casey. "Strike one," the um-
  pire said.

From the benches, black with people, there went up a
  muffled roar,
Like the beating of the storm waves on a stern and distant
  shore;
"Kill him! Kill the umpire!" shouted someone on the
  stand;   35
And it's likely they'd have killed him had not Casey
  raised his hand.

With a smile of Christian charity great Casey's visage
  shone;
He stilled the rising tumult; he bade the game go on;
He signaled to the pitcher, and once more the spheroid
  flew;
But Casey still ignored it, and the umpire said, "Strike
  two."   40

"Fraud!" cried the maddened thousands, and the echo answered, "Fraud!"
But a scornful look from Casey, and the audience was awed;
They saw his face grow stern and cold, they saw his muscles strain,
And they knew that Casey wouldn't let that ball go by again.

The sneer is gone from Casey's lips, his teeth are clenched in hate, 45
He pounds with cruel violence his bat upon the plate;
And now the pitcher holds the ball, and now he lets it go,
And now the air is shattered by the force of Casey's blow.

Oh! somewhere in this favored land the sun is shining bright;
The band is playing somewhere, and somewhere hearts are light; 50
And somewhere men are laughing, and somewhere children shout,
But there is no joy in Mudville—mighty Casey has struck out!

DEVELOPING SKILLS IN READING

Recognizing Humor in Language

Ernest Lawrence Thayer creates a humorous effect by using high-flown, or fancy, language to describe an ordinary event—a baseball game played in a town called Mudville. For example, in line 29, the poet doesn't say "baseball"; instead, he says "leather-covered sphere." What does the poet say instead of "baseball" in line 39?

Casey, Mudville's hero, is also described in high-flown, heroic language. What words and phrases in lines 20–30 describe him? How does Casey's own speech in line 32 differ from the heroic language used to describe him?

What image, or picture, is created in line 11? How is this image funny if you take it literally? What fancy simile is used in lines 33–34 to describe the crowd's roar?

DEVELOPING SKILLS OF EXPRESSION

Writing a Humorous Poem

Try your hand at writing a humorous poem similar to the story of Casey. Perhaps you can describe another sport (basketball, hockey, football, tiddlywinks) in elegant-sounding, heroic language. Perhaps you'll want to imitate the rhythm of Thayer's poem. Create a good title for your own sports saga.

Jabberwocky   *Lewis Carroll*

'Twas brillig, and the slithy toves
　　Did gyre and gimble in the wabe;
All mimsy were the borogoves,
　　And the mome raths outgrabe.

"Beware the Jabberwock, my son!　　　　　　5
　　The jaws that bite, the claws that catch!
Beware the Jubjub bird, and shun
　　The frumious Bandersnatch!"

He took his vorpal sword in hand;
　　Long time the manxome foe he sought—　10
So rested he by the Tumtum tree,
　　And stood awhile in thought.

And, as in uffish thought he stood,
　　The Jabberwock, with eyes of flame,
Came whiffling through the tulgey wood,　　15
　　And burbled as it came!

One, two! One, two! And through and through
　　The vorpal blade went snicker-snack!
He left it dead, and with its head
　　He went galumphing back.　　　　　　　20

"And hast thou slain the Jabberwock?
　　Come to my arms, my beamish boy!
O frabjous day! Callooh! Callay!"
　　He chortled in his joy.

'Twas brillig and the slithy toves　　　　　25
　　Did gyre and gimble in the wabe;
All mimsy were the borogoves,
　　And the mome raths outgrabe.

DEVELOPING VOCABULARY

Explaining Portmanteau Words

Alice asks Humpty Dumpty to explain "Jabberwocky." Here is their conversation.

"*Brillig* means four o'clock in the afternoon—the time when you begin *broiling* things for dinner."

"That'll do very well," said Alice; "and *slithy?*"

"Well, *slithy* means 'lithe and slimy.' *Lithe* is the same as 'active.' You see it's like a portmanteau—there are two meanings packed up into one word."

"I see it now," Alice remarked thoughtfully; "and what are *toves?*"

"Well, *toves* are something like badgers—they're something like lizards—and they're something like corkscrews."

"They must be very curious-looking creatures."

"They are that," said Humpty Dumpty; "also they make their nests under sundials—also they live on cheese."

"And what's to *gyre* and to *gimble?*"

"To *gyre* is to go round and round like a gyroscope. To *gimble* is to make holes like a gimlet."

"And *the wabe* is the grass plot round a sundial, I suppose?" said Alice, surprised at her own ingenuity.

"Of course it is. It's called *wabe*, you know, because it goes a long way before it, and a long way behind it—"

"And a long way beyond it on each side," Alice added.

"Exactly so. Well then, *mimsy* is 'flimsy and miserable' (there's another portmanteau for you). And a *borogove* is a thin, shabby-looking bird with its feathers sticking out all round—something like a live mop."

"And then *mome raths?*" said Alice. "I'm afraid I'm giving you a great deal of trouble."

"Well, a *rath* is a sort of green pig; but *mome* I'm not certain about. I think it's short for 'from home'—meaning that they'd lost their way, you know."

"And what does *outgrabe* mean?"

"Well, *outgribing* is something between bellowing and whistling, with a kind of sneeze in the middle; however, you'll hear it done, maybe—down in the wood yonder—and, when you've once heard it, you'll be *quite* content. Who's been repeating all that hard stuff to you?"

"I read it in a book," said Alice.

A *portmanteau* is a suitcase that opens into two parts. What does Humpty Dumpty say a *portmanteau word* is?

Try to explain the two meanings "packed up into" these common portmanteau words. Check your answers in your dictionary.

brunch   motel   smog   transistor

ABOUT THE AUTHOR

Lewis Carroll (1832–1898), whose real name was Charles Lutwidge Dodgson, was a mathematics teacher at Oxford University in England. He was friendly with a little girl named Alice Liddell, to whom he told stories. Out of this friendship came two of the most popular fantasies ever written, *Alice's Adventures in Wonderland* and *Through the Looking Glass*. Some of the other famous characters in these two books are the Mad Hatter, the March Hare, the Cheshire Cat, and Tweedledum and Tweedledee. Carroll once claimed that mathematics is the true wonderland, for "nothing is impossible" there.

Practice in Reading and Writing

POETRY

Reading Poetry

Here are some suggestions that can help you read poetry with more pleasure and understanding.

1. *Look for complete thoughts.*

The end of a complete thought in most poems is indicated by a period or semicolon. Sometimes these punctuation marks will come in the middle of a line. Sometimes you will have to read several lines before a thought is completed. Here is a little poem by Phyllis McGinley. You will probably recognize the children's chant it is based on.

A Choice of Weapons

Sticks and stones are hard on bones.
Aimed with angry art,
Words can sting like anything.
But silence breaks the heart.

How many sentences are contained in this poem? Where should you pause when you read these lines?

2. *Be aware of inverted (reversed) word order.*

Poets sometimes put words in an order that is not normal in English sentences. They do this for emphasis or to make their rhymes and rhythms work out. Look at line 39 from "The Raven" (page 441):

Not the least obeisance made he; not a minute stopped or stayed he;

In normal word order, the line would read this way:

He did not make the least obeisance; he did not stop or stay a minute;

Recite this line as part of the poem. What happens to the rhythm and rhyme? Put line 49 of "The Raven" in normal word order. How does the emphasis change?

3. *Interpret the figurative language.*

When the speaker in "Casey at the Bat" (page 456) says that Cooney "died at first," he is using a common figure of speech. Cooney, of course, didn't really fall over dead on first base. The speaker means that the possible run "died" at first base. Where is the figure of speech in these lines (9–10) from "Casey at the Bat"?

But Flynn preceded Casey, as did also Jimmy Blake,
And the former was a pudding, and the latter was a fake;

What picture does the figure of speech create? Do you think it is a good comparison?

4. *Try to paraphrase the poem, or difficult lines in the poem.*

Paraphrase means "to put in other words." Here are lines 3–4 of Phyllis McGinley's poem "Reflections Dental" (page 455), and a paraphrase:

No flutist flutes, no dancer twirls,
But comes equipped with matching pearls.

Every musician and every dancer has teeth that look like a pearl necklace.

How would you paraphrase these lines from "Casey at the Bat"?

So upon that stricken multitude grim melancholy sat,
For there seemed but little chance of Casey's getting to the bat.

Writing Poetry

Write four or more lines of poetry in which you use a figure of speech to describe a feeling or an idea about something. Do not worry about using rhyme and regular rhythm. (You might imitate the style used by Alice Walker on page 424.) Here are some suggestions:

The feeling you have when you run (or swim, or hike)
The way the earth smells after a rainfall
The way the streets look at night
What a dog sounds like when it eats
What a dripping faucet sounds like when you are trying to sleep

For Futher Reading

Baron, Virginia, *Here I Am!: An Anthology of Poems Written by Young People in Some of America's Minority Groups* (Dutton, 1969)

 Students from all over the United States write poems on things they care about most.

Benét, Rosemary, and Stephen Vincent Benét, *A Book of Americans* (Holt, Rinehart & Winston, 1933)

 These easy-to-read poems create "portraits" of fifty-six unusual Americans.

Bontemps, Arna, editor, *Golden Slippers: An Anthology of Negro Poetry for Young Readers* (Harper & Row, 1941)

 Arna Bontemps, a poet himself, chose these appealing poems from the works of America's black poets.

Brooks, Gwendolyn, *Selected Poems* (Harper & Row, 1963; paperback, Harper)

 The poet has selected these poems from her earlier books: *A Street in Bronzeville, Annie Allen,* and *The Bean Eaters.*

Browning, Robert, *The Pied Piper of Hamelin* (Coward-McCann & Geoghegan, 1971)

 This illustrated edition presents the funny story of the piper who has his revenge on the adults of Hamelin for breaking their promise.

Carroll, Lewis, *The Walrus and the Carpenter and Other Poems* (Dutton, 1969)

 Eleven of Lewis Carroll's best nonsense poems are illustrated here.

Dunning, Steven, Edward Lueders, and Hugh Smith, editors, *Reflections on a Gift of Watermelon Pickle and Other Modern Verse* (Lothrop, Lee & Shepard, 1967)

 If you think poetry is hard to understand, or only about "poetic" subjects, you should look into these modern poems especially chosen for young people. *Some Haystacks Don't Even Have Any Needle and Other Complete Modern Poems* (Lothrop, Lee & Shepard, 1969) is another gathering of poems, by the same editors, that are fun to read and think about.

Frost, Robert, *You Come Too: Favorite Poems for Young Readers* (Holt, 1959)

 Frost chose these fifty poems of his to please young people.

Jordan, June, *Who Look at Me* (Thomas Y. Crowell, 1969)

 Twenty-seven poems accompany paintings of black people by prominent American artists.

Lear, Edward, *Complete Nonsense Book* (Dodd, Mead, 1948; paperback, Dover)

 Here are limericks, nonsense rhymes, and silly poems designed to make you laugh.

Livingston, Myra Cohn, editor, *A Tune Beyond Us* (Harcourt Brace Jovanovich, 1968)

 These poems from all over the world were chosen by a writer of books for young people.

Merriam, Eve, *Independent Voices* (Atheneum, 1968)

 Read aloud these poems about Frederick Douglass, Henry David Thoreau, Lucretia Mott, and other famous Americans.

Peck, Richard, editor, *Sounds and Silences: Poetry for Now* (Delacorte 1970; paperback, Dell)

 Song lyrics are included in this collection of contemporary poems on such themes as isolation, illusion, communication, realities, and identity.

Swenson, May, *Poems to Solve* (Scribner, 1966; paperback, Scribner)

 Try to solve these thirty-five riddle poems and puzzling poems with hidden meanings.

Whitman, Walt, *Overhead the Sun: Lines from Walt Whitman* (Farrar, Straus & Giroux, 1969)

 Sixteen selections from *Leaves of Grass* are illustrated by Antonio Frasconi's bold woodcuts.

The heroic tales that open this unit come from many lands—from the cold lands of Scandinavia to the African tropics, from the plains of North America to the plains of Asia Minor. Some of these stories have become an important part of our heritage. Sigurd the dragon-slayer and Antigone, the young woman who defies a king, have lived in people's imaginations for hundreds of years.

People over the ages have also told very short stories to teach morals—lessons about how to get along in the world. Whether they come from the ancient world or the modern, the shrewd moral tales in this unit contain character types that everyone can recognize.

The unit ends with American folklore. Here are no knights or princesses, but a logger, a cowhand, a hunter, a steel driver, a miner, and even a schoolteacher. You'll find that most of these stories make use of humorous exaggeration—a characteristic of American humor. No ancient hero, for example, ever lassoed a cyclone, boiled split peas in the Great Lakes, or reared two coyotes who became members of Congress.

TALES FROM MANY LANDS

Tales of Heroes and Heroines

The most famous heroic legend of the Norse, or Scandinavian, people is the story of Sigurd the dragon-slayer. The legend begins in a mountain valley where Reidmar, the evil dwarf king, lived. Reidmar had used his magic to gather a great hoard of gold. When Reidmar died, his gold was taken by one of his evil sons, Fafnir. To guard the gold, Fafnir changed his form and became a huge dragon. For a thousand years, Fafnir lay sprawled over his treasure. His younger brother, Regin, longed for the gold and for Fafnir's magic. For a thousand years, Regin searched for a hero he could train to kill his brother. Finally, he found Sigurd, and prepared him for the murder.

As this part of the story opens, the innocent Sigurd and his wicked master approach the old dwarf king's hall.

Sigurd the Dragon-Slayer

Retold by Olivia Coolidge

The hall of the dwarf king, Reidmar, no longer blazed in the sun. The gilt had washed off its beams, the wide door was fallen from its hinges, and grass grew on the roof. "Look!" said Regin, pointing where a great track ran from the threshold down to the riverbank. It was ground through the dirt of the hillside to the depth of a tall man.

"That path must be made by Fafnir," said Sigurd, "and he uses it often, for no grass grows in it."

"Men say," answered Regin, "that the treasure still lies where my father piled it on the ground before his seat. Around it coils Fafnir, the serpent, gloating over it all day long. But when the moon shines down on him through the rents[1] in the ruined hall, he dreams of his youth, and the spring in the woodlands, and of the great gods he saw when the world was young. The gray morning wakens him early, and at that hour he loathes what he has become. He leaves his treasure and goes out to drink of the river, yet by dawn desire overcomes him once more, so that he returns to the gold."

"When he comes down the path in the morning before it is yet quite light, I will meet him and smite him," said Sigurd.

"His scales are as tough as steel, and it does no good to strike unless you can kill at a blow.

---

1. **rents:** openings, cracks.

Wound him, and he will crush you as you might step on an ant."

"I will dig a pit in the pathway and crouch there in the dark. When he comes, his eyes will be on the river and his mind still full of his dreams. Perhaps he will not see where I lie. Then as he rolls over me, I will thrust up through his belly where the scales are not so strong. This way I may reach his heart."

"But if he sees you?"

Sigurd laughed. "You will wait another thousand years for a dragon-slayer. That is all."

The moon was full and rose early. It took little time to dig the pit. Sigurd wrapped himself in his cloak and went to sleep while Regin stood on guard. He never stirred until Regin, weary of watching, touched his shoulder and whispered, "Hush! It is time."

Overhead at the edge of the mountains the sky was pale gray by now, but a river mist hung in the valley and clung to the grassy slope, so that low in the depths of Fafnir's track, it was still dark as the grave.

Sigurd crouched, his sword under his cloak, for he feared lest its gleam should be seen. No wind stirred in the trees by the river. A fox barked. The little clouds overhead turned white with the approach of day.

Something moved in the house. There was a scraping sound as though a log were being pushed over the floor. The scales of the monster rattled. A stone rolled down the track. The sounds came closer, and with them a strong, damp, musty smell. Sigurd saw through the thinning mist that a dark shape was filling the sunken pathway from side to side. The dawn was very close. He could see the huge head now almost on the edge of his hole. It was flat and scaly like a snake's, but the weary eyes were human, though of monstrous size. They stared straight through the gloom at Sigurd, whose grip tightened on his sword. For a moment the two seemed to look at each other, eye to eye, yet the monster moved on, dull and unseeing, heavy with sleep.

Black darkness rolled over Sigurd. Stench stifled him. Loose earth filled up the pit. Inch by inch the creature slid over him. Sigurd shut his eyes, set his teeth, and waited. He dared not strike too soon.

After what seemed minutes, he thought, I must risk it now. With that he straightened his knees and drove the sword upward with all his force. It tore up through the cloak, through the loose earth, and on with the force of his arm until it buried itself to the hilt. A great cry came from the monster. The echoing hills threw back and forth to each other a long succession of cries. Fafnir writhed. His huge body arched like a bow. Sigurd leaped from the pit. The tail lashed wildly after its slayer. Blood rolled down the track to the stream.

The sun was up behind the mountains, but the valley was still cold and gray. When the long death struggles were over, Regin crept from the bushes to look at the endless monster, the color of weathered stone. He gave a great sigh. "You have killed him," he said to Sigurd. "He was my brother once."

Sigurd laughed shortly. "It is late to think of that."

"Yet he was my brother, and you killed him. The fire which burned within me is quenched now in his blood. The long years of my waiting are over, the days of work and the endless wakeful nights. Now let me sleep for an hour, since I watched all this night for you. Kindle me a fire while I rest, and roast me Fafnir's heart. I will eat it and be wise, and after that, we will look on the ancient treasure which has waited so long for us."

"I will gladly do that," replied Sigurd. "You are old, and our journey was long."

Regin lay on the bank by the river. Sigurd

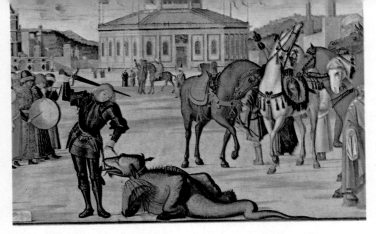

The Triumph of St. George. A detail from a painting by
Vittore Carpaccio (1455–1525) in St. George's Hospital, Venice.
Art Resource

lighted a fire in the glade. He spitted the monster's heart on a stick and thrust it into the flame. It hissed and crackled as he turned it from side to side. The sun came over the hills. Two woodpeckers sat in the trees calling to each other over his head. The meat blackened a little at the edges, and Sigurd thought it was nearly done. He put out his hand to turn it. It sputtered, and the hot fat seared his finger.

Sigurd put his hand to his mouth. As he tasted the fat with his tongue, all kinds of knowledge leaped suddenly into his head. The birds still chattered in the trees. Sigurd heard the first one say, "See how the hero, Sigurd, sits roasting Fafnir's heart."

"He roasts it for Regin," answered the other. "Does he not know that the wisdom and strength of the dragon go to him who eats?"

"Sigurd needs no strength from Fafnir, and he cares nothing for the wisdom of the dwarfs."

"Regin cares, for he covets[2] the wisdom, and he needs the strength to slay."

"To slay?"

---

2. **covets** (kŭv'ĭts): desires.

"Fool! To slay Sigurd. Is not Sigurd his tool to kill Fafnir? Is not his use over? Regin planned this murder when he first saw the dragon-slayer as a child in his mother's arms."

Sigurd turned from the fire to look at Regin. For the first time he understood the master of cunning who had reared him to this end. He saw how the love of gold burned in Regin, who must kill lest he have to divide. He understood the cold dwarfs who knew neither conscience nor pity, and who despised mankind for feeling these things.

Regin opened his eyes. The two stared a moment, and the truth was open to each. Regin snatched at his belt for a dagger and leaped at the young man, who sprang up and away, fumbling for his long sword. The dwarf struck too soon, and his dagger whistled savagely through the air. Again he jumped, like a wildcat, but this time the sword met him halfway. He gave a great cry as it pierced him, and he dropped twisting on the grass.

Sigurd looked soberly down on the two evil brothers, great serpent and scheming dwarf. He left them on the grass by the river and turned up to the hill to the crumbling house which hid the treasure he had won.

SEEKING MEANING

1. In this legend, a young and innocent hero fights for a gold treasure. What must be accomplished before the treasure can be won?

2. How does Sigurd's scheme to kill the dragon show his intelligence?

3. Fafnir's heart contains his magic powers. How does Sigurd accidentally receive these magic powers? How does the accident save his life?

DEVELOPING SKILLS IN LANGUAGE

Finding Names from Old Norse

The English language we speak today has been influenced by the Old Norse language. Several of the English names for the days of the week, for example, are based on Old Norse names. You might find the following information included with the dictionary definition of the word *Thursday*:

> [ME. *Thoresdai* <OE. *Thunres dæg* <ON. *Thorsdagr,* Thor's day]

The symbol < means "comes from." In other words, the word *Thursday* comes from the Middle English (ME.) word *Thoresdai*, which comes from the Old English (OE.) words *Thunres dæg*, which in turn come from the Old Norse (ON.) word *Thorsdagr*, meaning "Thor's day." Thor was a major god in Norse mythology. When his hammer struck, the Earth resounded with thunder.

People in Great Britain once called all the days of the week by their Old Norse names. Four of these names remain. In a dictionary, look up the names of the days of the week. Which three, besides Thursday, still carry the names of Old Norse gods? Where did the other names come from?

DEVELOPING SKILLS IN RESEARCH

Comparing Famous Monsters

Here is how Sigurd's enemy, the dragon Fafnir, is described:

> The scales of the monster rattled. . . . The sounds came closer, and with them a strong, damp, musty smell. Sigurd saw through the thinning mist that a dark shape was filling the sunken pathway from side to side. . . . He could see the huge head now almost on the edge of his hole. It was flat and scaly like a snake's, but the weary eyes were human, though of monstrous size. They stared straight through the gloom at Sigurd . . . For a moment the two seemed to look at each other, eye to eye, yet the monster moved on, dull and unseeing, heavy with sleep.
>
> Black darkness rolled over Sigurd. Stench stifled him.

In many heroic myths and legends, the enemy is as repulsive as the hero is admirable. Sometimes the enemies stink. Often they live in darkness and hate light. Their power usually comes from their monstrous size, never from their good hearts. Often they are cannibals.

Using a mythology book or an encyclopedia for reference, write a brief description of each of the following famous monsters. How does each one compare with Sigurd's enemy in this legend?

Cyclops (Greek)
Grendel (Old English and Norse)
Medusa (Greek)
Minotaur (Greek)

Nana Miriam

Retold by Hans Baumann

Fara Maka was a man of the Songai tribe, who lived by the River Niger.[1] He was taller than the other men and he was also stronger. Only he was very ugly. However, no one thought that important, because Fara Maka had a daughter who was very beautiful. Her name was Nana Miriam and she too was tall and strong. Her father instructed her in all kinds of things. He went with her to the sandbank and said, "Watch the fish!" And he told her the names of all the various kinds. Everything there is to know about fish he taught her. Then he asked her, "What kind is the one swimming here, and the other one over there?"

"This is a so-and-so," replied Nana Miriam. "And that is a such-and-such."

"Male or female?" asked Fara Maka.

"I don't know," said Nana Miriam.

"This one is a female, and so is the other one," explained Fara Maka. "But the third one over there is a male." And each time he pointed to a different fish.

That was how Nana Miriam came to learn so much. And in addition she had magic powers within her, which no one suspected. And because her father also taught her many magic spells, she grew stronger than anyone else in the Land of the Songai.

Beside the great river, the Niger, there lived a monster that took the form of a hippopotamus. The monster was insatiable.[2] It broke into the rice fields and devoured the crops, bringing famine to the Songai people. No one could tackle this hippopotamus, because it could change its shape. So the hunters had all their trouble for nothing and they returned to their villages in helpless despair. Times were so bad that many died of hunger.

One day, Fara Maka picked up all his lances and set out to kill the monster. When he saw it, he recoiled in fear, for huge pots of fire

---

1. **River Niger** (nī'jər): a long river in West Africa. The Songai people ruled an empire in the great bend of the Niger until the sixteenth century.

2. **insatiable** (ĭn-sā'shə-bəl): unable to be satisfied; always wanting more.

were hung around the animal's neck. Fara Maka hurled lance after lance, but each one was swallowed by the flames. The hippopotamus monster looked at Fara Maka with scorn. Then it turned its back on him and trotted away.

Fara Maka returned home furious, wondering who he could summon to help him. Now there was a man of the Tomma tribe who was a great hunter. His name was Kara-Digi-Mao-Fosi-Fasi, and Fara Maka asked him if he would hunt the hippopotamus with his one hundred and twenty dogs. "That I will," said Kara-Digi-Mao-Fosi-Fasi.

So Fara Maka invited him and his one hundred and twenty dogs to a great banquet. Before every dog, which had an iron chain around its neck, was placed a small mound of rice and meat. For the hunter, however, there was a huge mound of rice. None of the dogs left a single grain of rice uneaten, and neither did Kara-Digi-Mao-Fosi-Fasi. Well fortified, they set out for the place where the monster lived.

As soon as the dogs picked up the scent, Kara-Digi-Mao-Fosi-Fasi unchained the first one. The chain rattled as the dog leaped forward towards its quarry. One chain rattled after the other, as dog after dog sprang forward to attack the hippopotamus. But the hippopotamus took them on, one by one, and it gobbled them all up. The great hunter Kara-Digi-Mao-Fosi-Fasi took to his heels in terror. The hippopotamus charged into a rice field and ate that too.

When Fara Maka heard from the great hunter what had happened, he sat down in the shadow of a large tree and hung his head.

"Haven't you been able to kill the hippopotamus?" Nana Miriam asked him.

"No," said Fara Maka.

"And Kara-Digi-Mao-Fosi-Fasi couldn't drive it away either?"

"No."

"So there is no one who can get the better of it?"

"No," said Fara Maka.

"Then I'll not delay any longer," said Nana Miriam. "I'll go to its haunts and see what I can see."

"Yes, do," said her father.

Nana Miriam walked along the banks of the Niger, and she soon found the hippopotamus eating its way through a rice field. As soon as it saw the girl it stopped eating, raised its head and greeted her.

"Good morning," replied Nana Miriam.

"I know why you have come," said the hippopotamus. "You want to kill me. But no one can do that. Your father tried, and he lost all his lances. The great hunter Kara-Digi-Mao-Fosi-Fasi tried, and all his dogs paid with their lives for his presumption. And you are only a girl."

"We'll soon see," answered Nana Miriam. "Prepare to fight with me. Only one of us will be left to tell the tale."

"Right you are!" shouted the hippopotamus and with its breath it set the rice field afire. There it stood in a ring of flame through which no mortal could pass.

But Nana Miriam threw magic powder into the fire, and the flames turned to water.

"Right!" shouted the hippopotamus, and a wall of iron sprang up making a ring around the monster. But Nana Miriam plucked a magic hammer from the air, and shattered the iron wall into fragments.

Now for the first time the hippopotamus felt afraid, and it turned itself into a river that flowed into the Niger.

Again Nana Miriam sprinkled her magic powder. At once the river dried up and the water changed back into a hippopotamus. It grew more and more afraid and when Fara Maka came up to see what was happening, the monster charged him blindly. Nana Miriam ran after it, and when it was only ten bounds away from her father, she seized it by its left hind foot and flung it across the Niger. As it crashed against the opposite bank, its skull was split and it was dead. Then Fara Maka, who had seen the mighty throw, exclaimed, "What a daughter I have!"

Very soon, the whole tribe heard what had happened, and the Dialli, the minstrel folk, sang the song of Nana Miriam's adventure with the hippopotamus, which used to devastate the rice fields. And in the years that followed, no one in the Land of the Songai starved any more.

SEEKING MEANING

1. Nana Miriam's enemy is a hungry monster that has huge pots of fire hanging from its neck. What fate does Nana Miriam save the Songai people from when she destroys this monster?

2. The hero in a myth is usually different in some way from ordinary people. For example, Pecos Bill, in the American legend on page 505, was raised in the wilderness by coyotes. What is unusual about Nana Miriam and about her education?

3. What magic does Nana Miriam use to defeat her unusual enemy?

DEVELOPING SKILLS IN LANGUAGE

Discovering the Meaning of Names

Miriam is a form of an old Hebrew name meaning "bitter" or "rebellion."

Many first names have meanings: *Phyllis* comes from a Greek word for "green leaf," *Patrick* comes from the Latin word meaning "patrician," or "aristocrat," and *Leonard* comes from Germanic words meaning "hardy lion."

Family names, or surnames, often have meanings too. Many languages, for example, have a word element that means "son of": *Mac* or *Mc* (Gaelic), *Fitz-* (Norman-French), *-poulos* (Greek), *-wicz* (Polish), *-tse* (Chinese), *-ez* (Spanish). The names Hanson, McIan, O'Shea, and Ivanovich all mean—in different languages—"son of John."

In many countries, there are four traditional ways to produce a last name: by indicating parentage (Johnson); by indicating occupation (Cook); by indicating the place a person came from (Forest); or by indicating some special personal characteristic (Small).

What would each of the following names have once indicated about a person?

Armstrong	MacDonald
Fisher	Porter
Freeman	Smith
Jackson	Villanueva
Juarez	West
Lane	Wiseman

The Kamiah Monster

Retold by Fran Martin

Coyote was far from home, in the buffalo country, when Blue Racer suddenly appeared before him. This was a Snake, so tireless and swift that he was often used to carry important news. The very sight of this messenger brought Coyote to his feet.

"What news do you bring, Blue Racer?" he asked the Snake quickly.

"Coyote!" whispered the Snake, in a spent[1] voice, and his eyes bulged, and his shining sides were dull. "Never go home, Coyote!" he warned. "As you value your life, stay here in the East forever."

"What are you saying?" snapped Coyote. "Why should I do that?"

"They are gone, all the animals, swallowed up, sucked in on the breath of the Monster."

"What Monster, Blue Racer? What are you trying to say?"

"A Monster from the sky has fallen into the Kamiah Valley, and he fills it from rim to rim. His hot breath scorches the trees and the grass, and he sucks in living things with every breath."

Bear carved of cedar wood. Haida/Tlingit tribe. Lowie Museum of Anthropology. University of California, Berkeley.

---

1. **spent:** here, exhausted.

"Not the big things, certainly?" asked Coyote. "Mice, you mean, and rabbits, and chipmunks? Not Fox? Not Wolf? And never Bear?"

Blue Racer bent his head. "He's swallowed them, every one."

"How about yourself? Why hasn't he swallowed you?"

"I'm small and swift. I hid myself in the grass and slipped away. But heed my words, Coyote. You would not escape."

With that he was gone, and he left Coyote feeling badly shaken. But what was he to do? Stay in the East and never see a friend? It would be better to take his chances with the rest.

Coyote started bravely off, but the echo of the Snake's words checked[2] him. A Monster that filled the valley from rim to rim! He stopped, undecided.

Finally he summoned Meadowlark, and said to her, "Advise me!"

"Go you must," Meadowlark told him. "You are the only one that is left, and you must save your people. Take a bundle of pitch[3] and five sharp flint knives, and keep your wits about you."

So Coyote sharpened five flint knives, and on the way home he gathered a bundle of pitch pine, which burns fast and hot. As he started down the river he felt the first burning breath of the Monster. At last he climbed a tree at the top of a mountain and looked off toward the Kamiah Valley. But he could see nothing because of the range of mountains that lay between. Using his cherry stick from Walla-Walla, he hit the range of mountains and made a pass.

Then he saw the Monster.

From ridge to ridge the creature stretched, spanning the whole of the valley. The sun struck sparks from its burnished scales as it stirred its tail in sleep. Then it yawned. There was a hot gust as the huge red maw[4] came open—a terrrifying sight. Quick as a flash, Coyote scrambled down the tree. He bound himself to the trunk with several stout strands of grapevine, and lay on the side of the hill in the tall grass. Using his magic to speak in a mighty voice, he called out and woke the Monster.

"Ho, there, Monster!" called Coyote. "What are you doing in my valley?"

The Monster opened his dim little eyes and blinked across the mountains.

"Who's that?" he grumbled, and it was as if distant thunder rumbled across the valley.

"Can't you see? I am bigger than you!" Coyote stirred the grass and made it wave as if it hid another monster.

"No, I can't see you. My eyes are dim. But I can eat you, Coyote! I have swallowed all the others!"

"You won't eat me! My medicine-magic is many times more powerful than yours."

"Prove it then," the Monster rumbled. "Draw in your breath and swallow me down."

Coyote drew and drew in his breath, but the Monster shivered and clung with his claws, and never moved from the valley.

"It's my turn now," growled the Monster at last. "Now, Coyote, I'll draw you."

The Monster drew and drew in his breath, and it was as if a hot wind went whistling through the trees. Branches bent and broke and crashed to the ground, and Coyote was plucked from the tree and lashed about like a whip at the end of the grapevine. Fearing that

---

2. **checked:** here, stopped.
3. **pitch:** pitch pine, an evergreen that contains resin, which makes it burn quickly.

4. **maw:** the mouth of a devouring animal.

he would be dashed to pieces, he took out one of his flint knives and sawed away at the vine. It parted with a twang and off he went whizzing, toward the great red mouth of the Monster.

Over the valley, through the pass he flew, and then rows of teeth met with a snap above him and he found himself in darkness.

Luckily Coyote was able to see in the dark. He was in a long passage, in the Monster's throat, and a Rattlesnake came wriggling up beside him.

"I see he's swallowed you just like anyone else," hissed the Snake. "Fine medicine man you turned out to be."

Coyote trod on the Rattlesnake's head, and left it flat forever. Then he went on down the slippery passage until he came to the Monster's stomach. This was a huge, vaulted chamber, encased in the ribs of the Monster. On every side he saw piles of bones, and living animals among them, sighing with hunger. Fox was a shadow, and Wolf as well, and even little Black Bear had lost most of his fat.

"Now it's you, Coyote," they said to him bitterly, and they reproached him just as the Rattlesnake had for sharing their misfortunes. "Fine medicine man you are, to be sucked in too."

"Get up," Coyote told them. "Follow me."

Weary and sick and weak as they were, they did as Coyote told them, keeping close together in the dark, slippery passages. They came to another vaulted chamber, and high above them swung the Monster's heart. Here Coyote built a fire with the pitch pine. As soon as the Monster felt the heat below his heart, he started to stir in discomfort.

"Come out, Coyote!" he began to shout. "I'm sorry I ever swallowed you, Coyote! Come out, come out, Coyote! I'll let you go!"

But Coyote was climbing up the ribs of the roof, where he began to saw at the mighty cords that held the great swinging heart. The first knife broke, and the second, and the third, but Coyote continued to saw away with the fourth. Now the flame was burning hot below the Monster's heart and he writhed and snorted and bellowed in his pain.

"Coyote! Coyote! Come out! Come out!" he howled.

But Coyote only threw another stick on the fire.

Inside the Monster all was horrible confusion. The chamber rocked like a buffalo boat in the rapids. The animals were tossed from side to side, and deafened by his howls of pain. The fourth knife broke, and Coyote took up the fifth to hack at the last cord holding the giant heart. The Monster thrashed madly, the flames leaped high, the last heavy cord parted. Down fell the Monster's heart within him, and he rolled over, dead. As soon as the animals could pick themselves up, they built a ladder of the old dry bones and climbed out safely into the sunshine through the yawning mouth.

How good the air felt, how welcome was the sunlight, and the smell of the grass crushed down by the Monster's writhing! With never a word of gratitude, they shouted for joy as they leaped to the ground and set off about their business.

"You, there, come back!" Coyote shouted. "What are we going to do with the Monster's body?"

"Why do anything?" asked Fox, and the others agreed. "Just leave it there."

"Leave it there?" asked Coyote. "Don't you realize? Very soon now the human race will be coming! The valley must be cleared out and made ready for the people!"

So, using the last of his sharp flint knives, he started to carve up the Monster. He piled the meat on one side and the bones on the other, and each of the piles was like a little

Seal decoy, carved of wood.
© Peabody Museum, Harvard University. Photograph by Hillel Burger.

Bear mask, carved of wood. Kwakiutl tribe.
Museum of the American Indian, New York.

mountain. Then Coyote took the thighbone and flung it far over the Sawtooth Mountains, saying, "Here shall be born the tall, long-legged people." And in that land there sprang up the Blackfoot Indians, a tall, long-legged race. . . .

Coyote threw the fat over the Rocky Mountains and the great Sioux Indians came there. He threw the wide ribs into Montana, and the Flathead Indians came there.

So the piles were scattered over the earth, and at last the valley was clear.

"Well," sniffed Black Bear, "I hope you're satisfied. You haven't left a splinter for your own home valley."

It was true. Coyote had been working so hard, flinging the Monster's bones about the mountains, that he had forgotten to save a piece for the Idaho people. But a few drops of blood were left on his paws, and these he sprinkled on the ground, predicting, "The tribe that comes here will be small in numbers, but the bravest warriors of all."

And so it was. The Numipu came to Idaho, and they were the greatest fighters in the world. They conquered the Blackfeet; they conquered the Sioux; they conquered the Snakes and the Crows. But with all their triumphs in the art of war, they never forgot the Great Trickster, and even today, around the winter fires, they tell their children the stories of Coyote.

SEEKING MEANING

1. Tricksters use their wits to outsmart their enemies. What tricks does Coyote use to defeat the Kamiah Monster?

2. The Numipu and other American Indian peoples have used the term *medicine man* to indicate someone with magical or superhuman powers. What "medicine" does Coyote use in his battle?

3. This is a monster-slaying story, and it is also an origin myth. Which detail explains how the pass in the Walla-Walla mountains originated? Which passage explains why rattlesnakes have flat heads? What other origins, or beginnings, does this myth explain?

4. Do you think the coyote is an appropriate animal to cast as a trickster? Why or why not? Can you think of animals that would *not* qualify for the role?

5. In many myths and legends, a monster must be slain because it is eating up the population, or because it is burning the land and causing the people to starve. In killing the monster, the hero or heroine saves the people. How are the animals endangered in this Numipu myth? How does Coyote save his people?

DEVELOPING SKILLS IN LANGUAGE

Finding the Origins of Place Names

The study of names is called *onomastics*. You don't have to be an *onomast*, or name expert, to detect the influence of French, Spanish, Dutch, German, and Scandinavian languages on the map of America. But long before the first European settlers arrived, American Indians had their own names for rivers, mountains, and geographical areas. The influence of these American Indian languages can be seen in the following place names:

Oklahoma (from two Choctaw words: *okla*, "people," and *homma*, "red")

Chicago (from an Algonquian word: *sekongw* or *skekakwa*, "smell"—wild-onion smell, in this case)

Texas (from a Caddo word: *techas*, "friends" or "allies")

Use a dictionary to find the origin of these names:

Arkansas	Missouri
Connecticut	Nebraska
Kentucky	North Dakota
Massachusetts	Ozark Mountains
Mississippi	Saratoga

What can you conclude about names of cities and states that begin with the word *New*, such as New Mexico and New Hampshire?

DEVELOPING SKILLS IN RESEARCH

Finding American Indian Myths

The heroes and heroines in the Norse, African, and Greek myths and legends in this unit are humans. The hero in this Numipu tale, however, is an animal, a coyote.

The myths told by the American Indians often cast certain animals as heroes and even as gods. The American Indians who created these myths looked at the world differently from the way we do today. In general, they did not separate life into human, animal, vegetable, and mineral categories. In their imagination, all life was one.

Look up "Raven" and "Thunderbird" in a book about American Indian mythology. What deeds do these animal-heroes perform? A source that might be helpful is *Tales of the North American Indians* by Stith Thompson.

For centuries, people have told legends about a fabulous ancient city named Troy. Until the nineteenth century, most people thought Troy was imaginary. But then archaeologists found the ruins of a great city that had been burned to the ground between 1250 and 1150 B.C. This city was located exactly where Troy was supposed to have been. No one knows why this city was destroyed. But the legends tell us that a wooden horse and a trick brought Troy down.

The Wooden Horse

Retold by Bella Koral

About four thousand years ago, a great city stood on the shores of the Aegean Sea, near the mouth of the Hellespont. That great city is entirely gone, and people in our time have found relics of it by digging deep into the ground. And the name Hellespont, like the name of the city—Troy—is part of ancient legends and writings. The actual waterway still exists and is called the Dardanelles, which you can find on the map; but Troy is no more.

The walls of this great city were so high that no enemy could climb over them. And they were so thick and strong that no enemy could break through them or batter them down. And the gates of the city were well defended by its ablest and bravest soldiers.

Yet, proud and glorious though its history had been and confident as the Trojans were that their city would live forever, Troy at last fell upon evil days. This was because Paris, a prince of Troy, stole Helen, the most beautiful woman in the world, away from her husband Menelaus,[1] a king of the Greeks.

To avenge this great wrong, Menelaus called together all the heroes and great warriors of his country, among them the wise and courageous Ulysses. In two years of preparation, the Greeks assembled a tremendous army. They set sail for Troy in a fleet of a thousand ships. They landed on the beaches of the coastal plain before the city, and there the heroes made camp. The Trojans, too, were well prepared for battle, and their old King, Priam,[2] gathered many brave fighters and chieftains about him. The Greeks defied the Trojans to engage in battle.

For nine long years the Greeks laid siege to Troy. Many fierce battles were fought outside the gates, and many were the noble heroes who were slain on both sides, for the chief warriors would engage in single combat as their armies stood by, and the old people and children of Troy would come out to watch the contests from the city's walls. On both sides, the warriors were equally valiant, so that the Trojans could not rid their beaches of the invaders, nor could the Greeks force their way

1. **Menelaus** (měn′ə-lā′əs).

2. **Priam** (prī′əm).

into the city. Both sides suffered and struggled, and the weary siege dragged on and on. Finally the Greeks began to despair of ever conquering Troy in outright battle.

"For nine years we have been laying siege to Troy. Our bravest comrades are dead. Still the city is not ours, and Menelaus has not been avenged for the theft of Helen," the Greek soldiers grumbled.

"To fight any longer is useless. Let us give up this hopeless struggle! Our wives and children will learn to forget their husbands and fathers. We long to see our homes once more," they whispered at night among themselves.

Agamemnon,[3] chief of the Greek army, came to Ulysses. "Surely you, with your great cleverness and wisdom, can find a way to subdue the Trojans and save us," he urged.

After long consideration, Ulysses thought of a plan which the Greek chieftains decided to carry out.

Ulysses ordered his men, with the aid of a

Greek sculptor, to build a colossal horse of wood. It was so huge and spacious that it could hold a hundred armed men within its hollow body. It was fitted with a door so skillfully concealed that no one could possibly notice it. One night, under the cloak of darkness, Ulysses, Menelaus, Agamemnon, and others of the Greek heroes, fully armed, crept into the wooden figure. The door was shut upon them, and the rest of the Greek army broke up camp and set sail, leaving the enormous wooden horse on the beach.

The Greeks pretended they were abandoning the siege and were sailing for home. But once out of sight of Troy, they anchored behind a somewhat distant neighboring island where they were well hidden from their enemies.

When the sun rose the next morning, there was not a Greek ship to be seen on the shore and not a single tent on the plain. Only the huge wooden horse remained. Like wildfire, the exciting news spread throughout the city. "The Greeks have fled! The Greeks have fled! They have left at last!" cried the people.

---

3. **Agamemnon** (ăg'ə-měm'nŏn): the brother of King Menelaus.

Hundreds of eager men, women, and children ran toward the city's walls and gazed with happy, straining eyes toward the last straggling ship as it disappeared around the bend of the distant island.

Then the Trojans went wild with delight. The long years of siege were over, they thought. Everywhere there were embraces, kisses, and joyous shouts of laughter.

The newly found peace and liberty were wonderful to a people long besieged. They surged forward to the city gates, which were soon flung wide open, and quickly the crowds streamed over the site of the deserted enemy camp.

Now they saw the great wooden figure of the horse, resting on a wide platform of wood. Slowly they drew near it. Gazing and wondering, they walked round and round the colossal image. Touching it curiously, as little children will a strange object, they marveled at its tremendous height and girth.

"Perhaps it is a peace offering from the Greeks to the goddess Athene,"[4] said one Trojan to another. A few cautious ones continued to be afraid of the strange wooden creature, but others, becoming bolder, thought it should be carried back into the city as a war trophy.

At this, Laocoon,[5] priest of Neptune, god of the sea, came forward. "Trojans," warned the old man, "put no trust in this horse. Have you so soon forgotton the sad years of siege and suffering? Whatever this is, I fear the Greeks, even when they bear gifts," he cried.

Suddenly a great uproar was heard; the priest's warning was drowned in the hubbub that followed. "It's a Greek! A Greek!" A poor wretched fellow wearing Greek garments was dragged forward, his hands tightly bound. The ragged, badly beaten captive had been found by some shepherds, hiding among the reeds along the shore.

The captured Greek in reality was Sinon,[6] a trusted friend of the crafty Ulysses, and he had been left behind by his companions to deceive the Trojans into taking the wooden horse within their gates.

"Do not kill me," he begged his Trojan captors. "It is true that I am a Greek, but I escaped from my cruel countrymen when they were about to sacrifice me to the gods."

Sinon was brought before the Trojan chiefs, who promised to spare his life if he would tell them the truth about the wooden horse. "The wooden horse," he told them, "was built by my countrymen as an offering to appease the goddess Athene. It was made so large so that you would be unable to take it within your walls. For," he went on lying craftily, "those who own this wooden horse will gain the favor and protection of Athene. If once the horse stands within the walls of Troy, the city can never be captured!"

At first the Trojans doubted the spy's story, but after a while Sinon convinced them that if they took the sacred object the Greeks had left behind them into their city, they would have happiness and prosperity forever.

Soon they devised a scheme for taking the huge figure into the city. Putting rollers under the wooden platform on which the horse stood, they fastened long ropes about its legs and began dragging the immense image across the plain toward the walls of Troy.

Again, out of the crowd, came the voice of the aged priest, Laocoon. "Men of Troy," he cried, "beware, beware of the treacherous

---

4. **Athene** (ə-thē′nē): goddess of wisdom, who aided the Greeks during the war.
5. **Laocoon** (lā-ŏk′ō-ŏn′).

6. **Sinon** (sī′nŏn).

Greeks. Cast the horse into the sea or burn it, for it will bring you only misery and ruin!" As he spoke, he hurled his spear against the side of the horse, and it resounded with a hollow clang of armor.

While some people were again persuaded to doubt and were standing about discussing the priest's warning, an event occurred before their very eyes which seemed an omen direct from the gods. Out of the sea rose two immense serpents. With rearing heads, their eyes and tongues flashing flames before them, they swiftly glided through the terrified, panic-stricken crowd and made straight for Laocoon and his two sons.

Before they could escape, the two serpents entwined their coiling, slimy bodies about the three unfortunate men and crushed them to death. The monsters then slipped away again into the sea, as quickly and silently as they had come.

The Trojans, frozen with horror at this dreadful scene, were sure that this punishment had come to Laocoon for his words against the wooden horse. "He has been doomed for his sacrilege against this gift," they cried. "We will offer thanks to our protector Athene and bring the sacred image into our city."

Amid great acclaim, many willing hands dragged and pushed the great horse on its rolling platform over the plain, and little by little it approached the gate. When it was reached, they found that the opening was too narrow to admit the horse. So they pulled down part of the wall and made a breach to allow the wooden horse to be brought into the city. "Now," said the Trojans, "our city is safe from every enemy," and they draped wreaths and garlands of flowers around the horse.

That night they had a great feast of wild merrymaking to celebrate the end of nine years of anxious watching and suffering. For the first time in nine years, no one was on guard on the walls of Troy. On that night all went to sleep, secure in their belief that the gods were on their side.

When the noises of the city had died down and the streets were quiet and empty, Sinon, as had been planned, opened the cunningly concealed trapdoor in the side of the wooden horse. Out of it came the hero Ulysses, Menelaus, and the many other hidden Greeks. They set up a beacon light as a signal to the Greek army, for during the night the ships that had anchored behind the island had sailed back again toward the Trojan shore.

Soon, thousands of Greek soldiers swarmed through the streets of a proud city sunken in darkness and sleep. It was to the sounds of battle that the Trojans awoke from their dreams of peace. So the prophecy of Laocoon was fulfilled.

Priam, the King, and his noblest warriors were killed. Greek soldiers robbed the palaces and plundered the city of all its wealth and treasure. Helpless, the Trojans watched as their glorious city, set to the torch, burned to its very foundations.

Then the Greeks set sail for their own country, taking with them many Trojan captives. With them they took also the fair Helen, for whose sake the dreadful war had been waged. At last she had awakened from the spell that the goddess Venus[7] had cast upon her, and she was eager to behold again her native land.

But the glory of Troy was gone forever. Nothing but smoldering ruins and the everlasting renown of its valiant heroes remained of the wondrous, rich city on the shores of the Aegean.

---

7. **Venus:** goddess of love and beauty, who made Helen fall in love with Paris.

SEEKING MEANING

1. What is the conflict as this legend opens?
2. According to this legend, the Greeks' victory in the war depended entirely upon a trick thought up by one of their heroes, Ulysses. What was the trick?
3. What supernatural event convinced the Trojans to make the tragic decision to take the wooden horse into their city?

DEVELOPING SKILLS IN READING

Recognizing Allusions to a Legend

Several famous expressions allude to the legend of the Trojan War. For example, people often say that someone "worked like a Trojan." According to the legend, the Trojans worked for ten long years to keep the Greeks out of their city. Anyone who "works like a Trojan" works very hard and with great determination.

Here is another common expression: "I fear the Greeks, even when they bear gifts." Who says this in the legend? What does the expression mean?

Helen, whose abduction caused the Trojan War, was supposed to be the most beautiful woman in the world. The sixteenth-century poet Christopher Marlowe called her face "the face that launched a thousand ships." Find the passage early in this legend that explains this now-famous expression.

DEVELOPING SKILLS IN RESEARCH

Finding Out About Three Famous Epics

An *epic* is a very long poem that tells a story, often covering an extensive period of time and involving heroic characters and events. Usually an epic is important to a particular society because it embodies the society's most significant values and beliefs. (The longest epic in the world is the national epic of India, the *Mahabharata*, which is more than two hundred thousand lines long.)

There are three epics based on the legend of the Trojan War: the *Iliad* and the *Odyssey*, both composed by the Greek poet Homer, and the *Aeneid*, composed by the Roman poet Virgil.

The *Iliad* is set in the tenth and final year of the war. (*Iliad* means "the story of Ilium," which is another name for Troy.) The *Iliad* is a violent, action-filled war story. It centers on the character of Achilles, one of the Greek heroes. Homer says the *Iliad* is about Achilles' anger. In a mythology book or in an encyclopedia, look up "*Iliad*." What caused Achilles' anger? What happened to the Trojan prince Hector in the *Iliad*?

The *Odyssey* is the story of Odysseus, which is the Greek name for Ulysses. In "The Wooden Horse," Ulysses thinks up the trick that wins the war for the Greeks. Look up "*Odyssey*." Why did it take Odysseus ten years to sail home to his wife and son in Ithaca after Troy fell? What meaning does the word *odyssey* have today?

The *Aeneid* means "the story of Aeneas." Aeneas was a prince of Troy who fled the burning city, carrying his old father on his back and holding his young son by the hand. Look up "*Aeneid*." What connection does this Trojan prince have with the city of Rome?

Many Greek myths center on the ancient city of Thebes and its royal family. In this myth, Thebes has been torn by a civil war. The war was caused by two brothers who claimed the right to the throne. As the myth opens, the two brothers lie dead: they have killed each other in battle. Their uncle, Creon, has become king. Antigone is the sister of the two dead men.

In reading this story, you must know about the religious law of the ancient Greeks, which obliged them to perform burial rites for their dead. The Greeks believed that if burial rites were not performed, the soul of a dead person would wander forever in search of rest.

Antigone   *Retold by Rex Warner*

Creon became king of Thebes at a time when the city had lost half its army and at least half of its best warriors in civil war. The war was over. Eteocles,[1] the king, was dead; dead also was his brother Polynices,[2] who had come with the army of the Argives[3] to fight for his own right to the kingdom.

Creon, as the new king, decided first of all to show his people how unforgivable it was to make war upon one's own country. To Eteocles, who had reigned in Thebes, he gave a splendid burial; but he ordered that, upon pain of death, no one was to prepare for funeral or even sprinkle earth upon the body of Polynices. It was to lie as it had fallen in the plain for birds and beasts to devour. To make

certain that his orders should be carried out Creon set a patrol of men to watch the body night and day.

Antigone and Ismene,[4] sisters of Polynices, heard the king's orders with alarm and shame. They had loved both their brothers, and hated the thought that one of them should lie unburied, unable to join the world of the ghosts, mutilated and torn by the teeth of dogs and jackals and by the beaks and talons of birds. Ismene, in spite of her feelings, did not dare oppose the king; but Antigone stole out of the city by night, and, after searching among the piled-up bodies of those who had died in the great battle, found the body of her brother. She lightly covered it with dust, and said for it

---

1. **Eteocles** (ĭ-tē′ə-klēz′).
2. **Polynices** (pŏl′ĭ-nī′sēz).
3. **Argives** (är′gīvz′): people of the city of Argos.

4. **Ismene** (ĭs-mē′nē).

the prayers that ought to be said for the dead.

Next day it was reported to Creon that someone (the guards did not know who) had disobeyed the king's orders and scattered earth over the body of Polynices. Creon swore an oath that if the guilty person should be found, even though that person was a member of his own family, he or she should die for it. He threatened the guards also with death if they failed to find the criminal, and told them immediately to uncover the body and leave it to the birds and beasts of prey.

That day a hot wind blew from the south. Clouds of dust covered the plain, and Antigone again stole out of the city to complete her work of burying her brother. This time, however, the guards kept better watch. They seized her and brought her before King Creon.

Creon was moved by no other feelings than the feelings of one whose orders have been disobeyed. "Did you know," he asked Antigone, "the law that I made and the penalty that I laid down for those who broke the law?"

"I knew it," Antigone replied, "but there are other laws, made not by men but by the gods. There is a law of pity and of mercy. That law is to be obeyed first. After I have obeyed that, I will, if I may, obey the laws that are made by men."

"If you love your brother," said Creon, "more than the established laws of your country and your king, then you must bear the penalty of the laws, loving your brother in the world of the dead."

"You may kill me with your laws," Antigone replied, "but to me death is, in all these sufferings, less of an evil than would be treachery to my brother or cowardice when the time came to help him."

Her confident and calm words stirred Creon to even greater anger. Now her sister Ismene, who had at first been too frightened to help Antigone in her defiance of the law, came forward and asked to be allowed to share in Antigone's punishment; but Antigone would not permit her to claim a share with her in the deed or in its results. Nor would Creon listen to any appeal for mercy. Not wishing to have the blood of his niece upon his own hands, he gave orders that she should be put into an underground chamber, walled up from the light

and then left to die.

So Antigone was carried away to a slow and lingering death, willing to suffer it, since she had obeyed the promptings of her heart. She had been about to marry Haemon,[5] the king's son, but, instead of the palace that she would have entered as a bride, she was now going to the house of death.

Haemon himself came to beg his father to be merciful. He spoke mildly, but let it clearly be understood that neither he nor the rest of the people of Thebes approved of so savage a sentence. It was true that Antigone had broken the law; but it was also true that she had acted as a sister ought to act when her brother was unburied. And, Haemon said, though most people did not dare oppose the king in his anger, nevertheless most people in their hearts felt as *he* did.

Haemon's love for Antigone and even his good will toward his father only increased the fury of the king. With harsh words he drove his son from him.

Next came the blind prophet Tiresias[6] to warn King Creon that the gods were angry with him both for his merciless punishment of Antigone and for leaving the body of Polynices to be desecrated[7] by the wild beasts and birds. Creon might have remembered how often in the past the words of Tiresias had been fulfilled, but now, in his obstinate rage, he merely insulted the prophet. "You have been bribed," he said, "either by Haemon or by some traitor to try and save the life of a criminal by dishonest threats that have nothing to do with the gods at all."

Tiresias turned his sightless eyes on the king. "This very day," he said, "before the sun sets, you will pay twice, yes, with two dead bodies, for the sin which you could easily have avoided. As for me, I shall keep far away from one who, in his own pride, rejects the gods and is sure to suffer."

Tiresias went away, and now Creon for the first time began to feel that it was possible that his punishments had been too hard. For the first time, but too late, he was willing to listen to the advice of his council, who begged him to be merciful, to release Antigone and to give burial to the body of Polynices.

With no very good grace Creon consented to do as he had been advised. He gave orders for the burial of Polynices and went himself to release Antigone from the prison in which she had been walled away from the light. Joyfully his son Haemon went ahead of the rest with pickaxes and bars for breaking down the wall. But when they broke the stones of the wall they found that Antigone had made a

---

5. **Haemon** (hē′mŏn).

6. **Tiresias** (tī-rē′sē-əs).
7. **desecrated** (dĕs′ə-krāt′ĭd): treated in a way that did not show reverence.

noose out of the veil which she was wearing and had hanged herself. Haemon could not bear to outlive her. He drew his sword and plunged it into his heart before the eyes of his father. Then he fell forward dead on the body of the girl whom he had wished to be his wife.

As for Creon he had scarcely time to lament for his son when news reached him of another disaster. His wife had heard of Haemon's death and she too had taken her own life. So the words of Tiresias were fulfilled.

SEEKING MEANING

1. In heroic stories, a conflict takes place between the hero or heroine and an enemy. In many stories, the conflict involves physical strength (as in "Sigurd the Dragon-Slayer," page 466). However, in this myth, the conflict involves two strong wills. Why does Creon forbid burial to Polynices? Why does Antigone defy the king's law?

2. The tragedy that occurs could have been prevented if Creon had not been so proud and stubborn. Which two people come to Creon and ask him to show mercy to Antigone? How does each one try to persuade the king to change his mind?

3. What are the tragic results of Creon's stubbornness and pride?

4. In one sense, Antigone loses to Creon in their conflict of wills. But, in another sense, how does she also win?

5. Is Creon a loser or a winner or both at the end of this story? Explain your answer.

6. In most myths and legends, some characters have supernatural powers that set them apart from ordinary people. In this story, how does the prophet Tiresias show that he possesses such powers?

DEVELOPING SKILLS IN READING

Interpreting Values from a Myth

Myths are stories that reveal the important beliefs of a people. A myth like "Antigone" can tell us a great deal about what qualities the ancient Greek people valued and what kind of behavior they admired.

In this myth, two people obey two conflicting laws. The major problem in this myth is, which law must be obeyed?

Find the words spoken by Antigone that tell what laws she believes must be valued more than the king's laws. What does Antigone say on page 484 about reverence and family loyalty?

The blind prophet Tiresias is important in this myth. The prophet is a holy man who can interpret the will of the gods. According to the prophet, Creon is sure to suffer. Why? What does Creon value more than the will of the gods?

Tales with Morals

The Miller, the Son, and the Donkey

A Fable of Aesop
Retold by Louis Untermeyer

One day a Miller and his Son were driving their Donkey to market. They had not gone far when some girls saw them and broke out laughing. "Look!" cried one. "Look at those fools! How silly they are to be trudging along on foot when the Donkey might be carrying one of them on his back."

This seemed to make sense, so the Father lifted his Son on the Donkey and walked along contentedly by his side. They trod on for a while until they met some women who spoke to the Son scornfully. "You should be ashamed of yourself, you lazy rascal. What do you mean by riding when your poor old Father has to walk? It shows that no one respects age any more. The least you can do is get down and let your Father rest his old bones."

Red with shame, the Son dismounted and made his Father get on the Donkey's back.

They had gone only a little further when they met a group of young fellows who mocked them. "What a cruel old man!" jeered one of the fellows. "There he sits, selfish and comfortable, while the poor boy has to stumble along the dusty road to keep up with him."

So the Father lifted the Son up, and the two of them rode along.

However, before they reached the market-place, a townsman stopped them. "Have you no feelings for dumb creatures?" he shouted.

"The way that you load that little animal is a crime. You two men are better able to carry the poor little beast than he you!"

Wanting to do the right thing, the Miller and his Son got off the Donkey, tied his legs together, slung him on a pole, and carried him on their shoulders. When the crowd saw this spectacle the people laughed so loudly that the Donkey was frightened, kicked through the cords that bound him and, falling off the pole, fell into the river and was drowned.

He who tries to please everybody pleases nobody.

DEVELOPING SKILLS IN READING

Understanding Fables

Fables are little stories that contain lessons, or morals, about human conduct. The wisdom in fables is so practical that it can apply to life in almost any country, at almost any time.

The moral of this fable is stated at the end of the story. What modern situations could this moral be applied to?

The characters in fables generally show a single personality trait or quality. They are not fully developed in the way that characters are in short stories, novels, or plays. We call such characters *character types*. Fables might include such character types as fools, swindlers, sensible people, ambitious people, vain people, and so on. In some fables, these character types are represented by animals.

What type of characters are the Miller and his Son?

DEVELOPING VOCABULARY

Defining Words That Refer to Storytelling

This fable was supposedly told by Aesop, who is said to have been a slave in Greece. Aesop was so clever at storytelling that he often outsmarted his master with a clever tale.

Many words that refer to storytelling have come to refer also to falsehoods, or to something "not true." The word *fable* comes from the Latin word *fabula,* meaning "story." The word *fib* is a clipped form of *fable. Fib,* of course, means "a little white lie."

The word *fabulous* also comes from *fable.* It once meant "referring to a fable." What other meaning does *fabulous* have today?

Here are some other words that can refer to storytelling and to lying, or to something false. Use each word in two sentences to show its different meanings.

fiction   myth   storyteller   tale

Midas

Retold by Olivia Coolidge

Midas was King in Phrygia,[1] which is a land in Asia Minor, and he was both powerful and rich. Nevertheless, he was foolish, obstinate, and hasty, without the sense to appreciate good advice.

It happened one time that Dionysus with his dancing nymphs and satyrs[2] passed through Phrygia. As they went, the old, fat Silenus,[3] nodding on an ass, strayed from the others, who danced on without missing him. The ass took his half-conscious master wherever he wanted, until some hours later, as they came to a great rose garden, the old man tumbled off. The King's gardeners found him there and roused him, still sleepy and staggering, not quite sure who or where he was. Since, however, the revels[4] of Dionysus had spread throughout the land, they recognized him as the god's companion and made much of him. They wreathed his neck with roses and, one on each side and one behind, they supported him to the palace and up the steps, while another went to fetch Midas.

The King came out to meet Silenus, overjoyed at the honor done him. He clapped his hands for his servants and demanded such a feast as never was. There was much running to and fro, setting up of tables, fetching of wine, and bringing up of sweet-scented oil. While slaves festooned the hall with roses and made garlands for the feasters, Midas conducted his guest to the bath with all honor, that he might refresh himself and put on clean garments for the feast.

A magnificent celebration followed. For ten days, by daylight and by torchlight, the palace of the King stood open, and all the notables of Phrygia came up and down its steps. There were sounds of lyre and pipe and singing. There was dancing. Everywhere the scent of roses and of wine mingled with the costly perfumes of King Midas in the hot summer air. In ten days' time, as the revels were dying down from sheer exhaustion, Dionysus came in person to seek his friend. When he found how Silenus had been entertained and honored, he was greatly pleased and promised Midas any gift he cared to name, no matter what it was.

The King thought a little, glancing back through his doors at the chaos in his hall of scattered rose petals, overturned tables, bowls for the wine mixing, and drinking cups. It had been a good feast, the sort of feast a king should give, only he was very weary now and could not think. A king should entertain thus and give kingly presents to his guests, cups of

---

1. **Phrygia** (frĭj′ē-ə).
2. **Dionysus** (dī′ə-nī′səs); **nymphs** (nĭmfs); **satyrs** (sāt′ərz): Dionysus was the Greek god of wine. His worshipers joyfully danced and sang and often became frenzied on wine. The nymphs were beautiful goddesses of the mountains and woodlands. The satyrs were woodland creatures who were part goat and part man.
3. **Silenus** (sī-lē′nəs): one of Dionysus' followers. He almost always drank too much wine.
4. **revels** (rĕv′əlz): festivities; merrymakings.

beaten gold, such as he had seen once, with lifelike pictures of a hunt running round them or the golden honeycomb which Daedalus[5] made exactly as though it were the work of bees. Gods, like these guests, should have golden statues. Even a king never had enough.

"Give me," he said to Dionysus suddenly, "the power to turn all I touch to gold."

"That is a rash thing to ask," said Dionysus solemnly. "Think again." But Eastern kings are never contradicted, and Midas only felt annoyed.

"It is my wish," he answered coldly.

Dionysus nodded. "You shall have it," he said. "As you part from me here in the garden, it shall be yours."

Midas was so excited when he came back through the garden that he could not make up his mind what to touch first. Presently he decided on the branch of an oak tree which overhung his path. He took a look at it first, counting the leaves, noticing the little veins in them, the jagged edges, the fact that one of them had been eaten half away. He put out his hand to break it off. He never saw it change. One moment it was brown and green; the next it wasn't. There it was, stiff and shining, nibbled leaf and all. It was hard and satisfyingly heavy and more natural far than anything Daedalus ever made.

Now he was the greatest king in the world. Midas looked down at the grass he was walking over. It was still green; the touch was evidently in his hands. He picked up a stone to see; it became a lump of gold. He tried a clod of earth and found himself with another lump. Midas was beside himself with joy; he went into his palace to see what he could do. In the doorway he stopped at a sudden thought. He went outside again and walked down all the long row of pillars, laying his hands on each one. No king in the world had pillars of solid gold. He considered having a gold house but rejected the idea; the gold pillars looked better against the stone. Midas picked a gold apple and went inside again to eat.

His servants set his table for him, and he amused himself by turning the cups and dishes into gold. He touched the table too by mistake—not that it really mattered, but he would have to be careful. Absently he picked up a piece of bread and bit it and nearly broke his teeth.

Midas sat with the golden bread in his hand and looked at it a long time. He was horribly frightened. "I shall have to eat it without touching it with my hands," he said to himself after a while, and he put his head down on the table and tried that way. It was no good. The moment his lips touched the bread, he felt it turn hard and cold. In his shock he groped wildly for his winecup and took a big gulp. The stuff flowed into his mouth all right, but it wasn't wine any more. He spat it out hastily before he choked himself.

This time he was more than frightened; he was desperate. "Great Dionysus," he prayed earnestly with uplifted hands, "forgive my foolishness, and take away your gift."

"Go to the mountain of Tmolus,"[6] said the voice of the god into his ear, "and bathe in the stream that springs there so that the golden touch may be washed away. The next time think more carefully before you set your judgment against that of the gods."

Midas thanked the god with his whole heart, but he paid more attention to his promise than to his advice. He lost no time in jour-

---

5. **Daedalus** (dĕd′l-əs): in Greek mythology, a famous architect and craftsman.

6. **Tmolus** (tmō′ləs): a mountain god. The mountain is named for him.

neying to the mountain and dipping himself in the stream. There the golden touch was washed away from Midas, but the sand of the river bottom shone bright gold as the power passed into the water, so that the stream flowed over golden sand from that time on.

Midas had learned his lesson in a way but was still conceited. He had realized at least that gold was not the most important thing. Indeed, having had too much gold at one time, he took a violent dislike to it and to luxury in general. He spent his time in the open country now, listening to the music of the streams and the woodlands, while his kingdom ran itself as best it might. He wanted neither his elaborate palace, his embroidered robes, his splendid feasts, nor his trained dancers and musicians. Instead he wished to be at home in the woodlands with simple things that were natural and unspoiled.

It happened at the time that in the woods of Tmolus, the goat-god Pan[7] had made himself a pipe. It was a simple hollow reed with holes for stops cut in it, and the god played simple tunes on it like birdcalls and the various noises of the animals he had heard. Only he was very skillful and could play them fast and slow, mixed together or repeated, until the listener felt that the woods themselves were alive with little creatures. The birds and beasts made answer to the pipe so that it seemed the whole wood was an orchestra of music. Midas himself was charmed to ecstasy with the beauty of it and begged the shaggy god to play hour by hour till the very birds were weary of the calls. This Pan was quite ready to do, since he was proud of his invention. He even wanted to challenge Apollo[8]

7. **Pan:** a minor Greek nature god, associated with fields, forests, and shepherds. Like the satyrs, Pan had the body of a man and the legs of a goat.
8. **Apollo** (ə-pŏl′ō): one of the great Greek gods. He was the god of music, healing, the sun, and prophecy.

himself, sure that any judge would put his instrument above Apollo's golden lyre.

Apollo accepted the challenge, and Tmolus, the mountain, was himself to be the judge. Tmolus was naturally a woodland god and friendly to Pan, so he listened with solemn pleasure as the pipe trilled airs more varied and more natural than it had ever played before. The woods echoed, and the happy Midas, who had followed Pan to the contest, was almost beside himself with delight at the gaiety and abandon of it all. When, however, Tmolus heard Apollo play the music of gods and heroes, of love, longing, heroism, and the mighty dead, he forgot his own woods around him and the animals listening in their tiny nests and holes. He seemed to see into the hearts of men and understand the pity of their lives and the beauty that they longed for.

Even after the song had died away, Tmolus sat there in forgetful silence with his thoughts on the loves and struggles of the ages and the half-dried tears on his cheeks. There was a great quiet around him too, he realized, as he came to his senses. Even Pan had put down his pipe thoughtfully on the grass.

Tmolus gave the prize to Apollo, and in the whole woodland there was no one to protest but Midas. Midas had shut his ears to Apollo; he would neither listen nor care. Now he forgot where he was and in whose presence. All he remembered was that he was a great king who always gave his opinion and who, his courtiers told him, was always right. Leaping up, he protested loudly to Tmolus and was not even quiet when the mountain silently frowned on him. Getting no answer, he turned to Apollo, still objecting furiously to the unfairness of the judgment.

Apollo looked the insistent mortal up and down. "The fault is in your ears, O King. We must give them their true shape," he said.

hair began to grow so long and straggly that something had to be done. The royal barber had to be called.

The barber of King Midas was a royal slave, so it was easy enough to threaten him with the most horrible punishment if, whether waking or sleeping, he ever let fall the slightest hint of what was wrong with the King. The barber was thoroughly frightened. Unfortunately he was too frightened, and the King's threats preyed on his mind. He began to dream he had told his secret to somebody, and what was worse, his fellow servants began to complain that he was making noises in his sleep, so that he was desperately afraid he would talk. At last it seemed that if he could only tell somebody once and get it over, his mind would be at rest. Yet tell somebody was just what he dared not do.

Finally, he went down to a meadow which was seldom crossed because it was waterlogged, and there, where he could see there was no one around to hear him, he dug a hole in the ground, put his face close down, and whispered into the wet mud, "King Midas has asses' ears." Then he threw some earth on top and went away, feeling somehow much relieved.

Nothing happened for a while except that the hole filled up with water. Presently, though, some reeds began to grow in it. They grew taller and rustled as the wind went through them. After a while someone happened to go down that way and came racing back, half amused and half terrified. Everyone crowded around to listen to him. It was certainly queer, but it was a bit amusing too.

Everybody streamed down the path to investigate. Sure enough, as they came close to it, they could hear the whole thing distinctly. The reeds were not rustling in the wind; they were whispering to one another, "King Midas has asses' ears . . . asses' ears . . . asses' ears."

With that he turned away and was gone to Olympus,[9] while the unfortunate Midas put his hands to his ears and found them long and furry. He could even wriggle them about. Apollo had given him asses' ears in punishment for his folly.

From that time on King Midas wore a scarlet turban and tried to make it seem as though wearing this were a privilege that only the King could enjoy. He wore it day and night— he was so fond of it. Presently, however, his

---

9. **Olympus** (ō-lĭm′pəs): a mountain in northeastern Greece, where the gods were believed to live.

SEEKING MEANING

1. The opening paragraph describes Midas as "foolish, obstinate, and hasty, without the sense to appreciate good advice." How does Midas show his poor judgment and stubbornness?

2. Most myths do not contain "morals." This myth of Midas, however, has often been read as a story with a "moral." How would you state the lesson, or moral? What meaning do you think it has for people today?

3. Like many other myths, this story also explains the origins of two natural phenomena. Why is the sand of the river near Mount Tmolus gold-colored? Why do reeds seem to whisper in the wind?

DEVELOPING VOCABULARY

Recognizing How Word Meanings Change

In this myth, the god Apollo plays a golden *lyre,* an instrument that looks something like a small harp. In ancient Greece, poems were often recited to the music of a lyre. These poems came to be known as *lyric poems.*

The word *lyric* has acquired new meanings over the years. What do we mean by a *lyric poem* today?

What are song *lyrics?*

What do people mean when they say that someone's way of speaking is *lyrical?*

The word *panic* also has acquired a new meaning. It comes from a Greek word meaning "of Pan." In ancient Greece (just as today), people often had a sudden feeling of fear when they were alone outdoors at night. The Greeks believed that this sudden fear was caused by the presence of the god Pan.

Today we talk about "a *panic* on the stock market." We certainly do not mean that the shaggy god Pan is lurking among the brokers. What new meaning has *panic* acquired?

DEVELOPING SKILLS IN RESEARCH

Finding Stories About Metamorphosis

A change of form is called a *metamorphosis.* Scientists use the term *metamorphosis* to describe the changes that take place during the life cycles of the butterfly and the frog. In literature, however, metamorphosis is sudden and usually magical. Human beings become flowers, animals, and stars. Statues become living persons. Poor girls become princesses, mice become coachmen, and pumpkins become carriages.

What metamorphoses occur in this myth about Midas? Which one is a god's reward? Which is a god's punishment?

There are many famous stories about metamorphoses in literature. Each character in the first column of the following list undergoes a metamorphosis. Match each character with what he or she is transformed into in the second column. An encyclopedia or a mythology book will help you with most of them.

Narcissus	stone
Arachne	handsome prince
Daphne	flower
ugly frog	spider
Clark Kent	Mr. Hyde
Dr. Jekyll	Superman
Niobe	laurel tree

The Emperor's New Clothes

Hans Christian Andersen

Many years ago there lived an Emperor who was so exceedingly fond of fine new clothes that he spent all his money on being elaborately dressed. He took no interest in his soldiers, no interest in the theater, nor did he care to drive about in his state coach, unless it were to show off his new clothes. He had different robes for every hour of the day, and just as one says of a king that he is in his council chamber, people always said of him, "The Emperor is in his wardrobe!"

The great city in which he lived was full of gaiety. Strangers were always coming and going. One day two swindlers arrived; they made themselves out to be weavers, and said they knew how to weave the most magnificent fabric that one could imagine. Not only were the colors and patterns unusually beautiful, but the clothes that were made of this material had the extraordinary quality of becoming invisible to everyone who was either unfit for his post, or inexcusably stupid.

"What useful clothes to have!" thought the Emperor. "If I had some like that, I might find out which of the people in my empire are unfit for their posts. I should also be able to distinguish the wise from the fools. Yes, that material must be woven for me immediately!" Then he gave the swindlers large sums of money so that they could start work at once.

Quickly they set up two looms and pretended to weave, but there was not a trace of anything on the frames. They made no bones about demanding the finest silk and the purest gold thread. They stuffed everything into their bags, and continued to work at the empty looms until late into the night.

"I'm rather anxious to know how much of the material is finished," thought the Emperor, but to tell the truth, he felt a bit uneasy, remembering that anyone who was either a fool or unfit for his post would never be able to see it. He rather imagined that he need not have any fear for himself, yet he thought it wise to send someone else first to see how things were going. Everyone in the town knew about the exceptional powers of the material, and all were eager to know how incompetent or how stupid their neighbors might be.

"I will send my honest old Chamberlain[1] to the weavers," thought the Emperor. "He will be able to judge the fabric better than anyone else, for he has brains, and nobody fills his post better than he does."

So the nice old Chamberlain went into the hall where the two swindlers were sitting working at the empty looms.

"Upon my life!" he thought, opening his eyes very wide, "I can't see anything at all!" But he didn't say so.

Both the swindlers begged him to be good enough to come nearer, and asked how he liked the unusual design and the splendid colors. They pointed to the empty looms, and the poor old Chamberlain opened his eyes

---

1. **Chamberlain** (chăm′bər-lĭn): a high official in a royal court.

wider and wider, but he could see nothing, for there was nothing. "Heavens above!" he thought. "Could it possibly be that I am stupid? I have never thought that of myself, and not a soul must know it. Could it be that I am not fit for my post? It will never do for me to admit that I can't see the material!"

"Well, you don't say what you think of it," said one of the weavers.

"Oh, it's delightful—most exquisite!" said the old Chamberlain, looking through his spectacles. "What a wonderful design and what beautiful colors! I shall certainly tell the Emperor that I am enchanted with it."

"We're very pleased to hear that," said the two weavers, and they started describing the colors and the curious pattern. The old Chamberlain listened carefully in order to repeat, when he came home to the Emperor, exactly what he had heard, and he did so.

The swindlers now demanded more money, as well as more silk and gold thread, saying that they needed it for weaving. They put everything into their pockets and not a thread appeared upon the looms, but they kept on working at the empty frames as before.

Soon after this, the Emperor sent another nice official to see how the weaving was getting on, and to inquire whether the stuff would soon be ready. Exactly the same thing happened to him as to the Chamberlain. He looked and looked, but as there was nothing to be seen except the empty looms, he could see nothing.

"Isn't it a beautiful piece of material?" said the swindlers, showing and describing the pattern that did not exist at all.

"Stupid I certainly am not," thought the official; "then I must be unfit for my excellent post, I suppose. That seems rather funny—but I'll take great care that nobody gets wind of it." Then he praised the material he could not see, and assured them of his enthusiasm for the gorgeous colors and the beautiful pattern. "It's simply enchanting!" he said to the Emperor.

The whole town was talking about the splendid material.

And now the Emperor was curious to see it for himself while it was still upon the looms.

Accompanied by a great number of selected people, among whom were the two nice old officials who had already been there, the Emperor went forth to visit the two wily swindlers. They were now weaving madly, yet without a single thread upon the looms.

"Isn't it magnificent?" said the two nice officials. "Will Your Imperial Majesty deign to look at this splendid pattern and these glorious colors?" Then they pointed to the empty looms, for each thought that the others could probably see the material.

"What on earth can this mean?" thought the Emperor. "I don't see anything! This is terrible. Am I stupid? Am I unfit to be Emperor? That would be the most disastrous thing that could possibly befall me."—"Oh, it's perfectly wonderful!" he said. "It quite meets with my Imperial approval." And he nodded appreciatively and stared at the empty looms—he would not admit that he saw nothing. His whole suite looked and looked, but with as little result as the others; nevertheless, they all said, like the Emperor, "It's perfectly wonderful!" They advised him to have some new clothes made from this splendid stuff and to wear them for the first time in the next great procession.

"Magnificent!" "Excellent!" "Prodigious!"[2] went from mouth to mouth, and everyone was exceedingly pleased. The Emperor gave each of the swindlers a decoration to wear in his buttonhole, and the title of "Knight of the Loom."

---

2. **Prodigious** (prə-dĭj'əs): amazing.

Before the procession they worked all night, burning more than sixteen candles. People could see how busy they were finishing the Emperor's new clothes. They pretended to take the material from the looms, they slashed the air with great scissors, they sewed with needles without any thread, and finally they said, "The Emperor's clothes are ready!"

Then the Emperor himself arrived with his most distinguished courtiers, and each swindler raised an arm as if he were holding something, and said, "These are Your Imperial Majesty's knee breeches. This is Your Imperial Majesty's robe. This is Your Imperial Majesty's mantle," and so forth. "It is all as light as a spider's web, one might fancy one had nothing on, but that is just the beauty of it!"

"Yes, indeed," said all the courtiers, but they could see nothing, for there was nothing to be seen.

"If Your Imperial Majesty would graciously consent to take off your clothes," said the swindlers, "we could fit on the new ones in front of the long glass."

So the Emperor laid aside his clothes, and the swindlers pretended to hand him, piece by piece, the new ones they were supposed to have made, and they fitted him round the waist, and acted as if they were fastening something on — it was the train;[3] and the Emperor turned round and round in front of the long glass.

"How well the new robes suit Your Imperial Majesty! How well they fit!" they all said. "What a splendid design! What gorgeous colors! It's all magnificently regal!"

"The canopy which is to be held over Your Imperial Majesty in the procession is waiting

---

3. **train:** here, the part of the robe that trails behind.

outside," announced the Lord High Chamberlain.

"Well, I suppose I'm ready," said the Emperor. "Don't you think they are a nice fit?" And he looked at himself again in the glass, first on one side and then the other, as if he really were carefully examining his handsome attire.

The courtiers who were to carry the train groped about on the floor with fumbling fingers, and pretended to lift it; they walked on, holding their hands up in the air; nothing would have induced them to admit that they could not see anything.

And so the Emperor set off in the procession under the beautiful canopy, and everybody in the streets and at the windows said, "Oh! How superb the Emperor's new clothes are! What a gorgeous train! What a perfect fit!" No one would acknowledge that he didn't see anything, so proving that he was not fit for his post, or that he was very stupid.

None of the Emperor's clothes had ever met with such a success.

"But he hasn't got any clothes on!" gasped out a little child.

"Good heavens! Hark at the little innocent!" said the father, and people whispered to one another what the child had said. "But he hasn't got any clothes on! There's a little child saying he hasn't got any clothes on!"

"But he hasn't got any clothes on!" shouted the whole town at last. The Emperor had a creepy feeling down his spine, because it began to dawn upon him that the people were right. "All the same," he thought to himself, "I've got to go through with it as long as the procession lasts."

So he drew himself up and held his head higher than before, and the courtiers held on to the train that wasn't there at all.

SEEKING MEANING

1. How does the child show that he is more honest than all the adults in the story? What are the adults afraid of?
2. Who are the fools in this story? Who are the swindlers? Why are the swindlers able to get away with such an outrageous trick?
3. Nowhere in this story does the author state a moral. Yet clearly this story illustrates a lesson about human conduct. Try to state the lesson you find in this story.

ABOUT THE AUTHOR

The life of Hans Christian Andersen (1805–1875) reads like one of his fairy tales. He was born in a small fishing village in Denmark, the son of a poor shoemaker. At fourteen, he set out for Copenhagen to become an opera singer. But his audition was a humiliating failure, and for the next three years he lived in terrible poverty. He probably would have died unknown if he had not been rescued by a generous friend, who gave him a good education, money to travel, and the opportunity to write. Andersen's plays and novels were soon overshadowed by his fairy tales, which began to appear in 1835. Over the next forty years, Andersen wrote 156 of them. They were translated into dozens of languages, and brought Andersen fame and the friendship of the most famous people of his day, including some of the kings and queens of Europe. The title of A. A. Milne's play *The Ugly Duckling* is an allusion to one of Andersen's most famous stories. Other famous Andersen tales are "The Red Shoes," "The Nightingale," and "The Princess and the Pea," which was made into a musical called *Once upon a Mattress.*

The Princess and the Tin Box

James Thurber

Once upon a time, in a far country, there lived a king whose daughter was the prettiest princess in the world. Her eyes were like the cornflower, her hair was sweeter than the hyacinth, and her throat made the swan look dusty.

From the time she was a year old, the princess had been showered with presents. Her nursery looked like Cartier's[1] window. Her toys were all made of gold or platinum or diamonds or emeralds. She was not permitted to have wooden blocks or china dolls or rubber dogs or linen books, because such materials were considered cheap for the daughter of a king.

When she was seven, she was allowed to attend the wedding of her brother and throw real pearls at the bride instead of rice. Only the nightingale, with his lyre of gold, was permitted to sing for the princess. The common blackbird, with his boxwood flute, was kept out of the palace grounds. She walked in silver-and-samite[2] slippers to a sapphire-and-topaz bathroom and slept in an ivory bed inlaid with rubies.

On the day the princess was eighteen, the king sent a royal ambassador to the courts of five neighboring kingdoms to announce that he would give his daughter's hand in marriage to the prince who brought her the gift she liked the most.

The first prince to arrive at the palace rode a swift white stallion and laid at the feet of the princess an enormous apple made of solid gold which he had taken from a dragon who had guarded it for a thousand years. It was placed on a long ebony table set up to hold the gifts of the princess' suitors. The second prince, who came on a gray charger, brought her a nightingale made of a thousand diamonds, and it was placed beside the golden apple. The third prince, riding on a black horse, carried a great jewel box made of platinum and sapphires, and it was placed next to the diamond nightingale. The fourth prince, astride a fiery yellow horse, gave the princess a gigantic heart made of rubies and pierced by an emerald arrow. It was placed next to the platinum-and-sapphire jewel box.

Now the fifth prince was the strongest and handsomest of all the five suitors, but he was the son of a poor king whose realm had been overrun by mice and locusts and wizards and mining engineers so that there was nothing much of value left in it. He came plodding up to the palace of the princess on a plow horse and he brought her a small tin box filled with mica and feldspar and hornblende[3] which he had picked up on the way.

The other princes roared with disdainful laughter when they saw the tawdry[4] gift the fifth prince had brought to the princess. But

---

1. **Cartier's** (kär-tyāz′): a store that sells very expensive jewelry, located in New York City.
2. **samite** (sā′mĭt′): a silk fabric.

3. **mica; feldspar; hornblende:** three kinds of ordinary rock.
4. **tawdry** (tô′drē): cheap and flashy.

she examined it with great interest and squealed with delight, for all her life she had been glutted with precious stones and priceless metals, but she had never seen tin before or mica or feldspar or hornblende. The tin box was placed next to the ruby heart pierced with an emerald arrow.

"Now," the king said to his daughter, "you must select the gift you like best and marry the prince that brought it."

The princess smiled and walked up to the table and picked up the present she liked the most. It was the platinum-and-sapphire jewel box, the gift of the third prince.

"The way I figure it," she said, "is this. It is a very large and expensive box, and when I am married, I will meet many admirers who will give me precious gems with which to fill it to the top. Therefore, it is the most valuable of all the gifts my suitors have brought me and I like it the best."

The princess married the third prince that very day in the midst of great merriment and high revelry. More than a hundred thousand pearls were thrown at her and she loved it.

Moral: All those who thought that the princess was going to select the tin box filled with worthless stones instead of one of the other gifts will kindly stay after class and write one hundred times on the blackboard, "I would rather have a hunk of aluminum silicate than a diamond necklace."

SEEKING MEANING

1. James Thurber often gives funny, unexpected twists to old fairy tales and fables. In a traditional fairy tale, which gift would the princess choose?

2. The poor prince comes from a realm overrun by "mice and locusts and wizards and mining engineers." Which of these "pests" would be completely out of place in a traditional fairy tale?

3. Look back at the princess' announcement of her decision. What is surprising about the way she talks?

4. Some people believe that Thurber is mocking certain values of society in this tale. Do you agree? Why or why not?

DEVELOPING SKILLS OF EXPRESSION

Writing a Parody

A *parody* is a humorous imitation of a serious work of literature, art, or music. Writers may parody plots, characters, writing styles, or themes. In "The Princess and the Tin Box," Thurber mocks a typical fairy-tale plot: A rich princess marries a poor-but-handsome prince because he brings her a common rock that she has never seen before. As a reward for her indifference to wealth, the princess finds that the rock has been transformed into a pile of purest gold, and they live happily ever after. How does Thurber's story poke fun at this kind of fairy-tale plot?

Write a very brief parody of some familiar fairy tale, perhaps "The Three Little Pigs," "Jack and the Beanstalk," "Cinderella," or "Beauty and the Beast." Before you start to write, sum up the fairy-tale plot so you will be sure to cover every major part of the story. Here, for example, is a brief summary of the plot of "The Three Little Pigs":

Three pigs leave home, and each builds his own house. A wicked wolf destroys the first pig's straw house and the second pig's stick house, and the two pigs flee to the third pig's house. But the wolf cannot destroy the third pig's brick house. The wolf tries to trap the third pig outside his house, but the pig tricks him each time. Finally, the wolf falls down the chimney of the brick house into the pigs' pot of soup, and they eat him for supper.

Vary your story in some unexpected way. Can you change the happy-ever-after ending? Can you make some character stupid instead of wise, or cowardly instead of fearless? Suppose, for example, the wolf *did* blow down the brick house. What would you use as your moral?

American Folk Tales

Tales about Paul Bunyan, the giant logger, were first told in the northern lumber camps. Paul became popular with the general public when a logging company began using the stories in advertising brochures, to attract new workers. Since then, generations of storytellers have helped old Paul's tales grow taller and taller.

Paul Bunyan's Been There

Retold by Maurice Dolbier

Wherever you go in this big country, you're likely to find somebody who'll tell you that Paul Bunyan's been there. Been there and done things. Like digging the Great Lakes so that Babe would have watering troughs that wouldn't run dry, or digging a canal that turned out to be the Mississippi River.

You'll hear that the dirt he threw off to the right became the Rocky Mountains, and the dirt he threw off to the left became the Appalachians.

You'll hear that Kansas used to be full of mountains before Paul Bunyan came. He turned it upside-down. Now it's flat as a pancake because all its mountain peaks are inside the ground, pointing to the center of the earth.

You'll hear that Paul got so sad at what he saw going on in New York City that he fell to crying, and his tears started the Hudson River.

Western deserts or Southern swamps, Eastern shores or Northern forests, Paul is said to have been there and done things. And if by chance you can't find any stories about his having been in your neck of the woods, fix some up. Everybody else has.

Right now, let's stick to the Northern forests, because we know for sure that Paul was there. Paul and his men and the Blue Ox. They logged all through Michigan and Minnesota and the Dakotas, North and South, and they were always pushing westward to where the redwoods waited.

Maybe you'd like to know what life was like in those lumber camps of Paul Bunyan?

Well, the day started when the owls in the woods thought it was still night. The Little Chore Boy would blow his horn, and the men would tumble out of their bunks for chow.

There were always flapjacks for breakfast. These were made on a big round griddle about two city blocks wide. Before the batter was poured on, five men used to skate up and down and around on it with slabs of bacon tied on their feet. It'd take an ordinary man a week to eat one of the flapjacks that came off that griddle. Paul used to eat five or six every morning.

After breakfast came the work. The loggers tramped off to the woods. One crowd cleared the paths, another cut down the trees, another cut them up into logs, another piled them on carts or sledges. Then Babe the Blue Ox hauled the carts down to the water.

Soon after sunset, the men would all be back at the camp for supper. That was either baked beans or pea soup. Sometimes the cooks would surprise them, and serve pea soup or baked beans.

Sourdough Sam never liked to work very hard. One time he just dumped some split peas in the lake and then boiled the lake water and served it.

Matter of fact, Sam didn't stay with Paul Bunyan long. The men didn't mind that he was lazy, but they got almighty tired of sourdough. That's a kind of fermented dough that rises like yeast, and Sam used it in all his recipes. He put it in the coffee one morning. The Little Chore Boy drank a cup, and then started to rise into the air and float across the lake. They had to lasso him and pull him down.

After supper, they'd sit around and talk and sing and tell yarns so whopping that you'd never believe them.

Then, about nine o'clock, they turned in.

Of course, it wasn't all work at Paul's camp. The men would hunt and fish, and sometimes they'd have logrolling contests. That's when you stand on a log in the middle of the water and start the log rolling under you, trying to keep your balance as long as you can. Joe Murfraw used to win, mostly. Paul Bunyan himself never took part, except to demonstrate, because nobody could beat him anyway. He used to get the logs rolling so fast under foot that they set up a foam solid enough for him to walk to the shore on.

These are the things that went on fairly regularly, but I couldn't tell you what a typical day at Paul's camp was like. No day was typical. They were all special, and so was the weather.

There were fogs so thick that you could cut houses out of them, the way they do with snow and ice in the far north.

There were winds that blew up and down and in every direction at once.

There were thaws so quick that when the snow melted it just stayed there in big drifts of water for a week.

There was one time when all four seasons hit at once, and the whole camp came down with frostbite, sunstroke and spring fever.

There was another time when the rain didn't come from the skies at all. It came up from China, away underneath the world. Up from the ground it came, first in a drizzle and then in a pour, and it went straight up into the air. It got the sky so wet that the clouds were slipping and slopping around in the mud for a month.

But most of the stories you hear are about the winters that Paul Bunyan's loggers had to put up with. No one ever had winters like them before or since.

The cold was mighty intense. It went down to 70 degrees below zero, and each degree was 16 inches long. The men couldn't blow out the candles at night, because the flames were frozen, so they had to crack the flames off and toss them outdoors. (When the warm weather came, the flames melted and started quite a forest fire.)

It was so cold that the words froze in midair right after they'd come out of people's mouths, and all the next summer nobody had to talk. They had a winter's supply of conversation on hand.

The cold wasn't the only thing that was peculiar. Sometimes the snow was too. One winter it came down in big blue flakes, and Johnny Inkslinger used the icicles to write down the figures in his books. That's how he got the idea for inventing fountain pens. And the men used to have snowball fights until they were blue in the face.

Yes, the weather did all it could to upset Paul Bunyan's operations. And when the weather gave up, the mosquitoes tried.

One spring day, the men were working in a swamp, near a lake in northern Michigan, when they heard a droning noise. They looked up to see the whole stretch of western horizon black with flying creatures heading right toward them. The men didn't stop to inquire. They dropped their tools and went hotfoot back to the camp and locked themselves up in the bunkhouse.

Pretty soon they heard a terrible racket overhead, and then long things like sword blades began piercing through the tin roof. Paul Bunyan grabbed a sledgehammer and began pounding those stingers flat, so the mosquitoes couldn't get in or out. The rest of the mosquito army saw that it was no use and flew away.

Paul figured they'd be back with some new ideas, and he'd better have a new idea, too, just in case. So he sent Swede Charlie on a trip down into Indiana. He'd heard they had a special kind of monster bumblebee there. Charlie brought some of these back, and Paul trained them to fly in a protective circle around the camp. He thought that the next time the mosquitoes came they'd have a surprise. They did, and he did too. The bumblebees and the mosquitoes liked each other so much that they married and had children, and the children grew up with stingers in back and in front.

You won't hear anyone say that Paul Bunyan was ever stumped by any problem that came up. I won't say, either. But that section of timberland up in Michigan was the only place that Bunyan's men moved away from while there were still trees to be cut. I suppose they got a better offer.

SEEKING MEANING

1. Like the heroes of myths and legends, tall-tale figures often have superhuman characteristics. In tall tales, however, these characteristics are humorous. What exaggerated characteristics does the super-logger Paul Bunyan have?

2. Americans have become known as a people who are good problem-solvers. It isn't surprising that Paul Bunyan also has a reputation for being skilled at solving problems. How does he solve the mosquito problem?

3. Some tall-tale figures are so gigantic and powerful that their casual movements form lakes, rivers, deserts, and mountains. According to this tale, how did Paul Bunyan affect the geography of North America?

4. Tall-tale heroes of the frontier always live in the wilderness. Many of their stories show a distrust of city life and of the "city slicker." What passage in this story reveals that Paul dislikes city life?

DEVELOPING SKILLS IN READING

Recognizing Figures of Speech

Every language has expressions called *figures of speech*. Figures of speech are not literally, or factually, true. For example, the expression *on hand* in this sentence is used as a figure of speech:

> They had a winter's supply of conversation *on hand.*

The supply of conversation is not literally on top of anybody's hand. *On hand* here means "available; ready for use."

This story is told in a relaxed, informal style, the way that a storyteller might tell it aloud. It uses several figures of speech that are common in informal American usage. Explain the meaning of each of the italicized figures of speech in the following sentences from the story. Use your imagination to explain how each one might have originated.

> And if by chance you can't find any stories about his having been in *your neck of the woods,* fix some up.
> And the men used to have snowball fights until they were *blue in the face.*
> They dropped their tools and *went hotfoot* back to the camp and locked themselves up in the bunkhouse.

DEVELOPING SKILLS OF EXPRESSION

Writing a Tall Tale

The teller of these tall tales about Paul Bunyan says: "And if by chance you can't find any stories about his having been in your neck of the woods, fix some up. Everybody else has."

Make up a brief story about Paul Bunyan that is set in your state or community. What natural features (mountain, river, cave, lake, swamp, cliff) can you explain with a tall tale about Paul Bunyan? What problems are perplexing people in your area? What does ol' Paul do to solve them?

You might want to read more about Paul Bunyan. Two good collections are *Ol' Paul* by Glen Rounds and *Paul Bunyan* by Esther Shephard.

Before Pecos Bill came along, cowhands didn't know much about their jobs. The only way they knew to catch a steer was to hide behind a bush, lay a looped rope on the ground, and wait for the steer to step into the loop. Pecos Bill changed that the minute he reached the Dusty Dipper Ranch. But before that, he had lived as a coyote.

Pecos Bill, Coyote Cowboy

Retold by Adrien Stoutenburg

There aren't as many coyotes in Texas now as there were when Pecos Bill was born. But the ones that there are still do plenty of howling at night, sitting out under the sagebrush like thin, gray shadows, and pointing their noses at the moon.

Some of the cowboys around the Pecos River country claim that the oldest coyotes remember the time when Bill lived with them and are howling because they are lonesome for him. It's not often that coyotes have a boy grow up with them like one of their own family.

Bill had over a dozen older brothers and sisters for playmates, but they were ordinary boys and girls and no match for him. When Bill was two weeks old, his father found a half-grown bear and brought the bear home.

"You treat this bear nice, now," Bill's father said.

The bear didn't feel friendly and threatened to take a bite out of Bill. Bill wrestled the bear and tossed it around until the bear put its paws over its head and begged for mercy. Bill couldn't talk yet, but he patted the bear to show that he didn't have any hard feelings.

After that, the bear followed Bill around like a big, flat-footed puppy.

Pecos Bill's father was one of the first settlers in the West. There was lots of room in Texas, with so much sky that it seemed as if there couldn't be any sky left over for the rest of the United States. There weren't many people, and it was lonesome country, especially on nights when the wind came galloping over the land, rattling the bear grass and the yucca plants and carrying the tangy smell of greasewood. However, Bill didn't feel lonely often, with all the raccoons, badgers, and jack rabbits he had for friends. Once he made the mistake of trying to pet a skunk. The skunk sprayed Bill with its strongest scent. Bill's mother had to hang Bill on the clothesline for a week to let the smell blow off him.

Bill was a little over one year old when another family of pioneers moved into the country. The new family settled about fifty miles from where Bill's folks had built their homestead.

"The country's getting too crowded," said Bill's father. "We've got to move farther west."

So the family scrambled back into their big wagon and set out, the oxen puffing and snorting as they pulled the wagon toward the Pecos River. Bill was sitting in the rear of the wagon when it hit some rocks in a dry stream bed. There was a jolt, and Bill went flying out of the wagon. He landed so hard that the wind was knocked out of him and he couldn't even cry out to let his folks know. It might not have made any difference if he had, because all his brothers and sisters were making such a racket and the wagon wheels were creaking so loudly that no one could have heard him. In fact, with so many other children in the family besides Bill, it was four weeks before Bill's folks even missed him. Then, of course, it was too late to find him.

Young Bill sat there in the dry stream bed awhile, wondering what to do. Wherever he looked there was only the prairie and the sky, completely empty except for a sharp-shinned hawk floating overhead. Bill felt more lonely than he ever had in his life. Then, suddenly, he saw a pack of coyotes off in the distance, eating the remains of a dead deer. The coyotes looked at Bill, and Bill looked at them. These coyotes had never seen a human baby before, and they didn't know quite what to think. Apparently, they decided Bill was some new kind of hairless animal, for one of the female coyotes took a hunk of deer meat in her teeth and trotted over to Bill with it. She put it in front of him and stood back, waiting for him to eat it.

Bill had not eaten much raw meat before, but he knew that the female coyote meant well, and he didn't want to hurt her feelings. So he picked the meat up and began chewing. It tasted so good that he walked over and joined the other coyotes.

From that time on, Bill lived with the coyotes, going wherever they went, joining in their hunts, and even learning their language. Those years he lived with the coyotes were happy ones. He ran with them through the moonlit nights, curled up with them in their shady dens, and howled with them when they sang to the stars.

By the time Bill was ten years old, he could outrun and outhowl any coyote in the Southwest. And since he had not seen any other human beings in all that time, he thought he was a coyote himself.

He might have gone on believing this forever if one day a cowboy hadn't come riding through the sagebrush. The cowboy stopped, stared, and rubbed his eyes, because he could scarcely believe what he saw. There in front of him stood a ten-year-old boy, as naked as a cow's hoof, wrestling with a giant grizzly bear. Nearby sat a dozen coyotes, their tongues hanging out. Before the cowboy could say, "Yipee yi-yo!" or plain "Yipee!" the boy had hugged the bear to death.

When Pecos Bill saw the cowboy, he snarled like a coyote and put his head down between his shoulders, ready to fight.

"What's your name?" the cowboy asked. "What are you doing out here?"

Since Bill didn't know anything but coyote talk, he naturally didn't understand a word.

The cowboy tossed Bill a plug of tobacco. Bill ate it and decided it tasted pretty good, so when the cowboy came up close, Bill didn't bite him.

The cowboy stayed there for three days, teaching Bill to talk like a human. Then he tried to prove to Bill that Bill wasn't a coyote.

"I must be a coyote," Bill said. "I've got fleas, haven't I? And I can howl the moon out of the sky. And I can run a deer to death."

"All Texans have got fleas and can howl," the cowboy said. "In order to be a true coyote, you have to have a bushy tail."

Bill looked around and realized for the first time that he didn't have a nice bushy, waving tail like his coyote friends. "Maybe I lost it somewhere."

"No siree," the cowboy said. "You're a human being, sure as shooting. You'd better come along with me."

Being human was a hard thing for Bill to face up to, but he realized that the cowboy must be right. He told his coyote friends goodbye and thanked them for all that they had taught him. Then he straddled a mountain lion he had tamed and rode with the cowboy toward the cowboy's ranch. On the way to the ranch, a big rattlesnake reared up in front of them. The cowboy galloped off, but Bill jumped from his mount and faced the snake.

"I'll let you have the first three bites, Mister Rattler, just to be fair. Then I'm going to beat the poison out of you until you behave yourself!"

That is just what Bill did. He whipped the snake around until it stretched out like a thirty-foot rope. Bill looped the rattler-rope in one hand, got back on his lion, and caught up with the cowboy. To entertain himself, he made a loop out of the snake and tossed it over the head of an armadillo plodding along through the cactus. Next, he lassoed several Gila monsters.[1]

"I never saw anybody do anything like that before," said the cowboy.

"That's because nobody invented the lasso before," said Pecos Bill.

Before Pecos Bill came along, cowboys didn't know much about their job. They didn't know anything about rounding up cattle, or branding them, or even about ten-gallon hats. The only way they knew to catch a steer was to hide behind a bush, lay a looped rope on the ground, and wait for the steer to step into the loop.

---

1. **Gila** (hē′lə) **monsters:** large, poisonous lizards.

Pecos Bill changed all that the minute he reached the Dusty Dipper Ranch. He slid off his mountain lion and marched up to the biggest cowboy there.

"Who's the boss here?" he asked.

The man took one look at Bill's lion and at the rattlesnake-rope, and said, "I *was.*"

Young though he was, Bill took over. At the Dusty Dipper and at other ranches, Bill taught the cowboys almost everything they know today. He invented spurs for them to wear on their boots. He taught them how to round up the cattle and drive the herds to railroad stations where they could be shipped to market. One of the finest things Bill did was to teach the cowboys to sing cowboy songs.

Bill made himself a guitar. On a night when the moon was as reddish-yellow as a ripe peach, though fifty times as large, he led some of the fellows at the ranch out to the corral and set himself down on the top rail.

"I don't want to brag," he told the cowhands, "but I learned my singing from the coyotes, and that's about the best singing there is."

He sang a tune the coyotes had taught him, and made up his own words:

"My seat is in the saddle, and my saddle's in the sky,
And I'll quit punchin' cows in the sweet by and by."

He made up many more verses and sang many other songs. When Bill was through, the roughest cowboy of all, Hardnose Hal, sat wiping tears from his eyes because of the beauty of Bill's singing. Lefty Lightning, the smallest cowboy, put his head down on his arms and wept. All the cowboys there vowed they would learn to sing and make up songs. And they did make up hundreds of songs about the lone prairie, and the Texas sky, and the wind blowing over the plains. That's why

we have so many cowboy songs today.

Pecos Bill invented something else almost as useful as singing. This happened after a band of cattle rustlers came to the ranch and stole half a hundred cows.

"You boys," said Bill, "have to get something to protect yourselves with besides your fists. I can see I'll have to think up a six-shooter."

"What's a six-shooter?" asked Broncobusting Bertie. (Bill had taught horses how to buck and rear so that cowboys could learn broncobusting.)

"Why," said Bill, "that's a gun that holds six bullets."

Bill sat down in the shade of a yucca tree and figured out how to make a six-shooter. It was a useful invention, but it had its bad side. Some of the cowboys started shooting at each other. Some even went out and held up trains and stagecoaches.

One of the most exciting things Bill did was to find himself the wildest, strongest, most beautiful horse that ever kicked up the Texas dust. He was a mighty, golden mustang, and even Bill couldn't outrun that horse. To catch the mustang, Bill had the cowboys rig up a huge slingshot and shoot him high over the cactus and greasewood. When Bill landed in front of the mustang, the horse was so surprised he stopped short, thrusting out his front legs stiff as rifle barrels. The mustang had been going so fast that his hoofs drove into the ground, and he was stuck. Bill leaped on the animal's back, yanked on his golden mane, and pulled him free. The mustang was so thankful for being pulled from the trap that he swung his head around and gave Pecos Bill a smacking kiss. From then on, the horse was as gentle as a soft wind in a thatch of Jimson weed.

No one else could ride him, however. Most of the cowboys who tried ended up with

Comin' Through the Rye (1902). A bronze sculpture by Frederic Remington (1861–1909). The Thomas Gilcrease Institute of American History and Art, Tulsa, Oklahoma.

broken necks. That's why Bill called his mustang Widow-Maker.

Bill and Widow-Maker traveled all over the western range, starting new ranches and helping out in the long cattle drives. In stormy weather they often holed up with a band of coyotes. Bill would strum his guitar and the coyotes would sing with him.

Then came the year of the Terrible Drought. The land shriveled for lack of water, and the droves of cattle stood panting with thirst.

The cowboys and the ranch bosses from all around came to Bill, saying, "The whole country's going to dry up and blow away, Bill, unless you can figure out some way to bring us rain."

"I'm figuring," Bill told them. "But I've never tried making rain before, so I'll have to think a little."

While Bill thought, the country grew so dry it seemed that there would be nothing but bones and rocks left. Even cactus plants, which could stand a lot of dryness, began to turn brown. The pools where the cattle drank dried up and turned to cracked mud. All the snakes hid under the ground in order to keep from frying. Even the coyotes stopped howling, because their throats were too dry for them to make any sound.

Bill rode around on Widow-Maker, watching the clear, burning sky and hoping for the sight of a rain cloud. All he saw were whirls of dust, called dust devils, spinning up from the yellowing earth. Then, toward noon one day, he spied something over in Oklahoma which looked like a tall whirling tower of black bees. Widow-Maker reared up on his hind legs, his eyes rolling.

"It's just a cyclone," Pecos Bill told his horse, patting the golden neck.

But Widow-Maker was scared and began bucking around so hard that even Bill had a time staying in the saddle.

"Whoa there!" Bill commanded. "I could ride that cyclone as easy as I can ride you, the way you're carrying on."

That's when Bill had an idea. There might be rain mixed up in that cyclone tower. He nudged Widow-Maker with his spurs and yelled, "Giddap!"

What Bill planned to do was leap from his horse and grab the cyclone by the neck. But as he came near and saw how high the top of the whirling tower was, he knew he would have to do something better than that. Just as he and Widow-Maker came close enough to the cyclone to feel its hot breath, a knife of lightning streaked down into the ground. It stuck there, quivering, just long enough for Bill to

reach out and grab it. As the lightning bolt whipped back up into the sky, Bill held on. When he was as high as the top of the cyclone, he jumped and landed astraddle its black, spinning shoulders.

By then, everyone in Texas, New Mexico, Arizona, and Oklahoma was watching. They saw Bill grab hold of that cyclone's shoulders and haul them back. They saw him wrap his legs around the cyclone's belly and squeeze so hard the cyclone started to pant. Then Bill got out his lasso and slung it around the cyclone's neck. He pulled it tighter and tighter until the cyclone started to choke, spitting out rocks and dust. All the rain that was mixed up in it started to fall.

Down below, the cattle and the coyotes, the jack rabbits and the horned toads, stuck out their tongues and caught the sweet, blue, falling rain. Cowboys on the ranches and people in town ran around whooping and cheering, holding out pans and kettles to catch the raindrops.

Bill rode the cyclone across three states. By the time the cyclone reached California, it was all out of steam, and out of rain, too. It gave a big sigh, trembled weakly, and sank to earth. Bill didn't have time to jump off. He fell hard, scooping out a few thousand acres of sand and rock and leaving a big basin below sea level. That was what made Death Valley.

Bill was a greater hero than ever after that. Yet at times, he felt almost as lonely as on the day when he had bounced out of his folks' wagon and found himself sitting alone under the empty sky. Widow-Maker was good company most of the time, but Bill felt there was something missing in his life.

One day, he wandered down to the Rio Grande and stood watching the brown river flow slowly past. Suddenly, he saw a catfish as big as a whale jumping around on top of the water, its whiskers shining like broomsticks.

On top of the catfish was a brown-eyed, brown-haired girl.

Somebody beside Bill exclaimed, "Look at Slue-Foot Sue ride that fish!"

Pecos Bill felt his heart thump and tingle in a way it had never done before. "That's the girl I want to marry!" he said. He waded out into the Rio Grande, poked the catfish in the nose, and carried Slue-Foot Sue to a church. "You're going to be my bride," he said.

"That's fine with me," said Sue, looking Pecos Bill over and seeing that he was the biggest, boldest, smartest cowboy who had ever happened to come along beside the Rio Grande.

That was the beginning of a very happy life for Bill. He and Sue raised a large family. All of the boys grew up to be fine cowboys, and the girls grew up to be cowgirls. The only time Bill and Sue had any trouble was when Bill wanted to adopt a batch of baby coyotes who were orphans.

"We're human beings," Sue said, "and we can't be raising a bunch of varmints."

"I was a varmint once myself," said Bill. He argued so much that Sue agreed to take the coyotes in and raise them as members of the family. The coyotes grew to be so human that two of them were elected to the House of Representatives.

Pecos Bill grew old, as everyone and everything does in time. Even so, there wasn't a bronco he couldn't bust, or a steer he couldn't rope, or a bear he couldn't hug to death faster and better than anyone else.

No one knows, for sure, how he died, or even if he did die. Some say that he mixed barbed wire in his coffee to make it strong enough for his taste, and that the wire rusted in his stomach and poisoned him. Others say that one day he met a dude cowboy, all dressed up in fancy clothes, who didn't know the front end of a cow from the side of a boxcar. The dude asked so many silly questions about cowpunching that Pecos Bill lay down in the dust and laughed himself to death.

But the cowboys back in the Pecos River country say that every once in a while, when the moon is full and puffing its white cheeks out and the wind is crooning softly through the bear grass, Pecos Bill himself comes along and sits on his haunches and sings right along with the coyotes.

SEEKING MEANING

1. It is not surprising that a tall-tale figure, whose life is one long exaggeration, should have an extraordinary childhood. What was remarkable about Bill's younger years?
2. Pecos Bill is credited with inventing many of the cowhand's tools and skills. List all the things Pecos Bill is supposed to have done for his people.
3. According to the story, what natural wonders were caused by Bill's activities?
4. What disaster does Pecos Bill save his people from? What words on page 510 describe this enemy as if it were a living monster? How does Bill conquer this monster?

DEVELOPING VOCABULARY

Recognizing Words from Spanish

It is easy to see why many terms used by cowhands are direct borrowings of Spanish words. Many Spanish-speaking Mexican-Americans live in the Southwest, where the cowhands live and work. Here are three cowhand terms borrowed from Spanish:

mustang (from Mexican Spanish *mestengo*, "stray horse"): a wild horse.

lariat (from Spanish *la reata*, "the rope"): a long rope used to catch or tie up animals.

bronco (from Mexican Spanish *bronco*, "rough"): an untamed horse.

The following words are not all cowhand terms, but they all came into English from Spanish. Two go back originally to Nahuatl, an ancient Mexican Indian language, which was spoken before the Spanish came to Mexico. Use a dictionary to find the original meaning of each word. Have any of the words taken on new meanings?

alfalfa	chocolate	hurricane
bonanza	coyote	mesa

DEVELOPING SKILLS OF RESEARCH

Reporting on American Tall-Tale Heroes

Stories about Pecos Bill and Paul Bunyan are examples of occupational lore: stories about heroes associated with a particular kind of work. Here are some other tall-tale figures from American folk tales, and the work they are associated with:

Mike Fink, riverboatman
Casey Jones, railroad engineer
Joe Magarac, steelworker
Stormalong, sea captain

Choose one of these characters (or some other tall-tale figure you are interested in) and find one story about him. Write a brief report summing up the character's life and telling what impossible feats he achieved.

Information on these figures can be found in a book on American folklore or in an encyclopedia. A good source for stories of American folk heroes is *Yankee Doodle's Cousins* by Anne Malcolmson.

A Sensible Varmint

Davy Crockett

Some people become legends after they die, but the American frontiersman Davy Crockett (1786–1836) became a legend in his own time. Davy helped create his own legend with stories like this one, which is surely one of the tallest tales about hunting ever told. The story is written just as a back-country yarn spinner might write it.

Almost every boddy that knows the forrest, understands parfectly well that Davy Crockett never loses powder and ball, havin' ben brort up to blieve it a sin to throw away amminition, and that is the bennefit of a vartuous eddikation. I war out in the forrest won arternoon, and had jist got to a plaice called the grate gap, when I seed a rakkoon setting all alone upon a tree. I klapped the breech of Brown Betty to my sholder, and war jist a-going to put a piece of led between his sholders, when he lifted one paw, and sez he, "Is your name Crockett?"

Sez I, "You are rite for wonst, my name is Davy Crockett."

"Then," sez he, "you needn't take no further trubble, for I may as well cum down without another word"; and the cretur wauked rite down from the tree, for he considered himself shot.

I stoops down and pats him on the head, and sez I, "I hope I may be shot myself before I hurt a hare of your head, for I never had sich a kompliment in my life."

"Seeing as how you say that," sez he, "I'll jist walk off for the present, not doubting your word a bit, d'ye see, but lest you should kinder happen to change your mind."

John Henry was a real person, a steel driver, who is remembered for what he did and how he died. In 1870 John Henry raced an automatic steam drill in the Big Bend Tunnel of the Chesapeake and Ohio Railroad in the West Virginia mountains. What happened? The story is immortalized in this famous folk ballad.

John Henry

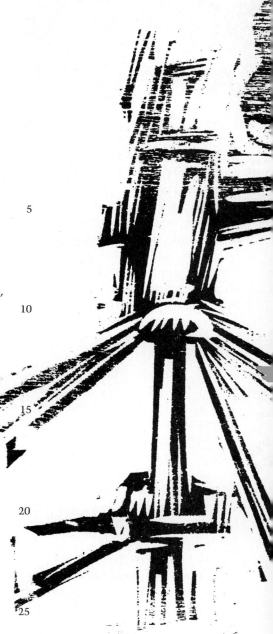

John Henry was a little baby boy,
You could hold him in the palm of your hand,
He gave a long and lonesome cry,
"Gonna be a steel-drivin' man, Lawd, Lawd,
Gonna be a steel-drivin' man."   5

They took John Henry to the tunnel,
Put him in the lead to drive,
The rock was so tall, John Henry so small,
That he lied down his hammer and he cried, Lawd, Lawd,
Lied down his hammer and he cried.   10

John Henry started on the right hand,
The steam drill started on the left,
"Fo' I'd let that steam drill beat me down,
I'd hammer my fool self to death, Lawd, Lawd,
I'd hammer my fool self to death."   15

John Henry told his Captain,
"A man ain't nothin' but a man,
Fo' I let your steam drill beat me down
I'll die with this hammer in my hand, Lawd, Lawd,
I'll die with this hammer in my hand."   20

John Henry had a little woman
Her name were Polly Anne,
John Henry took sick and he had to go to bed,
Polly Anne drove steel like a man, Lawd, Lawd,
Polly Anne drove steel like a man.   25

Now the Captain told John Henry,
"I b'lieve my tunnel's sinkin' in."
"Stand back, Captain, and doncha be afraid,
That's nothin' but my hammer catchin' wind, Lawd,
    Lawd,
That's nothin' but my hammer catchin' wind."   30

John Henry he told his shaker,°
"Now shaker, why don't you sing?
I'm throwin' nine pounds from my hips on down,
Just listen to the cold steel ring, Lawd, Lawd,
Just listen to the cold steel ring."   35

31. **shaker:** steel driver's assistant.

John Henry he told his shaker,
"Now shaker, why don't you pray?
For if I miss this six-foot steel
Tomorrow'll be your buryin' day, Lawd, Lawd,
Tomorrow'll be your buryin' day."   40

John Henry he told his Captain,
"Looky yonder, boy, what do I see?
Your drill's done broke and your hole's done choke,
And you can't drive steel like me, Lawd, Lawd,
And you can't drive steel like me."   45

John Henry hammerin' in the mountain
Till the handle of his hammer caught on fire,
He drove so hard till he broke his poor heart,
Then he lied down his hammer and he died, Lawd, Lawd,
Then he lied down his hammer and he died.   50

Women in the West heard of John Henry's death
They couldn't hardly stay in bed,
Stood in the rain, flagged that eastbound train
"Goin' where that man fell dead, Lawd, Lawd,
Goin' where that man fell dead."   55

They took John Henry to the tunnel,
And they buried him in the sand,
An' every locomotive come rollin' by
Say, "There lays a steel-drivin' man, Lawd, Lawd,
There lays a steel-drivin' man."   60

Now some say he come from England,
And some say he come from Spain,
But I say he's nothin' but a Lou'siana man,
Leader of a steel-drivin' gang, Lawd, Lawd,
Leader of a steel-drivin' gang.   65

SEEKING MEANING

1. Many folk heroes show unusual talents or promise when they are only babies. Pecos Bill, for example, was only two weeks old when he made a bear beg for mercy (page 505). What ambition did John Henry reveal when he was so little he could be held in the palm of a hand?

2. The famous contest with the machine starts in the third stanza. How was John Henry both a winner and a loser in that battle?

3. According to the next-to-last stanza, how is John Henry's memory kept alive?

4. How is Polly Anne also a heroic figure? How did the actions of other women show how people felt about John Henry's tragic death?

DEVELOPING SKILLS OF EXPRESSION

Writing a Ballad
Make up a brief song that tells a story about a colorful hero, perhaps Paul Bunyan, Pecos Bill, or someone else, real or imaginary. You might choose one of these episodes:

> Paul Bunyan's conquest of the giant mosquitoes
> Pecos Bill's life with the coyotes

The words to many ballads are composed to old melodies. Here are three good ones:

> "On Top of Old Smoky"
> "My Darling Clementine"
> "Sweet Betsy from Pike"

When Mark Twain went West to seek his fortune, he heard a tall tale about a jumping frog being told in Angel's Mining Camp, in Calaveras County, California. He used that tale in the following story, which made him an internationally famed humorist almost overnight. Europeans had never read anything quite like it.

Notice how Twain leads into the tall tale. The "I" telling the story is a dude.

The Celebrated Jumping Frog of Calaveras County

Mark Twain

In compliance with the request of a friend of mine, who wrote me from the East, I called on good-natured, garrulous[1] old Simon Wheeler and inquired after my friend's friend, Leonidas W. Smiley, as requested to do, and I hereunto append[2] the result. I have a lurking suspicion that *Leonidas W.* Smiley is a myth; that my friend never knew such a personage; and that he only conjectured[3] that if I asked old Wheeler about him, it would remind him of his infamous *Jim* Smiley, and he would go to work and bore me to death with some exasperating reminiscence of him as long and as tedious as it should be useless to me. If that was the design, it succeeded.

I found Simon Wheeler dozing comfortably by the barroom stove of the dilapidated tavern in the decayed mining camp of Angel's, and I noticed that he was fat and baldheaded, and

---

1. **garrulous** (găr′ə-ləs): long-winded; talkative.
2. **append:** attach.
3. **conjectured** (kən-jĕk′chərd): guessed.

had an expression of winning gentleness and simplicity upon his tranquil countenance. He roused up, and gave me good day. I told him that a friend of mine had commissioned me to make some inquiries about a cherished companion of his boyhood named *Leonidas W. Smiley—Reverend Leonidas W. Smiley*, a young minister of the gospel, who he had heard was at one time a resident of Angel's Camp. I added that if Mr. Wheeler could tell me anything about this Reverend Leonidas W. Smiley, I would feel under many obligations to him.

Simon Wheeler backed me into a corner and blockaded me there with his chair, and then he sat down and reeled off the monotonous narrative which follows this paragraph. He never smiled, he never frowned, he never changed his voice from the gentle-flowing key to which he tuned his initial sentence, and he never betrayed the slightest suspicion of enthusiasm; but all through the interminable narrative there ran a vein of impressive earnestness and sincerity, which showed me plainly that, so far from his imagining that there was anything ridiculous or funny about his story, he regarded it as a really important matter and admired its two heroes as men of transcendent[4] genius in finesse.[5] I let him go on in his own way and never interrupted him once.

"Reverend Leonidas W. H'm, Reverend Le—well, there was a feller here once by the name of *Jim* Smiley, in the winter of '49—or maybe it was the spring of '50—I don't recollect exactly, somehow, though what makes me think it was one or the other is because I remember the big flume[6] warn't finished when he first come to the camp; but anyway, he was the curiousest man about always betting on anything that turned up you ever see, if he could get anybody to bet on the other side; and if he couldn't he'd change sides. Any way that suited the other man would suit *him* —any way just so's he got a bet, *he* was satisfied. But still he was lucky, uncommon lucky; he most always come out winner. He was always ready and laying for a chance; there couldn't be no solit'ry thing mentioned but that feller'd offer to bet on it and take any side you please, as I was just telling you. If there was a horse race, you'd find him flush or you'd find him busted at the end of it; if there was a dogfight, he'd bet on it; if there was a catfight, he'd bet on it; if there was a chicken-fight, he'd bet on it; why, if there was two birds setting on a fence, he would bet you which one would fly first; or if there was a camp meeting, he would be there reg'lar to bet on Parson Walker, which he judged to be the best exhorter[7] about here, and so he was too, and a good man. If he even see a straddle-bug start to go anywheres, he would bet you how long it would take him to get to—to wherever he was going to, and if you took him up, he would foller that straddlebug to Mexico but what he would find out where he was bound for and how long he was on the road. Lots of the boys here has seen that Smiley and can tell you about him. Why, it never made no difference to *him*—he'd bet on *anything*— the dangdest feller. Parson Walker's wife laid very sick once, for a good while, and it seemed as if they warn't going to save her; but one morning he come in, and Smiley up and asked him how she was, and he said she was consid-

---

4. **transcendent** (trăn-sĕn′dənt): extraordinary; surpassing.
5. **finesse** (fĭ-nĕs′): trickiness; clever strategy.
6. **flume** (flo͞om): an inclined chute for carrying water.

7. **exhorter** (ĕg-zôrt′ər): here, preacher.

erable better—thank the Lord for his inf'nite mercy—and coming on so smart that with the blessing of Prov'dence she'd get well yet; and Smiley, before he thought, says, 'Well, I'll resk two and a half she don't anyway.'

"Thish-yer Smiley had a mare—the boys called her the fifteen-minute nag, but that was only in fun, you know, because of course she was faster than that—and he used to win money on that horse, for all she was so slow and always had the asthma, or the distemper, or the consumption, or something of that kind. They used to give her two or three hundred yards' start, and then pass her under way; but always at the end of the race she'd get excited and desperate like, and come cavorting and straddling up and scattering her legs around limber, sometimes in the air and sometimes out to one side among the fences, and kicking up m-o-r-e dust and raising m-o-r-e racket with her coughing and sneezing and blowing her nose—and *always* fetch up at the stand just about a neck ahead, as near as you could cipher it down.[8]

"And he had a little small bull pup, that to look at him you'd think he warn't worth a cent but to set around and look ornery and lay for a chance to steal something. But as soon as money was up on him he was a different dog; his underjaw'd begin to stick out like the fo'castle of a steamboat, and his teeth would uncover and shine like the furnaces. And a dog might tackle him and bullyrag him, and bite him, and throw him over his shoulder two or three times, and Andrew Jackson—which was the name of the pup—Andrew Jackson would never let on but what *he* was satisfied and hadn't expected nothing else—and the bets being doubled and doubled on the other side all the time, till the money was all up; and then all of a sudden he would grab that

other dog jest by the j'int of his hind leg and freeze to it—not chaw, you understand, but only just grip and hang on till they throwed up the sponge, if it was a year. Smiley always come out winner on that pup, till he harnessed a dog once that didn't have no hind legs, because they'd been sawed off in a circular saw, and when the thing had gone along far enough, and the money was all up, and he come to make a snatch for his pet holt, he see in a minute how he'd been imposed on and how the other dog had him in the door, so to speak, and he 'peared surprised, and then he looked sorter discouraged like, and didn't try no more to win the fight, and so he got shucked out bad. He give Smiley a look, as much as to say his heart was broke, and it was *his* fault for putting up a dog that hadn't no hind legs for him to take holt of, which was his main dependence in a fight, and then he limped off a piece and laid down and died. It was a good pup, was that Andrew Jackson, and would have made a name for hisself if he'd lived, for the stuff was in him and he had genius—I know it, because he hadn't no opportunities to speak of, and it don't stand to reason that a dog could make such a fight as he could under them circumstances if he hadn't no talent. It always makes me feel sorry when I think of that last fight of his'n, and the way it turned out.

"Well, thish-yer Smiley had rat tarriers, and chicken cocks, and tomcats and all them kind of things, till you couldn't rest, and you couldn't fetch nothing for him to bet on but he'd match you. He ketched a frog one day and took him home and said he cal'lated to educate him; and so he never done nothing for three months but set in his backyard and learn that frog to jump. And you bet you he *did* learn him, too. He'd give him a little punch behind, and the next minute you'd see that frog whirling in the air like a doughnut—

---

8. **cipher** (sī'fər) **it down:** calculate it.

see him turn one summerset, or maybe a couple, if he got a good start, and come down flat-footed and all right, like a cat. He got him up so in the matter of ketching flies and kep' him in practice so constant, that he'd nail a fly every time as fur as he could see him. Smiley said all a frog wanted was education, and he could do most anything—and I believe him. Why, I've seen him set Dan'l Webster down here on this floor—Dan'l Webster was the name of the frog—and sing out, 'Flies, Dan'l, flies!' and quicker'n you could wink he'd spring straight up and snake a fly off'n the counter there and flop down on the floor ag'in as solid as a gob of mud and fall to scratching the side of his head with his hind foot as indifferent as if he hadn't no idea he'd been doin' any more'n any frog might do. You never see a frog so modest and straightfor'ard as he was, for all he was so gifted. And when it come to fair and square jumping on a dead level, he could get over more ground at one straddle than any animal of his breed you ever see. Jumping on a dead level was his strong

suit, you understand; and when it come to that, Smiley would ante up money on him as long as he had a red. Smiley was monstrous proud of his frog, and well he might be, for fellers that had traveled and been everwheres all said he laid over any frog that ever *they* see.

"Well, Smiley kep' the beast in a little lattice box, and he used to fetch him downtown sometimes and lay for a bet. One day a feller—a stranger in the camp, he was—come acrost him with his box, and says: 'What might it be that you've got in the box?'

"And Smiley says, sorter indifferent like, 'It might be a parrot or it might be a canary, maybe, but it ain't—it's only just a frog.'

"And the feller took it, and looked at it careful, and turned it round this way and that, and says, 'H'm—so 'tis. Well, what's *he* good for?'

"'Well,' Smiley says, easy and careless, 'he's good enough for *one* thing, I should judge—he can outjump any frog in Calaveras County.'

"The feller took the box again and took another long, particular look and give it back to Smiley and says, very deliberate, 'Well,' he says, 'I don't see no p'ints[9] about that frog that's any better'n any other frog.'

"'Maybe you don't,' Smiley says. 'Maybe you understand frogs and maybe you don't understand 'em; maybe you've had experience, and maybe you ain't only a amature, as it were. Anyways, I've got *my* opinion, and I'll resk forty dollars that he can outjump any frog in Calaveras County.'

"And the feller studied a minute, and then says, kinder sad-like, 'Well, I'm only a stranger here, and I ain't got no frog; but if I had a frog, I'd bet you.'

"And then Smiley says, 'That's all right—

---

9. **p'ints:** a dialectal form of *points*, the qualities for which an animal is specially bred.

that's all right—if you'll hold my box a minute, I'll go and get you a frog.' And so the feller took the box and put up his forty dollars along with Smiley's and set down to wait.

"So he set there a good while thinking and thinking to himself, and then he got the frog out and prized his mouth open and took a teaspoon and filled him full of quail shot—filled him pretty near up to his chin—and set him on the floor.

"Smiley he went to the swamp and slopped around in the mud for a long time, and finally he ketched a frog, and fetched him in, and give him to this feller, and says: 'Now, if you're ready, set him alongside of Dan'l, with his forepaws just even with Dan'l's, and I'll give the word.' Then he says, 'One—two—three—*git!*' and him and the feller touched up the frogs from behind, and the new frog hopped off lively, but Dan'l give a heave, and hysted up his shoulders—so—like a Frenchman, but it warn't no use—he couldn't budge; he was planted as solid as a church, and he couldn't no more stir than if he was anchored out. Smiley was a good deal surprised, and he was disgusted too, but he didn't have no idea what the matter was, of course.

"The feller took the money and started away; and when he was going out at the door, he sorter jerked his thumb over his shoulder—so—at Dan'l, and says again, very deliberate, 'Well,' he says, '*I* don't see no p'ints about that frog that's any better'n any other frog.'

"Smiley he stood scratching his head and looking down at Dan'l a long time, and at last he says, 'I do wonder what in the nation that frog throw'd off for—I wonder if there ain't something the matter with him—he 'pears to look mighty baggy, somehow.' And he ketched Dan'l by the nap of the neck and hefted him and says, 'Why, blame my cats if he don't weigh five pound!' and turned him upside-down, and he belched out a double

handful of shot. And then he see how it was, and he was the maddest man—he set the frog down and took out after that feller, but he never ketched him. And——"

Here Simon Wheeler heard his name called from the front yard and got up to see what was wanted. And turning to me as he moved away, he said: "Just set where you are, stranger, and rest easy—I ain't going to be gone a second."

But, by your leave, I did not think that a continuation of the history of the enterprising vagabond *Jim* Smiley would be likely to afford me much information concerning the Reverend *Leonidas W.* Smiley, and so I started away.

At the door I met the sociable Wheeler returning, and he buttonholed me and recommenced: "Well, thish-yer Smiley had a yaller one-eyed cow that didn't have no tail, only a short stump like a bannanner, and——"

However, lacking both time and inclination, I did not wait to hear about the afflicted cow, but took my leave.

The Celebrated Jumping Frog of Calaveras County   521

SEEKING MEANING

1. In this story, Twain presents two different characters. One is the stiff and humorless narrator, the "I" in the first paragraph. The other is the old storyteller, Simon Wheeler. How does the stiff and humorless narrator become cornered by Simon Wheeler? How does this narrator describe Simon Wheeler?

2. Someone has probably played a joke on the narrator by asking him to call on Simon Wheeler. Where do you learn that Simon Wheeler's yarn doesn't seem funny to the narrator at all? Do you think that Simon Wheeler is also playing a joke on this narrator? Explain your answer.

3. Mark Twain once said that a humorous tale may be spun out at great length, wander about as much as it pleases, and arrive nowhere in particular. He said that the tale should be told gravely, as if the teller does not even dimly suspect that there is anything funny about it. How does Simon Wheeler show he is a master tale-spinner?

4. Find the passage in which Simon Wheeler goes on and on giving examples to show that Jim Smiley was a betting man. How many examples does he give? Which ones do you think are the funniest?

5. According to Wheeler's tale, how did the stranger outsmart Smiley?

DEVELOPING SKILLS OF EXPRESSION

Making an Oral Presentation

Mark Twain used to travel around the country, giving public readings of his works. His humor made him a popular favorite as a lecturer. Many years after Twain's death, the actor Hal Holbrook developed a one-man show in which he impersonated Twain giving his public readings. Holbrook was so convincing that the audience could easily imagine that they were actually watching Twain himself.

Suppose you were to deliver this humorous tale aloud for a public reading. One of your major problems would be to distinguish between the stuffy and humorless narrator, and the lovable old yarn-spinner, Simon Wheeler. How would you speak the narrator's part, which is that of a "straight man"? How would you change your delivery when you are speaking Simon Wheeler's part? For example, how would you deliver Wheeler's stretched-out word *m-o-r-e* on page 519?

A superstitious schoolmaster, a rich and pretty girl, a bold practical joker, and a mysterious headless horseman are the main characters in this famous American ghost story.

The Legend of Sleepy Hollow
Washington Irving

In the bosom of one of those spacious coves which indent the eastern shore of the Hudson, there lies a small market town, which by some is called Greensburgh, but which is more generally and properly known by the name of Tarrytown. This name was given by the good housewives of the adjacent country, from the tendency of their husbands to linger about the village tavern on market days. Not far from this village, perhaps about two miles, there is a little valley among high hills, which is one of the quietest places in the whole world. A small brook glides through it, with just murmur enough to lull one to repose, and the occasional whistle of a quail, or tapping of a woodpecker, is almost the only sound that ever breaks in upon the uniform tranquillity.[1]

From the listless repose of the place, and the peculiar character of its inhabitants, who are descendants from the original Dutch settlers, this glen has long been known by the name of Sleepy Hollow, and its lads are called the Sleepy Hollow Boys throughout all the neighboring country. A drowsy, dreamy influence seems to hang over the land. The whole neighborhood abounds with local tales, haunted spots, and twilight superstitions; and the nightmare seems to make it the favorite scene of her gambols.[2]

The dominant spirit, however, that haunts this enchanted region, and seems to be commander in chief of all the powers of the air, is the apparition of a figure on horseback without a head. It is said by some to be the ghost of a Hessian trooper[3] whose head had been carried away by a cannonball, in some nameless battle during the Revolutionary War, and who is ever and anon[4] seen by the country folk, hurrying along in the gloom of night, as if on the wings of the wind. His haunts are not confined to the valley, but extend at times to the adjacent roads, and especially to the vicinity of a church at no great distance. Certain historians of those parts claim that the body of the trooper having been buried in the churchyard, the ghost rides forth to the scene of battle in

---

1. **tranquillity** (trăn-kwĭl′ə-tē): peace and quiet.

2. **the nightmare . . . gambols:** People used to believe that nightmares were caused by an evil spirit, who often suffocated people while they slept. This spirit's gambols are frolics or "playful" activities.
3. **Hessian** (hĕsh′ən) **trooper:** a German soldier. German soldiers were hired by the British to fight the Americans during the Revolutionary War.
4. **ever and anon:** again and again; repeatedly.

nightly quest of his head; and that the rushing speed with which he sometimes passes along the Hollow, like a midnight blast, is owing to his being late, and in a hurry to get back to the churchyard before daybreak. The specter[5] is known, at all the country firesides, by the name of the Headless Horseman of Sleepy Hollow.

In this by-place of nature, there abode, some thirty years since,[6] a worthy fellow of the name of Ichabod Crane, who sojourned, or, as he expressed it, "tarried," in Sleepy Hollow, for the purpose of instructing the children of the vicinity. The name of Crane was not inapplicable to his person. He was tall, but exceedingly lank, with narrow shoulders, long arms and legs, hands that dangled a mile out of his sleeves, feet that might have served for shovels, and his whole frame most loosely hung together. His head was small, and flat at top, with huge ears, large green glassy eyes, and a long snipe nose,[7] so that it looked like a weathercock, perched upon his spindle neck, to tell which way the wind blew. To see him striding along the profile of a hill on a windy day, with his clothes bagging and fluttering about him, one might have mistaken him for the spirit of famine descending upon the earth, or some scarecrow eloped from a cornfield.

His schoolhouse was a low building of one large room, rudely constructed of logs; the windows partly glazed,[8] and partly patched with leaves of old copybooks. It stood in a rather lonely but pleasant situation, just at the foot of a woody hill, with a brook running close by, and a formidable birch tree growing at one end of it. From here the low murmur of his pupils' voices, conning over[9] their lessons, might be heard in a drowsy summer's day, like the hum of a beehive; interrupted now and then by the authoritative voice of the master, in the tone of menace or command; or, perhaps, by the appalling sound of the birch,[10] as he urged some tardy loiterer[11] along the flowery path of knowledge. Truth to say, he was a conscientious man, and ever bore in mind the golden maxim,[12] "Spare the rod and spoil the child."—Ichabod Crane's scholars certainly were not spoiled.

---

5. **specter:** ghost.
6. **abode . . . since:** lived or resided about thirty years ago. This story was written around 1820.
7. **snipe nose:** a nose resembling the long, slender bill of the snipe, a kind of bird.
8. **glazed:** fitted with glass.

9. **conning over:** memorizing.
10. **birch:** a stick or rod from a birch tree, used to punish pupils.
11. **tardy loiterer:** in other words, a slow learner.
12. **maxim** (măk'sĭm): a rule of conduct.

I would not have it imagined, however, that he was one of those cruel tyrants of the school who joy in the smart[13] of their subjects. On the contrary, he administered justice with discrimination[14] rather than severity, taking the burden off the backs of the weak and laying it on those of the strong. Your mere puny stripling[15] that winced at the least flourish of the rod was passed by. The claims of justice were satisfied by inflicting a double portion on some little, tough, wrongheaded Dutch urchin, who sulked and swelled and grew dogged[16] and sullen beneath the birch. All this he called "doing his duty by their parents," and he never inflicted a chastisement without following it by the assurance, so consoling to the smarting urchin, that "he would remember it, and thank him for it, the longest day he had to live."

When school hours were over, he was even the companion and playmate of the larger boys; and on holiday afternoons would convoy some of the smaller ones home who happened to have pretty sisters, or good housewives for mothers, noted for the comforts of the cupboard. Indeed it behooved him to keep on good terms with his pupils. The revenue arising from his school was small, and would have been scarcely sufficient to furnish him with daily bread, for he was a huge feeder. To help out his maintenance, he was, according to country custom in those parts, boarded and lodged at the houses of the farmers whose children he instructed. With these he lived successively a week at a time, thus going the rounds of the neighborhood, with all his worldly effects tied up in a cotton handkerchief.

That all this might not be too hard on the purses of his patrons, who are apt to consider the costs of schooling a grievous burden, and schoolmasters as mere drones, he had varied ways of rendering himself both useful and agreeable. He assisted the farmers occasionally in the lighter labors of their farms; helped to make hay; mended the fences; took the horses to water; drove the cows from pasture; and cut wood for the winter fire. He found favor in the eyes of the mothers by petting the children, particularly the youngest. He would sit with a child on one knee, and rock a cradle with his foot for whole hours together.

In addition to his other vocations, he was the singing master of the neighborhood, and picked up many bright shillings[17] by instructing the young folks in psalmody.[18] It was a matter of no little vanity to him, on Sundays, to take his station in front of the church gallery, with a band of chosen singers, where, in his own mind, he completely carried away the palm from the parson.[19] Certain it is, his voice resounded far above all the rest of the congregation; and there are peculiar quavers still to be heard in that church, and even half a mile off, quite to the opposite side of the millpond, on a still Sunday morning, which are said to be descended from the nose of Ichabod Crane. Thus, by various little makeshifts, the worthy pedagogue[20] got on tolerably enough, and was thought, by all who understood nothing of the labor of headwork, to have a wonderfully easy life of it.

---

13. **smart:** pain.
14. **discrimination** (dĭs-krĭm'ə-nā'shən): here, good judgment.
15. **stripling:** youth.
16. **dogged** (dô'gĭd): stubborn.

17. **shillings:** coins worth one twentieth of a pound, which is the basic unit of British money. Pounds and shillings were used for a time in America.
18. **psalmody** (säm'ə-dē): psalm singing.
19. **carried away . . . the parson:** in other words, took the triumph away from the parson. (The palm leaf is a symbol of triumph or victory.)
20. **pedagogue** (pĕd'ə-gŏg'): schoolteacher.

The schoolmaster is generally a man of some importance in the female circle of a rural neighborhood, being considered of vastly superior taste and accomplishments to the rough country swains,[21] and, indeed, inferior in learning only to the parson. Our man of letters, therefore, was peculiarly happy in the smiles of all the country damsels. How he would figure among them in the churchyard, between services on Sundays, gathering grapes for them from the wild vines that overran the surrounding trees; reciting for their amusement all the epitaphs on the tombstones; or sauntering, with a whole bevy[22] of them, along the banks of the adjacent millpond; while the more bashful country bumpkins hung sheepishly back, envying his superior elegance and address.[23]

From his half-itinerant life, also, he was a kind of traveling gazette,[24] carrying the whole store of local gossip from house to house, so that his appearance was always greeted with satisfaction. He was, moreover, esteemed by the women as a man of great learning, for he had read several books quite through, and was a perfect master of Cotton Mather's *History of New England Witchcraft*,[25] in which, by the way, he most firmly believed.

He was, in fact, an odd mixture of small shrewdness and simple credulity.[26] His appetite for the marvelous, and his powers of digesting it, were equally extraordinary; and both had been increased by his residence in this spellbound region. It was often his delight, after his school was dismissed in the afternoon, to stretch himself on the rich bed of clover bordering the little brook that whimpered by his schoolhouse, and there con over old Mather's direful tales, until the gathering dusk of the evening made the printed page a mere mist before his eyes. Then, as he took his way, by swamp and stream and awful[27] woodland, to the farmhouse where he happened to be quartered, every sound of nature, at that witching hour, fluttered his excited imagination: the moan of the whippoorwill from the hillside; the boding cry of the tree toad; the dreary hooting of the screech owl; or the sudden rustling in the thicket of birds frightened from their roost. His only resource on such occasions, either to drown thought, or drive away evil spirits, was to sing psalm tunes; and the good people of Sleepy Hollow, as they sat by their doors of an evening, were often filled with awe, at hearing his nasal melody, floating from the distant hill, or along the dusky road.

Another of his sources of fearful pleasure was to pass long winter evenings with the old Dutch wives, as they sat spinning by the fire, with a row of apples roasting and spluttering along the hearth, and listen to their marvelous tales of ghosts and goblins, and haunted fields, and haunted brooks, and haunted bridges, and haunted houses, and particularly of the headless horseman, or Galloping Hessian of the Hollow, as they sometimes called him. He would delight them equally by his anecdotes of witchcraft, and would frighten them woefully with speculations upon

---

21. **swains:** young men.
22. **bevy** (běv′ē): group.
23. **address:** here, manner of speaking.
24. **gazette:** newspaper.
25. **Cotton Mather . . . Witchcraft:** Cotton Mather (1663–1728), a famous preacher and scholar in colonial New England, wrote several books on witchcraft. However, no book with this title actually exists.
26. **credulity** (krĭ-dōō′lə-tē): readiness to believe.

27. **awful:** here, awe-inspiring.

comets and shooting stars, and with the alarming fact that the world did absolutely turn round, and that they were half the time topsy-turvy!

But if there was a pleasure in all this, while snugly cuddling in the chimney corner of a chamber that was all of a ruddy glow from the crackling wood fire, and where, of course, no specter dared to show his face, it was dearly purchased by the terrors of his walk homewards later. What fearful shapes and shadows beset his path amidst the dim and ghastly glare of a snowy night! — How often was he appalled by some shrub covered with snow, which, like a sheeted specter, beset his very path! — How often did he shrink with curdling awe at the sound of his own steps on the frosty crust beneath his feet, and dread to look over his shoulder, lest he should behold some uncouth being tramping close behind him! — And how often was he thrown into complete dismay by some rushing blast, howling among the trees, in the idea that it was the Galloping Hessian on one of his nightly scourings![28]

All these, however, were mere terrors of the night, phantoms of the mind that walk in darkness; and though he had seen many specters in his time, yet daylight put an end to all these evils. He would have passed a pleasant life of it, if his path had not been crossed by a being that causes more perplexity to mortal man than ghosts, goblins, and the whole race of witches put together, and that was — a woman.

Among the musical disciples who assembled, one evening in each week, to receive his instructions in psalmody was Katrina Van Tassel, the daughter and only child of a prosperous Dutch farmer. She was a blooming lass of fresh eighteen; plump as a partridge; ripe and melting and rosy-cheeked as one of her father's peaches; and universally famed, not merely as a beauty, but as an heiress. She was a little of a coquette,[29] as might be perceived even in her dress, which was a mixture of ancient and modern fashions, as most suited to set off her charms. She wore the ornaments of pure yellow gold which her great-great-grandmother had brought over from Holland; the tempting stomacher[30] of the olden time; and a provokingly short petticoat, to display the prettiest foot and ankle in the country round.

---

28. **scourings:** rides in search of something.

29. **coquette** (kō-kĕt′): a flirt.
30. **stomacher:** a fancy triangular piece of cloth, going around the waist and hanging over the stomach.

Ichabod Crane had a soft and foolish heart towards the sex; and it is not to be wondered at that so tempting a morsel soon found favor in his eyes, more especially after he had visited her in her paternal mansion. Old Baltus Van Tassel was a perfect picture of a thriving, contented, liberal-hearted farmer. He was satisfied with his wealth, but not proud of it, and prided himself upon the hearty abundance rather than the style in which he lived. His stronghold was situated on the banks of the Hudson, in one of those green, sheltered, fertile nooks, in which the Dutch farmers are so fond of nestling. A great elm tree spread its broad branches over it, at the foot of which bubbled up a spring of the softest and sweetest water, in a little well formed of a barrel. Close by the farmhouse was a vast barn that might have served for a church, every window and crevice of which seemed bursting forth with the treasures of the farm. Rows of pigeons were enjoying the sunshine on the roof. Sleek, unwieldy porkers were grunting in the repose and abundance of their pens. A stately squadron of snowy geese were riding in an adjoining pond, convoying whole fleets of ducks. Regiments of turkeys were gobbling through the farmyard and guinea fowls fretting about it with their peevish, discontented cry. Before the barn door strutted the gallant cock, clapping his burnished wings, and crowing in the pride and gladness of his heart—sometimes tearing up the earth with his feet, and then generously calling his ever-hungry family of wives and children to enjoy the rich morsel which he had discovered.

The pedagogue's mouth watered as he looked upon this sumptuous promise of luxurious winter fare. In his devouring mind's eye he pictured to himself every roasting-pig running about him with a pudding in his belly, and an apple in his mouth. The pigeons were snugly put to bed in a comfortable pie, and tucked in with a coverlet of crust; the geese were swimming in their own gravy; and the ducks pairing cozily in dishes, with a decent competency[31] of onion sauce. In the porkers he saw carved out the future sleek side of bacon, and juicy, relishing ham; not a turkey but he beheld daintily trussed up, with its gizzard under its wing, and, perhaps, a necklace of savory sausages; and even bright chanticleer[32] himself lay sprawling on his back, in a side dish, with uplifted claws.

As the enraptured Ichabod fancied[33] all this, and as he rolled his great green eyes over the fat meadowlands, the rich fields of wheat, of rye, of buckwheat, and Indian corn, and the orchard burdened with ruddy fruit, which surrounded the warm tenement[34] of Van Tassel, his heart yearned after the damsel who was to inherit these domains.

When he entered the house, the conquest of his heart was complete. It was one of those spacious farmhouses, with high-ridged but lowly sloping roofs, built in the style handed down from the first Dutch settlers, the low, projecting eaves forming a piazza[35] along the front, capable of being closed up in bad weather. Under this were hung flails,[36] harness, various utensils of husbandry,[37] and nets for fishing in the neighboring river. Benches were built along the sides for summer use; and a great spinning wheel at one end, and a churn at the other, showed the various uses to which this important porch might be devoted. From this piazza the wondering Ichabod entered the hall, which formed the center of the mansion and the place of usual residence.

---

31. **decent competency** (kŏm′pə-tən-sē): in other words, a decent amount.
32. **chanticleer** (chăn′tə-klîr′): a rooster.
33. **fancied:** imagined.
34. **tenement:** here, an estate or a dwelling.
35. **piazza** (pē-ăz′ə): a porch.
36. **flails:** tools for threshing grain.
37. **husbandry:** farming.

Here rows of resplendent pewter, ranged on a long dresser,[38] dazzled his eyes. In one corner stood a huge bag of wool ready to be spun; in another a quantity of linsey-woolsey[39] just from the loom; ears of Indian corn and strings of dried apples and peaches hung in gay festoons along the walls, mingled with red peppers; and a door left ajar gave him a peep into the best parlor, where the claw-footed chairs and dark mahogany tables shone like mirrors; and a corner cupboard, knowingly left open, displayed immense treasures of old silver and well-mended china.

From the moment that Ichabod laid his eyes upon these regions of delight, the peace of his mind was at an end, and his only study was how to gain the affections of the peerless[40] daughter of Van Tassel. In this enterprise, however, he had more real difficulties than generally fell to the lot of a knight-errant of yore, who seldom had anything but giants, enchanters, fiery dragons, and such like easily conquered adversaries to contend with. Ichabod, on the contrary, had to win his way to the heart of a country coquette, beset with whims and caprices[41] which were forever presenting new difficulties; and he had to encounter a host of fearful adversaries of real flesh and blood, the numerous admirers who beset every portal to her heart, keeping a watchful and angry eye upon each other, but ready to fly out in the common cause against any new competitor.

Among these the most formidable was a burly, roaring, roistering[42] blade, of the name of Abraham, or, according to the Dutch abbreviation, Brom Van Brunt, the hero of the country round, which rang with his feats of strength and hardihood. He was broad-shouldered and double-jointed, with short, curly

---

38. **dresser:** here, a large cupboard.
39. **linsey-woolsey:** a coarse cloth made from linen and wool, or from cotton and wool.
40. **peerless:** without equal.

41. **caprices** (kə-prēs′īz): sudden changes of heart or mind.
42. **roistering:** given to wild fun.

black hair, and a bluff but not unpleasant countenance, having a mingled air of fun and arrogance. From his Herculean[43] frame and great powers of limb, he had received the nickname of "Brom Bones," by which he was universally known. He was famed for great knowledge and skill in horsemanship. He was foremost at all races and cockfights. He was always ready for either a fight or a frolic, but had more mischief than ill will in his composition; and, with all his overbearing roughness, there was a strong dash of waggish[44] good humor at bottom. He had three or four boon companions,[45] who regarded him as their model, and at the head of whom he scoured the country, attending every scene of feud or merriment for miles round. In cold weather he was distinguished by a fur cap, surmounted with a flaunting[46] fox's tail; and when the folks at a country gathering spied this well-known crest at a distance, whisking about among a squad of hard riders, they always stood by for a squall.[47] Sometimes his crew would be heard dashing along past the farmhouses at midnight, with whoop and halloo; and the old dames, startled out of their sleep, would listen for a moment till the hurry-scurry had clattered by, and then exclaim, "Aye, there goes Brom Bones and his gang!" The neighbors looked upon him with a mixture of awe, admiration, and good will; and when any madcap prank or brawl occurred in the vicinity, always shook their heads, and warranted Brom Bones was at the bottom of it.

This reckless hero had for some time sin-

gled out the blooming Katrina for the object of his gallantries, and it was whispered that she did not altogether discourage his hopes. Certain it is, his advances were signals for rival candidates to retire. When his horse was seen tied to Van Tassel's paling,[48] on a Sunday night, a sure sign that his master was courting or, as it is termed, "sparking," within, all other suitors passed by in despair.

Such was the formidable rival with whom Ichabod Crane had to contend, and, considering all things, a stouter[49] man than he would have shrunk from the competition, and a wiser man would have despaired. He had,

---

43. **Herculean** (hûr′kyə-lē′ən): like Hercules, a hero in Greek mythology noted for his huge physique and his tremendous strength.
44. **waggish:** playful; joking.
45. **boon companions:** close friends who join him in seeking fun.
46. **flaunting:** showy.
47. **squall:** a storm; here, a disturbance.
48. **paling:** fence.
49. **stouter:** here, braver.

however, a happy mixture of pliability and perseverance in his nature.

To have taken the field openly against his rivals would have been madness. Ichabod, therefore, made his advances in a quiet and gently insinuating manner. Under cover of his character of singing master, he made frequent visits at the farmhouse; not that he had anything to fear from the meddlesome interference of parents, which is so often a stumbling block in the path of lovers. Balt Van Tassel was an easy, indulgent soul; he loved his daughter better even than his pipe, and, like a reasonable man and an excellent father, let her have her way in everything. His notable little wife, too, had enough to do to attend to her housekeeping and manage her poultry; for, as she sagely observed, ducks and geese are foolish things, and must be looked after, but girls can take care of themselves. Thus, while the busy dame bustled about the house, or plied her spinning wheel at one end of the piazza, honest Balt would sit smoking his evening pipe at the other. In the meantime, Ichabod would carry on his suit with the daughter by the side of the spring under the great elm, or sauntering along in the twilight—that hour so favorable to the lover's eloquence.

I profess not to know how women's hearts are wooed and won. To me they have always been matters of riddle and admiration. He who wins a thousand common hearts is entitled to some renown; but he who keeps undisputed sway over the heart of a coquette is indeed a hero. Certain it is, this was not the case with the redoubtable[50] Brom Bones. From the moment Ichabod Crane made his advances, the interests of the former evidently declined. His horse was no longer seen tied at the palings on Sunday nights, and a deadly feud gradually arose between him and the schoolmaster of Sleepy Hollow.

Brom, who had a degree of rough chivalry in his nature, would have carried matters to open warfare, and have settled their pretensions[51] to the lady according to the mode of the knights-errant of yore—by single combat; but Ichabod was too conscious of the superior might of his adversary to enter the lists[52] against him. He had overheard a boast of Bones, that he would "double the schoolmaster up, and lay him on a shelf of his own schoolhouse"; and he was too wary to give him an opportunity. There was something extremely provoking in this obstinately pacific[53] system; it left Brom no alternative but to play boorish practical jokes upon his rival. Ichabod became the object of whimsical persecution to Bones and his gang of roughriders. They harried his hitherto peaceful domains; smoked out his singing school, by stopping up the chimney; broke into the schoolhouse at night and turned everything topsy-turvy; so that the poor schoolmaster began to think all the witches in the country held their meetings there. But what was still more annoying, Brom took opportunities of turning him into ridicule in the presence of his mistress, and had a scoundrel dog whom he taught to whine in the most ludicrous manner and introduced as a rival of Ichabod's to instruct her in psalmody.

In this way matters went on for some time, without producing any material effect on the relative situation of the rivals. On a fine autumn afternoon, Ichabod, in pensive mood, sat enthroned on the lofty stool whence he usually watched all the concerns of his little

---

50. **redoubtable** (rĭ-dou′tə-bəl): causing fear and respect.

51. **pretensions:** claims.
52. **the lists:** a staked-out area of combat. Knights used to enter the lists as a competitive sport.
53. **pacific:** peaceful.

literary realm. In his hand he swayed a ferule,[54] that scepter of despotic power,[55] the birch of justice reposed on three nails, behind the throne, a constant terror to evildoers. Apparently there had been some appalling act of justice recently inflicted, for his scholars were all busily intent upon their books, or slyly whispering behind them with one eye kept upon the master; and a kind of buzzing stillness reigned throughout the schoolroom. It was suddenly interrupted by the appearance of a man who came clattering up to the school door with an invitation to Ichabod to attend a merrymaking, or "quilting frolic," to be held that evening at Mynheer[56] Van Tassel's.

All was now bustle and hubbub in the late quiet schoolroom. The scholars were hurried through their lessons, without stopping at trifles; those who were nimble skipped over half with impunity,[57] and those who were tardy had a smart application now and then in the rear, to quicken their speed, or help them over a tall word. Books were flung aside without being put away on the shelves, inkstands were overturned, benches thrown down, and the whole school was turned loose an hour before the usual time, bursting forth like a legion of young imps, yelping and racketing about the green, in joy of their early emancipation.

The gallant Ichabod now spent at least an extra half-hour at his toilet,[58] brushing up his best and indeed only suit of rusty black, and arranging his locks by a bit of broken looking glass that hung up in the schoolhouse. That he might make his appearance before his mistress in the true style of a cavalier,[59] he borrowed a horse from the farmer with whom he was living, a choleric[60] old Dutchman, of the name of Hans Van Ripper, and, thus gallantly mounted, issued forth, like a knight-errant in quest of adventures. But it is proper that I should, in the true spirit of romantic story, give some account of the looks and equipment of my hero and his steed. The animal he bestrode was a broken-down plow horse that had outlived almost everything but his viciousness. He was gaunt and shaggy, with a thin neck and a head like a hammer; his rusty mane and tail were tangled and knotted with burrs; one eye had lost its pupil, and was glaring and spectral; but the other had the gleam of a genuine devil in it. Still, he must have had fire and mettle[61] in his day, if we may judge from the name he bore of Gunpowder. Old and broken-down as he looked, there was more of the lurking devil in him than in any young filly in the country.

Ichabod was a suitable figure for such a steed. He rode with short stirrups, which brought his knees nearly up to the pommel of the saddle; his sharp elbows stuck out like grasshoppers'. He carried his whip perpendicularly in his hand, like a scepter, and, as his horse jogged on, the motion of his arms was not unlike the flapping of a pair of wings. A small wool hat rested on the top of his nose, for so his scanty strip of forehead might be called; and the skirts of his black coat fluttered out almost to the horse's tail. Such was the appearance of Ichabod and his steed as they shambled out of the gate of Hans Van

---

54. **ferule** (fĕr'əl): rod or ruler.
55. **scepter of despotic power:** a staff that symbolized absolute or tyrannical power.
56. **Mynheer** (mīn-hâr'): Dutch for "Mister."
57. **with impunity** (ĭm-pyōo'nə-tē): without fear of punishment.
58. **toilet:** here, the process of dressing up for an occasion.

59. **cavalier** (kăv'ə-lîr'): a knight.
60. **choleric** (kŏl'ə-rĭk): bad-tempered.
61. **mettle:** spirit.

Ripper, and it was altogether such an apparition as is seldom to be met with in broad daylight.

As Ichabod jogged slowly on his way, his eye ranged with delight over the treasures of jolly autumn. On all sides he beheld vast stores of apples: some hanging on the trees; some gathered into baskets and barrels for the market; others heaped up in rich piles for the cider press. Farther on he beheld great fields of Indian corn, with its golden ears peeping from their leafy coverts, and holding out the promise of cakes and hasty pudding; and the yellow pumpkins lying beneath them, turning up their fair round bellies to the sun, and giving ample prospects of the most luxurious of pies. Next he passed the fragrant buckwheat fields, breathing the odor of the beehive, and as he beheld them, soft anticipations stole over his mind of dainty slapjacks, well buttered and garnished with honey by the delicate little dimpled hands of Katrina Van Tassel.

It was toward evening that Ichabod arrived at the castle of the Heer Van Tassel, which he found thronged with the pride and flower of the adjacent country. Old farmers, a spare, leathern-faced race, in homespun coats and breeches, blue stockings, huge shoes, and magnificent pewter buckles. Their brisk, withered little dames, in close-crimped caps, long-waisted gowns, homespun petticoats, with scissors and pincushions and gay calico pockets hanging on the outside. Buxom lasses, almost as old-fashioned as their mothers, except for a straw hat, a fine ribbon, or perhaps a white frock. The sons, in short square-skirted coats with rows of stupendous brass buttons, and their hair generally queued[62] in the fashion of the times.

Brom Bones, however, was a hero of the scene, having come to the gathering on his favorite steed, Daredevil, a creature, like him-

---

62. **queued** (kyo̅o̅d): gathered in a pigtail.

self, full of mettle and mischief, which no one but himself could manage. He held a tractable,[63] well-broken horse as unworthy of a lad of spirit.

I pause to dwell upon the world of charms that burst upon the enraptured gaze of my hero as he entered the state parlor of Van Tassel's mansion. Not those of the bevy of buxom lasses, with their luxurious display of red and white; but the ample charms of a genuine Dutch country tea table, in the sumptuous time of autumn. Such heaped-up platters of cakes of various and almost indescribable kinds, known only to experienced Dutch housewives! There was the doughty[64] doughnut, the tenderer olykoek,[65] and the crisp and crumbling cruller; sweet cakes and short-cakes, ginger cakes and honey cakes, and the whole family of cakes. And then there were apple pies and peach pies and pumpkin pies; besides slices of ham and smoked beef; and moreover delectable dishes of preserved plums, and peaches, and pears, and quinces, not to mention broiled shad and roasted chickens; together with bowls of milk and cream; all mingled higgledy-piggledy, pretty much as I have enumerated them, with the motherly teapot sending up its clouds of vapor from the midst.

I want breath and time to discuss this banquet as it deserves, and am too eager to get on with my story. Happily, Ichabod Crane was not in so great a hurry as his historian, but did ample justice to every dainty.

He was a kind and thankful creature, whose heart dilated in proportion as his skin was filled with good cheer, and whose spirits rose with eating as some men's do with drink. He could not help, too, rolling his large eyes round him as he ate, and chuckling with the possibility that he might one day be lord of all this scene of almost unimaginable luxury and splendor. Then, he thought, how soon he'd turn his back upon the old schoolhouse, snap his fingers in the face of Hans Van Ripper and every other niggardly[66] patron, and kick any itinerant pedagogue out-of-doors that should dare to call him comrade!

Old Baltus Van Tassel moved about among his guests with a face dilated with content and good humor, round and jolly as the harvest moon. His hospitable attentions were brief, but expressive, being confined to a shake of the hand, a slap on the shoulder, a loud laugh, and a pressing invitation to fall to and help themselves.

And now the sound of the music from the common room, or hall, summoned to the dance. Ichabod prided himself upon his dancing as much as upon his vocal powers. Not a limb, not a fiber about him was idle; and to have seen his loosely hung frame in full motion, and clattering about the room, you would have thought Saint Vitus himself, that blessed patron of the dance,[67] was figuring before you in person. How could the flogger of urchins be otherwise than animated and joyous? The lady of his heart was his partner in the dance, and smiling graciously in reply to all his amorous looks, while Brom Bones, sorely smitten with love and jealousy, sat brooding by himself in one corner.

When the dance was at an end, Ichabod was attracted to a knot of the sager folks, who, with old Van Tassel, sat smoking at one end of the piazza, gossiping over former times,

---

63. **tractable** (trăk′tə-bəl): easily managed.
64. **doughty** (dou′tē): brave.
65. **olykoek** (äl′ə-kook′): a type of doughnut.

66. **niggardly:** stingy.
67. **Saint Vitus** (vī′təs) . . . **dance:** a reference to Saint Vitus' dance, a disease that causes sudden jerking movements.

and drawing out long stories about the war. But all these were nothing to the tales of ghosts and apparitions that succeeded. The neighborhood is rich in legendary treasures of the kind. The immediate cause of the prevalence of supernatural stories in these parts was doubtless owing to the vicinity of Sleepy Hollow. There was a contagion in the very air that blew from that haunted region; it breathed forth an atmosphere of dreams and fancies infecting all the land. Several of the Sleepy Hollow people were present at Van Tassel's, and, as usual, were doling out their wild and wonderful legends. Many dismal tales were told about funeral trains and mourning cries and wailings heard and seen about the great tree where the unfortunate Major André[68] was taken, and which stood in the neighborhood. Some mention was made also of the woman in white that haunted the dark glen at Raven Rock, and was often heard to shriek on winter nights before a storm, having perished there in the snow. The chief part of the stories, however, turned upon the favorite specter of Sleepy Hollow, the headless horseman, who had been heard several times of late, patrolling the country, and, it was said, tethered his horse nightly among the graves in the churchyard.

The lonely situation of this church seems always to have made it a favorite haunt of troubled spirits. It stands on a knoll, surrounded by locust trees and lofty elms, from among which its decent whitewashed walls shine modestly forth. A gentle slope descends from it to a silver sheet of water, bordered by high trees. To look upon its grass-grown yard, where the sunbeams seem to sleep so quietly, one would think that there at least the dead might rest in peace. On one side of the church extends a wide woody dell, along which pours a large brook among broken rocks and trunks of fallen trees. Over a deep black part of the stream, not far from the church, was formerly thrown a wooden bridge. The road that led to it, and the bridge itself, were thickly shaded by overhanging trees, which cast a gloom about it, even in the daytime, but caused a fearful darkness at night. This was one of the favorite haunts of the headless horseman, and the place where he was most frequently encountered. The tale was told of old Brouwer, a most heretical[69] disbeliever in ghosts, how he met the horseman returning from his foray into Sleepy Hollow, and was obliged to get up behind him; how they galloped over bush and brake,[70] over hill and swamp, until they reached the bridge, when the horseman suddenly turned into a skeleton, threw old Brouwer into a brook, and sprang away over the treetops with a clap of thunder.

This story was immediately matched by a thrice-marvelous adventure of Brom Bones, who made light of the Galloping Hessian as an arrant[71] jockey. He affirmed that, on returning one night from the neighboring village of Sing Sing, he had been overtaken by this midnight trooper; that he had offered to race with him for a bowl of punch, and should have won it, too, for Daredevil beat the goblin horse all hollow, but, just as they came to the church bridge, the Hessian bolted, and vanished in a flash of fire.

All these tales, told in that drowsy undertone with which men talk in the dark, the countenance of the listeners only now and then receiving a casual gleam from the glare of a pipe, sank deep in the mind of Ichabod.

---

68. **Major André:** a British officer during the Revolutionary War, hanged as a spy in 1780.

69. **heretical** (hə-rĕt′ĭ-kəl): holding an opinion that is opposed to established belief.
70. **brake:** a thicket or clump of briers.
71. **arrant:** notorious.

He repaid them in kind with large extracts from his invaluable author, Cotton Mather, and added many fearful sights which he had seen in his nightly walks about Sleepy Hollow.

The revel now gradually broke up. The old farmers gathered together their families in their wagons, and were heard for some time rattling along the hollow roads, and over the distant hills. The late scene of noise and frolic was all silent and deserted. Ichabod only lingered behind, according to the custom of country lovers, to have a tête-à-tête[72] with the heiress, fully convinced that he was now on the high road to success. What passed at this interview I will not pretend to say, for in fact I do not know. Something, however, must have gone wrong, for he certainly sallied forth, after no very great interval, with an air quite desolate and chopfallen.[73] — Oh, these women! these women! Could that girl have been playing any of her coquettish tricks? Was her encouragement to the poor pedagogue all a mere sham[74] to secure her conquest of his rival? — Heaven only knows, not I! — Let it suffice to say, Ichabod stole forth with the air of one who had been sacking[75] a hen roost rather than a fair lady's heart. Without looking to the right or left to notice the scene of rural wealth on which he had so often gloated, he went straight to the stable, and with several hearty cuffs and kicks, roused his steed most uncourteously from the comfortable quarters in which he was soundly sleeping, dreaming of mountains of corn and oats, and whole valleys of timothy and clover.

It was the very witching time of night that Ichabod, heavy-hearted and crestfallen, pursued his travel homewards, along the sides of the lofty hills which rise above Tarrytown, and which he had traversed so cheerily in the afternoon. The hour was as dismal as himself. In the dead hush of midnight, he could even hear the barking of the watchdog from the opposite shore of the Hudson; but it was so vague and faint as only to give an idea of his distance from this faithful companion of man. Now and then, too, the long-drawn crowing of a cock would sound far, far off, from some farmhouse away among the hills — but it was like a dreaming sound in his ear. No signs of life occurred near him but occasionally the melancholy chirp of a cricket, or perhaps the guttural twang of a bullfrog, from a neighboring marsh, as if sleeping uncomfortably and turning suddenly in his bed.

All the stories of ghosts and goblins that he had heard in the afternoon now came crowding upon his recollection. The night grew darker and darker; the stars seemed to sink deeper in the sky, and driving clouds occasionally hid them from his sight. He had never felt so lonely and dismal. He was, moreover, approaching the very place where many of the scenes of the ghost stories had been laid. In the center of the road stood an enormous tulip tree, which towered like a giant above all the other trees of the neighborhood, and formed a kind of landmark. Its limbs were gnarled and fantastic, large enough to form trunks for ordinary trees, twisting down almost to the earth, and rising again into the air. It was connected with the tragical story of the unfortunate André, who had been taken prisoner close by, and was universally known by the name of Major André's Tree. The common people regarded it with a mixture of respect and superstition, partly out of sympathy for the fate of its ill-starred namesake, and

---

72. **tête-à-tête** (tāt′ə-tāt′): private talk ("head to head" in French).
73. **chopfallen:** disappointed or humiliated. The word means that the "chop" (the jaw) has "fallen open" in surprised disappointment.
74. **sham:** a pretense.
75. **sacking:** robbing.

partly from the tales of strange sights and doleful lamentations told concerning it.

As Ichabod approached this fearful tree, he began to whistle; he thought his whistle was answered—it was but a blast sweeping sharply through the dry branches. As he approached a little nearer, he thought he saw something white, hanging in the midst of the tree—he paused and ceased whistling, but on looking more closely perceived that it was a place where the tree had been struck by lightning, and the white wood laid bare. Suddenly he heard a groan—his teeth chattered and his knees smote against his saddle; it was but the rubbing of one huge bough upon another as they were swayed about by the breeze. He passed the tree in safety; but new perils lay before him.

About two hundred yards from the tree a small brook crossed the road, and ran into a marshy and thickly wooded glen, known by the name of Wiley's Swamp. A few rough logs, laid side by side, served for a bridge over this stream. On that side of the road where the brook entered the wood, a group of oaks and chestnuts, matted thick with wild grapevines, threw a cavernous gloom over it. To pass this bridge was the severest trial. It was at this identical spot that the unfortunate André was captured, and under cover of those chestnuts and vines were the sturdy yeomen[76] concealed who surprised him. This has ever since been considered a haunted stream, and fearful are the feelings of the schoolboy who has to pass it alone after dark.

As he approached the stream his heart began to thump. He summoned up, however, all his resolution, gave his horse half a score of kicks in the ribs, and attempted to dash briskly across the bridge. But instead of starting forward, the perverse old animal made a lateral movement, and ran broadside against the fence. Ichabod, whose fears increased with the delay, jerked the reins on the other side and kicked lustily with the opposite foot. It was all in vain. His steed started, it is true, but it was only to plunge to the opposite side of the road into a thicket of brambles and alder bushes. The schoolmaster now bestowed both whip and heel upon the starveling ribs of old Gunpowder, who dashed forward, snuffing and snorting, but came to a stand just by the bridge, with a suddenness that had nearly sent his rider sprawling over his head. Just at this moment a splashing step by the side of the bridge caught the sensitive ear of Ichabod. In the dark shadow of the grove, on the margin of the brook, he beheld something huge, misshapen, black, and towering. It stirred not, but seemed gathered up in the gloom, like some gigantic monster ready to spring upon the traveler.

The hair of the affrighted pedagogue rose upon his head with terror. What was to be done? To turn and fly was now too late; and besides, what chance was there of escaping ghost or goblin, if such it was, which could ride upon the wings of the wind? Summoning up, therefore, a show of courage, he demanded in stammering accents, "Who are you?" He received no reply. He repeated his demand in a still more agitated voice. Still there was no answer. Once more he cudgeled the sides of the inflexible Gunpowder, and, shutting his eyes, broke forth with involuntary fervor into a psalm tune. Just then the shadowy object of alarm put itself in motion, and, with a scramble and a bound, stood at once in the middle of the road. Though the night was dark and dismal, yet the form of the unknown might now in some degree be made out. He appeared to be a horseman of large dimensions, and mounted on a black horse of powerful frame. He made no offer of harm or sociability, but

---

76. **yeomen** (yō'mən): here, farmers.

kept aloof on one side of the road, jogging along on the blind side of old Gunpowder, who had now got over his fright and waywardness.

Ichabod, who had no relish for this strange midnight companion, and bethought himself of the adventure of Brom Bones with the Galloping Hessian, now quickened his steed, in hopes of leaving him behind. The stranger, however, quickened his horse to an equal pace. Ichabod pulled up and fell into a walk, thinking to lag behind—the other did the same. His heart began to sink within him. He endeavored to resume his psalm tune, but his parched tongue clove[77] to the roof of his mouth, and he could not utter a stave.[78] There was something in the moody and dogged silence of this persistent companion that was mysterious and appalling. It was soon fearfully accounted for. On mounting a rising ground, which brought the figure of his fellow traveler in relief against the sky, gigantic in height, and muffled in a cloak, Ichabod was horror-struck on perceiving that he was headless—but his horror was still more increased on observing that the head, which should have rested on his shoulders, was carried before him on the pommel of the saddle. His terror rose to desperation. He rained a shower of kicks and blows upon Gunpowder, hoping, by a sudden movement, to give his companion the slip—but the specter started full jump with him. Away then they dashed through thick and thin, stones flying and sparks flashing at every bound. Ichabod's

---

77. **clove:** stuck.
78. **stave:** a stanza of music.

flimsy garments fluttered in the air as he stretched his long lank body away over his horse's head in the eagerness of his flight.

They had now reached the road which turns off to Sleepy Hollow; but Gunpowder, who seemed possessed with a demon, instead of keeping on it, made an opposite turn, and plunged headlong downhill to the left. This road leads through a sandy hollow, shaded by trees for about a quarter of a mile, where it crosses the bridge famous in goblin story, and just beyond swells the green knoll on which stands the whitewashed church.

As yet the panic of the steed had given his unskillful rider an apparent advantage in the chase; but just as he had got halfway through the hollow the girths of the saddle gave way, and he felt it slipping from under him. He seized it by the pommel, and endeavored to

hold it firm, but in vain; and he had just time to save himself by clasping old Gunpowder round the neck, when the saddle fell to the earth, and he heard it trampled underfoot by his pursuer. For a moment the terror of Hans Van Ripper's wrath passed across his mind — for it was his Sunday saddle; but this was no time for petty fears. The goblin was hard on his haunches; and (unskillful rider that he was!) he had much ado to maintain his seat, sometimes slipping on one side, sometimes on another, and sometimes jolted on the high ridge of his horse's backbone, with a violence that he feared would cleave him asunder.[79]

An opening in the trees now cheered him with the hopes that the church bridge was at hand. He saw the walls of the church dimly glaring under the trees beyond. He recollected the place where Brom Bones's ghostly competitor had disappeared. "If I can but reach that bridge," thought Ichabod, "I am safe." Just then he heard the black steed panting and blowing close behind him; he even fancied that he felt his hot breath. Another convulsive kick in the ribs, and old Gunpowder sprang upon the bridge; he thundered over the resounding planks; he gained the opposite side; and now Ichabod cast a look behind to see if his pursuer would vanish, according to the rule, in a flash of fire and brimstone. Just then he saw the goblin rising in his stirrups, and in the very act of hurling his head at him. Ichabod endeavored to dodge the horrible missile, but too late. It encountered his cranium with a tremendous crash — he was tumbled headlong into the dust, and Gunpowder, the black steed, and the goblin rider passed by like a whirlwind.

The next morning the old horse was found without his saddle, and with the bridle under

---

79. **cleave him asunder:** split him in two.

his feet, soberly cropping the grass at his master's gate. Ichabod did not make his appearance at breakfast—dinner hour came, but no Ichabod. The boys assembled at the schoolhouse, and strolled idly about the banks of the brook, but no schoolmaster. Hans Van Ripper now began to feel some uneasiness about the fate of poor Ichabod and his saddle. An inquiry was set on foot, and after diligent investigation they came upon his traces. In one part of the road leading to the church was found the saddle trampled in the dirt. The tracks of horses' hoofs deeply dented in the road, and evidently at furious speed, were traced to the bridge, beyond which, on the bank of a broad part of the brook, where the water ran deep and black, was found the hat of the unfortunate Ichabod, and close beside it a shattered pumpkin.

The brook was searched, but the body of the schoolmaster was not to be discovered. The mysterious event caused much speculation at the church on the following Sunday. Knots of gazers and gossips were collected in the churchyard, at the bridge, and at the spot where the hat and pumpkin had been found. The stories of Brouwer, of Bones, and a whole store of others, were called to mind; and when they had diligently considered them all, and compared them with the symptoms of the present case, they shook their heads, and came to the conclusion that Ichabod had been carried off by the Galloping Hessian. As he was a bachelor, and in nobody's debt, nobody troubled his head any more about him. The school was removed to a different quarter of the Hollow, and another pedagogue reigned in his stead.

It is true, an old farmer, who had been down to New York on a visit several years after, and from whom this account of the ghostly adventure was received, brought home word that Ichabod Crane was still alive; that he had left the neighborhood, partly through fear of the goblin and Hans Van Ripper and partly in mortification at having been suddenly dismissed by the heiress; that he had changed his quarters to a distant part of the country; had kept school and studied law at the same time, had been admitted to the bar, turned politician, electioneered, written for the newspapers, and finally had been made a justice of the Ten Pound Court.[80] Brom Bones, too, who shortly after his rival's disappearance conducted the blooming Katrina in triumph to the altar, was observed to look exceedingly knowing whenever the story of Ichabod was related, and always burst into a hearty laugh at the mention of the pumpkin, which led some to suspect that he knew more about the matter than he chose to tell.

The old country wives, however, who are the best judges of these matters, maintain to this day that Ichabod was spirited away by supernatural means; and it is a favorite story often told about the neighborhood round the winter-evening fire. The bridge became more than ever an object of superstitious awe, and that may be the reason why the road has been altered of late years, so as to approach the church by the border of the millpond. The schoolhouse, being deserted, soon fell to decay, and was reported to be haunted by the ghost of the unfortunate pedagogue; and the plowboy, loitering homeward of a still summer evening, has often fancied his voice at a distance, chanting a melancholy psalm tune among the tranquil solitudes[81] of Sleepy Hollow.

---

80. **Ten Pound Court:** a court that could try only minor cases and impose fines up to ten pounds.
81. **solitudes:** here, deserted places.

SEEKING MEANING

1. This legend is set in the Hudson Valley, in a place that is still called Sleepy Hollow. According to the storyteller, what is unusual about Sleepy Hollow and the people who live there?

2. The central character in this legend, Ichabod Crane, is introduced on page 524. Why is "Crane" a good name for him?

3. Reread the paragraph describing Ichabod's schoolhouse (page 524). How does it contrast with the Van Tassel dwelling?

4. The rich and pretty Katrina Van Tassel finds special favor with this lean and hungry hero. How does Ichabod go about wooing his lady fair? What do you think Katrina really thinks of him?

5. How does Ichabod contrast with Brom Bones? How does Ichabod's horse, Gunpowder, contrast with Bones's horse?

6. What does Brom Bones think of his rival? How does Brom Bones finally get rid of Ichabod?

7. According to the last paragraph, how is Ichabod Crane, who used to love to scare himself with ghost stories, still remembered by the country wives in Sleepy Hollow?

8. The old farmer, however, has another version of what became of Ichabod. According to his story, how did Ichabod prove that if you fail in one quest, you can always go on to find some success in another one?

DEVELOPING VOCABULARY

Using Context Clues

Suppose you do not know the meaning of the word *apparition* in this sentence. Context clues will help.

The dominant spirit, however, that haunts this enchanted region, and seems to be commander in chief of all the powers of the air, is the *apparition* of a figure on horseback without a head.

The context tells us that the apparition is a "spirit," and that its work appears to be "haunting." The sentence also tells us that this apparition is of a "figure on horseback without a head." These context clues seem to indicate that an *apparition*, in this sentence, is a kind of ghost. Check in your dictionary to see how the word is defined there.

Use context clues to figure out the meaning of each word in italics in the following sentences. Check your answers in a dictionary.

A small brook glides through it, with just murmur enough to lull one to *repose* . . . .

He made no offer of harm or sociability, but kept *aloof*, on one side of the road . . . .

But instead of starting forward, the perverse old animal made a *lateral* movement, and ran broadside against the fence.

ABOUT THE AUTHOR

Washington Irving (1783–1859) was the first major literary figure in America. He was a trained lawyer, but he hated the drudgery of business and always wanted to write. "The Legend of Sleepy Hollow" appeared in a collection called *The Sketch Book*, which also included "Rip Van Winkle," the story of the man who slept for twenty years. With the publication of *The Sketch Book*, Irving proved to the British that a writer of worth *could* come from their former colonies. Eventually, Irving settled in Tarrytown. There he built a remarkable house called "Sunnyside," which is now a museum.

Practice in Reading and Writing

WRITING BOOK REPORTS

When you are assigned to write a book report, you should ask yourself the following questions:

1. *What kind of book is it?*

If fiction, is the book a mystery, a romance, or an adventure story? Or is it about the problems of everyday life? If nonfiction, is the book a biography, an autobiography, a journal, or a diary? Or is it a book on history, science, or sports?

2. *What is the book about?*

If you are reporting on a novel, tell when and where the story is set and who the main characters are. Then tell, briefly, what the conflict (or problem) is and how it is resolved. If you are reporting on a nonfiction book, summarize its subject and note the most important events or people it tells about.

3. *What did you think of the book?*

Did you like it or dislike it? Why did you feel this way? Would you be interested in reading other books on the same topic, or other books by the same author?

Here is a sample of a book report on *The Diary of a Young Girl* by Anne Frank.

> *The Diary of a Young Girl* is an actual diary that was kept by Anne Frank, a Jewish girl living in Amsterdam during World War II. It begins on June 14, 1942, and ends on August 1, 1944. A few months after the diary ends, Anne died in a concentration camp.
>
> The book is about Anne's life in a secret hiding place in a warehouse, where her family fled to escape the Nazis. Some entries tell how the people quarrel and how Anne's father tries to keep her spirits up. Another interesting part of the diary tells about the love between Anne and Peter, a boy near her age, whose family is hiding in the warehouse too. In many entries Anne tells of her dreams for the future. Some of the important people in the diary, besides Anne and Peter, are her father, her mother, and her older sister, Margot.
>
> I thought the book was very sad, yet I am glad I read it. I believe that Anne's thoughts and feelings can be understood by every young person. Anne's diary is a book I will never

forget, because it tells about a young girl who had to face tragic things but who kept her spirits high.

Read a book from one of the reading lists in this book or from a list recommended by your teacher. Write a book report of three paragraphs. Organize the report around your answers to the three questions listed here.

For Further Reading

Arnott, Kathleen, *African Myths and Legends* (Walck, 1963)

Among these thirty-four tales from different parts of Africa are stories about a mother who frees her children from an elephant's stomach, and a spider who weaves a ladder to the sky.

Asimov, Isaac, *Words from the Myths* (Houghton Mifflin, 1961; paperback, New American Library)

Hypnotize, juvenile, somnambulist and hundreds of other words and phrases come from classical myths. The author explains the origins and briefly retells the myths.

Birch, Cyril, *Chinese Myths and Fantasies* (Walck, 1961)

This author retells strange stories of heroes, ghosts, and demons.

Blair, Walter, *Tall-Tale America: A Legendary History of Our Humorous Heroes* (Coward-McCann & Geoghegan, 1944)

Captain A. B. Stormalong, Windwagon Smith, Joe Magarac, and other fabulous folk heroes populate this collection.

Carmer, Carl, *The Screaming Ghost and Other Stories* (Knopf, 1956)

These twenty-one tales about ghosts and haunted places have been collected from all over America.

Colum, Padraic, *Myths of the World* (paperback, Grosset & Dunlap, 1959)

A superb storyteller narrates some of the world's most fascinating and mysterious myths. The tales come from such people as the ancient Egyptians, the Zuñis in America, the Celts in ancient Ireland, and the islanders of Polynesia.

Coolidge, Olivia E., *Legends of the North* (Houghton Mifflin, 1951)

Among the myths in this collection are stories of how mistletoe killed the young god Baldur and how the troublemaking Loki stole the apples that kept the gods forever young.

Courlander, Harold, editor, *A Treasury of African Folklore* (Crown, 1975)

This is a large collection of myths and folklore from all parts of Africa.

Feldman, Susan, editor, *The Storytelling Stone: Myths and Tales of the American Indians* (paperback, Dell, 1965)

Creation stories, trickster stories, and tales of heroes and supernatural journeys—these great imaginative narratives were handed down orally by the American Indian peoples.

Hazeltine, Alice, editor, *Hero Tales from Many Lands* (Abingdon Press, 1961)

Here are the stories of such great figures as King Arthur, the Blackfoot hero Scarface, the Irish hero Cuchulain, and the Danish monster-slayer Beowulf.

Lang, Andrew, editor, *Arabian Nights* (many editions)

The lovely bride Scheherazade is kept alive by the cruel Sultan (who wants to kill her) because he wants to hear the endings of her fascinating stories. Some of Scheherazade's tales include the stories of Ali Baba and the Forty Thieves, Sinbad the Sailor, and Aladdin and his magic lamp.

Picard, Barbara, *German Hero-Sagas and Folk Tales* (Walck, 1958)

Siegfried, the dragon slayer, and Till Eulenspiegel, the practical joker, are included in this collection of myths and folk tales.

Sutcliff, Rosemary, *Tristan and Iseult* (Dutton, 1971; paperback, Penguin)

The tragic tale of Tristan and Queen Iseult is one of the great love stories of all time.

Reading and Writing About Literature

INTRODUCTION

Many of the compositions you will be asked to write in English class will be about the literature you read. The writing may be in response to an examination question, a homework assignment, or a research project. At times you may be assigned a topic to work on; at other times you may be instructed to choose your own subject.

In writing about literature, you generally focus on some aspect of a work or group of works. For example, you may compare two characters in a story; you may discuss the conflict that is developed in a play; you may analyze the imagery in a poem. Such writing assignments are an important part of literary study, which aims at greater understanding and appreciation of the works you read.

Writing about a literary work brings you closer to it. Before you write a composition about a story, a poem, or a play, you must read and reread the selection carefully. You must sort out your thoughts and reach conclusions. In putting your thoughts down on paper, you become more fully involved with the work.

Throughout your studies you will become familiar with a great many elements that are useful in analyzing literary works. When you refer to the techniques a writer uses to create suspense, for instance, you may use the term *foreshadowing.* In discussing the attitude a writer takes toward a subject, you may concern yourself with *tone.* In examining the musical effects of a poem, you may point to patterns of *rhyme* and *rhythm.* These words are part of a common vocabulary used in writing about literature. You can assume that your readers will understand what you mean when you write about such elements. (See the *Guide to Literary Terms and Techniques,* page 609.)

The material on the following pages offers help in planning and writing papers about literature. Here you will find suggestions for reading and analyzing literature, answering examination questions, choosing topics, gathering evidence, organizing essays, and writing and revising papers. Also included are model essays and several new selections for study along with suggested writing topics.

READING LITERATURE

When you read a chapter in a social studies or science textbook, you read primarily to get the facts. Your purpose may be to understand the principles of American foreign policy stated in the Monroe Doctrine. Or your purpose may be to find out how ocean tides are caused by the gravitational attraction of the moon and sun. You read chiefly to gather information that is stated *directly* on the page.

Reading literature calls for more than understanding what all the words mean and getting the facts straight. Much of the meaning of a literary work may be stated *indirectly*. For example, a writer may not *tell* you directly that a character is frightened. However, by focusing on nervous mannerisms such as broken speech and the wringing of hands, or facial expressions of terror, the writer may *show* you the character's fear. In other words, when you read literature, you depend a good deal on *inference,* drawing conclusions from different kinds of evidence. To read literature critically and grasp its meaning, you have to be an active reader, aware of *what* the author is doing, *how* the author is doing it, and *why.*

When you are asked to write about a literary work, be sure to read it carefully before you begin writing. Read actively, asking yourself questions as you work through the selection.

Close Reading of a Short Story

A short story is made up of certain basic elements: plot (the sequence of related events); characters (persons, animals, or things presented as persons); point of view (the standpoint from which the writer tells the story); setting (the time and place of the action); and theme (the underlying idea about human life). The better you, the individual reader, understand how these elements work together, the better you will understand and appreciate the author's intent and meaning.

Here is a brief story that has been read carefully by an experienced reader. The notes in the margin show how this reader thinks in working through a story. Read the story at least twice before proceeding to the commentary on page 549. You may wish to make notes of your own on a separate sheet of paper as you read.

The Gift   *Ray Bradbury*

Tomorrow would be Christmas, and even while the three of them rode to the rocket port the mother and father were worried. It was the boy's first flight into space, his very first time in a rocket, and they wanted everything to be perfect. So when, at the customs table,[1] they were forced to leave behind his gift, which exceeded the weight limit by no more than a few ounces, and the little tree with the lovely white candles, they felt themselves deprived of the season and their love.

The boy was waiting for them in the Terminal room. Walking toward him, after their unsuccessful clash with the Interplanetary officials, the mother and father whispered to each other.

"What shall we do?"

"Nothing, nothing. What *can* we do?"

"Silly rules!"

"And he so wanted the tree!"

The siren gave a great howl and people pressed forward into the Mars Rocket. The mother and father walked at the very last, their small pale son between them, silent.

"I'll think of something," said the father.

"What . . .?" asked the boy.

And the rocket took off and they were flung headlong into dark space.

The rocket moved and left fire behind and left Earth behind on which the date was December 24, 2052, heading out into a place where there was no time at all, no month, no year, no hour. They slept away the rest of the first "day." Near midnight, by their Earth-time New York watches, the boy awoke and said, "I want to go look out the porthole."

There was only one port, a "window" of immensely thick glass of some size, up on the next deck.

"Not quite yet," said the father. "I'll take you up later."

"I want to see where we are and where we're going."

"I want you to wait for a reason," said the father.

He had been lying awake, turning this way and that, thinking of the abandoned gift, the problem of the season, the lost tree and the white candles. And at last, sitting up, no more than five minutes

---

First clue that this is science fiction. Space travel has become commonplace, even for children.

Opening paragraph brings together the old and the new —Christmas, with its tradition of gift-giving, and transportation by spaceship.

A problem develops when the boy's Christmas gift must be left behind.

How is the author going to make use of this problem in the story?

Why is the tree so important to the boy?

Special equipment for space travel is no longer required.

The concept of Earth time is not relevant in outer space, yet passengers still use their watches to tell time.

Space travelers are no longer troubled by weightlessness; they can move about freely.

---

1. **customs table:** an area in an airport or pier where goods and baggage coming into or leaving a country are inspected and duties are paid.

ago, he believed he had found a plan. He need only carry it out and this journey would be fine and joyous indeed.

"Son," he said, "in exactly one half hour it will be Christmas."

"Oh," said the mother, dismayed that he had mentioned it. Somehow she had rather hoped that the boy would forget.

The boy's face grew feverish and his lips trembled. "I know, I know. Will I get a present, will I? Will I have a tree? Will I have a tree? You promised——"

"Yes, yes, all that, and more," said the father.

The mother started. "But——"

"I mean it," said the father. "I really mean it. All and more, much more. Excuse me, now. I'll be back."

He left them for about twenty minutes. When he came back, he was smiling. "Almost time."

"Can I hold your watch?" asked the boy, and the watch was handed over and he held it ticking in his fingers as the rest of the hour drifted by in fire and silence and unfelt motion.

"It's Christmas *now!* Christmas! Where's my present?"

"Here we go," said the father and took his boy by the shoulder and led him from the room, down the hall, up a rampway, his wife following.

"I don't understand," she kept saying.

"You will. Here we are," said the father.

They had stopped at the closed door of a large cabin. The father tapped three times and then twice in a code. The door opened and the light in the cabin went out and there was a whisper of voices.

"Go on in, son," said the father.

"It's dark."

"I'll hold your hand. Come on, Mama."

They stepped into the room and the door shut, and the room was very dark indeed. And before them loomed a great glass eye, the porthole, a window four feet high and six feet wide, from which they could look out into space.

The boy gasped.

Behind him, the father and the mother gasped with him, and then in the dark room some people began to sing.

"Merry Christmas, son," said the father.

And the voices in the room sang the old, the familiar carols, and the boy moved forward slowly until his face was pressed against the cool glass of the port. And he stood there for a long, long time, just looking and looking out into space and the deep night at the burning and the burning of ten billion billion white and lovely candles. . . .

What is the father's plan?

How will the father keep his promise?

Where has he gone, and what has he done?

How will the family celebrate Christmas in deep space?

The code signals, darkness, and whispering suggest secrecy. What kind of surprise is coming?

Author builds suspense by recording the characters' reactions.

The climax, the most exciting part of the story, resolves the problem in a logical and satisfying way. The boy gets his wish.

A new concept of gift-giving emerges. The "gift" is the beauty of the stars.

Commentary on "The Gift"

In science-fiction stories, it is customary for human beings to encounter unusual life forms and strange experiences in outer space. In Ray Bradbury's story "The Gift," there are no fantastic creatures or time warps. Bradbury's concern is with what happens to old, familiar traditions as they pass into the world of the future. How will our civilization be transformed, and how will we be affected by the changes?

"The Gift" takes place in the middle of the twenty-first century. Interplanetary travel has become so commonplace that it is conducted very much as air travel is today. The problems caused by weightlessness in space have been solved; the passengers need no special equipment to make the trip to Mars. There are baggage limitations for the rocket ship, just as there are for commercial air carriers today. Space travel is safe enough for children.

The opening paragraph establishes the situation concisely. We learn that a family is going to spend the Christmas season away from Earth. This is obviously a special trip for the family, perhaps a holiday trip planned for the boy's first flight into space. A problem develops when their baggage is weighed and found to exceed the limit. The boy's Christmas present and a little tree with white candles must be left behind.

The Christmas tree is obviously important to the boy. Perhaps the Christmas tree has a special meaning to him because he is leaving Earth for Mars, and the tree reminds him of past holidays spent at home. Traditions are important to this boy. Later in the story he wishes to hold his father's watch so that he can mark the moment when Christmas arrives. Like most children, he can hardly wait for Christmas to come so that he can "open" his present. The parents, too, feel "deprived of the season and their love." They wish to give the boy what he wants.

The solution of this dilemma forms the main action of the story. The father puzzles over the problem for an entire day. Finally, he has a plan for a new gift to take the place of the tree. As the story builds toward the climax in the port cabin, there are hints of what the surprise will be. When the boy asks to look out the porthole, the father asks him to wait "for a reason." The father's plan takes into account the "abandoned gift" and the season. He promises his son that he will have a tree "and more."

At midnight the father leads the boy and his mother to a large cabin. He signals by a prearranged code, and the family is admitted to the port cabin. The father has arranged for a group of passengers to meet at twelve o'clock to celebrate Christmas. The "gift" to his son is a spectacular view of the galaxy, with the night sky lighted by innumerable brilliant stars.

The joyous ending of Bradbury's story resolves the problem in a logical and satisfying way. The boy gets his wish, but instead of an artificial tree with white candles, he is treated to a dazzling display of lighting effects that no celebration on Earth could equal. The ending also affirms the spirit of Christmas as a tradition that will continue to form a bond among future generations, whether they are earthbound or space travellers.

This analysis of "The Gift" tells more than the events of the story as they happen. It analyzes the *structure* of the story, making apparent the interconnection of setting, characters, and events. It explains how the major action of the story develops out of a problem—the abandoned Christmas gift—and how the ending of the story provides the solution for the problem. It also suggests that the underlying meaning of the story is concerned with the continuity and evolution of traditions.

The purpose of this exercise has been to demonstrate what is meant by the *close reading* of a story. When you read a story carefully, you read actively, responding to clues, anticipating outcomes, seeking to understand how different elements are related to the overall structure of the story.

With practice you can develop skill in reading and analyzing a literary work. Here are some guidelines for reading fiction.

Guidelines for Reading Fiction

1. *Look up unfamiliar words and references.* In Ray Bradbury's story, the phrase "customs table" is defined in a footnote. If you feel uncertain about the meaning of a word and cannot get the meaning from context clues, be sure to check in a standard dictionary or other reference work.

2. *Learn to draw inferences.* The author does not tell you directly that the boy is disappointed and upset. However, you are told that the boy enters the rocket ship "pale" and "silent." When his father announces that it is almost Christmas day, the boy's face grows "feverish," and his lips tremble.

3. *Actively question the author's purpose and method.* Ask yourself what significance there might be to details that the author gives you. Why, for example, does the father want the boy to wait before going up to the port? Where does the father go when he leaves the family for twenty minutes? As you read, try to anticipate what is coming.

4. *Probe for the central idea or point.* "The Gift," like many of the stories included in this textbook, has an underlying meaning, or *theme*, which makes a comment on human nature. The story suggests that human beings will hold on to their time-honored customs, and that traditions will continue to form a bond between future generations. Theme is seldom stated directly. Generally, it must be inferred from the characters and their actions.

Practice in Close Reading

The following passage is the opening of a short story. Read the passage carefully before answering the questions. If you need to, look up unfamiliar words or references.

"No; honest, now, Bob, I'm sure I was born too late. The twentieth century's no place for me. If I'd had my way——"

"You'd have been born in the sixteenth," I broke in, laughing, "with Drake and Hawkins and Raleigh and the rest of the sea kings."

"You're right!" Paul affirmed. He rolled over upon his back on the little afterdeck, with a long sigh of dissatisfaction.

It was a little past midnight, and, with the wind nearly astern, we were running down Lower San Francisco Bay to Bay Farm Island. Paul Fairfax and I went to the same school, lived next door to each other, and "chummed it" together. By saving money, by earning more, and by each of us foregoing a bicycle on his birthday, we had collected the purchase price of the *Mist*, a twenty-eight-footer, sloop-rigged, with baby topsail and centerboard. Paul's father was a yachtsman himself, and he had conducted the business for us, poking around, overhauling, sticking his penknife into the timbers, and testing the planks with the greatest care. In fact, it was on his schooner, the *Whim*, that Paul and I had picked up what we knew about boat sailing, and now that the *Mist* was ours, we were hard at work adding to our knowledge.

The *Mist,* being broad of beam, was comfortable and roomy. A man could stand upright in the cabin, and what with the stove, cooking utensils, and bunks, we were good for trips in her of a week at a time. And we were just starting out on the first of such trips, and it was because it was the first trip that we were sailing by night. Early in the evening we had beaten out from Oakland, and we were now off the mouth of Alameda Creek, a large salt-water estuary which fills and empties San Leandro Bay.

"Men lived in those days," Paul said, so suddenly as to startle me from my own thoughts. "In the days of the sea kings, I mean," he explained.

I said "Oh" sympathetically, and began to whistle "Captain Kidd."

"Now, I've my ideas about things," Paul went on. "They talk about romance and adventure and all that, but I say romance and adventure are dead. We're too civilized. We don't have adventures in the twentieth century. We go to the circus——"

"But——" I strove to interrupt, though he would not listen to me.

"You look here, Bob," he said. "In all the time you and I've gone together what adventures have we had? True, we were out in the hills once and didn't get back till late at night, and we were good and hungry, but we weren't even lost. We knew where we were all the time. It was only a case of walk. What I mean is, we've never had to fight for our lives. Understand? We've never had a pistol fired at us, or a cannon, or a sword waving over our heads, or—anything."

Jack London
from "To Repel Boarders"

FOR STUDY AND DISCUSSION

1. What is Paul's complaint about life in the twentieth century?
2. What does Paul mean by romance and adventure?
3. Identify Drake, Hawkins, and Raleigh. Why are they called "sea kings"? If necessary, consult a dictionary or encyclopedia.
4. What differences are there in the two boys?
5. Judging from the details of setting and the situation described in these opening paragraphs, what do you think is likely to happen in the story?

Close Reading of a Poem

Poets make use of many elements to communicate experience. They rely on the suggestive power of language and choose words for their emotional effect as well as for their literal meaning. They appeal to both the mind and the senses through images and figures of speech. Poets also make use of patterns, such as rhyme and rhythm, and special forms, such as the ballad.

It is a good idea to read a poem several times, and aloud at least once. Often it is helpful to write a prose paraphrase of a poem, restating all its ideas in plain language (see page 623).

Read the following poem several times. Then read the *explication*, a line-by-line examination of the poem's content and technique.

The Dark Hills   *E. A. Robinson*

Dark hills at evening in the west,
Where sunset hovers like a sound
Of golden horns that sang to rest
Old bones of warriors under ground,
Far now from all the bannered ways
Where flash the legions of the sun,
You fade — as if the last of days
Were fading, and all wars were done.

Explication of "The Dark Hills"

The speaker is watching a sunset. As the light fades, the hills grow dark. The real subject of the poem, however, is not the sunset but the thoughts and feelings that are set into motion by the dying day.

The poem is made up of a single sentence. In the opening line the speaker addresses the dark hills, but the subject and verb — "You fade" — do not appear until line 7. All the word groups in the first four lines modify the dark hills; all the word groups in lines 5–8 modify the verb *fade*.

The first four lines are devoted to a description of the hills at sunset. The poet describes the sunset in musical terms, drawing his simile from the fanfare of ancient warfare. The "golden horns" are trumpets that were played at a military cemetery to honor the "Old bones of warriors" laid to rest. The golden light of the setting sun seems to hover, or linger, over the scene the way the mellow sound of those "golden horns" once seemed to linger over the dead. Thus the reader is made to associate the final phase of the day with the calm of the grave.

Lines 5–6 also evoke military scenes from the past. The phrase "bannered ways" makes one think of roads or streets lined with flags. The "legions" refer to armies. The rays of the sun flashing across the sky during the day are the soldiers marching to battle. By drawing upon martial spectacles of the past, the speaker seems to be saying that throughout history human beings have made an elaborate and showy drama of war. At sunset, the dark hills seem remote from the heroics of battle.

In the final simile of lines 7–8, the speaker associates the peaceful mood of dusk with the "last of days." The speaker finds in the fading hills a symbol for the end of time and the end of human strife. What is not stated in the poem, but is clearly felt, is a longing on the part of the speaker for a world without war.

Guidelines for Reading a Poem

1. *Read the poem several times, and aloud at least once, following the author's clues for phrasing.* Punctuation marks tell you where to pause. Robinson does not expect the reader to pause at the end of each line. Lines 2 and 3, for example, are run-on lines, signifying that the author wishes no break in thought.

2. *Look up key words and references.* If you did not know the meaning of *legions* in line 6, you might miss the meaning of the metaphor in lines 5–6.

3. *Write a paraphrase of any lines that need clarification or simplification.* A paraphrase helps a reader understand imagery and figurative language. A paraphrase also puts into normal word order any inverted constructions. A paraphrase of lines 2–4 might read: "Where the glow of sunset lingers in the sky the way the mellow notes of trumpets, blown at the ceremonious burial of old soldiers, seemed to linger in the air."

4. *Arrive at the central idea or meaning of the poem.* Try to state this theme in one or two sentences: *In "The Dark Hills," watching the sun set in the west leads the speaker to reflect on the desire for peace and the inevitability of war.*

Practice in Close Reading

Read the following poem carefully; then answer the questions that
follow.

Stars   *Sara Teasdale*

Alone in the night
  On a dark hill
With pines around me
  Spicy and still,

And a heaven full of stars   5
  Over my head,
White and topaz
  And misty red;

Myriads° with beating
  Hearts of fire   10
That aeons°
  Cannot vex or tire;

Up the dome of heaven
  Like a great hill,
I watch them marching   15
  Stately and still,

And I know that I
  Am honored to be
Witness
  Of so much majesty.   20

9. **myriads** (mîr′ē-ədz): very large
numbers.

11. **aeons** (ē′ŏnz′): eons, very long periods
of time.

FOR STUDY AND DISCUSSION

1. What is the setting of the poem?
2. Describe the poet's feelings as she looks up at the stars.
3. What are the "beating/Hearts of fire" (lines 9–10)?
4. Which lines suggest a royal procession?
5. Lines 15–16 seem to be contradictory. What is the poet's meaning?

Close Reading of a Play

While many of the elements studied in connection with short stories and poetry are relevant to the study of drama, there are several additional elements that need to be taken into account. Dramatists frequently make use of stage directions to create setting and to give players instructions for acting. Sound effects are often important in creating setting and mood. Sometimes a dramatist may use a narrator to comment on the action, as Lucille Fletcher does in *The Hitchhiker* (page 270). Generally, however, dialogue is the dramatist's most important device for presenting character and for moving the action along.

The following scene is the opening of a one-act play by Van Dusen Rickert, Jr., called *The Bishop's Candlesticks*. The play is based on a famous episode in a nineteenth-century French novel, *Les Misérables (The Unfortunate Ones)*, by Victor Hugo. The central figure in this story is a man named Jean Valjean, who is sentenced to prison for stealing food. During this time, ex-convicts were required to carry yellow passports, which made it difficult for them to find shelter or to earn a living.

Read the scene several times, and aloud at least once. Then turn to the commentary on page 562.

from
The Bishop's Candlesticks

Van Dusen Rickert, Jr.

Characters

Monseigneur Bienvenu (môn-sĕ-nyœr′ byȧn′ və-nü′), Bishop of
  Digne (dēn′yə)[1]
Mademoiselle Baptistine (mȧd′mwȧ-zĕl′ bȧp′tē-stēn′), his sister
Madame Magloire (mȧ-dȧm′ mȧ-glwȧr′), their servant
Jean Valjean (zhäɴ vȧl-zhäɴ′), an ex-convict
A Sergeant and Two Police Officers

Scene: The home of the Bishop

Scene 1

The living room of the Bishop of Digne, *a large, oblong room plainly
furnished, scrupulously[2] neat. The walls are whitewashed. There is
no carpet. A fire burns in the fireplace down right; an alcove, closed
by portières,[3] occupies the upstage center. A door leading outdoors
is in the wall left of the alcove. Against the wall up left stands a
sturdy dresser. Down left a door leads to a passage.*

    The Bishop *and his* Sister *are finishing their supper. It is late
evening of a winter day. The room is lighted by firelight and two
candles which stand on the table in handsome silver candlesticks.*

Mlle.[4] Baptistine. Will you have coffee, brother?
The Bishop. If you please.
Mlle. Baptistine. I'll ring for Madame Magloire. . . .

[Mme.[5] Magloire *enters from the passage.*]

The Bishop. But here she is—and bringing our coffee. Madame
Magloire, you are wonderful; you read our minds.
Mme. Magloire. I should be able to, after all these years.

Setting gives impression of
simplicity, orderliness, and
no luxury.

This seems to be a peaceful
and happy household.

---

1. **Digne:** in southeast France, northeast of Marseilles.
2. **scrupulously** (skrōō′pyə-ləs-lē): with utmost care.
3. **portières**(pôr-tyȧrz′): heavy curtains.
4. **Mlle:** an abbreviation for mademoiselle.
5. **Mme.:** an abbreviation for madame.

The Bishop. Of faithful service — and mind reading.

Mme. Magloire. Thank you, my lord.

Mlle. Baptistine. We'll drink our coffee in front of the fire, Madame Magloire.

Mme. Magloire. Yes, mademoiselle. Let me stir up that fire a little. Such a cold night!

Mlle. Baptistine. I'm glad all our poor have fuel and food. (*Sits at fireplace and pours coffee*)

The Bishop. Not all, I'm afraid.

Mlle. Baptistine. I meant all in the parish.

The Bishop. If we could only help them all! My heart aches on a night like this to think of poor homeless wanderers, lonely, hungry —

Bishop sympathizes deeply with unfortunate human beings.

Mlle. Baptistine. Not all of them deserve help, I'm afraid. Some of them are good-for-nothing, ungrateful vagabonds.

Mme. Magloire. They say there's a tough-looking fellow in town now. He came along the boulevard and tried to get in to spend the night at the hotel. Of course they threw him out. A tramp with a sack over his shoulder and a terrible face. An ugly brute! (*She brings the candlesticks from the table and sets them on the mantelpiece above the fireplace.*)

The women are not as kind-hearted as the Bishop.

The Bishop. There are no human brutes; there are only miserable men who have been unfortunate.

Bishop gently chides the servant.

Mme. Magloire (*she is clearing the table*). You are as kindhearted as the good Lord himself, Bishop; but when there are fellows like that around, we say — mademoiselle and I . . .

Mlle. Baptistine. I have said nothing.

Mme. Magloire. Well . . . we say that his house isn't safe. If you don't mind, I'm going to send for the locksmith to put bolts on these doors. It's terrible to leave these doors unfastened, so that anybody can walk in. And the Bishop always calls "Come in!" the minute anyone knocks.

The Bishop is unconcerned about his safety.

[*There is a loud knock.*]

The Bishop. Come in.

[Jean Valjean *appears in the doorway*. Mlle. Baptistine *gasps;* Mme. Magloire *suppresses a cry. There is a silence.*]

Imagine the dramatic effect of this man's appearance.

Valjean. My name's Jean Valjean. I'm a convict. I've been nineteen years in prison at hard labor. I got out four days ago, and I'm on my way to Pontarlier.[6] I've come twenty-five miles on foot today, and

---

6. **Pontarlier** (pôn′tär-lyā′): in eastern France, near the Swiss border.

I'm tired and hungry. Nobody'll take me in, because I've got a convict's passport—yellow. See! They've kicked me out like a dog everywhere I stopped. I even went to the jail and asked for lodging, but the turnkey said, "Get yourself arrested, if you want to spend the night here." Then a good woman pointed out your door to me and said, "Knock there." So I did. I'm tired. Can I stay?

The Bishop. Madame Magloire, will you set another place and bring some food?

Valjean. Wait a minute. Did you understand? I'm a convict. There's my yellow passport. Take a look at it. It says nineteen years in prison—five years for burglary and fourteen for attempted escape. It says, "This man is dangerous." Dangerous! Well, are you going to take me in?

The Bishop. Won't you sit down, monsieur?[7] Madame Magloire, you may make up the bed in the alcove.

Valjean (*lowers his sack to the floor*). "Monsieur!" You call me "monsieur!" And you're not going to put me out! (Mme. Magloire *places food on the table.*) That looks good. (*He sits.*) I've been starving for four days. (*He begins to eat avidly.*) I'll pay you for this. I've got some money to pay you with. . . . You're an innkeeper, aren't you?

The Bishop. I'm a priest.

Valjean. Oh, a priest . . . a good priest. . . . That's a good one! Then you don't want me to pay——

The Bishop. No, no. Keep your money. How much have you?

Valjean. One hundred and nine francs.

The Bishop. And how long did it take you to earn that?

Valjean. Nineteen years.

The Bishop (*sighing*). Nineteen years.

Valjean. Yes, they pay us something for the work we do in prison. Not much, of course; but we get a little out of it. I really earned one hundred and seventy-one francs, but they didn't give me that much. I've still got all they paid me.

The Bishop. Madame Magloire, will you bring the candles to the table? It is a little dark over here.

Mlle. Baptistine (*timidly*). Did you . . . could you ever go to Mass while you were—in there?

Valjean. Yes, ma'am. They said Mass at an altar in the middle of the courtyard. You'll be interested in this, monsieur, since you're a priest. Once we had a bishop come to say Mass—"my lord," they called him. He's a priest who's over a lot of other priests. He said

	This is the "ugly brute" Mme. Magloire mentioned.
	The Bishop makes the stranger welcome.
	The man cannot believe that anyone will allow him to stay.
	The Bishop treats the man respectfully.
	The Bishop's sorrow indicates how small a sum it is.
	He implies that he was cheated.
	He doesn't realize that he is talking to a bishop.

---

7. **monsieur** (mə-syœ′): a title like "Mister" or "Sir" in English.

Mass and wore a pointed gold thing on his head. He wasn't close to us. We were drawn up in lines on three sides of the courtyard. We couldn't understand what he said. That was the only time we ever saw a bishop.

The Bishop. That's very interesting.

Mlle. Baptistine. How happy your family will be to see you again after so many years.

Valjean. I haven't got any family.

Mlle. Baptistine. Haven't you any relatives at all? Is there no one waiting for you?

Valjean. No, nobody. I had a sister. I used to live with her and her children, but I don't know what's become of her. She may have gone to Paris.

Mlle. Baptistine. Didn't she write to you sometimes?

Valjean. I haven't heard from her in twelve years. I'll never bother her again.

The Bishop. And you're going to Pontarlier. Do you know anyone there?

Valjean. No, I don't. It's not my part of the country; but I visited there once when I was young, and I liked it—high mountains, good air, and not too many people. I thought about it often in prison and made up my mind to go there if ever—if I ever was free.

The Bishop. You're going to a fine country, and there is plenty of work there: paper mills, tanneries, copper and iron foundries; and there are dairy farms all through the region. You'll have to find work, of course. What do you want to do?

Valjean. It doesn't matter. I can do any kind of work. I'm as tough as steel. But, with a yellow passport, I don't know whether I can get a job.

The Bishop (*writing*). Here, take this card. If you will give it to Monsieur Doumic from me . . . he has a tannery at Pontarlier and, what is more important, he has a heart. He will not ask you too many questions.

Valjean. Thank you, monsieur. You've been so kind, giving me this good dinner and taking me in—and all. . . . I ought to tell you my name.

The Bishop. You have a name I know without your telling me.

Valjean. Is that right? You already knew my name?

The Bishop. Yes. Your name is . . . my brother. You need not tell me who you are. Those who come to this door are not asked "What is your name?" but "What is your need . . . or sorrow?"

Valjean. I've seen plenty of that. There's nothing else in prison. If you complain—solitary confinement. Double chains, just for

the bishop's miter

Man is now all alone.

Bishop gives the ex-convict a recommendation.

Bishop reveals his humane nature.

nothing at all. A dog is better off than a convict! I had nineteen years of it—because I stole some food. And now I'm forty-six, and I have a yellow passport.

The Bishop. You have left behind you a sad and terrible place. If you have come from it with a little kindness or peace in your heart, then you are better than any one of us.

Mme. Magloire. The bed is made now.

The Bishop. Thank you, Madame Magloire. You may clear the table. And, monsieur, we know you are very tired. My sister and I will leave you to your rest. Do you need anything else?

Valjean. No . . . thanks.

The Bishop. Then good night, monsieur.

Mlle. Baptistine. Good night, monsieur.

[*Exit left, followed by the* Bishop. *Jean Valjean* carries his sack to the bed. *Mme. Magloire* comes from the kitchen carrying silver, which she puts away in the dresser. Jean Valjean watches her. When she leaves the room, he goes to the table and takes up one of the candlesticks. He looks toward the dresser. The *Bishop enters.*]

The Bishop. I've brought you an extra cover, monsieur. It is a doeskin I bought in Germany, in the Black Forest. This is better than a blanket for warmth.

[Jean Valjean *puts down the candlestick as the* Bishop *speaks.*]

Valjean (*harshly*). Are you going to let me sleep in your house like this? You'd better think it over. I'm a thief, you know. How do you know I'm not a murderer?

The Bishop. That is as God wills it, brother.

[*He blesses* Jean Valjean *and goes slowly out of the room.* Jean Valjean *looks after the* Bishop, *motionless and unyielding. Then he blows out the candles and goes to the alcove, where he lies down on the bed without undressing.*]

[*Curtain.*]

Punishment for crime was excessive.

Suspense mounts.

Is he going to steal the silver?

Valjean seems to be warning the Bishop.

The Bishop's strength is his faith.

Valjean remains unmoved.

Commentary on Scene from *The Bishop's Candlesticks*

The opening scene suggests that this is a play about the meaning of charity. The Bishop is shown to be a benevolent man. His humane nature is established in the opening lines of the play by his warm treatment of his servant and by his concern for wretched, poor, and homeless people. He does not agree with his sister and his servant that some human beings are undeserving of help. Rather, he believes that brutal behavior is the result of grave misfortunes. His home, like a church, is open to all.

The appearance of the ex-convict, Jean Valjean, is foreshadowed by Madame Magloire's mention of the stranger looking for lodging in town. To judge from her description, he is truly frightening: "tough-looking" with a "terrible face." She refers to him as a beast: "An ugly brute." We are prepared for the women's surprise and fear when Jean Valjean appears in the doorway.

The man speaks bluntly, getting to the point immediately. He has been traveling for four days. Because of his yellow passport, which he must present in order to prove his identity, no one will give him a lodging. He has a long prison record: nineteen years at hard labor.

When the Bishop offers him a place at the table, the ex-convict thinks that he has been misunderstood. He emphasizes that he has been labeled a dangerous man. He is stunned when the Bishop addresses him respectfully as "monsieur."

While the man eats greedily, the Bishop and his sister question him about his background. They learn that he no longer has any family, that he has no friends, and that he is virtually alone. He claims that he was imprisoned for nineteen years for stealing food. He tells of the excessive punishment in prison, and implies that he was exploited. Although he worked hard, he received very little money.

To help the man get a job in Pontarlier, the Bishop writes a recommendation for him. He brings him an extra cover for warmth. Before leaving for the night, he gives the man his blessing.

Despite the humane conduct of the Bishop, the scene ends ominously. When Madame Magloire puts away the silver, Jean Valjean watches her. After she leaves the room, he reaches for the candlestick and looks toward the dresser, where the silver is kept. He speaks harshly to the Bishop, warning him that he might be a murderer. Finally, his look at the end of the scene is "unyielding." We are not to expect that he has been softened or changed by the Bishop's kindness.

Guidelines for Reading a Play

1. *Note any information that establishes the setting and the situation that will start the plot moving.* The opening scene of the play shows us a simple and utilitarian room. Its humble character implies that the Bishop who lives there is uninterested in possessions and lavish furnishings. It is apparent from the Bishop's concern with ''poor homeless wanderers'' and the servant's fear of vagabonds that the play will focus in some way on the outcast.

2. *Note clues that tell you what the players are doing or how the lines are spoken.* Stage directions, such as *timidly* and *harshly*, tell you how some lines are delivered. Other speeches have clues built into them. We can tell from the short sentences and plain language of Jean Valjean's speeches that he speaks bluntly and roughly.

3. *Anticipate the action that will develop out of each scene.* There are several warnings of danger before the curtain falls. Jean Valjean watches the servant put away the silver. When no one is watching, he grasps one of the silver candlesticks. He says openly that the Bishop may be showing hospitality to a murderer. Finally, he goes to bed without undressing, suggesting that he means to leave in a hurry.

4. *Be alert to the mood of the play.* A somber mood is set by the many references to human suffering. We have the impression that Jean Valjean's character has been hardened by his life in prison and that he is untouched by the kindness and goodness of the Bishop.

Practice in Close Reading

Here is the conclusion of *The Bishop's Candlesticks.*

Scene 2

The room is dark. Jean Valjean *sits on the bed. After a moment he rises and takes up his pack and tiptoes toward the door. He hesitates, looking at the dresser; then he goes to it, opens it, and takes out silver; he crouches beside his pack, putting the silver into it. There is a sound as he thrusts the silver into the pack. Alarmed, he starts up, leaving the silver basket on the floor, catches up the pack, and goes hastily out of the door.*

[*Curtain.*]

Scene 3

It is morning. Mme. Magloire enters with dishes. Going directly to the table, she notices that the bed is unoccupied. Without seeing the basket, she runs to the dresser and finds that the silver is gone.

Mme. Magloire. Good heavens! Oh, good heavens! Mademoiselle! Monseigneur! What will the Bishop say! Oh, Mademoiselle!

[Mlle. Baptistine *enters.*]

Mlle. Baptistine. Good morning, Madame Magloire. What's the matter?
Mme. Magloire. Mademoiselle! The dresser is open—and that man is gone! The silver—all our knives and forks! Where are they?
Mlle. Baptistine. You put them away there last night?
Mme. Magloire. Yes, yes, just as I always do. And now there's nothing here! Oh, my lord.

[*The* Bishop *enters. He sees the silver basket and the empty alcove.*]

The Bishop. What is it, Madame Magloire?
Mme. Magloire. The silver! Does your lordship know where the silver basket is?
The Bishop. Yes.
Mme. Magloire. Oh, thank heaven! I didn't know what had become of it.
The Bishop (*picking up the empty basket and handing it to her*). Here it is.
Mme. Magloire. Well, but—there's nothing in it. Where's the silver?
The Bishop. Oh, then it's the silver you're worried about. I don't know where it is.
Mme. Magloire. Then it's stolen! Knives, forks, spoons—all gone. That vagabond stole them. He's gone, you see—cleared out before any of us were awake. The scoundrel!
The Bishop. Well, let's consider. In the first place, was the silver ours?
Mme. Magloire. Ours? And why not?
The Bishop. Madame Magloire, I had no right to keep that silver so long. It belonged to the poor. And this man was one of the poor, wasn't he?
Mme. Magloire. Oh, it isn't that I mind for myself—or mademoiselle. But, my lord, what will you eat with?
The Bishop. There are tin spoons.
Mme. Magloire (*with great disgust*). Tin smells.

The Bishop. And there are iron spoons.

Mme. Magloire. Iron tastes!

The Bishop (*chuckling*). Well, well—then there are wooden spoons. Tell me, sister, do you regret having given that poor fellow food and shelter?

Mlle. Baptistine. Not at all. I shall pray for him. Somehow I have a feeling that we may hear more of him.

[*They sit at the table.*]

Mme. Magloire. When I think of that cutthroat spending the night here! Suppose he had taken it into his head to kill us instead of stealing from us.

Mlle. Baptistine. He'll probably make haste to get as far away as he can. He wouldn't try to sell the silver in this neighborhood.

Mme. Magloire. I hope he'll take good care never to come this way again.

[*There is a knock at the door.* Mme. Magloire *and* Mlle. Baptistine *are startled.*]

The Bishop. Come in.

[*A* Sergeant *and two* Policemen, *guarding* Jean Valjean, *appear at the door.*]

Sergeant. Your excellency——

The Bishop. Come in, officer.

Valjean (*he looks up, surprised*). Excellency? Then he isn't a priest?

Policeman. Be quiet you. This is the Bishop.

The Bishop. Oh, it's you. I'm glad to see you. Why did you go off so early and without the candlesticks? They're solid silver and I gave them to you, as well as the other pieces. You can easily get two hundred francs for the pair.

Sergeant. Your excellency, we wanted to know if this fellow was telling the truth. We stopped him on suspicion and found that he had a yellow passport and this silver.

The Bishop. And he told you the silver was given him by a good old priest at whose house he spent last night.

Sergeant. He did, your excellency.

The Bishop. I see it all. Then you brought him back here. Well, it's just a misunderstanding.

Sergeant. Then we can let him go?

The Bishop. Of course, let him go.

[*The* Sergeant *hands the silver to* Valjean.]

Valjean. You mean I'm free?

Policeman. Yes, it's all right. You're free.

The Bishop. But, before you go, here are your candlesticks. Take them with you.

Valjean. Monsieur . . . monseigneur . . . I . . . (*He stands silent, with bowed head.*)

The Bishop. Ah—good morning, officer. You and your men were quite right in doing your duty. Good morning.

Sergeant. Good day, your excellency.

[*The* Sergeant *and* Policemen *close the door and leave.*]

Mlle. Baptistine (*very softly*). Come, Madame Magloire.

[*They slip discreetly out the door down left.*]

The Bishop. Now, Jean Valjean, you may go in peace. But never forget that you have promised to use that silver to make yourself an honest man.

Valjean (*slowly*). I didn't promise. . . . But I . . .

The Bishop. Jean Valjean, my brother, you no longer belong to evil, but to good. It is your soul that I am buying for you. It belongs to God. Will you give it to Him?

Valjean (*almost inaudibly*). Yes, Father. (*He kneels.*)

[*Curtain.*]

FOR STUDY AND DISCUSSION

1. Contrast the reactions of Madame Magloire and the Bishop to the theft of the silver. Are the reactions of both characters consistent with what you learned about them in the opening scene?

2. What do you think is the Bishop's motive in shielding Jean Valjean from the police?

3. Why does the Bishop give Jean Valjean the silver candlesticks?

4. How do you know at the end of the play that the Bishop has indeed saved Jean Valjean from continuing a life of crime?

WRITING ABOUT LITERATURE

The Writing Process

We often refer to writing an essay as a *process*, which consists of three key stages or phases: **prewriting, writing,** and **revising.** In this process, much of the crucial work precedes the actual writing of the paper. In the prewriting stage, the writer makes decisions about what to say and how to say it. Prewriting activities include choosing and limiting a topic, gathering ideas, organizing ideas, and arriving at a *thesis*—the controlling idea for the paper. In the next stage, the writer uses the working plan to write a first draft of the essay. In the revising stage, the writer rewrites the draft, several times perhaps, adding or deleting ideas, rearranging order, rephrasing for clarity, and proofreading for errors in spelling, punctuation, and grammar. The steps in this process are interdependent. For example, as ideas are developed on paper, the writer may find that the central idea of the paper needs to be restated or that a different organization is needed.

The amount of time devoted to each stage will vary with individual assignments. During a classroom examination, you will have limited time to plan your essay and to proofread your paper. For a term paper, you may have weeks or months to prepare your essay.

On the following pages the steps in this process are illustrated through the development of several model essays.

Answering Examination Questions

Often you may be asked to show your understanding of a literary work or topic by writing a short essay in class. Usually, your teacher will give you a specific question to answer. How well you do will depend not only on how carefully you have read and mastered the material, but on how carefully you read and interpret the essay question.

Before you begin to write, be sure you understand what the question calls for. If a question requires that you give *three* reasons for a character's actions, your answer will be incomplete if you supply only *two* reasons. If a question specifies that you deal with the *theme* of a work, take care not to give a summary of action or your answer will be unacceptable. Always take some time to read the essay question carefully in order to determine how it should be answered.

Remember that you are expected to demonstrate specific knowledge of the literature. Any general statement should be supported by evidence. If you wish to show that a character changes, for example, you should refer to specific actions, dialogue, thoughts and feelings, or direct comments by the author, in order to illustrate your point. If you are allowed to use your textbook during the examination, you may occasionally quote short passages or refer to a specific page in order to provide supporting evidence.

At the start, it may be helpful to jot down some notes to guide you in writing your essay. If you have four main points to make, you may then decide what the most effective order of presentation will be. You might build up to your strongest point, or you might present your points to develop a striking contrast. Aim for a logical organization.

Remember that length alone is not satisfactory. Your answer must be clearly related to the question, and it must be presented in acceptable, correct English. Always take some time to proofread your paper, checking for mistakes in spelling, punctuation, and usage.

Let us look briefly at some common instructions used in examinations.

ANALYSIS A question may ask you to *analyze* some aspect of a literary work. When you analyze something, you take it apart to see how each part works. In literary analysis you generally focus on some limited aspect of a work in order to better understand and appreciate the work as a whole. For example, you might analyze the technique of suspense in "The Sea Devil" (page 18); you might analyze O. Henry's use of irony in "A Retrieved Reformation" (page 215); you might analyze Twain's tone in "Cub Pilot on the Mississippi" (page 373).

COMPARISON CONTRAST A question may ask that you *compare* (or *contrast*) two characters, two settings, two ideas. When you *compare*, you point out likenesses; when you *contrast*, you point out differences. Sometimes you will be asked to *compare and contrast*. In that event, you will be expected to deal with similarities and differences. You might, for instance, compare and contrast the two fathers in "A Cap for Steve" (page 99); you might contrast the two settings in "Of Missing Persons" (page 203); you might compare the characters of the folk heroes in "Paul Bunyan's Been There" (page 501) and "Pecos Bill, Coyote Cowboy" (page 505). Sometimes the word *compare* is used to include both comparison and contrast. Always check with your teacher to make sure that you understand what the question calls for.

DESCRIPTION   If a question asks you to *describe* a setting or a character, you are expected to give a picture in words. In describing a setting, remember to include not only features of the physical locale, but those features that establish the historical period or evoke a mood. In describing a character, you should deal with both direct characterization and indirect characterization (see page 612). You might describe the setting in "The Legend of Sleepy Hollow" (page 523); you might describe Ichabod Crane in the same story.

DISCUSSION   The word *discuss* in a question is much more general than the other words we've looked at. When you are asked to discuss something, you are expected to examine it in detail. If you are asked to discuss the images in a poem, for example, you must deal with all major images; if asked to discuss the use of dialect in a story or poem, you must be sure to cover all significant examples. You might be asked to discuss humorous elements in a group of poems (pages 449–460).

EXPLANATION   A question may ask you to *explain* something. When you explain, you give the reasons for something being the way it is. You make clear a character's actions, or you show how something has come about. For example, you might explain what the talents are of "The No-Talent Kid" (page 2); you might explain the mystery of identity in "Charles" (page 94); you might explain how the author gives the appearance of authenticity to the story of "The Man Without a Country" (page 154).

ILLUSTRATION   The word *illustrate, demonstrate,* or *show* asks that you provide examples to support a point. You might be asked for examples of Harriet Tubman's courage illustrated in "They Called Her Moses" (page 27). You might be asked to demonstrate exaggerated characteristics of heroes in the American folk tales about Paul Bunyan, Pecos Bill, and Davy Crockett (pages 501–513).

INTERPRETATION   The word *interpret* in a question asks that you give the meaning or significance of something. You might, for example, be asked to interpret "The Road Not Taken" (page 430), a poem that is famous for its symbolism.

At times it will be useful to combine approaches. In discussing a subject, you may draw upon illustration, explanation, or analysis. In comparing or contrasting two works, you may rely on description or interpretation. However, an examination question generally will have a central purpose, and you should focus on this purpose in preparing your answer.

Here are some sample examination questions and answers for study and discussion. Note that the assignments (shown in italics) may be phrased as direct questions or as essay topics.

I

QUESTION   *The conflict in the myth of "Antigone" (page 483) involves two strong wills. In a single paragraph, explain the struggle between Antigone and Creon.*

METHOD OF ATTACK   Before writing, jot down some notes to guide you:

Both characters are obstinate and unyielding in their beliefs.
As king, Creon makes it a penalty for anyone to bury Polynices.
Antigone defies Creon's laws and buries her brother.
Creon holds the established laws of the country uppermost.
Antigone claims that the laws of the gods have a prior claim over the laws made by men.

In the opening sentence of your answer, state your *thesis*, your main point, wording it in such a way that you restate the key words of the question.

ANSWER

Main Idea

The struggle between Antigone and her uncle centers about the matter of law. As king, Creon makes it a penalty for anyone to bury Polynices, whom he considers a traitor. Antigone feels obligated to perform the burial rites for her brother Polynices; otherwise his soul will be unable to find rest. Creon accuses her of breaking the laws of the kingdom in disobeying his will. In defending her actions, Antigone claims that the laws of pity and mercy must be obeyed first, for those are the laws of the gods.

Supporting Statements

Length: 90 words

II

Discuss the clues that point to the true identity of Mr. Underhill in "The Rule of Names" (page 194). Refer to your textbook.

Mr. Underhill, in "The Rule of Names," is really a powerful dragon named Yevaud that has come to Sattins Island in disguise. Throughout the story there are clues that indicate Mr. Underhill is not what he seems to be. When he first appears in the story he is

Clue 1   breathing hard. The breath comes out of his nostrils "as a double puff of steam" (page 194). According to legend, dragons are fire-

Clue 2   breathing. Mr. Underhill has come to Sattins Island as a wizard, but he is not a great success. His magic remedies are weak, and his enchantments are a failure. Whenever a strange ship comes to the

Clue 3   island, Mr. Underhill stays out of sight. Another indication that he has something to hide is that he does not allow people to visit his

Clue 4   cave. Dragons keep their treasures in caves. When the boys try to pry open the door, they are greeted by a terrific roar and a "cloud of

Clue 5   purple steam" (page 195), a further clue to the wizard's true identity.

Clue 6   We learn that Mr. Underhill has an enormous appetite. After visiting Palani, the schoolteacher, and the children, he becomes very hungry. Dragons are known for devouring maidens. When we put these clues together, we are prepared for Mr. Underhill's transformation into a dragon.

Length: 213 words

III

Is the narrator of Poe's "The Tell-Tale Heart" (page 227) mad or sane? Give your interpretation, referring to specific details in the story. You may use your textbook.

Notes
The narrator is mad.
He claims to hear sounds in hell, the insects in the wall, the dead man's heart beating.
He is nervous; his broken speech shows he is in a state of excitement.
He has no rational motive for killing the old man.
He is obsessed by the old man's eye, which he calls the Evil Eye.
He has contradictory emotions: he pities the old man, but chuckles at the thought of murder; after he kills the old man, he smiles gaily.
He is unable to control himself, working himself up to an hysterical pitch in the presence of the police.
He keeps insisting on his sanity.

There is a considerable amount of information to organize here. You might try grouping the notes so that you can present the evidence under a few categories, perhaps 1) his sense of hearing; 2) his lack of motive for the murder; 3) his inability to control his emotions.

ANSWER

Main Idea

The narrator in Poe's "The Tell-Tale Heart" is incapable of distinguishing between reality and fantasy. Although he tries to convince his audience that he is sane, pointing to examples of his cleverness and cunning, his behavior throughout the story reveals a diseased mind.

Point 1

Supporting Statements

One significant piece of evidence is his claim that his sense of hearing is acute. In his very first speech, he says that he can hear "many things in hell" (page 227). A little later he says he has been in the habit of listening to the deathwatches in the wall (page 228). Before he suffocates the old man, he claims to hear the man's heart beating, and again, after the old man has been murdered and his body dismembered, the narrator claims to hear the heart beating in ever-increasing loudness.

Point 2

Supporting Statements

Another indication of his insanity is his admission that he has no rational motive for killing the old man. In fact, he loves the old man, but he is obsessed by the old man's blue eye, an "Evil Eye" which vexes him. For eight nights he postpones the murder, until the sight of the eye incites him to fury.

Point 3

Supporting Statements

Furthermore, the narrator is unable to control his emotions, and he seems to be constantly on the verge of hysteria. He admits to being "very dreadfully nervous" (page 227); his speech is broken, showing his state of excitement and tension. His emotions also are contradictory. He pities the old man, yet chuckles inwardly (page 228). After he smothers the old man, he smiles gaily (page 229). His behavior after murdering the old man also shows that he is emotionally unbalanced. He brings the police officers into the room where he has buried the body and places his own chair on the very spot where the dismembered corpse is concealed. He soon works himself up into a frenzy, foaming at the mouth, raving, swearing, and scraping his chair upon the boards. His confession is brought on by his delusion that the police actually know of the crime and hear the heart beating, but deliberately wish to mock him.

Length: 350 words

Writing on a Topic of Your Own

Choosing a Topic

At times you may be asked to choose a topic of your own. Often it will be necessary to read a work more than once before a suitable topic presents itself.

A topic may focus on one element or technique in a work. If you are writing about fiction, you might concentrate on some aspect of a plot, such as conflict. Or you might concentrate on character, setting, or theme. If you are writing about poetry, you might choose to analyze imagery or figurative language. A topic may deal with more than one aspect of a work. You might, for example, discuss several elements of a short story in order to show how an idea or theme is developed.

Once you have a topic in mind, your object is to form it into a *thesis*, a controlling idea that represents the conclusion of your findings. You would then need to present the evidence supporting your position. It may be necessary to read a work several times before you can formulate a thesis. Here are some examples:

''Shane'' (page 60)

Topic	Analyzing the character of Shane
Thesis	Shane is a noble, heroic figure who cannot overcome some tragedy in his past.

''The Apprentice'' (page 37) and ''Weep No More, My Lady'' (page 46)

Topic	Comparing characters of Peg and Skeeter
Thesis	Both Peg and Skeeter ''come of age'' by learning to handle responsibility.

''Flowers for Algernon'' (page 241)

Topic	Explaining the effect of increasing intelligence on Charlie's life
Thesis	As Charlie becomes more intelligent, he finds himself becoming more isolated from other people.

"The Dog That Bit People" (page 388)

Topic Describing Muggs

Thesis Muggs was a big, irritable, moody dog, who intimidated everyone with whom he came into contact.

"The Road Not Taken" (page 430)

Topic Explaining significance of title

Thesis The speaker emphasizes the choice he made in life by not taking the easier and more conventional path.

"The Raven" (page 441)

Topic Discussing the responses of the speaker to the raven

Thesis The speaker, at first seemingly assured, becomes increasingly distracted and loses emotional control.

"The Emperor's New Clothes" (page 494)

Topic Interpreting the theme of the story

Thesis When he is stripped of his finery—all the trappings that proclaim his rank—the Emperor is seen for what he really is—a vain and foolish man.

Gathering Evidence

It is a good idea to take notes as you read, even if you do not yet have a topic in mind. Later on, when you have settled on a topic, you can discard any notes that are not relevant. Some people prefer a worksheet, others index cards. In the beginning, you should record all your reactions. A topic may emerge during this early stage. As you continue to read, you will shape your topic into a rough thesis.

When you take notes, make an effort to state ideas in your own words. If a specific phrase or line is so important that it deserves to be quoted directly, be sure to enclose the words in quotation marks. When you transfer your notes to your final paper, be sure to copy quotations exactly.

In working with a short poem, you may cite phrases and lines without identifying the quotations by line numbers. If you cite lines in a long poem, you should enclose the line numbers in parentheses following the quotation. The following note, which is for "Elizabeth Blackwell" (page 12), shows you how to do this:

> When the ladies of Geneva hypocritically began to flatter her, Elizabeth "wrapped her shawl/against the praise" (lines 140–141).

The slash (/) shows the reader where line 140 ends and line 141 begins.

If you cite three or more lines, you should separate the quotation from your own text. The following note, which is for "Paul Revere's Ride" (page 148), shows you how to do this:

> After he climbs the North Church tower, Revere's friend looks into the distance and sees the British crossing by water:
>
> Where the river widens to meet the bay—
> A line of black, that bends and floats
> On the rising tide, like a bridge of boats.
> (lines 54–56)

Let us suppose that you have chosen to contrast the characters of the narrator and his Uncle Wash in the following story.

Thanksgiving Hunter   *Jesse Stuart*

"Hold your rifle like this," Uncle Wash said, changing the position of my rifle. "When I throw this marble into the air, follow it with your bead;[1] at the right time gently squeeze the trigger!"

Uncle Wash threw the marble high into the air and I lined my sights with the tiny moving marble, gently squeezing the trigger, timing the speed of my object until it slowed in the air ready to drop to earth again. Just as it reached its height, my rifle cracked and the marble was broken into tiny pieces.

Uncle Wash was a tall man with a hard leathery face, dark discolored teeth and blue eyes that had a faraway look in them. He hunted the year round; he violated all the hunting laws. He knew every path, creek, river and rock cliff within a radius of ten miles. Since he was a great hunter, he wanted to make a great hunter out of me. And tomorrow, Thanksgiving Day, would be the day for Uncle Wash to take me on my first hunt.

Uncle Wash woke me long before daylight.

"Oil your double-barrel," he said. "Oil it just like I've showed you."

---

1. **bead:** the sight at the muzzle end of a gun barrel.

I had to clean the barrel with an oily rag tied to a long string with a knot in the end. I dropped the heavy knot down the barrel and pulled the oily rag through the barrel. I did this many times to each barrel. Then I rubbed a meat-rind over both barrels and shined them with a dry rag. After this was done I polished the gunstock.

"Love the feel of your gun," Uncle Wash had often told me. "There's nothing like the feel of a gun. Know how far it will shoot. Know your gun better than you know your own self; know it and love it."

Before the sun had melted the frost from the multicolored trees and from the fields of stubble and dead grasses, we had cleaned our guns, had eaten our breakfasts and were on our way. Uncle Wash, Dave Pratt, Steve Blevins walked ahead of me along the path and talked about the great hunts they had taken and the game they had killed. And while they talked, words that Uncle Wash had told me about loving the feel of a gun kept going through my head. Maybe it is because Uncle Wash speaks of a gun like it was a living person is why he is such a good marksman, I thought.

"This is the dove country," Uncle Wash said soon as we had reached the cattle barn on the west side of our farm. "Doves are feeding here. They nest in these pines and feed around this barn fall and winter. Plenty of wheat grains, rye grains, and timothy seed here for doves."

Uncle Wash is right about the doves, I thought. I had seen them fly in pairs all summer long into the pine grove that covered the knoll east of our barn. I had heard their mournful songs. I had seen them in early April carrying straws in their bills to build their nests; I had seen them flying through the blue spring air after each other; I had seen them in the summer carrying food in their bills for their tiny young. I had heard their young ones crying for more food from the nests among the pines when the winds didn't sough[2] among the pine boughs to drown their sounds. And when the leaves started turning brown I had seen whole flocks of doves, young and old ones, fly down from the tall pines to our barnyard to pick up the wasted grain. I had seen them often and been so close to them that they were no longer afraid of me.

"Doves are fat now," Uncle Wash said to Dave Pratt.

"Doves are wonderful to eat," Dave said.

And then I remembered when I had watched them in the spring and summer, I had never thought about killing and eating them. I had thought of them as birds that lived in the tops of pine trees and that hunted their food from the earth. I remembered their mournful songs that had often made me feel lonely when I worked in the cornfield near the barn. I had thought of them as flying over the deep hollows in pairs in the bright sunlight air chasing each other as they flew toward their nests in pines.

"Now we must get good shooting into this flock of doves," Uncle Wash said to us, "before they get wild. They've not been shot among this season."

Then Uncle Wash, to show his skill in hunting, sent us in different directions so that when the doves flew up from our barn lot, they would have to fly over one of our guns. He gave us orders to close in toward the barn, and when the doves saw us, they would take to the air and we would do our shooting.

"And if they get away," Uncle Wash said, "follow them up and talk to them in their own language."

Each of us went his separate way. I walked

---

2. **sough** (sŭf, sou): make a murmuring sound; sigh.

toward the pine grove, carrying my gun just as Uncle Wash had instructed me. I was ready to start shooting as soon as I heard the flutter of dove wings. I walked over the frosted white grass and the wheat stubble until I came to the fringe of pine woods. And when I walked slowly over the needles of pines that covered the autumn earth, I heard the flutter of many wings and the barking of guns. The doves didn't come my way. I saw many fall from the bright autumn air to the brown crab-grass-colored earth.

I saw these hunters pick up the doves they had killed and cram their limp, lifeless, bleeding bodies with tousled feathers into their brown hunting coats. They picked them up as fast as they could, trying to watch the way the doves went.

"Which way did they go, Wash?" Dave asked soon as he had picked up his kill.

"That way," Uncle Wash pointed to the low hill on the west.

"Let's be after 'em, men," Steve said.

The seasoned hunters hurried after their prey while I stood under a tall pine and kicked the toe of my brogan[3] shoe against the brown pine needles that had carpeted the ground. I saw these men hurry over the hill, cross the ravine and climb the hill over which the doves had flown.

I watched them reach the summit of the hill, stop and call to the doves in tones not unlike the doves' own calling. I saw them with guns poised against the sky. Soon they had disappeared the way the doves had gone.

I sat down on the edge of a lichened[4] rock that emerged from the rugged hill. I laid my double-barrel down beside me, and sunlight

fingered through the pine boughs above me in pencil-sized streaks of light. And when one of these shifting pencil-sized streaks of light touched my gun barrels, they shone brightly in the light. My gun was cleaned and oiled and the little pine needles stuck to its meat-rind-greased barrels. Over my head the wind soughed lonely among the pine needles. And from under these pines I could see the vast open fields where the corn stubble stood knee-high, where the wheat stubble would have shown plainly had it not been for the great growth of crab grass after we had cut the wheat; crab grass that had been blighted by autumn frost and shone brilliantly brown in the sun.

Even the air was cool to breathe into the lungs; I could feel it deep down when I breathed and it tasted of the green pine boughs that flavored it as it seethed through their thick tops. This was a clean cool autumn earth that both men and birds loved. And as I sat on the lichened rock with pine needles at my feet, with the soughing pine boughs above me, I thought the doves had chosen a fine place to find food, to nest and raise their young. But while I sat looking at the earth about me, I heard the thunder of the seasoned hunters' guns beyond the low ridge. I knew that they had talked to the doves until they had got close enough to shoot again.

As I sat on the rock, listening to the guns in the distance, I thought Uncle Wash might be right after all. It was better to shoot and kill with a gun than to kill with one's hands or with a club. I remembered the time I went over the hill to see how our young corn was growing after we had plowed it the last time. And while I stood looking over the corn whose long ears were in tender blisters, I watched a groundhog come from the edge of the woods, ride down a stalk of corn, and start eating a blister-ear. I found a dead sassa-

---

3. **brogan** (brō′gən): a heavy work shoe, fitting ankle-high.
4. **lichened** (lī′kənd): covered with lichen, a type of plant that grows in colored patches on wood or rock.

fras[5] stick near me, tiptoed quietly behind the groundhog and hit him over the head. I didn't finish him with that lick. It took many licks.

When I left the cornfield, I left the groundhog dead beside his ear of corn. I couldn't forget killing the groundhog over an ear of corn and leaving him dead, his gray-furred clean body to waste on the lonely hill.

I can't disappoint Uncle Wash, I thought. He has trained me to shoot. He says that I will make a great hunter. He wants me to hunt like my father, cousins and uncles. He says that I will be the greatest marksman among them.

I thought about the way my people had hunted and how they had loved their guns. I thought about how Uncle Wash had taken care of his gun, how he had treated it like a living thing and how he had told me to love the feel of it. And now my gun lay beside me with pine needles sticking to it. If Uncle Wash were near he would make me pick the gun up, brush away the pine needles and wipe the gun barrels with my handkerchief. If I had lost my handkerchief as I had seen Uncle Wash often do, he would make me pull out my shirttail to wipe my gun with it. Uncle Wash didn't object to wearing dirty clothes or to wiping his face with a dirty bandanna; he didn't mind living in a dirty house—but never, never would he allow a speck of rust or dirt on his gun.

It was comfortable to sit on the rock since the sun was directly above me. It warmed with a glow of autumn. I felt the sun's rays against my face and the sun was good to feel. But the good fresh autumn air was no longer cool as the frost that covered the autumn grass that morning, nor could I feel it go deep into my lungs; the autumn air was warmer and it was flavored more with the scent of pines.

Now that the shooting had long been over near our cattle barn, I heard the lazy murmur of the woodcock in the pine woods nearby. Uncle Wash said that woodcocks were game birds and he killed them wherever he found them. Once I thought I would follow the sound and kill the woodcock. I picked up my gun but laid it aside again. I wanted to kill something to show Uncle Wash. I didn't want him to be disappointed in me.

Instead of trying to find a rabbit sitting behind a broom-sedge[6] cluster or in a briar thicket as Uncle Wash had trained me to do, I felt relaxed and lazy in the autumn sun that had now penetrated the pine boughs from directly overhead. I looked over the brown, vast autumn earth about me where I had worked when everything was green and growing, where birds sang in the spring air as they built their nests. I looked at the tops of barren trees and thought how a few months ago they were waving clouds of green. And now it was a sad world, a dying world. There was so much death in the world that I had known: flowers were dead, leaves were dead, and the frosted grass was lifeless in the wind. Everything was dead and dying but a few wild birds and rabbits. I had almost grown into the rock where I sat but I didn't want to stir. I wanted to glimpse the life about me before it all was covered with winter snows. I hated to think of killing in this autumn world. When I picked up my gun, I didn't feel life in it—I felt death.

I didn't hear the old hunters' guns now but

---

5. **sassafras** (săs′ə-frăs′): a type of tree having a fragrant bark.

6. **broom sedge:** a type of beard grass, also known as broom grass.

I knew that, wherever they were, they were hunting for something to shoot. I thought they would return to the barn if the doves came back, as they surely would, for the pine grove where I sat was one place in this autumn world that was a home to the doves. And while I sat on the rock, I thought I would practice the dove whistle that Uncle Wash had taught me. I thought a dove would come close and I would shoot the dove so that I could go home with something in my hunting coat.

As I sat whistling a dove call, I heard the distant thunder of their guns beyond the low ridge. Then I knew they were coming back toward the cattle barn.

And, as I sat whistling my dove calls, I heard a dove answer me. I called gently to the dove. Again it answered. This time it was closer to me. I picked up my gun from the rock and gently brushed the pine needles from its stock and barrels. And as I did this, I called pensively to the dove, and it answered plaintively.

I aimed my gun soon as I saw the dove walking toward me. When it walked toward my gun so unafraid, I thought it was a pet dove. I lowered my gun; laid it across my lap. Never had a dove come this close to me. When I called again, it answered at my feet. Then it fanned its wings and flew upon the rock beside me trying to reach the sound of my voice. It called, but I didn't answer. I looked at the dove when it turned its head to one side to try to see me. Its eye was gone, with the mark of a shot across its face. Then it turned the other side of its head toward me to try to see. The other eye was gone.

As I looked at the dove the shooting grew louder; the hunters were getting closer. I heard the fanning of dove wings above the pines. And I heard doves batting their wings against the pine boughs. And the dove beside me called to them. It knew the sounds of their wings. Maybe it knows each dove by the sound of his wings, I thought. And then the dove spoke beside me. I was afraid to answer. I could have reached out my hand and picked this dove up from the rock. Though it was blind, I couldn't kill it, and yet I knew it would have a hard time to live.

When the dove beside me called again, I heard an answer from a pine bough nearby. The dove beside me spoke, and the dove in the pine bough answered. Soon they were talking to each other as the guns grew louder. Suddenly, the blind dove fluttered through the treetops, chirruping its plaintive melancholy notes, toward the sound of its mate's voice. I heard its wings batting the wind-shaken pine boughs as it ascended, struggling, toward the beckoning voice.

Contrast, as you recall, focuses on differences. However, you must be selective about the differences you choose to point out. There wouldn't be much point, for example, in noting that Uncle Wash is older than the narrator, since age is not an essential feature in the story. If you have read the story carefully, you have no doubt concluded that the story points out a difference in attitudes toward hunting and killing. In other words, the story makes you, the reader, look closely at different *values.*

You might work out a chart of this kind for taking notes:

Uncle Wash

He is described as a "tall man with a hard leathery face." He is a seasoned sportsman, used to the outdoors.

He is a "great hunter" and wants his nephew to follow in his footsteps.

He takes better care of his guns than of his person or his home. He never allows his gun to be dirty or rusty. He tells the narrator to know and love his gun. He speaks of his weapon "like it was a living person."

He has no respect for hunting laws. He hunts all year round. He has no attachment to the things he kills. He talks about the doves being fat and making "good shooting."

He likes to show his skill as a hunter. He teaches his nephew how to shoot. He shows others how to close in around the doves, how to follow them, and how to call to them.

The Narrator

He is a beginner. This is to be his first hunt.

He doesn't want to disappoint his uncle. He has never openly questioned his uncle's ideas. He has followed his uncle's advice in cleaning his rifle, in shooting at targets.

He has a sensitivity to nature that the others lack. He has observed the doves all summer. He talks about their "mournful songs." He has watched them building nests and feeding their young. They are not afraid of him. He had never thought about killing and eating them.

He loves the feel of the cool autumn earth. He prefers enjoying nature to joining the hunt.

He once killed a groundhog, and the memory of the killing has haunted him.

There is so much death in the autumn world that he hates the thought of killing.

The dove, blinded by a hunter, becomes a symbol for nature misused by people. The narrator's decision not to kill the bird shows that he has rejected the code of the hunters.

You might find at this point that a thesis statement has begun to emerge: *Uncle Wash views nature as a challenge to the hunter's skill, while the narrator feels protective toward the natural world and its creatures.* You would continue to study the story, gathering additional evidence and refining your ideas. The next step is organizing the material.

Organizing the Material

Before you begin writing, organize your main ideas into an outline. Your outline should provide for an introduction, a body, and a conclusion. The introduction should identify the author (or authors, if you are dealing with two or more works), the work (or works), or the problem that is under study. It should contain a statement of your thesis as well. The body of your paper should present the evidence supporting your thesis. The conclusion should bring together your main ideas.

This is one kind of outline you might use for a short paper. It indicates the main idea of each paragraph.

INTRODUCTION

Paragraph 1   *Thesis* Uncle Wash views nature as a challenge to the hunter's skill, while the narrator feels protective toward the natural world and its creatures.

BODY

Paragraph 2   Uncle Wash, whose skill as a hunter is greatly admired, has no qualms about hunting and killing wildlife.

Paragraph 3   The narrator, who is sensitive to the mystery and beauty of nature, finds hunting and killing distasteful.

CONCLUSION

Paragraph 4   In making the decision not to kill the blind dove, in fact—not to kill any of the creatures in the woods, the narrator resists the pressures of the hunters and listens to his own, inner sense of right and wrong.

Writing the Essay

Here is a model essay based on the outline.

TITLE

CONTRASTING ATTITUDES TOWARD NATURE IN
"THANKSGIVING HUNTER"

INTRODUCTION
Identify the selection
and the subject.

Thesis

In Jesse Stuart's "Thanksgiving Hunter," the two main characters, Uncle Wash and the narrator, represent contrasting attitudes toward nature. *Uncle Wash views nature as a challenge to the hunter's skill, while the narrator feels protective toward the natural world and its creatures.* The situation that the story presents, the narrator's first hunt, brings these two attitudes into conflict.

BODY
Topic Sentence

Supporting Evidence

Uncle Wash, whose skill as a hunter is greatly admired, has no qualms about hunting and killing wildlife. His "hard leathery face" shows that he is a seasoned sportsman, used to the outdoors. He does not allow anything to interfere with his pleasure in hunting. He has no respect for hunting laws and violates them by hunting out of season. To him, doves are not gentle creatures but fat birds that make "good shooting." He enjoys hunting and enjoys teaching others how to close in around the doves and how to call to them. He considers his weapon to be a living thing and tells the narrator to know and love his gun.

Topic Sentence

Show evidence of
close reading.

The narrator, by contrast, is sensitive to the mystery and beauty of nature, and finds hunting and killing distasteful. This Thanksgiving hunt is an important occasion. It is his first hunt, and a great deal is expected of him. Although he doesn't want to disappoint his uncle, he cannot bring himself to use his gun to inflict pain and death. There is so much death in autumn that he hates the thought of killing. He has observed the doves all summer; he has listened to their songs and watched them building their nests and feeding their young. He feels he cannot betray their trust. Moreover, he remembers killing a groundhog once, and the memory of that killing has haunted him.

CONCLUSION

Stuart presents these characters without drawing moral judgments about them. The resolution of the conflict, however, seems to say that Stuart's sympathies lie with the narrator. The dove that has been blinded by a hunter becomes a symbol for nature misused by people. In its innocence the dove answers the narrator's call. He knows that the dove will have a hard time trying to survive, yet he cannot kill it. His decision not to kill—to face Uncle Wash with his hunting coat empty—shows that the narrator has resisted the pressures of the hunters and has trust in his own sense of right and wrong.

Length: 397 words

Revising Papers

When you write an essay in class, you have a limited amount of time to plan and develop your essay. Nevertheless, you should save a few minutes to read over your work and make necessary corrections.

When an essay is assigned as homework, you have more time to prepare it carefully. Get into the habit of revising your work. A first draft of an essay should be treated as a rough copy of your manuscript. Chances are that reworking your first draft will result in a clearer and stronger paper.

When you revise your paper, examine it critically for awkward sentences, inexact language, errors in capitalization, punctuation, and spelling. Rewrite any passages that are unclear or incomplete.

Here are some guidelines for revision.

Guidelines for Revising a Paper

1. *Check to see that your major point, a thesis, is clearly stated.* In a short essay, the thesis should be stated in the first sentence. In a longer composition, the thesis should appear in the introduction.
2. *Follow a logical organization.* A long composition should have an introduction, a body, and a conclusion. Each part of the essay should be clearly related to the thesis.
3. *Make sure that ideas are adequately developed.* Support any generalization with specific evidence.
4. *Check for errors in capitalization, punctuation, spelling, and sentence structure.*

Here is an early draft of the essay on pages 582–583, showing how it
was revised for greater clarity, accuracy, and conciseness.

In Jesse Stuart's ~~short story~~ "Thanksgiving Hunter," Uncle Wash
and the narrator ~~are~~ the two main characters. ~~They~~ represent contrasting
attitudes toward nature. Uncle Wash views nature as a challenge to
the hunter's skill, while the narrator feels protective toward the
natural world and its creatures. The situation that the story presents, the narrator's first hunt, brings These two attitudes ~~are brought~~
into conflict, ~~during the hunt.~~

Uncle Wash, whose skill as a hunter is greatly admired, has no
qualms about hunting and killing wildlife. ~~We are told that he has~~
His "~~a~~ hard leathery face," ~~which~~ shows that he is a seasoned sportsman,
used to the outdoors. He does not allow anything to ~~Nothing~~ interfere with his pleasure in hunting.

~~He is a "great hunter" and wants his nephew to follow in his footsteps.~~

He considers his weapon to be a living thing and tells the narrator
to know and love his gun. He has no respect for hunting laws, and He
violates ~~the~~ them ~~laws~~ by hunting out of season. To him, Doves are not gentle
creatures but fat birds that make "good shooting." He enjoys hunting
and teaches enjoys ing others how to close in around the doves and how to call
to them.

The narrator, ~~who~~ *by contrast,* is sensitive to the mystery and beauty of

nature, *and* finds hunting and killing distasteful. This *Thanksgiving* hunt is an

important occasion. It is his first hunt, and a great deal is

expected of him. *Although* ~~He~~ doesn't want to disappoint his uncle, *he cannot bring himself*

to use his gun to inflict pain and death. ~~He has never openly questioned his uncle's ideas.~~ There is so much death in

autumn that he hates the thought of killing. He has observed the ~~birds~~ *doves*

he has listened to their songs and watched them building their nests and feeding their young,

all summer; ~~and~~ he feels he cannot betray their trust. ~~He once killed~~

Moreover, he remembers killing a groundhog *once,* and the memory of that killing has haunted him.

Stuart presents these characters ~~in the story~~ without drawing

moral judgments about them. The ~~end of the story~~ *resolution of the conflict, however,* seems to say that

Stuart's sympathies lie with the narrator. The ~~blind~~ dove *that has been blinded by a hunter* becomes a

symbol for nature misused by people. *In its innocence* The dove ~~innocently~~ answers the

narrator's call. He knows that the dove will have a hard time trying

to survive, yet he cannot kill it. ~~In making the~~ *His* decision not to

kill ~~any of the creatures in the woods~~ *— to face Uncle Wash with his hunting coat empty — shows that*, the narrator *has* resist~~s~~*ed* the

pressures of the hunters and ~~listens to~~ *has trust in* his own ~~inner~~ sense of right

and wrong.

ADDITIONAL SELECTIONS

Too Soon a Woman   *Dorothy M. Johnson*

We left the home place behind, mile by slow mile, heading for the mountains, across the prairie where the wind blew forever.

At first there were four of us with the one-horse wagon and its skimpy load. Pa and I walked, because I was a big boy of eleven. My two little sisters romped and trotted until they got tired and had to be boosted up into the wagon bed.

That was no covered Conestoga,[1] like Pa's folks came West in, but just an old farm wagon, drawn by one weary horse, creaking and rumbling westward to the mountains, toward the little woods town where Pa thought he had an old uncle who owned a little two-bit sawmill.

Two weeks we had been moving when we picked up Mary, who had run away from somewhere that she wouldn't tell. Pa didn't want her along, but she stood up to him with no fear in her voice.

"I'd rather go with a family and look after kids," she said, "but I ain't going back. If you won't take me, I'll travel with any wagon that will."

Pa scowled at her, and her wide blue eyes stared back.

"How old are you?" he demanded.

"Eighteen," she said. "There's teamsters come this way sometimes. I'd rather go with you folks. But I won't go back."

"We're prid'near out of grub," my father told her. "We're clean out of money. I got all I can handle without taking anybody else." He turned away as if he hated the sight of her. "You'll have to walk," he said.

So she went along with us and looked after the little girls, but Pa wouldn't talk to her.

On the prairie, the wind blew. But in the mountains, there was rain. When we stopped at little timber claims along the way, the homesteaders said it had rained all summer. Crops among the blackened stumps were rotted and spoiled. There was no cheer anywhere, and little hospitality. The people we talked to were past worrying. They were scared and desperate.

So was Pa. He traveled twice as far each day as the wagon, ranging through the woods with his rifle, but he never saw game. He had been depending on venison,[2] but we never got any except as a grudging gift from the homesteaders.

He brought in a porcupine once, and that

---

1. **Conestoga** (kŏn′ ĭs-tō′gə): a covered wagon with broad wheels, used by American pioneers in crossing the prairies.

2. **venison** (vĕn′ə-sən, -zən): deer meat.

was fat meat and good. Mary roasted it in chunks over the fire, half crying with the smoke. Pa and I rigged up the tarp sheet for a shelter to keep the rain from putting the fire clean out.

The porcupine was long gone, except for some of the tried-out fat[3] that Mary had saved, when we came to an old, empty cabin. Pa said we'd have to stop. The horse was wore out, couldn't pull anymore up those grades on the deep-rutted roads in the mountains.

At the cabin, at least there was shelter. We had a few potatoes left and some corn meal. There was a creek that probably had fish in it, if a person could catch them. Pa tried it for half a day before he gave up. To this day I don't care for fishing. I remember my father's sunken eyes in his gaunt, grim face.

He took Mary and me outside the cabin to talk. Rain dripped on us from branches overhead.

"I think I know where we are," he said. "I calculate to get to old John's and back in about four days. There'll be grub in the town, and they'll let me have some whether old John's still there or not."

He looked at me. "You do like she tells you," he warned. It was the first time he had admitted Mary was on earth since we picked her up two weeks before.

"You're my pardner," he said to me, "but it might be she's got more brains. You mind what she says."

He burst out with bitterness. "There ain't anything good left in the world, or people to care if you live or die. But I'll get grub in the town and come back with it."

He took a deep breath and added, "If you get too all-fired hungry, butcher the horse. It'll be better than starvin'."

---

3. **tried-out fat:** fat that is rendered, or melted down.

He kissed the little girls goodbye and plodded off through the woods with one blanket and the rifle.

The cabin was moldy and had no floor. We kept a fire going under a hole in the roof, so it was full of blinding smoke, but we had to keep the fire so as to dry out the wood.

The third night we lost the horse. A bear scared him. We heard the racket, and Mary and I ran out, but we couldn't see anything in the pitch-dark.

In gray daylight I went looking for him, and I must have walked fifteen miles. It seemed like I had to have that horse at the cabin when Pa came or he'd whip me. I got plumb lost two or three times and thought maybe I was going to die there alone and nobody would ever know it, but I found the way back to the clearing.

That was the fourth day, and Pa didn't come. That was the day we ate up the last of the grub.

The fifth day, Mary went looking for the horse. My sisters whimpered, huddled in a quilt by the fire, because they were scared and hungry.

I never did get dried out, always having to bring in more damp wood and going out to yell to see if Mary would hear me and not get lost. But I couldn't cry like the little girls did, because I was a big boy, eleven years old.

It was near dark when there was an answer to my yelling, and Mary came into the clearing.

Mary didn't have the horse—we never saw hide nor hair of that old horse again—but she was carrying something big and white that looked like a pumpkin with no color to it.

She didn't say anything, just looked around and saw Pa wasn't there yet, at the end of the fifth day.

"What's that thing?" my sister Elizabeth demanded.

"Mushroom," Mary answered. "I bet it hefts[4] ten pounds."

"What are you going to do with it now?" I sneered. "Play football here?"

"Eat it—maybe," she said, putting it in a corner. Her wet hair hung over her shoulders. She huddled by the fire.

My sister Sarah began to whimper again. "I'm hungry!" she kept saying.

"Mushrooms ain't good eating," I said. "They can kill you."

"Maybe," Mary answered. "Maybe they can. I don't set up to know all about everything, like some people."

"What's that mark on your shoulder?" I asked her. "You tore your dress on the brush."

"What do you think it is?" she said, her head bowed in the smoke.

"Looks like scars," I guessed.

"'Tis scars. They whipped me. Now mind your own business. I want to think."

Elizabeth whimpered, "Why don't Pa come back?"

"He's coming," Mary promised. "Can't come in the dark. Your pa'll take care of you soon's he can."

She got up and rummaged around in the grub box.

"Nothing there but empty dishes," I growled. "If there was anything, we'd know it."

Mary stood up. She was holding the can with the porcupine grease.

"I'm going to have something to eat," she said coolly. "You kids can't have any yet. And I don't want any squalling, mind."

It was a cruel thing, what she did then. She sliced that big, solid mushroom and heated grease in a pan.

The smell of it brought the little girls out

of their quilt, but she told them to go back in so fierce a voice that they obeyed. They cried to break your heart.

I didn't cry. I watched, hating her.

I endured the smell of the mushroom frying as long as I could. Then I said, "Give me some."

"Tomorrow," Mary answered. "Tomorrow, maybe. But not tonight." She turned to me with a sharp command: "Don't bother me! Just leave me be."

She knelt there by the fire and finished frying the slice of mushroom.

If I'd had Pa's rifle, I'd have been willing to kill her right then and there.

She didn't eat right away. She looked at the brown, fried slice for a while and said, "By tomorrow morning, I guess you can tell whether you want any."

The little girls stared at her as she ate. Sarah was chewing an old leather glove.

When Mary crawled into the quilts with them, they moved away as far as they could get.

I was so scared that my stomach heaved, empty as it was.

Mary didn't stay in the quilts long. She took a drink out of the water bucket and sat down by the fire and looked through the smoke at me.

She said in a low voice, "I don't know how it will be if it's poison. Just do the best you can with the girls. Because your pa will come back, you know. . . . You better go to bed. I'm going to sit up."

And so would you sit up. If it might be your last night on earth and the pain of death might seize you at any moment, you would sit up by the smoky fire, wide-awake, remembering whatever you had to remember, savoring life.

We sat in silence after the girls had gone to sleep. Once I asked, "How long does it take?"

---

4. **hefts:** weighs.

"I never heard," she answered. "Don't think about it."

I slept after a while, with my chin on my chest. Maybe Peter[5] dozed that way at Gethsemane[6] as the Lord knelt praying.

Mary's moving around brought me wide-awake. The black of night was fading.

"I guess it's all right," Mary said. "I'd be able to tell by now, wouldn't I?"

I answered gruffly, "I don't know."

Mary stood in the doorway for a while, looking out at the dripping world as if she found it beautiful. Then she fried slices of the mushroom while the little girls danced with anxiety.

We feasted, we three, my sisters and I, until

---

5. **Peter:** one of the twelve apostles, also called Simon Peter or Saint Peter.
6. **Gethsemane** (gĕth-sĕm′ə-nē): the garden outside Jerusalem where Jesus was arrested (Matthew 26:36–57).

Mary ruled, "That'll hold you," and would not cook any more. She didn't touch any of the mushroom herself.

That was a strange day in the moldy cabin. Mary laughed and was gay; she told stories, and we played "Who's Got the Thimble?" with a pine cone.

In the afternoon we heard a shout, and my sisters screamed and I ran ahead of them across the clearing.

The rain had stopped. My father came plunging out of the woods leading a pack horse—and well I remember the treasures of food in that pack.

He glanced at us anxiously as he tore at the ropes that bound the pack.

"Where's the other one?" he demanded.

Mary came out of the cabin then, walking sedately. As she came toward us, the sun began to shine.

My stepmother was a wonderful woman.

FOR STUDY AND DISCUSSION

1. Pa allows Mary to travel with his wagon. Why, then, won't he speak to her?

2. Why is it difficult for the family to find food?

3. Why is the father forced to leave his family in Mary's care?

4. Consider Mary's behavior after she finds the mushroom. Why is her harsh treatment of the children necessary?

5. How are you prepared early in the story for the strength in Mary's character?

6. Were you surprised by the conclusion of the story? Tell why or why not.

SUGGESTIONS FOR WRITING

1. In a short essay, show how this story reveals the hardships faced by many early settlers in moving west across the prairie.

2. Compare the character of Mary with the character of the girl in "The Oklahoma Land Run" (page 172). Show how both women display courage and strength of will.

This story is from a collection of stories called Grandfather's Chair, *by Nathaniel Hawthorne. Grandfather's chair is an antique chair in which the old man sits, telling stories about New England to his grandchildren.*

The Pine-Tree Shillings   *Nathaniel Hawthorne*

Captain John Hull was the mintmaster of Massachusetts and coined all the money that was made there. This was a new line of business; for, in the earlier days of the colony, the current coinage consisted of gold and silver money of England, Portugal, and Spain. These coins being scarce, the people were often forced to barter their commodities instead of selling them.

For instance, if a man wanted to buy a coat, he perhaps exchanged a bearskin for it. If he wished for a barrel of molasses, he might purchase it with a pile of pine boards. Musket bullets were used instead of farthings.[1] The Indians had a sort of money, called wampum, which was made of clamshells; and this strange sort of specie[2] was likewise taken in payment of debts by the English settlers. Bank bills had never been heard of. There was not money enough of any kind, in many parts of the country, to pay the salaries of the ministers; so that they sometimes had to take quintals[3] of fish, bushels of corn, or cords of wood, instead of silver or gold.

As the people grew more numerous, and their trade with one another increased, the want of current money was still more sensibly felt. To supply the demand, the General Court passed a law for establishing a coinage of shillings, sixpences, and threepences. Captain John Hull was appointed to manufacture this money, and was to have about one shilling out of every twenty to pay him for the trouble of making them.

Hereupon all the old silver in the colony was handed over to Captain John Hull. The battered silver cans and tankards,[4] I suppose, and silver buckles, and broken spoons, and silver buttons of worn-out coats, and silver hilts of swords that had figured at court—all such curious old articles were doubtless thrown into the melting pot together. But by far the greater part of the silver consisted of bullion[5] from the mines of South America, which the English buccaneers—who were little better than pirates—had taken from the Spaniards, and brought to Massachusetts.

All this old and new silver being melted

---

1. **farthings** (fär'*th*ingz): A farthing was a British coin, worth one-fourth of a penny.
2. **specie** (spē'shē, -sē): here, coin.
3. **quintals** (kwĭnt'lz): a quintal is equal to 100 kilograms.

4. **tankards** (tăng'kərdz): A tankard was a large drinking cup with one handle and, frequently, a hinged lid.
5. **bullion** (bŏŏl'yən): gold or silver, usually in bars.

down and coined, the result was an immense amount of splendid shillings, sixpences, and threepences. Each had the date, 1652, on the one side, and the figure of a pine tree on the other. Hence they were called pine-tree shillings. And for every twenty shillings that he coined, you will remember, Captain John Hull was entitled to put one shilling into his own pocket.

The magistrates soon began to suspect that the mintmaster would have the best of the bargain. They offered him a large sum of money if he would but give up that twentieth shilling which he was continually dropping into his own pocket. But Captain Hull declared himself perfectly satisfied with the shilling. And well he might be; for so diligently did he labor, that, in a few years, his pockets, his moneybags, and his strong box were overflowing with pine-tree shillings. This was probably the case when he came into possession of Grandfather's chair; and, as he had worked so hard at the mint, it was certainly proper that he should have a comfortable chair to rest himself in.

When the mintmaster had grown very rich, a young man, Samuel Sewall[6] by name, came a-courting to his only daughter. His daughter —whose name I do not know, but we will call her Betsey—was a fine, hearty damsel, by no means so slender as some young ladies of our own days. On the contrary, having always fed heartily on pumpkin pies, doughnuts, Indian puddings, and other Puritan dainties, she was as round and plump as a pudding herself. With this round, rosy Miss Betsey did Samuel Sewall fall in love. As he was a young man of good character, industrious in his business, and a member of the church, the mintmaster very readily gave his consent.

"Yes, you may take her," said he, in his rough way, "and you'll find her a heavy burden enough!"

On the wedding day, we may suppose that honest John Hull dressed himself in a plum-colored coat, all the buttons of which were made of pine-tree shillings. The buttons of his waistcoat were sixpences; and the knees of his smallclothes[7] were buttoned with silver threepences. Thus attired, he sat with great dignity in Grandfather's chair; and being a portly old gentleman, he completely filled it from elbow to elbow. On the opposite side of the room, between her bridesmaids, sat Miss Betsey. She was blushing with all her might, and looked like a full-blown peony, or a great red apple.

There, too, was the bridegroom, dressed in a fine purple coat and gold-lace waistcoat, with as much other finery as the Puritan laws and customs would allow him to put on. His hair was cropped close to his head, because Governor Endicott[8] had forbidden any man to wear it below the ears. But he was a very personable young man; and so thought the bridesmaids and Miss Betsey herself.

The mintmaster also was pleased with his new son-in-law; especially as he had courted Miss Betsey out of pure love, and had said nothing at all about her portion.[9] So, when the marriage ceremony was over, Captain Hull whispered a word to two of his menservants, who immediately went out, and soon returned, lugging in a large pair of scales. They

---

6. **Samuel Sewall:** He became chief justice of Massachusetts and presided over witchcraft trials at Salem.

7. **smallclothes:** close-fitting knee breeches.
8. **Governor Endicott:** John Endicott (1589?–1665), first governor of Massachusetts Bay Colony.
9. **portion:** dowry, the money or property contributed by a bride.

were such a pair as wholesale merchants use for weighing bulky commodities; and quite a bulky commodity was now to be weighed in them.

"Daughter Betsey," said the mintmaster, "get into one side of these scales."

Miss Betsey—or Mrs. Sewall, as we now must call her—did as she was bid, like a dutiful child, without any question of the why and wherefore. But what her father could mean, unless to make her husband pay for her by the pound (in which case she would have been a dear bargain), she had not the least idea.

"And now," said honest John Hull to the servants, "bring that box hither."

The box to which the mintmaster pointed was a huge, square, iron-bound, oaken chest; it was big enough, my children, for all four of you to play at hide-and-seek in. The servants tugged with might and main, but could not lift this enormous receptacle, and were finally obliged to drag it across the floor. Captain Hull then took a key from his girdle,[10] unlocked the chest, and lifted its ponderous lid. Behold! It was full to the brim of bright pine-tree shillings, fresh from the mint; and Samuel Sewall began to think that his father-in-law had got possession of all the money in the Massachusetts treasury. But it was only the mintmaster's honest share of the coinage.

Then the servants, at Captain Hull's command, heaped double handfuls of shillings into one side of the scales, while Betsey remained in the other. Jingle, jingle, went the shillings, as handful after handful was thrown in, till, plump and ponderous as she was, they fairly weighed the young lady from the floor.

"There, son Sewall!" cried the honest mintmaster, resuming his seat in Grandfather's chair, "take these shillings for my daughter's portion. Use her kindly, and thank Heaven for her. It is not every wife that's worth her weight in silver!"

------

10. **girdle:** belt.

FOR STUDY AND DISCUSSION

1. Which parts of this story are based on actual fact? Which parts, do you suspect, have been invented by the author?
2. In literature, the Puritans are often depicted as stern and humorless people. What qualities of the early Puritans are emphasized in Hawthorne's story?

SUGGESTIONS FOR WRITING

1. Write a short essay giving your impression of Captain Hull's character. In your discussion refer to specific details in the story.
2. Compare the character of Betsey in Hawthorne's story with that of Katrina Van Tassel in "The Legend of Sleepy Hollow" (page 523). How are these characters alike, and how are they different?
3. Discuss the author's use of fact and fiction to give readers a sense of life in colonial New England.

Calling in the Cat   *Elizabeth Coatsworth*

Now from the dark, a deeper dark,
The cat slides,
Furtive and aware,
His eyes still shine with meteor spark
The cold dew weights his hair.   5
Suspicious,
Hesitant, he comes
Stepping morosely from the night,
Held but repelled,
Repelled but held,   10
By lamp and firelight.

Now call your blandest,
Offer up
The sacrifice of meat,
And snare the wandering soul with greeds,   15
Give him to drink and eat,
And he shall walk fastidiously
Into the trap of old
On feet that still smell delicately
Of withered ferns and mould.   20

FOR STUDY AND DISCUSSION

1. What characteristics of the cat are emphasized in this poem? Refer to specific lines in formulating your answer.
2. Why is the cat both held and repelled?
3. What words and phrases in the second stanza emphasize that the cat must be lured indoors?

SUGGESTION FOR WRITING

From earliest times the cat has been associated with magic. One superstition, for example, claimed that witches were attended by cats that were spirits in animal form. Discuss the elements in the poem that give the cat a fascinating and mysterious character.

The First Spring Day
Christina Rossetti

I wonder if the sap is stirring yet,
If wintry birds are dreaming of a mate,
If frozen snowdrops feel as yet the sun
And crocus fires are kindling one by one:
   Sing, robin, sing;   5
I still am sore in doubt concerning Spring.

I wonder if the Springtide of this year
Will bring another Spring both lost and dear;
If heart and spirit will find out their Spring,
Or if the world alone will bud and sing: 10
   Sing, hope, to me;
Sweet notes, my hope, soft notes for memory.

The sap will surely quicken soon or late,
The tardiest bird will twitter to a mate;
So Spring must dawn again with warmth and bloom,   15
Or in this world, or° in the world to come:
   Sing, voice of Spring,
Till I too blossom and rejoice and sing.

16. **Or . . . or:** either or.

FOR STUDY AND DISCUSSION

1. In the first stanza, what are five signs of spring that the speaker is waiting for? Why is she in doubt?
2. Springtime is often a symbol for rebirth. What personal experience do you think the speaker refers to in lines 7–9?
3. How are the speaker's doubts resolved in the last stanza?

SUGGESTION FOR WRITING

A *symbol* is something that has meaning in itself and which also stands for something else. Discuss the symbolic meaning of spring in Rossetti's poem.

In Shakespeare's comedy A Midsummer Night's Dream, *a group of workingmen plan a play as entertainment for the wedding of their ruler, the Duke of Athens. The men can hardly read or write. They have difficulty figuring out the meaning of their lines and memorizing them. These amateur actors take themselves very seriously, and they decide to dramatize a tragic story that was well known in Shakespeare's day—a tale of two young lovers named Pyramus and Thisby. The result is hilarious, as you will see.*

Pyramus and Thisby   *William Shakespeare*

Characters

Peter Quince, a carpenter, the director of the play, who also delivers
  the Prologue
Nick Bottom, a weaver, who takes the part of the lover Pyramus
Francis Flute, a bellows-mender, who takes the part of Thisby
Robin Starveling, a tailor, who presents Moonshine
Tom Snout, a tinker, who plays the Wall
Snug, a joiner, or cabinetmaker, who plays the Lion
Theseus (thē′sē-əs,-syo͞os′), Duke of Athens
Hippolyta (hǐ-pŏl′ə-tə), queen of the Amazons and bride of Theseus
Philostrate (fǐ′lŏs-strä′tē), master of the revels
Courtiers, Ladies, and Attendants

Scene 1

    [Quince's *house. Enter* Quince, Snug, Bottom, Flute, Snout, *and* Starveling.]

Quince. Is all our company here?
Bottom. You were best to call them generally,° man by man, according to the scrip.°
Quince. Here is the scroll of every man's name which is thought fit, through all Athens,
    to play in our interlude° before the Duke and the Duchess on his wedding day at
    night.   5

---

2. **generally:** Bottom means "severally" or "separately." **scrip:** list. 4. **interlude:** play.

Bottom. First, good Peter Quince, say what the play treats on. Then read the names of the actors, and so grow to a point.°

Quince. Marry,° our play is *The most lamentable comedy and most cruel death of Pyramus and Thisby.*

Bottom. A very good piece of work, I assure you, and a merry. Now, good Peter Quince, call forth your actors by the scroll. Masters, spread yourselves.   10

Quince. Answer as I call you. Nick Bottom, the weaver.

Bottom. Ready. Name what part I am for, and proceed.

Quince. You, Nick Bottom, are set down for Pyramus.

Bottom. What is Pyramus? A lover, or a tyrant?   15

Quince. A lover, that kills himself most gallant for love.

Bottom. That will ask some tears in the true performing of it. If I do it, let the audience look to their eyes, I will move storms, I will condole° in some measure. To the rest. Yet my chief humor° is for a tyrant. I could play Ercles° rarely, or a part to tear a cat in,° to make all split.   20

　　"The raging rocks
　　And shivering shocks
　　Shall break the locks
　　　Of prison gates.
　　And Phibbus' car°   25
　　Shall shine from far,
　　And make and mar
　　　The foolish Fates."

This was lofty! Now name the rest of the players. This is Ercles' vein, a tyrant's vein.° A lover is more condoling.   30

Quince. Francis Flute, the bellows-mender.

Flute. Here, Peter Quince.

Quince. Flute, you must take Thisby on you.

Flute. What is Thisby? A wandering knight?

Quince. It is the lady that Pyramus must love.   35

Flute. Nay, faith, let not me play a woman. I have a beard coming.

Quince. That's all one. You shall play it in a mask, and you may speak as small° as you will.

Bottom. An° I may hide my face, let me play Thisby too. I'll speak in a monstrous little voice, "Thisne, Thisne." "Ah Pyramus, my lover dear! Thy Thisby dear, and lady dear!"   40

Quince. No, no. You must play Pyramus, and Flute, you Thisby.

Bottom. Well, proceed.

---

7. **grow to a point:** conclude.   8. **Marry:** an exclamation.   18. **condole:** Bottom means "lament."   19. **humor:** whim. **Ercles:** Hercules.   20. **tear a cat in:** to overact.   25. **Phibbus' car:** the chariot of Phoebus, the sun god.   29. **tyrant's vein:** In the old drama, Hercules was portrayed as a ranting character.   37. **small:** shrilly.   39. **An:** if.

Quince. Robin Starveling, the tailor.

Starveling. Here, Peter Quince. 45

Quince. Robin Starveling, you must play Thisby's mother. Tom Snout, the tinker.

Snout. Here, Peter Quince.

Quince. You, Pyramus' father. Myself, Thisby's father. Snug, the joiner, you, the lion's part. And, I hope, here is a play fitted.

Snug. Have you the lion's part written? Pray you, if it be, give it me, for I am slow of 50 study.

Quince. You may do it extempore, for it is nothing but roaring.

Bottom. Let me play the lion too. I will roar that I will do any man's heart good to hear me; I will roar that I will make the Duke say, "Let him roar again, let him roar again." 55

Quince. An you should do it too terribly, you would fright the Duchess and the ladies, that they would shriek; and that were enough to hang us all.

All. That would hang us, every mother's son.

Bottom. I grant you, friends, if you should fright the ladies out of their wits, they would have no more discretion but to hang us. But I will aggravate° my voice so that 60 I will roar you as gently as any sucking dove, I will roar you an 'twere any nightingale.

Quince. You can play no part but Pyramus; for Pyramus is a sweet-faced man, a proper° man as one shall see in a summer's day, a most lovely, gentlemanlike man. Therefore you must needs play Pyramus. 65

Bottom. Well, I will undertake it. What beard were I best to play it in?

Quince. Why, what you will.

Bottom. I will discharge it in either your straw-color beard, your orange-tawny beard, your purple-in-grain° beard, or your French-crown-color beard, your perfect yellow. 70

Quince. Masters, here are your parts. And I am to entreat you, request you, and desire you, to con° them by tomorrow night; and meet me in the palace wood, a mile without the town, by moonlight. There will we rehearse, for if we meet in the city, we shall be dogged with company, and our devices known. In the meantime I will draw a bill of properties such as our play wants. I pray you, fail me 75 not.

Bottom. We will meet, and there we may rehearse most obscenely° and courageously. Take pains, be perfect. Adieu.

Quince. At the Duke's Oak we meet.

---

60. **aggravate:** Bottom means "restrain." 63. **proper:** handsome. 69. **purple-in-grain:** dyed purple. 72. **con:** learn. 77. **obscenely:** Bottom means "obscurely" or "off the scene."

Scene 2

[*A wood near Athens. Enter* Quince, Snug, Bottom, Flute, Snout, *and* Starveling.]

Bottom. Are we all met?

Quince. Pat,° pat, and here's a marvelous convenient place for our rehearsal. This green plot shall be our stage, this hawthorn brake° our tiring-house;° and we will do it in action as we will do it before the Duke.

Bottom. Peter Quince ——   5

Quince. What sayest thou, bully Bottom?

Bottom. There are things in this comedy of Pyramus and Thisby that will never please. First, Pyramus must draw a sword to kill himself, which the ladies cannot abide. How answer you that?

Snout. By'r lakin, a parlous° fear!   10

Starveling. I believe we must leave the killing out, when all is done.

Bottom. Not a whit. I have a device to make all well. Write me a prologue, and let the prologue seem to say we will do no harm with our swords, and that Pyramus is not killed indeed. And, for the more better assurance, tell them that I Pyramus am not Pyramus, but Bottom, the weaver. This will put them out of   15 fear.

Quince. Well, we will have such a prologue, and it shall be written in eight and six.°

Bottom. No, make it two more. Let it be written in eight and eight.

Snout. Will not the ladies be afeard of the lion?   20

Starveling. I fear it, I promise you.

Bottom. Masters, you ought to consider with yourselves. To bring in — God shield us — a lion among ladies is a most dreadful thing; for there is not a more fearful wildfowl than your lion living, and we ought to look to 't.

Snout. Therefore another prologue must tell he is not a lion.   25

Bottom. Nay, you must name his name, and half his face must be seen through the lion's neck. And he himself must speak through, saying thus, or to the same defect°— "Ladies"—or "Fair ladies—I would wish you"—or "I would request you"—or "I would entreat you—not to fear, not to tremble. My life for yours. If you think I come hither as a lion, it were pity of my life. No, I am no such thing. I am a man as other   30 men are." And there indeed let him name his name, and tell them plainly he is Snug the joiner.

Quince. Well, it shall be so. But there is two hard things: that is, to bring the moonlight into a chamber, for, you know, Pyramus and Thisby meet by moonlight.   35

Snout. Doth the moon shine that night we play our play?

---

2. **pat:** right on time.   3. **hawthorn brake:** thicket of hawthorn bushes.   **tiring-house:** dressing room.   10. **parlous:** perilous.   17–18. **eight and six:** Ballads were written in alternate lines of eight and six syllables.   27. **defect:** Bottom means "effect."

Bottom. A calendar, a calendar! Look in the almanac, find out moonshine, find out moonshine!

Quince. Yes, it doth shine that night.

Bottom. Why, then may you leave a casement of the great-chamber° window, where we play, open, and the moon may shine in at the casement.   40

Quince. Aye, or else one must come in with a bush of thorns and a lantern,° and say he comes to disfigure,° or to present, the person of moonshine. Then, there is another thing. We must have a wall in the great chamber, for Pyramus and Thisby, says the story, did talk through the chink of a wall.   45

Snout. You can never bring in a wall. What say you, Bottom?

Bottom. Some man or other must present wall. And let him have some plaster, or some loam, or some roughcast° about him, to signify wall. And let him hold his fingers thus, and through that cranny shall Pyramus and Thisby whisper.

Quince. If that may be, then all is well. Come, sit down, every mother's son, and   50
rehearse your parts. Pyramus, you begin. When you have spoken your speech, enter into that brake. And so everyone according to his cue. Speak, Pyramus. Thisby, stand forth.

Bottom (*as* **Pyramus**). "Thisby, the flowers of odious savors sweet——"

Quince. Odors, odors.   55

Bottom (*as* **Pyramus**). "——odors savors sweet.
    So hath thy breath, my dearest Thisby dear.
    But hark, a voice! Stay thou but here awhile,
    And by and by I will to thee appear."   [*Exit.*]

Flute. Must I speak now?   60

Quince. Aye, marry must you, for you must understand he goes but to see a noise that he heard, and is to come again.

Flute (*as* **Thisby**). "Most radiant Pyramus, most lily-white of hue,
    Of color like the red rose on triumphant brier,
    Most briskly juvenal,° and eke° most lovely too,   65
    As true as truest horse, that yet would never tire,
    I'll meet thee, Pyramus, at Ninny's tomb."

Quince. "Ninus' tomb," man. Why, you must not speak that yet. That you answer to Pyramus. You speak all your part at once, cues and all. Pyramus enter. Your cue is past. It is "never tire."   70

Flute (*as* **Thisby**). Oh—
    "As true as truest horse, that yet would never tire."

                                            [*Reenter* Bottom.]

Bottom (*as* **Pyramus**). "If I were fair, Thisby, I were only thine."

[*At this point the rehearsal is broken up and the players scatter. They next meet to perform their play before the Duke and his court.*]

---

40. **great-chamber:** hall of a great house.   42. **bush . . . lantern:** supposedly carried by the man in the moon.   43. **disfigure:** Quince means "figure" or "portray."   48. **roughcast:** rough plaster.   65. **juvenal:** youthful. **eke:** also.

Scene 3

[*Athens. The palace of* Theseus. *Enter* Theseus, Hippolyta, Philostrate, Lords, *and* Attendants.]

Theseus. Where is our usual manager of mirth?
    What revels are in hand? Is there no play?
    Call Philostrate.
Philostrate.   Here, mighty Theseus.
Theseus. Say, what abridgment° have you for this evening?
    What masque?° What music? How shall we beguile   5
    The lazy time, if not with some delight?
Philostrate. A play there is, my lord, some ten words long,
    Which is as brief as I have known a play.
    But by ten words, my lord, it is too long,
    Which makes it tedious; for in all the play   10
    There is not one word apt, one player fitted.
    And tragical, my noble lord, it is,
    For Pyramus therein doth kill himself.
    Which, when I saw rehearsed, I must confess,
    Made mine eyes water, but more merry tears   15
    The passion of loud laughter never shed.
Theseus. What are they that do play it?
Philostrate. Hard-handed men that work in Athens here,
    Which never labored in their minds till now.
    And now have toiled their unbreathed° memories   20
    With this same play, against° your nuptial.
Theseus. I will hear that play,
    For never anything can be amiss,
    When simpleness and duty tender it.
    Go, bring them in, and take your places, ladies.   25

[*As Philostrate leaves to get the players,* Theseus *and the others arrange themselves on the side of the stage as an audience.* Philostrate *reenters.*]

Philostrate. So please your Grace, the Prologue is addressed.°

        [*Flourish of trumpets. Enter* Quince *for the* Prologue.]

Quince (*as* **Prologue**). If° we offend, it is with our good will.
    That you should think, we come not to offend,

---

4. **abridgment:** entertainment (to abridge, or shorten, the evening). 5. **masque:** court entertainment. 20. **unbreathed:** unpracticed, inexperienced. 21. **against:** in anticipation of. 26. **addressed:** ready. 27. **If . . .:** Because the prologue is mispunctuated, the meaning of Quince's speech is comically distorted.

But with good will. To show our simple skill,
That is the true beginning of our end.
Consider, then, we come but in despite.° 30
We do not come, as minding to content you,
Our true intent is. All for your delight,
We are not here. That you should here repent you,
The actors are at hand, and, by their show,
You shall know all, that you are like to know. 35

Theseus. This fellow does not stand upon points.°

First Courtier. He hath rid° his prologue like a rough colt, he knows not the stop. A good
moral, my lord. It is not enough to speak, but to speak true.

Hippolyta. Indeed he hath played on his prologue like a child on a recorder—a sound, 40
but not in government.°

Theseus. His speech was like a tangled chain—nothing impaired, but all disordered.
Who is next?

[*Enter* Pyramus *and* Thisby, Wall, Moonshine, *and* Lion.]

Quince (*as* **Prologue**). Gentles, perchance you wonder at this show,
But wonder on, till truth makes all things plain. 45
This man is Pyramus, if you would know.
This beauteous lady, Thisby is certáin.
This man, with lime and roughcast, doth present
Wall, that vile Wall which did these lovers sunder,°
And through Wall's chink, poor souls, they are content 50
To whisper. At the which let no man wonder.
This man, with lantern, dog, and bush of thorn,
Presenteth Moonshine; for, if you will know,
By moonshine did these lovers think no scorn
To meet at Ninus' tomb, there, there to woo. 55
This grisly beast, which Lion hight° by name,
The trusty Thisby, coming first by night,
Did scare away, or rather did affright.
And, as she fled, her mantle she did fall,
Which Lion vile with bloody mouth did stain. 60
Anon comes Pyramus, sweet youth and tall,
And finds his trusty Thisby's mantle slain.
Whereat, with blade, with bloody blameful blade,
He bravely broached° his boiling bloody breast.
And Thisby, tarrying in mulberry shade, 65
His dagger drew, and died. For all the rest,

---

31. **despite:** ill will.   37. **stand upon points:** pay attention to punctuation marks.   38. **rid:** ridden.   41. **not in govern-**
ment: undisciplined.   49. **sunder:** separate.   56. **hight:** is called.   64. **broached:** stabbed.

Let Lion, Moonshine, Wall, and lovers twain
At large° discourse, while here they do remain.
[*Exeunt* Prologue, Pyramus, Thisby, Lion, *and* Moonshine.]
Theseus. I wonder if the lion be to speak.
Second Courtier. No wonder, my Lord. One lion may, when many asses do.   70
Snout (*as* **Wall**). In this same interlude it doth befall
    That I, one Snout by name, present a wall,
    And such a wall, as I would have you think,
    That had in it a crannied hole or chink,
    Through which the lovers, Pyramus and Thisby,   75
    Did whisper often very secretly.
    This loam, this roughcast, and this stone doth show
    That I am that same wall. The truth is so.
    And this the cranny is, right and siníster,°
    Through which the fearful lovers are to whisper.   80
Theseus. Would you desire lime and hair to speak better?
Second Courtier. It is the wittiest partition that I ever heard discourse, my lord.
Theseus. Pyramus draws near the wall! Silence!

[*Reenter* Pyramus.]

Bottom (*as* **Pyramus**). O grim-looked night! O night with hue so black!
    O night, which ever art when day is not!   85
    O night, O night! alack, alack, alack,
    I fear my Thisby's promise is forgot!
    And thou, O wall, O sweet, O lovely wall,
    That stand'st between her father's ground and mine!
    Thou wall, O wall, O sweet and lovely wall,   90
    Show me thy chink, to blink through with mine eyne!

[Wall *holds up his fingers.*]

Thanks, courteous wall. Jove shield thee well for this!
    But what see I? No Thisby do I see.
    O wicked wall, through whom I see no bliss!
    Cursed be thy stones for thus deceiving me!   95
Theseus. The wall, methinks, being sensible,° should curse again.
Bottom. No, in truth, sir, he should not. "Deceiving me" is Thisby's cue. She is to enter now, and I am to spy her through the wall. You should see it will fall pat as I told you. Yonder she comes.

---

68. **at large:** in full.   79. **sinister:** left.   96. **being sensible:** having feeling.

[*Reenter* Thisby.]

Flute (*as* **Thisby**). O wall, full often has thou heard my moans,   100
    For parting my fair Pyramus and me!
    My cherry lips have often kissed thy stones,
    Thy stones with lime and hair knit up in thee.
Bottom (*as* **Pyramus**). I see a voice. Now will I to the chink,
    To spy an I can hear my Thisby's face.   105
    Thisby!
Flute (*as* **Thisby**). My love thou art, my love I think.
Bottom (*as* **Pyramus**). Think what thou wilt, I am thy lover's grace;
    And like Limander,° am I trusty still.
Flute (*as* **Thisby**). And I, like Helen,° till the Fates° me kill.   110
Bottom (*as* **Pyramus**). Oh, kiss me through the hole of this vile wall!
Flute (*as* **Thisby**). I kiss the wall's hole, not your lips at all.
Bottom (*as* **Pyramus**). Wilt thou at Ninny's tomb meet me straightway?
Flute (*as* **Thisby**). 'Tide° life, 'tide death, I come without delay.

                             [*Exeunt* Pyramus and Thisby.]

Snout (*as* **Wall**). Thus have I, Wall, my part dischargèd so;   115
    And, being done, thus Wall away doth go.   [*Exit* Wall.]
Theseus. Now is the mural° down between the two neighbors.
Second Courtier. No remedy, my lord, when walls are so willful to hear without
    warning.
Hippolyta. This is the silliest stuff that I ever heard.   120
Theseus. The best in this kind are but shadows, and the worst are no worse if imagina-
    tion amend them.
Hippolyta. It must be your imagination then, and not theirs.
Theseus. If we imagine no worse of them than they of themselves, they may pass for
    excellent men. Here come two noble beasts in, a man and a lion.   125

[*Reenter* Lion *and* Moonshine.]

Snug (*as* **Lion**). You, ladies, you, whose gentle hearts do fear
    The smallest monstrous mouse that creeps on floor,
    May now perchance° both quake and tremble here,
    When lion rough in wildest rage doth roar.
    Then know that I, one Snug, the joiner, am   130
    A lion fell,° nor else no lion's dam;

---

109. **Limander:** instead of *Leander,* a legendary Greek lover.   110. **Helen:** instead of *Hero,* Leander's love. Helen was in another legend.   **Fates:** in Greek mythology, the three goddesses who controlled the future.   114. **'tide:** betide; happen.   117. **mural:** wall.   128. **perchance:** perhaps.   131. **fell:** fierce. *Fell* also refers to an animal's hide or skin.

For, if I should as lion come in strife
Into this place, 'twere pity on my life.°
Theseus. A very gentle beast, and of a good conscience.
Second Courtier. The very best at a beast, my lord, that e'er I saw.   135
First Courtier. This lion is a very fox for his valor.
Starveling (*as* **Moonshine**). This lantern doth the hornèd moon present,
    Myself the man i' the moon do seem to be.
Theseus. This is the greatest error of all the rest. The man should be put into the lantern.
    How is it else the man i' the moon?   140
First Courtier. Proceed, Moon.
Starveling. All that I have to say is, to tell you that the lantern is the moon; I, the man
    i' the moon; this thornbush, my thornbush; and this dog, my dog.
Second Courtier. Why, all these should be in the lantern, for all these are in the moon.
    But silence! Here comes Thisby.   145

[*Reenter* Thisby.]

Flute (*as* **Thisby**). This is old Ninny's tomb. Where is my love?
Snug (*as* **Lion,** *roaring*). Oh —   [Thisby *runs off.*]
Second Courtier. Well roared, Lion!
Theseus. Well run, Thisby!
Hippolyta. Well shone, Moon! Truly, the moon shines with a good grace.   150
                    [*Lion shakes* Thisby's *mantle and exits.*]
Theseus. Well moused, Lion!
First Courtier. And so the lion vanished.
Second Courtier. And then came Pyramus.

[*Reenter* Pyramus.]

Bottom (*as* **Pyramus**). Sweet Moon, I thank thee for thy sunny beams,
    I thank thee, Moon, for shining now so bright.   155
    For, by thy gracious, golden, glittering gleams,
    I trust to take of truest Thisby sight.
        But stay, oh spite!
        But mark, poor knight,
        What dreadful dole° is here!   160
        Eyes, do you see?
        How can it be?
        Oh dainty duck! Oh dear!
        Thy mantle good,

---

133. **'twere . . . life:** I should be hanged for it.   160. **dole:** sorrow.

What, stained with blood! 165
Approach, ye Furies fell!°
O Fates, come, come,
Cut thread and thrum°
Quail, crush, conclude, and quell!°

Theseus. This passion,° and the death of a dear friend, would go near to make a man 170
look sad.

Hippolyta. Beshrew my heart, but I pity the man.

Bottom (*as* **Pyramus**). O wherefore, Nature, didst thou lions frame?
Since lion vile hath here deflowered my dear,
Which is—no, no—which was the fairest dame 175
That lived, that loved, that liked, that looked with cheer.
Come, tears, confound!°
Out, sword, and wound
The pap° of Pyramus.
Aye, that left pap, 180
Where heart doth hop. [*Stabs himself.*]
Thus die I, thus, thus, thus.
Now am I dead,
Now am I fled,
My soul is in the sky. 185
Tongue, lose thy light,
Moon, take thy flight, [*Exit* Moonshine.]
Now die, die, die, die, die. [*Dies.*]

Theseus. With the help of a surgeon he might yet recover, and prove an ass.

Hippolyta. How chance Moonshine is gone before Thisby comes back and finds her 190
lover?

Theseus. She will find him by starlight. Here she comes, and her passion ends the
play.

[*Reenter* Thisby.]

Flute (*as* **Thisby**). Asleep, my love?
What, dead, my dove? 195
O Pyramus, arise!
Speak, speak. Quite dumb?
Dead, dead? A tomb
Must cover thy sweet eyes.
These lily lips, 200

---

166. **Furies fell:** In Greek mythology, the Furies avenged unpunished crimes.   168. **thrum:** the very end of the thread.
One of the goddesses spun the thread of life, a second goddess determined its length, and a third cut it.   169. **quell:**
slay.   170. **passion:** display of sorrow.   177. **confound:** destroy.   179. **pap:** breast.

This cherry nose,
These yellow cowslip cheeks,
Are gone, are gone.
Lovers, make moan.
His eyes were green as leeks.   205
O Sisters Three,°
Come, come to me,
With hands as pale as milk;
Lay them in gore,
Since you have shore°   210
With shears his thread of silk.
Tongue, not a word.
Come, trusty sword,
Come, blade, my breast imbrue!° [*Stabs herself.*]
And, farewell, friends.   215
Thus Thisby ends.
Adieu, adieu, adieu! [*Dies.*]

Theseus. Moonshine and Lion are left to bury the dead.

Second Courtier. Aye, and Wall too.

Bottom (*starting up*). No, I assure you; the wall is down that parted their fathers. Will it   220
please you to see the epilogue?

Theseus. No epilogue, I pray you, for your play needs no excuse. Never excuse, for when
the players are all dead, there need none to be blamed. Marry, if he that writ it had
played Pyramus and hanged himself in Thisby's garter, it would have been a fine
tragedy. And so it is, truly, and very notably discharged.   225

---

206. **Sisters Three:** the Fates.   210. **shore:** cut.   214. **imbrue:** drench with blood.

FOR STUDY AND DISCUSSION

Scene 1

1. How can you tell that these workingmen are simple and uneducated?
2. How does the title of the interlude contribute to the humor of this scene?
3. Bottom often uses words without understanding what they mean. For example, in line 60 he says he will *aggravate* his voice when he means that he will *restrain* it. Find several comic examples of his misuse of language.
4. How does Bottom show that he is a "ham," a performer who tends to exaggerate his roles?
5. In lines 21–28, Bottom treats us to poetry in the "lofty" vein. Why is this speech so comical?

Scene 2

1. What fears does Bottom express about the audience's reaction to certain parts of the play? What solution does he offer to these problems?
2. Quince says in line 33 that there are "two hard things" to present in the interlude. How do the actors decide to handle these difficulties?
3. What problems does Quince have in directing the rehearsal?

Scene 3

1. Why does Philostrate try to dissuade Theseus from having the play performed? Why does Theseus decide, nevertheless, to hear it? What does his decision reveal about him as a ruler?
2. The story of Pyramus and Thisby was a well-known tragic legend in Shakespeare's day. Retell the story in your own words. Be sure to include the role played by the wall and by the lion.
3. *Parody* is a humorous imitation of a serious work or style of writing for the purpose of amusement. In this play Shakespeare parodies certain techniques of his contemporaries. Find instances where he pokes fun at flowery language and ridiculous comparisons.
4. Read aloud Bottom's speech, lines 154–169. How does Bottom overuse such poetic devices as alliteration and rhyme?
5. How do the various members of the audience react to the production?
6. Find instances where the actors drop out of character to address members of the audience. Why do these interruptions add to the comedy?

SUGGESTIONS FOR WRITING

1. Shakespeare was an actor as well as a playwright. What aspects of his profession might he be poking fun at in this "interlude?" In your discussion refer to specific speeches.
2. Bottom is one of Shakespeare's great comic characters. Write an analysis of Bottom's character. Be sure to include his treatment of language.
3. All the workingmen are simple and uneducated. However, they are presented as individuals with distinguishing characteristics. Explain the differences you note in this group.

ABOUT THE AUTHORS

Dorothy M. Johnson (1905–   ) was born in Iowa and grew up in Montana. She attended the University of Montana and after graduation worked as a secretary and as an editor. She has written many stories about the Western frontier. Several of her works, including "The Man Who Shot Liberty Valance" and "A Man Called Horse," have been adapted for the movies. She is an honorary member of the Blackfeet tribe in Montana.

Nathaniel Hawthorne (1804–1864) was born in Salem, Massachusetts. His father was a ship's captain. One of his ancestors was a judge who presided at the Salem witch trials. After graduating from Bowdoin College in Maine, Hawthorne returned to Salem and began writing stories based on New England's past. In 1837 his first volume of *Twice-Told Tales* was published. In 1850 he won recognition for *The Scarlet Letter,* a novel set in the Puritan period. In addition to novels and short stories, he wrote books for young children. He is generally acknowledged to be one of America's major writers.

Elizabeth Coatsworth (1893–   ) was born in Buffalo. Her work is known for blending the natural and supernatural. She first achieved recognition with *The Cat Who Went to Heaven* (1930), a story based on Japanese folklore. This book was awarded the Newbery Medal for 1931. She has written many books for children.

Christina Rossetti (1830–1894) is considered one of the finest lyrical poets of the nineteenth century. She was born in London. Her distinguished family included her brothers, Dante Gabriel Rossetti, a poet and painter, and William Michael Rossetti, a biographer and editor, both of whom were leading spirits of an artistic group known as the Pre-Raphaelites. Her first volume of poetry was printed privately when she was twelve. She was extremely devout and on two separate occasions refused to marry because of religious differences. In later life she became quite ill and was preoccupied with the idea of death. Her principal works include *Goblin Market and Other Poems, The Prince's Progress and Other Poems,* and *Sing Song,* a book of poems for children.

Guide to Literary Terms and Techniques

ALLITERATION *The repetition of a sound in a group of words.* Alliteration is used in many common expressions: "safe and sound," "over and out," "do or die." Most alliteration occurs at the beginning of words, but sometimes we also find alliteration in the middle or at the end of words, as in "tickled pink" and "dribs and drabs."

Two uses of alliteration seem to be to gain emphasis and to aid our memory. This is why many advertising jingles depend on alliteration and why so many products are given names that are alliterated.

Politicians often use alliteration. When we are asked to put up with hardship, we are asked to "tighten our belts," or to "bite the bullet." A famous political slogan during a presidential campaign went "Tippecanoe and Tyler too!"

Poets use alliteration to the most obvious and memorable effect. Here are some examples of alliteration in poetry:

Mere prattle, without practice,
Is all his soldiership.

> William Shakespeare
> *Othello*

Open here I flung the shutter, when, with
    many a flirt and flutter,
In there stepped a stately Raven of the
    saintly days of yore.

> Edgar Allan Poe
> "The Raven"

I like to see it lap the miles,
And lick the valleys up,

> Emily Dickinson

Sometimes alliteration is used simply for the fun of it. One poet, Algernon Charles Swinburne, wrote a poem that made fun of his own style. He had been criticized for using too much alliteration. So he composed "Nephelidia" (little clouds), which is complicated and funny nonsense. It starts this way:

> From the depth of the dreamy decline of the
>   dawn through a notable nimbus of neb-
>   ulous noonshine,
> Pallid and pink as the palm of the flag-
>   flower that flickers with fear of the flies
>   as they float,

Swinburne makes the amusing point that heavily alliterated poetry can seem to mean more than it does.

Prose writers use alliteration, too, but they have to be careful not to sound too artificial. Mary O'Hara's story "My Friend Flicka" uses alliteration in its title. Some of the most memorable expressions from the King James translation of the Bible are alliterated: "Let there be light: and there was light" (Genesis), and "There is no new thing under the sun" (Ecclesiastes).

See page 437.

ALLUSION *A reference to a work of literature or to an actual event, person, or place, which the speaker expects the audience to recognize.* Allusions are used in everyday conversation, as well as in prose and poetry. The great danger with an allusion is that the reader or listener won't understand it. People can seem snobbish if they allude to very obscure works or events.

Writers often allude to other works of literature. James Street, for example, has entitled a story "Weep No More, My Lady," which is the title of a sad song by Stephen Foster. In titling one of his plays *The Ugly Duckling*, A. A. Milne alludes to the fairy tale by Hans Christian Andersen.

Literature contains many allusions to the Bible. Emily Dickinson expects us to recognize her allusion to a thunderous speaker in the New Testament when she says that a train "roared like Boanerges." The title of a section of a biography about Harriet Tubman is "They Called Her Moses," which alludes to the Biblical leader Moses. In that case, we are expected to make the connection between Moses and Harriet Tubman, both deliverers of their people.

Allusions to the myths of ancient Greece and Rome are also common in literature. The great writers used to be carefully trained to read both Latin and Greek. We do not study these languages as intensely nowadays, so we miss many of the allusions that writers like William Shakespeare, John Milton, William Wordsworth, and Alfred, Lord Tennyson took for granted. When the speaker in Edgar Allan Poe's poem "The Raven" thinks that the Raven came from "Night's Plutonian shore," he expects us to know that he is alluding to the shore of the underworld ruled by Pluto, a Roman god identified with night and darkness.

Allusions to the media are growing more and more common, though these are not as lasting as allusions to the Bible and classical literature. Squeaky, in the story "Raymond's Run" by Toni Cade Bambara, describes an encounter with some unfriendly girls as "one of those Dodge City scenes." This is an allusion to the television series "Gunsmoke," a Western that was popular in the 1950's and 1960's.

See pages 448, 482.

ANECDOTE *A very short story which is told to make a point.* Many anecdotes are funny; some are jokes. Originally, anecdotes were little-known, entertaining facts about a person or about a historical event. Anecdotes are used in nearly all kinds of literature. Mark Twain uses several anecdotes in his tale

"The Celebrated Jumping Frog of Calaveras County." Twain tells this anecdote to prove that a man named Jim Smiley would bet on *anything*:

Why, it never made no difference to *him*—he'd bet on *anything*—the dangdest feller. Parson Walker's wife laid very sick once, for a good while, and it seemed as if they warn't going to save her; but one morning he come in, and Smiley up and asked him how she was, and he said she was considerable better—thank the Lord for his inf'nite mercy—and coming on so smart that with the blessing of Prov'dence she'd get well yet; and Smiley, before he thought, says, "Well, I'll resk two and a half she don't anyway."

ATMOSPHERE *The general mood or feeling established in a piece of literature.* Atmosphere can be gloomy, peaceful, frightful, tense, etc. Atmosphere is usually achieved through description. Landscapes, such as dark, dank moors that ooze a steaming mist, often lend themselves to creating atmosphere. Edgar Allan Poe is famous for the creation of gloomy atmospheres, as in this opening passage of his story "The Fall of the House of Usher." Notice how the italicized words make us sense the atmosphere:

During the whole of a *dull, dark* and soundless day in the *autumn* of the year, when the clouds *hung oppresively low* in the heavens, I had been passing alone, on horseback, through a singularly *dreary* tract of country, and at length found myself, as the *shades of the evening* drew on, within view of the *melancholy* House of Usher.

Atmosphere doesn't always have to be spooky and frightening. Notice how the italicized words create an atmosphere of comfort and well-being in this passage from Washington Irving's "The Legend of Sleepy Hollow":

His stronghold was situated on the banks of the Hudson, in one of those *green, sheltered, fertile nooks* in which the Dutch farmers are so fond of *nestling*. A great elm tree spread its broad branches over it. At the foot of the tree *bubbled* up a *spring* of the *softest* and *sweetest water*, in a little well formed of a barrel. The spring then stole *sparkling* away through the *grass* to a neighboring *brook* that *bubbled* along among alders and dwarf willows. Close by the farmhouse was a vast barn, which might have served for a church, every window and crevice of which seemed *bursting* forth with the *treasures* of the farm.

See page 231.

BALLAD *A storytelling poem that uses regular patterns of rhythm and strong rhymes. Most ballads are meant to be sung.* Folk ballads, in fact, are sung long before they are written down. Others, the so-called "literary" ballads, are composed by writers and are not specifically intended for singing. Most ballads are full of adventure, action, and romance, such as you find in Sir Walter Scott's rousing "Lochinvar." Many ballads tell stories of famous villains, like Jesse James and Billy the Kid. One very famous folk ballad, "John Henry," celebrates the heroic railroad worker who raced a machine. There are often several versions of folk ballads, since they change a bit as people sing them and pass them on.

See page 516.

BIOGRAPHY *The life story of a person written by someone else.* When a person writes his or her own biography, it is called an *autobiography*. Ann Petry wrote a biography called *Harriet Tubman: Conductor on the Underground Railroad*. Richard Wright wrote his own life story in an autobiography called *Black Boy*. Biography and autobiography are two of the most popular forms of nonfiction, and most libraries have a section set aside for them. Almost every famous person has been the subject of a biography. Some famous people have had three or four biographies written about them, by different people.

CHARACTERIZATION *The methods used to present the personality of a character in a narrative.* A writer can create a character by: (1) giving a physical description of the character; (2) showing the character's actions and letting the character speak; (3) revealing the character's thoughts; (4) revealing what others think of the character; and (5) commenting directly on the character. Characterization can be sketchy, particularly if the character does not take an important role in a story. Or, characterization can be extraordinarily full, as when the character is the main focus of a story.

Washington Irving describes Ichabod Crane in "The Legend of Sleepy Hollow" in many ways to reveal his character. Here is a physical description:

> The name of Crane was not inapplicable to his person. He was tall, but exceedingly lank, with narrow shoulders, long arms and legs, hands that dangled a mile out of his sleeves, feet that might have served for shovels, and his whole frame most loosely hung together.

Here Irving tells about Ichabod's thoughts and fears:

> How often did he shrink with curdling awe at the sound of his own steps on the frosty crust beneath his feet, and dread to look over his shoulder, lest he should behold some uncouth being tramping close behind him!

Here he reveals what others think of Ichabod:

> He was, moreover, esteemed by the women as a man of great learning, for he had read several books quite through. . . .

And here Irving gives his own evaluation of his hero:

> He was, in fact, an odd mixture of small shrewdness and simple credulity.

Sometimes animals can be characterized, using the same techniques. Rudyard Kipling's famous story "Rikki-tikki-tavi" has as its hero a little mongoose, who is characterized as if he were a person.

See pages 108, 117, 226, 296, 360, 488.

COMEDY *A literary work with a generally happy ending. A comedy can be funny and, sometimes, rather serious under it all.* Any narrative can be a comedy—a short story, novel, play, or narrative poem, though the term is most often applied to plays. One of the typical plots of comedies is the one involving young lovers who almost don't get together. The plot of such a comedy always ends happily, often with a marriage, and the theme usually has something to do with the power of love. A comedy that has these characteristics is A. A. Milne's play *The Ugly Duckling*. Many movies and novels are also based on this kind of plot.

Television features a great many situation comedies—weekly episodes about funny complications that take place in the lives of the same group of characters. Slapstick comedy, with a lot of roughhousing and knockabout humor, was popular in early movies. The films of Abbott and Costello, Laurel and Hardy, and the Three Stooges are examples.

See page 296.

CONFLICT *The struggle that takes place between two opposing forces.* A conflict can take place between a character and a natural force, like a bear or a hurricane; between two characters; or between opposing views held by separate characters or groups of characters. Such conflicts are external conflicts. Conflict can also be internal — it can exist within the mind of a character who must make a difficult decision or overcome a fear.

Usually, a conflict arises when a character's wishes or desires are blocked. In Sir Walter Scott's poem "Lochinvar," Ellen's father is marrying her to someone else, and so Lochinvar is blocked from wedding the maiden he loves. Lochinvar resolves this conflict by stealing Ellen away from her own bridal feast. We might expect this to produce new conflict, but as the poem tells us, Lochinvar and Ellen escape and are never seen again.

In Arthur Gordon's story "The Sea Devil," a man struggles with a manta ray which nearly drowns him. In Dorothy Canfield's story "The Apprentice," a girl's views on how she should behave clash with her parents' views. In Langston Hughes's story "Thank You, M'am," the character Roger has an internal conflict: he must decide whether to respect someone's trust in him, or do the easy thing and run away.

In many types of literature, especially in novels and dramas, there are two or more kinds of conflict. In the play *The Diary of Anne Frank*, for example, there is the conflict between the "family" in hiding and the hostile outside world which seeks to destroy them; there is the conflict of views between Anne and the adults; there is also the internal conflict within Anne's mind, between her feelings of love for her parents and her desire to please them, and her need to grow up and be herself.

See **Plot**.
See also page 221.

CONNOTATION *All the emotions and associations that a word or phrase arouses.* Connotation is different from *denotation*, which is the strict literal (or "dictionary") definition of a word. For example, the word *springtime* literally means "the season of the year between the vernal equinox and the summer solstice." But *springtime* usually makes most people think of love, rebirth, youth, and romance.

Poets are especially sensitive to the connotations of words. An example is Gwendolyn Brooks's poem about two old people called "The Bean Eaters." Literally, beans are merely the edible seeds of a kind of legume. But the word *beans* has certain connotations. When most people hear the word *beans* they think of a quick, cheap food. They might even picture campers cooking a can of beans over an outdoor fire. Thus the word *beans* in this poem is meant to suggest poverty. You can imagine how different it would be if the poet had called the old couple in her poem "The Legume Eaters."

DESCRIPTION *The kind of writing that creates pictures of persons, places, things, or actions. Description may also tell how something sounds, smells, tastes, or feels.* Washington Irving, a master of description, gives us this picture of Ichabod Crane's route homeward. Notice how he uses words like *barking*, *crowing*, *chirp*, and *twang*, which help us hear certain sounds.

The hour was as dismal as himself. Far below him, the Tappan Zee spread its dusky and indistinct waste of waters, with here and there the tall mast of a sloop riding quietly at anchor under the land. In the dead hush of midnight he could even hear the barking of the watchdog from the opposite shore of the Hudson, but it was so vague and faint as only to give an idea of his distance from this faithful companion of man. Now and then, too, the long-drawn crowing of a cock, accidentally awakened, would sound far, far off, from some farmhouse away among the hills — but it was like a dreaming sound in his ear. No signs of life occurred near him, but occasionally the melancholy chirp of a cricket or, perhaps, the guttural twang of a bullfrog from a neighboring marsh, as if sleeping uncomfortably and turning suddenly in his bed.

See **Atmosphere, Imagery.**
See also pages 86-87.

DIALECT   *A representation of the speech patterns of a particular region or social group.* Dialect is often used to make a character or place seem authentic. Some of the regional dialects in the United States are the Downeast dialect of Maine; the Cajun dialect of Louisiana; and the dialects of the South and West.

Hosea Bigelow was one of the great American humorists who used dialect simply for the fun of it — and sometimes to make a point. Here is a letter he wrote to the editor of a Down-east newspaper about a debate in the United States Senate:

To Mr. Buckenam.
  Mr. Editer, As i wuz kinder prunin round, in a little nussry sot out a year of 2 a go, the Dbait in the sennit cum inter my mine. An so i took & Sot it to wut I call a nussry rime. I hev made sum onnable Gentlemun speak that dident speak in a Kin uv Poetikul lie sense the seeson is dreffle backerd up This way.
    ewers as ushul
    Hosea Bigelow.

See page 59.

DIALOGUE   *Talk or conversation between two or more characters.* Dialogue usually attempts to present the speech of characters in a realistic fashion. It is used in almost all literary forms: biography, essays, fiction and nonfiction, poetry, and drama. Dialogue is especially important in drama, where it forwards *all* the action of the play. Dialogue must move the plot of a play, reveal the characters, and even help establish some of the mood. When dialogue appears in a play, there are no quotation marks to set it apart, since — besides stage directions — a play is nothing but dialogue.

When dialogue appears in a prose work, or in a poem, it is usually set apart with quotation marks. Since actual life is conducted almost entirely in dialogue, a short story that uses a lot of dialogue will not only move fast, but it will also seem realistic.

See **Dialect.**
See also pages 109, 361, 363.

DRAMA   *A story written to be acted out on a stage, with actors and actresses taking the parts of specific characters.* The word *drama* comes from a Greek word meaning "act," so it is important to stress the idea of action in a drama. While reading a drama, we have to try to imagine real people as they would play the parts on stage.

We usually think of two main kinds of drama. *Tragedies* are serious plays in which a hero or heroine suffers defeat or death. William Shakespeare's *Hamlet* and *Macbeth* are tragedies, as is *The Diary of Anne Frank*. *Comedies* are lighter plays which usually end happily and are often funny. A. A. Milne's play *The Ugly Duckling* is a comedy.

Drama involves the use of *plot,* the series of related events that make up the story.

Conflict, the most important element in the plot, pits the characters in a play against one another, or against forces that are powerful and sometimes greater than they are. The characters carry forward the plot of a play by means of *dialogue*.

Most playwrights include *stage directions*, which tell the actors and actresses what to do or what feelings to project when certain lines are spoken. The stage directions are useful to the director, who must help the actors and actresses interpret their lines. The director decides things like the timing of a line, the speed of delivery, the way the actors and actresses stand or move when speaking their lines, and what they do when they are not speaking their lines. The director really interprets the way the whole play should go. In many productions, the director is as important as the author of the play.

Most plays are presented on stages with *sets*. The set is a representation of the room, landscape, or other locale in which the play takes place. *Props* are important items used in the drama, such as a telephone, a sword, a book, a glass of water, or any other item that figures in the action. *Lighting* helps to establish the desired moods, or the time of day or the season.

Each *act* of a play is usually composed of several *scenes*. The end of each act often includes a *climax*, which is an emotional or suspenseful moment, designed to keep the audience interested so it will come back after the intermission. The final act of the drama usually builds to a final climax or crisis, which is greater than any that went before. The end of the drama involves the resolution of the conflict: usually by death in a tragedy, or by marriage in a comedy.

See **Dialogue.**
See also pages 280, 296–297, 360–361, 362.

ELEGY *A mournful poem or lament, usually a meditation on the death of someone famous or of someone important to the writer.* Elegies may also be laments on the nature of death itself, or on the loss of youth and beauty. The most famous elegy is probably "Elegy Written in a Country Churchyard," by the English poet Thomas Gray. One of its frequently quoted stanzas is:

> The boast of heraldry, the pomp of power,
> And all that beauty, all that wealth e'er
>   gave,
> Awaits alike the inevitable hour.
> The paths of glory lead but to the grave.

Walt Whitman's poem "O Captain! My Captain!" is one of several elegies he wrote mourning the death of Abraham Lincoln.

ESSAY *A short piece of prose writing which discusses a subject in a limited way and which usually expresses a particular point of view.* The word *essay* means "an evaluation or consideration of something." Most essays tend to be thoughtful considerations about a subject of interest to the writer. Most essays are *expository* in nature, which simply means that they do not tell a story, but explain or give information about a situation, an event, or a process. J. Frank Dobie's "Bandanna" is a good example of an expository essay.

See **Exposition.**

EXPOSITION *The kind of writing that explains something or gives information about something.* Exposition can be used in fiction and nonfiction, but its most familiar form is the *essay*. A typical example of exposition is this passage from Henry David Thoreau's *Walden*, in which Thoreau explains why he decided to spend some time alone in a cabin in the woods:

I went to the woods because I wished to live deliberately, to front only the essential facts of life, and see if I could not learn what it had to teach, and not, when I came to die, discover that I had not lived. I did not wish to live what was not life, living is so dear; nor did I wish to practice resignation, unless it was quite necessary. I wanted to live deep and suck out all the marrow of life, to live so sturdily and Spartan-like as to put to rout all that was not life. . . .

Exposition is also that part of a play or other narrative that helps the reader understand important background information. For example, in *The Diary of Anne Frank* the authors provide background information, or exposition, in the first scene. Here the audience is told how the Frank family and others were forced to go into hiding in a warehouse in Amsterdam, to escape the Nazis.

See **Essay**.
See also pages 190–191.

FABLE　*A brief story with a moral, written in either prose or poetry.* The characters in fables are often animals who speak and act like human beings. The most famous fables are those of Aesop, who was said to be a Greek slave living in the sixth century B.C. Almost as famous are the fables of the seventeenth-century French writer, La Fontaine.

A typical fable is Aesop's "Belling the Cat," the story of the mice who decided to put a bell around a cat's neck so they'd hear it coming. It was a wonderful solution that every mouse applauded. Then came the obvious problem: Who would actually put the bell on the cat? Their solution had merely gotten them another problem. The moral of the story is "It is easy to propose impossible remedies."

See page 488.

FICTION　*A prose account which is invented and not a record of things as they actually happened.* Much fiction is based on real personal experience, but it almost always involves invented characters, or invented actions or settings, or other details which are made up for the sake of the story itself. Fiction can be brief, as a fable or short story is, or it can be book length, as a novel is.

FIGURATIVE LANGUAGE　*Any language that is not intended to be interpreted in a strict literal sense.*

When we call a car a "lemon," we use figurative language. We do not mean that the car is really a citrus fruit, but that its performance is "sour" — it will cause its owner to lose money. When we refer to someone as a lamb, or a peach, or a rock, or an angel, we know that the person is none of those things. Instead, we mean simply that the person shares some quality with those other things.

The main form of figurative language used in literature is *metaphor*. Metaphor makes a comparison between two different things. The father in Mary O'Hara's story "My Friend Flicka" uses metaphors when he says that the mares are hellions and the stallions outlaws. He is comparing the mares to ghastly creatures from hell. They are not *really* from hell, as we know, but the comparison makes us realize how troublesome they can be. To say the stallions are outlaws is also a metaphor, because it compares the horses to human outlaws. Horses do not have legal institutions: that's reserved for humankind. By comparing the stallions to human outlaws, this speaker shows how bad they are and how hard they are to control.

These metaphors are stated clearly: "The mares *are* hellions," etc. But sometimes a metaphor does not state the comparison so directly. We also use a metaphor when we say something like: "Kate's sunny smile enchanted us." We are actually comparing her smile with the brightness and the welcoming warmth of the sun. When Control Houston, in the dialogue with Apollo 8, says to the astronauts, "You are riding the best bird we can find," the control tower is using metaphor. We know the astronauts are not riding a bird. The Control Tower is comparing the flight of the rocket to the flight of a bird, and the metaphor puts an interesting picture in our minds.

Similes are another form of figurative language. Similes are easy to recognize because they always use special words to state their comparisons. When the poet Robert Burns says "My luve is like a red, red rose," he uses a simile. It is a comparison and it is, indeed, like a metaphor. But it's different because it uses a special word to state the comparison. That word is *like*. Other words and phrases used in similes are *as, as if, than, such as,* and *resembles*—all of which state a comparison directly. Just as with metaphor, the simile does not use *all* the points of comparison for its force. It only uses some. For instance, the comparison of "my luve" to "a rose" does not necessarily mean that the loved one is thorny, nor that she lives in a garden, nor that she has a green neck. Rather, it means that "my luve" is delicate, fragrant, rare, and beautiful, as the flower is.

Emily Dickinson uses a simile in "I Like to See It Lap the Miles" when she says that the train is "punctual as a star." But she also uses a metaphor in this poem, since she makes other comparisons between the train and an animal, which seems to be a horse. The verbs in particular suggest this metaphor: she tells us that the train *laps, licks, feeds itself, steps, peers, crawls, chases,* and *neighs at its own stable door.* All of these verbs describe actions that we know a train cannot perform, but an animal can.

Similes in everyday language are common. "He was madder than a hornet." She roared like a bull." "Louie laughed like a hyena." "Float like a butterfly, sting like a bee." "Be as firm as Gibralter and as cool as a cucumber." "She resembles Wonder Woman."

See **Metaphor, Simile, Symbol.**
See also pages 397, 423, 428, 462, 504.

FLASHBACK *An interruption of the action in a story to tell about something that happened earlier in time.* The usual plot moves in chronological order: it starts at a given moment, progresses through time, and ends at some later moment. A flashback interrupts that flow by suddenly shifting to past time and narrating important incidents that make the present action more understandable. Usually there is a signal to indicate the flashback, but occasionally a writer will leave out the signal. The reader must pay very close attention to find the point where the narrative picks up the action again.

The play *The Diary of Anne Frank* is almost entirely a flashback. In the opening scene, when Mr. Frank enters the warehouse, it is 1945. The play then flashes back to 1942, and not until the final scene are we brought back to 1945 again.

See page 361.

FOLK TALE *A story that was not originally written down, but was passed on orally from one storyteller to another.* Folk tales often exist in several forms because they are carried by storytellers to different parts of the world. Over the years, and according to changing local customs, the same tale can take on slightly different qualities. Many fairy tales, such as the story of Cinderella and the story of Jack and the Beanstalk, are folk tales that originated in Europe, and versions of them later appeared in the Appalachian Mountains of the New World. Folk tales often involve unreal creatures, like dragons, cannibalistic giants, and chatty animals.

In the United States, folk tales have grown up about such figures as the frontiersman Davy Crockett, the steel-drivin' man John Henry, and the original cowhand Pecos Bill.

FORESHADOWING *The use of hints or clues in a narrative to suggest action that is to come.* Foreshadowing helps to build suspense in a story because it alerts the reader to what is about to happen. It also helps the reader enjoy all the details of the buildup. Lewis Carroll uses a bit of foreshadowing in his poem "Jabberwocky" when he has the old man warn: "Beware of the Jabberwock, my son! / The jaws that bite, the claws that catch!" But foreshadowing is more common in short stories, longer fiction, and drama. It is often said that if a loaded gun is presented in Act One of a play, it should go off before Act Five. In other words, the gun in the first act usually foreshadows some danger to come.

See pages 202, 407.

HERO / HEROINE *The chief character in a story or drama.* In older heroic stories, the heroes and heroines often embody qualities that their society thought were best and most desirable. The heroines and heroes in such stories are often of noble blood and are usually physically strong, courageous, and intelligent, characteristics that are shown by the great hero of Norse mythology, Sigurd. Often the conflict involves the hero or heroine with a monster or with a force that threatens the entire social group, a detail found in the African legend about Nana Miriam, in which the heroine saves her people from a hippopotamus.

Folk heroes like Daniel Boone and John Henry, and the heroes of tall tales like Paul Bunyan and Pecos Bill, share most of these heroic qualities with their counterparts in myth.

Nowadays, we use the term *hero* or *heroine* to mean the main character in any narrative. At times, this person might be admirable, as in the poem "Elizabeth Blackwell" by Eve Merriam, in which a young woman makes a heroic decision to study medicine, even though her society disapproves. At times, however, the hero or heroine in modern stories is not entirely admirable. Some of them might even show ordinary human weaknesses, such as fear or poor judgment. For example, in Mary O'Hara's story "My Friend Flicka," the hero, Kennie, seems to be a failure in everything but his devotion to his horse. In some stories, the hero or heroine might even be "unheroic" and not admirable at all. In Washington Irving's "The Legend of Sleepy Hollow," the hero, Ichabod, is cowardly and superstitious, just the opposite of the noble, strong, intelligent heroes of old.

IMAGERY *Words and phrases that describe something in a way that creates pictures, or images, that appeal to the reader's senses.* Most images tend to be visual, though many times a writer will also use words that suggest the way things sound, smell, taste, or feel to the touch. Images appear in all kinds of writing: poetry, nonfiction, fiction, and drama. Not all writers use imagery extensively. But those who do, use it in an effort to make an experience in literature more intense for us. Because good images involve our sensory awareness, they help us to be more responsive readers.

Washington Irving, in "The Legend of Sleepy Hollow," describes something (a phantom?) as if it were a wind that could be felt and heard: "some rushing blast, howling among the trees." Katrina Van Tassel is described in images that appeal to our sense of taste: "a blooming lass of fresh eighteen, plump as a partridge, ripe and melting and rosy cheeked as one of her father's peaches." The Van Tassel barnyard is described in visual images that also make our mouths water: "he pictured to himself every roasting-pig running about with a pudding in his belly, and an apple in his mouth. The pigeons were snugly put to bed in a comfortable pie, and tucked in with a coverlet of crust; the geese were swimming in their own gravy."

See **Description.**
See also page 419.

INFERENCE *A reasonable conclusion made about something based on certain clues or facts.* Often the writer of a piece of literature will not tell us everything there is to tell. At times, we have the pleasure of drawing an inference about a scene, a character, or an action. The process of drawing an inference is pleasurable, because we are actually making a discovery on our own.

In her poem "I Like to See It Lap the Miles," Emily Dickinson never tells us that she is describing a train. Yet readers have inferred that she is talking about a train from clues given in the poem: it speeds over the miles, goes around mountains and through passages hewn out of rocks, hoots and makes other noises, "chases itself" downhill, and when it stops, it is quiet.

In "Casey at the Bat," Ernest Lawrence Thayer never tells us directly that Casey is a fellow who is very sure of himself. He lets us infer that his character is enormously confident—perhaps even overconfident—when Casey lets a perfectly good ball go by and says, "That ain't my style." By that point in the poem, we also infer that Casey's pride and confidence are going to do him in.

See page 69.

INVERSION *A reversal of the normal order of words in a sentence, usually for some kind of emphasis.* The normal word order in an English sentence is subject-verb-complement. When writers and speakers invert, or reverse, this pattern, the word or phrase that is placed out of order usually receives more emphasis. The device often appears in poetry, but it occurs in prose and in speech as well. In poetry, inversion is often used to make a line's rhythm beat out in a certain way, or to achieve a certain end-rhyme.

Edgar Allan Poe used inversion in many of his poems. In these lines from "The Raven," we find inversion in the clause in the second line. Poe probably used inversion here so that he could get a word to rhyme with *nevermore*:

But the Raven, sitting lonely on the placid bust, spoke only
That one word, as if his soul in that one word he did outpour.

The normal word order of the last clause would be:

. . . as if he did outpour his soul in that one word.

At times, inversion can make a passage sound too literary or poetical, or even old-fashioned. Its use must be cautious, since too much inversion makes a passage seem artificial.

See pages 440, 462.

IRONY *A contrast between what is stated and what is really meant, or between what is expected to happen and what actually does happen.* Irony is used in everyday conversation. When we say, "It's not at all warm here," when we're standing in the desert in July, we are using irony.

There are three kinds of irony used in literature: (1) *Verbal irony* occurs when a writer or speaker says one thing and means something entirely different; (2) *Irony of situation* occurs when a situation turns out to be completely different from what we expect; (3) *Dramatic irony* occurs when a reader or an audience knows something that a character in a play or story does not know. Irony is used in literature for all kinds of effects, from humor to serious comments on the unpredictable nature of life.

A humorous example of *verbal irony* is found in this short verse by Lewis Carroll:

The Crocodile

How doth the little crocodile
   Improve his shining tail,
And pour the waters of the Nile
   On every shining scale!

How cheerfully he seems to grin,
   How neatly spread his claws,
And welcomes little fishes in
   With gently smiling jaws!

This speaker says one thing but really means something else. He says that the crocodile "welcomes" little fish into his "gently" smiling jaws. He really means that the crocodile is eating the fish and that his massive, toothy jaws are anything but gentle.

One of the most famous examples of *irony of situation* is the ending of William Shakespeare's tragedy *King Lear*. After a terrible struggle and a mighty battle, King Lear is saved by his faithful daughter, Cordelia. We expect her to be able to enjoy her victory, but just the reverse happens: she is executed after the battle is won. She lies dead in Lear's arms, and, instead of enjoying his new-found freedom and safety, Lear dies too. This unpleasant ending is so ironic that throughout the eighteenth century, people insisted that the play be performed with a happy ending.

A good example of *dramatic irony* is found in the play *The Diary of Anne Frank*. We, the audience, are told at the beginning of the play that no one but Mr. Frank survives the Nazi prison camps. Thus, we watch the play knowing what the main characters themselves don't know: that only one of them will survive the war.

See page 221.

LEGEND *A story handed down from the past. Legends seem to have some basis in history.* A legend usually centers on some historical incident, such as a battle or a journey in search of a treasure or the founding of a city or nation. A legend usually features a great hero or heroine who struggles against some powerful force to achieve the desired goal. Most legends were passed on orally long before they were written down, so the characters became larger than life, and their actions became fantastic and unbelievable. An example of a famous legend is the story "The Wooden Horse," which tells how the Greeks won the war against Troy almost four thousand years ago.

See page 482.

LIMERICK *A comic poem written in five lines, rhymed in the pattern a a b b a, and having a definite pattern of rhythm.* Writing limericks is a great popular pastime. Much of the fun comes in finding rhymes to match the name of a person or place. A typical limerick begins like this: "There was a young girl from St. Paul." What comes later is up to the writer.

Sometimes writers of limericks twist the spellings of the rhyming words to build more humor. The following limerick plays on the Irish spelling of a town south of Dublin, *Dun Laoghaire*, pronounced "dun leery."

An ancient old man of Dun Laoghaire
Said, "Of pleasure and joy I've grown
    waoghaire.
  The life that is pure,
  Will suit me I'm sure,
It's healthy and noble though draghaire."

You can see that the pattern of rhythm for lines 1, 2, and 5 is the same and that the pattern for lines 3 and 4 is the same.

See page 449.

LYRIC POEM *A brief poem which expresses an emotion and which usually represents the poet as "I."* (A lyric poem does *not* tell a story. A poem that tells a story is called a *narrative poem.*) The word *lyric* is derived from the word *lyre,* a musical instrument. The lyre is a stringed instrument remotely related to our guitar. It was struck in chords by the ancient Greek lyric poets, who sang their poems in a chant-like fashion. The lyre was used to help build up the emotional effects and to help the listener respond to the poem. Today we do not necessarily associate the lyric poem with music, although we do call the words to songs "lyrics."

English poet Leigh Hunt expresses a number of emotions in this lyric poem:

Jenny Kissed Me

Jenny kissed me when we met,
  Jumping from the chair she sat in;
Time, you thief, who love to get
  Sweets into your list, put that in!
Say I'm weary, say I'm sad,
  Say that health and wealth have missed
  me,
Say I'm growing old, but add,
  Jenny kissed me.

METAMORPHOSIS *In literature, a fantastic change, mainly of shape or form.* Myths often use metamorphosis to suggest a close relationship among gods, humans, and the world of nature. The Greek goddess Aphrodite, for instance, sprang from the foam of the sea. The goddess Athena appeared to the Greek hero Odysseus in the form of a mist. She also assumed the form of an owl when it suited her. Such metamorphoses reflected the ancient Greeks' wonder about the nature of the world, by suggesting that the shapes of things were not necessarily true indications of what the things really were. If an owl could be a goddess, then it was only wise for a Greek to be cautious of the owl and to respect it. Many people other than the ancient Greeks have had this sense of wonder and respect for all aspects of the world. The early American Indians are one example. In the myth "The Kamiah Monster," we read that the Blackfoot, Sioux, and Flathead peoples took their forms from the bone and flesh of a huge sky monster.

In A.D. 8, a Roman poet named Ovid collected the Greek and Roman myths of shape-changing into a book called *The Metamorphoses.* One of the famous stories from Ovid's collection is "Midas," in which a king is given the power to change everything he touches into gold. *The Metamorphoses* influenced many later writers to introduce sudden changes of form or shape into their works. Metamorphoses are found in many popular European folktales, in which handsome princes are often reduced to ugly and repellent creatures. In "The Princess and the Frog," a frog is transformed back into a beautiful prince, and in "Beauty and the Beast," a prince is transformed into a beast and then returned to his original form.

Metamorphoses are used in modern literature as well. In "Flowers for Algernon," Daniel Keyes writes about a scientifically-induced metamorphosis, in which a retarded man is transformed into a mental giant as a result of a surgical procedure. In fact, metamorphoses are found in many works of science fiction.

See page 493.

METAPHOR *A comparison made between two different things, as in the saying "Life is a dream," "You are my sunshine," or "He is a peach."* The intention of a metaphor is to give added meaning to one of the things being compared. A metaphor is one of the most important forms of *figurative language*. It is used in virtually all forms of language, including everyday speech, formal prose, and all forms of fiction and poetry.

If we say, "He was a gem to help me out," we use a metaphor, because we say a person is a gem. Gems are stones; they are hard; they glisten; they are often quite small. But these are *not* the qualities which the metaphor wants us to consider. We rely on our listener to understand that the metaphor is comparing the person's *value* to a gem's value.

If we say, "Misers have hearts of flint," we do not mean that their hearts are small dark stones that are bloodless and nonfunctioning. Rather, we mean that misers cannot show sympathy and kindness, just as the piece of stone cannot.

Metaphors are not always stated directly. When James Street, in "Weep No More, My Lady," calls the sounds of the swamp animals a "moonlight symphony," he uses a metaphor that compares the sounds of the creatures to the sounds of a symphony: they are musical and rhythmic. Street may also expect us to see another, less obvious metaphor, when he tells us it is a *"moonlight"* symphony." He may expect us to remember Beethoven's piano piece, the "Moonlight Sonata."

A poet will sometimes *extend* a metaphor throughout a poem. Langston Hughes does this in his poem "Mother to Son." In the first line, the mother compares life to a stairway, and throughout the poem she talks of life as if it *were* a stairway. A metaphor is also extended throughout the following poem by Emily Dickinson. In the first line, the poet compares hope to a bird: Throughout the poem, she continues to describe hope as if it were a bird:

> Hope is the thing with feathers
> That perches in the soul,
> And sings the tune without the words,
> And never stops at all,
>
> And sweetest in the gale is heard;
> And sore must be the storm
> That could abash the little bird
> That kept so many warm.
>
> I've heard it in the chillest land,
> And on the strangest sea;
> Yet, never, in extremity,
> It asked a crumb of me.

See **Figurative Language, Simile.**
See also pages 428–429.

MYTH *A story, often about gods and goddesses, that attempts to give meaning to the world.* Almost every society has myths which explain the beginnings of the world, the beginnings of the human race, and the origins of evil. Myths tell people other things that they are concerned about: who their gods are, what their most sacred beliefs are, who their heroes are, and what their purpose in life is.

The term "classical mythology" refers to the myths told by the ancient Greeks and Romans. Most of the classical myths have to do with divinities who lived on Olympus, such as Zeus, Aphrodite, Apollo, Athena, and many others. Some of the classical myths have to do with the histories of great families. The myth "Antigone" is one of several stories told about the family of a king named Oedipus.

See pages 469, 477, 486.

NARRATION *The kind of writing or speaking that relates a story (a narrative).* Narration tells about a series of connected events, explaining what happened, when it happened, and to whom it happened. Narration can be fictional, or it can be based on actual events. Narration can take the form of prose or poetry. It can be as long as a novel, or it can be as brief as an anecdote, which may be only a paragraph. Short stories, narrative poems, myths, fables, and legends are all examples of narration.

See **Point of View.**
See also pages 137, 152, 266.

NARRATIVE POETRY *Poetry that tells a story.* Well-known narrative poems included in this anthology are Henry Wadsworth Longfellow's "Paul Revere's Ride," Sir Walter Scott's "Lochinvar," Edgar Allan Poe's "The Raven," Ernest Lawrence Thayer's "Casey at the Bat," and Lewis Carroll's "Jabberwocky."

See **Ballad, Narration, Point of View.**
See also page 152.

NONFICTION *Any prose account that tells about something that actually happened or that presents factual information about something.* One of the chief kinds of nonfiction is the history of someone's life. When a person writes his own personal life history, we call it *autobiography* (such as Richard Wright's *Black Boy*). When someone else writes a person's history, we call it *biog-*

raphy (such as Ann Petry's book *Harriet Tubman: Conductor on the Underground Railroad*). Another kind of nonfiction is the *essay* (such as J. Frank Dobie's account of the uses of the bandanna). News stories, editorials, letters to the editor, travel accounts, personal journals, and diaries, such as the one kept by Anaïs Nin, are all forms of nonfiction.

See **Biography, Essay.**
See also pages 365, 414.

NOVEL *A fictional narrative in prose, generally longer than a short story.* The novel allows for greater complexity of character and plot development than the short story. The forms the novel may take cover a wide range. For example, there are the *historical novel*, in which historical characters, settings, and periods are drawn in detail; the *picaresque novel*, presenting the adventures of a rogue; and the *psychological novel*, which focuses on characters' emotions and thoughts. Other forms of the novel include the detective story, the spy thriller, the Western, and the science-fiction novel.

PARAPHRASE *A summary or restatement of a piece of writing, which expresses its meaning in other words.* A paraphrase of Ernest Lawrence Thayer's poem "Casey at the Bat" might go this way:

> The Mudville baseball team was behind in the last inning, and it looked as if Casey would not even get a chance at bat. But, when some batters before him actually got on base, everyone had high hopes that Casey could win the game with one of his famous home runs. But Casey showed off, did not swing at the first two good pitches, and struck out on the third one.

It is clear that such a paraphrase takes all the fun out of the original poem. The purpose of the paraphrase is to see that we understand just what really did happen in the poem.

PARODY *The humorous imitation of a serious piece of literature, or of some other art form, for the sake of amusement or ridicule.* In literature, a parody can be made of a character, a plot, a writer's style, or a theme.

Casey, in Ernest Lawrence Thayer's "Casey at the Bat," is a parody of the great heroes of old, like Sigurd or King Arthur, who never fail to come to the rescue of their people. The last and highest hopes of the home-team crowd are focused on Casey, their conquering hero. But all hopes die, and the hero fails the home team after all.

Ichabod Crane, in Washington Irving's "The Legend of Sleepy Hollow," is also a parody of the knights of old. Here is a passage describing Ichabod—notice how he is just the opposite of those strong and handsome heroes who always ride beautiful, fleet, and loyal horses.

That he might make his appearance before his mistress in the true style of a cavalier, he borrowed a horse from the farmer with whom he was living . . . and, thus gallantly mounted, issued forth, like a knight-errant in quest of adventures. But it is proper that I should, in the true spirit of romantic story, give some account of the looks and equipment of my hero and his steed. The animal he bestrode was a broken-down plow horse that had outlived almost everything but his viciousness. He was gaunt and shaggy, with a thin neck and a head like a hammer; his rusty mane and tail were tangled and knotted with burrs: one eye had lost its pupil and was glaring and spectral; but the other had the gleam of a genuine devil in it. Still,

he must have had fire and mettle in his day, if we may judge from the name he bore of Gunpowder.

The following verse is a parody of the style of Edgar Allan Poe's "The Raven," a poem which has been often parodied over the years:

Once upon a midnight dreary, while I
    shivered eerie, bleary,
    Full of teary leer-y, fear-y,
Thinking of my lost Lenore, my lost Le-
    nore . . .
Lenore and nothing more!
Not the oaken door, the grocery store, the
    dreadful bore, the apple core, the golf
    fore, the marine corps, or the Lakers'
    score:
My lost Lenore and nothing more.
While I shivered nearly freezing, in my
    thin pajamas sneezing,
    Who should wing right in a-breezing
    but a bristling Raven wheezing,
Wheezing, wheezing right above my
    chamber door.

Such parodies are fun and harmless, even if they do make us laugh a bit at some of the techniques used by a respected poet like Poe.

PLOT *The sequence of events that take place in a story.* Short stories, novels, dramas, and narrative poems all have plots.

The major element in a plot is a *conflict,* or a struggle of some kind that takes place between the characters and their environment, or between warring desires in the characters' own minds. A plot will introduce the characters, reveal the nature of their conflict, and show us how the conflict is resolved.

624 *Guide to Literary Terms and Techniques*

Many times, especially in novels and plays, there will be more than one plot. In *The Diary of Anne Frank*, the main plot tells what happens as the "family" hides from their enemies; the *subplot* tells what happens to Anne and her growing love for Peter.

See **Conflict**.
See also pages 221, 296, 360.

POETRY *Traditional poetry is language arranged in lines, with a regular rhythm and often with a definite rhyme scheme. Nontraditional poetry does away with regular rhythm and rhyme, though it usually is set up in lines.* There is no satisfactory way of defining poetry, although most people have little trouble knowing when they read it. Some definitions offered by those concerned with poetry may help us. The English poet William Wordsworth called it "the spontaneous overflow of powerful feelings." Matthew Arnold, an English writer and poet of the nineteenth century, defined it in this way: "Poetry is simply the most beautiful, impressive and widely effective mode of saying things."

Poetry uses *figurative language* and *imagery* extensively. It is often divided into *stanzas*. Poetry often uses *rhyme* in order to create a kind of music or to emphasize certain moods or effects. Poetry depends heavily on strong *rhythms*, even when the rhythms are not regular. Techniques like *alliteration* and *inversion* are often considered especially poetic.

There are two general categories of poetry: *narrative poetry*, which tells a story, and *lyric poetry*, which does not tell a story but expresses some personal emotion. Some of the well-known poetic forms are the *ballad*, the *elegy*, and the *limerick*.

See **Figurative Language, Rhyme, Rhythm**.
See also pages 119, 152, 448, 454, 462–463.

POINT OF VIEW *The vantage point from which a story is told.* Every story has to have a point of view, since it has to be told to us by some "voice." Writers may tell their stories from a third-person point of view, or they may use a first-person point of view.

(1) The *third-person point of view* is one of the most common in literature. In this point of view, a story is told by someone not in the story at all. The following paragraph is an example of the third-person point of view. We are told here that a character, Hester Martin, has made a decision. She is referred to in the third person ("she"), which is how this point of view gets its name:

> Hester Martin could let the insult get her down. She could reply rudely or call for the manager and make a formal complaint. But she decided against both courses. Instead, she took the man aside and explained to him what it felt like to have a total stranger say something cruel, even if the man did not intend to be insulting. The man did not intend to be insulting at all, and once Hester told him how she felt, he changed his manner entirely. Hester had done the right thing. She had educated someone.

This is an example of an *omniscient*, or *all-knowing, third-person point of view*. The narrator tells us things that Hester Martin does not directly think or observe. The narrator tells us also that Hester made the right decision.

A third-person point of view might *not* be all-knowing. A *limited third-person point of view* only tells us what one character sees, feels, and thinks. This same scene written from a limited third-person point of view might go this way:

> Hester Martin felt her face flush. Did he notice it, too? Should she go to his manager?

Should she insult him back? She took a moment to bring her emotions back under control, but when she collected herself she drew the man aside and lectured him carefully and patiently on the subject of insulting a patron. His apologies and his extraordinary politeness and caution gave her a small measure of satisfaction.

This limited third-person point of view tells the story from the point of view of one character only. The narrator does not tell us what other characters are thinking or feeling.

(2) The *first-person point of view* tells everything from the vantage point of a narrator who is usually a character in the story. We can be told only what this narrator knows and feels. We cannot be told what any other character thinks, except when the narrator may guess about that character's feelings or thoughts. The first-person is a very limited point of view, but its popularity is secure since we all identify with "I" in a story. The passage about Hester Martin's decision might be told like this by a first-person narrator:

> I felt my face burn with the insult. I wondered if he noticed it. Should I go to his manager? No, I thought. And I won't stoop to his level and return the comment. When I thought I could control myself, I took the man aside and I told him in no uncertain terms that I did not like being insulted by a stranger. The only satisfaction I got was watching him try to squirm out of it, telling me he didn't mean it as an insult. But at least I got him to admit he was wrong. Maybe he learned a lesson.

The first-person point of view is much like our own view of life. It is limited to what one person knows and is controlled by that one person's thoughts and feelings.

See pages 45, 117, 264.

PROSE *All literature which is not written as poetry.* Essays, short stories, novels, biographies, and most dramas are written in prose. Prose styles differ widely, from the simple and direct style of a story like Mary O'Hara's "My Friend Flicka," to the more ornate and colorful style of Washington Irving's story "The Legend of Sleepy Hollow." One of the most remarkable pieces of prose is Abraham Lincoln's "Gettysburg Address," which was so short that very few people who were present when Lincoln spoke actually remembered hearing it.

REFRAIN *A word, phrase, line, or group of lines that is repeated regularly in a poem or song, usually at the end of each stanza.* Refrains are sometimes used to emphasize a particularly important idea. In Poe's "The Raven," for example, the sentence "Quoth the Raven, 'Nevermore' " is a refrain. It helps to build up the mood of despair, and it reminds us continually of the sound of the name of the dead Lenore.

Sometimes the refrain in a poem or song is repeated exactly the same way, and sometimes it is varied slightly for effect. One of the delights in refrains is in anticipating their return.

RHYME *The repetition of sounds in words that appear close to each other in a poem.* One of the primary uses of rhyme seems to be as an aid to memory. You may have used some of the simpler rhymes for this purpose yourself, such as the one about months, beginning: "Thirty days hath September, April, June, and November." A rhyme that might help you remember a spelling rule is the one beginning: "*I* before *e* except after *c*."

The most familiar form of rhyme is *end rhyme*. This simply means that the rhymes come at the ends of the lines. The following lines are from a long poem on music, by the English poet Alexander Pope. In this part of the poem, Pope is trying to re-create the sounds of the underworld when Orpheus sings there in an attempt to rescue his beloved Euridyce:

What sounds are heard,
What scenes appeared,
    O'er all the dreary coasts!
        Dreadful gleams,
        Dismal screams,
        Fires that glow,
        Shrieks of woe,
        Sullen moans,
        Hollow groans,
    And cries of tortured ghosts!

Each of these rhymes is an exact rhyme, although we would now pronounce *heard* differently from *appeared*.

Rhyme that occurs within a line is called *internal rhyme*. One of the masters of internal rhyme is Edgar Allan Poe, who uses it in the first line of "The Raven": "Once upon a midnight *dreary*, while I pondered, weak and *weary*." One of Poe's clever internal rhymes is "lattice" and "thereat is" (lines 33-34).

Clearly, in poetry, rhymes are used for more than an aid to memory. Rhymes in the works of Pope or Poe, or any other careful poet, serve many purposes. One is to increase the musicality of the poem. (Songwriters also do this.) Another purpose of rhyme is to give delight by rewarding our anticipation of a returning sound, as in Pope's "coasts" / "ghosts" rhyme. Rhyme is also used for humor. *Limericks*, for instance, would not be half so funny if they did not rhyme. The English poet George Gordon, Lord Byron invented one of the funniest rhymes in English when he rhymed "intellectual" with "hen-pecked you all."

See **Poetry**.
See also pages 435, 448, 451.

RHYTHM *The pattern of stressed and unstressed sounds in a line of poetry.* All language has rhythm of some sort or another, but rhythm is most important in poetry, where it is carefully controlled for effect.

There are several effects of rhythm in poetry. Rhythm lends poetry a musical quality, which gives the reader or listener pleasure. Rhythm can also be used to imitate the action being described in a poem. For example, in Robert Browning's poem "How They Brought the Good News from Ghent to Aix," the rhythm actually imitates the galloping rhythm of horses' hoofs.

And there was my Roland to bear the whole weight,
Of the news which alone could save Aix from her fate,
With his nostrils like pits full of blood to the brim,
And with circles of red for his eye sockets' rim.

One thing to remember is that good poets usually put the stress on the most important words in the line. If you say a line to yourself in a natural voice, you will hear that the most important words demand stress.

In addition to using a pattern of stressed and unstressed syllables, a poet has another powerful means of building rhythm. This is by the use of *repetition*. In this passage from "The Bells," Edgar Allan Poe repeats the word *bells* eighteen times. He echoes the word three more times with the repetition of the rhyming word *knells*. He also repeats the word *time* six times, and echoes it twice more with the rhyming word *rhyme*. All of this repetition builds up a kind of pounding rhythm, which might remind us of the repeated ringing of bells themselves:

Keeping time, time, time,
In a sort of runic rhyme,
    To the throbbing of the bells,

Of the bells, bells, bells—
   To the sobbing of the bells;
Keeping time, time, time,
   As he knells, knells, knells,
In a happy runic rhyme,
   To the rolling of the bells,
Of the bells, bells, bells:
   To the tolling of the bells,
Of the bells, bells, bells, bells,
   Bells, bells, bells—
To the moaning and the groaning of the
   bells.

See **Alliteration, Rhyme.**
See also pages 429, 440.

SETTING *The time and place in which the events of a story take place.* In short stories, novels, poems, and nonfiction, setting is established by *description.* In dramas, setting is usually established by *stage directions,* but since dramas normally have *sets* which appear before the audience, elaborate descriptions of setting are unnecessary.

In some stories, setting is not important at all, but in other stories setting is very significant. Washington Irving's story "The Legend of Sleepy Hollow," for example, could only happen in one setting—a "spellbound" region, where people believe in ghosts:

A drowsy, dreamy influence seems to hang over the land. The whole neighborhood abounds with local tales, haunted spots, and twilight superstitions; and the nightmare seems to make it the favorite scene of her gambols.

Setting can serve simply as the physical background of a story, or it can be used to establish atmosphere. In his poem "The Raven," Edgar Allan Poe uses setting to establish an atmosphere of gloom and mystery. He does this by telling us what time it is (a "midnight dreary"), what month it is ("bleak De-

cember"), what the study looks like ("each separate dying ember wrought its ghost upon the floor"), and what sounds are heard ("the silken, sad, uncertain rustling of each purple curtain").

See **Atmosphere.**
See also page 214.

SIMILE *A comparison made between two different things, using a word such as* like *or* as. Similes are *figures of speech* and are common in everyday language and in most forms of literature. We use similes when we say, "He fought like a tiger"; "He was as mild as a dove"; "She was as cool as a cucumber." A more poetic use of simile is this, from George Gordon, Lord Byron's "Stanzas for Music":

There will be none of Beauty's daughters
   With a magic like thee;
And like music on the waters
   Is thy sweet voice to me.

See **Figurative Language.**
See also page 423.

STANZA *A group of lines forming a unit in a poem.* Some poems, such as limericks, consist of a single stanza. "Lochinvar" by Sir Walter Scott is divided into eight stanzas, each of which has six lines and the same rhyme scheme.

See **Poetry.**

SUSPENSE *That quality in a literary work that makes the reader or audience uncertain or tense about what is to come next.* Suspense is a kind of "suspending" of our emotions. We know something is about to happen, and the longer the writer can keep us guessing, the greater the suspense. Suspense is popular in any kind of literature that involves *plot,* whether it be nonfiction, drama, short stories, novels, or narrative poems.

Every reader of Ernest Lawrence Thayer's "Casey at the Bat," for example, wants to find out if the hero of the poem will come to the rescue of the Mudville Nine. Holding the reader off for as long as possible is part of the poet's strategy of building suspense.

Suspense is possible even when the reader *knows* what to expect. Even though we know in Edward Everett Hale's "The Man Without a Country" that Philip Nolan has died in exile, we want to keep on reading to find out what his life at sea was like. We also are kept in suspense over Nolan's feelings; we want to know if he changed his mind about his country during his exile.

See **Foreshadowing, Plot.**
See also pages 202, 407.

SYMBOL *Any person, place, or thing which has meaning in itself but which is made to represent, or stand for, something else as well.* A symbol can be an object, a person, an action, a place, or a situation. Writers sometimes rely on commonly used symbols: most people know, for example, that an old man with a scythe usually is a symbol for time, that a dove is a symbol for peace, that a snake is often a symbol for evil, that ice is often a symbol for hatred, and that red is often a symbol for passion. But often we have to be on our toes in order to understand what something in literature is supposed to symbolize.

Symbols are often personal. In Robert Frost's poem "The Road Not Taken," we know that the road symbolizes a choice, but we do not know exactly what choice the poet has in mind. Frost purposely leaves its full meaning indefinite, so that the road can take on any number of symbolic meanings. For Frost, it may have symbolized a choice of careers—should he be a schoolteacher or a poet, for example. For us, it may symbolize other choices. Frost's road works well as a symbol

because everybody has choices to make and nobody can make all of them. There has to be "a road not taken" in everyone's life.

A symbol is like a rock thrown in a pond: we see the splash right away, but then we notice that the ripples go much further than we expected. As we reflect on a symbol, its suggested meanings move out like the ripples, slowly and ever more widely.

See page 432.

TALL TALE *A highly improbable, humorous story that stretches facts beyond any hope of belief.* Tall tales feature things like people as high as mountains, pancake griddles two city blocks wide, and lakes used for boiling vegetables. Tall tales seem to have been extremely popular in the American West, where even nature seemed to assume gigantic proportions. The tales of Mike Fink, the keelboatman, John Henry, the railroad man, and Paul Bunyan, the logger, were the delight of the evening campfire. Some tall tales continue to become taller as generations of new storytellers add to them.

See pages 504, 512.

THEME *The main idea expressed in a literary work.* Many stories, such as some murder mysteries and sports stories, seem to have little to say about life or about human nature. Such stories are told chiefly for entertainment, and theme is of little or no importance in them. But other stories do try to make a comment on the human condition, and in those stories, theme is of great importance.

Because themes are rarely expressed directly, they are not always obvious to the reader. Theme is one of those qualities which must be dug out and thought about. One of the rewards of reading is the pleasure of coming upon the theme of a literary work on our own.

Usually, however, careful writers plan their stories so that readers can pick out sentences or events that point toward the theme. Such "key passages" are recognizable because they seem to speak directly to us as readers. They make direct, thoughtful statements, discussing the meaning of an action or a lesson the characters may have learned.

For example, Dorothy Canfield's story "The Apprentice" is a story with a strong theme. Its theme has to do with a young person's coming-of-age, or achieving adult status. A key passage in this story explicitly tells us that when the young heroine realizes what unendurable tragedy is, she becomes a mature adult.

Often the title of a story will also help us arrive at its theme. This is the case with "The Apprentice." The title reminds us of the old custom of apprenticeship, where young people learn a particular skill that prepares them to earn their living as adults.

Some simple themes can be stated in a single sentence. But sometimes a literary work is so rich and complex that a paragraph or essay is needed to state the theme satisfactorily.

See pages 25, 45, 240, 296, 360.

TONE *The attitude the writer takes toward his or her subject.* A writer may approach a subject with absolute seriousness, as Abraham Lincoln approached the subject of the war dead in his speech "The Gettysburg Address." Or, a writer can approach a subject with humor and mockery, as Ernest Lawrence Thayer approaches Casey in "Casey at the Bat." We get the feeling that Thayer is mocking Casey because he presents him as a proud and vain hero whose overconfidence prevents him from winning the ball game.

Tone is present in all kinds of writing. It is very important for a reader to recognize the tone of a biography. A biographer who loves his or her subject may not be completely objective or truthful. The same is true of a biographer who does *not* think well of his or her subject. In poetry, tone can sometimes change our entire view of a subject. Arthur Guiterman has written a poem called "The Vanity of Earthly Greatness," which is a very serious topic. But Guiterman only pretends to be solemn about this "deep" subject. His tone makes us laugh at something that most people treat very seriously. On the other hand, Edgar Allan Poe's "The Raven" is totally serious in tone. If we make fun of the poem (see the example under **Parody**), we can see how tone can change our entire view of a situation.

See page 380.

TRAGEDY *A serious literary work which portrays a heroic, dignified, or courageous character who comes to a terrible end, such as death or exile.* Any narrative can be a tragedy—short stories, novels, narrative poems, and plays, though the term is most often applied to plays. Some famous tragedies are the dramas of ancient Greece, such as *Agamemnon, Oedipus Rex,* and *Antigone.* The tragedies written by William Shakespeare are also famous. They include such plays as *Romeo and Juliet, Julius Caesar, Hamlet,* and *Macbeth.* All of these titles are the names of people, and this is appropriate, since tragedies usually tell of the downfall of one person. In older tragedies (such as the Greek tragedies and Shakespeare's tragedies), this person is usually a noble character, perhaps a king, queen, prince, or princess. This tragic hero or heroine often falls because of a defect in character, which gives way under the stress of events. Or, a tragic hero or heroine might fall because a series of outside events just cannot be controlled. The outcome of the action in a tragedy is always terrible. Tragedies are not usually depressing, however, because they show us how human dignity and courage can be maintained, even in the face of defeat.

See page 360.

YARN *An exaggerated story that seems to go on and on, like a ball of yarn.* A yarn is a story told in the tradition of the *folktale,* often handed down orally from teller to listener. A yarn seems to be built out of many episodes, which gradually are added on to the central core of a story. The origins of the yarn are connected to the sea and to stories told by sailors.

The old storyteller Simon Wheeler, in Mark Twain's story "The Celebrated Jumping Frog of Calaveras County," is a good example of an expert yarn-spinner. Wheeler would never have stopped yarn-spinning if the narrator had not walked out on him.

See page 522.

Glossary

The words listed in the glossary in the following pages are found in the selections in this textbook. You can use this glossary to look up words that are unfamiliar to you. Strictly speaking, the word *glossary* means a collection of technical, obscure, or foreign words found in a certain field of work. Of course, the words in this glossary are not "technical, obscure, or foreign," but are those that might present difficulty as you read the selections in this textbook.

Many words in the English language have several meanings. This glossary does not give all the meanings of a word. The meanings given here are the ones that apply to the words as they are used in the selections in the textbook. Words closely related in form and meaning are frequently listed together in one entry (**afflict** and **affliction**), and the defintion is given for the first form. Regular adverbs (ending in *-ly*) are defined in their adjective form, with the adverb form shown at the end of the definition.

The following abbreviations are used:

adj., adjective   *n.,* noun
adv., adverb   *v.,* verb

For more information about the words in this glossary, consult a dictionary.

A

abate (ə-bāt′) *v.* To lessen.

abdominal (ăb-dŏm′ə-nəl) *adj.* In the abdomen, the part of the body between the chest and the hips.

abominable (ə-bŏm′ə-nə-bəl) *adj.* Hateful.

abound (ə-bound′) *v.* To have a plentiful supply of.

abrupt (ə-brŭpt′) *adj.* Sudden. —**abruptly** *adv.*

absorption (ăb-sôrp′shən, ăb-zôrp′-) *n.* The passing of matter into the bloodstream.

abundance (ə-bŭn′dəns) *n.* A great supply.

accelerate (ăk-sĕl′ə-rāt′) *v.* To make something happen more quickly than usual.

access (ăk′sĕs′) *n.* **1.** A way of approaching or getting something. **2.** An outburst.

acclaim (ə-klām′) *n.* General approval.

acute (ə-kyōōt′) *adj.* Severe.

adjacent (ə-jā′sənt) *adj.* Next to.

adjourn (ə-jûrn′) *v.* To end a meeting.

adversary (ăd′vər-sĕr′ē) *n.* An enemy.

affable (ăf′ə-bəl) *adj.* Friendly; agreeable.

affect (ə-fĕkt′) *v.* To pretend.

affinity (ə-fĭn′ə-tē) *n.* **1.** A close relationship. **2.** An attraction.

affirm (ə-fûrm′) *v.* To declare something to be true.

afflict (ə-flĭkt′) *v.* To cause to suffer. —**afflicted** *adj.*

aggravate (ăg′rə-vāt′) *v.* To annoy; irritate. —**aggravating** *adj.*

aggressive (ə-grĕs′ĭv) *adj.* **1.** Hostile. **2.** Bold.

aghast (ə-găst′, ə-gäst′) *adj.* Shocked.

agitated (aj′ə-tāt′əd) *adj.* Upset; disturbed.

alien (ā′lē-ən, āl′yən) *adj.* **1.** Foreign. **2.** Strange and unfriendly.

allure (ə-lŏŏr′) *v.* To tempt; attract.

allusion (ə-lōō′zhən) *n.* A reference; mention.

aloof (ə-lōōf′) *adv.* Apart; separate.

altitude (ăl′tə-tōōd′, -tyōōd′) *n.* Height above sea level.

amble (ăm′bəl) *v.* To walk in a slow, relaxed way.

amiable (ā′mē-ə-bəl) *adj.* Friendly.

amnesia (ăm-nē′zhə) *n.* A loss of memory.

ă pat/ā pay/âr care/ä father/b bib/ch church/d deed/ĕ pet/ē be/f fife/g gag/h hat/hw which/ĭ pit/ī pie/îr pier/j judge/k kick/l lid, needle/m mum/ n no, sudden/ng thing/ŏ pot/ō toe/ô paw, for/oi noise/ou out/ŏŏ took/ōō boot/p pop/r roar/s sauce/sh ship, dish/t tight/th thin, path/th this, bathe/ ŭ cut/ûr urge/v valve/w with/y yes/z zebra, size/zh vision/ə about, item, edible, gallop, circus/ à Fr. ami/œ Fr. feu, Ger. schön/ü Fr. tu, Ger. über/ ᴋʜ Ger. ich, Scot. loch/ɴ Fr. bon.

ample (ăm′pəl) *adj.* Plentiful.

amputate (ăm′pyōō-tāt′) *v.* To cut off. — **amputation** *n.*

anatomical (ăn′ə-tŏm′ĭ-kəl) *adj.* Referring to the structure of the body.

anatomy (ə-năt′ə-mē) *n.* The study of the shape and structure of animals and plants.

anecdote (ăn′ĭk-dōt′) *n.* A brief story.

anguish (ăng′gwĭsh) *n.* Great suffering.

animated (ăn′ə-mā′tĭd) *adj.* Lively.

anteroom (ăn′tĭ-rōōm′, -rŏōm′) *n.* A small room that leads into a larger room.

anticipation (ăn-tĭs′ə-pā′shən) *n.* An expectation.

apologetic (ə-pŏl′ə-jĕt′ĭk) *adj.* Showing or expressing regret for a wrong. — **apologetically** *adv.*

appall (ə-pôl′) *v.* To shock; horrify. — **appalling** *adj.*

apparatus (ăp′ə-rā′təs, -răt′əs) *n.* Equipment.

apparition (ăp′ə-rĭsh′ən) *n.* A ghostly shape or figure.

appease (ə-pēz′) *v.* To satisfy; soothe.

appendix (ə-pĕn′dĭks) *n.* Additional material at the end of a book or article.

appraise (ə-prāz′) *v.* To judge the quality or value of. — **appraisingly** *adv.*

apprehensive (ăp′rĭ-hĕn′sĭv) *adj.* Fearful. — **apprehensively** *adv.*

appropriation (ə-prō′prē-ā′shən) *n.* Money given for a certain purpose.

apt (ăpt) *adj.* Suitable. — **aptly** *adv.*

ardent (är′dənt) *adj.* Passionate. — **ardently** *adv.*

arid (ăr′ĭd) *adj.* Very dry.

arrogance (ăr′ə-gəns) *n.* Overbearing pride. — **arrogant** *adj.*

ascend (ə-sĕnd′) *v.* To move upward. — **ascending** *adj.*

assault (ə-sôlt′) *n.* An attack.

assess (ə-sĕs′) *v.* To judge the importance or value of.

assiduous (ə-sĭj′ōō-əs) *adj.* Hardworking. — **assiduously** *adv.*

attire (ə-tīr′) *n.* Clothing.

auspicious (ô-spĭsh′əs) *adj.* Favorable.

authoritative (ə-thôr′ə-tā′tĭv, ə-thŏr′-) *adj.* Official; reliable.

avail (ə-vāl′) *v.* To make use of.

avenge (ə-vĕnj′) *v.* To get revenge for.

avert (ə-vûrt′) *v.* To turn away.

awed (ôd) *adj.* Filled with respect and wonder.

B

badger (băj′ər) *v.* To nag. — **badgering** *n.*

baffle (băf′əl) *v.* To puzzle.

balk (bôk) *v.* To refuse.

bar (bär) *v.* To prevent.

barometer (bə-rŏm′ə-tər) *n.* An instrument that measures air pressure and is used to predict changes in the weather.

barren (băr′ən) *adj.* **1.** Empty. **2.** Without plant life.

barter (bär′tər) *v.* To trade.

bayou (bī′ōō, bī′ō) *n.* A swamp.

beacon (bē′kən) *n.* A warning signal.

bearing (bâr′ĭng) *n.* A determination of someone's or something's position.

beguile (bĭ-gīl′) *v.* To charm or amuse.

behoove (bĭ-hōōv′) *v.* To be necessary or right for.

belfry (bĕl′frē) *n.* A tower in which a bell is hung.

belligerent (bə-lĭj′ər-ənt) *adj.* Ready to fight. — **belligerently** *adv.*

beseech (bĭ-sēch′) *v.* To beg.

besiege (bĭ-sēj′) *v.* To surround in order to attack and capture. — **besieged** *adj.*

betray (bĭ-trā′) *v.* **1.** To be disloyal to. **2.** To reveal. — **betraying** *adj.*

bevy (bĕv′ē) *n.* A large group.

bilk (bĭlk) *v.* To cheat.

billow (bĭl′ō) *v.* To cause to swell out.

blackjack (blăk′jăk′) *n.* A kind of oak tree with a black bark.

blunt (blŭnt) *adj.* Abrupt. — **bluntly** *adv.*

blurt (blûrt) *v.* To speak suddenly without thought.

bluster (blŭs′tər) *n.* **1.** Empty threats. **2.** Loud, noisy talk.

breach (brēch) *n.* An opening.

burnish (bûr′nĭsh) *v.* To make shiny. — **burnished** *adj.*

C

cajole (kə-jōl′) *v.* To coax.

candid (kăn′dĭd) *adj.* Honest.

canopy (kăn′ə-pē) *n.* A cloth that serves as a roof or cover.

caper (kā′pər) *v.* To jump about playfully.

captor (kăp′tər, -tôr′) *n.* Someone or something that holds a person or an animal prisoner.

carillon (kăr′ə-lŏn′, kə-rĭl′yən) *n.* A set of bells that can be played from a keyboard.

carp (kärp) *n.* A kind of fish.

cascade (kăs-kād′) *v.* To fall in great amounts.

causeway (kôz′wā′) *n.* A raised road, often above water.

cavernous (kăv′ər-nəs) *adj.* Like a cave.

cavort (kə-vôrt′) *v.* To run and jump in a playful manner.

chaos (kā′ŏs′) *n.* Complete disorder.

charger (chär′jər) *n.* A horse trained for battle.

chastise (chăs-tīz′) *v.* To punish. — **chastisement** *n.*

chortle (chôrt′l) *n.* A laugh, midway between a chuckle and a snort.

chronicle (krŏn′ĭ-kəl) *v.* To record; list.

circumference (sər-kŭm′fər-əns) *n.* The measurement of the outer edge of a circular object.

clemency (klĕm′ən-sē) *n.* Mercy.

coax (kōks) *v.* To persuade by using soothing words and an agreeable manner.

colossal (kə-lŏs′əl) *adj.* Gigantic.

commend (kə-mĕnd′) *v.* To recommend.

commission (kə-mĭsh′ən) *v.* To give someone a job to do.

common (kŏm′ən) *n.* A public park in a village or town.

competent (kŏm′pə-tənt) *adj.* Able; capable.

compliance (kəm-plī′əns) *n.* The act of following a request.

compromise (kŏm′prə-mīz′) *v.* **1.** To settle by concessions from both sides. **2.** To put someone's good reputation in danger.

compulsory (kəm-pŭl′sə-rē) *adj.* Required.

conceive (kən-sēv′) *v.* To think of.

condense (kən-dĕns′) *v.* To put in a briefer form.

condescend (kŏn′dĭ-sĕnd′) *v.* **1.** To lower oneself willingly. **2.** To deal with others in a proud or overbearing way.

conical (kŏn′ĭ-kəl) *adj.* Shaped like a cone.

conscientious (kŏn′shē-ĕn′shəs) *adj.* Careful; painstaking.

consciousness (kŏn′shəs-nĭs) *n.* An awareness of one's thoughts, feelings, and sensory impressions.

consecrate (kŏn′sə-krāt′) *v.* To dedicate as something sacred.

conspicuous (kən-spĭk′yōō-əs) *adj.* Easily seen; noticeable.

constancy (kŏn′stən-sē) *n.* Steadfastness; firmness of purpose.

consul (kŏn′səl) *n.* An official representative of a government.

contagion (kən-tā′jən) *n.* A tendency to spread by contact.

contemplate (kŏn′təm-plāt′) *v.* **1.** To look at thoughtfully. **2.** To think about intently.

contend (kən-tĕnd′) *v.* **1.** To compete. **2.** To hold to be a fact.

contort (kən-tôrt′) *v.* To twist into unusual shapes. — **contorted** *adj.*

convene (kən-vēn′) *v.* To come together, as for a meeting. — **convened** *adj.*

converge (kən-vûrj′) *v.* To come together at a point; meet.

convey (kən-vā′) *v.* **1.** To carry from one place to another. **2.** To make known.

conviction (kən-vĭk′shən) *n.* A belief.

convoy (kŏn′voi′, kən-voi′) *v.* To accompany in order to protect.

convulsion (kən-vŭl′shən) *n.* A violent muscle spasm; a fit.

convulsive (kən-vŭl′sĭv) *adj.* Like a convulsion.

coordination (kō-ôr′də-nā′shən) *n.* The ability of the muscles to act together and result in a smooth action.

countenance (koun′tə-nəns) *n.* A face.

counteract (koun′tər-ăkt′) *v.* To act against.

courtier (kôr′tē-ər, kōr′-, -tyər) *n.* One who serves a king or queen at court.

cove (kōv) *n.* A bay.

covet (kŭv′ĭt) *v.* To envy.

cower (kou′ər) *v.* To shrink back, as in fear.

cranium (krā′nē-əm) *n.* The skull.

credible (krĕd′ə-bəl) *adj.* Believable.

creed (krēd) *n.* A statement of belief.

crescent (krĕs′ənt) *n.* The moon in its first or last quarter, when its shape is thin and not rounded.

crest (krĕst) *n.* A crownlike growth on the head of some birds.

crystallize (krĭs′tə-līz′) *v.* To take definite shape. — **crystallized** *adj.*

cudgel (kŭj′əl) *v.* To strike, as with a club.

cunning (kŭn′ĭng) *adj.* Clever in a tricky way. — *n.* Cleverness; trickery. — **cunningly** *adv.*

curvaceous (kûr-vā′shəs) *adj.* Pleasingly curved.

D

dauntless (dônt′lĭs, dänt′-) *adj.* Fearless; courageous.

dawdle (dôd′l) *v.* To spend time aimlessly.

daybed (dā′bĕd′) *n.* A couch that can also be used as a bed.

decorum (dĭ-kôr′əm, dĭ-kōr′əm) *n.* Proper appearance.

deem (dēm) *v.* To judge.

default (dĭ-fôlt′) *n.* Failure to do something.

deign (dān) *v.* To stoop to do something beneath one's dignity.

dejection (dĭ-jĕk′shən) *n.* Sadness.

ă pat/ā pay/âr care/ä father/b bib/ch church/d deed/ĕ pet/ē be/f fife/g gag/h hat/hw which/ĭ pit/ī pie/îr pier/j judge/k kick/l lid, needle/m mum/ n no, sudden/ng thing/ŏ pot/ō toe/ô paw, for/oi noise/ou out/ŏŏ took/ōŏ boot/p pop/r roar/s sauce/sh ship, dish/t tight/th thin, path/*th* this, bathe/ ŭ cut/ûr urge/v valve/w with/y yes/z zebra, size/zh vision/ə about, item, edible, gallop, circus/ ä *Fr.* ami/œ *Fr.* feu, *Ger.* schön/ü *Fr.* tu, *Ger.* über/ ᴋʜ *Ger.* ich, *Scot.* loch/ɴ *Fr.* bon.

delectable (dĭ-lĕk'tə-bəl) *adj.* Delicious.

denizen (dĕn'ə-zən) *n.* One who lives in a certain place.

deprive (dĭ-prīv') *v.* To take something away from; dispossess.

depute (dĭ-pyoot') *v.* To assign.

descend (dĭ-sĕnd') *v.* To go down.

deteriorate (dĭ-tîr'ē-ə-rāt') *v.* To become worse. — **deterioration** *n.*

detract (dĭ-trăkt') *v.* To take away; subtract.

devise (dĭ-vīz') *v.* To plan.

dexterity (dĕk-stĕr'ə-tē) *n.* Skill.

diameter (dī-ăm'ə-tər) *n.* Width; the distance across the center of a circular object.

dilapidated (dĭ-lăp'ə-dā'tĭd) *adj.* In very bad condition.

dilate (dī-lāt', dī'lāt', dĭ-lāt') *v.* To expand.

diligent (dĭl'-ə-jənt) *adj.* Careful.

dinghy (dĭng'ē) *n.* A small rowboat.

direful (dīr'fəl) *adj.* Fearful; terrible.

dirge (dûrj) *n.* **1.** A funeral song. **2.** Any sad piece of music.

discard (dĭs-kärd') *v.* To remove from use. — **discarded** *adj.*

disciple (dĭ-sī'pəl) *n.* A pupil.

disconcert (dĭs'kən-sûrt') *v.* To confuse; upset. — **disconcerted** *adj.*

disconsolate (dĭs-kŏn'sə-lĭt) *adj.* Very sad.

discord (dĭs'kôrd) *n.* **1.** A disagreement. **2.** In music, a lack of harmony.

discourse (dĭs'kôrs', -kōrs') *v.* To speak.

discrimination (dĭs-krĭm'ə-nā'shən) *n.* Prejudice.

disdain (dĭs-dān') *n.* Scorn. — **disdainful** *adj.*

disheveled (dĭ-shĕv'əld) *adj.* Disorderly in appearance.

dismember (dĭs-mĕm'bər) *v.* To cut the arms and legs off.

dispassionate (dĭs-păsh'ən-ĭt) *adj.* Fair; not partial.

dispel (dĭs-pĕl') *v.* To get rid of.

dispirit (dĭs-pĭr'ĭt) *v.* To make unhappy; depress. — **dispirited** *adj.*

dispute (dĭs-pyoot') *n.* An argument.

dissolution (dĭs'ə-loo'shən) *n.* The process of dissolving into nothingness.

divine (dĭ-vīn') *v.* To guess; figure out.

docile (dŏs'əl) *adj.* Tame; easily handled.

doff (dôf, dŏf) *v.* To take off.

dogged (dô'gĭd, dŏg'ĭd) *adj.* Persistent; stubborn. — **doggedly** *adv.*

doleful (dōl'fəl) *adj.* Sad.

drab (drăb) *adj.* Dull; colorless.

drone (drōn) *n.* **1.** A lazy person. **2.** A low, continuing sound.

drone (drōn) *v.* To make a low, continuing sound. — **droning** *adj.*

drudgery (drŭj'ə-rē) *n.* Hard work.

E

ebb (ĕb) *v.* **1.** To become less. **2.** To recede; flow back.

ebony (ĕb'ə-nē) *adj.* Black.

ecstasy (ĕk'stə-sē) *n.* Great joy.

ejaculation (ĭ-jăk'yə-lā'shən) *n.* A sudden shout.

elation (ĭ-lā'shən) *n.* Great joy.

eloquence (ĕl'ə-kwəns) *n.* Forceful and graceful speech.

elude (ĭ-lood') *v.* To escape from being noticed.

elusive (ĭ-loo'sĭv) *adj.* Hard to find or catch.

emancipate (ĭ-măn'sə-pāt') *v.* To free someone. — **emancipation** *n.* — **emancipated** *adj.*

emerge (ĭ-mûrj') *v.* To come out.

emigrate (ĕm'ĭ-grāt') *v.* To leave one's country to live elsewhere. — **emigration** *n.*

eminent (ĕm'ə-nənt) *adj.* Outstanding.

engulf (ĕn-gŭlf', ĭn-) *v.* To cover completely.

enrapture (ĕn-răp'chər, ĭn-) *v.* To fill with joy. — **enraptured** *adj.*

enterprising (ĕn'tər-prī'zĭng) *adj.* Ambitious and imaginative.

entrance (ĕn-trăns', -träns', ĭn-) *v.* To fill with delight. — **entranced** *adj.*

entreat (ĕn-trēt', ĭn-) *v.* To plead; beg.

enumerate (ĭ-noo'mə-rāt', ĭ-nyoo'-) *v.* To list.

envelop (ĕn-vĕl'əp, ĭn-) *v.* To cover completely.

envision (ĕn-vĭzh'ən) *v.* To picture in the imagination.

epitaph (ĕp'ə-tăf', -täf') *n.* The writing on a tombstone.

era (îr'ə, ĕr'ə) *n.* An important period of time.

esteem (ĕ-stēm', ĭ-stēm') *v.* To hold in high regard.

etch (ĕch) *v.* **1.** To draw; outline. **2.** To make a clear impression.

etiquette (ĕt'ə-kĕt', -kĭt) *n.* Proper social or official behavior.

evolve (ĭ-vŏlv') *v.* To develop.

exact (ĕg-zăkt', ĭg-) *v.* To demand.

exalt (ĕg-zôlt', ĭg-) *v.* To raise in importance. — **exalted** *adj.*

exasperate (ĕg-zăs'pə-rāt', ĭg-) *v.* To annoy greatly. — **exasperating** *adj.*

exasperation (ĕg-zăs'pə-rā'shən, ĭg-) *n.* A feeling of great annoyance.

exhiliration (ĕg-zĭl'ə-rā'shən, ĭg-) *n.* Excitement.

exotic (ĕg-zŏt'ĭk, ĭg-) *adj.* **1.** Interestingly different. **2.** Foreign.

expire (ĕk-spīr', ĭk-) *v.* To die.

extinguish (ĕk-stĭng'gwĭsh, ĭk-) *v.* To put out.

extract (ĕk-străkt', ĭk-) *v.* To draw out or pull out.

exult (ĕg-zŭlt', ĭg-) *v.* To rejoice.

F

fanatical (fə-năt'ĭ-kəl) *adj.* Enthusiastic beyond reason.

farce (färs) *n.* Something ridiculous and laughable.

fastidious (fă-stĭd′ē-əs, fə-) *adj.* Fussy; not easily pleased.

ferment (fər′mĕnt′) *v.* To undergo a chemical reaction that changes sugar into other compounds. — **fermented** *adj.*

fervent (fûr′vənt) *adj.* Showing great warmth of feeling; intense. — **fervently** *adv.*

fervor (fûr′vər) *n.* Intense feeling.

fester (fĕs′tər) *v.* To produce pus. — **festering** *adj.*

festoon (fĕs-tōōn′) *n.* A wreath. — *v.* To decorate with wreathes of flowers or leaves.

finicky (fĭn′ĭ-kē) *adj.* Hard to please.

flay (flā) *v.* To beat wildly, without aim.

flinch (flĭnch) *v.* To draw back or make a face, as if in pain.

flog (flŏg, flôg) *v.* To whip. — **flogger** *n.*

florid (flôr′ĭd) *adj.* Red-faced; ruddy.

flounder (floun′dər) *v.* To move clumsily. — **floundering** *adj.*

foray (fôr′ā′) *n.* A raid.

ford (fôrd, fōrd) *n.* A place in the river that is shallow enough to be crossed on foot.

formidable (fôr′mə-də-bəl) *adj.* **1.** Causing fear or wonder. **2.** Commanding respect and admiration.

formula (fôr′myə-lə) *n.* A statement expressed in symbols and numbers.

fortify (fôr′tə-fī′) *v.* To build up strength. — **fortified** *adj.*

front (frŭnt) *v.* To face.

fumigate (fyōō′mĭ-gāt′) *v.* To disinfect. — **fumigated** *adj.*

furrow (fûr′ō) *n.* A groove.

G

gait (gāt) *n.* Step; way of walking.

gallant (gə-lănt′, -länt′, găl′ənt) *n.* An attentive, courteous man.

gape (gāp, găp) *v.* To be wide open. — **gaping** *adj.*

gaunt (gônt) *adj.* Thin; underfed-looking. — **gauntly** *adv.*

genial (jēn′yəl, jē′nē-əl) *adj.* Friendly. — **genially** *adv.*

ghastly (găst′lē, gäst′-) *adj.* **1.** Like a ghost. **2.** Horrible.

gilt (gĭlt) *n.* Gold applied in a thin layer.

girth (gûrth) *n.* The measurement around something.

glacial (glā′shəl) *adj.* Produced by glaciers — huge masses of ice and snow.

gland (glănd) *n.* One of many organs, cells, or groups of cells that produce a secretion.

glandular (glăn′jə-lər) *adj.* Referring to the activity of the glands.

glib (glĭb) *adj.* Speaking easily and smoothly, often in a way that is not convincing. — **glibly** *adv.*

gloat (glōt) *v.* To take great pleasure in.

glut (glŭt) *v.* To supply or fill to excess.

grate (grāt) *v.* To rub something noisily against another object.

grenadier (grĕn′ə-dîr′) *n.* Originally, a soldier trained to use grenades.

grille (grĭl) *n.* A metal grating.

grotesque (grō-tĕsk′) *adj.* Strangely misshapen. — **grotesquely** *adv.*

grovel (grŭv′əl, grŏv′-) *v.* To assume a humble position; cringe.

gullible (gŭl′ə-bəl) *adj.* Easily fooled or cheated.

gully (gŭl′lē) *n.* A deep ditch.

gutter (gŭt′ər) *v.* To melt quickly and run off in a stream as the wax of a burning candle does.

guttural (gŭt′ər-əl) *adj.* Coming from the throat.

H

hallow (hăl′ō) *v.* To make holy.

hamlet (hăm′lĭt) *n.* A small village.

harken (här′kən) *v.* To listen carefully.

harass (hăr′əs, hə-răs′) *v.* To worry; trouble. — **harassed** *adj.*

harry (hăr′ē) *v.* To torment.

hassock (hăs′ək) *n.* A large, padded footstool.

haughty (hô′tē) *adj.* Proud.

haunch (hônch, hänch) *n.* The hip and upper thigh.

haunt (hônt, hänt) *n.* A favorite place.

heed (hēd) *v.* To pay attention to.

hew (hyōō) *v.* To carve or shape.

hoist (hoist) *v.* To lift; raise.

homestead (hōm′stĕd′) *n.* Farm property.

horde (hôrd, hōrd) *n.* A large, disorderly group.

hostile (hŏs′təl) *adj.* Unfriendly.

hoyden (hoid′n) *n.* A tomboy.

hull (hŭl) *n.* The frame of a ship.

hussy (hŭz′ē, hŭs′ē) *n.* A bold, immoral woman.

hybrid (hī′brĭd) *adj.* Produced from a mixture of parent plants.

ă pat/ā pay/âr care/ä father/b bib/ch church/d deed/ĕ pet/ē be/f fife/g gag/h hat/hw which/ĭ pit/ī pie/îr pier/j judge/k kick/l lid, needle/m mum/
n no, sudden/ng thing/ŏ pot/ō toe/ô paw, for/oi noise/ou out/ŏŏ took/ōō boot/p pop/r roar/s sauce/sh ship, dish/t tight/th thin, path/*th* this, bathe/
ŭ cut/ûr urge/v valve/w with/y yes/z zebra, size/zh vision/ə about, item, edible, gallop, circus/à *Fr.* ami/œ *Fr.* feu, *Ger.* schön/ü *Fr.* tu, *Ger.* über/
ᴋʜ *Ger.* ich, *Scot.* loch/ɴ *Fr.* bon.

hypocrite (hĭp′ə-krĭt′) n. One who pretends to have qualities he or she does not have. — **hypocritical** adj.

hypodermic syringe (hī′pə-dûr′mĭk sə-rĭnj′, sîr′ĭnj) n. A glass tube with attached needle, used for giving injections.

hypothesis (hī-pŏth′ə-sĭs) n. A theory; a possible explanation.

I

illiteracy (ĭ-lĭt′ər-ə-sē) n. The inability to read and write.

imminent (ĭm′ə-nənt) adj. About to happen.

impact (ĭm′păkt′) n. Force.

impair (ĭm-pâr′) v. To weaken; damage.

impassioned (ĭm-păsh′ənd) adj. Very emotional.

impede (ĭm-pēd′) v. To interfere with.

impend (ĭm-pĕnd′) v. To be about to happen. — **impending** adj.

imperceptible (ĭm′pər-sĕp′tə-bəl) adj. Barely noticeable.

imperial (ĭm-pîr′ē-əl) adj. Referring to an emperor.

imperious (ĭm-pîr′ē-əs) adj. Domineering; arrogant (like an emperor).

impetuous (ĭm-pĕch′ōō-əs) adj. Eager to act; impatient.

implement (ĭm′plə-mənt) n. A tool.

implicit (ĭm-plĭs′ĭt) adj. Without doubt; absolute. — **implicitly** adv.

implore (ĭm-plôr′, -plōr′) v. To beg; ask. — **imploring** adj. — **imploringly** adv.

imply (ĭm-plī′) v. To suggest; hint.

inarticulate (ĭn′är-tĭk′yə-lĭt) adj. **1.** Unable to speak. **2.** Not clearly spoken.

inaudible (ĭn-ô′də-bəl) adj. Not able to be heard.

incentive (ĭn-sĕn′tĭv) n. Something that stimulates one to action.

incision (ĭn-sĭzh′ən) n. A cut.

incisor (ĭn-sī′zər) n. A tooth shaped for cutting — the middle four upper and middle four lower teeth.

inclination (ĭn′klə-nā′shən) n. A desire to do something.

incompetent (ĭn-kŏm′pə-tənt) adj. Not capable.

incomprehensible (ĭn′kŏm-prĭ-hĕn′sə-bəl) adj. Not able to be understood.

incredible (ĭn-krĕd′ə-bəl) adj. Unbelievable.

indecorous (ĭn-dĕk′ər-əs) adj. Not proper.

indelible (ĭn-dĕl′ə-bəl) adj. Not able to be erased.

indignant (ĭn-dĭg′nənt) adj. Very angry. — **indignantly** adv.

indignation (ĭn′dĭg-nā′shən) n. Great anger; outrage.

indistinct (ĭn′dĭs-tĭngkt′) adj. Not clear.

indomitable (ĭn-dŏm′ə-tə-bəl) adj. Not easily defeated or discouraged.

indubitable (ĭn-dōō′bə-tə-bəl, ĭn-dyōō′-) adj. Definite; without a doubt. — **indubitably** adv.

induce (ĭn-dōōs′, -dyōōs′) v. To persuade.

indulgent (ĭn-dŭl′jənt) adj. Overly considerate or generous. — **indulgently** adv.

inevitable (ĭn-ĕv′ə-tə-bəl) adj. Sure to happen. — **inevitability** n.

infamous (ĭn′fə-məs) adj. Having a bad reputation.

infectious (ĭn-fĕk′shəs) adj. Catching.

infernal (ĭn-fûr′nəl) adj. Evil.

infinite (ĭn′fə-nĭt) adj. Limitless; endless (like infinity).

inflexible (ĭn-flĕk′sə-bəl) adj. Unchanging; firm.

inflict (ĭn-flĭkt′) v. To force something unpleasant on someone. — **inflicted** adj.

infuse (ĭn-fyōōz′) v. To fill with.

ingenious (ĭn-jēn′yəs) adj. Very clever.

inimitable (ĭn-ĭm′ĭ-tə-bəl) adj. Not able to be imitated; matchless.

inquest (ĭn′kwĕst′) n. An investigation.

insignia (ĭn-sĭg′nē-ə) n. A badge; emblem.

insinuate (ĭn-sĭn′yōō-āt′) v. To hint at or suggest something in an indirect way. — **insinuating** adj.

insistent (ĭn-sĭs′tənt) adj. Demanding.

insolent (ĭn′sə-lənt) adj. Disrespectful. — **insolently** adv.

instinctive (ĭn-stĭngk′tĭv) adj. Inborn; not learned.

insufferable (ĭn-sŭf′ər-ə-bəl) adj. Impossible to put up with.

intercourse (ĭn′tər-kôrs′, -kōrs′) n. Association with others, as in conversation.

interminable (ĭn-tûr′mə-nə-bəl) adj. Endless.

intimate (ĭn′tə-mĭt) adj. Close in affection; very friendly. — **intimately** adv.

intimate (ĭn′tə-māt′) v. To hint. — **intimation** n.

intolerable (ĭn-tŏl′ər-ə-bəl) adj. Unbearable.

intolerant (ĭn-tŏl′ər-ənt) adj. Unwilling to put up with.

invariable (ĭn-vâr′ē-ə-bəl) adj. Unchanging; constant. — **invariably** adv.

inventory (ĭn′vən-tôr′ē, -tōr′ē) n. A list of supplies on hand.

involuntary (ĭn-vŏl′ən-tĕr′ē) adj. Done without conscious thought.

invulnerable (ĭn-vŭl′nər-ə-bəl) adj. Not able to be harmed.

irresolute (ĭ-rĕz′ə-lōōt′) adj. Undecided; uncertain.

itinerant (ī-tĭn′ər-ənt, ĭ-tĭn′-) adj. Going from place to place in order to work.

J

jaunt (jônt, jänt) n. A short trip.

jest (jĕst) v. To joke. — **jestingly** adv.

jostle (jŏs′əl) v. To push and shove.

jovial (jō′vē-əl) adj. Good-humored. — **jovially** adv.

jubilation (joo′bə-lā′shən) *n*. Rejoicing.

judicious (joo-dĭsh′əs) *adj*. Wise (like a judge).

K

kindle (kĭnd′l) *v*. To start (a fire).

knoll (nōl) *n*. A small hill.

L

lacerate (lăs′ə-rāt′) *v*. To tear, or cut jaggedly. — **lacerated** *adj*.

lament (lə-mĕnt′) *v*. To grieve; mourn. — *n*. An expression of grief.

lamentation (lăm′ən-tā′shən) *n*. An expression of grief.

lank (lăngk) *adj*. Tall and thin.

lateral (lăt′ər-əl) *adj*. Sideways.

lattice (lăt′ĭs) *adj*. Woven like a screen.

leer (lîr) *v*. To look at slyly or evilly.

legion (lē′jən) *n*. A large group; band.

liberality (lĭb′ə-răl′ə-tē) *n*. Generosity.

limber (lĭm′bər) *v*. To loosen up by exercise.

listless (lĭst′lĭs) *adj*. Showing a lack of energy or interest. — **listlessly** *adv*.

literate (lĭt′ər-ĭt) *adj*. Able to read and write.

loathe (lōth) *v*. To hate intensely.

loll (lŏl) *v*. **1.** To lounge about in a relaxed way. **2.** To hang out loosely.

lope (lōp) *v*. To run with a long stride.

low (lō) *v*. Moo. — **lowing** *n*.

ludicrous (loo′dĭ-krəs) *adj*. Ridiculous; laughable.

lumber (lŭm′bər) *v*. To move slowly and clumsily.

luminous (loo′mə-nəs) *adj*. **1.** Able to shine in the dark; glowing. **2.** Filled with light.

M

makeshift (māk′shĭft′) *adj*. Made quickly and used as a substitute.

malice (măl′ĭs) *n*. A desire to hurt others.

maneuver (mə-noo′vər, -nyoo′-) *v*. To move.

manifold (măn′ə-fōld) *adj*. Many and different; various.

mantle (măn′təl) *n*. A sleeveless cape or cloak.

mast (măst, mäst) *n*. A pole used to support the sails and rigging of a ship.

mastodon (măs′tə-dŏn′) *n*. An extinct animal that resembled an elephant.

matron (mā′trən) *n*. A married woman, especially one mature in age and appearance. — **matronly** *adv*.

melancholy (mĕl′ən-kŏl′ē) *n*. Great sadness. — *adj*. Very sad.

mellow (mĕl′ō) *adj*. Rich. — **mellowness** *n*.

mercurial (mər-kyoor′ē-əl) *adj*. Changing quickly (like mercury).

merge (mûrj) *v*. To blend in.

mesa (mā′sə) *n*. A hill or plateau having steep sides and a flat top, especially in the southwestern United States.

meticulous (mə-tĭk′yə-ləs) *adj*. Extremely precise about minor details; fussy.

minstrel (mĭn′strəl) *n*. Poet-musician.

mobile (mō′bəl, -bēl, -bīl′) *adj*. Movable.

mobilize (mō′bə-līz′) *v*. To move into action.

molest (mə-lĕst′) *v*. To bother or to harm.

monotony (mə-nŏt′n-ē) *n*. Sameness.

mooring (moor′ĭng) *n*. The place where a boat is tied up.

morass (mə-răs′, mô-) *n*. A swamp.

mortal (môrt′l) *n*. A human being.

mottled (mŏt′ld) *adj*. Covered with spots of different colors and shapes.

muster (mŭs′tər) *v*. To assemble; gather together.

mutilate (myoot′l-āt′) *v*. To cut off or otherwise destroy a part of the body. — **mutilated** *adj*.

mutinous (myoot′n-əs) *adj*. Rebellious.

N

naiveté (nä′ēv-tā′) *n*. Simplicity; lack of worldliness.

neurosurgeon (noor′ō-sûr′jən, nyoo′-) *n*. A doctor who specializes in surgery involving the nervous system.

nonchalant (nŏn′shə-länt′) *adj*. Unconcerned; casual. — **nonchalantly** *adv*.

nondescript (nŏn′dĭ-skrĭpt′) *adj*. Commonplace; uninteresting.

nontransferable (nŏn-trăns-fûr′ə-bəl) *adj*. Not usable by anyone else.

novelty (nŏv′əl-tē) *n*. Something new or unusual.

O

oblivious (ə-blĭv′ē-əs) *adj*. Not aware.

obnoxious (ŏb-nŏk′shəs, əb-) *adj*. Highly unlikable; hateful.

obscure (ŏb-skyoor′, əb-) *adj*. Little known.

obsession (əb-sĕsh′ən, ŏb-) *n*. An idea or thought that is impossible to get rid of.

ă pat/ā pay/âr care/ä father/b bib/ch church/d deed/ĕ pet/ē be/f fife/g gag/h hat/hw which/ĭ pit/ī pie/îr pier/j judge/k kick/l lid, needle/m mum/ n no, sudden/ng thing/ŏ pot/ō toe/ô paw, for/oi noise/ou out/oo took/oo boot/p pop/r roar/s sauce/sh ship, dish/t tight/th thin, path/*th* this, bathe/ ŭ cut/ûr urge/v valve/w with/y yes/z zebra, size/zh vision/ə about, item, edible, gallop, circus/ à *Fr.* ami/œ *Fr.* feu, *Ger.* schön/ü *Fr.* tu, *Ger.* über/ ᴋʜ *Ger.* ich, *Scot.* loch/ɴ *Fr.* bon.

obstinate (ŏb'stə-nĭt) *adj.* Stubborn. — **obstinately** *adv.*

omen (ō'mən) *n.* A sign of something to come.

ominous (ŏm'ə-nəs) *adj.* Warning; threatening.

onslaught (ŏn'slôt', ôn'-) *n.* An attack.

opportunist (ŏp'ər-tōo'nĭst, -tyōo'nĭst) *n.* One who takes unfair advantage of another or of a situation.

oppression (ə-prĕsh'ən) *n.* Power used to crush or to persecute.

ordeal (ôr-dēl') *n.* A very unpleasant experience.

orthodontist (ôr'thə-dŏn'tĭst) *n.* A dentist who specializes in straightening teeth.

ostentatious (ŏs'tĕn-tā'shəs, ŏs'tən-) *adj.* Showy. — **ostentatiously** *adv.*

P

pandemonium (păn'də-mō'nē-əm) *n.* Noisy confusion.

passionate (păsh'ən-ĭt) *adj.* Intense. — **passionately** *adv.*

paternal (pə-tûr'nəl) *adj.* Referring to a father.

patron (pā'trən) *n.* **1.** A customer. **2.** A person who supports an artist or musician.

pensive (pĕn'sĭv) *adj.* Thoughtful.

percussion (pər-kŭsh'ən) *n.* A musical instrument, such as a drum, that is played by striking.

perimeter (pə-rĭm'ə-tər) *n.* The outer boundary of something.

periscope (pĕr'ə-skōp') *n.* A tubelike instrument with lenses and mirrors that enables one to see an area otherwise not viewable.

permeate (pûr'mē-āt') *v.* To spread through. — **permeated** *adj.*

perpendicular (pûr'pən-dĭk'yə-lər) *adj.* At a right angle. — **perpendicularly** *adv.*

perplexity (pər-plĕk'sə-tē) *n.* Confusion.

persistent (pər-sĭs'tənt) *adj.* Repeated; continued. — **persistently** *adv.*

perverse (pər-vûrs') *adj.* Stubbornly difficult.

petition (pə-tĭsh'ən) *n.* A formal request signed by a number of people.

pewter (pyōo'tər) *n.* Objects made from pewter, a mixture of tin and other metals.

phobia (fō'bē-ə) *n.* An exaggerated fear.

phonetic (fə-nĕt'ĭk) *adj.* Referring to the sounds of language.

photostat (fō'tə-stăt') *v.* To make a copy of something using a certain kind of machine.

pinion (pĭn'yən) *v.* To tie or bind. — **pinioned** *adj.*

piston (pĭs'tən) *n.* A disk or cylinder fitted into a tube and moved back and forth by pressure, as in an engine.

placid (plăs'ĭd) *adj.* Quiet; peaceful.

pliable (plī'ə-bəl) *adj.* Flexible. — **pliability** *n.*

pliant (plī'ənt) *adj.* Easily bent; flexible.

pluck (plŭk) *n.* Courage.

plunder (plŭn'dər) *v.* To rob.

poise (poiz) *v.* To be balanced in a certain position. — **poised** *adj.*

ponder (pŏn'dər) *v.* To think deeply about.

portal (pôrt'l, pōrt'l) *n.* An entrance; door.

posterity (pŏ-stĕr'ə-tē) *n.* All those yet to be born.

potent (pōt'nt) *adj.* Powerful; strong.

potentiality (pə-tĕn'shē-ăl'ə-tē) *n.* A possible ability.

predecessor (prĕd'ə-sĕs'ər, prē'də-) *n.* One who comes before another, as in a job or a political office.

predominant (prĭ-dŏm'ə-nənt) *adj.* Most important — **predominantly** *adv.*

preeminence (prē-ĕm'ə-nəns) *n.* The condition of holding first place in a particular grouping.

preliminary (prĭ-lĭm'ə-nĕr'ē) *n.* Something that comes before or introduces something else.

prestige (prĕ-stēzh', -stēj) *n.* High standing in the eyes of others.

presumption (prĭ-zŭmp'shən) *n.* The act of taking something for granted.

pretext (prē'tĕkst') *n.* An excuse.

prevalence (prĕv'ə-ləns) *n.* The state of being widespread.

prim (prĭm) *adj.* Formal; stiff. — **primly** *adv.*

prodigious (prə-dĭj'əs) *adj.* **1.** Amazing. **2.** Huge.

prodigy (prŏd'ə-jē) *n.* An unusually gifted child.

profound (prə-found', prō-) *adj.* **1.** Deep. **2.** Wise. — **profoundly** *adv.*

progressive (prə-grĕs'ĭv) *adj.* Ever-increasing.

proposition (prŏp'ə-zĭsh'ən) *n.* A statement that something is true.

propound (prə-pound') *v.* To offer for consideration.

provocation (prŏv'ə-kā'shən) *n.* An action that annoys or irritates.

prudent (prōod'ənt) *adj.* Cautious.

pry (prī) *v.* To examine in a nosy way.

pungent (pŭn'jənt) *adj.* Sharp-smelling.

Q

quarry (kwôr'ē, kwŏr'ē) *n.* **1.** A mine from which marble and other kinds of stone are taken. **2.** A hunted object or person.

quash (kwŏsh) *v.* To suppress or put down.

quaver (kwā'vər) *v.* To shake; tremble. — *n.* A vibration. — **quavering** *adj.*

quicksilver (kwĭk'sĭl'vər) *n.* Mercury, a metal that moves very quickly in its liquid form.

quizzical (kwĭz'ĭ-kəl) *adj.* Puzzled; questioning. — **quizzically** *adv.*

R

rash (răsh) *adj.* Unthinking; reckless. — **rashly** *adv.*

rasp (răsp, räsp) *v.* To scrape with a harsh sound.

rave (rāv) *v.* To talk like an insane person.

ravenous (răv′ən-əs) *adj.* Extremely hungry.

ravine (rə-vēn′) *n.* A deep, narrow valley.

rear (rîr) *v.* To bring up (a child).

rebuke (rĭ-byook′) *v.* To show disapproval.

recede (rĭ-sēd′) *v.* To become farther away; withdraw.

recoil (rĭ-koil′) *v.* To spring back.

recommence (rē′kə-měns′) *v.* To begin again.

reformation (rĕf′ər-mā′shən) *n.* A change to a better way of behaving.

refrain (rĭ-frān′) *v.* To keep someone from doing something.

regal (rē′gəl) *adj.* Kingly.

regression (rĭ-grĕsh′ən) *n.* A return to an earlier, less-advanced state.

rehabilitate (rē′hə-bĭl′ə-tāt′) *v.* To return someone or something to a useful condition.

relent (rĭ-lĕnt′) *v.* To become less firm or strict about something. — **relenting** *adj.*

relevant (rĕl′ə-vənt) *adj.* To the point. — **relevancy** *n.*

relic (rĕl′ĭk) *n.* A fragment of something that no longer exists.

reluctance (rĭ-lŭk′təns) *n.* Unwillingness. — **reluctant** *adj.*

reminiscence (rĕm′ə-nĭs′əns) *n.* A memory.

remorse (rĭ-môrs′) *n.* Regret over something.

render (rĕn′dər) *v.* **1.** To give or hand over. **2.** To make.

rendezvous (rän′dā-voo′, rän′də-) *n.* A meeting place.

renown (rĭ-noun′) *n.* Fame.

repast (rĭ-păst′, -päst′) *n.* A feast; meal.

repercussion (rē′pər-kŭsh′ən) *n.* A result, often an unpleasant one.

repose (rĭ-pōz′) *v.* To lie at rest.

reproach (rĭ-prōch′) *v.* To blame; scold. — **reproachfully** *adv.*

resigned (rĭ-zīnd′) *adj.* Giving in; accepting without complaint. — **resignedly** *adv.*

resolute (rĕz′ə-loot′) *adj.* Firm; determined. — **resolutely** *adv.*

resolution (rĕz′ə-loo′shən) *n.* Firmness; determination.

resonant (rĕz′ə-nənt) *adj.* Rich-sounding.

resound (rĭ-zound′) *v.* To sound loudly.

resource (rē′sôrs′) *n.* A source of support or help.

respirator (rĕs′pə-rā′tər) *n.* **1.** A mask worn to keep substances in the air from being breathed in. **2.** A machine that gives artifical respiration.

resplendent (rĭ-splĕn′dənt) *adj.* Shining.

restriction (rĭ-strĭk′shən) *n.* A limit.

resurrect (rĕz′ə-rĕkt′) *v.* To bring back into life or into use.

retaliate (rĭ-tăl′ē-āt′) *v.* To strike back.

retard (rĭ-tärd′) *v.* To slow down.

revel (rĕv′əl) *n.* A celebration.

revelry (rĕv′əl-rē) *n.* A noisy celebration.

revere (rĭ-vîr′) *v.* To respect.

rouse (rouz) *v.* To awaken.

rucksack (rŭk′săk′, rook′-) *n.* A backpack; knapsack.

S

sacrilege (săk′-rə-lĭj) *n.* A lack of respect for a sacred person or object.

sage (sāj) *adj.* Wise. — **sagely** *adv.*

sally (săl′ē) *v.* To come out.

sarcastic (sär-kăs′tĭk) *adj.* Given to sharp, biting humor. — **sarcastically** *adv.*

saunter (sôn′tər) *v.* To walk in a leisurely way.

savor (sā′vər) *v.* To enjoy.

scan (skăn) *v.* To look at carefully.

scuttle (skŭt′l) *v.* To run off in haste; hurry.

scythe (sī*th*) *n.* A long-handled blade used to cut grass.

sear (sîr) *v.* To burn.

securities (sĭ-kyoor′ə-tēz) *n.* Stock certificates or bonds.

self-assurance (sĕlf′ə-shoor′əns) *n.* Confidence.

semantic (sə-măn′tĭk) *adj.* Referring to the relationships between words and meanings.

senility (sĭ-nĭl′ə-tē) *n.* A condition, usually occurring in old people, in which the mental powers are weakened.

sensibility (sĕn′sə-bĭl′ə-tē) *n.* The ability to respond emotionally.

shake (shāk) *n.* A rough shingle.

shamble (shăm′bəl) *v.* To walk in an awkward way.

shimmer (shĭm′ər) *v.* To shine. — **shimmering** *adj.*

shrew (shroo) *n.* A woman who scolds a lot.

sidle (sīd′l) *v.* To move sideways, often in a sneaky way.

siege (sēj) *n.* An organized attack.

simultaneous (sī′məl-tā′nē-əs) *adj.* Happening at the same time. — **simultaneously** *adv.*

ă pat/ā pay/âr care/ä father/b bib/ch church/d deed/ĕ pet/ē be/f fife/g gag/h hat/hw which/ĭ pit/ī pie/îr pier/j judge/k kick/l lid, needle/m mum/ n no, sudden/ng thing/ŏ pot/ō toe/ô paw, for/oi noise/ou out/oo took/oo boot/p pop/r roar/s sauce/sh ship, dish/t tight/th thin, path/*th* this, bathe/ ŭ cut/ûr urge/v valve/w with/y yes/z zebra, size/zh vision/ə about, item, edible, gallop, circus/ à *Fr.* ami/œ *Fr.* feu, *Ger.* schön/ü *Fr.* tu, *Ger.* über/ ᴋʜ *Ger.* ich, *Scot.* loch/ɴ *Fr.* bon.

singular (sĭng'gyə-lər) *adj.* Unusual; peculiar.—
singularly *adv.*

sinister (sĭn'ĭ-stər) *adj.* Evil-seeming.

skiff (skĭf) *n.* A small boat.

slacken (slăk'ən) *v.* To slow up.

smite (smīt) *v.* **1.** To hit. **2.** To attack.

smolder (smōl'dər) *v.* To burn without a flame.—
smoldering *adj.*

sojourn (sō'jûrn, sō-jûrn') *v.* To stay for a short
time.

solicitude (sə-lĭs'ə-tōōd', -tyōōd') *n.* Care; concern.

solitude (sŏl'ə-tōōd', -tyōōd') *n.* Aloneness.

sovereignty (sŏv'ər-ən-tē) *n.* Independence.

span (spăn) *v.* To stretch completely across, as a
bridge spans a body of water.

spar (spär) *n.* A pole used to support a ship's rigging.

specter (spĕk'tər) *n.* **1.** A ghost. **2.** Something that
causes fear or terror.

spectral (spĕk'trəl) *adj.* Ghost-like.

speculation (spĕk'yə-lā'shən) *n.* An unproved explanation; thought.

spontaneous (spŏn-tā'nē-əs) *adj.* Not planned.

spume (spyōōm) *n.* The foamy part of a wave.

staple (stā'pəl) *n.* A basic food, such as flour, sugar,
or salt.

stark (stärk) *adj.* Unrelieved; complete.

starveling (stärv'lĭng) *adj.* Starving.

stately (stāt'lē) *adj.* Dignified.

stethoscope (stĕth'ə-skōp') *n.* An instrument used to
listen to pulse beats.

stifle (stī'fəl) *v.* **1.** To smother. **2.** To hold back.—
stifled *adj.*

still (stĭl) *v.* To quiet; calm.

stilted (stĭl'tĭd) *adj.* Stiff; formal.

stimulant (stĭm'yə-lənt) *n.* A substance that speeds
up bodily activity.

stoical (stō-ĭ-kəl) *adj.* Not caring about either pain
or pleasure.

stolid (stŏl'ĭd) *adj.* Dull; lacking in imagination.—**stolidly** *adv.*

stout (stout) *adj.* **1.** Brave. **2.** Thick.—**stoutly** *adv.*

stupendous (stōō-pĕn'dəs, styōō-) *adj.* **1.** Amazing.
2. Huge.

succeed (sək-sēd') *v.* **1.** To come after; follow. **2.** To
have success.

succession (sək-sesh'ən) *n.* A series.

successor (sək-sĕs'ər) *n.* One who comes after another, as in a job or a political office.

suite (swēt) *n.* A group of attendants.

sullen (sŭl'ən) *adj.* Glum; ill-humored.

sumptuous (sŭmp'chōō-əs) *adj.* Magnificent.

supposition (sŭp'ə-zĭsh'ən) *n.* Something that is
supposed, or considered to be true.

surmount (sər-mount') *n.* **1.** To overcome. **2.** To be
on top of.

surreptitious (sûr'əp-tĭsh'əs) *adj.* Secret.—**surreptitiously** *adv.*

sustain (sə-stān') *v.* **1.** To keep up; keep in effect. **2.**
To experience; undergo.—**sustained** *adj.*

swagger (swăg'ər) *v.* To walk in a proud, self-impor-
tant way.

syndrome (sĭn'drōm') *n.* A group of symptoms that
occur together in a particular illness.

T

tactful (tăkt'fəl) *adj.* Considerate of another's feelings.—**tactfully** *adv.*

talon (tăl'ən) *n.* A sharp claw.

tangible (tăn'jə-bəl) *adj.* Real; definite.

tarry (tăr'ē) *v.* To stay longer than planned; linger.

taunt (tônt) *v.* To make fun of; mock.

taut (tôt) *adj.* **1.** Tight. **2.** Tense.

tawny (tô'nē) *adj.* Golden brown in color.

tedious (tē'dē-əs) *adj.* Boring.

teem (tēm) *v.* To be crowded or full of.—**teeming**
adj.

temper (tĕm'pər) *v.* To treat steel to make it hard
and flexible.—**tempered** *adj.*

tempest (tĕm'pĭst) *n.* A severe storm.

tenacious (tə-nā'shəs) *adj.* **1.** Hard to get rid of. **2.**
Stubborn.—**tenaciously** *adv.*

tentative (tĕn'tə-tĭv) *adj.* Not definite.

terse (tûrs) *adj.* Brief and to the point.

theory (thē'ə-rē, thîr'ē) *n.* An idea offered to explain
a happening.

thrash (thrăsh) *v.* To move about wildly.

threshold (thrĕsh'ōld', thrĕsh'hōld') *n.* A doorway.

tiller (tĭl'ər) *n.* A part of a boat used in steering.

tolerable (tŏl'ər-ə-bəl) *adj.* Fairly good.—**tolerably**
adv.

tourniquet (tōōr'nĭ-kĭt, -kā', tûr'-) *n.* Any device tied
around a part of the body (over an artery) to stop
bleeding.

tousle (tou'zəl) *v.* To make untidy.—**tousled** *adj.*

tranquil (trăn'kwəl) *adj.* Peaceful.

transfusion (trăns-fyōō'zhən) *n.* The injection of
large amounts of blood into the body.

transgression (trăns-grĕsh'ən, trănz-) *n.* The breaking of a law.

transparent (trăns-pâr'ənt, păr'ənt) *adj.* Clear; able
to be seen through.

traverse (trăv'ərs, trə-vûrs') *v.* To cross; travel.

tread (trĕd) *n.* Step.

tresses (trĕs'əz) *n.* Hair.

tribute (trĭb'yōōt) *n.* Money paid (out of fear) by one
nation to another.

troubadour (trōō'bə-dôr', -dōr', -dōōr') *n.* A traveling poet-musician.

trough (trôf, trŏf) *n.* A long narrow container used
for water or feed for animals.

tumbler (tŭm'blər) *n.* **1.** An acrobat. **2.** A drinking glass. **3.** A part of a lock.

tumult (tōō'məlt, tyōō'-) *n.* A noisy disturbance.

tyranny (tĭr'ə-nē) *n.* Power that is used cruelly or unjustly.

U

ultimate (ŭl'tə-mĭt) *adj.* Final.

unabashed (ŭn'ə-basht') *adj.* Not embarrassed.

unassuming (ŭn'ə-sōō'mĭng) *adj.* Humble; modest.

uncanny (ŭn'kăn'ē) *adj.* Strange; weird.

uncouth (ŭn'kōōth') *adj.* **1.** *Archaic* Unfamiliar. **2.** Not refined; crude.

undaunted (ŭn'dôn'tĭd) *adj.* Not discouraged; not giving up.

unhygienic (ŭn'hī'jē-ĕn'ĭk) *adj.* Not healthful.

unperceived (ŭn'pər-sēvd') *adj.* Unseen; not noticed.

urchin (ûr'chĭn) *n.* A mischievous youngster.

V

vacuous (văk'yōō-əs) *adj.* **1.** Empty. **2.** Showing lack of intelligence or interest. **3.** Meaningless.

vagabond (văg'ə-bŏnd') *n.* A tramp.

vain (vān) *adj.* Not successful. — **in vain.** To no use.

valiant (văl'yənt) *adj.* Brave.

valid (văl'ĭd) *adj.* True.

validate (văl'ə-dāt') *v.* To declare something legal.

vanity (văn'ə-tē) *n.* **1.** The state of being overly proud and concerned about oneself. **2.** Uselessness.

vaulted (vôlt'əd) *adj.* Having an arched ceiling.

veer (vîr) *v.* To turn.

vehement (vē'ə-mənt) *adj.* Very emotional; intense. — **vehemently** *adv.*

venture (vĕn'chər) *v.* **1.** To say at the risk of another's disapproval. **2.** To dare.

verify (vĕr'ə-fī) *v.* To prove that something is true.

vex (vĕks) *v.* To annoy.

vibrant (vī'brənt) *adj.* Full of life.

virtuosity (vûr'chōō-ŏs'ə-tē) *n.* Skill.

visage (vĭz'ĭj) *n.* The face.

vocation (vō-kā'shən) *n.* A type of work.

void (void) *adj.* Not usable. *n.* Total emptiness; nothingness.

W

wanton (wŏn'tən) *adj.* Without cause; reckless. — **wantonly** *adv.*

warrant (wôr'ənt, wŏr'-) *v.* To state; declare.

wayward (wā'wərd) *adj.* Not able to be controlled. — **waywardness** *n.*

wedge (wĕj) *n.* Anything that separates people or things.

well (wĕl) *v.* To pour forth.

wily (wī'lē) *adj.* Tricky.

wince (wĭns) *v.* To shrink back or make a face, as if in pain.

windbreak (wĭnd'brāk') *n.* A row of trees planted as a shelter from the wind.

winsome (wĭn'səm) *adj.* Pleasing; attractive.

wiry (wīr'ē) *adj.* Lean and strong.

wistful (wĭst'fəl) *adj.* Sad with longing. — **wistfully** *adv.*

wont (wônt, wōnt, wŭnt) *adj.* Used; accustomed.

woolgathering (wŏŏl'găth'ər-ĭng) *n.* Daydreaming.

wrath (răth, räth) *n.* Great anger.

writhe (rīth) *v.* To squirm. — **writhing** *adj.*

wrought (rôt) *v.* Formed.

ă pat/ā pay/âr care/ä father/b bib/ch church/d deed/ē pet/ē be/f fife/g gag/h hat/hw which/ĭ pit/ī pie/îr pier/j judge/k kick/l lid, needle/m mum/
n no, sudden/ng thing/ŏ pot/ō toe/ô paw, for/oi noise/ou out/ōō took/ōō boot/p pop/r roar/s sauce/sh ship, dish/t tight/th thin, path/*th* this, bathe/
ŭ cut/ûr urge/v valve/w with/y yes/z zebra, size/zh vision/ə about, item, edible, gallop, circus/ä *Fr.* ami/œ *Fr.* feu, *Ger.* schön/ü *Fr.* tu, *Ger.* über/
кн *Ger.* ich, *Scot.* loch/N *Fr.* bon.

Outline of Skills

Page numbers in italics refer to entries in the Guide to Literary Terms and Techniques.

Reading / Literary Skills

Expression Skills

COMPOSITION

OTHER EXPRESSION EXERCISES

SPEECH AND ARTWORK

Index of Contents by Types

Myths, Legends, Fables, Folklore

Short Stories

Nonfiction

Selections from Novels

Plays

Poetry

Index of Fine Art

Photo Credits

Art Credits

Index of Authors and Titles

The page numbers in italics indicate where a brief
biography of the author is located.

6
D 7
E 8
F 9
G 0
H 1
I 2
J 3